EXAM PREP

SPHR

Dr. Larry Phillips, SPHR

PUBLISHER
Paul Boger

EXECUTIVE EDITOR
Jeff Riley

ACQUISITIONS EDITOR
Steve Rowe

DEVELOPMENT EDITOR
Steve Rowe

MANAGING EDITOR
Charlotte Clapp

PROJECT EDITOR
Dan Knott

COPY EDITOR
Mike Henry

INDEXER
Aaron Black

PROOFREADER
Brad Engels

TECHNICAL EDITOR
Dawn Denvir

PUBLISHING COORDINATOR
Cindy Teeters

MULTIMEDIA DEVELOPER
Dan Scherf

BOOK DESIGNER
Ann Jones

PAGE LAYOUT
Nonie Ratcliff

Contents at a Glance

Table of Contents

Chapter Three:
Workforce Planning and Employment **135**

Chapter Six:
Employee and Labor Relations **437**

About the Author

Dr. Larry Phillips (SPHR) has extensive experience as a Human Resource Management (HRM) manager at both the operational and strategic levels. At the operational level he has managed small HR organizations with as few as ten employees servicing 800 clients as well as large HR organizations with 100 employees and more than 10,000 clients. At the strategic level he has been the program manager for the process reengineering of benefits services for a large federal agency. In addition he has managed consolidations of both personnel processing and training functions at the regional level, again for a large federal agency. He was the project manager for the creation of a corporate university of a mid-sized corporation in the private sector.

Dr. Phillips is on the faculty of Indiana University South Bend where he teaches both graduate and undergraduate classes in human resource management, compensation and benefits, labor and employee relations, organizational behavior, management, and leadership. He has previously taught courses in training and development, interviewing techniques, customer service strategies, and marketing at the higher-education level. Dr. Phillips publishes frequently in these areas. In addition he has taught numerous PHR/SPHR certification classes under the auspices of the Society for Human Resource Management.

His educational background includes an Ed.D. from Indiana University, an MPA from the University of West Florida, and a BS from the University of South Carolina. He is a member of the Society for Human Resource Management.

Dr. Phillips is an experienced HR consultant in both the private and public sector and is affiliated with Ergo Resource Management, Inc., a regional management consulting firm based in Syracuse, IN. He can be reached via email at lwphilli@iusb.edu.

Dedication

This book is dedicated to my lovely wife, Dr. Joyce Phillips. Our dual careers have often kept us apart, but our commitment and love have always kept us together.

Acknowledgments

I wish to acknowledge Steve Rowe, Development Editor of Que Certification, for his assistance, trust, and confidence.

We Want to Hear from You!

As the reader of this book, *you* are our most important critic and commentator. We value your opinion and want to know what we're doing right, what we could do better, what areas you'd like to see us publish in, and any other words of wisdom you're willing to pass our way.

As an executive editor for Que Publishing, I welcome your comments. You can email or write me directly to let me know what you did or didn't like about this book—as well as what we can do to make our books better.

Please note that I cannot help you with technical problems related to the topic of this book. We do have a User Services group, however, where I will forward specific technical questions related to the book.

When you write, please be sure to include this book's title and author as well as your name, email address, and phone number. I will carefully review your comments and share them with the author and editors who worked on the book.

Email: feedback@quepublishing.com

Mail: Jeff Riley
          Executive Editor
          Que Publishing
          800 East 96th Street
          Indianapolis, IN 46240 USA

For more information about this book or another Que Certification title, visit our website at www.examcram.com. Type the ISBN (excluding hyphens) or the title of a book in the Search field to find the page you're looking for.

Introduction

The purpose of this book is to assist you in preparing to take and pass the Senior Professional in Human Resources (SPHR) examination. The SPHR is generally recognized as the highest level of certification available to the HR professional and is a symbol and credential indicating mastery of the domestic body of knowledge of the profession.

The Society for Human Resource Management (SHRM), through its affiliate the Human Resource Certification Institute (HRCI), has determined that the HR body of knowledge consists of six functional areas:

- ▶ Strategic Management
- ▶ Workforce Planning and Employment
- ▶ Human Resource Development
- ▶ Compensation and Benefits
- ▶ Employee and Labor Relations
- ▶ Occupational Health, Safety, and Security

This book has been created around those six functional areas with a major chapter devoted to each area. The material has been presented in the same relative proportions as represented by the number of test questions on the examination. In other words, there is much more material on Strategic Management and Employee and Labor Relations, which compose about 50% of the test questions, as opposed to Occupational Health, Safety, and Security, which represents only about 5% of the examination test items.

The SPHR candidate should not only understand the technical information and HR practices associated with each area but also be able to integrate that knowledge and practice from multiple areas into viable HR strategy. An understanding of the interdependence of the various functional areas is required. Although the book contains a huge amount of material, some of the technical minutia has been left out. The SPHR is not a day-to-day tactical operative, but understands and is responsible for strategic programmatic planning and direction. To that end, interspersed throughout the text are discussions of the potential strategic implications of decisions and activities in the functional areas.

The HR professional lives in a dynamic world of change. Certification is only the beginning. New challenges confront the professional on a daily basis. Constant study and engagement with the larger body of HR professionals is the only way to keep current in the evolving, often turbulent world of the profession. Active involvement in professional organizations such as SHRM is a big step to maintaining one's competency.

I congratulate you on your decision to sit for the SPHR examination and hope that this book is of major assistance in achieving your goal of joining a very elite group of HR professionals who are certified as Senior Professionals in Human Resources.

How This Book Helps You

This book gives a self-guided tour of all the areas that are covered by the SPHR exam. The goal is to teach you the specific skills and knowledge you need to achieve your SPHR certification. You'll also find helpful hints, tips, examples, exercises, and references to additional study materials.

Organization

As mentioned earlier, this book is organized around the six functional areas of the HR body of knowledge. Each functional area has a full chapter of coverage and the book also includes the following features:

▶ The "Study Strategies" section helps you develop study strategies. It also provides you with valuable exam-day tips and information. You should read it early on.

▶ Each chapter starts with a list of objectives that are covered in that chapter.

▶ Each chapter also begins with an outline that provides an overview of the material for that chapter as well as the page numbers where specific topics can be found.

▶ Each objective is repeated in the text where it is covered in detail.

Instructional Features

This book is designed to provide you with multiple ways to learn and reinforce the exam material. Here are some of the instructional features you'll find inside:

▶ **Objective explanations**   As mentioned previously, each chapter begins with a list of the objectives covered in the chapter. In addition, each objective has a detailed explanation that puts the objective in the context of the product.

▶ **Study strategies**   Each chapter offers a selected list of study strategies: exercises to try or additional material to read that will help you learn and retain the material in the chapter.

► **Exam Alerts**   Exam Alerts appear in the margins and provide specific exam-related advice. Exam Alerts address what material is likely to be covered (or not covered) on the exam, how to remember it, or particular exam quirks.

► **Chapter summaries**   Crucial information is summarized, at various points in the book, in lists of key points you need to remember. Each chapter ends with an overall summary of the material covered in that chapter as well.

► **Key terms**   A list of key terms appears at the end of each chapter.

► **Notes**   Notes appears in the margins and contain various kinds of useful information, such as tips on technology, historical background, side commentary, or notes on where to go for more detailed coverage of a particular topic.

► **Exercises**   Found at the end of each chapter in the "Apply Your Knowledge" section, the exercises include chances to practice the skills that you learned in the chapter.

Extensive Practice Test Options

The book provides numerous opportunities for you to assess your knowledge and practice for the exam. The practice options include the following:

► **Review questions**   These open-ended questions appear in the "Apply Your Knowledge" section at the end of each chapter. They allow you to quickly assess your comprehension of what you just read in the chapter. The answers are provided later in the section.

► **Exam questions**   These questions appear in the "Apply Your Knowledge" section. They reflect the kinds of multiple-choice questions that appear on the SPHR exam. You should use them to practice for the exam and to help determine what you know and what you might need to review or study further. Answers and explanations are provided later in the section.

► **Practice exam**   The "Final Review" section includes a complete exam that you can use to practice for the real thing. The "Final Review" section and the practice exam are discussed in more detail later in this introduction.

► **MeasureUp**   The MeasureUp software included on the CD-ROM provides further practice questions.

Final Review

The "Final Review" section of the book provides a valuable tool for preparing for the exam:

▶ **Practice exam**   A full practice test for the exam is included in this book. Questions are written in the style and format used on the actual SPHR exam. You should use the practice exam to assess your readiness for the real thing.

This book includes several valuable appendixes, including details about the content of the CD-ROM (Appendix A) and a glossary of terms and definitions used throughout the book (Appendix B).

These and all the other book features mentioned previously will provide you with thorough preparation for the exam.

Objectives Matrix

(continues)

(continues)

(continues)

Study and Exam Prep Tips

Imagine yourself in this situation: It's the day before you're scheduled to take the SPHR exam. Your legs, arms, and fingertips tingle as you experience a rush of adrenaline. Beads of sweat dot your forehead. If you've scheduled the exam on a workday, or on a day that follows a workday, you might find yourself cursing the tasks you normally enjoy because, in the back of your mind, you're wishing you could read just a few more pages…or review your notes just one more time…or complete just a couple more practice questions….

Fear not: If you use this book, along with your other preparation resources, you can develop an evenly paced study plan that will help you avoid (most of) these pre-test day jitters.

This section of the book provides you with some general guidelines for preparing for any certification exam and for the Senior Professional in Human Resources (SPHR) exam in particular. It's organized into three sections. The first section addresses learning styles and how they affect the way you should prepare for the exam. The second section covers exam-preparation activities and as well as general study and test-taking tips. This is followed by a closer look at the SPHR certification exam, including SPHR-specific study and test-taking tips.

Learning Styles

To best understand the nature of preparation for the test, it is important to understand the learning process. You're probably already aware of how you best learn new material. If you're not, now's a great time to figure it out. You might find that outlining works best for you. If you're more of a visual learner, you might need to see things for them to sink in. If you're a kinesthetic learner, the hands-on approach will serve you best.

Whatever your preferred learning style, test preparation is always more effective when it takes place over a period of time. You obviously wouldn't start studying for a certification exam by pulling an all-nighter the night before the exam or postponing your study until the week before the exam. But solid preparation means even more than that. It requires *consistent* preparation—at a steady pace, over a period of months, not days or weeks. As you begin your preparation, it's important to really appreciate that learning is a developmental process. It will help you focus on what you know well, what you need to know better, and on what you still need to learn.

Learning takes place when you incorporate new information into your existing knowledge base. And remember, with confidence, that even if this book is the first SPHR study tool you've looked at so far, you do have an existing knowledge base! How can you be certain of that? Because you're required to have two years exempt-level experience to sit for the SPHR exam. In fact, six to eight years of exempt experience is recommended. If you have that amount of experience, you've already got a good background from which to begin your preparation.

> **NOTE**
>
> Don't rely on any single resource—even this book—to prepare for the SPHR exam. No matter how good a resource might be, it only provides one perspective, and it can provide only a limited amount of material. This *Exam Prep* should serve as a supplement to your other study resources, not as a replacement for them. There is more knowledge and skill required to pass the SPHR exam than could ever be found in this book or any other single book. And nothing, of course, can replace practical experience.

As you prepare for the SPHR exam, this book (along with all other study materials you use) will serve four purposes:

- ▶ First, it adds incrementally to your existing knowledge base.

- ▶ Second, it facilitates the process of drawing meaningful connections between the test content and your own professional experience.

- ▶ Third, it enables you to restructure your existing knowledge and experience into a format that's consistent with the SPHR exam.

- ▶ Fourth, and probably most importantly, it reminds you to think strategically in terms of systems and interdependencies. The SPHR must be able to integrate multiple laws, regulations, and programs into activities that are aligned with each other.

So, perhaps without even realizing it, you'll add new information into your existing knowledge base—all of which will then be organized around the framework of the six functional areas of HR on which the exam is designed. This process will lead you to a more comprehensive understanding of important concepts, relevant techniques, and of the human resources profession in general. Again, all of this will happen only as a result of a repetitive process, not as the product of a single study session.

Keep this model of learning in the forefront of your mind as you prepare for the SPHR exam. It will help you make better decisions about what to study and about how much more studying you need to do.

General Study Tips

There's no one best way to study for any exam. There are, however, some general test prepa-ration strategies and guidelines that have worked well for many test-takers and that might work well for you, too.

Study Strategies

Although each of us learns and processes information somewhat differently, certain basic learning principles apply to everyone. As you develop your own personal study plan, try to incorporate some of the strategies that are built on these principles. One of these principles is that learning can be broken into various depths:

▶ Recognition (of terms, for example) exemplifies a rather surface level of learning in which you rely on a prompt of some sort to elicit recall.

▶ Comprehension or understanding (of the concepts behind the terms, for example) represents a deeper level of learning than recognition.

▶ The ability to analyze a concept and apply your understanding of it represents further depth of learning.

▶ Finally, the ability to synthesize material is required for those at the SPHR level. This is a higher level of learning that represents the ability to combine seemingly diverse and unrelated bits of information into a new whole.

This is not to say that recognition isn't important. However, in addition to ensuring that you recognize terms, your study strategy should also ensure that you absorb the material at a level or two deeper than that. In that way, you'll know the material so thoroughly that you can per-form well on questions that require you to apply your knowledge to problems as well as on recognition-level types of questions. In fact, synthesis is needed for the SPHR exam. In prac-tical terms, it represents the skill to take a multitude of HR programmatic activities and concepts and integrate them into a strategic HR plan that facilitates the achievement of orga-nizational goals.

Macro and Micro Study Strategies

One strategy that can enhance and support learning at multiple levels of depth is outlining. Creating your own outline that covers all the objectives and subobjectives of the SPHR exam supports your efforts to absorb and understand the content more fully. Specifically, it helps you make connections between the 19 core areas of knowledge, HR-related responsibilities, and the HR-related knowledge associated with each of the six functional areas on the SPHR exam. It also helps you dig a bit deeper into the material by including a level or two of detail beyond what you might find on most generic, pre-prepared, summary-style study tools. You can add even more to your outline by expanding it to include a statement of definition—or a summary of a particular approach—for each point in the outline.

An outline provides two approaches to studying. First, you can study the outline by focusing on the organization of the material. As you build the points and subpoints of your outline, you'll be able to better appreciate how they relate to one another. You'll also gain a better understanding of how each of the main objective areas for the SPHR exam is similar to—and different from—the other main objective areas. Then do the same thing with the subobjectives; be sure that you understand how subobjectives pertain to each objective and how they relate to one another. It's also important to understand how each of the HR-related responsibilities is similar to—or different from—the others. The same also holds true for the HR-related knowledge required for each of the functional areas, and the 19 core areas of knowledge that span the six functional areas.

Next, work through your completed outline. Focus on learning the details. Take time to memorize and understand terms, definitions, facts, laws, cases, and so on. In this pass-through of the outline, you should attempt to learn details rather than the big picture (you focused on that as you built your outline).

Research has shown that attempting to assimilate both types of information (macro and micro) at the same time interferes with the overall learning process. If you separate your studying into these two approaches, you are likely to perform better on the exam.

Active Study Strategies

The process of writing down and defining objectives, subobjectives, terms, facts, and definitions promotes a more active learning strategy than merely reading the material does. In human information-processing terms, writing forces you to engage in more active encoding of the information. Simply reading the information leads to more passive processing. Using this study strategy, focus on writing down the items that are highlighted in the book's bulleted or numbered lists, exam alerts, notes, cautions, and review sections.

Another active study strategy involves applying the information you learned by creating your own examples and scenarios. Think about how or where you could apply the concepts you are learning. You could even try your hand at writing your own questions, which you could then consider sharing with a study partner or group. Once again, write everything down to help you process the facts and concepts in an active fashion.

Finally, consistently compare what you learn in a particular chapter with what you already know and what you learned in previous chapters. The SPHR examination requires you to understand the interdependencies of programs. So, think about what the impact is to other program areas if you implement the activity or strategy that you are currently studying.

The multiple review and exam questions at the end of each chapter provide additional opportunities to actively reinforce the concepts you are learning...so don't skip them!

Common-Sense Strategies

Follow common-sense practices when studying: study when you are alert, reduce or eliminate distractions, and take breaks when you become fatigued.

Design Your Own Personal Study Plan

And do it now. There is no single best way to prepare for any exam. Different people learn best in different ways, so it's important to develop a personal study plan that's right for you. As you do so, establish long-term and short-term goals for yourself. Know exactly what you will accomplish and by what date. There is good motivation theory that indicates self-reward is a powerful method of sustaining your effort. So, reward yourself when you have attained an objective or finished a good session of studying. You'll experience a sense of accomplishment each time you reach a milestone.

Questions to Ask Yourself

As you develop your personal study plan, ask yourself the following questions:

- ▶ If I've taken this test before, and didn't pass, what was effective about my original study plan? What was ineffective?

- ▶ How much time do I have to invest in preparing for the exam?

- ▶ How much money do I have to invest in preparing for the exam?

- ▶ Do I learn better on my own or when I have the chance to interact with others? Or does some combination of both approaches work best for me?

- ▶ Am I comfortable with an online study environment or do I prefer a traditional classroom setting?

- ▶ Does my schedule afford me the opportunity to attend regularly scheduled classroom-based workshops?

- ▶ What is/are my preferred learning style/s?

Pretesting

One of the most important aspects of learning is what has been called *meta-learning*. Meta-learning has to do with realizing when you know something well or when you need to study some more. In other words, you recognize how thoroughly (or not) you have learned the material you are studying.

For most people, this can be difficult to assess independently in the absence of study tools. Pretesting allows you to assess the overall effectiveness of your study strategies. Pretesting tools such as review questions, practice questions, and practice tests are useful in that they objectively assess what you have successfully learned as well as what you have not yet learned.

You can use the insights you obtain from assessment tools to guide and direct your studying because developmental learning takes place as you cycle through studying. So, assess how well you learned a particular topic. Use that assessment to decide what you need to review more. Then conduct another assessment followed by more review. Repeat this cycle until you feel ready to take the exam.

You might have already noticed that there is a practice exam included in this book. You should use it as part of your learning process. The test-simulation software included on this book's CD-ROM also provides you with a tool with which to assess your knowledge.

Set a goal for your pretesting. A reasonable goal is to score consistently in the 90% range.

Please see Appendix A, "CD Contents and Installation Instructions," for further explanation of the test-simulation software.

General Test-Taking Tips

Taking exams can be stressful! This is especially true if it's been a while since you've been in school or taken tests. As you prepare for the test—and answer lots of practice questions—your comfort level with test-taking will likely increase. Be patient with yourself; your rustiness will fade away.

The structure, format, and style of the exam might be unfamiliar to you. Test-taking is a skill all on its own and every test is different. This is why so many individuals offer test-preparation services. You've probably seen the advertisements—SAT, LSAT, GRE, GMAT—the alphabet soup of test-taking goes on and on. The specific attributes of each exam, however, are unique. Be patient with yourself.

SPHR-Specific Information, Study, and Test-Taking Tips

We've all heard the phrase "the fear of the unknown." Well, knowledge dispels fear (at least it helps). Knowing as much as possible about how the SPHR exam is designed, formatted, administered, and delivered helps you as you prepare to take the exam.

How Is the SPHR Exam Administered?

HRCI contracts with the Professional Examination Service (PES) to handle a variety of administrative responsibilities, including

▶ Determining whether PHR, SPHR, and GPHR candidates meet exam eligibility requirements.

▶ Handling payments.

▶ Issuing authorization to test (ATT) letters after a candidate's eligibility to take the test and earn the credential are confirmed. (You have to bring the letter with you to the test site.)

▶ Tabulating and communicating (in writing) PHR, SPHR, and GPHR test scores.

HRCI contracts with Thomson Prometric for exam delivery services. These services include scheduling, administering, and proctoring exams.

How Is the SPHR Exam Put Together?

It's helpful to understand how the SPHR exam was developed—and how it's updated. This insight can help you maintain your focus on what's truly most important to study.

Since 1976, HRCI has defined the HR body of knowledge for the SPHR exam. This body of knowledge has evolved and changed over time, and the SPHR exam has evolved and changed with it. This body of knowledge also translates directly into the SPHR exam test specifications.

EXAM ALERT

At times, the changes to the SPHR exam have been relatively subtle. Such changes can result from information gleaned through literature review and/or environmental scans. Four times since 1976, however, the body of knowledge has been completely revised. Make sure that you periodically check the HRCI website to monitor whether—and how—the SPHR exam test specifications have changed or evolved, and modify your preparation accordingly.

SPHR Exam Format

In addition to studying each of the six functional areas, you also need to be familiar with the format of the SPHR exam. The SPHR exam is a computerized test comprising 225 multiple-choice questions. You'll have four hours to complete the exam, which is administered only in English.

Of the 225 test questions, only 200 are actual exam questions that count toward your overall score. Twenty-five of the 225 questions are being "tested" for possible use in future exams. Your responses to these pretest questions do not count toward your overall score. Pretest questions, however, aren't identified as such. You won't know which questions count toward your overall score and which won't—so your best bet is to assume that every question is a scored question.

Each question has four possible answers. Often, more than one answer makes sense or might initially seem correct. You must, however, choose the best possible answer.

> **EXAM ALERT**
>
> It has been said that "close only counts in horseshoes and hand grenades." Close doesn't count on the SPHR exam, either. Take your time and evaluate all four options before selecting the best possible answer.
>
> Be particularly careful not to choose the response that is the closest to how your employer would handle a particular situation. Every organization has its own way of handling HR-related situations; however, *your* employer's way of handling a situation isn't necessarily the *best* way.

Examples of multiple-choice questions appear at the end of each chapter in this book.

SPHR Preparation Options

There are many options from which to choose as you prepare for the SPHR exam. Here is a sampling of some of those options:

▶ **Classroom courses**   A variety of classroom options exist, including

  ▶ College/university preparatory courses   More than 200 colleges/universities offer the SHRM preparatory course. The SHRM Learning System—valued at more than $500—is included with most of these programs. Visit http://www.shrm.org/ to find a college/university program offered near you.

  ▶ SHRM certification test courses   SHRM sponsors intensive three-day preparatory courses throughout the country. This immersion program allows a condensed training opportunity for test takers, and might offer a valuable option for those who cannot attend a semester-long college/university based program. The SHRM Learning System is included with the three-day program.

  ▶ Chapter-level course   From time to time, certain chapters affiliated with SHRM offer preparatory courses. Contact your local chapter to find out whether it offers the preparatory course. A list of SHRM-affiliated chapters can be found at http://www.shrm.org/.

  ▶ In-house company courses   If enough individuals at your company are interested in earning PHR or SPHR certification, your company might decide to bring SHRM onsite to deliver a preparatory course to you and your co-workers. Normally, only individuals within the sponsoring organization can participate in these programs.

▶ **Online course**   You might want to consider a college/university-based online prep course instead, especially if a traditional classroom setting is not the most appropriate option for you. Through the Internet, you'll become part of a virtual class that prepares together for the SPHR exam.

CAUTION

Check out online college/university programs carefully before signing up to ensure that you choose a format that's right for you. Be particularly alert to real-time participation requirements if you have limited time availability, or are available to study only during nontraditional classroom hours.

▶ **Self-study**   If being part of a cohort group isn't the best choice for you, you might want to consider a self-study option. SHRM offers a self-study learning system, which contains prep books on each functional area as well as software that includes

  ▶ Diagnostic pre-test

  ▶ Application exercises for each module

  ▶ Electronic flashcards

  ▶ Electronic glossary

  ▶ Diagnostic post-test

The self-study format allows you maximum flexibility to prepare for the SPHR at a time and a place that's most convenient for you.

▶ **"Study Buddies"**   Whether you're preparing for the SPHR using a classroom, online, or self-study format, you might find it helpful to find another test-taker with whom you can partner as you prepare for the test. Ideally, you'll want to find someone whose schedule and learning style are similar to your own. Even more important is to look for a buddy who has strengths in those functional areas in which you need the most development, and who needs someone to help him or her in those functional areas in which you are strongest. You can look for a buddy to work with in person, or someone with whom you will confer online. Buddies can be found through colleagues at work, through a prep course, or through other reputable sources.

▶ **Online study groups**   If you're an SHRM member (and who shouldn't be?), check out http://www.shrm.org/ to look for others with whom you can form a study group that's right for you.

SPHR-Specific Test Preparation Tips

Make no mistake: The SPHR exam challenges your knowledge, your HR skills, and your test-taking skills. Here are some tips to help you as you prepare for the SPHR exam:

▶ *Be prepared to combine your skill sets with your experience and identify solutions.* The SPHR exam tests your knowledge as well as your skill. You will be called on to resolve a problem that might involve different dimensions of the material covered. For example, you could be presented with a realistic workplace scenario about a layoff that requires you to understand when—and how—the Age Discrimination in Employment Act (ADEA) needs to be taken into consideration. Why is this type of question likely to appear? Because it's reflective of real life. And it's necessary to be able to make these applications if you're going to be an effective HR professional. In this particular example, it's one thing to know the provisions of the ADEA, but it's something else entirely to understand its application and relevance to a layoff situation.

▶ *Practice delving into minute details.* Each exam question can incorporate a multitude of details. Some of this information is ancillary. Some of it will help you rule out possible issues, but not necessary enable you to identify the best possible response. Some of it will provide you with a more complete picture. Still, you might be called on to combine this information with what you know and with what you have experienced to identify the best possible response. If you don't pay attention to how the information that you're given helps you to eliminate certain responses, the correct answer might elude you completely.

▶ *Practice with a time limit.* The SPHR exam must be completed within four hours. To get used to time limits, use a timer when you take practice tests. Learn to pace yourself.

▶ *Peruse the HRCI website at http://www.hrci.org/.* It contains valuable information and materials, such as the PHR/SPHR/GPHR Handbook.

▶ *Talk with others who have already taken the SPHR exam—whether or not they passed.* Although PHR test-takers are prohibited from sharing specific parts of the exam with you, they can tell you about their experiences with it. You might find that their information, ideas, and suggestions help as you get ready to take the test.

Strategies and Tips for SPHR Exam Day

Your studying is done, you've familiarized yourself with the test center, you're wearing comfortable clothing, and you've arrived at least 30 minutes early with ID in hand. Now what? First, breathe. Remember that you have thoroughly prepared yourself for the SPHR exam. You are ready for this.

Now, prepare yourself mentally. Focus on your feelings of confidence. There's no one right way to do this. Some people, however, find it helpful to consider—and hang onto—one (or perhaps both) of the following two mindsets:

"If you can see it, you can be it": Visualize yourself confidently answering test questions. See yourself leaving the test center, a smile on your face, just having learned that you have passed the exam.

"What's the worst that can happen?": Remind yourself that the very worst thing that could possibly happen is that you do not pass the exam. If that does happen, there are many choices available to you, the most obvious of which is retaking the test. So, even if the very worst thing possible happens, you'll get through it.

Here are some additional suggestions to consider as you sit down to take the SPHR exam:

- **Take your time** Determine how much time you can spend on each question and still allow yourself time to check your responses afterward. Most importantly, read every question—and every answer—deliberately and completely. You need to identify the *best* response, not just a *good* response.

- **Collect yourself** After you actually sit down at the computer terminal, take a few moments to collect yourself before you jump right into the test. Once again, breathe. Set aside any internal distractions and focus on the exam.

- **Take a break if you need one** You have four hours to complete the exam, so give yourself some time to get some air, stretch your legs, and just reenergize yourself.

- **Remember that you might be audiotaped or videotaped** Don't allow this to distract you; instead, just remember that taping test-takers is business as usual for Prometric testing facility. Don't take it personally. Just let it go. You have more important things to focus on than a camera or microphone.

- **Don't rush, but don't linger on difficult questions, either** The questions vary in degree of difficulty. Don't let yourself be flustered by a particularly difficult, wordy, or (seemingly) tricky question.

- **Read every word of every question** Just as in real life, one word or one minute detail can make all the difference in selecting the best possible answer.

- **Don't look for patterns in answer selections** There aren't any.

- **Don't assume that the longest answer is the best answer** Don't assume that the shortest answer is the best answer, either.

- **Answer every question** Unanswered questions are 100% likely to be wrong. If you make a guess, you have a 25% chance of getting it right. If, however, you can narrow down your choices to three possible responses, you've doubled or tripled your chances of answering the question correctly.

▶ **Take advantage of the fact that you can return to and review skipped or previously answered questions** When you reach the end of the exam, return to the more difficult questions.

▶ **If you have session time remaining after you complete all the questions, review your answers** Pay particular attention to questions that seem to contain a lot of detail.

▶ **Don't second-guess yourself too much** When rechecking your responses, you might be tempted to question every answer you made. If you read the question carefully and completely and you felt like you knew the right answer, you probably did. If, however, as you check your answers, a response clearly stands out as incorrect, change it. You also might want to consider changing a response if you misread or misinterpreted details in the questions the first time around, or if you jumped to a clearly incorrect conclusion. If you are at all unsure, however, go with your first impression.

PART I

Exam Preparation

CHAPTER ONE

The SPHR Certification Process

Objectives

In this chapter you will cover some fundamental ideas surrounding the SPHR certification process. Understanding what is required of you for registration and how to register for the exam is critical.

Understand the SPHR Certification Process

Discover How to Apply for the Exam

Learn What Is Required of You to Be Able to Sign Up for the SPHR Exam

Understand Recertification

Outline

Study Strategies

Because this chapter does not have any content that you need to know to correctly answer exam questions, there are no study strategies to discuss. However, in the coming chapters look to this section for study hints and tips you can use to absorb that chapter's SPHR content.

Welcome to *SPHR Exam Prep*. The material in this chapter is an introduction to the SPHR exam and the process you, as the testing candidate, will encounter in your endeavor to become SPHR certified. The content of this chapter is largely taken from the *PHR/SPHR/GPHR Certification Handbook* and expanded by the author's own experience of many years teaching and assisting candidates in successfully passing the certification examination. The handbook is available online at the Human Resource Certification Institute's (*HRCI*) website (www.hrci. org) or through a link at the website of the Society for Human Resource Management (www.shrm.org). The prospective SPHR candidate should consult this resource, as well as other resources available on both organizations' websites; this chapter gives merely a summary of the process.

Is This the Correct Certification for Me?

Three certifications are available through HRCI: the *Professional in Human Resources (PHR)*, *Senior Professional in Human Resources (SPHR)*, and *Global Professional in Human Resources (GPHR)*. Assuming that your major duties do not involve the HR management of foreign operations (which is what a GPHR candidate is involved in), the decision is really between the PHR and the SPHR. Although you could hold both a GPHR and an SPHR or PHR, you cannot hold the PHR and SPHR simultaneously. The SPHR is the higher level of the two, but that does not necessarily mean that it is preferable. It is important that the certification fit your current job, your aspirations, and your knowledge and experience level. A PHR might be the more preferred credential for the new HR professional in that, more than the SPHR, it indicates a mastery of the body of knowledge at the operational level and is more aligned with the job responsibilities at that level. For more experienced HR professionals desiring to move to middle and upper management, the SPHR is probably preferable. The SPHR is the certification of choice at the upper levels of the profession and, in fact, more and more a requirement for entry.

Am I Eligible?

To be eligible, the candidate must be actively engaged in HR management and have two years of exempt-level experience. Exempt-level employees are exempt from the minimum wage and overtime requirements of the Fair Labor Standards Act. The definition of exempt employment is covered elsewhere in this book in Chapter 5, "Compensation and Benefits," and can be found at www.dol.gov/elaws/flsa.htm. However, a quick definition is that the work is executive, administrative, or professional in nature and requires the consistent exercise of discretion and independent judgment with respect to issues of significance. Most HR professional positions, those engaged in teaching HR at the higher education level, HR researchers, and HR consultants are generally considered exempt-level jobs.

Actively engaged is defined as at least 51% of a candidate's daily tasks are within the human resource function. Candidates must document their work duties on the application and, in some cases, attach their job description.

Students and recent graduates might be eligible to take the examination, but cannot use the SPHR designation until they have met the experience requirements. The certification handbook provides additional guidance and procedures for students and recent graduates who want to consider taking the examination before gaining two years of experience at the exempt level.

Although the earlier limit is the minimum standard for eligibility to take the SPHR examination, HRCI recommends strongly that candidates have substantial exempt-level work experience. Its recommendation is six to eight years of experience.

What Is the Application Process?

There are two testing windows for the examination: May 1 to June 30 and December 1 to January 31. Application deadlines vary but can be as much as two months before the testing window. You should consult the most current certification handbook for the exact dates.

The application can be submitted via mail by completing a scannable application form using a #2 pencil. The application is available with the printed certification handbook. The handbook contains directions as to how to fill out the form and where to mail the completed application. HRCI recommends that you use certified or registered mail. If eligible, you will receive an Authorization to Test (*ATT*) letter in approximately two to three weeks. The ATT will contain an HRCI ID number and password. These are needed both to schedule the examination and for communication purposes regarding your application. After the ATT letter has been received, you may then contact a convenient Thomson Prometric testing center to schedule the examination during the testing period. A little later in the chapter you'll discover how to contact Thomson Prometric. Note that candidates determined to be ineligible will be notified and the examination fee refunded.

You can also apply online at www.hrci.org. If applying online, you will receive a confirmation email confirming that the application has been received. It does not confirm eligibility to take the test. Receipt of the ATT letter by mail is confirmation of eligibility.

You should apply early and submit all required documentation. When applying online with www.hrci.org, you have five working days to fax any additional documentation that might be required. Early and complete applications will avoid late and resubmission fees.

Applicants with disabilities can request accommodation by submitting a form that is included in the printed certification handbook and is also found online. Those requesting accommodation will also have to provide documentation from a professional who has the appropriate credential or license to treat the disability for which the accommodation is requested. There is a form for the professional to complete also.

Payment is due with the application. Online applications require payment through a Visa, MasterCard, or American Express credit card. Applications that are mailed in may be paid by credit card, money order, certified check, or organizational check. Cash and personal checks are not accepted. The cost to take the examination is $375 for SHRM members and $425 for nonmembers.

> **EXAM ALERT**
>
> HRCI recommends an online application to receive faster processing.

How Do I Schedule the Examination?

The examination can be scheduled during the testing period online at www.prometric.com or by calling Thomson Prometric's toll-free number: 800-467-9582. HRCI recommends that you schedule your exam as soon as you receive your ATT letter to ensure that you receive a test time that is convenient for you. Remember that you will need your HRCI ID and password to schedule the exam. Thomson Prometric will provide you with a confirmation number after the test date and time have been set. Thomson Prometric has more than 250 test centers throughout the United States, United States territories, and Canada. There is likely a center within a convenient driving distance from your home, your place of employment, or both.

What Is the Examination Like?

The SPHR examination is a computer-based test that covers the body of knowledge expected of a senior HR professional. The percentage of questions coming from each of the functional areas is as follows:

Strategic Management	26%
Workforce Planning and Employment	16%
Human Resource Development	13%
Compensation and Benefits	16%
Employee and Labor Relations	24%
Occupational Health, Safety, and Security	5%

There are 225 questions on the examination of which 200 are scored and 25 are being tested for future examinations. Although the questions query technical knowledge, they tend to be oriented toward strategy and policy as opposed to direct tactical, day-to-day application of that technical knowledge. Therefore you will be required to integrate multiple concepts, regulations, and laws in formulating one answer. The test is multiple choice with four possible answers per question. You must choose the best answer. You are allowed four hours to complete the test.

How Should I Study?

Studying for the exam is like climbing a mountain. It takes much preparation and a lot of hard work. Your goal is to reach the summit (have the maximum amount of knowledge) on test day.

Preparation is obviously facilitated if you have a challenging HR position in which you are constantly faced with new situations and issues. Your ongoing study of the profession and growth in the position will enhance your knowledge and ability to pass the test. However, even HR generalists at relatively high levels in the organization are not likely to encounter all concepts in the functional areas that are being tested. Consequently, the candidate must begin a process of familiarization with the full range of the body of knowledge of the HR profession. That process should be systematic and ongoing and should start months before the test date.

EXAM ALERT

Discipline is really the main point when it comes to studying for the SPHR exam. You should develop a study plan that helps you learn best and stick to it.

How then should the candidate study for the exam? There is no one correct answer to this question because everybody learns differently. In general, the greater the variety of your learning experiences and techniques, the more likely you are to encounter the depth and breadth of information needed, and the more likely you are to retain it.

Even though you must study all six functional areas of the body of knowledge, it is wise to concentrate on those areas in which you have less knowledge or experience. Pre-tests and self assessments are excellent ways of determining where you might need to concentrate you efforts. The HRCI certification handbook has a practice exam and the HRCI website has an online assessment for the SPHR, which is available for a fee. Other pre-test and study materials are available through SHRM and various online sites.

SHRM offers a certification preparation course that is available in many areas. Local SHRM chapters might offer training courses or study groups to assist in preparation. You might want to invest in one or more current textbooks on HR subjects. Many good references are listed in the "Suggested Readings and Resources" section at the end of each chapter. Taking an HR course at the graduate or undergraduate level at your local college or university is also a way to review the body of knowledge and come up to speed on recent developments in the profession. You can establish your own study group with one or more of your colleagues who are also studying for the test. Finally, you can do it alone, but that approach takes a great deal of self-discipline.

The percentage of questions devoted to each functional area is given earlier in this section. That information should be a good indicator of the relative time you should spend studying in each area, modified by your comfort level in that area. For example, if your background and expertise are in employee and labor relations, you might not need to spend as much time studying that area even though it composes about a quarter of the examination.

You are not tested on dates, so do not try to memorize them. However, the chronological relationship of laws and events might be important. For example, you will need to know that the Wagner Act preceded the Taft-Hartley Act, as well as the significance and provisions of the two acts. Additionally, you do not need to know specific state laws for the examination.

I recommend that you use multiple methods to study for the course. Most importantly, you must be disciplined and committed. You must set aside specific amounts of time and religiously adhere to your study schedule.

What Should I Do on Examination Day and During the Exam?

You should show up at the testing site about 30 minutes early with an unexpired government-issued photo identification card that contains your signature. You should be well rested. Do not get over-stimulated on sugar or caffeine thinking that doing so will improve your performance; it will likely wear off during the examination period, causing you to crash. Do not bring study materials, calculators, cell phones, recording or photographic devices, food and drinks, or other extraneous items into the testing center. Smoking is not allowed in the testing area. Although you may take a break and leave the test area, you will not be allowed any additional time to complete the examination. Remember that you have four hours to complete the examination and many people require the whole four hours. A restroom stop prior to entering the test facility is a good idea.

The best possible advice I can provide you is to be prepared for frustration during and after the exam. The feedback from literally hundreds of persons who have taken the exam is that they found it very difficult and were not sure of the answer on many of the questions. This is normal, so do not let it concern you. The pass rate for the test is typically about 60%, so there is better than a 50/50 chance that you passed it.

The standard practice in constructing multiple-choice tests containing four answers is, obviously, to include one correct answer and three distractors. Often, two of the distractors are patently wrong or obviously less right. However, the third distractor might be correct and quite close in content and accuracy to the correct answer. The real difficulty is in discerning which of the possibly correct answers (usually two) is most correct. Good test-taking practices under this scenario are

> ▸ Read the question first and try to answer it prior to reading the answer. If the answer you came up with is included in the possible answers, select it and go to the next question. The answer you select under this scenario is very frequently the correct one.

▶ If you did not immediately come up with an answer, read all the answers. If you believe one answer is clearly correct, select it and go on. First impressions are generally accurate.

▶ If you do not know the correct answer but know that one or more of the answers are incorrect, discard them from consideration. Remember, every time you eliminate a potential answer you have theoretically improved your potential for choosing the correct answer by 25%. If, after you have eliminated one or more of the distractors, you believe you now can choose the best answer, do so. If not, go to the next question.

▶ Do not dwell on a question if you don't know the answer or you will get bogged down. Come back to those questions that you have not answered after you have gone through the whole test. Eliminate obviously wrong answers and make your best guess as to the correct one. Do not let your concern about not being familiar with the information being tested affect your performance. No one knows the whole body of knowledge of HR. You are being tested at a very high level and are not expected to get all the questions correct.

▶ After you have gone through all the questions, go back and make sure that you have answered every one. If you do not know the answer, pick your best guess and go forward.

▶ Don't overwork the test. After you have decided that an answer is correct, it is generally best to not return to that question other than to make sure that you have answered it. You can always talk yourself out of a correct answer by going back over it and second-guessing yourself.

EXAM ALERT

Remember, there is no penalty for guessing, so answer every question.

The computer will monitor your progress and give you an indication as to whether you are on schedule to complete the test. Do not rush through the exam and do not dwell on a question that you do not know the answer to, but rather skip it and go to the next one. Work at a steady pace and, if possible, take several quick breaks at the computer terminal during the exam. Clear your mind, close your eyes, and relax for a few seconds when you become a bit stressed. This will enable you to get back to the test and concentrate effectively on the questions.

How Is Passing Determined?

When you have completed the test, you will receive immediate preliminary feedback as to whether you have passed. Official results providing your actual score and how well you did in each functional area will be sent to your home mailing address in two to three weeks.

To pass the test, you must receive a scaled score of 500. The range of possible scaled scores is from 100 to 700. In simple terms, a scaled score of 500 reflects performance on the test of a minimally qualified professional entitled to be certified. This is determined by evaluating the difficulty of test questions and the likelihood that a minimally qualified individual would get the question right. This evaluation is done by trained HR content experts. No set number of correct answers out of the 200 scored answers equals a passing grade. It is dependent on the difficulty of questions included in the particular test form that you take.

What About Recertification?

Certification is good for three years. You can recertify by taking the examination again, but most SPHRs recertify through professional development activities and continuing education. Sixty contact hours are required and can be achieved in a variety of endeavors. Full information on recertification is available on HRCI's website.

Summary

This chapter covered the SPHR certification process, including application procedures and test-taking hints. It is highly recommended that you obtain a copy of the certification handbook because procedures are subject to modification and change.

Apply Your Knowledge

In coming chapters look for exercises, key terms, review questions, and practice exam questions that are designed to help you drill and practice your knowledge.

CHAPTER TWO

Strategic Management

Objectives

This chapter helps you to prepare for the SPHR examination by covering the concepts and strategies associated with strategic management. This section composes **26%** of the SPHR examination.

Gain an Understanding of the Profession of HR

- ▶ Understand the history or HR

- ▶ Understand the various roles HR fulfills

- ▶ Be familiar with the various professional associations allied with the HR profession

- ▶ Understand the relationship between the functions of management and the roles of HR

- ▶ Understand the evolving issues impacting HR and their strategic significance

- ▶ Understand project planning and project management

- ▶ Understand the outsourcing process and management of outsourced programs and outsourcing vendors

- ▶ Understand the impact of technology on the practice of HR

Gain an Understanding of the Strategic Planning Process

- ▶ Understand the four-step strategic planning process

- ▶ Understand HR strategic planning and its relationship to the organizational strategic plan

Gain an Understanding of Environmental Scanning

- ▶ Understand the components of the environment and the impact they have on strategic planning

- ▶ Understanding the environmental scanning process and its outcomes

Gain an Understanding of Organizations

- ▶ Understand the common functional components of organizations

- ▶ Understand basic financial statements and financial ratios

- ▸ **Understand the four P's of marketing**
- ▸ **Understand the six elements of organizational structure**
- ▸ **Understand various types of organizational models and their alignment with organizational strategy**

Gain an Understanding of Measuring HR Effectiveness

- ▸ **Understand the HR audit and its purpose and outcomes**
- ▸ **Understand the concept of the balanced scorecard and HR scorecard and their implications for aligning organizational members with the organizational strategy**
- ▸ **Understand various types of metrics and their usage**
- ▸ **Understand basic concepts associated with research methods**
- ▸ **Understand the scientific method**
- ▸ **Understand basic statistical concepts**

Gain an Understanding of the Role of HR in Organizational Ethics

- ▸ **Understand common ethical issues in the workplace**
- ▸ **Understand the components of an effective workplace ethics programs**
- ▸ **Understand concepts associated with organizational social responsibility**

Gain an Understanding of the Legislative Environment

- ▸ **Understand the legislative process**
- ▸ **Understand how to effectively communicate with legislators and monitor the legislative environment**

Outline

Study Strategies

This chapter forms the basis and lens through which the SPHR should view all subsequent chapters. You should study this chapter with the intent of beginning to think strategically using the concepts that are covered. The subsequent chapters should be studied with constant vigilance as to how the concepts and practices being discussed fit into the big picture. How can compensation, or human resource development, or employee and labor relations, and so on facilitate the strategic goals of the organization, and how do activities in one program area affect activities in another area?

As you proceed through the subsequent chapters with a strategic perspective, you will not only gain increased technical knowledge in the particular area of practice, but will begin to grasp the concept of the larger whole that is the body of knowledge and practice of HR. The SPHR must understand the interdependence and interrelatedness of all program areas to develop and implement HR programs that are strategic in nature.

Introduction

Human resource management professionals have historically been considered staff. The staff function is one of assisting the operating functions achieve their goals after those goals have been strategically developed. This is no longer the case. As human capital increasingly becomes the core competency and distinctiveness of the organization, the HR function is taking on a critical role in determining the organization's future and its ultimate success.

This new role, however, does not come easily to HR, nor has it been accepted unconditionally by the other functions of the organization. HR professionals continually talk about earning a "seat at the table" or "acceptance in the corner office" or similar metaphors for achieving full partnership in the executive suite. However, this new position must be earned through credible performance and strategic leadership. That is what this chapter of this book is about.

The HR function must expand its influence in leading the organization toward a better future. HR professionals must understand the impact that HR programs can have throughout the whole organization in assisting the various functions achieve their objectives. HR must be proactively involved in partnering with those functions in developing the objectives and associated programs and practices that will facilitate their achievement. HR must understand the strategic planning process and be attuned to changes internally or externally that will affect the organization. HR must understand the "business of business"; that is, understand the basic concepts, language, and strategic importance of the various departments and functions within the organization. HR must earn its "seat at the table" by proving it can affect the bottom line in terms of organizational efficiency, effectiveness, profitability, or other measures of organizational success. HR must not only affect organizational success, but it must do so in an ethical manner. The practice of HR is constantly affected by new legislation, judicial rulings, and issuances of regulation. To be a strategic partner, HR must not only react to these changes but also anticipate and even influence governmental and judicial actions. It is the responsibility of the SPHR to lead this transformation.

The issues introduced in the previous paragraphs are discussed fully in this chapter. If HR performs effectively in its strategic role in the dynamic environment in which many organizations exist today (and in which many more organizations will exist in the future), HR will become not only a strategic partner, but a "first among equals" in the executive suite!

The Role of HR in Organizations

Objective:
Gain an Understanding of the Profession of HR

Human Resource *(HR)* management, also referred to as *HRM*, is the design and implementation of organizational systems to efficiently and effectively use people to accomplish organizational goals. The practice of HR is multidisciplinary and includes many roles and diverse activities, all of which must be coordinated to affect organizational success. HR has evolved from its early beginnings as a clerical function to one that is strategic in nature in many organizations. In this section, we discuss a wide array of issues that are related to the HR profession and its role in the organization. We begin by discussing the history of HR, followed by the roles that HR currently assumes in organizations. We then discuss professional associations and professional certification. Next we discuss the criteria for classification as a profession based on guidance from the Department of Labor, and then the relationship of HR roles to the functions of management. We then turn our attention to a discussion of the changing nature of the HR profession, and finally introduce some basic concepts associated with managing projects. The concepts of organizational change and change management are mentioned briefly and covered more fully in a subsequent chapter.

History of HR

The history of HR as a management function can be traced back to the Industrial Revolution when, for the first time, it became economically and technologically feasible to mass-produce products in large factories employing many people. HR or *personnel management*, as it was known then, was largely a clerical function maintaining employee records and ensuring that employees were paid.

HR roles have largely been impacted by external events. HR became increasing involved in employee selection after WWI when psychological testing, used initially during the war, became available for nongovernmental purposes. Next HR took on both a control and advisory role as a result of the significant social and labor legislation of the New Deal in the 1930s. The human relations movement of the 1950s affected the practice of HR as issues such as motivation, job satisfaction, participative management, and performance evaluation became important in the workplace. The 1960s began a period of significant employment legislative activity that largely dominated HR programs until the 1990s. During this period, many organizations changed the name of the function from Personnel to Human Resource Management. The name change reflects a broader program perspective that includes not only personnel, but also training and development, organizational development, and career and employee counseling initiatives.

Currently the HR function has become or is attempting to become a strategic partner. As the people of the organization increasing become its core competence and differentiation, HR programs such as recruitment, retention, employee involvement, and high performance work systems are critical to organizational success.

Current Roles of HR

HR roles can be classified into three categories: administrative, operational/employee advocate, and strategic. The role of HR in its infancy was clerical and administrative in nature. As laws and regulations became more numerous and as HR became more professionalized, the operational role came into prominence and occupied a large percentage, but not a majority, of HR staff time. In recent decades, HR has become more involved in the strategic role. Many HR practitioners and researchers predict that in the relatively near future the strategic role will occupy a majority of staff time, with the operational/employee advocate role constituting most of the remainder. As administrative tasks are increasingly performed by automated systems or outsourced, that role will diminish to a very small percentage. Current research indicates that this migration to a predominantly strategic role is in fact occurring, but at a considerably slower pace than predicted. Although the reasons for this slow transformation are many, HR as a profession has not always proven its ability to understand the "business of business" or to prove its effect on organizational success. These issues are discussed in other sections of this chapter. The three current roles are discussed in further detail in the following sections.

Administrative Role

As previously discussed, this is the traditional and historical role of HR. It involves clerical administration, personnel processing, and record keeping. Maintaining personnel and payroll records and processing payroll are major tasks to be accomplished in this role. HR staff needed to provide these services are relatively low-level administrative and clerical employees.

Although the administrative role is critical to the efficient operation of HR and the organization, the advent of automated systems has brought about a huge decrease in the number of employees required to provide this role. Computerized payroll and human resource management information systems *(HRISs)* can now efficiently and effectively perform many of the tasks in this role. HRISs also permit employees themselves to provide their own services that previously required HR administrative staff. Employees or prospective employees can now access the HRIS or other automated systems through the Internet or the organization's intranet for employment applications, benefits information, enrollment and changes, application for promotion or transfer, input of timecards and leave information, training modules, and so on without HR staff intervention.

Another issue that has profoundly affected the administrative role, and one which is expected to continue to have an even greater effect, is outsourcing. Payroll, workers' compensation, and unemployment insurance processing are frequently outsourced, as are benefits administration, employee assistance and career counseling programs, and training. Often organizations can save money by taking advantage of the economies of scale, imbedded expertise, and superior technology that outsourcing vendors and subcontractors can provide.

The administrative role has traditionally occupied a large percentage of HR staff time and in many organizations, particularly small ones, still does. However, predictions are that the role will increasingly become automated and outsourced so that it occupies a very small percentage of overall HR staff activity. This percentage might drop to 10–15% of total HR staff time allocations.

Operational/Employee Advocate Role

The operational/employee advocate role has been an important one, beginning with the rapid increase in HR related legislation in the 1930s and continuing until today. The role is likely to remain important and occupy substantial HR staff time into the future.

The operational role involves the planning, implementation, and evaluation of various HR programmatic activities in support of the organization's strategic goals. This role has traditionally been reactive in terms of supporting the strategic plan after the plan has been developed, rather than proactive in terms of being intimately involved in the development of the organization's strategic plan. The operational role involves the traditional HR programs that one thinks of when visualizing the HR profession. Recruitment, selection, performance management, training and development, compensation and benefits, employee and labor relations, and occupational health, safety, and security programs are all included in the operational role. These programs must be developed and implemented within a complex maze of federal, state, and local laws and regulations. It is HR's responsibility to ensure that programs assist in achieving organization goals while remaining legally compliant. These programs are tactical versus strategic in nature, providing support for organizational leadership. Oftentimes, management evaluation of these programs and the operational role as a whole is based on efficiency perceptions rather than effectiveness perceptions. For example, the speed with which a position is filled is often the evaluative factor rather than the eventual performance and retention of the person who fills the job.

The other factor in the role is that of employee advocate. Although this might be considered by some, particularly operational managers, as the "soft side" of HR, the advocacy role is undertaken as a management function to facilitate the achievement of management goals. EEO compliance, career counseling, employee assistance programs, grievance and complaint administration, employee involvement programs, and quality of work life issues are examples of programs that might be considered part of this role. Programmatic activities are evaluated and undertaken in the context of facilitating organizational goals. Positive outcomes such as complaint and litigation avoidance, improved job satisfaction, greater commitment, better quality, and increased productivity are some of the goals.

Strategic Role

The strategic role sets the stage for the future for HR and, in many organizations today, is a vitally important function. The strategic role is a proactive planning approach to assist the organization in designing its future. In this role, HR becomes a strategic business partner in determining the strategic direction of the organization and in developing a strategic HR plan that supports that direction. In many organizations, where competitiveness and success are based on the capabilities of its human capital, HR has become or will become the "first among equals," taking a lead role in the strategic planning process. Activities such as workforce planning, organizational change, designing and supporting restructuring, merger, or acquisition initiatives, and developing strategic compensation, benefits, and performance management strategies are all included in the strategic role.

HR Professional Associations

As an SPHR, you should be familiar with the various professional associations that are allied with the practice of HR. The broad range of activities and programs under the umbrella of human resource management requires specific in-depth knowledge of a variety of separate, but interdependent, bodies of knowledge. Membership and participation in these associations is one way to improve your knowledge and, at the same time, forward the profession. Because the purpose of this book is to prepare you to take the certification examination for SPHR, you should be familiar with the Society for Human Resource Management *(SHRM)*. However, SHRM is not the only HR-related professional organization, and the PHR/SPHR/GPHR certifications are not the only professional certifications available.

Society for Human Resource Management

SHRM was founded as the American Society for Personnel Administration *(ASPA)* in 1948 by a group of 28 professionals who wanted to create an organization that provided professional development, networking opportunities, and generally contributed to the advancement of the profession. Today, SHRM has more than 200,000 members in more than 120 countries, and is the largest professional organization devoted to human resource management in the world. There are more than 550 local chapters around the globe. SHRM has more than 200 employees based in its Washington, D.C. offices who are organized in more than 20 specialized departments to serve the needs of its members.

The mission of SHRM is to provide a wide variety of services and resources to the HR professional. The mission also includes the advancement of the HR profession and the capabilities of HR professionals to ensure that HR is an essential and effective partner in developing and executing organizational strategy. More information can be found at http://www.shrm.org/.

Other HR Professional Organizations

Other HR-related professional organizations, the certification (if any) each administers, and their websites are provided in Table 2.1.

TABLE 2.1   HR Professional Organizations

Professional Organization	Certification	Website
American Society for Training and Development *(ASTD)*	Certified Performance Technician *(CPT)*—jointly sponsored with the International Society for Performance Improvement	http://www.astd.org/
World at Work Association	Certified Compensation Specialist *(CCP)*	http://www.worldatwork.org/
World at Work Association	Certified Employee Benefits Specialist *(CEBS)*	http://www.worldatwork.org/
Board of Certified Safety Specialists	Certified Safety Professional *(CSP)*	http://www.bcsp.org/
American Board of Industrial Hygiene	Occupational Health and Safety Technologist *(OHST)*—jointly sponsored with the Board of Certified Safety Specialists	http://www.abih.org/
Academy of Management		http://www.aom.pace.edu/
American Psychological Association		http://www.apa.org/
International Personnel Management Association		http://www.impa-hr.org/

NOTE

The list in Table 2.1 is not all-inclusive. A number of additional professional organizations are allied with the practice of HR and its subspecialties.

HR As a Profession

In the mid-1960s, SHRM (then ASPA) and a group representing Cornell University asked the Department of Labor *(DOL)* to define exactly what constituted a profession. The DOL responded that a profession must possess five characteristics. Based on the response, HR is a profession because it meets all five of the criteria. The five criteria and characteristics of HR that meet those criteria are discussed in the following list:

▸ **A national organization**   A profession must have a national organization that can collectively speak for it members and advocate on behalf of the profession. SHRM clearly provides that service.

▶ **A code of ethics**   A profession must have a written code of ethics that provides guidance to its members as to appropriate standards of behavior. Again, SHRM has a code of ethics to which members must pledge as a condition of membership in the organization.

▶ **Research**   A profession must engage in applied research to advance knowledge in the field. There are many journals that publish HR-related research and a large number of academics and HR practitioners who are actively engaged in both theoretical and applied research. In addition, the SHRM Foundation funds research projects.

▶ **Body of knowledge**   A profession must be recognizable as a discipline with a defined body of knowledge. That task is accomplished by the Human Resource Certification Institute *(HRCI)*, which collects this information and uses it to define the body of knowledge that must be tested in order to obtain certification.

Professional Certification

A profession must have a credentialing body that sets professional standards of practice. This criterion is met through the testing and certification process conducted by HRCI.

EXAM ALERT

Even though the criteria for a profession might seem a bit self-serving and self-justifying; they are important to SHRM and HRCI. Expect a question regarding the five criteria of a profession and how HR meets those criteria.

Integrating HR Roles and HR Management Functions

We have discussed the various roles that HR undertakes to support the line function and facilitate achievement of organizational goals. However, HR must be managed internally just as the line function is managed. We can define *management* as the process used to achieve organizational goals through people and resources. Henri Fayol studied the practice of management in the first part of the twentieth century and attempted to classify management activities into functions. He determined that managers engaged in five functions: planning, organizing, coordinating, directing, and controlling. Modern management theory has collapsed the coordinating and directing functions into one function called *leading*. The SPHR as a manager uses these functions to strategically manage the HR function. Table 2.2 lists and describes the four management functions and provides an example of how the HR manager might use them in development of a compensation program.

TABLE 2.2   Management Functions

Management Function	Description	Example: Compensation Program
Planning	Determining the goals of the organization and deciding on activities required to accomplish them.	Evaluating the strategic plan and organizational culture to determine an appropriate compensation strategy. Scanning the environment for potential changes affecting compensation strategy. Developing baseline metrics and determining the need for change.
Organizing	Assembling the resources necessary to achieve goals.	Allocating HR staff and resources to the development and implementation of the compensation strategy. Creating a project team.
Leading	Directing and motivating employees to achieve goals.	Providing day-to-day guidance and motivation to the HR project team. Developing support and enthusiasm for the program from the line function.
Controlling	Monitoring progress toward goals and making changes when necessary.	Monitoring the project action plans, timelines, and budgets. Evaluating success of the compensation program after implementation.

EXAM ALERT

Know the four functions of management and how they apply to the management of HR internally.

Evolving Issues in HR Management

Most organizations reside in a dynamic environment and are affected by changes in competitive practices, economic conditions, social goals, economic conditions, technology, employee and customer demographics, and government regulations. All of these changes and pressures affect the design and implementation of HR programs and require new and innovative approaches to assist the organization in adapting and, ultimately, in being successful. The issues faced by HR professionals are ever-evolving and are discussed next.

Movement of HR from an Administrative to a Strategic Role

The concept of the strategic role was introduced in a previous section. In addition, the subject is covered with respect to specific program areas in the chapter covering that program. Suffice it to say that the movement from an administrative and operational role to a strategic and operational one brings many challenges for the HR profession and the SPHR who must lead this transformation. The role requires new skill sets, new knowledge, and a different way of thinking and approaching the HR practice. To become a strategic partner with the other functions of the organization, HR must be able to document its performance and effect on organizational success. This will increasingly require sophisticated metrics. This subject is covered later in this chapter, and specific metrics appropriate for specific program areas are also discussed in the chapters covering those programs.

Workforce Demographics

The workforce today is increasingly female, diverse, and older. Each of these characteristics brings special challenges to the HR profession. The increase in the percentages of females in the workforce has driven new programmatic challenges to provide flexibility in work hours and workplaces. Increasing diversity has driven new challenges in terms of valuing diverse cultures and preventing discrimination. An older workforce brings about issues of health insurance coverage and skill obsolescence. On the other hand, many of these older workers, who have valuable and needed skills, might elect to retire, leaving a potential void in terms of knowledge and experience in the workplace.

Occupational Shifts

The change from a manufacturing to a service to a knowledge economy has dramatically affected the types of jobs that are required. There is a bimodal demand for jobs in today's economy with increased demand for relatively high-paying, technology-oriented jobs such as those in the computer field, and increases in demand for relatively low-paying service jobs such as food service workers and retail clerks. The challenge for HR lies at both ends of the spectrum: in attracting and retaining employees in high skill jobs where demand is likely to exceed supply, and attracting and retaining employees at the other end of the spectrum where jobs are less desirable.

Globalization of Business

Increasingly HR must deal with the issue of *offshoring*; that is, the movement of jobs to foreign countries. Organizations are finding that they can produce products or services of equal quality at greatly reduced labor costs by establishing facilities in other countries. Not only does this bring complexity to the HR function by having to deal with different cultures and foreign rules and regulations, but it also brings about numerous ethical dilemmas such as working conditions, child labor in the offshore operation, and the loss of jobs in this country.

Growth in Contracting Out and Use of the Contingent Workforce

Why buy when you can lease? Why do it internally when you can contract it out for less? These are common issues faced by HR today and they are expected to be even more prevalent in the future. Many organizations have elected to operate with a small core group of employees with skills critical to the success of the organization and either augment the permanent staff with temporary, leased, contract, or part-time workers or to contract the work out to external vendors. These activities often result in significant cost savings and release the organization from the expense of such obligations as benefits and taxes. In addition, these activities limit the organization's exposure to litigation and complaints to regulatory agencies regarding their employment policies, practices, and decisions. However, these practices result in new challenges for HR in terms of monitoring and administering contracts and maintaining quality and productivity standards.

Technology Changes

Technology changes bring about new ways of doing the organization's work, freeing the work and workers from the constraints of time and place. Workers are now often literally connected to the workplace 24 hours a day through the Internet, cell phones, personal digital assistants, and other wireless technology. The result is that many employees work more hours and are presented with the issue of being constantly available, requiring new ways of managing and new or modified HR programs and policies to accommodate these changes. Technology also brings about rapid changes in the methods of work and skill sets required, resulting in the need for constant training, retraining, and developmental programs.

Workforce and Skill Shortages

The Baby Boomers are expected to begin retiring in great numbers in the near future. The worker cohorts replacing them are smaller in absolute numbers. Many experts predict significant shortages of available workers in the next several decades, bringing recruitment and employee retention challenges for HR. This shortage will be compounded by the fact that many new workers are entering the workforce with substantial skill deficits. As the nature of work becomes more complex, entering worker skill levels are not keeping pace. If workers with the requisite skills are not available, HR will be forced to increasingly engage in remedial skills training.

Mergers and Acquisitions

Because of competitive pressures, many organizations will explore opportunities to either merge or acquire another organization or organizations. HR should be intimately involved in the exploration and due diligence stages and, subsequently, in the implementation stage. A major issue in these stages is cultural fit. Research indicates that many mergers and acquisitions that fail or do not achieve anticipated objectives do so because of conflicting and incompatible cultures. *Implementation challenges* involve the integration of two separate companies and their policies and procedures that might not be compatible. Often compensation systems, retirement programs, and other benefit must be merged. A frequent challenge in the implementation stage is redundancy in positions, which often requires termination or redeployment of employees.

Decentralization and Centralization

Many HR functions and the organizations they support are becoming both centralized and decentralized at the same time. Both initiatives are largely driven by technology. Many HR functions are placing day-to-day HR operational responsibilities at the field level. HR professionals stationed in the field are better able to understand the needs of the organization and the demographics of the workforce in order to customize HR programs. Because of technology, these field-level professionals are connected in real time to higher-level HR managers and experts should they need assistance.

At the same time that decentralization is occurring, many parts of HR are being centralized. There are some processes that can be most effectively and efficiently conducted at headquarters or at some other centralized location. Strategic planning and policy development are best centralized. Many repetitive processes (payroll, workers' compensa tion, and unemployment claim processing, for example) are most efficiently and effectively conducted in either a centralized environment, often called an *HR service center*, or outsourced to specialized vendors where economies of scale, expert knowledge, and access to specialized and expensive automation equipment are available.

> ### EXAM ALERT
> The SPHR should be familiar with the evolving issues that are driving change in the practice of HR and their strategic implications. Expect at least one question in this area.

> ### NOTE
> Part of the decentralization process also includes giving more authority and responsibility to field management. Automated systems permit managers to classify jobs, input payroll changes and performance evaluation results, and so on.

Managing Projects

The nature of work is increasingly project based. Contingent workers are often employed on a project basis. New and innovative ideas involving organizational, cultural, and work processes change are often developed in committees or task forces and then converted to projects at the implementation stage. The work of the organization is increasingly project based, using cross-functional and cross-hierarchical temporary organizational structures. Therefore, a critical skill of the HR professional, and particularly the SPHR, is the ability to manage projects. A *project* is a set of coordinated activities and tasks having a definite beginning and ending point. Projects are different from programs and processes in that projects are one-time-only events. Characteristics of a project are

- Has an objective that is specifically defined
- Has funding and resource allocations and limits
- Has defined start and end dates
- Consumes resources

Projects have a defined lifecycle based on the starting and ending dates that are assigned. The cycle moves from project conception and approval, to project planning, project management, and finally, project evaluation. Organizational members can conceive great ideas, but they must be elevated to the decision-making level where support and allocation of required resources can be obtained and then the project can be effectively managed until the project objective is achieved.

To obtain resources, a project sponsor must be obtained. A *sponsor* is typically a high-level executive who controls resources and agrees to fund the project. A project also needs a champion. A *champion* is an individual who is committed to the project and communicates its value throughout the organization. The champion is often the one who obtains the support of the sponsor, might also be the project team leader, and otherwise attempts to gain support and resources for the project. A project is frequently planned and managed by a project team headed by a project team leader.

After the project is conceived and approved, it needs to be planned and then implemented. The process of planning and monitoring project activities is referred to as *project management*. Both project planning and project management are critical to project success and are discussed next.

Project Planning

Project planning is the process of determining project tasks to be accomplished and the resources needed to accomplish those tasks. Planning also includes the determination of who is to accomplish those tasks and when they need to be done. Planning involves determining the most effective and efficient schedule and developing contingency plans should the original plan not be executed as expected. A number of tools are available to assist in the planning process and they are discussed next.

Statement of Work

A *statement of work* is a broad written description of work required to complete the project. It includes the objectives to be achieved, deliverables, and a generalized schedule. Also included are resource requirements and resource constraints, if any. The statement of work is a broad summation of the project.

> **NOTE**
>
> As the nature of work becomes more flexible, it is possible that job descriptions will increasingly look very similar to statements of work.

Work Breakdown Structure

The statement of work provides little in specifics and is the top-level first step in the planning process. The work breakdown structure *(WBS)* is a planning document that shows the total project divided into the tasks that need to be completed. The document also identifies the time required to complete each task and who is responsible for completing it. Table 2.3 is a very simple example of a work breakdown structure, consisting of several tasks and associated activities. Complex projects might require multiple levels to capture the many activities and subcomponents of those activities. The WBS can include a fourth column that provides the estimated cost. This is referred to as a *costed* WBS. The WBS is indispensable in the project planning process, particularly if the project is somewhat complex.

TABLE 2.3   Sample WBS

Name of Project		
Task	**Estimated Time (Days or Weeks)**	**Responsible Unit or Person**
Task 1: (*description*)	5.0	Bill
Activity 1.1: (*description*)	2.5	John
Activity 1.2: (*description*)	1.5	Bill
Activity 1.3: (*description*)	1.0	John
Task 2: (*description*)	10.0	Sue
Activity 2.1: (*description*)	2.0	Mary
Activity 2.2: (*description*)	3.0	Mary
Activity 2.3: (*description*)	5.0	Sue
Task 3: (*description*)	1.0	Joe
Activity 3.1: (*description*)	0.3	Joe
Activity 3.2: (*description*)	0.3	Joe
Activity 3.3: (*description*)	0.4	Joe

Program Evaluation and Review Technique/Critical Path Method

The WBS provides the tasks that must be completed to finish a project, but it does not provide critical information as to the order in which the tasks and activities must be completed. Tasks are often sequential in that one cannot be started until the other is completed. On the other hand, some tasks are independent and can be completed at anytime during the project. When projects are relatively simple, determining the order in which the tasks must be completed is not difficult. However, what if the project is extremely complex, such as constructing a large building or a jet airliner? Luckily, many computerized project management programs are now available.

Program Evaluation and Review Technique *(PERT)* is a system first used by the U.S. Navy in 1958. It was developed for planning and monitoring huge weapons systems projects. A similar methodology was introduced at about the same time by the DuPont Company and is called the *critical path method (CPM)*. The two methods are very similar and newer project management software programs use essentially the same logic.

The outcome of any of these methods is a determination of the proper flow of activities based on the interrelationship between them. A very simple PERT/CPM diagram is shown in Figure 2.1. The circles are called *nodes* and they represent the beginning and ending of tasks. The line between the nodes represents the time it takes to complete a task. For example, task 1,3 takes 9 days and task 1,2 takes 3 days. This time can be obtained from the WBS. Activity 4,7 requires 0 days. This activity is referred to as a *dummy* activity and means that activity 7,8 cannot begin until activity 1,4 is complete. The important concept to understand in this explanation is the *critical path*; that is, the order of activities depicted by the solid arrows connecting 1, 2, 3, 5, 6, 7, and 8. In this case, activity 2,3 cannot begin until 1,2 is complete, activity 3,5 cannot begin until 2,3 is complete, and so forth. This critical path depicts the mandatory order in which activities must be completed, and represents the least possible time in which the project can be competed. In this case, the critical path indicates that the project can be completed in 23 days. Any delay in completion of tasks on the critical path will delay the entire project. All activities on the critical path must begin and end on time for the project to be completed as planned. Thus, the critical path is the path that must be most closely monitored.

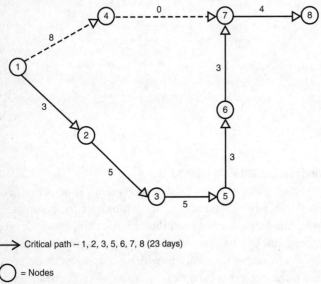

→ Critical path – 1, 2, 3, 5, 6, 7, 8 (23 days)

◯ = Nodes

→ or --▷ = Time required (days)

FIGURE 2.1 Sample PERT/CPM diagram.

A final concept associated with the critical path is that of *slack* (or *float*). You will notice that the path 1,4,7 takes 8 days and, as stated before, activity 7,8 cannot begin until 1,4 is complete. However the critical path (1, 2, 3, 5, 6, 7) requires 19 days to complete before activity 7,8 can begin. The difference of 11 days between the two paths is called *slack* or *float* and provides some room for the project team leader or project manager to divert resources to the critical path. In this case, activity 1,8 has a slack or float of 11 days and can begin anytime between day 1 and day 11 without delaying the project. Those resources devoted to activity 1,8 can be used to assist in other activities during the slack, presenting flexibility in the planning process. In complex projects there are typically many activities that do not fall on the critical path, generating substantial slack or float that facilitates the efficient use of available resources. On some days, all employees will be required to work on activities on the critical path. On other days, very few employees might be required to work on the critical path. The slack or float allows the project planner to level the resources so that the number of employees required on each day of the project is the same or close to the same, rather than requiring a large number of employees one day and few the next.

Gantt Charts

Project activities can be visually displayed using Gantt charts. The charts depict the starting and ending times of all activities and show how each activity fits into the overall schedule. The actual beginning and ending dates can be overlaid on the projected dates to provide an indication as to whether the project is on schedule. Figure 2.2 depicts a Gantt chart. In this case, the project was behind schedule for activities A, B, and C, but back on schedule at the completion of activity D.

EXAM ALERT
You should be familiar with the concepts discussed in regard to project planning. The most likely subjects are PERT/CPM and Gantt charts.

Project Monitoring

A great plan poorly executed is not likely to succeed. When project planning ends and project activities begin, the process of project monitoring also begins. Project monitoring consists of the following activities:

- Tracking progress
- Comparing actual to predicted
- Making corrections

Progress must be tracked to make sure that all activities are accomplished. The WBS and Gantt charts can be modified and used for that purpose, as can action plans. These methods, however, become quite difficult to use on complex projects. In those cases, project management software is needed.

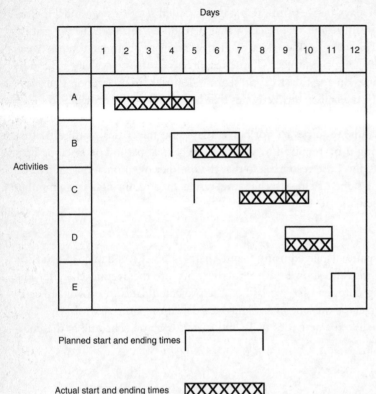

FIGURE 2.2 Sample Gantt chart.

Time and resources (people, money, supplies, and so on) must be monitored for expected usage versus actual usage. The objective of project monitoring is to ensure not only that the project is completed on time, but also that it is completed within the allocation of resources. For relatively simple projects, a combination of Gantt charts, action plans, and budgets might suffice to provide the necessary data. Large projects require sophisticated project management software that integrates activity and budget tracking, a process called *cost/schedule integration*.

Off-budget or off-schedule situations require analysis of the cause. After causation is determined, various options can be explored to get the project back on track. When corrective action is initiated, project monitoring continues to ensure that the corrections have the desired effect and that the project is back on schedule and within budget.

Project monitoring is more than tracking progress. It incorporates many other issues discussed in this book. For example, project teams are often cross-functional and cross-hierarchal. They might be organized as concentrated structures. Project monitoring requires leadership. Projects often involve organizational change that must be communicated throughout the organization, and resistance to the change must be overcome if the project is to be successful.

Managing Organizational Change

Change is the alteration of the status quo of an individual, group, or organization. *Organizational change* is the transformation of the structure, culture, or work processes in response to internal or external forces. Organizational change can be reactive or proactive, externally or internally driven. Strategic planning facilitates positive, adaptive change in that it is proactive and internally driven.

The change process, change theory, and overcoming resistance to change are all issues with which the SPHR must be familiar. They are discussed in Chapter 4, "Human Resource Development."

Managing Outsourcing Vendors

The subject of outsourcing is discussed throughout this book. *Outsourcing* is the process of contracting for services or products externally rather than producing them internally. Virtually every function within HR comprises activities that are candidates for being performed by third-party vendors. In fact, many organizations contract out the whole HR function. However, activities comprising the administrative role of HR are the most likely to be outsourced because they are often rather mundane and repetitive processes that can be accomplished in a mass or batch processing manner, frequently using automation.

Outsourcing in this case tends to provide significant cost savings either through economies of scale or use of sophisticated specialized software. Outsourcing often provides access to expertise that the organization does not have, either because it is too small to be able to devote resources to the development of that expertise or because it elects not to. In addition, outsourcing provides flexibility in that the organization is committed for only the contractual period and is free to shop around for a better deal.

As the HR function continues to move toward a strategic orientation, many predict that most of the administrative function will be outsourced. In fact, some research studies show that around 50% of the administrative role is currently being outsourced. Activities and programs that are subject to outsourcing include, but are not limited to the following:

- Payroll processing
- Benefits administration
- Recruitment
- HRIS
- Outplacement
- Workers' compensation
- Training

- Employee assistance programs
- Career counseling
- Salary and benefits surveys
- Health insurance and claim administration
- Relocation
- 401(k) administration

- ▶ Fitness and wellness programs
- ▶ Background checks
- ▶ Temporary staffing

HR is not the only function of the organization that is engaging in outsourcing. Virtually every activity that the organization conducts is subject to outsourcing and offshoring (see the discussion regarding virtual organizations later in this chapter). Outsourcing activities of other functions has implications for the HR function as well. These activities often result in the need to redeploy or lay off employees. Also, outsourcing initiatives might have a negative effect on overall organizational commitment because employees could begin to question job security.

Outsourcing of HR functional areas has disadvantages as well as advantages. Potential loss of organizational commitment was mentioned earlier. Concern about job security often manifests itself in lower productivity, reduced quality, and increased turnover. Outsourcing frequently brings about a diminution of organizational skills and overall organizational capabilities as internal development of human capital in those areas is not undertaken. It results in overall loss of control of the means of accomplishing the work as only the outcomes are normally specified in outsourcing agreements. Outsourcing requires that contracts be intelligently negotiated and properly monitored and enforced. These subjects will be explored briefly in the sections that follow.

Outsourcing Process

The outsourcing process is similar to any other procurement or contractual process and consists of the following steps:

- ▶ Analyze current operations, identify potential for improvement, and define goals. The first step is to understand how an operation is currently being performed and its efficiency and effectiveness. Understanding current operations in relationship to desired outcomes will identify whether there is a need for improvement; that is, a performance gap. Improvement goals in terms of cost savings, improved services, and so on can then be defined.

- ▶ Various alternatives for achieving the goals are considered in terms of projected cost benefits. If outsourcing is considered a viable option, the process continues.

- ▶ The organization creates and issues a request for proposal (RFP). Development of an RFP is an extremely crucial step. The RFP must be explicit as to the types of services desired and the deliverables to be contracted. A badly developed RFP will likely result in lack of desired outcomes and, potentially, contract renegotiation after it has been agreed on. The outcome of renegotiation frequently is additional cost.

- ▶ The responses are evaluated in terms of compliance with the RFP. This evaluation includes cost, company capabilities and reputation, and many other considerations.

▶ The contractor is chosen and a contract is negotiated.

▶ The contract is implemented, administered, and monitored.

▶ The outsourcing strategy is evaluated periodically to determine whether the original goals are being reached in an effective and efficient manner.

EXAM ALERT

Outsourcing is an issue in which the SPHR will become increasingly involved. Expect a question regarding the outsourcing process and the benefits and disadvantages of outsourcing HR functions.

Contract Law

To administer and monitor outsourcing contracts, the SPHR must understand the basic concepts of contracts. This will assist the SPHR in determining when legal counsel is needed. A *contract* is a binding and legally enforceable agreement between two or more people or parties. To be enforceable, the contract must meet the following conditions:

▶ An offer must be made to do something or provide a product or service.

▶ The offer must be voluntarily accepted.

▶ Both parties must give and receive something of value.

▶ Both parties must be competent. They must be of legal age and capable of making sound decisions. A minor cannot enter into a contract, neither can persons who have been declared mentally incompetent, nor persons who are temporarily incompetent; for example, those whose capabilities are impaired by drug or alcohol use.

▶ The contract must be for legal purposes. A contract to kill another person, for example, is not legal and, therefore, not enforceable. Neither is one for the purchase of illegal drugs.

▶ The contract must be in a proper legal form. For example, contracts extending beyond one year, contracts for real estate, and contracts worth a substantial amount of money must be in writing.

If a party fails to live up to the agreement, breach of contract has occurred, which often requires intervention of the court systems. Failure to follow the terms of the contract can result in a judicial order for specific performance, which means that the court orders the violator to live up to the terms of the agreement. The courts might require the violator to pay damages based on costs or lost income caused by the breach of contract. Finally, the court can discharge the nonviolator from any obligations under the contract.

HR and Technology

Technology is having a major impact on the practice of HR and will continue to do so. In this section, we discuss how technology is affecting HR in terms of strategic management, decision-making, employee self-service, productivity, systems security, and outsourcing. In the final section, we discuss the software programs that facilitate all these changes: the Human Resource Information System.

Strategic HR

As discussed earlier, automation of processing and other lower-level HR programmatic work has facilitated the transformation from an administrative emphasis to a strategic emphasis in many organizations. Freed from the burdensome tasks of repetitive processes, HR professionals can now concentrate on becoming a strategic partner in the organization. In addition, as discussed later, technology enhances the ability to make strategic decisions by providing analyzed information and the capability to measure effectiveness through metrics.

Decision-Making

Immense amounts of data are now available to enhance decision-making. Technology permits the establishment of huge databases of relevant information, referred to as data warehouses. Sophisticated HR software systems can access and analyze that data, providing appropriate metrics and statistical analysis that facilitate a rational decision-making process.

Employee Self-Service

Employee self-service improves HR productivity because paper processing in many areas has been replaced with online, real-time processing. Self-service also improves the accuracy and timeliness of service to the employee. The advent of inexpensive, high-powered personal computers, web portals, and wireless networks has increased employee access to computer technology. New internal or outsourced programs allow employees to provide many traditional HR services for themselves. Employees in many organizations can now apply for job promotions or transfers, sign up for benefits, update personal information, input time and attendance information, take training courses, request information, and perform many other tasks online. In many cases, the requested action completes in real-time and the employee receives instant verification.

Technology also improves the amount of information available to the employee. Web portals often provide immediate access to retirement information, health insurance claim processing, and other services provided by outsourced vendors. Internally, employees might be able to access their personnel files and payroll records.

Productivity

Huge increases in productivity have been obtained by using technology. This is particularly true with respect to the traditional HR administrative responsibilities. Payroll, timekeeping, job application and other processes are subject to automation, virtually eliminating the need for employee processing in these areas. Employee self-service has eliminated paperwork and the need for HR staff to process it. Technology permits the transfer of HR-related tasks to the field, improving the internal productivity of the HR function. For example, software programs permit line managers to draft job descriptions, perform job evaluations, and set pay without HR intervention, but with HR oversight. In addition, productivity is enhanced by the use of electronic signatures. This permits the instantaneous processing of HR activities without requiring a physical signature.

Systems Security

This issue is also discussed in Chapter 7, "Occupational Health, Safety, and Security." Technology brings many benefits, but not without a cost in terms of potential exposure of confidential employee data and proprietary organizational information. The combination of increased internal access (particularly with wireless systems) and increased connectivity with the external world compounds the security problems. Systems must have proper password control, firewalls, anti-virus software, and other protections to safeguard organizational systems and data from hackers, destructive unauthorized access, and the infusion of spam. In addition, technology has brought about new issues regarding employee privacy and policy issues with respect to personal use. The issues are compounded if the organization does not internally run the software, but uses application service providers *(ASPs)* that host the hardware and software on their premises.

Outsourcing

Technology enables the outsourcing of many HR programs and enhances the efficiency and effectiveness of such programs. Outsourced applications can be seamlessly accessed by employees via web portals. In addition, outsourcing vendors can have real-time access to the organization's internal computer systems and databases. For example, an outsourced payroll vendor can process the employee wage payment while simultaneously posting that action to the employee database and accounting systems. At the same time, the employee can view his or her own payroll records via the vendor's web portal.

> **EXAM ALERT**
>
> Technology is having a huge effect on the practice of HR. The SPHR should be familiar with this issue. Expect a question.

Human Resource Information System

A *Human Resource Information System (HRIS)* is an integrated computer application that collects, processes, stores and analyzes human resource data to support HR activities. An HRIS might also be called a Human *Resource Management System (HRMS)*. An HRIS improves the efficiency of processing by not only automating many processes, but also by integrating them with other automated systems. For example, the automated recruitment system might send information on a selection to the personnel database, payroll processing system, and financial/accounting systems. The HRIS improves decision-making by providing relevant information to the decision maker. The HRIS frees up staff resources for high-level work and provides statistical analysis and metrics that facilitate the strategic role of HR.

All of this capability comes with a price. We have previously discussed issues with respect to the security and privacy of data, but there are other significant issues associated with implementation and maintenance of an HRIS. The first one is cost. Large integrated systems can run well into seven figures for large organizations. In addition, the cost of capturing data or of transferring data to a new HRIS can be enormous. Maintenance and updating can also be costly, as can initial and recurrent training. Many of the systems are not user friendly, contrary to the claims of the vendors. In those cases, there might be significant inefficiencies while employees learn the new system and become both comfortable and proficient. In addition, employee and manager resistance often hampers system implementation. For example, managers might resist having to input employee performance evaluation ratings into the system if that process is perceived to be cumbersome or difficult. The following are just some of the processes and activities that might be integrated into an HRIS:

- Recruitment
- Applicant tracking
- EEO reporting and complaint tracking
- Grievance tracking
- Payroll, including merit or other increases and variable pay
- Benefits administration
- Time and attendance reporting
- Job analysis

- Job evaluation
- 401(k) or other pension system contribution tracking
- Turnover
- Internal promotions
- Labor scheduling
- Overtime
- Temporary/leased labor usage and cost

EXAM ALERT

sophisticated human resource information systems.

Table 2.4 provides additional explanations of some of the technology-related terms with which the SPHR should be familiar.

TABLE 2.4   Technology-Related Terms

Term	Explanation
Data warehouses	Large databases containing HR and employee information.
Application service providers *(ASPs)*	Firms that host and manage hardware and/or HR software for the organization.
Electronic signatures	Permit the use of digital signatures for processing of HR and other activities without the cumbersome process of having to obtain an actual hand signature.
Web portals	Allow users to access HR programs from a personal computer.
Mobile/wireless nets	Allow access to systems without the costs and restrictions of cabling.
Synchronization systems	Allow cell phones, personal digital assistants, personal computers, and similar equipment to communicate with each other and access web portals.
Service center	A place where HR processing is centralized. It usually yields economies of scale.
Streaming video	Allows training and development programs to be delivered directly to the employee's desktop computer.

The Strategic Planning Process

Objective
Gain an Understanding of the Strategic Planning Process

Strategic planning is the process of making decisions regarding the organization's long-term goals and strategies. The purpose of planning is to match the organization's capabilities to its environment to maximize organizational success and goal achievement. Strategic planning is a process that is circular and iterative. Organizations must continually evaluate the effectiveness of their strategies in an ever-changing environment and adjust as necessary. The strategic planning process can be broken down into several steps. Various authorities use different terminology and varying numbers of steps in the process, but basically describe it very much in the same manner. For our purposes, we will use a four-step strategic planning process. The steps are strategy formulation, development of strategic objectives, strategy implementation, and strategy evaluation. Each is discussed in greater detail in the pages that follow. In this section, we also briefly address the benefits and potential problems associated with strategic planning, along with HR strategic planning.

Strategy Formulation

Strategy formulation is the first step in the strategic planning process. This is where the organization decides what business it is in and what its basic mission and values are. The strategy formulation step involves answering two basic questions: "What is the organization's purpose currently?" and given organizational capabilities in relationship to its environment "Is that purpose viable in the future?" The answer will lead to the development or modification of the organization's vision, mission, and values statements as discussed next. Taken together, the vision, mission, and values statements provide direction for the strategic planning process, guiding decisions regarding the development of appropriate strategic objectives.

Vision Statement

The vision statement describes the organization's desired future state. It is a general statement as to where the organization is headed in the future and what it will look like. Vision statements are broad and designed to evoke an emotional appeal from the various stakeholders, particularly employees. It describes what the organization can become in the future.

Mission Statement

The mission statement describes the fundamental purpose of the organization. It defines why the organization exists, what it does, and where it is headed. Whereas the vision statement is a global statement of some desired future state, the mission statement is more specific and describes the organization's current status, providing additional guidance for developing plans that can be implemented.

Values Statement

The values statement describes the basic beliefs of the organization. These statements help to define the organization and provide guidance as to expected standards of behavior for all organizational members.

Development of Strategic Objectives

In this step, the organization performs an internal and external analysis to translate its mission and vision into strategic goals and develops strategies to achieve those goals. The analytical process is normally referred to as *SWOT* and is discussed next, as are some basic concepts surrounding strategic objectives.

SWOT

SWOT is the acronym for an analytic process that is frequently associated with strategic planning. In fact, it has become the universal explanation for what happens in the strategic planning process. SWOT refers to

- **Strengths**   Internal strengths of the organization
- **Weaknesses**   Internal weaknesses of the organization
- **Opportunities**   Opportunities present in the environment
- **Threats**   Threats present in the environment

The determination of strengths and weaknesses is made through an analysis of the organization internally. This must be an objective review of the organization as it currently exists, including a realistic appraisal of such items as financial resources, technology, human capital, leadership, culture, plant and equipment, quality of product or service, core competencies, brand image, and market share.

Opportunities and threats are in the organization's environment. They are appraised through the process of environmental scanning, which is discussed later in this chapter. An analysis of competitor strategies, economic trends, changes in customer needs and wants, and potential legislative and regulatory action can provide rich information as to what is likely to occur or is occurring in the environment.

EXAM ALERT

Remember the acronym SWOT and concepts associated with it. It is likely to be the subject of a test question.

Strategic Objectives

The SWOT analysis permits strategic planners to evaluate the organization's capabilities, or lack thereof, against environmental trends and conditions. The simple explanation of the process is that it allows the organization to develop strategic objectives that best match the organization's capabilities (strengths) against opportunities in the environment. In practice, it is obviously a bit more complex. Internally, the organization must eliminate or minimize its weaknesses or find a way to turn those weaknesses into strengths. An example might be developing a new use for or dramatically improving an old product. Externally, it must attempt to avoid environmental threats or make them into strengths. Here an example might be acquiring or merging with a competitor or vigorously engaging in lobbying to prevent passage of legislation deemed to be harmful.

Strategic objectives are what the organization plans to achieve in the long-term. *Long-term* might mean different things to different organizations. In stable environments, organizations may be able to develop objectives for five or more years out into the future. Some organizations in extremely volatile environments might not be able to plan strategically at all. In general, strategic objectives cover three to five years in the future. The objectives developed must be in alignment with the vision, mission, and values statements.

After objectives are determined, strategies must be developed to achieve them. A *strategy* is a course of action that directs organizational activities toward achievement of its objectives. The strategy provides direction and guidance as to how the organization plans to get from its current status to the status identified in the objectives. Strategies are formulated at various levels of the organization to guide action and decision-making.

What has been discussed so far is the overall or corporate strategy. But this strategy needs to be translated into more specificity at the operating levels. In large organizations, the next level of strategy formulation might be at the strategic business unit or group level. For example, subsidiaries of a conglomerate might develop individual strategic plans. The next level of development is usually referred to as the *functional strategic plan*. Here, each of the operating functions (operations, marketing, finance, and so on) develops its respective plan. The HR functional strategic planning is discussed further in this chapter. Regardless of the level of strategic planning, the objectives and strategies must be in alignment with those of the organizational entity above it and with the vision, mission, and values of the organization. If not, mixed messages will be transmitted throughout the organization, which will likely result in confusion, dysfunction, and failure to achieve the objectives.

NOTE

The issue of alignment of all strategic plans with the organization's vision, mission, and values is critical.

Strategy Implementation

Strategy implementation is the process by which strategic objectives are achieved. It requires the development of operational plans that are short-term in nature. Operational plans define specific activities to be undertaken, usually in the coming year, to achieve the strategic objectives. It involves such managerial activities as creating action plans, committing resources, and directing and motivating employees. Increasingly organizations are realizing that execution is the key to strategic success. Grand plans poorly executed do not facilitate the achievement of strategic objectives. Successful implementation requires organizational commitment and coordinated effort so that the decisions and activities of all organizational subentities are in alignment with the strategy and are directed toward achieving strategic objectives.

Strategy Evaluation

Strategy evaluation is the process of determining progress toward achievement of the strategic objectives and, if required, taking corrective action. First, progress toward strategic objectives must be evaluated. This can often be measured by completion of action plan milestones or expenditure of resources. Most critical, however, is measurement of organizational performance in relationship to its strategic objectives. This requires metrics, which are discussed later in this chapter.

Traditionally organizations have established objectives, strategies to achieve those objectives, and actions necessary to achieve the strategy. They then have measured performance against action plan milestones at periodic intervals. If the measurements indicated a lack of appropriate progress, the organization then attempted to resolve this by making midcourse corrections. As discussed in Chapter 4, this is known as *single-loop learning*. It often results in escalation of commitment, committing more resources to objectives without reconsidering them. Learning organizations also engage in *double-loop learning*, evaluating not only progress toward the objectives but the objectives themselves, adapting their strategic plans to changes in both internal capabilities and the dynamics of the environment.

> **EXAM ALERT**
>
> You should be familiar with the four-step strategic planning process just described. It will almost certainly be the subject of an exam question.

Advantages and Disadvantages of Strategic Planning

Strategic planning can provide a forceful message throughout the organization as to where the organization is heading, what its priorities are, and what it values. When clearly communicated, it provides guidance for action, commitment to goals, and facilitates cooperation and collaboration. Well-articulated vision, mission, and values statements often contribute to customer loyalty, ease of recruitment, employee retention, and access to resources. The planning process forces the organization, particularly upper management, to be forward-thinking. Research reveals a positive correlation between the quality of planning and organizational success.

However, many organizations do not engage in strategic planning. The reasons for not doing so are many. But most often organizational leaders put the lack of planning down to not having time to do so given the intense pressures of day-to-day management.

Strategic planning, if not done well, however, can be detrimental to organizational success. Plans based on a less-than-thorough understanding of the capabilities of the organization and the nature of the environment will likely result in improper positioning of the organization. Planning is a process, not a project. Plans that are formulated but not continuously reviewed and updated might result in the organization missing opportunities in the environment and pursuing strategies that are no longer viable. Plans and the planning process can create rigidity if they are not flexible. Strategic planning often tends to rely too heavily on assumptions that have proven successful in the past rather than those that might be needed in the future. Finally, many argue that some environments are too turbulent and that strategic planning, with its long-range focus, is wasted effort.

HR Strategic Planning

Traditionally, HR strategic planning has been at the functional level. That is, after the organization's strategic planning process has been completed, it is the responsibility of HR and, for that matter, other functional units to develop strategic plans that support the organization's plan.

The HR strategic planning process itself is virtually the same as the overall organizational strategic planning process. HR must initially determine just what its role is in relation to the organization. This might result in the development of HR's own vision, mission, and values statements that are different from, but aligned with, those of the organization. These statements provide guidance for the rest of the process. Next the HR function performs a SWOT analysis to determine its own internal capabilities and evaluate the current and future conditions in the environment that will affect its ability to accomplish its tasks. HR then develops strategic objectives aligned with the strategic objectives of the organization. The HR strategic objectives are designed to directly support and facilitate the achievement of the organization's overall objectives. Strategies are then developed to achieve the HR objectives. The strategies lead to development of specific programmatic activities that must be implemented, monitored, and controlled. After implementation, progress toward achievement of the HR objectives is monitored and corrections are made as necessary. Evaluations are made at two levels. The first is the extent of accomplishment of the HR objectives. More importantly, evaluations must be made as to the effect of the HR strategy and strategic planning process on the accomplishment of organizational goals.

The process just described is second-tier in nature. It is reactive to the overall organizational strategic plan and does not include the HR function as a strategic partner. However, in many organizations, HR is integrally involved in the strategic formulation process. As the organization's future and success increasingly are integrally intertwined with its human capital, HR must become directly involved in the strategic planning process in a proactive, first-tier manner. In fact, if the differentiation of the organization in the market is to be based on the capabilities of the workforce, the organizational strategic planning process and strategic plan and the HR strategic planning process and strategic plan are effectively one and the same. At this point, HR has earned its much-desired "seat at the table."

EXAM ALERT
Understand the concept of the HR strategic plan being directly aligned with the organizational strategic plan in order to support it. You can expect a question in this area.

Environmental Scanning

Objective:

Gain an Understanding of Environmental Scanning

The environment is composed of institutions, forces, and stakeholders external to the organization that directly or potentially affect its performance, success, and survivability. *Environmental scanning* is the process of collecting and interpreting information to determine conditions, trends, and changes in the environment that might create opportunities or impose threats on the organization. Environmental scanning is integral to the SWOT analysis and the strategic planning process and can be conducted at the organizational or functional level. In this section, we discuss environmental scanning with respect to the HR function. Three issues regarding environmental scanning are discussed. Prior to scanning the environment, we must first understand the components and dimensions of the environment. Next, we determine what actions and processes are included in environmental scanning. Finally, we discuss the uses or outputs of environmental scanning.

Components of the Environment

The environment is composed of a number of factors, or segments, that affect the development of HR strategy and should be included in the environmental scan. Seven factors are discussed: political/legal, global, economic, social, competitive, demographic, and technology.

Political/Legal

Various governmental, legislative, and regulatory bodies at the local, state, and federal level are continually passing new laws or amending old ones and issuing new regulatory requirements. HR must not only be aware of these actions but must also attempt to anticipate future actions of these bodies and, in some cases, attempt to influence those actions.

The courts routinely issue rulings that affect HR. As with laws and regulations, HR not only must be aware of these rulings and their effect now and in the future, but might in some situations be in a position to affect the outcome of court proceedings either by instituting legal proceedings, vigorously defending itself if the organization is the defendant, or by intervening in juridical proceedings if the organization is not a party though the filing of *amicus curiae* (friend of the court) briefs.

Global

In this globalized society, environmental scanning must take in what is occurring around the world. Importation of low-cost products affects the organization's capability to compete in domestic markets; at the same time, opportunities both to export products or services and to take advantage of low-cost labor might present themselves.

The economies of many countries are, to some extent, interdependent. Scanning must reveal what global international economic changes might affect the organization. Changes in political power and legislation in other countries might also affect the strategic planning process of the organization.

International integration, such as the European Union, and trade arrangements, such as NAFTA and GATT, affect the organization's capability to operate both globally and domestically. These organizations and trade agreements are discussed in further detail in Chapter 6, "Employee and Labor Relations."

Economic

The economy affects a number of issues of importance to HR. Overall economic conditions and interest rates affect availability of resources to conduct operations and to implement the strategic plan. Overall economic conditions influence both the availability and cost of labor. Inflation, the overall increase in cost of goods and services over time, affects wage rates and the cost of benefits, particularly health insurance and retirement plans. Several statistics that should be included in the environmental scan are

- **Unemployment rate**   Provides a general indicator of the availability of labor and influence its cost. A high unemployment rate generally indicates good availability of high quality workers at relatively low wages, whereas low unemployment rates have the opposite implication. However, it is the unemployment rates of areas in which the organization has operations and of those types of employees that the organization use that are critical (as opposed to national rates).

- **Consumer price index** *(CPI)*   Measures the change in cost of about 400 goods and services and is used to measure inflation.

- **Gross domestic product** *(GDP)*   The total value of goods and services produced by a country in a given year. It is an overall measure of a country's economic production and standing. Increases in GDP indicate that an economy is growing.

Social

The social environment encompasses societal expectations as to the responsibilities of organizations. Trends and changes in these expectations must be monitored. Such issues as fair treatment for employees, organizational ethics, corporate responsibility, and environmental responsibility, among others, must be monitored because they could affect strategic planning. The issue of an organization's social responsibility is discussed later in this chapter.

Competitive

The organization must know what strategies its competitors are following. This allows the organization to adjust its strategies in compensation, benefits, and other programs. This is often referred to as *competitive intelligence*.

Demographic

Demographic changes in the workforce affect planning in a wide variety of areas. The organization must be able to forecast the availability of workers and their skill levels. In addition, changes in the makeup of the workforce require planning to develop strategies that will attract and retain the type of employees that the organization needs to be successful. Changes in the age, ethnicity, and/or gender of the workforce all affect HR program requirements.

Technology

Scanning the environment for trends and new developments in technology is critical. Technology affects both the way and where work is done. Technology facilitates and, in some cases, permits global operations, outsourcing, and increased customer service and support. Technology influences the skills required to do the job, affecting recruitment and training programs.

EXAM ALERT

The SPHR should know the components of the environment that must be monitored and be able to discuss their effect on strategic planning. Expect to be tested on this knowledge.

Environmental Scanning Process

Environmental scanning might be very simplistic, very sophisticated, or somewhere in between. In small organizations, environmental scanning could comprise of talking to customers, suppliers, competitors, and reading the local newspaper. Leaders in many small organizations engage in environmental scanning without knowing they are doing so. Large organizations might devote substantial resources to environmental scanning and could have a separate department devoted exclusively to the process. Also, there are a number of consulting firms that specialize exclusively in providing this service on a contract basis. Small organizational leaders might analyze the data in their heads, whereas large organizations might have sophisticated data warehouses and analytical software to accomplish the same task. The Internet has had a profound effect on environmental scanning, making large amounts of external data immediately available.

Sources of relevant environmental scanning data are limited only by the creativity and resourcefulness of those engaged in doing it. Common sources of information are

- ▶ Customers.
- ▶ Suppliers.
- ▶ Employees. One of the best sources. Employees are often those who interact the most with the environment.
- ▶ Media. TV, radio, newspapers, magazines, and so on.
- ▶ Internet. Competitor websites, governmental databases, online research, and so on.
- ▶ Professional organizations and their publications.
- ▶ Professional, trade, and academic journals.
- ▶ Internal data and statistics.

- ▶ Competitor advertising, annual reports, publications, and so on.
- ▶ Tradeshows.
- ▶ Governmental reports and governmental databases.

Environmental Scanning Outcomes

The data collected from the environment must be analyzed and put into some form that can be used by those engaged in strategic planning. Common outcomes of the scanning process are forecasts, competitive intelligence, scenarios, and benchmarks. Each is discussed in the following sections.

Forecasts

Forecasts are predictions as to how a particular measure will change in the future. Common forecasts are revenue, sales, profit, staffing requirements, benefit costs, skills needed, and changes in technology. Forecasts provide valuable input into the strategic planning process.

Forecasts are often developed from historical data and analysis of trends in that data. For example, if revenue has been increasing at the rate of 5% for the last several years, a forecast can be based on that data. However, such forecasts are accurate only to the extent that the environmental factors stay relatively stable.

Competitive Intelligence

Competitive intelligence is information about competitors that enables the organization to adjust its strategies to compete in the environment. Competitive intelligence provides information on who the organization's current and potential competitors are, what strategies they are currently pursuing or are likely to pursue, and how those strategies are likely to affect the competitiveness of the organization.

Scenario

A *scenario* is a general description of what the future is likely to be. As strategic planners contemplate the future, they often take environmental scanning information and combine it in different ways using a variety of assumptions. In this way, alternative scenarios are developed that describe various views of the future. This facilitates two processes: the development of strategic plans under the most likely scenario and the development of contingency plans for the alternative scenarios.

Benchmarking

Benchmarking is the process of comparing the organization's operations against those of other organizations. Environmental scans might reveal best practices that are a source of competitive advantage for other organizations. In that case, the organization examines its practices in relation to the best practices to determine the need for change.

Understanding the Organization

Objective:
Gain an Understanding of Organizations

To operate at the strategic level, the HR function must form partnerships with the various parts of the organization. But to do so requires an understanding of the mission, language, culture, work processes, and technology of these various entities. In addition, the SPHR must understand how these various departments or organizational subparts come together to create a functioning whole and how various organizational designs support various strategies. This section discusses both the functions of the individual units of an organization and also the concepts associated with an organization as an entire entity.

Functions of an Organization

Most organizations, whether for-profit or not-for-profit, have common organizational functions. All provide a service or product and, thus, must manage their operations. All need some sort of finance and accounting function to manage money and resources. All need to gain access to resources, whether that is through sales and marketing or through some sort of development office. Finally, in this rapidly evolving digitized world, organizations are becoming increasingly dependent on the ability to manage data, information, and knowledge through technology systems. Each of the functions is discussed in the following sections.

Operations Management

Operations management is a relatively new term that has evolved from production management. It better describes the function in an environment in which knowledge and services, rather than products, are the core competencies of the organization. It can be defined as the planning and analysis of those activities by which the organization transforms its inputs to outputs. The output might be a product, service, or knowledge. Increasingly it is a combination of all three. Operations management includes such activities as production scheduling, quality control, purchasing, and inventory and supply management. Some of the concepts associated with operations management in today's world are

▶ **Facility location and layout**   The selection of geographic location and physical design that best facilitates the achievement of customer satisfaction and organizational goals.

- **Process planning**   Designing internal processes to produce the organization's goods, services, or knowledge.

- **Total quality management**   A comprehensive approach to achieving customer satisfaction though the process of continuous improvement. The process involves statistical controls on quality, employee involvement in quality improvement, and an organizational culture that is customer-oriented.

- **ISO certification**   Certification by the International Organization for Standardization that the organization's processes meet certain standards designed to ensure product or service quality and/or protect the environment.

- **Mass customization**   Applies to all industry sectors and uses technology to incorporate the efficiencies of mass production yet customize the product, service, or provision of knowledge to the customer's exact needs.

- **Lean manufacturing**   Programs designed to achieve maximum quality and productivity by eliminating unnecessary steps, minimizing inventory, engaging in just-in-time production and supply, and using teams or cells.

Financial Management

Financial information is critical to the organization. Resources are the organization's lifeblood and accounting has been called "the language of business." Those responsible for managing resources must be accountable for efficient and effective usage. *Financial management* is those activities designed to account for and control the organization's resources so that it can achieve its goals and objectives. Two important processes associated with financial management are accounting and budgeting.

Accounting

Accounting is the process of collecting, recording, summarizing, and analyzing financial data. Accounting includes several specialized areas:

- **Financial accounting**   Analysis of financial data, largely for regulatory and external use. Financial accountants prepare such documents as the balance sheet and income statement.

- **Tax accounting**   Preparation of required tax forms and documents. Tax accountants also analyze the tax implications of potential managerial actions and develop organizational tax strategies.

- **Managerial accounting**   Provides financial data for internal use in decision-making, such as production costs, sales costs, and marketing costs.

▶ **Auditing**   Comprises two related processes, both of which review the accuracy of internal accounting practices:

   ▶ **Internal auditing**   Internal review of the accuracy and usefulness of financial data for the purpose of evaluating the organization's operations and making recommendations for improvement.

   ▶ **External auditing**   Typically performed by an external accounting firm, it provides an independent evaluation of the accuracy of the organization's financial statements.

NOTE

In the aftermath of the Enron accounting scandal, among others, the Sarbanes-Oxley Act of 2002 created the Public Company Accounting Oversight Board *(PCAOB)*. The PCAOB oversees auditors of public companies to protect the interests of investors and further the public interest in the preparation of informative, fair, and independent audit reports.

Accounting systems produce a number of reports that are used to determine the financial health of the organization. The SPHR should have a basic understanding of the fundamental accounting equation, balance sheet, income statement, statement of cash flows, and commonly used financial ratios.

NOTE

The Financial Accounting Standards Board *(FASB)* is a private entity that derives its authority from the federal Securities and Exchange Commission. The FASB issues rules, which are to be followed by the accounting profession, regarding how certain transactions are to be recorded and how financial information is to be reported to stockholders and the public. FASB rules particularly affect the practice of HR in the area of compensation and benefits.

The Fundamental Accounting Equation

The fundamental accounting equation is the basis for the balance sheet. The equation is

   Assets = Liabilities + Owners' Equity

Assets are economic resources owned by the organization. Assets can be tangible, such as cash and buildings, or intangible, such as goodwill. Some assets are referred to as *fixed*, such as buildings. These assets are relatively permanent and might take a period of time to turn into cash should the need arise. Other assets, such as accounts receivable and cash, are referred to as *current* assets. They are cash or assets that can be converted to cash in a short period of time, such as notes receivable.

Liabilities are financial obligations of the organization. They include such items as accounts payable, notes payable, and bonds payable. Obligations that are due in less than a year are current liabilities, whereas those with due dates in excess of a year are long-term liabilities.

Owners' equity is the difference between the assets and liabilities of the organization and represents the value of what is owned by the owners. If stockholders own the organization, this is called *stockholders' equity*; if owned by partners, it is called *partners' equity*.

EXAM ALERT

You should memorize this simple formula and know that it is the basis for preparation of the balance sheet.

Balance Sheet

The *balance sheet* is a financial statement that reports the organization's financial condition at a certain date and is a measure of the organization's overall financial health. It is called a balance sheet because it uses the fundamental accounting equation as its basis and, as indicated earlier, assets must equal the summation of liabilities plus owners' equity. Table 2.5 is a balance sheet for ABC Corporation, reporting its financial condition as of December 31, 20__. Because it is a corporation, the owners' equity is reported as stockholders' equity.

TABLE 2.5   Sample Balance Sheet

ABC Corporation Balance Sheet December 31, 20__			
Assets			
Current Assets			
Cash		$ 10,000	
Accounts Receivable		20,000	
Inventory		120,000	
Total Current Assets			$150,000
Fixed Assets			
Land		$100,000	
Buildings	$200,000		
Less Accumulated Depreciation	−50,000		
		150,000	
Furniture and Fixtures	100,000		
Less Accumulated Depreciation	75,000		
		25,000	

TABLE 2.5 *Continued*

ABC Corporation Balance Sheet December 31, 20__			
Equipment and Vehicles	300,000		
Less Accumulated Depreciation	175,000		
		125,000	
Total Fixed Assets			500,000
Intangible Assets			
Goodwill		$ 20,000	
Total Intangible Assets			20,000
Total Assets			$670,000
Liabilities and Owners' Equity			
Liabilities			
Current Liabilities			
Accounts Payable		$ 50,000	
Notes Payable		50,000	
Wages Payable		25,000	
Taxes Payable		5,000	
Total Current Liabilities			$180,000
Long-term Liabilities			
Notes Payable (Due March, 2010)		390,000	
Total Long-term Liabilities			390,000
Total Liabilities			$570,000
Stockholders' Equity			
Common Stock (50,000 Shares)		$ 50,000	
Retained Earnings		$ 50,000	
Total Stockholders' Equity			$100,000
Total Liabilities & Stockholders Equity			$670,000

Income Statement

The income statement is used to show profit or loss for a particular period of time, usually a quarter or fiscal or calendar year. The *income statement* summarizes all revenue coming into the organization and expenses going out, which result in a net income or net loss. Several formulae are used in the preparation of the statement:

Gross Margin = Revenue – Cost of Goods Sold (or Manufactured)

Net Income Before Taxes = Gross Margin – Operating Expenses

Net Income After Taxes = Net Income Before Taxes – Taxes

Table 2.6 is an example of a simple income statement for ABC, Inc. Note that the firm made a net profit after taxes of $190,000 on sales of $800,000.

TABLE 2.6 Sample Income Statement

ABC, Inc. Income Statement For the Year Ended December 31, 20__			
Revenues			
Cash		$ 10,000	
Gross Sales		$820,000	
Less: Sales Returns and Allowances	$ 25,000		
Sales Discounts	5,000	–30,000	
Net Sales			$800,000
Cost of Goods Sold			
Beginning Inventory, January 1, 20__		$200,000	
Merchandise Purchased	$400,000		
Freight	20,000		
Net Purchases		420,000	
Cost of Goods Available for Sale	$620,000		
Ending Inventory, December 31, 20__		–300,000	
Cost of Goods Sold			–320,000
Gross Margin			$480,000

TABLE 2.6 *Continued*

ABC, Inc. Income Statement For the Year Ended December 31, 20__			
Operating Expenses			
Selling Expenses			
Salaries	$100,000		
Advertising	45,000		
Supplies	5,000		
Total Selling Expenses		$150,000	
General Expenses			
Administrative Salaries	$100,000		
Insurance	10,000		
Rent	30,000		
Utilities	10,000		
Total General Expenses		100,000	
Total Operating Expenses			250,000
Net Income Before Taxes			$230,000
Less Income Tax Expense			40,000
Net Income After Taxes			$190,000

Statement of Cash Flows

The *statement of cash flows* reports all cash receipts and disbursements during a specified period. Cash flow is critical to a business. The income statement can show a profit based on sales and expenses, but the money from the sales must actually be collected and turned into cash. An organization can show a profit but have insufficient funds to pay its bills, potentially causing bankruptcy or discontinuation of operations. This could occur if the organization extended credit to its customers and then was unable to collect accounts or notes receivable in a timely manner. The organization might then be forced to borrow funds to pay its own accounts payable. If the cycle continued long enough, the organization's credit limit could be reached and its source of funds cut off by its own creditors, resulting in an inability to pay its obligations even though the income statement reported high sales and profits. The statement of cash flows for ABC, Inc. is shown in Table 2.7. Note that cash flow is positive and that the cash balance has increased during the year of the report.

TABLE 2.7 Sample Statement of Cash Flows

ABC, Inc. Statement of Cash Flows For the Year Ended December 31, 20__		
Cash Flows from Operating Activities		
Cash Received from Customers	$250,000	
Cash Paid to Suppliers and Employees	−150,000	
Interest Paid	−10,000	
Income Tax Paid	−40,000	
Interest Received	0	
Net Cash from Operating Activities		$ 50,000
Cash Flows from Investing Activities		
Proceeds from Sale of Vehicles	$ 50,000	
Payments for Purchase of Vehicles	−45,000	
Net Cash from Investing Activities		$5,000
Cash Flows from Financing Activities		
Proceeds from Issuance of Short-term Note	$ 25,000	
Payment of Dividends to Stockholders	−50,000	
Net Cash from Financing Activities		$−25,000
Net Change in Cash		$30,000
Cash Balance December 31, 20__ (Prior Year)		$5,000
Cash Balance December 31, 20__ (Current Year)		$ 35,000

EXAM ALERT

You should be familiar with what the balance sheet, income statement, and statement of cash flows each tells us about the financial condition of the organization. Remember, an organization can be profitable but still not survive if it doesn't have adequate cash flow or sources of credit.

Financial Ratios

An in-depth discussion of ratios is beyond the scope of this text. However, a basic understanding of the concept of some of the more common ratios will give the SPHR some familiarity with ratios and how they can be used to better understand the financial performance of the organization. *Financial ratios* are statistical measures used to evaluate the financial performance of the organization, especially in relationship to other organizations in its particular industry. Common ratios are business activity, profitability, debt, and liquidity. They are briefly discussed in the sections that follow. Often, it is not the absolute value of the ratio that is important, it is the value of the ratio in comparison with industry averages. For example, some industries are less profitable that others. A low value in relation to the average of all industries is not particularly important, but a low value in relation to the average for the organization's particular industry would be reason for further analysis.

▸ **Business activity** Business activity ratios measure the organization's efficiency in using its assets. The inventory turnover ratio is an example. The firm wants to balance sales performance with adequate availability of inventory to satisfy customer demand. Low turnover ratios might indicate poor purchasing practices, resulting in inventory that the customer does not value. However, high turnover ratios might indicate lack of product availability and the potential for lost sales. Inventory turnover ratio is calculated as follows:

Inventory Turnover Ratio = Cost of Goods Sold / Average Inventory

▸ **Profitability** Profitability ratios measure the effectiveness of the organization in turning resources into profits. Common profitability ratios are earnings per share, earnings per diluted share, return on sales, and return on equity. The difference between the first two ratios is that the earnings per diluted share includes not only current common stock outstanding but also various instruments that could be turned into common stock, such as convertible preferred stock and stock options. This gives a truer picture of profitability in an era in which executives, particularly the CEO, are given lucrative equity-based compensation packages. Rather than provide the calculation for all the ratios, return on equity is used as a sample equation. It measures profitability as a percentage of the owners' investment in the organization.

Return on Equity = Net Income After Taxes / Owners' Equity

▸ **Debt** Debt ratios, also called *leverage ratios*, measure the extent to which the organization relies on borrowed money. The debt of owners' equity ratio is frequently used. A ratio above 1 indicates that the organization has more debt than equity (a not uncommon condition in growing organizations and organizations in some industries). This ratio is calculated as shown here:

Debt of Owners' Equity = Total Liabilities / Owners' Equity

▸ **Liquidity** *Liquidity* is a measure of how quickly the organization is turning assets into cash. Recall from the discussion on the statement of cash flows that an organization could have high income, but not be able to turn that income into cash to pay its obligations. There are two important and commonly used liquidity ratios: current ratio and acid test ratio. Both are used to evaluate the capability of the organization to pay its short-term debts (those that are coming due within a year).

▶ **Current Ratio**   The *current ratio* evaluates the organization's current assets in relationship to its current liabilities. The higher the current ratio, the more credit worthy an organization is and the more likely financial institutions will be willing to loan it money. The formula for current ratio is

> Current Ratio = Current Assets / Current Liabilities

▶ **Acid-Test Ratio**   The acid-test is another measure of the organization's ability to pay its short-term debts, but takes the organization's current inventory of product or goods for sale out of the calculation. This might provide a better indicator of actual capability to pay if the inventory is of a type that would be difficult to quickly turn into cash. The formula is

> Acid-test ratio = (cash + marketable securities + receivables) / current liabilities

---

NOTE

Information needed to prepare financial ratios is available on the balance sheet or can be computed from information listed on the balance sheet.

Budgeting

Budgeting is the process of estimating revenues and allocating them for specific purposes. After they're established, budgets become financial control devices through monitoring budget execution and any difference between budgeted and actual expenditures. There are a wide variety of budget types (cash budget, sales budget, master budget, and project budget, for example). However, the development process to create any of the budgets tends to follow one of the methodologies discussed here:

▶ **Incremental budgeting**   This is the traditional way of developing a budget and involves using the previous budget as a base or reference point. The new budget is then developed by adjusting individual budget items either upward or downward. This type of budget is easier to develop than other types, but it assumes that all budget items continue to be valid needs, and this might not be correct.

▶ **Formula budgeting**   This is actually a type of incremental budgeting in which a specific percentage increase (or, less likely, decrease) is applied to the whole budget. Again, the assumption is that all budgeted items in the past budget are still valid.

▶ **Zero-based budgeting**   This method involves developing the entire budget from scratch. Each budget item must be justified during each cycle. The advantage to this type of budgeting is that each budget item is specifically addressed in terms of its value to the organization. The disadvantage, particularly with large budgets, is that it is very time-consuming.

▶ **Activity-based budgeting**   Rather than allocating resources to organizational functions or departments, this method allocates funds to processes or projects. Activity-based budgeting better links resources to organizational goals, but it becomes a bit cumbersome when allocating overhead costs. For example, a decision must be made as to how to allocate utility expenses among multiple processes.

Regardless of the method used, the budget can be developed in one of two ways: bottom-up or top-down. The bottom-up methods requires all levels of the organization to develop estimates for resources and, in some cases, revenue. These estimates are then aggregated into a budget. This process tends to develop better commitment to executing the budget as developed, but it might miss identifying critical organizational needs that cross functional boundaries. It also tends to take longer than the top-down process. The top-down process is just the opposite, with top management developing and executing the budget. The advantage here is that it is a quicker process and might better link the budget with organizational goals. The disadvantage is that top management often is not aware of valid resource needs at the lower levels of the organization.

EXAM ALERT

You should expect a question regarding the various types of budgeting methods.

Sales and Marketing

Marketing is the process of developing, pricing, promoting, and distributing products, services, and knowledge that satisfy customer needs while facilitating the achievement of organizational goals. Sales are the outcome of marketing and result in the transfer of ownership or usage of the product, service, or knowledge. Sales are a part of the promotion component of marketing.

The marketing strategy must support the strategic goals of the organization. Successful marketing involves identification of customer needs and wants. Customers will not purchase an outstanding product, elegant in design and functionality, if it does not fill a perceived need. Rather than produce products or services that the organization thinks the customer will value, many organizations engage in extensive marketing research to determine customer needs and wants. This practice has led to what is called the *marketing concept*. According to this concept, the organization should attempt to engage in a mutually satisfying relationship with the customer, simultaneously solving customer needs and wants while achieving organizational goals.

Successful marketing involves determining the correct marketing mix for targeted customers (called *market segment*). The marketing mix is the appropriate combination of the four elements of marketing (discussed next) for the particular market segment. Because organizations might have multiple targeted market segments and because the marketing environment is often dynamic and volatile, marketing mixes have to be customized for each market segment and frequently adjusted as the environment changes. The four elements of marketing that make up the marketing mix are often characterized as the four "P's" and are discussed next.

Product

A *product* can be a good, service, or idea (knowledge). Products must serve a perceived need or want based on market research. The product element includes development of the product, determination of its potential profitability, determination of the product mix that the organization is going to market, testing of the product concept to determine customer demand, building in product differentiation to set it apart from other similar products, and product packaging and labeling, among many other activities.

Place

Placement is used to make the element a "P," but *distribution* is more descriptive. A product must be available to customers, when, where, and how they want it. Place activities include selecting the correct marketing channel (wholesale, retail, Internet, and so on) and distribution network.

Promotion

Promotion informs potential customers about the product and the organization. It can promote product demand, increase public awareness of the product, and create and maintain the organization's public image. Promotion includes advertising, public relations, personal selling, and sales promotion.

Pricing

Pricing, as the title suggests, involves strategic decisions regarding product price in relationship to organizational goals. This involves analyses of the relationship among market demand, price, and profitability and a determination of the method of setting product price. Although the strategy of determining product price is beyond the scope of this book, price is set to obtain certain objectives. For example, product price would be different if the objective were to maximize market share as opposed to maximizing profit.

> **EXAM ALERT**
>
> The four P's are always a good test question area.

Information Technology

Information technology is the computer systems that improve work processes, communication, and decision-making. Initial applications of computers in the workplace were used to automate routine processes including transmission of information. Today, information technology is transforming how the organization achieves its goals. It has become a strategic rather than a tactical tool. The Internet and intranets allow organizations to conduct their activities free of the constraints of time and place. Information technology allows for instant communication and information transfer. Increasingly, information technology is being replaced by knowledge technology, which places analyzed and relevant information (knowledge) at the disposal of organizational members when they need it. This technology must be planned and managed effectively by the organization, typically by an information technology (or knowledge management) department, so that technology strategies are in alignment with and support the achievement of organizational goals.

Organizational Design

Form must follow function. The proper organizational design facilitates the effective and efficient operation of the organization and enhances goal achievement. *Organizational design* can be defined as the process of determining the appropriate organizational structure based on organizational goals and culture. In this section, we discuss organizational structure and organizational designs, or models, using the various structural elements in different ways. Then we discuss several organizational strategies and their implication for organizational design. First, however, we briefly discuss the building blocks of an organization, its people, and the concept of an organizational lifecycle.

People

Just as organizational design is dictated by organizational strategy, so too is the composition of the workforce. The ability of the people and their commitment to organizational goals are critical for organizational success. The concept of human capital is fully explored in Chapter 4, but needs to be touched on briefly here in the context of organizational design.

Organizational design and human capital are interdependent activities. The capabilities of organizational members can be tapped to their fullest extent only if the organizational structure is designed to do so. Inversely, a particular organizational design will not achieve its goals if the wrong people are placed in that structure. These concepts will be explored further in this section. However, a quick example might be appropriate. The organization wants to explore a strategy of innovation and creativity. What are the implications for alignment of people and structure? First, we know that organic structures (discussed later in this section) facilitate organizational creativity and innovation. Organic organizational models include team-based designs, empowerment, and the free flow of information both vertically and laterally throughout the organization. To be effective, this organizational design requires human capital with decision-making and interpersonal skills that like to work in a decentralized environment with little managerial direction.

Organizational Lifecycle

Organizations tend to follow a predictable lifecycle; one that is similar to living organisms. The organizational design for one lifecycle might not be appropriate for another. In fact, organizational structure changes might be appropriate even within the same stage of the lifecycle. If organizations follow a somewhat predictable lifecycle, why have some organizations been around for hundreds of years? The answer is quite simple: Organizations can renew themselves. An organization can change its mission, product, or service, often starting the lifecycle over again. The organizational lifecycle is often described in terms of these four stages:

▶ **Introduction** The organization is simple and flat, following the guidance of the founder. Rules are few and policies and procedures minimal. Organizational goals are often centered on surviving and growing. Cash flow and access to resources might be minimal. Employee compensation is often low, but supported with equity provisions designed to increase commitment and performance.

▶ **Growth** The organization expands in terms of market share, employee population, plant and equipment, and (hopefully) profitability. The objectives are often to maximize market share and profitability. Because of the growth, there is need to begin formalization of the organization through the development of policies and procedures. Job responsibilities are codified and incentive plans are increasingly designed to encourage efficiency of operations.

▶ **Maturity** The organization reaches its maximum size. Revenue is often at maximum, but profitability may be declining because of increased internal costs of hierarchy and increased competition. The organization often becomes bureaucratic and somewhat inflexible and less adaptive to the environment. The organization might lose touch with the environment and changes that are occurring in the market. Compensation systems become fixed and often follow an entitlement philosophy. Incentives tend to be short-term in nature, and based on achieving cost savings or productivity increases.

▶ **Decline** The organization has become uncompetitive in the market. The structure has become highly formalized and centralized with rigid departmentalization, poor lateral communications, and an incapability to change. Compensation systems tend to become fixed in order to control costs. At this point, if organizational leadership is unable to turn the organization around through significant cultural or mission changes, the organization will fail or continue to grow smaller. In that case, significant employee layoffs are likely to occur and profitability cannot be sustained.

Organizational Structure

The organizational structure is composed of six elements that together define how the organization functions. The elements are job specialization, formalization, departmentation, chain of command, span of control, and centralization. Each is discussed in the following sections.

Job Specialization

Job specialization, also referred to as *division of labor*, is the extent to which work is broken down into its component parts with each part being the primary task assignment of a separate job. The concept of job specialization is based on Taylor's principles of scientific management. The more the tasks are separated and assigned to separate jobs, the greater the specialization and, under many circumstances, the greater the productivity because workers become very proficient at doing rather simple repetitive tasks. However, as discussed in Chapter 4, simplified jobs tend to lead to job dissatisfaction. There are diseconomies of simplification where the job becomes too boring and production increases based on increased simplification tend to level off or decline.

Formalization

Formalization is the extent to which work assignments in an organization are standardized. The formalization process is implemented through tightly written job descriptions, policies, and standard operating procedures. In a highly formalized structure, employee discretion in the performance of the job is kept to a minimum. Formalization facilitates centralization in that many decisions are already made and codified in the policies and procedures. Thus, important decisions can flow to the top. Formalization limits flexibility, however. In dynamic environments, formalized policies and procedures prevent the organization from adapting and prevent employees from undertaking activities customized to the needs of the organization's customers.

Departmentation

Departmentation, also referred to as *departmentalization*, is the framework by which jobs are grouped in the organization. There are three common ways of grouping jobs: function, division, and matrix. Each has its own advantages and disadvantages.

Function

Departmentation by functions performed is the most common and traditional way of grouping jobs. Typical functions are human resources, finance, accounting, production, research and development, engineering, and so on. There are several good reasons for creating a structure in which all jobs performing similar work are placed in the same organizational unit. When many similar jobs are grouped together, there is a potential for efficiency because of economies of scale. This type of grouping also might lead to effectiveness because, with many jobs grouped together, specialist positions can be created that facilitate the development of a high degree of expertise. There is a problem, however, with departmentation by function. Such an organizational structure tends to create loyalty to the function instead of accountability for achieving the organization's goals. In addition, communication across functions tends to be stifled. Figure 2.3a is an example of a functional organizational structure. In this case, the organization has four functions: marketing, production, administration, and finance. All marketing employees are assigned to the marketing function, all production employees to the production function, and so forth.

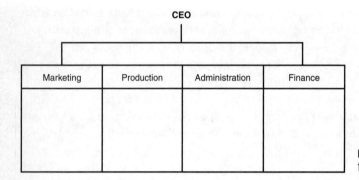

FIGURE 2.3a Departmentation by function.

Division

Departmentation by function is not the only option. The organization can elect to departmentalize by division. Divisional departmentation can be done is several ways: product, process, geography, customer, or some other system. Product departmentation is done by product or product line (for example: washers and dryers, refrigerators, stoves, and vacuum cleaners). Geography departmentation is typically done by dividing the service market up into segments (for example: northeast states, mid-Atlantic states, southern states, and western states). Process departmentation is done by the type of work or work process being done (for example: logging operations, sawmill operations, finished lumber operations, and retail operations). Customer departmentation structures the organization around the type of customer (for example: retail customers, business customers, and governmental customers). Figure 2.3b is an example of departmentation by division. The divisional structure overcomes some of the obstacles of departmentation by function, but creates others. Departmentation by division creates accountability to organizational outcomes and goals. It encourages cross-functional communication and cooperation because representatives of all functions are located in the same organizational subentity. However, this type of departmentation dilutes the amount of expertise that is available and limits the ability to create efficiency through economies of scale, often creating duplication of activities and associated increases in costs across the divisions.

Matrix

The matrix structure is a combination of departmentation by function and departmentation by division. Figure 2.3c illustrates a matrix departmentation structure using the same functions that were used in the preceding discussion. In a matrix organization, jobs are assigned to both the function and the division. Employees have two supervisors. The advantages of such a structure are those of both the functional and divisional structures. Grouping all jobs performing similar functions creates the potential for economy of scale efficiencies and facilitates the development of expertise. Grouping jobs supporting a division creates accountability and commitment and facilitates cross-functional communication and support. However, the matrix has certain disadvantages. It creates confusion and violates the unity of command principle (discussed in the next session) because employees must be responsive to more than one supervisor. Another disadvantage is that a matrix organization can often cause turf battles and conflicts between the function and the division regarding assignment of work and resources.

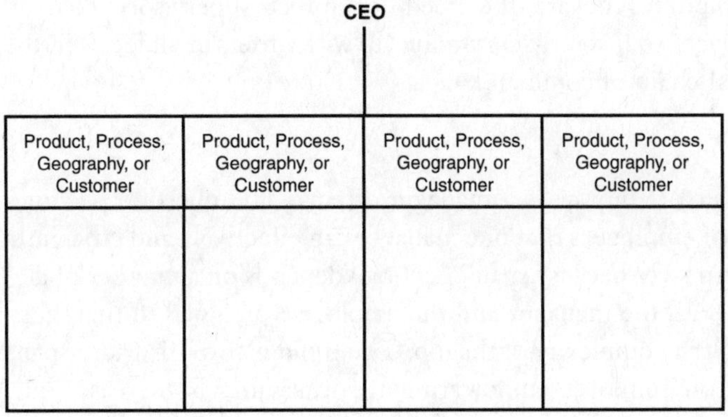

CEO

Product, Process, Geography, or Customer	Product, Process, Geography, or Customer	Product, Process, Geography, or Customer	Product, Process, Geography, or Customer

FIGURE 2.3b Departmentation by division.

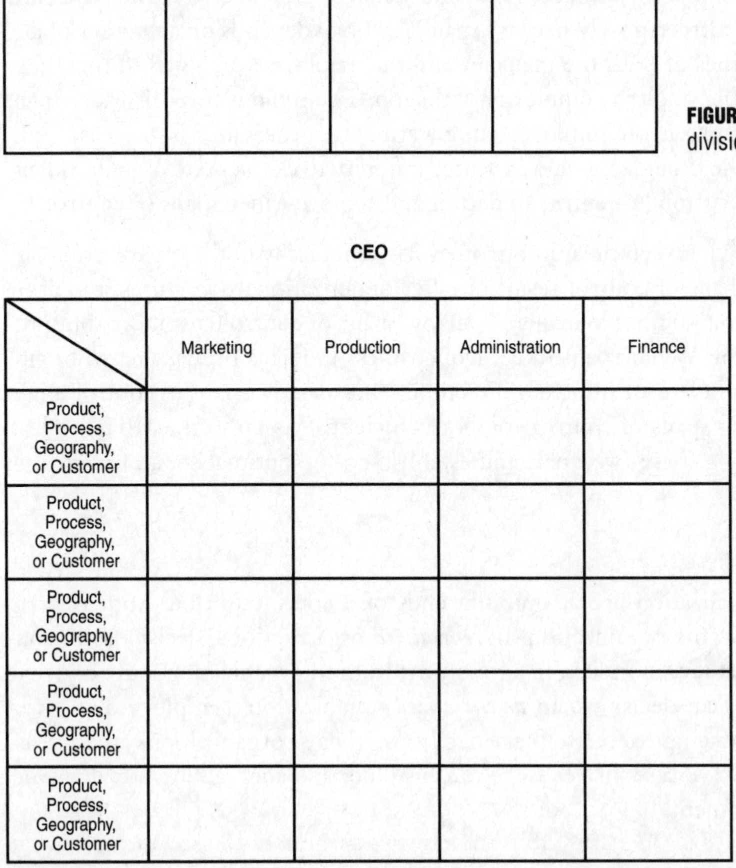

CEO

	Marketing	Production	Administration	Finance
Product, Process, Geography, or Customer				
Product, Process, Geography, or Customer				
Product, Process, Geography, or Customer				
Product, Process, Geography, or Customer				
Product, Process, Geography, or Customer				

FIGURE 2.3c Matrix structure.

Chain of Command

Chain of command is the hierarchical arrangement of authority. This authority flows from the highest executive to the lowest employee in an unbroken line. The chain of command defines who reports to whom. *Authority* is the right of superiors to give orders to those below them in the chain of command and expect that those orders be carried out. Incorporated in chain of command is the principle of unity of command, which states that each employee has only one person to whom he or she reports. The matrix structure violates the unity of command principle as discussed earlier. However, neither the chain of command nor the unity of command concept no longer necessarily reflects the reality of organizational structure. Empowerment and increased use of teams sometimes negate the need for direct supervisory control. Technology advances allow employees to instantly communicate with others at all levels in the hierarchy without using the formal chain of command.

Span of Control

Span of control refers to the number of employees a manager directs. The question becomes "What is the limit on the number of employees that one manager can effectively and efficiently manage?" There is no one correct answer because span of control depends on a number of factors, including the capabilities of both the manager and the employees assigned to that manager, the technology available, and the complexity of the job. The trend is towards wider spans of control. The current emphasis on employee empowerment, cost savings to increase competitiveness, flattening of the organizational structure, and initiatives to create organic, adaptable organizations that are customer-centric all permit and require wider spans of control.

There is a direct correlation between the number of levels of hierarchy in the organization and span of control. Narrow spans of control result in taller organizational structures, requiring more levels of management and more managers. Narrow spans of control cost more, but provide more direct supervision. Wider spans of control cost less in terms of management compensation, but might result in lack of sufficient direction. Thus narrow spans of control might be more effective, but wider spans of control are more efficient. It is up to the SPHR to lead the organization in balancing these two goals and establishing the optimal span of control in each organizational unit.

Centralization

Centralization and decentralization are at opposite ends of a continuum, but both refer to where decisions are made in the organization. In *centralized* organizations, decisions are concentrated at the very highest levels. In fact, in a totally centralized organization, only one person has the authority to make decisions. In *decentralized* organizations, employees at lower levels of the organization are empowered to make decisions. Today's organizations are increasingly decentralizing to improve responsiveness to the customer and adaptability to a dynamic, volatile market and environment.

Organizational Models

Elements of the organizational structure can be combined in a variety of ways to create organizational models possessing a variety of characteristics. There is nothing inherently good or bad, functional or dysfunctional about these models. They are appropriate if they permit the organization to achieve its goals in an effective and efficient manner. Keep in mind that organizations can be designed in an infinite variety of ways and the description of each model usually represents one end of a continuum. Furthermore, one organization might have characteristics of more than one of the models discussed in the following sections. The simple structure, bureaucracy, virtual organization, boundaryless organization, mechanistic organization, organic organization, and concentrated structures are discussed next.

Simple Structure

The simple structure, depicted in Figure 2.4a, is characteristic of small organizations and of many organizations at the introduction phase of their lifecycle. Simple structures typically are not departmentalized, spans of control are wide, the chain of command is simplistic with few levels or hierarchy, formalization is virtually nonexistent, jobs responsibilities are fluid, and decision-making is centralized. The structure is flat and is both efficient and effective for relatively small organizations.

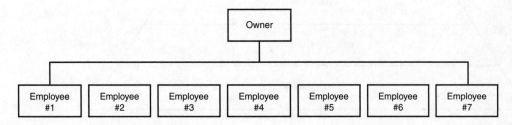

FIGURE 2.4A Simple structure.

However, this structure quickly becomes dysfunctional as the organization grows. Without the guidance of the procedures and policies of formalization, all information and requirements for decisions flow to the centralized top. This slows down operations because all levels must wait for the decision to flow back down the organization so that action can be taken.

Furthermore, this type of model does not permit empowerment and does not facilitate employee growth. The success of the organization is based on the capabilities of the founder or entrepreneur. If something happens to that individual, the organization might not be able to survive. At some point, successful founders and entrepreneurs come to the realization that they can no longer do it all and that the structure must be modified for the organization to continue to grow and be successful.

Bureaucracy

The bureaucracy model, depicted in Figure 2.4b, is characteristic of many large organizations, including governmental entities. Bureaucracies are characterized by a high degree of job specialization, highly formalized procedures and policies, centralization, rigid departmentation (usually by function), small spans of control, and multiple levels of hierarchy. Bureaucracies can be described as pyramidal organizational structures.

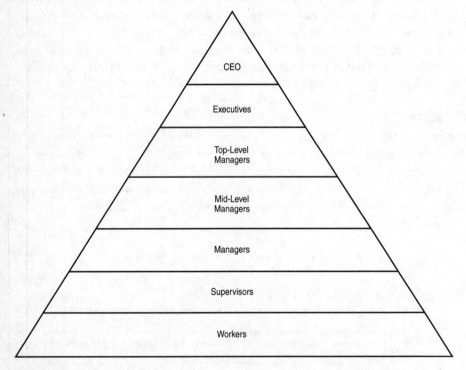

FIGURE 2.4b Bureaucracy model.

The terms *bureaucracy* and *bureaucratic* are often used in a pejorative sense, but not all bureaucracies are inefficient and ineffective. Bureaucracies are very efficient in providing products or services when the work is repetitive and the environment is relatively stable. Because of a high degree of job specialization, bureaucracies develop high levels of expert knowledge in relatively narrow areas. Because many similar jobs are grouped together, bureaucracies are often able to attain significant economies of scale in their operations. In addition, the high degree of formalization often permits bureaucracies to perform well with less talented and less expensive management. Under those same circumstances, they can be very effective in accomplishing their mission.

However, bureaucracies are effective and efficient only under the circumstances just described. They are highly resistant to change, and are not effective in dynamic environments or where the nature of work and technology is constantly in flux. Centralization slows down decision-making. Formalization and job specialization do not facilitate dealing with unique work situations, and rigid functional departmentalization limits cross-functional cooperation and communication.

Virtual Organization

Is it possible to create an organization with a revenue stream of a billion dollars a year that has only one employee? The answer is a qualified yes. In today's connected environment, an organization can subcontract for all of its organizational functions. Why have permanent staffs of production workers, accountants, HR professionals, engineers, and so on when it can all be rented, leased, or contracted?

The creation of such an organization, frequently referred to as a *virtual organization*, and depicted in Figure 2.4c, has distinct advantages. It can be created quickly and just as easily disbanded. It can be highly flexible and adaptive to the environment and may contain very high levels of expertise. Issues such as employment taxes, employee benefits, and employment law requirements can be avoided. However, there are disadvantages, the first and foremost of which is loss of managerial control. This issue is discussed at further length in Chapter 5, "Compensation and Benefits." Another issue is commitment and shared goals. The primary goals of a subcontracted advertising agency might not be the same as those of the organization, nor shared with other parts of the virtual organization such as the manufacturing contractors.

Boundaryless Organizations

A *boundaryless organization* is a construct or concept that defines how large organizations can become adaptive and organic. The object is to remove the vertical boundaries of hierarchy, the horizontal boundaries of rigid functional departmentalization, and the external organizational boundaries that preclude free interaction with suppliers and customers. Boundaryless organizations will likely never become a reality, but many organizations are making great strides in attempting to do so. Characteristics of boundaryless organizations include sophisticated communications and information technology systems that permit rapid dissemination of information vertically and horizontally both within and external to the organization, empowered cross-functional and cross-hierarchical teams, and strategic alliances and joint ventures with suppliers and customer integration systems.

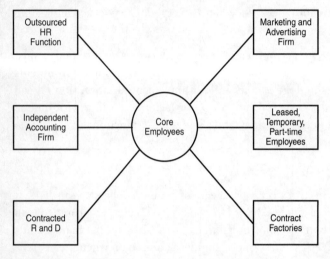

FIGURE 2.4C Virtual organization.

Mechanistic Organizations

Mechanistic organizations are rigid and highly structured and fall at one end of a continuum with organic structures falling at the other. Bureaucracies are one example of such a model. They are characterized by high formalization, high job specialization, centralized decision-making, narrow spans of control, and a high degree of departmentalization. The concepts of mechanistic and organic organizations are interrelated with all other organizational designs. They are often used to describe how organizations operate, as opposed to how they are designed. For example, highly adaptive organizations can be made more efficient and mechanistic and highly stable organizations can be made more organic and adaptive through design changes. All organizations must be a bit mechanistic to get their work done.

Organic Organizations

Organic organizations are highly adaptive. They interact with the environment and provide information regarding the dynamics of the environment throughout the organization using rapid lateral and vertical channels. They tend to be composed of a loose configuration of cross-functional and cross-hierarchal teams with decision-making being decentralized. They have few levels of hierarchy and little formalization. Virtual and boundaryless organizations are examples of this type of organization. Adaptation is both the strength and weakness of this type of organization. At the far end of the continuum, organic organizations can be chaotic, with rapid, uncoordinated changes occurring in various parts of the organization.

Concentrated Structures

Concentrated structures is the term used to refer to specific organizational substructures that are created to make mechanistic organizations more organic. External to the actual organizational structure, their work outputs might be funneled back into the mechanistic structure to take advantage of its efficiencies. The term *skunkworks* is sometimes used with respect to these entities. Project teams, task forces, and committees (often cross-functional and cross-hierarchical) are all examples of concentrated structures. Employee involvement programs, as discussed in Chapter 6, are also examples. The purpose of concentrated structures is to create organizational entities that are external to the permanent organizational structure and, to some extent, free of the formalization, specialization, departmentation, and centralization of that structure. In this way, the concentrated structures can interact with the environment and, freed from the constraints of the organization, can be innovative and creative. Rather than operating entirely independently, innovations are then driven back into the mechanistic organization for implementation.

Organizational Strategy

The organizational design and structure must align with and support the organization's strategic plan. Various researchers have categorized the types of strategies that organizations might pursue (Miles and Snow, and Porter, for example). They have essentially identified three types of common strategies. The structural implications for two—differentiation/innovation and cost-minimization/leadership—are discussed next because they are at opposite ends of the continuum. The third strategy, often referred to as *imitation*, is at the middle of the continuum, and the implications for this strategy are a combination of the other two.

> **NOTE**
>
> It is quite possible that one part of the organization can be pursuing one type of strategy while another part is pursuing a different strategy. The obvious implication is that the two parts of the organization should have different structural components that are aligned with the strategy being pursued.

Innovation or Differentiation

An *innovation* or *differentiation* strategy involves being first to the market with new and exciting products or services that are valued by the customer. To do that, the organization must be flexible, adaptive, and close to the customer; in other words, organic. Thus low formalization, decentralization, flat hierarchical design, lack of rigid departmentation, and low job specialization are all indicated.

Cost Minimization or Cost Leadership

A *cost-minimization* or *cost-leadership* strategy requires an organization that is efficient. In other words, the organization should be mechanistic. This requires, in particular, the efficiencies and high productivity of job specialization. Also supporting such a strategy are centralization, formalization, functional departmentation, and a narrow span of control.

> **NOTE**
>
> All HR programs are interdependent. The organizational strategies above are discussed in Chapter 5 with respect to their implications for compensation. The same could be said for HRD, recruitment, performance management, or any other program. All the various elements must support the strategic plan. A change in one program often dictates a compensating change in other programs.

Measuring HR Effectiveness

Objective:
Gain an Understanding of Measuring HR Effectiveness

As HR moves from a staff-supporting function to a strategic partner, it must be able to prove the effectiveness and efficiency of its operations. *Effectiveness* is the extent to which goals are met and the needs of stakeholders satisfied. *Efficiency* is the ratio of inputs to outputs and the cost per unit of production. It is possible for the HR function to be effective but not efficient, or efficient but not effective. HR must be able to prove that it is both.

The HR function must develop metrics and processes to evaluate its internal operations and, more importantly, how those operations affect the success of the organization. First we discuss evaluation of internal operations through a process known as the *HR audit*. We next discuss a method of linking organizational activities to strategic success—the balanced scorecard and its direct application to HR—the HR scorecard. The organization must develop specific quantitative and objective ways of measuring effectiveness and efficiency. These measures are referred to as *metrics*, and we next discuss various types of metrics that can be used. Finally, HR must be able to demonstrate a relationship between its activities and organizational outcomes by engaging in research. This requires knowledge of basic statistical measures, the scientific method, and experimental design, which are the subjects of the final discussion in this section.

HR Audit

The HR audit is a formal and systematic process of evaluating the current effectiveness and efficiency of the HR function and determining what activities need to be taken to improve it.

Most organizations routinely audit their accounting and financial records, but many organizations do not do the same with other functions, particularly HR. HR audits review current HR programs and policies such as regulatory compliance, performance against stated goals and organizational expectations, and integration with the strategic plan. The outcome of the audit is an extensive report, evaluating the effectiveness and efficiency of the HR function as a whole and each major program area individually. The audit identifies gaps in performance and typically makes recommendations as to how to close those gaps. HR audits can be specialized and review only a specific programmatic area, particularly if the organizational or HR leadership believes that area is not contributing to organizational success. However, most frequently the audit is of the total function and typically focuses on the following areas:

- ▶ **Payroll**   Whether done internally or externally, accuracy, timeliness, and so on

- ▶ **Compensation**   Strategy, equity, and so on

- ▶ **Mandatory benefits**   Compliance

- ▶ **Voluntary benefits**   Breadth and depth, meeting of employee needs, cost-effectiveness, and so on

- ▶ **Employee and labor relations**   Contract compliance and administration, performance management, employee discipline, employee involvement, rewards and recognition programs, and so on

- ▶ **Employee communications**   Employee handbook, policies, and so on

- ▶ **Use of technology**   HRIS and other automated systems

- ▶ **Training and development**   OJT, orientation, career planning, mentoring, coaching, and so on

- ▶ **HR planning**   Linkage with strategic plan, metrics, and so on

- ▶ **Health, safety, and security**   Regulatory compliance, proactive planning and intervention strategies, and so on

- ▶ **Recruitment and Selection**   Capability of programs to meet organizational needs, capability of methods to predict future performance, and so on

Large organizations often have the capability of performing the HR audit internally, whereas smaller organizations typically employ outside auditors to evaluate the HR function. The HR audit can have a positive effect on HR effectiveness and efficiency by identifying areas for improvement. In practice, the typical audit tends to be operationally oriented as opposed to strategically oriented. Audits often provide an excellent technical review of HR programs, but less often link that review to HR's contribution to organizational success.

Balanced Scorecard and HR Scorecard

The *balanced scorecard* is a process for translating strategic goals into operational plans and metrics. It is a method of evaluating the overall effectiveness of the organization as opposed to the effectiveness of HR specifically. However, part of the scorecard evaluation process includes evaluation of measures specifically related to the HR function. The balanced scorecard is largely the work of Robert Kaplan and David Norton. Organizations have traditionally been evaluated using only financial measures. However, these measures are historical in nature and indicate what the organization has done in the past, not its current performance level; nor do they provide adequate information to make decisions in volatile environments. In addition, financial measures often place too much emphasis on short-term performance to the detriment of the types of long-term planning that are essential for organizational growth and future success. The balanced scorecard balances the importance of financial measures by providing additional measures that attempt to evaluate future rather than past performance. The scorecard includes the following measures:

▶ **Financial**   These are the traditional measures of organizational success; market share, cash flow, profitability, return on capital invested, and so on

▶ **Customers**   Share of the wallet, customer retention and repurchase, new customer acquisition, per customer profitability, and so on

▶ **Internal business processes**   Innovation in new product and service development, quality, cycle time, cost reduction, and so on

▶ **Learning and growth**   Employee satisfaction, employee productivity, employee skill levels, employee retention, and so on

After the strategic objectives of the organization are developed, they are communicated throughout the organization. Managers and employees then work together to create tactical and operational objectives, including appropriate metrics in each of the scorecard areas. Much like the MBO process, these objectives are distilled throughout the organization, with lower levels and even individual employees developing their own scorecards. Progress toward scorecard objectives is then monitored and corrections made if necessary. Proponents of the balanced scorecard believe that it aligns organizational activities to the strategic plan, increases employee knowledge of and commitment to organizational goals, provides performance feedback, and facilitates organizational learning.

Many HR functions have begun the process of developing HR scorecards, either as part of the larger process of a balanced scorecard approach or independently. An HR scorecard is a method of evaluating the effectiveness and efficiency of the HR function by using a series of measures or metrics of employee behaviors and HR program outcomes that are believed to be related to organizational success. The development of an HR scorecard follows the same process as the development of a balanced scorecard.

The process begins with a thorough understanding of the strategic goals of the organization. HR must be able to identify employee behaviors and HR program goals that are causally related to the achievement of those organizational goals and then develop methods to measure these behaviors and program outcomes. These measures become the basis for the HR scorecard and goals are set in each relevant area. HR strategies and activities are developed to achieve the goals. These activities are then implemented, and accomplishments in relation to the goals are periodically evaluated with corrective activity taken as appropriate. Finally, the HR scorecard results are compared with and linked to achievement of the organization's strategic objectives.

Metrics

Metrics are quantitative measures of performance. The number of metrics that can be conceived, computed, and reported is limited only by the creativity and imagination of HR leadership. Too many metrics becomes confusing and a wasteful use of valuable staff resources. The important consideration is to choose metrics that are of direct importance to the organization externally and HR internally. Too often, HR leaders develop metrics based on counting of activities: number of training classes held, number of applications received, number of job descriptions written and classified, and so on. Rather, metrics directly related to strategic objectives and HR functional strategies are those of critical importance. If absenteeism is virtually nonexistent, tracking and reporting it might not be important. However, if turnover is believed to be a problem, tracking the rate and costs of turnover and benchmarking it against competitors might be of critical importance. Discussed next are three universal metrics—cost-benefit analysis, return on investment, and break-even analysis—each of which can be applied and used in a wide variety of circumstances. Also discussed are more specific metrics that are directly applicable to the HR function.

Cost-Benefit Analysis

Cost-benefit analysis can be used both as a reporting methodology and in the decision-making process. It is a quantitative method of evaluating the financial value of program outcomes in relation to program costs. As a reporting metric, actual benefits of a specific program can be compared against actual costs. As a decision-making tool, expected benefits can be compared against expected costs by using a variety of scenarios or options.

A simple example as a reporting metric should suffice. The organization decides that providing a sales training course to all salespersons can increase sales. After the training is completed, sales on an annualized basis increased by $200,000 whereas the costs of the training was $50,000. The cost-benefit ratio for this activity is calculated to be 4:1. That means each dollar invested in the program yielded four dollars in benefits. The calculation and determination of costs are given here:

Cost-Benefit Ratio = Benefits / Costs

$200,000/$50,000 = 4 (ratio is 4:1)

Benefits		Costs	
Increased sales	$200,000	Trainer's salary for conducting and developing training	$20,000
		Trainee's salary	$ 2,000
		Lost sales during training	$27,000
		Cost of training facility and equipments	$ 1,000
Totals	**$200,000**		**$50,000**

There are two issues associated with cost-benefit analysis that should be examined. The first, and most important, is that the benefits that are reported might or might not have been directly a result of the HR program. In the preceding example, the $200,000 gain in sales could be been a result of many factors other than the training program; improved economic conditions, for example. Second, it is often difficult to quantify both the costs and benefits of programs that are qualitative in nature. In this example, the training might have had an effect on employee job satisfaction, organizational commitment, or customer satisfaction—all outcomes that are difficult to quantify.

Break-Even Analysis

Break-even analysis is more frequently used in the marketing function to determine product pricing. It allows marketers to determine the amount of sales volume that is required at various price points to make a profit. However, it can be used in the HR function to determine at what point the benefits from a particular activity begin to exceed the investment in the activity. The break-even point is that point in time when benefits exactly equal costs. It is another form or method of cost-benefit analysis. Using the cost-benefit example shown earlier, and assuming that increased sales are uniformly spread across the year, the break-even point would be three months as illustrated in the following equations. At the three-month point, total costs equal total benefits. Because there are no additional costs in this program beyond the initial training costs, the organization has earned back its investment at the three-month point. Only benefits accrue after that period.

BE = Costs (Per Year) / Benefits (Per Year)

BE = 50,000/200,000

BE = .25

.25 ¥ 12 (Months in a Year) = 3 Months

Return on Investment

Return on investment is a financial tool that measures the productivity of assets. Specifically, in HR, it is used to evaluate the benefits that accrue from the allocation of resources to a particular activity. For example, HR decides to upgrade its HRIS system to provide self-service for employee benefit elections and changes. The cost of the total program is estimated to be $250,000 over two years, with first-year costs of $150,000. First year savings realized through the reduction of staff time required to manually process benefit elections and changes is $50,000. The return on investment is 33%.

($50,000/$150,000) ¥ 100 = 33%

HR-Specific Metrics

Table 2.8 lists some of the many metrics that can be used. The SHRM website (http://www.shrm.org/) contains a large number of sample metrics, along with spreadsheets preformatted with appropriate input cells and formulae for metric calculation. A perusal of those web pages provides additional insight into the vast array of potential metrics that are applicable to the HR function.

TABLE 2.8 HR-Specific Metrics

HR Metric	Explanation/Usage
Workers' Compensation Costs/Employee	Total WC Costs / Avg. # of Workers Current versus historical costs can be used to evaluate programs designed to reduce on-the-job injuries and illnesses.
Turnover Rate	(# of Separations / Avg. # of Employees) ¥ 100 Reports turnover percentages. Can be compared against industry averages or against organizational historical rates to evaluate the effect of program activities designed to improve retention.
Cost Per Hire	Total Expenses of Recruitment and Selection / # of New Hires Total expenses include a number of factors, such as recruitment expenses (advertising, recruiter travel and salary, and so on), management salary costs for interviewing, HR staff salaries involved in processing the recruit action, relocations expenses, and so on. Used to evaluate program initiatives to automate, streamline, or otherwise reduce costs.
HR Cost Factor	Total Cost of HR Function / Total Organizational Expenditures Provides data on the efficiency of HR operations and can be compared against benchmarks or organizational baseline data.
HR Cost Per Employee	Total Cost of HR Function / Avg. # of Employees Another way of evaluating the efficiency of the HR function.
Human Capitol ROI	Net Income / Compensation Costs (Wages + Benefits) Evaluates the return on investment in employees. Can be compared with historical data to determine whether HR programs are affecting the bottom line.

(continues)

TABLE 2.8 *Continued*

HR Metric	Explanation/Usage
Training Investment Factor	Total Training Cost / Avg. # of Employees
	Evaluates training expenditures per employee. Can be used against industry benchmarks or organizational historical data. Can be correlated with other organizational metrics such as profitability or productivity.

Research

In simple terms, *research* can be defined as the process of finding answers to questions. HR uses the findings of and engages in social sciences research. The purpose of this research is to describe, predict, and control behavior. For example, HR practitioners might engage in research to describe the overall concept of employee turnover, determine the causes of turnover, and predict when turnover is likely to occur, and then engage in programmatic activities that are designed to control turnover behavior.

Research can either be qualitative or quantitative. *Qualitative* research produces findings that are not arrived at by statistical procedures or other types of quantification. *Qualitative* research uses observation and interviews to develop themes and theories to explain the behavior that is being studied. Qualitative research findings only describe behavior. However, the findings of qualitative research often lead to the development of theories of behavior that can be proved or disproved through quantitative research.

Quantitative research involves the use of statistical procedures to determine the relationship, including causation, between two or more variables. It is empirical in nature and uses the scientific method (described later in this section).

Research must have data to analyze. Data can be collected from two sources. Primary data are those which are collected directly from the group being studied in the particular experiment being conducted; examples include interviews, direct observation, test scores, and surveys. Secondary data are those that are collected from sources other than the group being studied; examples include other research findings, professional journals, and third-party interviews.

Quantitative research uses the scientific method, which is discussed next. The scientific method uses statistical methods to test hypotheses. Basic statistical methods are discussed in the final part of this section.

Scientific Method

The scientific method is a systematic process of testing a hypothesis regarding the relationship between two or more variables. It is a five-step methodology that includes

1. Problem identification and analysis

2. Hypothesis development

3. Research design

4. Data collection

5. Data analysis

Each of the five steps is discussed in greater detail in the following sections.

Problem Identification and Analysis

The initial action in research is identifying what issue or problem the researcher is going to explore. Obviously, the issue should be something that is important to the organization and one whose resolution would contribute to the organization's success. To deal with unimportant matters might result in a successful research project, but would be a waste of resources for the organization. Issues that are ripe for research are those that present a current and continuing problem for the organization. The more critical the issue is to organizational success, the more important the issue is in terms of research.

After the problem or issue is identified, it becomes the dependent variable in the research. A *dependent variable* is something that is affected by or caused by an independent variable. For example, assume that the organization is a bank and the issue is low production rates in the mortgage processing unit; low productivity in that unit becomes the dependent variable. Whatever causes this low productivity and makes it either increase or decrease is the independent variable or variables.

Problem analysis is the process of understanding the dependent variable and determining under what conditions it changes. This thorough analysis and understanding allows the researcher to begin the process of determining potential independent variables that might affect the dependent variable. Assuming that low productivity in the mortgage processing unit is the issue, the researcher attempts to determine what conditions could potentially be causing low mortgage processing rates. The researcher might consider compensation levels, management philosophy, lack of training, low job satisfaction, or many other potential causes. Thoroughly researching the issue, including secondary research in professional publications, might lead the researcher to conclude that the mortgage processing staff lacks adequate training. Training then becomes the independent variable. The independent variable is what the researcher manipulated or measured to determine whether it affects the dependent variable.

Hypothesis Development

A *hypothesis* is a tentative statement describing the relationship between the independent and dependent variables. It is tentative because the accuracy of the statement must be tested. A simple hypothesis (continuing the banking scenario) might be the following:

> *Productivity as measured by number of mortgages processed per day by the mortgage processing unit is positively related to training as measured by the number of hours of job specific training received.*

Research Design

The research design is used to test the hypothesis. A true scientific design in the social sciences involves manipulating or measuring the independent variable with one group but not with another, the control group. The dependent variable for both groups is then measured for both groups. Because the hypothesis in our example is that training will positively affect productivity, the research design would be to select two groups that are statistically similar (an issue discussed later in this section), determine their current productivity, provide training for one group (the experimental group) but not for the other (the control group), and then measure productivity again after the training has been conducted.

The ultimate purpose of the research, as previously mentioned, is to be able to make predictions about behavior and to be able to control it. To do this and to be able to say that the findings apply to the whole population, not just the groups included in the experiment, the experimental design must provide reliable and valid data.

Reliability

Reliability is the consistency or dependability of a measurement. A reliable measure yields the same results on multiple measurements. There are many ways to measure the reliability of the data that are obtained. They include the following:

▶ **Test/retest** The same measurement is administered to the same group on more than one occasion. Reliability is determined by the degree of correlation between one measurement and the other.

▶ **Parallel forms** Two separate forms of the same measurement are administered to the same group. Reliability is determined by the degree of correlation between the two forms.

▶ **Internal consistency** The measurement instrument is divided into two separate but equivalent parts and the scores on the two parts are correlated. The degree of correlation measures reliability.

▶ **Inter-rater reliability** Some measurements involve observation and evaluation by individuals (raters). For example, a researcher might be conducting an experiment to see whether a training course on conflict management affects the ability of employees to handle such situations in a simulated situation. Several raters might observe the employee in the simulated conflict role-play and evaluate the employee's ability to correctly handle the situation. The degree of agreement in ratings is a measure of reliability.

Validity

Data that are reliable are not necessarily valid. The researcher might get consistent measurements, but measure the wrong thing. *Validity* is the capability of the measurement to measure what it is intended to measure. Valid data are also reliable. Valid data permit the researcher to make predictions (generalize) about the population based on the analysis of data from a sample of the population.

A *population* is the total group to which the research being conducted applies. For example, the population might include all employees in the organization. However, it might be impractical in terms of time, expense, or availability to apply the independent variable to the whole population. Consequently, most research projects use a sample of the population. A *sample* is a subset of the population. For the data to be valid, the sample must be randomly selected and accurately replicate the characteristics of the population as a whole. After these criteria are met, the findings of the research can be generalized to the entire population. Other measures of validity are

- ▶ **Content validity**   The extent to which the measurement contains actual elements of what it is intended to measure. For example, does a job simulation test actually contain important components of the job?

- ▶ **Construct validity**   Does the measurement actually measure that which cannot be directly observed? *Constructs* are theoretical traits or characteristics such as intelligence or dependability.

- ▶ **Criterion-related validity**   Does the measurement accurately predict performance? There are two types of criterion-related validity:

  - ▶ **Concurrent validity**   A group is simultaneously measured on the independent and dependent variables, and the two measures are correlated. This correlation can then be the basis for generalizing to the entire population. For example, current employees are given an aptitude test and their score on the aptitude test is then correlated with current performance ratings. If there is a statistically significant correlation between high scores on the test and high performance ratings, that correlation can be generalized to the population and the test could be used in the selection process to predict performance levels.

  - ▶ **Predictive validity**   A group is measured on the independent variable and then, at some later time, measured on the dependent variable. For example, new employees are given the aptitude test and performance is measured at some later date. If the correlation is statistically significant, the findings can be generalized to the population and the test could be used in the selection process as a valid predictor of on-the-job performance.

EXAM ALERT

The SPHR should be familiar with the concepts of reliability and validity. You should also be able to define the various types of validity and explain the difference between concurrent and predictive validity. Expect one or more questions in this area.

Data Collection

Data are collected in a variety of ways. Data are raw, unanalyzed facts. After the data are collected, the process of data analysis transforms the data into information. Relevant information is knowledge. Data can be collected in a number of ways:

- ▶ **Interviews**   These should be conducted by a trained interviewer or a panel of interviewers, and can be an expensive method of data collection. Although interviews yield deep information, the data are often difficult to quantify. Interviews are more frequently used in qualitative research where the in-depth information can be used to develop themes that can potentially lead to theory development. In quantitative research, interviews can be used to assist in the development of questionnaires or surveys.

- ▶ **Surveys/questionnaires**   These yield quantifiable data that can be statistically analyzed. Survey and questionnaire methodology is relatively inexpensive in relation to interviews or observations.

- ▶ **Observations**   These might be the best way to judge performance of higher-level tasks, but require trained observers. Observation is an expensive way to collect data.

- ▶ **Tests/organizational records**   Both of these methods typically yield quantifiable data. Tests can be given to measure learning or skill development. Organizational records such as turnover rates, absenteeism, productivity, quality, and scrap are often used to collect data regarding either the independent or dependent variable.

Continuing with our example, we can measure skill and learning levels with a test at the completion of the training for both the experimental group that received the training and the control group that did not. We can then, at some future date, obtain data from production records that are already maintained for both groups and compare the productivity of the two groups.

Data Analysis

After the data are collected, they are analyzed to determine whether relationships exist between the independent and dependent variables. The analysis differs between qualitative studies and quantitative studies. The analytical processes of each type of research are discussed in the following sections.

Qualitative Studies

Data are analyzed using both inductive and deductive reasoning in qualitative studies to develop themes. *Inductive* reasoning involves creating the whole from its parts, whereas *deductive* reasoning involves the application of the whole to a specific part. Inductive reasoning moves from the particular to the general, whereas deductive reasoning does just the opposite.

Qualitative data analysis involves the coding and classifying of huge amounts of written data, frequently accumulated by interviews. As the data is analyzed, certain commonalities emerge; these commonalities are called *themes*. In other words, many of the interviewees consistently say the same thing about an issue. These themes become the basis for making an observational statement about the relationship between two variables. The themes might be specific in nature, in which case the researcher might be able to use inductive reasoning to make observations about the general case or whole. If the themes are general in nature, deductive reasoning might be used to make observations about how the whole is related to its parts.

Qualitative analysis is limited to the case being studied. In other words, findings and observations are limited to the group under study and cannot be generalized to other groups. However, those findings (themes) might be the basis for developing a hypothesis.

Quantitative Studies

Data are analyzed to prove or disprove a hypothesis. In the sample research study, data are analyzed to determine whether the stated positive relationship between training and production in the mortgage processing unit is verified. Not only do we want to prove that a relationship exists, we want to prove that the training influences or causes the performance or increase in performance. Quantitative studies use statistical techniques to perform these analyses. Those concepts are discussed next.

An in-depth discussion of statistics is beyond the scope of this book. However, the SPHR should have a basic understanding of statistics and how they are used. Statistics are the result of mathematical processes that collect, analyze, interpret, and describe data. Statistics can be categorized into two types: descriptive and inferential. Each type is described in the following sections along with associated concepts and methods.

Descriptive statistics are used to organize, summarize, and describe the data. Descriptive statistics provide a summarization and description of data that were collected during the research project or study, and present an overall picture of the data as a whole that represent the results of the research study. Techniques and concepts associated with descriptive statistics are discussed next.

Frequency Distributions

We can use various types of charts and graphs to visually display and summarize how the data are arrayed. Bar charts, histograms, frequency polygons, and percentile scales are all frequently used methods.

Measures of Central Tendency and Variability

Even though frequency distributions provide a visual presentation of the data, they provide too much information to allow for definitive interpretation. What is needed is a way to describe the important characteristics of the data. This is accomplished by measures of central tendency and measures of variability. Measures of central tendency (mode, median, and mean) and measures of variability (range, standard deviation, and variance) are briefly described next.

Measures of Central Tendency

Measures of central tendency describe the typical score in the distribution of data. Put another way, these measures describe the center of the distribution. Measures of central tendency are mode, median, and mean:

▶ **Mode**   The *mode* is the score that is obtained most often in the distribution. In the distribution depicted in the later table, the mode is 12, which is the score that has the most occurrences.

▶ **Median**   The *median* is the score below which 50% of all scores fall. The median is that score which divides the distribution in half. In the sample data distribution here, the median is 14.

▶ **Mean**   The *mean* is the most basic and frequently used measure of central tendency. It is the average score; that is, it is the sum of the scores divided by the number of scores. The mean is very sensitive to extreme scores. Thus, all three measures of central tendency should be considered when analyzing central tendency. In the sample data distribution, the mean is 13.

Sample Data Distribution

1	
12	
12	Mode
12	
13	Mean
14	Median
15	
15	
16	
16	
17	

EXAM ALERT

Given a sample distribution, the SPHR should be able to determine the mean, mode, and median. Expect a question asking you to do so.

Measures of Variability

Measures of variability of data describe the spread of scores in a distribution. Common measures of variability are range and standard deviation.

Range

The *range* is the difference between the highest score and lowest score in the distribution. In the sample distribution shown earlier, the range is 16 (17 – 1 = 16).

Standard Deviation

Although the range provides some data, we do not know how the scores are distributed around the measures of central tendency. The most common measure of variability is the standard deviation. The *standard deviation* is an index of the spread of scores in the distribution about the mean. A larger absolute value of the standard deviation indicates that scores are distributed more widely around the mean. Additional explanation of the standard deviation is given later in this section.

The Normal Distribution (Bell Curve)

Socialh science data, when summarized and plotted, frequently take the form of a bell-shaped curve. The bell-shaped curved is mathematically modeled by the normal distribution. The *normal distribution* is one in which the mean, mode, and median are the same numerical value, and scores in the distribution are symmetrically arranged on either side with most scores occurring near the measure of central tendency. Figure 2.5 is a depiction of a normal distribution.

All scores are depicted in the area below the curve. The median, mode, and mean all have the same value and fall at the center of the distribution. Approximately two-thirds of all scores fall within one standard deviation above and one standard deviation below the mean (.3413 + .3413 = .6826 or 68. 26%), about 95% of all scores fall within two standard deviations, and 99.9% fall within three standard deviations. The calculations are shown in the following equations and are based on the values shown in Figure 2.5. If the absolute value of the standard deviation is high, the curve becomes flatter and the scores are more spread out. If the absolute value of the standard deviation is low, the curve becomes very steep and concentrated around the center.

Two standard deviations = (.3413 + .1359) ¥ 2 = .9544 or 95.44 %

Three standard deviations = (.3413 + .1359 + .0215) ¥ 2 = .9974 or 99.74%

> **EXAM ALERT**
>
> Expect a question regarding the bell curve (normal distribution). You should understand the positioning of the mean, mode, and median, and the fact that virtually all scores are located within two (95.44%) or three (99.74%) standard deviations of the mean.

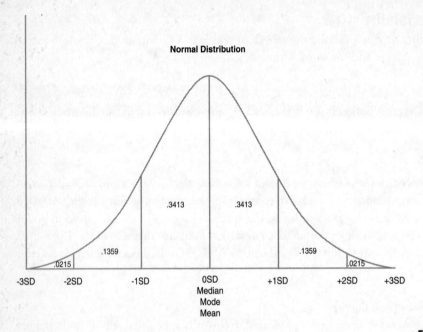

Normal Distribution

.3413 .3413

.1359 .1359

.0215 .0215

-3SD   -2SD   -1SD   0SD   +1SD   +2SD   +3SD
                        Median
                        Mode
                        Mean

SD = Standard Deviation

FIGURE 2.5 The normal distribution curve.

Measures of Association

Measures of association indicate the nature and strength of the relationship between two or more variables. Common methods used are joint distributions, correlation coefficient, and linear regression.

Joint Distributions

A *joint distribution* is the graphical or tabular display of two pairs of scores in one presentation. The most common joint distribution is a scatter plot in which the values from one distribution are placed on the x-axis and those from the other distribution on the y-axis. This provides a visual representation of the relationship between the two variables.

Correlation Coefficient

The *correlation coefficient* is a measure of the strength of association between two variables. The correlation coefficient also measures the direction of the relationship. If the scores on variable x increase with increases in the scores on variable y, a positive relationship exists. If the scores on variable x decrease with increases in the scores on variable y, a negative relationship exists.

Correlation coefficients range on a continuum from −1 to +1. If there is a direct linear relationship between an increase in y and an increase in x, the correlation coefficient is +1 and there is obviously a strong positive association between the two variables. If there is a direct linear relationship between an increase in y and a decrease in x the correlation coefficient is −1, and there is a strong negative relationship between the variables.

> **EXAM ALERT**
>
> You are likely to be asked a question regarding the meaning of the correlation coefficient as just explained.

> **NOTE**
>
> A correlation coefficient, even one of +1 or −1, indicates only association. It does not indicate causation. Causation can only be proven and predicted through inferential statistics.

Linear Regression

Linear regression permits the prediction of one variable based on the systematic relationship between it and another variable. Multiple linear regression permits the prediction of one variable based on the systematic relationship between it and two or more variables. Multiple linear regression permits the testing of many independent variables to determine their impact on the dependent variable.

Inferential Statistics

Inferential statistics permit inferences to be made about a larger group, the population, based on data collected from a representative subset of that group, the sample. Inferential statistics allow researchers to predict with confidence the behavior of the larger group based on the behavior of the smaller one. T-test and chi-square statistics are examples of inferential statistics that can be used. In-depth discussion of inferential statistics is beyond the scope of this book.

> **NOTE**
>
> The reader should consult a basic text on statistics for more information on both descriptive and inferential statistics.

The Role of HR in Organizational Ethics

Objective:

Gain an Understanding of the Role of HR in Organizational Ethics

Recent highly publicized corporate scandals involving Enron, Arthur Andersen, WorldCom, and others have raised public awareness and cynicism regarding the ethical conduct of organizations in both the private and public sector. For the purposes of this discussion, we define *ethics* as a system of rules and values that govern the conduct of individuals or groups. Ethics drive decisions as to what should be done, not what is required to be done by law. Much has been made of the problems experienced by the organizations mentioned and the costs the scandal imposed on the organization, its leaders, its employees, its stockholders, its suppliers, and its customers. So, the question is, "If bad ethics result in negative outcomes, do good ethics result in positive organizational outcomes?" The answer is yes. Many research studies show a positive correlation between an organization's reputation for proper ethical practices and such positive factors as

- ▶ Improved capability to meet strategic goals
- ▶ Profitability
- ▶ Increased employee commitment and retention
- ▶ Customer loyalty
- ▶ Positive image in the community
- ▶ Capability to recruit employees

If there are positive outcomes to proper ethical behavior, what is the SPHR's responsibility in guiding the organization? Briefly discussed in the following sections are HR's responsibilities with respect to organizational ethics, types of ethical issues encountered by HR, ethics programs, the impact of organizational culture on organizational ethics, and the concept or organizational social responsibility.

HR's Role in Ethics

HR has traditionally been thought of as the organization's conscience. In its various roles, HR is responsible for ensuring compliance with a multitude of laws and regulations that form the foundation of good ethical behavior. More importantly, HR is responsible for developing policies, procedures, and rules that guide decision-making in the organization. These documents must support and facilitate achievement of the organization's strategic objectives. They must not only be compliant with law, but must also be in alignment with the organizational culture and meet professional standards of ethical behavior. Policies that are fair, balanced, and go beyond the mere requirements of the law have been proven to be effective in influencing the overall success of the organization.

NOTE

The SPHR is obligated to follow the Society for Human Resource Management Code of Ethics, which can be found at the SHRM website, http://www.shrm.org/.

Ethical Issues in the Workplace

The SPHR is constantly bombarded with ethical dilemmas. Not only must the SPHR work through these issues, but he or she must assist the organization and its managers and employees in making good ethical decisions. The possibilities for ethical dilemmas in today's highly competitive environment are virtually unlimited, but some of the more common ones are discussed here.

Reorganizations

Rightsizing, downsizing, mergers, and acquisitions occur frequently in today's competitive environment. One of the main rationales for such activities is increased efficiency. Increased efficiency, defined as output per employee, can most easily be achieved by elimination of employees. Although there have been successes associated with these activities, many studies indicate that these activities frequently do not achieve the desired results. Many employees lose their jobs and those that remain are required to pick up the extra work while worrying about when they might lose their jobs. In addition, workers who keep their jobs often suffer from "survivor guilt" because they still are working while others aren't and become disillusioned with the organization. The SPHR must be involved in the decision-making process to ensure that the decision is sound from both a business and an ethical perspective.

Whistle Blowing

Are employees protected when they disclose improper or illegal activities of the organization? Although ethically it seems that such a disclosure is required and should be protected, legally it might not be. Employees disclosing improprieties regarding federal contracts are likely to be covered by the False Claims Act of 1863. Employee disclosing improprieties related to state contracts might be covered by similar state laws, and employees reporting improprieties with respect to securities regulations are covered by Sarbanes-Oxley (2002). It is also possible that certain whistle-blowing activities might be interpreted as an exception to employment-at-will. However, other whistle-blowing activities might violate the loyalty principle of common law and subject the employee to disciplinary action up to and including termination. In these situations, the SPHR must assist the organization in making ethical decisions that balance the rights of employees and other stakeholders with those of the organization.

Business Practices

Global organizations are often faced with common business practices in foreign countries that would be illegal in the United States. Many countries permit, or at least ignore, payoffs, bribes, and kickbacks as the normal way to get something done or to close a deal. U.S. organizations are often faced with the moral dilemma of engaging in these types of activities or facing the possibility of not being competitive in a particular country. The pressures are immense. However, the Foreign Corrupt Practices Act (1977) prohibits such activities with the exception of minor types of expediting fees that are paid to officials to quicken the receipt of governmental services (obtaining a phone line, for example). There is a large gray area between what is permitted and what violates the Foreign Corrupt Practices Act.

There are many other business- and employment-related practices that are legal in foreign countries that are not prohibited by the Foreign Corrupt Practices Act. Should the organization employ children and work them long hours? Should an organization pay workers $1.00 a day to work a 60-hour week? Should practices be permitted that would violate safety and environmental laws in the United States? The quick reaction to these ethical dilemmas is no. But what if the wages that the child is earning are needed to provide food for the family? What if raising wages or engaging in better environmental or safety practices would make the organization uncompetitive, resulting in a loss of jobs? The SPHR must develop and implement policies and practices that guide organizational members in decision-making in these situations.

Discipline and Termination

Discipline and termination actions must be compliant with a variety of employment laws, yet there is a great deal of discretion remaining with management as to whether to take an action and what type of action to take. The SPHR must develop procedures and oversight in these areas to ensure that disciplinary action is not only legal but also that it is ethical in its outcome and aligned with achievement of organizational goals.

Employee Privacy

A major ethical issue in today's technologically driven workplace is employee privacy. The issue is discussed further in Chapter 7, but needs to be addressed briefly here as well. Employee privacy must be balanced with the needs of the organization in terms of achieving its goals and protecting its assets. Thus, many HR programs involve a balancing of these two rights and obligations. Examples are

▶ **Surveillance** The organization has a right and obligation to protect its property. Surveillance cameras and taping, inspections of bags and briefcases, and security guard presence in the workplace are all examples of the types of activities that may be conducted in the workplace. Most activities are legal, but can be intrusive. For example, is it appropriate to have surveillance cameras in locker rooms and restrooms? When might it be appropriate to monitor employee activities off the job?

▶ **Monitoring of electronic systems** Is it appropriate to monitor employee use of the telephone, computer, email systems, and intranet? In general, such monitoring and practices are legal under the Electronic Communications Privacy Act (1986), but are they appropriate and balanced?

> **NOTE**
>
> Surveillance of employee activities associated with rights protected under the Wagner Act (1935) as amended might be illegal. For example, photographing employees as they exit an offsite union organizing meeting would be illegal. This issue is covered in Chapter 6, "Employee and Labor Relations."

Employment Practices

Should the information contained in an employee's employment file be divulged to interested third parties? In general, unless the organization is a federal employer or the state has enacted a specific law, privacy laws do not protect this information. Should employees be subject to pre-employment and/or post-employment drug testing? Is it important to obtain an employee's credit history? These are among the many issues that the SPHR must assist the organization in dealing with in an ethical manner.

> **NOTE**
>
> Employment practices are discussed extensively in Chapter 3, "Workforce Planning and Employment."

Releasing Employee Personnel Information

This is one of the most frequently occurring ethical dilemmas the SPHR faces. To the extent possible, the organization wants to preserve the employee's privacy. Yet, in many instances, the ethically right thing to do is to reveal information either to assist the employee or provide a third party with information it needs to make a decision. Historically the issue has been resolved based on risk management. Very little information is revealed, even if positive, to prevent potential legal action by the employee for defamation of character. Yet there might also be an ethical and, in some cases, legal reason for providing personnel information. For example, if the employee was terminated for violence in the workplace, is it ethical not to reveal that to a prospective employer? Furthermore, if the employee subsequently commits violence on a third party, it is possible that the tort liability for negligent hiring could be transferred from the hiring organization to the former organization that failed to provide relevant information.

Drug Testing

Drug testing is legal but mandated only in limited circumstances, usually under Department of Transportation (DOT) regulations. Does drug testing violate the privacy expectations of the employee, does it support organizational goals, and what message does it send to both employees and the public?

Credit and Background Checks

Credit investigations and background checks done by third parties are regulated by the Fair Credit Reporting Act (1970). Both are legal activities, but do they balance the rights of employees and achieve organizational purposes?

Lie Detector Tests

Polygraph testing in the private sector is prohibited for pre-employment screening by the Employee Polygraph Protection Act (1988) except in specific situations. However, polygraph testing is permitted in certain investigations in the private sector. What message does polygraph testing send to employees? Does it serve organizational purposes?

Ethics Programs

Many organizations today have created ethics programs in an attempt to ensure ethical behavior by organizational members. Common components of programs judged to be effective are

- ▶ **Commitment from the top** Nothing is more critical than commitment at the executive level regarding proper behavior. The CEO, COO, CFO, and other top executives must model good ethical behavior at all times and insist that organizational members behave in an ethical manner.

- ▶ **Organization code of ethics and/or code of conduct** This document should clearly define the values of the organization and what is acceptable and unacceptable behavior.

- ▶ **Training on ethical behavior** Everyone from the CEO to the lowest-level employee should receive training on the code of ethics/conduct and its meaning and application to workplace decisions. This should be repeated at periodic intervals.

- ▶ **Swift and sure investigation and discipline** As appropriate, for ethical violations. The program will be undermined if bad ethical behavior is tolerated.

- ▶ **An office specifically responsible for organizational ethics** This is often HR, but could be an ethics officer or an ombudsman. The purpose of this office is to have a confidential process that organizational members can use to obtain advice and guidance on ethical issues and where they can go to anonymously report unethical or questionable behavior.

EXAM ALERT

Expect a question regarding the components of an effective ethics program.

NOTE

The SPHR is obligated to follow the Society for Human Resource Management Code of Ethics which can be found at the SHRM website, http://www.shrm.org/.

Impact of the Organization's Culture on Ethics

Organizational culture is discussed more fully in Chapter 4. An organizational culture guides organizational members on what is acceptable behavior. A strong culture has a significant effect on impacting individual, group, and organizational behavior. A culture that permits unethical and questionable ethical behavior results in exactly that type of behavior. One of the roles of the SPHR and the HR function is to understand the organization's culture and to engage in activities that properly align the culture with organizational goals and vice versa. However, cultural change is often a difficult and time-consuming process.

Organizational Social Responsibility

Social responsibility can be defined as the organization's long-term commitment to the welfare of society. Much the same as individuals, organizations can be conceptualized as operating at varying levels of ethical behavior. Various researchers and writers (Paine, Robbins, Nickels, et al.) have put different titles on these levels, but their findings are very similar and are discussed next.

Indifference/Benign Neglect/Reactive Philanthropy

There is little commitment to ethical behavior or the needs of society. The philosophy is that most behaviors, within obvious limits, are okay as long as the individual or organization doesn't get caught. The organization might engage in limited philanthropic activity, largely to satisfy social obligations of senior executives.

Social Obligation/Compliance/Strategic Philanthropy

The organization meets its legal obligations and no more. Social welfare programs are pursued only to the extent that they might have a positive impact on the organization's economic condition. Philanthropic activity is limited and focused on improving the long-term economic condition of the organization and its public image.

Social Responsiveness/Cooperation/Mainstream Involvement

Organizations not only obey the letter of the law, but also engage in activities in the spirit and intent of the law. They adapt to changes in social conditions and modify organizational activities to be coincident with current social standards before those requirements are codified into law. Philanthropic activity is broadened to include multiple causes that are of importance to the organization or its stakeholders.

Social Responsibility/Contribution/Corporate Accountability

Only a few organizations actually operate at this level. Here the organization operates on the ethical imperative to make society better. It pursues activities that are good for society as opposed to being good for the organization and, sometimes, even to the detriment of the organization. The organization engages in activities to improve and monitor its behavior to ensure that it is meeting the highest possible ethical standards.

The Legislative Environment

Objective:

Gain an Understanding of the Legislative Environment

At the strategic level, the organization not only endeavors to be compliant with the law, but to influence outcomes of the legislative process. To do so, the SPHR must have a basic understanding of legislative process, understand how to communicate views to legislative officials, and be aware of what is happening within the legislative environment.

The Legislative Process

The legislative process of the U.S. Congress is briefly described in the following list. Similar processes are followed in the state legislatures, although some states have a unicameral system in which there is only one legislative chamber. The passage of a law involves a number of steps:

1. A member of the legislature submits a bill.

2. The bill is referred to a committee. However, there is no obligation for the committee to act and the bill can be killed at this point.

3. The bill is often referred to a subcommittee for hearings.

4. When the hearings are complete, the subcommittee can elect to kill the bill by failing to report it back to the full committee, can report the bill back to the committee without changes, or can report it back with changes (called *marking it up*).

5. The full committee can conduct further hearings and debate prior to making its recommendation. The committee then votes to whether to *report the bill*.

6. A written report of the bill is then prepared, which delineates the purpose of the bill and its impact on current law.

7. The bill is sent to the chamber in which it originated and is placed on the calendar.

8. If the bill reaches the floor of the chamber, it is debated.

9. After completion of the debate, the bill and its amendments (if any) are either passed or defeated via a vote.

10. If the bill is passed, it is referred to the other chamber for action. The process in the other chamber is similar in terms of committee and subcommittee actions leading to a vote of passage or defeat.

11. If the second chamber makes major modifications to the bill, it is sent to a conference committee made up of members of both chambers to attempt to resolve the differences. If the differences cannot be resolved, the bill dies. If agreement is reached, a conference report describing the changes is prepared and both chambers must approve the report.

12. The bill is then sent to the president for approval. The president can sign the bill, veto the bill, or take no action. If Congress is in session and the president takes no action, the bill becomes law. However, if Congress is not in session, the bill does not become law. This is called a *pocket veto*.

Communicating with Legislators

There are many methods with which to communicate with legislators. Email and letters explaining your position on an issue are two popular and effective means of conveying your views. Written correspondence should be concise and courteous. You should state your purpose for communicating, your view on the legislation, and specifically identify the bill (HR__ or S __) in the first paragraph. Telephone calls are also appropriate, but you will likely speak to a staff member, not the legislator. You should be very succinct, giving the same information that would be contained in the first paragraph of a written communication. SHRM and other professional organizations often provide drafts of letters or emails that can be used to communicate with legislators.

You can engage in lobbying activities by making an appointment with the legislator or with staff members. Federal legislators typically maintain one or more offices within the district that they represent, so travel to Washington, D.C. is not always necessary. Appointments must generally be made well in advance and are subject to cancellation due to pressing business. The appointment will be very short, so you must be well prepared to present your position in a very short time.

Monitoring the Legislative Environment

There are a number of ways to remain aware of what is going on within the legislative body. Obviously, the media is one excellent source. This is where an effective program of environmental scanning, discussed earlier in this chapter, is important. However, many HR-related bills might not be of interest to the larger public and be reported in the newspapers or on radio or TV. More current information affecting HR is better obtained through membership in professional organizations. Most of these organizations provide electronic email newsletters reporting current legislative activity. Their websites also often contain current information.

Strategic Considerations for the SPHR

A section on the strategic considerations of strategic planning might seem a bit redundant. However, this section is incorporated to underscore the importance of strategic planning and strategic planning. Every subsequent chapter in the book contains a section with the same title just to remind the SPHR that systems and strategic thinking is the SPHR's domain and responsibility. It is the area in which the SPHR adds value to the organization.

The HR function is composed of multiple programs and activities that are interrelated and interdependent. The SPHR must think in terms of systems, not in terms solely of the individual HR function being contemplated or managed. In subsequent chapters, we discuss the main program areas of HR. As a prospective SPHR, you must view the remaining chapters in light of this one, always contemplating the strategic importance and implications of the issues being discussed.

Chapter Summary

This chapter covers a broad range of subjects associated with the concept of strategic management. The actual processes—strategic planning process and environmental scanning—were introduced and discussed. But strategic management cannot occur in a vacuum. It must be undertaken within the context of understanding organizations, their cultures, functions, and structures.

Environmental scanning includes more than determining trends in the environment. Those trends must be analyzed in terms of their impact on the organization and on HR both as a function and as a profession. Politics and legislative action are a major factor in the environment affecting both HR and the organization. The HR professional must understand the legislative process and be able to interpret and affect it.

Strategic plans must be monitored to determine whether organizational goals are being reached. Thus strategic management includes strategic monitoring of organizational activities. This requires the development of metrics.

Finally, the organization has options with respect to compliance with appropriate laws and the kind of activities it undertakes. The HR function is often the conscience of the organization, and can affect organizational ethics and the extent to which the organization treats all stakeholders fairly and accepts its social responsibility.

Key Terms

- Human resource (HR) management
- Administrative role
- Operational/employee advocate role
- Strategic role
- Society for Human Resource Management (SHRM)
- Human Resources Certification Institute (HRCI)
- Management
- Planning
- Organizing
- Leading
- Controlling
- Project
- Project sponsor
- Project champion
- Project management
- Project planning
- Statement of work
- Work breakdown structure
- Performance evaluation review technique
- Critical path method
- Gantt charts
- Project monitoring
- Outsourcing

- Contract
- Human Resource Information System (HRIS)
- Strategic planning
- Vision statement
- Mission statement
- Values statement
- Strategy formulation
- Development of strategic objectives
- SWOT
- Strategy
- Environment
- Environmental scanning
- Consumer price index (CPI)
- Gross domestic product
- Forecasts
- Competitive intelligence
- Scenario
- Benchmark
- Operations management
- Total quality management
- Accounting
- Financial Accounting Standards Board (FASB)
- Fundamental accounting equation
- Balance sheet
- Income statement
- Statement of cash flows
- Financial ratios
- Budgeting
- Incremental budgets
- Formula budgets
- Zero-based budgets
- Activity-based budgets
- Organizational design
- Organizational structure
- Specialization
- Formalization
- Departmentation
- Chain of command
- Span of control
- Centralization
- Decentralization
- Simple structure
- Bureaucracy
- Virtual organizations
- Boundaryless organizations
- Mechanistic organizations
- Organic organizations
- Concentrated structures
- Effectiveness
- Efficiency
- HR audit
- Balanced scorecard
- HR scorecard
- Metrics
- Cost-benefit analysis

- ▶ Break-even analysis
- ▶ Return on investment
- ▶ Research
- ▶ Qualitative research
- ▶ Quantitative research
- ▶ Scientific method
- ▶ Hypothesis
- ▶ Validity
- ▶ Reliability
- ▶ Induction
- ▶ Deduction

- ▶ Statistics
- ▶ Descriptive statistics
- ▶ Mode
- ▶ Median
- ▶ Mean
- ▶ Range
- ▶ Standard deviation
- ▶ Correlation coefficient
- ▶ Inferential statistics
- ▶ Ethics
- ▶ Social responsibility

Apply Your Knowledge

Exercises

2.1 Organizational Structure

The board of directors of your organization, a public service organization serving four small cities, is considering going to a matrix organizational structure and has asked you to do two things. First, the board would like you to draw a simple picture of what the matrix structure would look like so that they can better visualize it. Your organization is currently departmentalized by function, of which there are four: Operations, Administration, Development, and Volunteer Relations. The board wants to continue this functional arrangement, but would like to create accountability to the towns (Northville, Southville, Westville, and Eastville) through the matrix structure.

Second, the board would like you to brief its members on the advantages and disadvantages of a move to this type of structure.

Draw the structure and then fill in the following table.

Advantages and Disadvantages of a Matrix Organizational Structure

Advantages	Disadvantages

Advantages and Disadvantages of a Matrix Organizational Structure

Advantages	Disadvantages

4.2 Cost-Benefit Analysis

The CEO of your organization has asked you to justify the continuance of a wellness program that was initiated last year. She believes the program is too expensive. You decide to do a cost-benefit analysis based on first-year data. Sick leave usage for the year went down 10%, which translates to a decrease in usage of 500 hours. The average wage in the organization is $10.00 per hour. You also estimate that the decrease in sick leave usage resulted in a savings of 20 hours of overtime at time and one-half. The wellness program consists of eight one-half hour educational programs a year that are mandatory for all employees. The program is contracted out at a cost of $10,000 per year. You estimate that loss of productivity during the mandatory sessions cost the organization about $5,000 per hour. What is the estimated cost-benefit of the program?

Review Questions

1. You are the HR Director of SuperTech, Inc. SuperTech competes in a highly volatile market designing software for cellular phones. To survive and grow, SuperTech must be highly innovative and first to the market with new and creative software applications. What are the implications for organizational design of SuperTech?

2. Your organization has recently experienced some ethically questionable behavior by several employees. In these instances, the CEO was able to correct the issue before major problems arose. She is now wondering whether the organization should begin an ethics program for employees to provide them with better guidance as to what is acceptable and unacceptable behavior. She asks you to research the issue and provide her with a briefing as to what should be included in an ethics program. What do you tell her?

3. You are the HR Director of a for-profit medical group. The CEO is a physician who has little training in or knowledge of business practices. He asks you to provide him an overview of what information is provided by common financial statements. Specifically, he wants to know about the balance sheet, income statement, and statement of cash flows. How do you respond?

4. As the HR Director of a small service organization, you have decided it is time to do a complete review of the HR function and want to contract out the process with a consulting firm that specializes in HR audits. You are to brief the CEO and board of directors on the concept of an HR audit. What do you tell them? What is your rationale for contracting out the process?

5. You are the HR Director of a small not-for-profit organization that has been growing rather rapidly in the last several years. The CEO now realizes that the organization is in a position where it needs to begin planning for the future. He asks you to come up with a basic outline for a strategic planning process and brief him and the board of directors in two weeks. What do you say at the briefing?

Exam Questions

1. Which of the following is the financial statement that shows whether an organization is operating at a profit or loss?

   - ○ **A.** Balance sheet
   - ○ **B.** Income statement
   - ○ **C.** Statement of cash flows
   - ○ **D.** Acid test

2. Which of the following is not a criterion that the Department of Labor determined to be a necessary characteristic of a profession?

   - ○ **A.** State and local professional organizations
   - ○ **B.** Credentialing body
   - ○ **C.** Applied research in the field
   - ○ **D.** Code of ethics

3. You are a section chief in HR and have been assigned the task of designing and implementing a new performance evaluation system. In managing the project, you monitor project action plans and budget execution. Which of the four management functions are you performing when you engage in these activities?

   - ○ **A.** Planning
   - ○ **B.** Organizing
   - ○ **C.** Leading
   - ○ **D.** Controlling

4. You are the HR Director of a not-for-profit organization that has just installed an HRIS to automate some payroll and benefit processes. The cost of the new system is expected to more than offset the reduction in HR staff during the first year. The Executive Director wants to know when the HRIS will have paid for itself in staff compensation savings. What metric would you use to calculate the answer?

   ○ **A.** Cost-benefit analysis

   ○ **B.** Break-even analysis

   ○ **C.** Return on investment

   ○ **D.** HR cost per employee

5. The HR department processes the payroll each week. Which of the HR roles is being performed by conducting this activity?

   ○ **A.** Administrative

   ○ **B.** Operational

   ○ **C.** Employee advocate

   ○ **D.** Strategic

6. Which of the following is not part of the acronym SWOT?

   ○ **A.** Strengths

   ○ **B.** Wants or needs

   ○ **C.** Opportunities

   ○ **D.** Threats

7. Which of the following is the process of planning and analyzing those activities through which an organization converts inputs into outputs?

   ○ **A.** Operations management

   ○ **B.** Financial management

   ○ **C.** Sales and marketing management

   ○ **D.** Organizational design

8. The CEO of your organization makes virtually all decisions of any importance. With respect to organizational structure, your organization is classified as which of the following?

○ **A.** Formalized

○ **B.** Centralized

○ **C.** Departmentalized

○ **D.** Specialized

9. Which of the following is the process of comparing the organization's operations against those of other organizations?

○ **A.** Forecasting

○ **B.** Competitive intelligence development

○ **C.** Scenario development

○ **D.** Benchmarking

10. Which of the following is not a characteristic of a project?

○ **A.** Consumes resources

○ **B.** Has funding and resource limits

○ **C.** Has a specific objective

○ **D.** Is ongoing

Answers to Exercises

2.1 Organizational Structure

A matrix organization would look like the design shown here.

	Operations	Administration	Development	Volunteer Relations
Northville				
Southville				
Westville				
Eastville				

Advantages and Disadvantages of a Matrix Organizational Structure

Advantages	Disadvantages
Grouping of functional jobs creates potential of economies of scale	Violation of unity of command principle can create confusion
Grouping of functional jobs creates opportunities to create special expertise	Can cause turf wars and conflict between the functional and divisional managers over allocation of resources and the assignment of work
Grouping of jobs supporting the division creates commitment to goals	
Grouping of jobs supporting division creates accountability to goal achievement	
Cross-functional communication and cooperation is facilitated	

2.2 Cost-Benefit Analysis

Cost and benefits are contained in the following table. The cost-benefit is computed by dividing the benefits by the costs of the program as shown. The cost-benefit analysis indicates that each dollar spent on the program returns $1.68 in benefits. You must remember, however, that this relationship might not be causal. The reduced use of sick leave and overtime could be associated with other factors, and not the wellness program.

Cost-benefit ratio = Benefits / Costs

Cost-benefit ratio = $50,300/$30,000

Cost-benefit ratio = 1.68

Benefits		Costs	
Decrease in Sick Leave	$50,000	Vendor Costs	$10,000
500 ¥ $10	$ 300	Lost Production 4 Hours ¥ $5,000	$20,000
Overtime savings 10 ¥ $15	$50,300	Total	$30,000

Answers to Review Questions

1. SuperTech is pursuing a differentiation/innovation strategy. The organizational design and structure must support the strategy by creating an organic organization that is flexible and quick to adapt to the dynamics of its environment. The implications for design are

   ▶ **Low job specialization** General work assignments facilitate creativity and innovation, as opposed to high job specialization that restricts freedom to explore new ways of doing things.

   ▶ **Low formalization** Permits experimenting with new and innovative approaches, as opposed to high formalization characterized by restrictive policies and procedures.

- ▶ **Wide spans of control** Empowers employees to make decisions and take risks.

- ▶ **Decentralization** Allows employees to make decisions regarding their jobs.

- ▶ **Flat hierarchy** Encourages free flow of information internally and externally, potentially resulting in collaboration and a better understanding of the needs and wants of customers.

- ▶ **Lack of rigid departmentalization** Permits cross-functional communication and cooperation.

2. You can tell her that common components of ethics programs judged to be effective are

- ▶ **Commitment from the top** Nothing is more critical than commitment at the executive level regarding proper behavior. The CEO, COO, CFO, and other top executives must model good ethical behavior at all times and insist that organizational members behave in an ethical manner.

- ▶ **Organization code of ethics and/or code of conduct** This document should clearly define the values of the organization and what acceptable and unacceptable behavior is.

- ▶ **Training on ethical behavior** Everyone from the CEO to the lowest-level employee should receive training on the code of ethics/conduct. This should be repeated at periodic intervals.

- ▶ **Swift and sure investigation and discipline, if appropriate, for ethical violations** The program will be undermined if bad ethical behavior is tolerated.

- ▶ **Establishment of an office specifically responsible for organizational ethics** This is often HR, but could be an ethics officer or an ombudsman. The purpose of this office is to have a confidential process that organizational members can use to obtain advice and guidance on ethical issues and where they can go to anonymously report unethical or questionable behavior.

3. You can tell him that the balance sheet is based on the fundamental accounting equation: (assets = liabilities + owners' equity). The balance sheet reports the organization's financial condition as of a certain date and can be used to evaluate the overall financial health of the organization. The income statement summarizes revenue coming into the organization and payment going out. It is used to show whether the organization has made a profit or loss during a specific period of time, usually a quarter or fiscal or calendar year. The statement of cash flows reports all cash receipts and disbursements during a specified period. It is used to evaluate the cash balance of the organization. Although an organization can be making a profit as shown on the income statement, it might not be converting that revenue into cash. Cash flow is critical to have sufficient funds to operate the organization.

4. An HR audit is a formal and systematic process that evaluates the current effectiveness and efficiency of the HR function and provides guidance on how to improve it. The audit will review current programs for regulatory compliance, goal achievement, and alignment with the strategic plan. The outcome of the audit is an extensive report that identifies any gaps in performance and makes specific recommendations for future activities and strategies to rectify them.

There are two justifications that you can give for subcontracting this activity. The first is that a firm that specializes in doing HR audits brings additional expertise and objectivity to the process. The second is that it is unlikely your team will be able to do the project internally without substantially affecting current operations.

5. You can tell the CEO and the board of directors that the strategic planning process can be described in four steps. The first step is strategy formulation, in which the organization makes basic decisions regarding why it exists and what its mission is. Work products of this step are the creation or potential amendment of the organization's vision, mission, and values statements. The second step involves development of strategic objectives. This often involves a SWOT analysis (internal strengths and weaknesses, external opportunities and threats) that permits the organization to develop objectives that match its capabilities to the opportunities available in the environment. During the third step, operational plans are developed and implemented to achieve the objectives. The final step is strategy evaluation. Progress toward achieving the objectives is monitored and corrective action taken if necessary.

Answers to Exam Questions

1. The correct answer is **B**. The income statement is used to show profit or loss during a stated period of time, usually a quarter or a year. The balance sheet (answer A) gives the financial condition of an organization as of a certain date and is used to evaluate the organization's overall financial health. The statement of cash flows (answer C) provides information on the flow of cash into and out of the organization during a specified period of time. The acid test (answer D) is a financial ratio that measures the organization's capability to pay its short-term debts, but takes the organization's current inventory of product or goods for sale out of the calculation.

2. The correct answer is **A**. DOL indicated that a national organization, not a state or local organization was required. A credentialing body (answer B), applied research in the field (answer C), and a code of ethics (answer D) are all criteria of a profession that DOL enumerated and are met by HR.

3. The correct answer is **D**. The controlling function involves monitoring progress towards goal achievement. Planning (answer A) involves determining goals and objectives. Organizing (answer B) involves assembling the necessary people and resources to achievement the goal. Leading (answer C) involves motivating and directing people towards goal achievement.

4. The correct answer is **B**. Break-even analysis is used to determine at what point in time the benefits from a program will exceed the costs. Cost-benefit analysis (answer A) is used to evaluate the ratio of program benefits to program costs. Return on investment (answer C) is a financial tool that is used to evaluate the benefits that accrue from the allocation of resources to a particular activity. HR cost per employee (answer D) is one way of evaluating the overall efficiency of the HR function and is computed by dividing the total costs of the HR function by the average number of employees in the organization.

5. The correct answer is **A**. Processing payroll is part of the administrative role. The operational role (answer B) involves the planning and implementation of traditional HR programs such as recruitment and training. The employee advocate role (answer C) involves ensuring fair treatment for organizational members. The strategic role (answer D) is one of assisting the organization in planning and achieving its overall strategies.

6. The correct answer is **B**. Wants or needs are not part of the acronym. The *W* stands for *weaknesses* and is part of the internal analysis of the organization. Strengths (answer A) is the other part of the internal analysis. Opportunities (answer C) and threats (answer D) are part of the analysis of the environment and are all included in a SWOT analysis.

7. The correct answer is **A**. Operations management involves managing internal processes that convert inputs into the product, service, or knowledge that the organization produces. Financial management (answer B) is the process of accounting for and controlling the organization's resources. Sales and marketing management (answer C) is the process of developing, pricing, promoting, and distributing products of services. Organizational design (answer D) is the process of determining the correct organizational structure to support organizational strategy and goal achievement.

8. The correct answer is **B**. In a centralized organization, decisions are concentrated at the top of the organization. A formalized organization (answer A) is characterized by tightly written job descriptions, policies, and standard operation procedures. A departmentalized organization (answer C) has jobs grouped together, typically by function. A specialized organization (answer D) has broken the jobs down into their component parts, making them the primary tasks of a separate job assignment.

9. The correct answer is **D**. Benchmarking is the process of comparing the organization's operations against those of others. Forecasting (answer A) is the process of making predictions as to how a particular measure will change in the future. Competitive intelligence development (answer B) is the process of developing information regarding competitors that will enable the organization to adjust its strategies appropriately. Scenario development (answer C) is the process of developing descriptions of what the future will look like.

10. The correct answer is **D**. Projects, as opposed to programs for example, have defined start and ending times. Projects do consume resources (answer A), have resource limits (answer B), and have a specific objective (answer C).

Suggested Readings and Resources

1. Books and Papers

▶ Bateman, T. S. & Snell, S. A. (2004). *Management: The New Competitive Landscape* (6th edition). New York: McGraw-Hill/Irwin.

▶ Dessler, G. (2005). *Human Resource Management* (10th edition). Upper Saddle River, NJ: Pearson Education.

▶ Gravett, L. (2003). *HRM Ethics: Perspectives for a New Millennium*. Cincinnati: Atomic Dog Publishing.

▶ Hellriegel, D., Slocum, J. W., Jr. & Woodman, R. W. (2001). *Organizational Behavior* (9th edition). Cincinnati: South-Western.

▶ Johnson, C. E. (2001). *Meeting the Ethical Challenges of Leadership*. Thousand Oaks, CA: Sage Publications.

▸ Kaplan, Robert S. & Norton, David P. (1996). *The Balanced Scorecard: Translating Strategy into Action*. Boston, MA: Harvard Business School Press.

▸ Mathis, R. L. & Jackson, J. H. (2006). *Human Resource Management* (11th edition). Mason, OH: Thomson South-Western.

▸ Nickels, W. G., McHugh, J. M. & McHugh, S. M. (2002). *Understanding Business* (6th edition). New York: McGraw-Hill.

▸ Paine, L. (2005, June). *Creating Companies That Do the Right Thing: Character or Competence*. Paper presented at the 57th Annual Conference and Exposition of the Society for Human Resource Management, San Diego, CA.

▸ Pride, W. M. & Ferrell, O. C. (2000). *Marketing: Concepts and Strategy* (2000). Boston: Houghton Mifflin.

▸ Quinn, R. E., Faerman, S. R., Thompson, M. P. & McGrath, M. R. (2003). *Becoming a Master Manager: A Competency Approach* (3rd edition). Hoboken, NJ: John Wiley and Sons.

▸ Robbins, S. P. (2005). *Organizational Behavior* (11th edition). Upper Saddle River, NJ: Pearson Education.

▸ Shavelson, R. J. (1988). *Statistical Reasoning in the Behavioral Sciences* (2nd edition). Needham Heights, MA: Allyn & Baker.

▸ Werner, J. M. & DeSimone, R. L. (2006). *Human Resource Development* (4th edition). Mason, OH: Thompson South-Western.

2. Websites

▸ http://www.abih.org/

▸ http://www.aom.pace.edu/

▸ http://www.apa.org/

▸ http://www.astd.org/

▸ http://www.bcsp.org/

▸ http://www.impa-hr.org/

▸ http://www.shrm.org/

▸ http://www.worldatwork.org/

CHAPTER THREE

Workforce Planning and Employment

Objectives

This chapter helps you prepare for the SPHR examination by covering concepts and strategies associated with workforce planning and employment. This section composes **16%** of the SPHR examination.

Gain a Strategic Understanding of Workforce Planning and Employment

▸ **Understand the importance of workforce planning and employment to organizational success**

Gain an Understanding of Workforce Planning and Employment Law

▸ **Understand the implications of these laws, regulations, and precedent cases in the design of workforce planning and employment programs**

Gain an Understanding of Affirmative Action and Equal Employment Opportunity

▸ **Understand affirmative action plans**

▸ **Understand the EEO complaint process**

Gain an Understanding of Gender Discrimination

▸ **Understand the two types of sexual discrimination**

▸ **Understand the broad scope of hostile environment**

▸ **Understand how to develop effective harassment prevention programs**

Gain an Understanding of Workforce Planning

▸ **Understand how to forecast workforce needs**

▸ **Understand how to forecast workforce supply**

Gain an Understanding of Job Analysis

▸ **Understand the job analysis process**

▸ **Understand how to collect data needed for job analysis**

▸ **Understand how to write job descriptions and job specifications**

▸ **Understand job analysis using competencies**

Gain an Understanding of Recruitment

▶ **Understand internal recruitment methods**

▶ **Understand external recruitment methods**

▶ **Understand how to evaluate recruitment program effectiveness**

Gain an Understanding of the Contingent Workforce

Gain an Understanding of Selection

▶ **Understand the development of selection criteria**

▶ **Understand the selection process**

▶ **Understand the evaluation of the selection process**

Gain an Understanding of Post-Offer Employment Practices

▶ **Understand employment offers**

▶ **Understand employment contracts**

▶ **Under employer practices with respect to relocation benefits and requirements for medical tests**

Gain an Understanding of Organizational Exit

▶ **Understand concepts associated with organizational exit such as layoffs, exit interviews, and wrongful terminations**

Gain an Understanding of the Management of Employment Records

▶ **Understand legal requirements for the retention of employment and payroll related records**

Outline

Study Strategies

As with all chapters in this book, the objective is to understand the strategic implications of HR programmatic activities through grounding in the law, concepts, and practices associated with them. In this case, you should begin with the strategic plan of the organization and understand how the various employment practices facilitate its achievement. It is not enough to know the basics of recruitment or job analysis or workforce planning in isolation. The SPHR must approach the study of these and other concepts through an integrative approach understanding the interdependencies. You should attempt to understand how workforce planning, EEO strategies, recruitment, selection, organizational exit, and so forth are must be integrated into one comprehensive strategy that support the organizational goals and mission. You should also approach the study of this material by attempting to understand the interdependency of the various sections and the practices discussed in them. For example, how does workforce planning affect recruitment strategies, affirmative action plans, and exit strategies?

Introduction

Objective:
Gain a Strategic Understanding of Workforce Planning and Employment

There are a number of dynamics that increasingly make workforce planning and employment critical components of the organization's strategic plan. The United States economy has transitioned from a manufacturing base to a service base and is in the process of transitioning to a knowledge base. As the economy moves along this continuum, the success of the organization is increasingly based on the quality of its *human capital*, which is defined as the total current and potential capabilities of the organization's workforce. As this transition occurs, organizational strategies increasingly must be developed to develop the organization's primary resource: people. The quality of its human capital will allow an organization to differentiate itself in the market place, much as innovative products and services now do. In fact, for many organizations, human capital will become their *core competency*—the unique capability that distinguishes them from their competitors. To create this competency, an organization must be able to attract the right kinds of people in the right place at the right time.

The nature of competition has changed and is global. Markets and environments are frequently dynamic and volatile, and organizations have been downsized and right-sized to improve cost efficiencies. Globalization requires the organization to understand multiple cultures and how to attract, retain, and motivate persons from those cultures. The dynamics of the environment often require flexibility and adaptation at the lower levels of the organization. All this affects the workforce planning and employment practices.

Technology has not only changed the way work is done, it has also changed the knowledge, skills, and abilities needed to do the work. Organizations must plan to either attract those with the right skills to the organization or to develop those skills internally. The latter requires hiring individuals who have the capacity to learn and to grow.

Workforce demographics in the United States are changing. The workforce is aging and contains an increasing percentage of both women and members of minority groups. In addition, workers often come to the organization with deficient skill sets. The organization must plan how to replace the impending retirement of the "Baby Boomers" while developing the skills of those that follow.

The organization must be actively engaged in planning to determine how to react to the dynamics just discussed to develop an internal workforce that is capable of accomplishing the organization's strategic goals. That is the essence of workforce planning and employment.

Workforce Planning and Employment Law

Objective:

Gain an Understanding of Workforce Planning and Employment Law

Since the early 1960s there has been great legislative activity in the area of employment law. Most of this legislation has been enacted to prevent employment discrimination. The SPHR should be familiar with these laws and guide the organization in not only compliance with the legal requirements of the law, but also in its intent. The following regulations, executive orders, laws, and precedent case law are discussed in this section:

- Civil Rights Act of 1866
- United States Constitution
- Equal Pay Act (1963)
- Civil Rights Act of 1964
- Executive Orders 11246 (1965) and 1375 (1967) and 11478 (1969)
- Age Discrimination in Employment Act (1967)
- Consumer Credit Protection Act (1968)
- Fair Credit Reporting Act (1970)
- Rehabilitation Act (1973)
- Vietnam Era Veterans' Readjustment Assistance Act (1974)
- Privacy Act of 1974
- Pregnancy Discrimination Act (1978)
- Uniform Guidelines on Employee Selection Procedures (1978)
- Immigration Reform and Control Act (1986)
- Worker Adjustment and Retraining Notification Act (1988)
- Employee Polygraph Protection Act (1988)
- Americans with Disabilities Act (1990)
- Civil Rights Act of 1991
- Uniformed Services Employment and Reemployment Act (1994)
- Congressional Accountability Act (1995)
- Fair and Accurate Credit Transactions Act (2003)

▶ Precedent Case Law

    ▶ *Griggs v. Duke Power* (1971)

    ▶ *McDonnell-Douglas Corp v. Green* (1973)

    ▶ *Abermarle Paper Company v. Moody* (1975)

    ▶ *Washington v. Davis* (1976)

Civil Rights Act of 1866

The Thirteenth Amendment to the United States Constitution was passed in 1865 at the end of the Civil War and abolished slavery. However, it did not guarantee equal rights for all groups and states began passing laws limiting the rights of newly emancipated slaves in a number of areas, including employment. In response, the Civil Rights Act of 1866 was passed. It prohibits illegal discrimination based on race or ethnicity in the formation or enforcement of contracts. The act also allows for punitive and compensatory damages in cases of intentional racial discrimination. Its impact on preventing discrimination is limited to cases in which an actual employment contract exists and it doesn't cover other types of illegal discrimination based on sex, age, and so forth.

United States Constitution

The Fourteenth Amendment of the United States Constitution was passed in 1868 largely because the states were not complying with the provisions of the Civil Rights Act of 1866. It states, in part:

> *No state shall make or enforce any law which shall abridge the privileges or immunities of citizens of the United States; not shall any State deprive any person of life, liberty, or property, without due process of law; nor deny to any person within its jurisdiction the equal protection of the law.*

This seems to imply that all persons should be treated fairly and equally in matters of employment because the courts consider employment to be a property right. Had all employers and governments abided by this requirement and complied with the intent of the Civil Rights Act of 1866, the massive employment legislation of the twentieth century would not have been necessary.

Equal Pay Act (1963)

The Equal Pay Act of 1963, which is an amendment to the Fair Labor Standards Act, is covered comprehensively in Chapter 5, "Compensation and Benefits." The act prohibits discrimination in the payment of compensation based on sex for jobs that are similar in terms of skill, effort, responsibility, and working conditions.

Civil Rights Act of 1964

The Civil Rights Act of 1964 is the most comprehensive and far reaching legislation dealing with employee relations. Title VII of the act prohibits discrimination in employment as follows:

It shall be an unlawful employment practice for an employer—

1. *To fail or refuse to hire or to discharge any individual or otherwise discriminate against any individual with respect to his compensation, terms, conditions, or privileges of employment, because of such individual's race, color, religion, sex, or national origin; or*

2. *To limit, segregate, or classify his employees or applicants for employment in any way which would deprive or tend to deprive any individual of employment opportunities or otherwise adversely affect his status as an employee, because of such individual's race, color, religion, sex, or national origin.*

The outcome of the act, along with its amendments, has been to create *protected classes*. Those are groups specifically identified in the law for special protection from illegal discrimination. They are as follows:

▶ Race (African-American, Native American, Hispanic-American, and Asian-American)

▶ Color

▶ Religion

▶ Sex (women)

▶ National origin

▶ Employees over 40 (Age Discrimination in Employment Act)

▶ Disabled (Americans with Disabilities Act)

The act creates the Equal Employment Opportunity Commission *(EEOC)* in the Department of Labor to administer and enforce the act. The act prohibits retaliation against individuals exercising their rights under the act. This includes both voicing opposition to the organization's employment practices and filing complaints with the EEOC.

Employers covered by the act are

▶ Those that have 15 or more employees for each working day in each of 20 or more weeks in the current or preceding calendar year

▶ All private and public educational institutions

▶ Federal, state, and local governments

- ▶ Public and private employment agencies
- ▶ Labor unions with 15 or more members
- ▶ Joint labor/management committees for apprenticeships and training

The act also imposed certain record-keeping and reporting requirements on employers. Covered employers must keep employment-related records that can be requested by either the Equal Employment Opportunity Commission or the Office of Contract Compliance Programs. Those records include documents associated with recruitment and selection, promotions, discipline, compensation and benefits, training, and so forth. Retention requirements for the documents are discussed later in this chapter.

In addition certain employers are required to submit an annual report to EEOC. The most common annual report is the EEO-1, which is required to be submitted by the following employers:

- ▶ Employers with 100 or more employees, except for state and local governments
- ▶ Federal contractors with at least 50 employees and contracts of $50,000 or more
- ▶ Financial institutions with at least 50 employees and that hold government funds or issue savings bonds

The EEO-1 requires the workforce be reported by race and gender for nine categories of employees:

- ▶ Officials and managers
- ▶ Professionals
- ▶ Technicians
- ▶ Sales workers
- ▶ Office and clerical
- ▶ Craft workers (skilled)
- ▶ Operatives (semiskilled)
- ▶ Laborers (unskilled)
- ▶ Service workers

NOTE

EEO-1 is required for private businesses. Other industries might also be required to report on a different form, but the reporting requirements vary. For example, EEO-4 is a similar form for state and local governments, but is only required biannually.

Several exceptions in the law permit discrimination that would otherwise be prohibited. They are as follows:

▶ **Business necessity**   A practice that is job-related and necessary for the safe and efficient operation of the organization may be permitted even if it negatively affects certain employees covered under the act. For example, a Ph.D. in physics may be required for research physicist positions even though some groups might be less likely to possess that degree.

▶ **Bona fide occupational qualification** *(BFOQ)*   Permits an organization to exclude persons from consideration on a basis that would otherwise be illegal. For example, a film company wanting to hire an actor to play the female lead role could exclude all males from consideration.

▶ **Seniority systems**   Systems giving preferential treatment based on seniority are generally legal.

EXAM ALERT

You should expect at least one question on the Civil Rights Act of 1964. Remember that employers with fewer than 15 employees are not covered under the federal statute although they could be covered under local or state laws. Remember the concepts of job relatedness, business necessity, and BFOQ. They will be discussed again in this chapter and are critical to understanding employer obligations under the law.

Executive Orders 11246 (1965), 11375 (1967), and 11478 (1969)

Executive Order 11246, as amended by Executive Order 11375, requires federal contractors and subcontractors with contracts in excess of $10,000 in any 12-month period to comply with Title VII of the Civil Rights Act of 1964 and to take positive steps to eliminate employment barriers for women and minorities.

NOTE

A 2002 amendment to the executive order permits contractors and subcontractors that are religious organizations to hire only individuals of a particular religion. This amendment is controversial and is subject to being overturned by congressional action.

A contractor with contracts of more than $50,000 and 50 or more employees must develop and implement a written affirmative action plan to increase the participation of protected classes in the workforce. Executive Order 11246 creates the Office of Federal Contract Compliance Programs *(OFCCP)* within the Department of Labor to implement and monitor compliance under the orders. Noncompliance can result in cancellation of current contracts and ineligibility for future contracts with the federal government. Affirmative action is further discussed later in this chapter.

Executive Order 11478 prohibits discrimination in employment practices by the United States Postal Service and federal government agencies on the basis of race, color, religion, sex, national origin, handicap, or age. The executive order also requires federal agencies to prepare and implement affirmative action plans for federal employees.

EXAM ALERT

You should know that affirmative action plans are required of certain federal contractors by Executive Order 11246, as amended, and the OFCCP enforces the order. Expect a question on one or both of these items.

NOTE

States and local governments often have additional requirements for affirmative action activities with respect to governmental contracts issued at that level.

Age Discrimination in Employment Act of 1967

This act, commonly referred to as *ADEA*, prohibits employment discrimination against employees who are at least 40 years of age. It has been amended several times, including the Older Workers' Benefit Protection Act of 1990, which is discussed in Chapter 5.

The act covers employers that have 20 or more employees in each working day for 20 or more weeks in the current or preceding year and is administered and enforced by the EEOC. The act prohibits discrimination against employees over 40 in hiring, promotion, compensation, retirement, layoff, discharge, and any other terms, conditions, or privileges of employment. Employers may not retaliate against employees for exercising their rights under the law. In general, an employer may not require a mandatory retirement age. However, certain groups of employees—airline pilots, for example—may be subject to mandatory retirement based on safety requirements. In addition, highly paid executives over the age of 65 may be subject to involuntary retirement if they were in the position at least two years before the retirement and are entitled to immediate retirement benefits of at least $44,000.

Exceptions to the act are as follows:

▶ Bona fide seniority systems, even though they might adversely affect workers over 40, are generally allowed. For example, an employee who is 35 years of age with 15 years of service might be entitled to certain employment rights and benefits over an employee who is 55 but has worked with the company for only 5 years.

▶ Certain benefits may be adjusted based on age on the principle of equal costs or equal benefits. For example, an employer may provide less life insurance coverage to an older employee as long as the cost of the insurance is equal to what is spent on employees less than 40 years of age.

▶ The employer may take appropriate disciplinary action against covered employees if it does so for good cause.

▶ The employer may discriminate against persons over 40 using the requirements of BFOQ. For example, an advertising agency could discriminate against someone over 40 when hiring a model for children's clothing.

EXAM ALERT

You should expect a question on ADEA. Be familiar with its provisions and remember that the employer must have 20 employees, as opposed to the 15 employees required in most other discrimination laws. You should also be familiar with the act's exceptions.

Consumer Credit Protection Act (1968)

This act is discussed in depth in Chapter 5. It provides protections for employees whose wages have been garnished.

Fair Credit Reporting Act (1970)

This act, often referred to as the *FCRA*, regulates the process of obtaining and using credit and other types of information on employees. Consumer reporting agencies *(CRAs)* are businesses or persons that are paid a fee to assemble, analyze, evaluate, or report information on individuals for third parties. These reports are referred to in the regulations as *consumer reports*. The most common use of CRAs is to obtain credit reports on current or prospective employees. However, other vendors who provide background checks or perform investigations for a fee are also covered by the act. The employer must certify to the CRA that it is in compliance with all applicable provisions of the FCRA.

An employer that wants to obtain a consumer report on a current employee or applicant must advise the person of its intent. In addition, the employer must obtain written consent from the employee or applicant to obtain the report. There are certain exemptions to the pre-investigation notice and consent that are covered later in the discussion regarding the Fair and Accurate Credit Transactions Act.

An employer making a decision based wholly or in part on the consumer report that negatively affects the employee or applicant (failure to hire, termination, disciplinary action and so forth) must provide that individual with a *pre-adverse action disclosure*. Included in the disclosure is a document, prescribed by the Federal Trade Commission *(FTC)*, which provides employees with information on their rights and a copy of the report. In general, the employer must then provide a reasonable amount of time, usually five business days, to refute the findings. After the final decision is made and effected, the employer must give the employee or applicant another notice that includes

- ▶ The name, address, and telephone number of the CRA

- ▶ A statement indicating that the employer, not the CRA, made the decision regarding the adverse action and that the CRA would not be able to provide specific reasons why the action was taken

- ▶ Notice of the right of the individual's right to obtain a free copy of the report from the CRA within 60 days

- ▶ Notice of the right of the individual to contact the CRA to dispute the accuracy of the information and to provide more complete information

Rehabilitation Act of 1973

This act prohibits employment discrimination based on disability. Those covered by the act are as follows:

- ▶ Contractors or subcontractors that have federal contracts in excess of $2,500

- ▶ Depositories of federal funds

- ▶ Organizations receiving federal grants or aid assistance

Contractors that have contracts in excess of $10,000 must take affirmative action to hire the disabled, and contractors with contracts of more than $50,000 and at least 50 employees must also develop and implement affirmative action plans to hire qualified individuals with a disability. These plans may be integrated with affirmative action plans required under Executive Order 11246 and the Vietnam Era Veterans' Readjustment Assistance Act. The OFCCP monitors compliance with the law. Failure to comply can result in cancellation of current contracts and ineligibility for future federal contacts.

NOTE

As amended, the Rehabilitation Act definitions of handicap and requirements for accommodation are very similar to those of the Americans with Disabilities Act, which are discussed in greater depth later in this section.

Vietnam Era Veterans' Readjustment Assistance Act (1974)

This act prohibits discrimination against disabled veterans, veterans of the Vietnam era, veterans who served on active duty in during a war, campaign, expedition, or military operation and recently separated veterans. *Recently separated veterans* are those that have been released from active duty less than three years. The act applies to the federal government and employers having at least $50,000 worth of federal contracts and 50 or more employees. Contractors meeting this threshold are required to

▶ Develop and implement a written affirmative action plan to employee covered veterans.

▶ List job opportunities with the local unemployment office. Exceptions are temporary positions lasting less than four days, jobs that are to be filled internally, and certain top-level positions.

▶ Prepare and submit an annual report (VETS-100) that reports hiring practices with respect to covered veterans.

NOTE

The requirement for filing a VETS-100 report has been changed so that only employers with $100,000 or more in federal contracts are required to file the report.

The act is administered by the OFCCP. Failure to comply with the provision of the act can lead to contract cancellation and disbarment from future federal contracts.

Privacy Act of 1974

This act applies only to federal government employees and prohibits the release of information contained in an employee's personnel file, with limited exceptions, without the employee's written release. Federal employees also have the right to review their personnel files.

NOTE

In general, employees other than those of the federal government have no such rights. State and local laws may impose restrictions on the release of employee information, both for private and public sector employees. The Health Insurance Portability and Accountability Act *(HIPAA)*, discussed in Chapter 5, protects disclosure of medical information.

Employers must be very careful in releasing employment-related information on employees. Release could subject the employer to tort action under common law for invasion of privacy, defamation of character, and so forth.

Pregnancy Discrimination Act (1978)

This act is an amendment to the Civil Rights Act of 1964 and prohibits discrimination in employment matters based on pregnancy, childbirth, or related medical conditions. An employer must treat pregnant women the same for all employment purposes, including fringe benefits, as other employees who are similar in their ability or inability to work. Employer policies must apply equally to pregnant employees as to other employees. For example, if the employer provides temporary disability insurance for its employees, pregnancy must be considered the same as any other temporary disability. Employers may not require a pregnant employee to leave work because of the pregnancy if she is able to perform the essential function of the job. However, the act does not require any special accommodations or benefits for pregnant employees that are not provided to other employees.

> **EXAM ALERT**
>
> You can expect a question regarding the Pregnancy Discrimination Act. You should know that the act does not require any special provisions for pregnancy other than to treat it as any other temporary disability.

> **NOTE**
>
> The Pregnancy Discrimination Act might present problems when the pregnant employee is employed in hazardous occupations or subject to exposure to chemicals that could impose health risks for the fetus. Although the employer might believe it wise to temporarily transfer the employee to another position, to do so involuntarily is a violation of the act. The Supreme Court has ruled that the health of the fetus is the responsibility of the employee.

Uniform Guidelines on Employee Selection Procedures (1978)

The Uniform Guidelines on Employee Selection Procedures *(UGESP)* is considered to be the most comprehensive document regarding the legality of employee selection procedures. They are administrative regulations published in the *Code of Federal Regulations*. The document provides guidance as to how employers should manage their various employment systems (recruitment, testing, selection, promotion, discipline, and so forth) to comply with federal employment law prohibiting discrimination. Two approaches for proving that illegal discrimination has not occurred are addressed in the guidelines: no disparate impact and job relatedness/business necessity. These approaches are discussed next.

No Disparate Impact

The regulations provide guidance on the determination of adverse impact, also referred to as *disparate impact*. Adverse impact occurs when members of a protected class are negatively affected by employment decisions. As will be discussed later in this chapter, employees alleging illegal discrimination must prove first that they are a member of a protected class and then that they have been the victim of disparate treatment or adverse impact. *Disparate treatment* is a relatively simple concept; it means that members of a protected class are treated differently from others. For example, requiring a woman to take a strength test but not requiring the same of a man. Disparate treatment is discussed further later in this chapter.

The determination of adverse impact is a bit more complicated and there are many statistical methods of doing so. However, UGESP provides a relatively simple way of determining whether adverse impact has occurred. The methodology is referred to as the *4/5ths rule* and can be used for analysis both internally and externally. Internally it can be used to determine whether an employer procedure or policy is adversely impacting a protected class. It also can be used to analyze the organization's workforce in relation to the external workforce to determine whether underutilization exists. Both methods are described in the following sections.

Internal Analysis of Employment Practices

Under UGESP, adverse impact occurs when the selection rate for a protected class is lower than 80% of the selection rate of the group with the highest selection rate. Selection rate is a broad term and can be applied to a number of practices. For example:

- Selection for an interview
- Passing an interview
- Selection for a position
- Selection for promotion
- Selection for training
- Performance awards and bonuses

As an example, an organization just finished a large recruitment effort that resulted in the hiring of 200 employees. The data regarding the number of employees interviewed and the number hired are shown in Table 3.1. The organization wants to determine whether its hiring practices resulted in adverse impact.

TABLE 3.1 Internal Adverse Impact Analysis

Group	# Interviewed	# Hired	Selection Rate
Hispanic Males	30	20	60%
White Males	100	80	80%
African-American Females	100	65	65%
Asian-American Females	50	35	70%
Totals	310	200	

To determine whether the selection rates identified in the table resulted in adverse impact, the adverse impact threshold must be determined. This is determined by calculating 4/5ths (80%) of the highest selection rate. In this case, the highest selection rate is that of white males and is 80%. The adverse impact threshold is 4/5ths of 80% or 64% (.80 ¥ .80). Any selection rate below 64% is an indication of adverse impact. In this case, Hispanic males have been adversely impacted. At this point the organization might elect to modify the practice, abandon the practice, or justify the practice using job relatedness and business necessity.

NOTE

Application forms cannot ask about an individual's protected class status, but the employer might be required to prove that such employment practices as the application process, prescreening process, and inventory process do not create adverse impact. This is referred to as *applicant flow data*.

There are two ways to collect this data. The first, and preferable, way is to request that the applicant complete a separate EEO information form. The form must be kept separate from the application. The second way is visual inspection. For example, a receptionist can record perceptions of race and gender when the individual reports for an interview.

Analysis of the Workforce Against the External Labor Market

The organization might want to know whether the internal workforce mirrors the demographics of the external workforce. This analysis is required if the employer is required to prepare affirmative action plans and otherwise can be used to evaluate the organization's diversity efforts.

Table 3.2 compares the composition of the organization's workforce, in percentages, with the composition of the relevant labor market. The organization wants to know whether its practices have resulted in adverse impact and underutilization of a protected class.

TABLE 3.2   External Adverse Impact Analysis

Group	% of Internal Workforce	% of Labor Market	4/5ths of Labor Market
African-Americans	15	20	16
Asian-Americans	10	8	6.4
Native Americans	4	4	3.2
Hispanic-Americans	21	25	20

In this example adverse impact and underutilization are shown for African-Americans because they compose 15% of the internal workforce, but the adverse impact threshold is 16%. Note that Hispanic-Americans compose 21% of the workforce when they compose 25% of the external labor market. However, 21% is above the adverse impact threshold of 20%.

NOTE

Remember that it is the outcome of an employer's practices, not the intent, which determines whether adverse impact and potentially illegal discrimination has occurred. A seemingly neutral practice engaged in with good intent can be found to be illegal.

EXAM ALERT

Given a scenario, you should be able to determine whether adverse impact has occurred based on either internal or external analysis.

Job Relatedness / Business Necessity

An employer might not be illegally discriminating against a protected class, even if its employment practices result in adverse action for a protected class. For the purposes of UGESP, practices are referred to as *tests*. Recruitment, interviews, job simulations, and actual tests are all referred to as tests. All tests must be job-related and they must be valid predictors of performance on the job. Two types of validity are used, as was discussed at length in Chapter 2, "Strategic Management."

Content validity is used to prove that the practice is job-related. *Job-related* means that the practice (test) actually contains elements of the knowledge, skills, and ability required in the job. *Criterion validity* is used to prove that the test or practice is a valid predictor of future performance. Concurrent validity and predictive validity are two methods of validating the capability of a test to predict future performance. Those methods were discussed in Chapter 2.

However, it is not enough to prove that the tests are job-related. The practices must also be reasonably related to the safe and efficient operation of the organization. This concept is known as *business necessity*. The organization must prove that it would incur significant expenses, or suffer some harm, if it did not use the particular practice. For example, an organization could argue that a mathematical aptitude test is highly correlated with performance on a particular job and that not using it would cause the organization to select employees who would fail on the job, thus resulting in increased cost associated with high turnover. The organization could also argue that high error rates caused by these employees result in expensive rework.

Immigration Reform and Control Act (1986)

This act, often referred to as *IRCA*, was passed for two purposes. The first is to prohibit employers from hiring persons who are not permitted to work in the United States. Passed largely to reduce illegal immigration, the act prohibits the hiring, recruiting, and referral of undocumented workers and unauthorized aliens for a fee. Compliance with the act requires that the employer

▶ Not knowingly hire unauthorized aliens

▶ Verify the employee's identity and work status

▶ Maintain records regarding the employee's identity

Employers must verify the identity of the employee and eligibility to work in the United States by completing and signing a Form I-9. The form must be completed within 72 hours of hiring and kept for a minimum of three years or one year after the employee leaves employment, whichever is greater.

The second purpose of the act is to prohibit discrimination in hiring and termination based on national origin or citizenship status. Employers may not discriminate in the hiring or termination of individuals based on

▶ National origin

▶ Citizenship status

    ▶ As a citizen

    ▶ As an alien lawfully admitted for either temporary and permanent residence

    ▶ As a refugee granted asylum

The employer may not retaliate against an employee for exercising any rights under the act. In addition, an employer may not refuse to honor documents that show immigration status nor may the employer require additional documentation beyond that required in the act. Finally, the act does not prohibit employers from giving preference in employment to a United States citizen over an alien if the two have equal qualifications.

With very limited exceptions—union hiring halls, for example—the act applies to all employers. However, the discrimination provisions of the act apply only to employers with four or more employees. The act originally was enforced by the United States Immigration and Naturalization Service *(INS)*, but responsibility has now been transferred to the Department of Homeland Security.

Employers who fail to comply with the form I-9 requirements can be subject to fines ranging from $100 to $1,000 per violation. Each instance of not documenting an employee can be found to be a separate violation. Additional fines can be imposed for falsification of documents and knowingly accepting fraudulent documents. These fines can range up to $5,000 per incident for repeated incidents. Repeated hiring of unauthorized aliens can result in fines up to $10,000 for each alien hired. Finally, employers who consistently violate the act can be subject to criminal prosecution.

EXAM ALERT

You should expect a question regarding IRCA. Remember that it has dual purposes: to prevent discrimination based on national origin or citizenship status, and to prevent the employment of undocumented workers. Also remember that the I-9 must be completed within 72 hours of employment.

NOTE

Although other antidiscrimination laws apply to almost all personnel actions, IRCA coverage is limited to the hiring and termination process.

Worker Adjustment and Retraining Notification Act (1988)

This act, most frequently referred to as the *WARN act*, requires advance notification to employees in the event of mass layoffs and plant closings. The act applies to employers that employ 100 or employees (excluding part-time employees) or 100 or more employees that in the aggregate work 4,000 hours per week, excluding overtime. Subsidiaries and independent contractors may be considered in the calculation for coverage if they have common ownership.

The employer must provide 60 days advance notice to employees, their designated representative, the dislocated worker unit (unemployment office), and the chief elected official in the governmental unit to which the organization pays the highest taxes when any of the following events occurs at a single site of employment during any 30-day period:

▶ The permanent or temporary shutdown of a plant that results in 50 or more employees, excluding part-time employees, losing their jobs

▶ A mass layoff if

   ▶ 50 or more employees, excluding part-time employees, are laid off and the layoffs constitute at least 33% of the workforce or

   ▶ 500 or more employees, excluding part-time employees

There are exceptions to the notification requirements that might permit less than a 60-day advance notice in the cases of

▶ Natural disasters

▶ Business conditions that could not have been reasonably foreseen

However, if a reduced notice exception exists, the employer must give the notice as soon as it is practical to do so. The notice must include an explanation for the shortened notice.

Failure to provide notice can result in significant costs to the employer. Former employees or their designated representative (a union) may sue the employer for back wages, including health benefits, for each day of violation up to the full 60 days. For example, if the employer provided notice but closed the plant or executed the layoff 30 days after the notice, it could be liable for an additional 30 days of compensation. The actual amount that can be awarded is reduced by any compensation or severance payments made during the violation period. Employers may also be subject to fines for violation of the act.

> **EXAM ALERT**
>
> You should be familiar with the conditions under which WARN notification is required.

Employee Polygraph Protection Act (1988)

The act, often referred to as *EPPA*, restricts most private employers from conducting polygraph (lie detector) tests on prospective and current employees. It is enforced by the Wage and Hour Division of the Department of Labor. Pre-employment polygraph tests are not permitted, with the following exceptions:

▶ Local, state, or federal governments and certain federal contractors involved in law enforcement or national security

▶ Private employers who provide certain security services (armored cars, security alarm systems, private guards, and so forth)

▶ Private employers that are involved in manufacturing, distributing, or dispensing controlled substances

Private employers, however, may administer polygraph tests to employees that are subjects of investigations regarding economic loss or injury suffered by the employer. For example, an employer may administer a polygraph to an employee suspected of theft, misappropriation of funds, embezzlement, and so forth.

This employer right is not without limitation. The employer must have a reasonable cause to believe that the employee was involved in the activity being investigated and had access to the lost, stolen, or damaged property. The employee does not have to take the polygraph and, if he or she elects to, may terminate the test at any time. The employer must provide the employee with a statement indicating why the test is requested and the questions that will be asked. The employer is prohibited from taking a personnel action based on the employee's refusal to take the test. Furthermore, the employer cannot use the polygraph test results as the sole determinant of a personnel action. There must be other evidence that the employee was involved in the alleged infraction.

Americans with Disabilities Act (1990)

This act, commonly referred to as *ADA*, is the major federal legislative act that prohibits employment discrimination against the disabled. Title I of the act prohibits discrimination in employment decisions against qualified individuals with a disability. This includes job application procedures, hiring, firing, promotion, compensation, selection for training and any other terms, conditions, or privileges of employment.

The act is enforced by the EEOC and covers employers that have 15 or more employees for 20 or more calendar weeks in the current of preceding year, employment agencies, labor unions with fifteen or more employees, state and local governments, and joint labor-management apprenticeship committees. These are the same employers covered by the Civil Rights Act of 1964.

For an employee to be covered by the act, the individual must be disabled and qualified for the job. After that is determined, the employer might have an obligation to engage in reasonable accommodation. These subjects are covered in the following sections.

What Is a Disability?

The act covers a disabled individual that

▶ Has a physical or mental impairment that substantially limits one or more major life function

▶ Has a record of such impairment

▶ Is regarded or treated as having an impairment

NOTE

The courts have also included into coverage under the act those that have an association or relationship with a disabled individual. For example, an employer could not fail to hire an individual who has a disabled child on the basis that that person might miss too much work in caring for the child.

Physical impairment refers to any physiological condition or loss of one or more body systems (neurological, respiratory, speech organs, cardiovascular, digestive, and so forth). *Mental impairment* encompasses such conditions as mental retardation, mental or emotional illness, and learning disabilities. The Supreme Court has ruled that correction or control of an impairment by medicine or medical device to the level of normal functioning may remove the individual from coverage under the act. For example, eyeglasses that restore vision to the normal range or medicine that controls blood pressure may return the employee to normal functional capacity, thus eliminating the limitation on a major life activity. Major life functions include

▶ Caring for oneself
▶ Breathing

▶ Reproduction
▶ Learning

▶ Performing manual tasks
▶ Sitting or standing

▶ Walking
▶ Lifting or reaching

▶ Seeing
▶ Thinking or concentrating

▶ Hearing
▶ Interacting with others

▶ Speaking

NOTE

Case law is ever-changing in this area. The definitions of impairment and major life function are constantly evolving.

However, certain conditions are specifically exempted from the definition of disability in the act. They are as follows:

- ▶ Homosexuality and bisexuality

- ▶ Sexual behavior disorders (such as pedophilia and exhibitionism)

- ▶ Gender identity disorders not resulting from physical impairments

- ▶ Compulsive gambling

- ▶ Pyromania

- ▶ Kleptomania

- ▶ Current illegal use of drugs

> **NOTE**
>
> Although illegal drug use is not covered under ADA, drug addiction itself might be if the employee has undergone or is undergoing drug rehabilitation and is not currently using illegal drugs. The same is true for alcohol addiction. An employee can be disciplined for on-the-job use of alcohol, but comes under the protection of the law if the individual is a recovering alcoholic.

What Is a Qualified Individual?

A disabled person, to be a qualified individual, must be able to perform the essential functions of the job with or without accommodation. Job analysis, discussed later in this chapter, is a critical process for determining those tasks that are essential for successfully performing in the job. A function is essential if the following conditions are true:

- ▶ **It is the reason why the job exists**. In other words, the job was created specifically to perform the function in question.

- ▶ **The function cannot be assigned to another employee**. If assignment of a particular task would disrupt the primary purpose of the job, it is not an essential function. For example, the primary job responsibility of the job is to load trucks with a forklift whereas a minor function is to perform periodic maintenance on the forklift, such as changing the tires. If the organization has a department that performs other maintenance on the forklifts, the function of changing tires could likely be easily reassigned to that department without disturbing the primary purpose of the job. Thus, changing tires would not be an essential function.

- ▶ **The function requires a great deal of skill not found in employees in other job categories**. The more skill required, the more difficult it is to assign the function to another employee and, consequently, the more likely that function would be considered an essential function.

What Is Reasonable Accommodation?

An employee or applicant that is disabled but qualified to perform the essential functions of the job is entitled to reasonable accommodations by the employer. The intent of the law is that this be an interactive process with the employee or applicant requesting the accommodation and the employer responding in an appropriate manner. However, it is good practice for the SPHR to be proactive in this area, particularly if it is obvious that accommodation is needed and the nature of the disability might prevent the employee from asking for the accommodation. The employer can require documentation for disabilities or requests for accommodation that are not obvious. Failure to do so relieves the employer from responsibility and the employee is not entitled to accommodation under the law.

Reasonable accommodation is the modification of the workplace or work requirements to permit the individual to perform the essential functions of the job unless those accommodations would create and undue hardship on the employer. There are no legislative rules that clearly define reasonable accommodation as opposed to undue hardship. Each situation must be determined individually. Often the determination is based on the resources available to the employer. A reasonable accommodation for a large corporation might very well be undue hardship for a smaller one. The EEOC has determined that there are three categories of accommodation. They are as follows:

▶ **Job application process**   The job application and selection process must not be discriminatory. Accommodations such sign language interpreters, modification of testing procedures, applications in Braille, and so forth might be appropriate in certain circumstances.

▶ **Work environment**   Accommodations in the work environment are virtually unlimited. Accommodations can be made to the physical layout itself such as making the restroom handicapped-accessible, widening aisles for wheelchair access, providing teletype phone capabilities, and so forth. The nature of the work and the work flow itself can be modified by eliminating nonessential job functions or assigning those tasks to another individual. Finally, the work schedule itself can be modified as an accommodation.

▶ **Benefits and privileges of employment**   In some circumstances accommodations can be made to allow the employee to continue to work or to deal with the medical treatment associated with the disability. If the employee can no longer perform the essential function of the job, reassignment to another job is often preferable to termination. However, there is no obligation under the law to create a special position for the employee. In addition, leaves of absences to attend to medical issues might be appropriate.

NOTE

The EEOC has issued guidance regarding reasonable accommodation and undue hardship, which can be found on its website at http://www.eeoc.gov/.

ADA restricts the use of pre-employment medical examinations and medical inquiries. An employer cannot inquire into the medical conditions and medical history of an individual prior to employment. The employer, however, may ask whether the employee can perform the essential functions of the job. Pre-employment medical examinations are prohibited. However, medical examinations can be required after a conditional offer of employment is given to the applicant.

Medical examinations must be nondiscriminatory in that either all applicants or all applicants in a given job category can be required to have a pre-employment medical examination. Requiring medical examinations for only those whom the employer believes might be incapable of performing the job is a violation of the act. Medical examinations for current employees may be required if they are clearly job-related, required by law, required to determine whether a disability exists or a particular accommodation is required and, in limited circumstances, to determine whether the employee can perform the job (fitness for duty examinations).

After the employee has received a conditional job offer, medical information necessary for normal processing may be collected. For example, medical information needed for health and life insurance or by the occupational health nurse may be collected. The employer is responsible for maintaining the confidentiality of any medical information collected. Access to medical records must be restricted to those who need to know, and the records themselves must be kept separate from other employment-related records.

> **NOTE**
>
> Drug tests are not medical examinations under ADA and they can be used in the employment prescreening process.

Employment discrimination is not the only prohibition covered by the act. Title II of the act prohibits discrimination against the disabled in government programs and public transportation. Title III requires access for the disabled to public and commercial facilities, and Title IV requires closed-captioning services in television broadcasts for those who are hearing impaired. Finally, the act prohibits retaliation against an employee for exercising any right provided by the act.

> **EXAM ALERT**
>
> You most definitely will receive one or more questions regarding ADA. Remember that the individual must be disabled or thought to be disabled and qualified to perform the essential functions of the job. When that threshold is reached, the employer has an obligation to provide reasonable accommodations. You should know the definition of disability and when an individual is qualified under the act. In addition, you should be familiar with reasonable accommodations and undue hardship.

Civil Rights Act of 1991

The Civil Rights Act of 1991 is an amendment to the Civil Rights Act of 1964. It was passed largely to offset some conservative judicial decisions by the Supreme Court in the late 1980s, often called the *Reagan Court*. Major provisions of the act are as follows:

- **Returned the burden of proof to the original standard**. The Supreme Court had, in the late 1980s, issued a decision that placed the burden of proof on the employee to prove that the employer had engaged in illegal discrimination. The act changed the burden of proof back to the original standard. An employee has the burden to prove that he or she is a member of a protected class and that the employer's employment practices have resulted in adverse impact on members of the protected class. After passage of the act, the burden of proof then switches to the employer to prove that the adverse impact was not a result of illegal discrimination.

- **Allowed for jury trials and compensatory and punitive damages**. The Civil Rights Act of 1964 permits only actual damages. That is damages for lost wages, attorney fees, and court costs. The Civil Rights Act of 1866 provides for additional damages but only in specified situations. The Civil Rights Act of 1991 permits damages to compensate the employee for pain and suffering, mental anguish, and other intangible damages. It also permits the courts to award punitive damages designed to punish the employer for egregious instances of intentional discrimination.

- **Prevents the use of a "mixed motive" defense**. Prior to the act, employers could defend discriminatory action by proving that the action was justified in the absence of discriminatory intent. For example, the employer could argue that the employee's performance was so poor that termination would have occurred in any event. The act prohibits such defenses and requires the plaintiff only to prove that protected class status was a factor in the decision to take an action.

- **Prohibits the practice of race-norming**. Many employers began the process of adjusting the scores of protected classes on tests used in the employment process either by adding to the score or establishing different passing scores for protected classes. The process was used to level the playing field when statistics revealed that certain protected classes scored lower on the particular test. The act prohibits such practices.

- **Extended protection of the Civil Rights Act of 1964**. Protection was extended to include certain federal and state government employees not previously covered under the act. Protection was also granted to United States citizens working for United States organizations in foreign countries except where those rights conflict with local law or customs.

EXAM ALERT

Expect a question regarding the Civil Rights Act of 1991, most likely regarding provisions for compensatory and punitive damages.

NOTE

Under the Civil Rights Act of 1991, compensatory and punitive damages are limited based on the size of the organization as depicted in Table 3.3.

TABLE 3.3 Compensatory and Punitive Damage Limitations (Civil Rights Act of 1991)

Size of Organization	Limit
15–100 employees	$ 50,000
101–200 employees	$100,000
201–500 employees	$200,000
More than 500 employees	$300,000

Uniformed Services Employment and Reemployment Act (1994)

This act prohibits discrimination in employment actions based on military service. It is discussed in further depth in Chapter 5.

Congressional Accountability Act (1995)

This act brought employees of the United States Congress under coverage of 11 major employee relations and employment-related laws. Those laws are as follows:

- Fair Labor Standards Act (1938)
- Civil Rights Act of 1964, as amended
- Age Discrimination in Employment Act (1967)
- Occupational Safety and Health Act of 1970
- Rehabilitation Act of 1973
- Civil Service Reform Act (1978)
- Employee Polygraph Protection Act (1988)
- Worker Adjustment and Retraining Notification Act of 1988

- Americans with Disabilities Act (1990)
- Family and Medical Leave Act (1993)
- Veterans Reemployment Act (1994)

Fair and Accurate Credit Transactions Act (2003)

This act, frequently referred to as *FACTA*, amended the Fair Credit Reporting Act discussed earlier. The act was passed largely in reaction to the increasing problem of identity theft. It provides certain rights for consumers, such as the right to get a free copy of their credit report annually, and mandates a number of obligations for providers, resellers, and users of credit reports. As a user of credit reports and other third-party information, FACTA predominantly affects HR in two ways:

- Pre-investigation notification and consent are no longer required when contracting with a third party for certain types of investigations, such as allegations of employee misconduct, violations of law, or violations of employer policies. The post-investigatory notification requirements are still mandated.

- The employer cannot maintain credit reports on employees. After an employment decision is made, based in whole or in part on a credit report, the report must be removed from the files and disposed of.

Precedent Case Law

Court decisions regarding employment and antidiscrimination law are constantly interpreting and modifying the current statues. As discussed earlier, Supreme Court rulings become the law of the land. Where those rulings differ from the current intent of the legislative body, they can be overturned only by congressional action as in the case of the Civil Rights Act of 1991. The following sections compose a list of precedent cases with which the SPHR should be familiar.

Griggs v. Duke Power (1971)

The Supreme Court decision in *Griggs* created the judicial concept of adverse impact and established two major points:

- Discrimination does not need to be overt or intentional to violate the Civil Rights Act of 1964. It is the outcome of the practices that is in question. If a practice results in differential effect (adverse impact), it is a potential violation of the law.

- The employer must prove that a practice is job-related as a business necessity if that practice creates adverse impact.

NOTE

The concept of adverse impact is discussed later in this chapter.

McDonnell-Douglas Corp. v. Green (1973)

This Supreme Court ruling established the concept of disparate treatment and created what is known as the *McDonnell-Douglas test*. Disparate treatment, by definition, is intentional discrimination. To establish a *prima facie* case of disparate treatment, the court set the following conditions:

▶ The person belongs to a protected class.

▶ The individual applied for a job and was qualified for the job for which the employer was seeking applicants.

▶ The individual was rejected for the job.

▶ After the rejection, the employer continued to seek applications from persons with the same or similar qualifications of the individual.

EXAM ALERT

You should be familiar with both *Griggs* and *McDonnell-Douglas* because they are the two precedent cases for adverse impact and disparate treatment.

Abermarle Paper Company v. Moody (1975)

The Supreme Court decision in *Abermarle* expanded the guidance provided in *Griggs* by clarifying that employment tests, including performance evaluation systems, used to make employment decisions must not only be job-related but that they must also be valid predictors of performance on the job. The effect of the ruling was essentially to make the federal regulations contained in the Uniform Guidelines for Employee Selection Procedures take on the impact of law.

Chandler v. Roudebush (1976)

The Supreme Court ruled that federal employees have the same rights under federal employment discrimination statutes as private sector employees.

Washington v. Davis (1976)

The Supreme Court ruled in *Washington* that an employer practice, in this case a verbal skills test for police officers, can be job-related even if it creates adverse impact for a protected class. To be job-related, a practice must be a valid predictor of performance.

Regents of the University of California v. Bakke (1978)

The Supreme Court ruled that a medical school could legitimately consider race in its admission procedures but that race could not be the only factor considered.

EXAM ALERT

Bakke is the most well-known precedent case regarding reverse discrimination. You might expect a question here. The ruling actually is somewhat mixed in that it establishes the principle that race can be a factor in decisions, but it cannot be the only factor.

United Steelworkers v. Weber (1979)

The Supreme Court ruled that voluntary affirmative action quotas agreed to by an employer and a union are legal. However, the court indicated that such agreements can be used within very narrow limitations so as to not trammel the interest of nonprotected groups.

Meritor Savings Bank v. Vinson (1986)

The Supreme Court ruled that a hostile work environment was a violation of Title VII even if there are no negative employment consequences and that an economic effect is not required for sexual discrimination to occur.

Johnson v. Santa Clara County Transportation Agency (1987)

The Supreme Court ruled that gender could be used as one factor in an employment decision if under-representation is shown and the affirmative action plan does not have firm quotas.

Martin v. Wilks (1988)

The Supreme Court ruled that reverse discrimination could occur if the nonprotected class is not consulted in the negotiations for a consent decree giving a protected class employment preferences.

City of Richmond v. J. A. Croson Company (1989)

The Supreme Court ruled that rigid numerical quota systems were unconstitutional when past discrimination was not documented.

Taxman v. Board of Education of Piscataway (1993)

The United States Court of Appeals ruled that a nonremedial affirmative action plan cannot violate the nondiscrimination mandate of the Civil Rights Act of 1964.

Harris v. Forklift Systems, Inc. (1993)

The Supreme Court ruled that a "reasonable person" test must be used to determine the existence of a hostile work environment that violates Title VII.

Hopwood v. State of Texas (1996)

The United States Court of Appeals ruled that taking race into account, even as a means of achieving diversity, violates the Fourteenth Amendment guarantee of equal protection. The Supreme Court refused to hear this case on appeal.

Ocale v. Sundowner Offshore Services, Inc. (1998)

The Supreme Court ruled that Title VII prohibitions against discrimination based on sex includes same sex harassment.

Faragher v. City of Boca Raton (1998)

The Supreme Court ruled that the employer has vicarious, as opposed to strict, liability for the hostile environment created by a supervisor unless it establishes and clearly communicates procedures for handling sexual harassment complaints and the employee fails to follow those procedures. The Court further stated that if the harassment results in a tangible employment action, there is no defense and the employer is strictly liable.

Ellerth v. Burlington Northern (1998)

The Supreme Court defined *a tangible employment action* as a significant change in employment status such as hiring, firing, failing to promote, reassignment with significantly different responsibilities, or a decision causing a significant change in benefits.

Grutter v. Bollinger et al. (2003)

The Supreme Court ruled that narrowly tailored use of race in admission decisions to a law school does not violate the Fourteenth Amendment guarantee of equal protection when it is used to further a compelling governmental interest in the educational benefits that flow from a diverse student body. The Court ruled that the decision must be made based on a highly individualized review of each applicant; that no decision can be based automatically on one variable such as race; and that the process must ensure that all factors contributing to diversity are meaningfully considered.

Gratz et al. v. Bollinger et al. (2003)

The Supreme Court ruled that giving preference to minorities for admission to a college undergraduate program serves a governmental interest in the educational benefits that result from a racially and ethnically diverse student body. However, the Court ruled that the procedures used in this case violated the Fourteenth Amendment guarantee of equal protection because they were not sufficiently narrowly tailored.

NOTE

Grutter and *Gratz* were decided on the same day by the Supreme Court.

General Dynamics Land Systems, Inc. v. Cline (2004)

The Supreme Court ruled that the Age Discrimination in Employment Act does not protect younger workers who are over 40 years of age from employment decisions that favor older workers (reverse age discrimination).

Affirmative Action and Equal Employment Opportunity

Objective:

Gain an Understanding of Affirmative Action and Equal Employment Opportunity

Laws, regulations, and executive orders require various employers to engage in affirmative action to increase the applicant supply of individuals in protected classes that are under-represented. Employees that believe they are victims of illegal discrimination have the legal right to bring those complaints to the Equal Employment Opportunity Commission. These two important processes are discussed in the following section.

Affirmative Action

Affirmative action is the process by which employers engage in employment practices designed to eliminate the present effects of past discrimination. Affirmative action can be voluntary or involuntary. Voluntary affirmative action is engaged in by organizations that realize that is good business practice and the right thing to do. These employers understand that diversity in the workforce often creates a positive image for the organization, which could result in improved organizational performance, increased customer loyalty, and improved employee recruitment and retention programs. In these cases, a written formal affirmative action plan might or might not be developed.

> **NOTE**
>
> Voluntary affirmative action plans can be a problem and result in complaints of reverse discrimination, particularly where there is no history of past discrimination in the organization.

However, as discussed previously, many organizations are required to develop and implement, if indicated, formal affirmative action plans as required by Executive Order 11246, the Rehabilitation Act of 1973, and the Vietnam Era Veterans' Readjustment Act of 1974. In general, the following employers must develop and implement, if appropriate, written affirmative action plans *(AAPs)* and submit them to the Office of Federal Contract Compliance Programs on an annual basis:

▶ Federal contractors and subcontractors with 50 or more employees and $50,000 in government contracts during any 12-month period

▶ Depositories of federal funds

▶ Issuing or paying agents for United States savings bonds and savings notes

In addition, certain other employers might also be required to submit written affirmative action plans. The courts can require employers in certain instances to prepare and implement AAPs. Also, employers might agree or be required to submit affirmative action plans as part of consent agreements negotiated under the auspices of state or federal courts.

> **NOTE**
>
> The threshold for coverage under the Vietnam Veterans' Readjustment Act has been raised to employers that have contracts of at least $100,000.

In November of 2000, the OFCCP issued new regulations designed to simplify the AAP development process. The new regulations require an organizational profile using either a workforce analysis or an organizational display, a job group analysis, an availability analysis, a utilization analysis, and goals and actions, if appropriate. These topics are discussed in the following sections, as are several judicial issues dealing with affirmative action.

Organizational Profile

An organizational *profile* displays information on the composition of the organization by gender and ethnicity. It provides an overall view of the composition of the organization. An organizational *display* is a graphical presentation by organizational unit. An *organizational unit* is defined as one that has one or more managers that have authority to make employment decisions such as hiring and firing. Each managerial/supervisory level is listed along with the gender and ethnicity of the manager(s)/supervisor(s). The numbers of employees supervised by each manager are listed along with each employee's gender and ethnicity.

A workforce analysis was the required method of presenting the organizational profile prior to the new regulations in 2000. It provides the number of employees in an organizational unit by job title, ordered by rate of pay, and each employee's gender and ethnicity.

Job Group Analysis

A *job group analysis* aggregates the information from the organizational profile based on job titles, regardless of which organizational unit they are assigned to. Thus the job group analysis provides an overall picture of the organization by job title. The difference between the organizational profile and the job group analysis is often explained with the analogy that the workforce analysis provides a vertical slice of the organization by departmental unit, whereas the job group analysis provides a horizontal view by job groups.

Availability Analysis

An *availability analysis* is a two-factor examination in which the organization evaluates the availability of minority and women candidates potentially available for the job groups determined in the job group analysis. It is called a *two-factor* analysis because two distinct factors or sources of workers must be considered. The first factor is those internal employees that could be promoted or transferred to the job with appropriate training. The second factor is the availability of workers with appropriate skills from the relevant recruitment area. An availability analysis shows the candidate pool potentially available to fill jobs in each job group by gender and ethnicity.

Utilization Analysis

A *utilization analysis* compares the availability analysis for each job group with the job group analysis. The purpose of the comparison is to determine whether underutilization exists. Underutilization exists if a protected class constitutes a lesser percentage in the organization's workforce than it does in the availability analysis. Underutilization can be determined using a variety of methods, including

- ▶ Any difference rule in which underutilization is determined to exist any time the current workforce percentage for a protected class does not equal the availability analysis percentage in a particular job group

- ▶ The 4/5ths rule previously discussed in which the current workforce percentage of a protected class must be at least 4/5ths (80%) of the availability analysis percentage in a particular group

- ▶ The two standard deviations rule in which the current workforce percentage of a protected class cannot vary from the availability analysis percentage by more that two standard deviations

Goals and Actions

If underutilization is indicated in any protected class, goals must be set for bringing the utilization up to parity and action decided on to achieve those goals. In the case of multiple areas of underutilization, multiple goals are required.

The issue of goals has gathered considerable controversy over the years. The regulations consider goals to be targets that the organization will make reasonable good-faith efforts to achieve. They are not to be mandatory quotas. However, many argue that goals are, in fact, de facto quotas.

The organization must develop action plans to achieve the goals, including appropriate programmatic activities. Activities typically include targeted recruiting and training and development programs designed to increase the applicant supply pool of underutilized protected groups.

The organization must develop internal auditing and reporting systems to monitor its progress toward achieving goals. After a goal is reached, affirmative action activities with respect to that goal must cease.

EXAM ALERT

The SPHR should be familiar with AAPs because the components and process will likely be the subject of an exam question.

Judicial Issues and Affirmative Action

Three issues raised in the courts should be discussed: reverse discrimination, quotas, and the "glass ceiling." The issues are interrelated in that quotas create reverse discrimination. Precedent case law was discussed earlier in this chapter. Case law is often conflicting and confusing, and is still evolving. As a general statement, current court decisions trend toward conservatism in the use of affirmative action programs, limiting the situations in which such programs can be engaged in largely to those in which past discrimination is evident.

Reverse discrimination occurs when an equally qualified or more qualified member of a non-protected class (generally white male) is not hired or promoted in favor of a member of a protected class. Preferential treatment and quota systems can create situations in which reverse discrimination is created. Court decisions in this area tend to strongly support prohibitions against reverse discrimination and protect valid affirmative action initiatives. Obviously this is a gray area and dependent on the situation in each instance.

Quotas are created when all individuals that are not members of a targeted protected class are excluded from consideration for a position. In the absence of a valid bona fide occupational qualification, case law prohibits firm quotas in affirmative action plans. In general, law and the courts permit the consideration of protected class status as one factor in employment decisions if there is evidence of past discrimination. However, protected class status cannot be the only criteria except in very narrowly defined situations.

Nothing in affirmative action law and regulations requires organizations to hire unqualified candidates. Affirmative action activities where there is no underutilization or history of past discrimination are generally found to violate Title VII. Affirmative action plans and activities are designed to be temporary in nature. Affirmative action means that employers attempt to place protected class members in jobs in which the class is under-represented. Continuation of these activities after the goal is achieved is illegal.

Glass ceilings and glass walls (also referred to as glass elevators) are concepts associated with affirmative action and illegal discrimination. Whereas affirmative action activities might result in hiring members of under-represented protected classes, such actions do not guarantee that those individuals will rise to the highest levels of the organization. *Glass ceilings* is a concept that means that protected class individuals are promoted only so far in the organization and then reach a seemingly impenetrable barrier in which they can see the top of the organization but cannot achieve promotion to it. The Civil Rights Act of 1991 created a Glass Ceiling Commission to study barriers to the advancement of women and minorities in the workforce and to recommend means of overcoming those barriers.

Glass walls or *glass elevators* is the phenomenon that occurs when women and minorities are hired into nonrevenue-producing staff functions that do not normally lead to high-level executive positions and are prohibited from transferring into other occupations within the organization. Public relations, corporate communications, and HR are often given as examples of nonrevenue-producing functions.

Affirmative action plans, consequently, must be concerned not only with getting protected classes into the organization, but also with moving them up the organization. Activities such as mentor programs, lateral transfers to revenue-producing departments, and developmental programs are often implemented by organizations to improve the potential for promotion of members of protected classes to alleviate both glass ceilings and glass walls.

EXAM ALERT

You should understand the concept of reverse discrimination, the fact that quotas but not goals are generally prohibited, and be familiar with the concepts of glass ceilings and glass walls.

NOTE

The courts are constantly wrestling with the issue of preferences for protected classes, quotas versus goals, and reverse discrimination. For example, following the series of reverse discrimination cases from *Bakke* to *Gratz* and *Grutter* provides a perspective as to the thinking of the Supreme Court. As new justices are appointed, that thinking might be modified or significantly changed.

EEOC Complaint Process

The SPHR must have a general understanding of how the EEOC processes complaints. An in-depth discussion is beyond the scope of this book and the SPHR is advised to seek legal counsel to comply with EEOC regulations and properly defend the organization. Following the discussion of the complaint process itself is a brief discussion regarding employer response to a complaint. The process has been amended several times by law or new regulations issued by the EEOC. The process can be summarized as follows:

▶ **Initiation of the complaint**   What might seem simple can be a bit complex in that the complainant often is covered under two or more separate antidiscrimination laws. The basic rule is that an employer must file a complaint within 180 days of the alleged discrimination. However, the EEOC permits local and state equal employment opportunity agencies to process and attempt to settle federal discrimination complaints. In these cases, the local or state agency typically has exclusive jurisdiction for the first 60 days after complaint filing. If a state or local agency has jurisdiction, the individual has 300 days from the date of the alleged discriminatory action or 30 days from the date of receipt that the state or local agency has terminated its processing to file a charge with the EEOC, whichever is earlier.

NOTE

Discriminatory acts that are continuing in nature, such as a hostile work environment (discussed later in this chapter), do not all have to occur within the stated time period (180 or 300 days). However, at least one of the acts must. When that occurs, acts outside the time period may be considered for determining employer liability.

NOTE

For simplicity and because state or local laws may differ, the following description of the complaint process addresses only EEOC procedures. These are the procedures that the SPHR must be familiar with and those that could be tested.

▶ **Determination of jurisdiction**   The EEOC determines whether it has jurisdiction. If not, the complaint is rejected. For example, a complaint against an organization that has five employees is not covered under the Civil Rights Act of 1964.

▶ **Initial acceptance and request for information**   If the EEOC has jurisdiction, it accepts the complaint and advises the employer that a complaint has been filed against it, generally within 10 days of receipt of the complaint. It simultaneously sends the organization a Request for Information form that the employer must complete and return.

▶ **EEOC investigation**   The EEOC next determines the level of investigation that it wants to pursue base on a priority lists. Full investigations are normally conducted on charges that appear to involve matters that have been targeted as priorities. Lesser levels of investigation are required for complaints that appear to have some merit, but require additional information and little or no investigation might be done on complaints that appear to require dismissal.

Depending on the level of investigation, the EEOC requires the organization to produce certain records. In full investigations, the EEOC often requires the production of voluminous records. The organization, in addition to the records required, provides an explanation and its defense of the alleged violation. In complex or priority cases, an EEOC investigator might visit the organization to review records or talk to individuals having knowledge of the complaint.

If the investigation reveals that no discrimination has taken place, the EEOC issues a Dismissal and Notice of Rights Letter. The complainant may then pursue the case in the court system. If there appears to be reasonable cause to believe that illegal discrimination has occurred, the EEOC issues a Letter of Determination, also referred to as a *cause letter*.

▶ **Conciliation**   After the Letter of Determination is issued, the EEOC attempts to get the organization and complainant to settle the case. This often involves continuing negotiation and conciliation efforts. The EEOC has begun a program of offering the parties voluntary mediation (a process discussed in Chapter 6, "Employee and Labor Relations") to speed up complaint processing and settlement.

▶ **Final action**   If attempts at conciliation fail, the EEOC has two options. First it can initiate suit against the employer. As a practical matter, the EEOC is likely to undertake this action only when the complaint involves a number of employees. The second option is more likely and that is the issuance of a Right-to-Sue letter. This permits the complainant to purse the case in court.

Employer Response to a Complaint

On receipt of notification that a complaint has been filed with the EEOC, an organization should take the following steps:

▶ Review the complaint and the employment records of the complainant.

▶ Take no retaliatory action against the complainant.

▶ Conduct an internal investigation regarding the allegations contained in the complaint.

▶ Cooperate, to the extent possible, with the EEOC. EEOC investigations can be quite burdensome for the employer with massive and, sometimes, seemingly irrelevant requests for information and analysis. The scope of these requests can often be reduced through negotiation with the EEOC investigators.

▶ If the agency issues a cause letter, the organization must determine whether to settle or to fight the complaint in the court system. The decision is often a difficult one, taking into consideration the merits of the complaint, costs of defense, and ethical implications. An organization might elect to defend itself in court even though the costs of such a defense might run much more than the cost of settlement. The SPHR must lead the organization in these matters, attempting to determine the importance of the case to the organization and the message the decision will send to stakeholders and, most importantly, the employees.

> **EXAM ALERT**
>
> The SPHR should be familiar with the EEOC complaint process and the appropriate employer response when advised by the EEOC that a complaint has been filed. You will likely receive a test question on one of the two topics, with the complaint process being the more likely test question subject.

Gender Discrimination

Objective:

Gain an Understanding of Gender Discrimination

Title VII of the Civil Rights Act of 1964 prohibits discrimination in employment based on sex. However, the definition of what defines discrimination has been the subject of much judicial interpretation. In this section, the following issues are discussed:

▶ Sexual harassment

▶ The broad scope of hostile environment

▶ Harassment prevention programs and affirmative defense

▶ Sexual orientation issues

Sexual Harassment

Sexual harassment is a violation of Title VII. The EEOC first issued its *Guidelines on Sex Discrimination* in 1980 defining sexual harassment as a violation of Title VII prohibitions against discrimination based on sex. The EEOC defines sexual harassment as *unwelcome sexual advances, requests for sexual favors, and other verbal or physical conduct of a sexual nature that takes place under any of the following conditions:*

▶ *Submission to such conduct is made either explicitly or implicitly a term or condition of employment.*

▶ *Submission to or rejection of such conduct by an individual is used as the basis for employment decision affecting the individual.*

▶ *Such conduct has the purpose or effect of unreasonably interfering with an individual's work performance or creating an intimidating, hostile, or offensive work environment.*

For the employer to be held liable for sexual harassment, the individual making the claim must prove

▶ There was unwelcome conduct or communication of a sexual nature (harassment).

▶ The harassment was based on a person's sex.

▶ The harassment affected a term, condition, or privilege of the person's employment.

▶ The employer is legally responsible for the harassment.

Both the EEOC and the courts recognize two distinct types of sexual harassment: quid pro quo and hostile environment. They are discussed next.

Quid Pro Quo

Quid pro quo means *this for that* and occurs when an employee is forced to choose between submitting to sexual advances or forfeiting employment opportunities or benefits. It is harassment in which employment outcomes are linked to the granting of sexual favors. By definition, the harasser must be in a position or perceived to be in a position to, in fact, create the employment opportunities and tangible employments promised. Consequently, quid pro quo harassment must be perpetrated by a supervisor or manager. EEOC guidelines provide that the employer is strictly responsible for the actions of its supervisors, regardless of whether the employer knew or should have known of their occurrence. Nevertheless, it is possible for the employer to avoid legal liability in some cases of quid pro quo sexual harassment by using an affirmative defense. This issue is discussed later in this section.

Hostile Environment

The Supreme Court decision in *Meritor Savings Bank* discussed earlier in the chapter established the concept of hostile workplace environment. A hostile workplace environment can violate Title VII even if there are no employment or economic effects if that environment unreasonably interferes with an individual's work or work performance or creates an intimidating, hostile, or offensive working environment.

As opposed to quid pro quo sexual harassment, the employer is liable only if it knew or should have known that the conditions existed. Also as opposed to quid pro quo, the harassers do not have to be supervisors for the organization to be found guilty. In fact, the harassers do not even have to be employees of the organization. Customers, suppliers, independent contractors, and so forth can all create a hostile work environment. Activities such as sexual or derogatory jokes or remarks, offensive physical contact, sexually oriented horseplay, posting of offensive or pornographic material, inappropriate emails, solicitation of sexual favors, and so forth might lead to hostile environment claims.

The courts have consistently ruled that such behaviors and activities must be severe or pervasive to be considered harassment. In its *Harris* decision, discussed earlier, the Supreme Court ruled that a "reasonable person" test must be used to determine whether harassment has occurred. This means that the environment must be one that a "reasonable person" would find abusive. Examples of environments that might be considered abusive are ones that

- ▶ Prevent advancement in one's career.

- ▶ Result in constructive discharge. *Constructive discharge* occurs when the work environment is so hostile that a reasonable person would quit.

- ▶ Affect the psychological well-being of the victim.

- ▶ Detract from the individual's work performance.

As stated before, the employer has strict liability in quid pro quo cases because that type of harassment must be perpetrated by an agent of the organization—a manager or supervisor. However, what happens if the hostile environment is a result of managerial behavior? There are two Supreme Court decisions that together address the issue, both of which were discussed earlier in this chapter. *Faragher v. City of Boca Raton* provides the basis for an employer's defense of actions of its managers as long as a tangible employment action has not occurred. This argument is referred to as an *affirmative defense* and is discussed later in this section. *Ellerth v. Burlington Northern* defines what types of actions are to be considered tangible employment actions.

> **EXAM ALERT**
>
> You can be assured that sexual harassment with be covered on the SPHR examination. Be familiar with the two types of sexual harassment discussed and with the difference in liability that the employer incurs (vicarious versus strict).

The Broad Scope of Hostile Environment

In 1999, the EEOC provided new and comprehensive guidance on the subject of harassment and hostile environment. This guidance is included in the EEOC's *Compliance Manual*, which is available on its website at http//www.eeoc.gov/. The guidance expands the concept of hostile environment from prohibition against sexual harassment to include prohibition against national origin harassment. EEOC defines actions that might include a hostile or abusive work environment based on national origin to include ethnic slurs, workplace graffiti, or other offensive conduct directed toward an individual's birthplace, ethnicity, culture, or foreign accent. The EEOC indicates that the following factors should be considered in determining whether the national origin harassment rises to the level of creating a hostile work environment.

- ▶ Whether the conduct was physically threatening or intimidating
- ▶ How frequently the conduct was repeated
- ▶ Whether the conduct was hostile and/or patently offensive
- ▶ The context in which the harassment occurred
- ▶ Whether management responded appropriately when it learned of the harassment

EXAM ALERT

The expanded concept of harassment is often a question on the examination.

Harassment Prevention Programs and Affirmative Defense

To defend itself against complaints of harassment, either quid pro quo or hostile environment, the organization must first have a proactive harassment prevention program in place. Critical components of an effective program are as follows:

- ▶ Establishment of a harassment policy covering all protected classes
- ▶ Executive-level support and commitment to the policy
- ▶ Training of managers on the policy
- ▶ Communication of the policy throughout the organization
- ▶ Providing a procedure for employees to bring issues of sexual or other types of harassment to the organization's attention
- ▶ Protection of complainants from retaliation
- ▶ Quick and thorough investigations of complaints
- ▶ Taking timely and effective action if indicated by the results of the investigation

If the organization has a viable harassment protection program and can demonstrate that it took reasonable care to prevent harassment, it might be able to raise an affirmative defense against allegations of quid pro quo sexual harassment or national origin or sexual discrimination based on hostile environment. The critical issue in this defense is that the organization followed its procedures and policies as indicated in its harassment prevention policies. An affirmative defense must be based on two factors:

- ▶ The organization exercised reasonable care to prevent and promptly correct any harassing behavior.

▶ The complainant unreasonably failed to take advantage of any preventive or corrective opportunities provided.

If the employee suffered no tangible employment action, an organization that has developed, implemented, and rigorously followed its harassment prevention plan might be able to avoid liability, even with respect to the actions of its managers, in a discrimination complaint. However, if a tangible employment action has occurred as part of the harassment, the organization has no viable defense.

> **EXAM ALERT**
>
> You should be familiar with the elements necessary in an effective harassment prevention program and with the concept of an affirmative defense. Remember that a tangible employment action negates an affirmative defense. Be prepared for a question in this area.

Sexual Orientation Issues

Sexual orientation is not recognized or protected under Title VII. Although the *Oncale v. Sundowner Offshore Services* decision, discussed earlier, protects individuals from discrimination and harassment by the same sex, it does not provide protection based on sexual preference or orientation. However, many state and local laws and ordinances do prevent discrimination based on sexual preference.

Workforce Planning

Objective:
Gain an Understanding of Workforce Planning

The SPHR must lead an organization through the process of determining how many employees the organization needs and the characteristics that those employees should have to facilitate the accomplishment of organizational. *Workforce planning* is the process of determining how to staff the organization with the right employees at the right time and in the right place. As discussed in Chapter 2, workforce planning is increasingly indistinguishable from organizational strategic planning in those organizations where human capital is the critical factor in organizational success. For the purposes of discussion and explanation in this section, it is assumed that organization has completed its strategic-planning process and determined its strategic goals and objectives.

The purpose of workforce planning then becomes to determine the characteristics needed in the organization's workforce to facilitate achievement of those objectives. In this scenario, workforce planning is strategic planning at the HR level and involves similar processes, including a SWOT analysis, which occurs at the organizational level. In simplistic terms, the HR function, under the leadership of the SPHR, must determine the numbers and types of employees needed and evaluate the availability of both internal and external individuals having the correct characteristics. Based on these analyses, a determination can be made as to the proper HR programmatic activities required to achieve the correct workforce composition. Workforce planning then involves three stages: forecasting workforce needs, determining internal and external supply of employees, and developing appropriate strategies to achieve forecasted needs in relationship to projected supply. These three processes are discussed in the following sections.

Forecasting Workforce Needs

The organization's strategic plan and allied business plan provide guidance as to the number and type of employees that the organization needs during the planning period. Expansion, retrenchment, new products or services, introduction of new technology, entrance of new competitors in the market, economic conditions, employee retirements, workforce turnover, and so forth must be considered when forecasting workforce needs. *Forecasting* is the process of using both historical data and predicted scenarios to determine workforce needs during a stated planning period. Following is a discussion of several forecasting methods that are often used.

Trend Analysis

Trend analysis involves studying historical organizational employment levels to predict future employment levels. For example: If, on average, employment levels in the organization have increase 5% per year, it might be logical to forecast a 5% increase for the next planning period. A more accurate forecast using this method might be to evaluate trends in separate departments or other organizational subentities and then aggregate the increases (or, potentially, decreases) at the organizational level. Doing so provides more specificity as to not only the numbers of employees but also the types of employees needed.

Trend analysis assumes that history will repeat itself. In today's more volatile times that might not be the case. However, trend analysis provides some data on which a final forecast can be made.

Ratio Analysis

Ratio analysis is a forecasting technique that assumes a set relationship between one variable and another, and that the relationship allows for the prediction of workforce needs. Assuming no increases in productivity, an organization might be able to predict total workforce requirements based on predicted total sales or total productivity. For example: If, historically, it takes five employees for each 100,000 unit of product produced, a projected increase of 1,000,000 units per year will require an additional 50 employees.

Organizations often have standard staffing tables that can be used in ratio analysis. As an example, a restaurant chain would know how many servers, cooks, managers, and so forth are needed to staff a restaurant. Based on a projected expansion in terms of number of restaurants, increase in workforce needs can be forecast.

Turnover

Analysis of historical turnover—in reality a type of trend analysis—provides additional data for forecasts. Average turnover rates provide an indication of the number of new employees required just to maintain current employment levels. Obviously, turnover is affected by many environmental factors, most notably unemployment rates, so other variables must be considered when using these data for forecasting.

Nominal Group Technique

The *nominal group technique* is a group-forecasting and decision-making method that requires each member of the group to make an independent forecast prior to discussion of any forecasts. Members of the group meet and independently develop a forecast. Each member must present his or her forecast before any of the forecasts are discussed. After all presentations are made and clarifying questions addressed, the group works to come up with a final forecast.

Delphi Technique

The Delphi technique is another group forecasting method in which experts independently develop forecasts that are shared with each other, but in this approach the experts never actually meet. Each of the members refines his or her forecasts until a group consensus is reached.

> **NOTE**
>
> The nominal group and Delphi techniques are used to avoid the phenomenon known as group think. *Group think* occurs when group members, in the interest of developing group cohesiveness, reach consensus without fully considering what might be divergent forecasts.

Managerial Judgment

Managers and executives are asked, based on their experience and knowledge, to develop forecasts. Forecasts, like budgets, can be a top-level overall estimate or a bottom-up aggregation of multiple departmental estimates. Top-level forecasts provide a gross indicator of needed employment levels, but do not indicate where those employees should be allocated in the organization. Bottom-up forecasts, provided by managers in the various departments, provide a better idea of allocation of the workforce and the types of employees that are needed. However, bottom-up forecasts tend to overestimate workforce needs as each manager tries to increase staff size.

Statistical Forecasts

Statistical analysis was discussed in Chapter 2 in the section on research. Various statistical procedures, including regression analyses, can be used to develop forecasts based on scenarios or theorized relationships between variables.

Computer Modeling

Many organizations use sophisticated forecasting software. This permits the organizations to evaluate workforce needs under various scenarios.

Multiple Methods

In the final analysis, no single forecasting method is likely to be accurate every time. Most organizations use multiple methods to develop different forecasts. Ultimately, it is likely to be a top-level manager, using intuition based on accumulated knowledge and years of experience, that makes the final determination of the most likely forecast.

Determining Internal and External Supply of Employees

Not only must the demand for employees be determined, but workforce planning must include an analysis of the potential supply. Forecasts must be made of the supply of candidates for jobs within the organization and the supply external to the organization in the relevant labor market. Methods of forecasting supply, internally and externally, are discussed in the following section.

Internal Supply

The internal supply of candidates can be determined using a number of methods, such as replacement charts, succession plans, human resource management information systems, and departmental estimates. A brief discussion of each of these methods follows.

Replacement Charts

Replacement charts are manual or automated records indicating which employees are currently ready for promotion to a specific position. If needs are forecasted for a particular job, replacement charts provide data with which to determine the supply of internal candidates to fill the openings.

Succession Planning

The concept of succession planning is similar to replacement charting except the time perspective is different. *Succession planning* is the process of identifying candidates for future openings. It is a longer-term plan for developing candidates to fill positions. Traditionally, succession planning has been reserved for only high-level positions. However, because of the increased importance of human capital in many organizations, succession plans are being developed for the orderly replacement of lower-level employees.

Human Resource Management Information Systems

Many human resource management information systems frequently contain data on qualifications or skills of current employees. After workforce demand is forecast, the database can be queried regarding the supply of potential internal candidates that possess the necessary qualifications or skills.

Departmental Estimates

Organizations are not static. Most organizations and their component departments experience constant flows of employees both in and out. Analysis of this movement provides valuable information to forecast internal supply. Table 3.4 provides the formula used to forecast internal supply within a particular department in the organization and common sources of employee movement in and out.

TABLE 3.4   Estimated Internal Labor Supply for a Department

Current Staffing Level – Outflows + Inflows = Internal Supply

Inflows	Outflows
▶ Transfers from other departments	▶ Retirements
▶ Hires from the external labor market	▶ Resignations
▶ Recalls from layoffs	▶ Death
▶ Returns from leaves of absence and sabbaticals	▶ Promotions to other departments
	▶ Transfers to other departments
	▶ Terminations

External Supply

There is a huge amount of information available to assist in the forecasting external supplies of labor. State and local economic and workforce development agencies typically can provide data on the labor supply availability. The United States Department of Labor (http://www.dol.gov/) has data available for virtually any location and publishes annual forecasts of labor supply by occupation, and the Bureau of Labor Statistics (http://www.bls.gov/) provides a wide variety of labor force information that is available online. In addition, various professional organizations regularly analyze labor availability within their respective professions. The availability of external candidates is affected by

▶ Economic conditions

▶ Unemployment rates

▶ College and high school graduation rates in the relevant labor market

▶ Net migration in or out of the area

- ▶ Relative skill levels of potential candidates in the labor market

- ▶ Competition for labor in the labor market

- ▶ Changes in the skill requirements of the organization's potential job openings

EXAM ALERT

You should be familiar with the various methods of forecasting both demand for and supply of employees and candidates.

Determination of Strategies

The analysis of demand and supply for labor leads the SPHR to develop appropriate strategies to achieve the planned level of employment. The result of the analysis can result in one of three conditions:

- ▶ **Equality**   In which case the strategy becomes one of retaining current employees

- ▶ **Insufficient number of employees**   In which case the strategy becomes recruitment

- ▶ **Too many employees**   In which case the strategy becomes decruitment

Retention of employees involves strategies designed to maintain or improve job satisfaction and organizational commitment. They are discussed throughout this entire book as they apply to a particular program area. For example, retention strategies involve creating pay equity and providing desired benefits when compensation and benefits strategies are being developed. Both recruitment and decruitment (organizational exit) are discussed later in this chapter.

It would be very similar if the analysis reveals that only one of the conditions from the preceding list exists. However, that is not often the case and the SPHR frequently finds that some departments are currently staffed appropriately for future needs during the planning period, whereas some departments have too many employees and others too few. Thus, strategies of recruitment, decruitment, and retention must be developed simultaneously and interdependently because the recruitment objectives of one department can often serve to fulfill the decruitment objectives of another.

The diagram in Figure 3.1 is often referred to as a *yield funnel*. It provides a basis for understanding two major programmatic activities that are discussed later in this chapter: recruitment and selection. Assuming that an expansion of the workforce is required, strategy determination is affected by the forecasts of yield rates and the timeframes required for each step in the recruitment and selection process. *Yield rates* are a comparison of the number of applicants or potential applicants at one stage in the recruitment/selection process with the number of applicants that remain available at the next stage. To determine programmatic activities and action plans, the SPHR must work backward from the total number and types of employees that will be needed, including dates on which they will be needed. Based on experience, moderated by any projected changes in timeframes or yield rates, the planning process must incorporate an evaluation of the scope and timing of activities to produce the desired results. In the case of the example in Figure 3.1, the SPHR must lead the organization in a determination as to the timing of recruitment efforts and the number of actual contacts that must be made to produce the 10 new employees at the appropriate time. The various stages of this process are discussed in subsequent sections of this chapter.

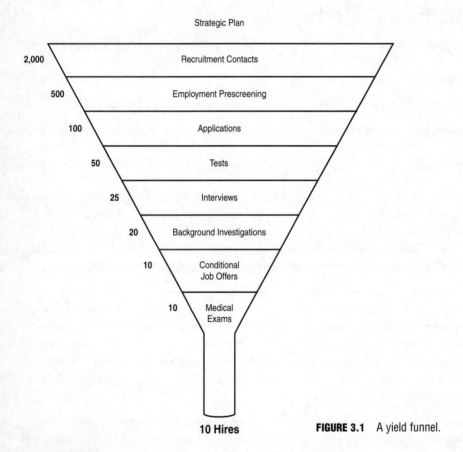

Employment Yield Ratios

Strategic Plan

2,000 — Recruitment Contacts

500 — Employment Prescreening

100 — Applications

50 — Tests

25 — Interviews

20 — Background Investigations

10 — Conditional Job Offers

10 — Medical Exams

10 Hires

FIGURE 3.1   A yield funnel.

NOTE

The strategic plan drives all activities depicted in Figure 3.1.

Job Analysis

Objective:
Gain an Understanding of Job Analysis

Job analysis is the systematic process of gathering information regarding the duties required of a job and the human characteristics necessary to successfully perform those duties. The work products of job analysis are job descriptions, which describe the job, and job specifications, which describe what kind of person to hire for the job. Job analysis can be described as the foundation of human resource management because it the basis for so many HR programmatic activities. Job analysis is used for

▶ **Recruitment**   Provides information about the nature of the job to guide recruitment activities

▶ **Selection**   Provides information on the knowledge, skills, and abilities required of persons that can successfully perform the job

▶ **Training**   Provides information regarding the tasks to be performed and the skills and knowledge required in order to guide the development of training programs

▶ **Performance evaluation**   Provides information on the level of proficiency of various tasks that are required in order to develop performance standards

▶ **Compensation**   Provides information necessary to evaluate the internal worth of the job to the organization and to compare it with jobs in the relevant job market in order to determine appropriate wage and benefit levels

▶ **EEO compliance**   Forms the basis for determining whether employment practices and decisions are job-related

The SPHR should be familiar with a number of concepts regarding the process of job analysis. Discussed in the following sections are

▶ Job analysis process

▶ Job analysis information requirements

▶ Data collection methods

▶ Writing job descriptions and job specifications

▶ Competencies and the future of job analysis

The Job Analysis Process

Job analysis can be described as a six-step process as follows:

1. **Determine the purpose for conducting job analysis**. The purpose should be clearly linked to organizational success and the organizational strategic plan. A frequent reason for conducting job analysis projects is that jobs are much more dynamic than ever before. Technology and the demands of a competitive environment frequently change the nature of the job requiring reevaluation. Rapid organizational growth often means new types of jobs requiring job descriptions. High turnover or low job satisfaction might be other indicators of the need for job analysis projects. High turnover might indicate that jobs are not properly priced in relation to the external job market. Because job analysis drives compensation decisions, old job analysis results might need to be updated. Low job satisfaction is often the result of boring or repetitive jobs. Job analysis can identify new ways to design jobs to make them more interesting and challenging.

2. **Identify the jobs to be analyzed**. After the purpose is identified, it provides some indication as to which jobs should be included in the job analysis. Often, however, time and resource constraints limit the total number of jobs that can be included in the process. For example, if the organization as a whole is experiencing turnover, that data should be analyzed to determine the particular departments in which the problem seems to be the worst. That analysis indicates the direction for the project. The same is true if the organization is growing or experiencing significant change in only certain areas. Those are the jobs that are most appropriate for job analysis.

   When a large number of employees encumber the same job, a determination must be made as to how many of the positions will be included in the project. Statistical sampling might be appropriate if the number is large.

   This is also the time in the project in which communication with both employees and managers begins to take place. They should be advised as to the purpose of the project and provided a general overview of the process.

3. **Review relevant background data**. Efficient and effective job analysis often builds from previous work and data that are already corrected. A review of current job descriptions and organizational charts provides basic information with which to begin the project. Analysis of workflow assists in understanding the responsibilities of the job and how it fits into the total work process.

4. **Plan and execute the job analysis project**. Planning is the key to successful projects. The appropriate data-gathering methodologies must be determined and an action plan developed as to project activities and milestones. Data collection methods are covered in the next section.

5. **Write the job description and job specifications**. After the data are collected and analyzed, they must be turned into the written work outputs, job descriptions, and job specifications. Before these documents are finalized, they should be reviewed with a representative sample of both the affected employees and their managers. If modifications to the documents are required, they should be made and the appropriate final approvals obtained.

6. **Periodic review**. It is good HR practice to engage in a planned process of periodic review of job descriptions and job specifications. Many organizations use a revolving process, reviewing a portion of the organization each year so that the entire organization is reviewed in a cycle—usually three, four, or five years. During the review, managers in that portion of the organization under review are required to verify the accuracy of the job descriptions and job specifications. If managers indicate job descriptions are out of date, those descriptions are included in the job analysis review. In addition, a random sample of jobs is also included for review.

> **EXAM ALERT**
>
> You should be familiar with the basic process, purpose, and uses of job analysis because it is often a question on the examination.

Job Analysis Information Requirements

The job analysis process requires the collection of sufficient information to fully understand the job, its functions, and how it fits in both the workflow and organizational structure of the organization to produce the job description and job specifications. The following information is representative of the types of data collected during the job analysis process:

▶ **Work activities** Information must be collected on the tasks performed by the job and what is to be accomplished (work outputs). The data should include how, why, and when the activity is performed.

▶ **Worker activities** These data include worker behaviors such as decision-making, communicating, and performing physical actions such as lifting heavy weights.

▶ **Machines, tools, and equipment** Data here include information regarding the types of equipment that are used in the job. This might include computers, safety equipment, machines, and other devices that facilitate accomplishment of the work.

▶ **Job-related tangible and intangibles** Information is required on the types of materials used and the products made or services rendered. In addition, information is needed on the type of knowledge dealt with (chemistry or accounting, for example).

▶ **Performance standards** Information is needed about requirements for productivity and quality required for successful performance of the job. Work standards, production records, and so forth are collected.

▶ **Job context** A wide variety of information is collected here. Examples include reporting relationships, type of employees supervised (if any), working conditions, financial incentives, and types of contacts the job has with other jobs and the purposes of those contacts.

▶ **Human requirements** These include job-related knowledge and skills such as education, training, credentials, and work experience. In addition, information is needed on required personal attributes such as aptitudes, physical characteristics, and personality.

Data Collection Methods

Information regarding the tasks performed and the human characteristics needed to successfully perform them can be gathered in many ways. The most common are as follows:

▶ **Observation** The observer watches the individual that is performing the job and takes notes as to what is occurring. The advantage of such an approach is that the individual doing the job analysis sees for him or herself exactly what is being done. However, there are several disadvantages. The first is that this method might be appropriate only for what are referred to as *short-cycle jobs*; that is, those that are repetitive in nature and in which the full range of job responsibilities is repeated at relatively short intervals. Otherwise, the observer is liable to miss some of the tasks that are essential to the job. Observation cannot really capture work that is not observable, such as decision-making, thinking, and analysis. Another issue is time. Observation methods are very time-consuming, and, thus, expensive to do. Some types of observation methods are

> ▶ **Time and motion studies** These are normally performed by industrial engineers and involve determining the most efficient way to perform a particular task and the normal time required to do so. Time and motion studies can be used to not only develop job descriptions and job specifications, but also to develop piece rate compensation programs.

> ▶ **Work sampling** This process involves statistically sampling what is being done by the worker during random periods of the day. These are recorded and analyzed. This method is typically more efficient than continuous observation and is most appropriate for repetitive jobs.

> ▶ **Critical incidents** Critical incidents are discussed in Chapter 6. They are the recordation of positive and negative job performance. Critical incidents can be used to develop the job description and job specifications and also to develop the associated performance standards.

▶ **Employee logs**   The employee can observe him or herself by completing a diary or log, recording exactly what is being done at periodic intervals during the day. In addition to the obvious interruption of work, other issues associated with this method are that the employee might often forget to record activities and might indicate what he or she thinks should be done as opposed to exactly what is being done.

▶ **Interviews**   The job analyst can interview the employee inquiring as exactly what activities are engaged and what knowledge, skills, and abilities are required. To cover all aspects of the job and provide a basis for analysis, good practice is to develop a standardized and structured interview protocol that is used in all interviews. Interviews provide in-depth information and might be appropriate when there are only a few persons occupying the job or when the data can be used to develop a survey instrument to be given to a larger number of employees. The disadvantage of using interviews is that they are very staff-intensive and can be costly.

▶ **Questionnaires and checklists**   Surveys can be developed and given to a large number of employees. This is an efficient way of gathering data when a large number of individuals occupy the same job and when the employees are widely dispersed geographically. In addition, data gathered in this method can often be statistically analyzed.

However, questionnaires are only as good as the questions they ask. Poorly developed questionnaires do not yield the data required to accurately prepare job descriptions and specifications. In addition, some employees might not have the literacy skills to properly complete the questionnaire, and others might purposefully answer the questions inaccurately. There are numerous off-the-shelf questionnaires and checklists that can be purchased from vendors or that are available from governmental agencies. Some of the more frequently used ones are

> ▶ **Position analysis questionnaire**   This is a specialized checklist, usually referred to as *PAQ*, which analyzes the job in six dimensions based on responses to nearly 200 questions. It can be used both for job analysis and job evaluation (discussed in Chapter 5). The dimensions analyzed are
>
>> ▶ Information input
>>
>> ▶ Mental processes
>>
>> ▶ Work output
>>
>> ▶ Relationships with other persons
>>
>> ▶ Job context
>>
>> ▶ Other job characteristics

▶ **Function job analysis**   Referred to as *FJA*, this is a comprehensive approach to job analysis that incorporates the goals of the organization, what workers do to achieve those goals, level and orientation of what the workers do, performance standards, and training content. The FJA evaluates the function of the job in three classifications: data, people, and things.

▶ **Management position description questionnaire**   This instrument is similar to the PAQ, but has been developed specifically to describe managerial jobs.

▶ **O*Net Online**   This is a resource provided by the Department of Labor, which is available on the Internet at http://www.onetcenter.org/. It is a huge database, providing standardized job descriptions for a large number of jobs and incorporates the DOL's *Dictionary of Occupational Titles*.

▶ **Computer-based systems**   A huge number of computer-based job analysis systems can be obtained from a variety of vendors. These systems frequently contain large databases of descriptive statements that can be used to describe various tasks, based on responses to questions. These systems can often dramatically decrease the time required for job analysis and can facilitate decentralization of the process to management.

▶ **Multiple methods**   It is often good practice to use multiple methods of data collection. For example, interviews can often be used to develop a basic understanding of the job under evaluation and can be used to develop a questionnaire used to capture data from many employees. The data can then be analyzed and entered into another system prior to developing the job descriptions and job specifications. This often provides a deeper understanding of the job and more defensible job description and job specifications should either be an issue in a complaint process being heard before a third party.

EXAM ALERT

You should be familiar with the basic methods of data collection, knowing that a combination of methods often yields the best result. This is often a question on the examination.

NOTE

Job analysis data collection is extremely important in regard to compliance with the Americans with Disabilities Act. Analysis of the data must reveal what the essential functions (as opposed to marginal functions) of the job are. The essential functions, as previously discussed, are those that a disabled individual must be able to perform to be considered qualified for the job. Disqualification of an individual based on an inaccurate determination of the essential functions of the job might be a violation of the ADA.

NOTE

Job analysis is also critical is complying with the Fair Labor Standards Act, discussed in Chapter 5. Job analysis data should provide information necessary to make a determination as to whether the job is exempt or nonexempt—concepts also discussed in Chapter 5.

Writing Job Descriptions and Job Specifications

Job *descriptions* are written documents that describe the functions and working conditions of a job. Job *specifications* are the human characteristics necessary to successfully perform the job. Job specifications are typically a subsection of a job description. In general, federal law does not require job descriptions. One exception is employees that handle or dispose of certain types of hazardous chemicals. However, job descriptions are desirable for a number of reasons:

▶ They assist employers in complying with the Americans with Disabilities Act and Fair Labor Standards Act as discussed earlier.

▶ They assist in compliance with antidiscrimination laws that require employment practices and decisions be job-related as they define the job.

▶ They assign work and document work assignments.

▶ They help clarify the mission through the types of work assigned.

▶ They provide the basis for developing training and performance evaluation programs.

Job descriptions should use action verbs to specifically describe the essential functions and duties. These descriptions should be logical, concise, and specific as to exactly what is to be done by the employee. A simple format for a job description and job specifications is shown in Table 3.5. It contains the following components, which are typically included in job descriptions:

▶ **Identification section**   This section provides general information regarding the job including the job title, where the position is located in terms of geography, the department in which the job is located, whether the job is exempt or nonexempt under the Fair Labor Standards Act, the pay grade of classification of the job, the EEOC classification required for the EEO-1 report, and whether the job is included in the bargaining unit (a concept discussed in Chapter 6). In addition, this section often includes a job code or other identifying number used for identification in the human resource information system *(HRIS)*. The HRIS might permit or require the entry of skill codes that identify the type of skills used in the job. If so, those codes are often placed in the identification section. Finally, the section might include information regarding the name of the individual that wrote the job description and job specifications and the name of the manager that approved them. The amount of information placed in this section depends on the needs of the organization and might range from merely identifying the job to a rather extensive section with large amounts of identifying information.

▶ **Position summary**   This section is a concise statement indicating what the job does, why it exists, and what makes it different from other jobs. The statement is generally only one or two sentences.

▶ **Essential functions**   This section is the meat of the job description and specifies clearly what the major functions of the job are. This is the most important section of the job description and the most difficult and time-consuming to write.

▶ **Nonessential functions**   This section lists other duties of the job that are minor in nature. For the purposes of the ADA, these are the duties that could potentially be assigned elsewhere in the organization as a reasonable accommodation.

▶ **Job specifications**   As previously stated, job specifications are normally included within the job description. This section should list the knowledge, skills, and abilities that a job incumbent should possess to perform the job successfully. Such characteristics as experience, education, and physical abilities are included in this section if they are requirements of the job. For example, "B.S. degree in biology," "two years of directly related experience," and "able to lift 100 pounds above the shoulders" are examples of explanatory statements that might be used in this section.

▶ **Working conditions**   This section describes the environment in which the work is performed. Such issues as exposure to weather, fumes, heat or cold, noise, and so forth should be described in this section. If the job is not performed in a difficult environment, the conditions under which the work is performed should still be described. For example, "the work is performed in an office environment with no disagreeable conditions" might be appropriate in those situations.

▶ **Disclaimers**   Many organizations put a variety of disclaimers in this section. These statements often include information that the management reserves the right to change the nature of the job and that the job description does not describe all tasks and responsibilities of the job. The purpose of these statements is to clarify that the employee might be required by management to perform other tasks. Often employers include this concept in a statement under the functions section using the terminology "other duties as assigned." However, the courts find this a bit problematic, especially if placed in the essential functions section, because the essential functions have to be clearly defined. A disclaimer section at the end of the job description is preferable. A final disclaimer often used is a statement to the effect that the job description does not constitute a contract for employment and may be changed at the discretion of the employer.

> **NOTE**
>
> A common error in writing job descriptions and job specifications is to base them on the person currently doing the job as opposed to what the actual requirements of the job are in terms of duties and human abilities. Incumbents often take on additional responsibilities and bring special skills to the job, neither of which is a requirement.

TABLE 3.5   Sample Job Description Format

Position Title:	Job Code:
Location:	FLSA Status:
Department:	Bargaining Unit Status:
Reports To:	Skill Codes:
Pay Grade:	EEOC Class:

Position Summary

Essential Functions

1.

2.

3.

4.

5.

Nonessential Functions

1.

2.

3.

4.

5.

Job Specifications

KSAs

Experience

Education

Working Conditions

Disclaimers

Competencies and the Future of Job Analysis

Job analysis, job specifications, and job descriptions meet the needs of organizations experiencing stable environments and stable markets. The process allows the organization to describe its jobs in relation to its mission and specify exactly what tasks must be performed to facilitate achievement of organizational goals. These processes are recognized by the court systems, which provide guidance through case law as to the characteristics of legally defensible activities. However, more and more frequently organizations are affected by a dynamic and volatile environment with rapidly changing technology, increased competition, and fluctuating customer demands. This has led to the "dejobbing of America."

Dejobbing refers to the fact that jobs often change every day and cannot be specifically described in the traditional ways. Increased competition has often resulted in a flattening of the traditional hierarchy, removing multiple layers of management. When this occurs, employees at the bottom of the organization often are required to manage themselves and are empowered to make decisions. To be quickly adaptive to the market and customer wants, employees must be able to make instantaneous decisions and engage in a variety of new and innovative behaviors. The nature of work has often become one of teams, projects, and task forces, requiring new skills and ever-changing job responsibilities.

Many organizations engage in the practice of enriching jobs by increasing the skill variety, task identity, task significance, autonomy, and feedback. This practice makes the jobs more flexible and increases responsibilities for planning and decision-making. High-performance work systems and employee involvement programs provide for more employee input into their jobs and more flexibility as to how jobs are performed. To deal with these new dynamics, many organizations are beginning the transition or have already transitioned to using competencies rather than tasks, duties, and responsibilities. Rather than task-based, job analysis has become competency-based. Competencies and competency-based job analysis are discussed in the sections that follow.

Competencies

Competencies are personal or organizational capabilities that are linked to successful performance outcomes. For the individual, competencies can be defined as characteristics of the person that enable performance. Competencies also consider how the knowledge, skills, and abilities are used. No single definition of competency has emerged as the standard because this is a relatively new area of study and practice. However, competencies include knowledge, skills, and abilities but are more than that. There is a component of behavior, performance outcomes, motivation, and attitude included in the concept. Many organizations believe that the use of competencies is a more strategic approach and better aligns employee behavior with the organization's mission and values than do description of tasks and functions.

Competencies can be categorized as technical, general, and leadership. Technical competencies apply to the particular job being analyzed. General (also called *behavioral*) competencies are required in varying amounts throughout the workforce. Leadership competencies are required by supervisors, managers, and others that have leadership responsibilities. Table 3.6 provides some commonly used competencies.

TABLE 3.6 Competencies

Developing subordinates	Resolving conflicts
Focusing on customer satisfaction	Working creatively
Communicating effectively	Leading decisively
Working with others	Thinking
Listening	Understanding technology

Competency-based analysis follows essentially the same process as described previously, but its purpose is to determine competencies needed to successfully perform the job rather than the functions performed in the job. There is a difference in emphasis between the two processes: Traditional or task-based job analysis focuses on the job and what is actually being done, whereas competency-based analysis focuses on the person and how the job outcomes are to be accomplished.

NOTE

Focusing on the "how" and the person is problematical. Discrimination law and associated case law is based on "what" is being done and the job itself. As discussed previously, one of the basic concepts is that of job-relatedness. There is very little case law on competencies at this point in time.

NOTE

A transition to competency-based job analysis has implications for many other programs. If the jobs descriptions describe the work in terms of competencies it means that associated training plans, performance management systems, compensation strategies, and so forth must be aligned.

EXAM ALERT

You should understand the concept and implications of a competency approach to job analysis. Because this is an emerging issue, it is likely to be covered on the test.

Recruitment

Objective:
Gain an Understanding of Recruitment

The outcome of the workforce strategic-planning process provides the organization with information as to how many employees and what types will be needed in the future. One of the possibilities is that fewer employees will be needed. That process is often referred to as *decruitment*. It is also possible, and frequently likely, that the organization might need additional employees but that the current workforce does not have and is not likely to be able to develop the skills needed. In that case, the organization might be involved in both recruitment and decruitment at the same time. Decruitment strategies and actions are discussed later, in the "Organizational Exit" section.

Recruitment is the process of attracting qualified applicants for the organization to consider when filling its positions. Two strategic determinations must be made initially before the process begins. The first is whether the organizations want to do its own recruiting or to contract it out. Organizations lacking internal expertise might want to have an outside vendor do the recruiting for them. The vendor might be used for all recruiting or only for specified jobs. Some organizations find that it is cost-effective to outsource all recruiting gaining access to expertise and efficiencies of scale. Other organizations find that using vendors to recruit for specific jobs is most effective and efficient.

There are several scenarios in which having a vendor perform the recruiting and initial screening might be advantageous to the organization. The first scenario involves hard-to-fill jobs. Recruitment firms often specialize in filling specific positions, such as CEO or research scientist. In these cases, outside vendors may be in a better position that the organization to attract qualified candidates. The second scenario deals with entry-level workers. Organizations often find it cost-effective to deal with employment and temporary agencies to find these types of workers.

The second strategic issue is "make or buy." The organization must decide whether to engage in a practice of internal promotions and transfers (make) to fill its positions or to go to the external labor market (buy) to fill them. The decision is driven by the outcome of the strategic workforce-planning process, which evaluates the availability and skill levels of internal applicants. It is the SPHR's responsibility to ensure that the recruitment strategy is in alignment with organizational goals and objectives. For example, an emerging organization in a highly technical field might engage in predominantly external recruitment because it does not have the time or capability to develop expertise internally and because the technical skills required are constantly changing. However, an organization operating in a relatively stable environment and attempting to compete based on cost-leadership and efficiency might find that internal recruitment is more in alignment. Also, organizations are often constrained by labor agreements that require an internal process prior to looking for applicants externally. The decision, in practice, is not an either/or choice. Organizations often pursue both strategies, frequently simultaneously. Table 3.7 summarizes the advantages and disadvantages of internal versus external recruitment.

TABLE 3.7   Advantages and Disadvantages of Internal Versus External Recruiting

Internal Recruiting	External Recruiting
Advantages	**Advantages**
▶ Promotes high morale.	▶ Brings new ideas and methods into the workplace.
▶ Employees are familiar with the organization.	
▶ Employee's performance and skill levels are already known.	▶ Might facilitate diversity and affirmative action initiatives.
▶ Promotes employee commitment.	▶ Might bring in expertise not currently available internally.
▶ Provides a career path for employees.	
▶ Provides opportunities for the employee to increase his or her salary.	▶ A lack of knowledge of current internal processes and procedures might facilitate innovation.
▶ Reduces recruiting costs.	
▶ Reduces orientation costs because the employee already is familiar with the job and organizational culture.	▶ Employee starts with a clean slate and has no internal political affiliations.
▶ Reduces training costs because the employee likely has already learned some of the requirements of the job through exposure to the job.	▶ Might reduce training costs and time if the employee comes to the organization with skills to do the job.
Disadvantages	**Disadvantages**
▶ Can negatively affect morale and commitment of those not promoted.	▶ Individual might not be a good fit with the organization and organizational culture.
▶ Does not encourage new and innovative ways of doing things.	▶ Might lower morale and commitment of current employees that are deprived of promotion opportunities.
▶ Promotes individual competition for promotion, which can affect cooperation and collaboration.	▶ Must be oriented into organization, potentially resulting in increased time to adjust and reach full performance level.

EXAM ALERT

You should be familiar with the advantages and disadvantages of external and internal recruitment. It is an issue of HR strategy and almost assuredly to be a question on the exam.

EXAM ALERT

The SPHR should be familiar with the concept of a realistic job preview, often referred to as an *RJP*. An RJP provides the applicant with an accurate description of the job and the work environment. The realistic job preview process can actually start well before recruitment ever begins as the individual becomes familiar with the organization, its culture, and image. This can occur through organizational advertisements and public relations or just from the fact that the individual lives in the community where the organization is located. The RJP is reaffirmed by recruiters accurately portraying the requirements of the job and the conditions under which it is performed. The RJP process continues during selection interviewing and actually continues after the employee is hired, and through orientation and subsequent continuous socialization. Realistic job previews have been shown by numerous research studies to be positively correlated with employee retention, particularly during the first several months of employment. You should expect a question regarding realistic job preview.

NOTE

The concept of employer branding is increasingly being discussed in relation to recruitment. *Branding* is a marketing concept that refers to customer perceptions of an organization or its products that differentiate it from it competitors. In a recruitment context, branding is the process by which an employer becomes the employer of choice in its relevant labor markets. Employer branding is tied to the perception and popularity of the organization and its products or services. Recruitment activities can leverage that image to facilitate attracting applicants.

To be effective, the recruitment strategy must be in alignment with the brand. If the organization has innovative products and a creative culture, the recruitment strategies should be a bit innovative and "out of the box." For example, recruitment strategies for Yahoo! would be considerably different than those for Wells Fargo bank in order to align themselves with the organizational and product image. A critical issue in employee branding is the selection and training of recruiters. Recruiters must not only have the appropriate skills and attitude, but they must also reflect the culture and image of the organization. Continuing with the preceding example, a recruiter for Yahoo! should act, dress and, in general, reflect a different attitude than one from Wells Fargo.

If the organization decides to not contract out recruitment, it must determine what types of recruitment activities to engage in and it must evaluate the effectiveness of those activities. The following sections discuss the potential methods that an organization can use to recruit both internally and externally. Also discussed are recruitment metrics used to evaluate recruitment activities.

Internal Recruiting

Internal recruiting involves recruiting current or former employees for job openings in the organization along with soliciting referrals from current employees. Various methods are discussed in this section.

Human Resource Management Information System

Sophisticated HRISs and employee databases are excellent sources of applicants. Many of these systems include data on employee training, education, and skills. In addition, some systems also include information on employee career goals and employee performance ratings. The system is able to match the requirements of a job with the characteristics and career goals of an employee to instantaneously create a potential applicant list. These employees can then be contacted, often by an automated email system, regarding their interest in a job opening.

Job Posting

Job posting is the process of advertising and publicizing job openings to employees. This might be accomplished by physically posting the opening on bulletin boards or by electronically posting them on the company's intranet or Internet. It is then up to the employee to actually apply for the position.

Job Bidding

Job bidding is similar to job posting and is more common in unionized environments. *Job bidding* permits an employee to apply for a position even if no openings exist. The employee's application is then held for a period of time, usually for a year, and the employee receives automatic consideration should the position come open. The process is often referred to as *automatic consideration*. Job bidding might be more efficient when openings for a job come open quite frequently. The employer can go to the job bid list without having to post each opening separately.

Former Employees

Former employees are often a good source of applicants. Former employees include three categories:

▶ **Employees that have temporarily dropped out of the workforce** For example, individuals that have elected to stay home with their young children. Often these former employees are ready to come back to the workforce or are willing to accept part-time employment.

▶ **Retirees that might be willing to come back to the employer on a consultant or contract basis.**

▶ **Employees that have left the organization for work in another organization.**

Assuming that these employees were good performers prior to their exit from the organization, they are likely to be good performers on their return. Many organizations have alumni and retiree clubs and groups to keep in touch with former employees. This frequently provides a rich base from which to recruit. Often employees leave thinking that a new organization provides a better working environment, better pay, or more challenging work, only to be disappointed. They often can be enticed back to the organization.

Former Applicants

Applicants that previously applied for positions with the organization are to some extent known quantities, depending on how far they got in the selection process. Good applicants should be reconsidered. Many organizations keep files on excellent candidates that were not selected for prior openings and re-recruit them for current positions. This method is both efficient and effective. Much of the screening might have already been done and, if the applicants were previously interviewed, they might have already been judged as acceptable.

> **NOTE**
>
> Keeping in touch with prior applicants and making them feel good about the recruitment and selection process is good practice and an extension of the branding process discussed earlier. Applicants should be kept informed of their status throughout the hiring process and given feedback.

Employee Referrals

Many organizations have active formal employee referral programs, particularly in tight job markets or where the employer has difficult-to-fill or high-turnover positions. These programs reward employees for referring applicants to the organization. Other organizations have less formal programs and encourage employees to refer potential applicants, but do not provide an incentive for doing so.

Experience and research show considerable benefit to the employee referral type of recruitment. First, employees are not likely to refer applicants that would not be good employees. They do not want to be embarrassed by the performance or conduct of their referral. Also, candidates that are referred by employees typically already have begun the orientation process and have somewhat of a realistic job preview via their relationship with the current employee. Finally, there is a positive correlation between employee referral and employee retention of those hired as a result.

There is, however, one potential problem that can associated with employee referrals. Employees tend to refer their relative and friends, who most likely are of the same ethnicity or sex as themselves. Therefore, this type of recruitment does not normally facilitate the achievement of diversity and affirmative action plan goals and can create adverse impact. This is particularly true if the organization has a past practice of discrimination.

External Recruiting

External recruiting involves obtaining applications from individual external to the organization. A threshold strategic issue for the SPHR is the determination of the appropriate external labor market from which to recruit. For lower-level jobs, the appropriate market is most likely to be the local labor market—defined as the geographical area from which most people are willing to commute. This subject is discussed in greater depth in Chapter 5.

However, a sufficient applicant pool might not be available in the local labor market for many jobs. For certain types of jobs, particularly professional jobs, the appropriate labor market is determined in terms of the profession. Recruiting is often most effective when performed inside the profession, using professional organizations and professional journals for example. For mid-level types of positions, a regional labor market might produce a better applicant pool, whereas many top-level and highly specialized jobs require recruiting nationally and even internationally.

Of course, use of the Internet, which is discussed later, facilitates a broader recruiting area. However, Internet recruiting often is not appropriate, effective, or efficient for many jobs and the critical decision affecting the success of a recruitment effort remains in the selection of the appropriate labor market from which to recruit. External recruiting can involve many methods, the most common of which are discussed in this section.

Media Advertising

Media advertising refers to recruitment using radio, television, newspapers, and so forth. This is a technical area requiring expertise not normally available within the HR function. Writing effective advertisements frequently calls for professionals in the field. Professionally done media advertising can be an extremely effective and cost-efficient recruitment method. It allows the organization to reach a large number of potential applicants, often resulting in significant savings in hiring costs. By use of appropriate outlets targeted protected groups can be reached, which facilitates diversity and affirmative action efforts. However, when poorly done media advertising can be extremely expensive.

College and School Recruiting

College and university recruiting is a good source of entry- and mid-level managers and professionals. In general, college recruiting requires a continuing relationship with the organization and its placement office, and a history of hiring the college's graduates. These together tend to put the organization at the front of the referral queue. However, this is often an expensive proposition requiring expenditure of both staff and financial resources. Sponsoring professional clubs and providing scholarships and internships can be expensive if the organization never hires individuals from the college. Many organizations have scaled down their college recruiting efforts to focus on a few schools where they can maintain a continuing presence and hire excellent candidates in a cost-effective manner.

Two-year colleges (junior and community colleges) and technical schools can be good sources for entry-level, para-technical, and para-professional positions. The strategies associated with recruiting at these institutions are the same as for higher-level institutions—only the type of positions being recruited for is different.

High schools are a good source of blue-collar, clerical, and retail entry-level positions. Many organizations do not realize the potential of recruiting at this level, often assuming that graduates will pursue higher education. Good relationships with school counselors and athletic departments often facilitate this type of recruitment.

Labor Unions

Labor union hiring halls are often a good, and sometimes the only, source of applicants. This is particularly true in the construction trades.

Employment Agencies

As mentioned earlier in the discussion of outsourced recruitment, employment agencies and job search firms often are good sources of job candidates. First, all states have unemployment offices, displaced worker units, or similar agencies performing the same function. These are often sources of applicants.

Private employment agencies can be viable sources of applicants. These firms most frequently charge the organization a fee for referral of candidates, either on a contingency or retainer basis. Contingency-based firms receive the fee only if the applicant is hired, whereas retainer-based firms receive a fee for engaging in the search even if no one is hired. Employment agencies normally prescreen the applicants for the organization and refer only those that are qualified. The agencies often have contacts and relationships that the organization does not, and might be able to locate excellent candidates for higher-level managerial and hard-to-fill technical and professional positions. Although using employment agencies and search firms might be cost-effective and yield results that the organization could not achieve on its own, doing so can be extremely expensive. Costs for using these types of firms often run 25–30% of the yearly salary for the position being recruited.

Temporary Employment Agencies

Many private employment agencies provide temporary, part-time, or just-in-time workers. These employees are paid by the temporary agency and are not employees of the organization. Temporary agencies screen these workers and often provide training. These agencies have traditionally provided lower-level blue-collar and clerical workers, but that is no longer the case. There are now temporary employment agencies that specialize in providing technical, professional, and managerial temporary workers. There are even agencies that specialize in temporary executives up to and including CEOs.

The advantage of these agencies is in their flexibility. The employer has no continuing obligation to the employee and can, within limits, rotate them in and out of the organization. This is especially important to firms than have frequent variations in demand or are seasonal in nature. Employers pay a fee to the temporary agency and do not have to worry about employee benefits or employment taxes. In addition, organizations often use the temporary employment as a probationary period. The temporary agency permits the organization to hire these temporary workers as permanent employees for a fee.

Customers

Loyal customers are pleased with the organization's product or services. To some extent they have made a commitment to the organization, and might be familiar with the culture, the responsibilities of some of the jobs, and the working conditions. In other words, they have a realistic job preview. Many organizations have found customers to be an excellent source of candidates. They frequently recruit actively in their retail establishments, taking job applications on the spot and providing easy access to employment information and application procedures on their websites.

Suppliers and Competitors

Employees of suppliers and competitors are often good sources of applicants. They are familiar with the industry and frequently familiar with the organization itself.

Professional and Trade Associations

Virtually all professional and trade associations provide placement services for their members and allow employers to post job openings on their website, typically for a fee. In addition, these associations normally publish newsletters or journals in which the organization can place recruiting advertisements. Most associations also have annual meetings or conventions that provide additional opportunities for the organization to recruit in person. Organizations have found professional and trade associations to be excellent sources of applicants, particularly for specialized types of jobs such as banking, finance, human resource management, and so forth. Some associations are organized around gender or ethnicity. They are good sources of candidates for organizations engaging in diversity or affirmative action initiatives.

Walk-Ins

Many organizations accept applications from individuals that visit the organization for the express purpose of inquiring about job opportunities. Walk-ins have been found to be good sources of entry-level employees. The mere fact that they have taken the time and effort to visit the organization shows some level of interest and commitment.

Job Fairs and Special Events

Job fairs held by other organizations—for example, the local chamber of commerce—tend to attract a wide variety of applicants and might provide the organization with numerous recruiting leads and applicants. However, many organizations have found that some individuals attending these types of events are merely shopping and are not really interested in changing jobs. In addition, many of the individuals tend to have low skills and might be largely unemployable. That being said, job fairs held by organizations such as professional associations (for example, the Society for Human Resource Management) can be an excellent source of candidates.

Internally held job fairs have proven to be an effective means of recruitment, particularly for entry-level blue-collar and clerical employees. Organizations often open up their facilities during the evening or on the weekend and provide free food and prizes as an incentive for potential applicants to visit. Actually visiting the work site begins the realistic job preview process and might result in better retention of applicants who are actually hired.

Organizations have also found that using special events as a recruiting tool has proven effective. A booth or kiosk at sporting and civic events could produce viable candidates.

Internet

The Internet has opened up all sorts of possibilities and associated challenges in recruiting. It provides access to a worldwide population of potential applicants. There are essentially three major sources of applicants using e-recruiting: commercial job boards, professional/trade association websites, and the employer's website.

Many organizations have successfully used commercial job boards such as Monster.com and Hotjobs.com where, for a fee, employers can post job opportunities. Job boards have been found to provide access to a large number of qualified candidates. However, because of ease of access many of the candidates often are not seriously looking for a new job but are merely testing their competitiveness in the job market or trying to determine current compensation rates.

As discussed previously, many professional and trade associations publish job openings on their website. These can provide viable candidates for specialized positions.

Most larger employers now provide employment information on their websites. They typically find this to be an effective and efficient means of generating applications. To be effective, access to job information must be easy. Most employers provide a button on the home page that leads prospective applicant to the information. Effectiveness is increased if the web page for employment information continues the same format and theme as the home page and is consistent with the organization's image and culture. This is an important continuation of the employer branding previously discussed.

Internet recruiting can save time because the application forms and/or resumes are readily available. Applicants can be immediately contacted via email. Internet recruiting is typically much less expensive than media advertising or onsite recruiting initiatives. Internet recruiting expands the relevant job market to the globe and has the potential to generate a large number of qualified candidates.

However, the ease of application in Internet recruiting and the wide exposure of job opening information often generate applications from those that are not qualified or that are not seriously looking for work. In fact, Internet recruiting might generate too many applications that must be screened and applicants that must be contacted, thus increasing the workload on HR. Fortunately, there are now software packages that can largely automate many of these processes.

Internet recruiting poses problems for the tracking of applicant flow data. However, recent rulings by both the EEOC and OFCCP have clarified the issue somewhat. As a general overview of that guidance, employers have to consider applications received on the Internet as applicants for applicant flow data only if the organization actually considers the applicant for an open position, if the applicant maintains continued interest and follows the organization's standard application process, and if the applicant expresses interest and is basically qualified for a particular position.

A final concern about Internet recruiting is the potential for adverse impact caused by what is known as the *digital divide*. Although access to the Internet has increased dramatically, certain minority groups might have less access than other groups.

Outplacement Firms

Many organizations have formed alliances with outplacement firms. These firms provide placement assistance to individuals, many of whom have been involuntarily separated from their former employer through no fault of their own. These individuals are often excellent candidates.

> **EXAM ALERT**
>
> The SPHR should be familiar with the various types of recruiting methods available, the advantages and disadvantages associated with them (if applicable), and which are considered internal and external methods.

Evaluating Recruitment Effectiveness

The SPHR provides leadership in evaluating the efficiency and effectiveness of recruitment activities. Efficiency evaluation is largely operational in nature, whereas effectiveness evaluation is strategic. Unfortunately, organizations tend to do a rather good job at developing efficiency metrics, but a poor job of developing effectiveness measures. The efficiency metrics provide information regarding the accomplishments of short-term objectives. However, the critical issue is the long-term strategic impact of recruitment activities on the success of the organization (effectiveness metrics).

Typical efficiency metrics are as follows:

- ▶ **Quantity of applications** This is a gross measure of the effect of recruitment activities with the philosophy that the more applications an organizations gets, the more likely it is to fill its openings with highly qualified individuals. Quantities can be evaluated by source, giving a gross estimate of the cost-effectiveness of television versus newspaper advertising, for example.

- ▶ **Quality of applications** Organizations might want to evaluate the percentage of applications that were considered qualified for the job or that were actually offered an interview. Again, this is a gross measure of the impact of the recruitment program and can be analyzed by the source of the application.

▸ **Time to fill**   Most organizations evaluate the time it takes to fill a position, typically in terms of the number of days from the date the request is received in the HR department until new employee actually reports onboard. These data are then compared against goals, historical averages, and benchmarks to evaluate recruitment efficiency.

▸ **Yield rates**   Yield rates were discussed earlier in this chapter. Recruitment is often evaluated in terms of yield rates from one stage of the process to another. For example, the organization needs to know what percentage of applicants were actually considered to be qualified for the job, what percentage that were qualified passed the initial screening, what percentage passing the initial screening also passed the pre-employment tests, what percentage passing the pre-employment test were offered in-person interviews, and so forth. This provides an additional measure of efficiency in that higher yield ratios reduce wasted staff effort and produce more viable candidates for the organization to consider.

▸ **Cost per hire**   Many organizations track the average cost to hire employees, typically by dividing all recruitment-related expenses by the number of actual hires. The measure provides an indication of the efficiency of the recruitment program in terms of costs, but yields little information regarding effectiveness. Also, the calculation of recruitment costs is often difficult.

▸ **Selection rates**   Selection rate provide some indication of efficiency because they evaluate the number of new hires against the total number of applicants. For example, if 50 hires were made from an application pool of 100, the selection rate is 50%.

However, one cannot really necessarily evaluate that metric in terms of effectiveness. Presumably, the higher the selection rate, the more efficient and effective recruitment process. But are selections being made using the "any warm body" philosophy because positions must be filled with any applicant that is minimally qualified? Selection rates along with other measures of efficiency do not give the organization any indication of the actual performance of an individual after being hired, nor do they tell the organization anything about employee retention.

▸ **Acceptance rates**   Some organizations track selection rates, which are typically evaluated as the number of applicants that accept the position divided by the number of applicants that were offered the position. The higher the ratio, the more efficient the recruitment program is considered to be. However, acceptance rates can be significantly affected by outside influences that have nothing to do with the quality of recruitment efforts. For example, acceptance rates could be expected to be appreciably higher during periods of high unemployment.

This metric is frequently used to evaluate both individual recruiter and recruitment sources. When evaluating individual recruiters, the interest is in how effective the recruiter is in actually convincing the applicant to accept the job. This might be a critical issue, especially with higher-level jobs where the costs of recruiting are substantial. The organization is also interested in knowing whether the acceptance rate differs among the various recruitment methods so that it can adjust its strategies.

Effectiveness measures are those that evaluate the long-term strategic impact of the recruitment program. As discussed in Chapter 4, "Human Resource Development," in the context of evaluation of training and development there is often an inverse relationship between the value of data and analysis and its difficulty. However, this is the value added by the SPHR. The SPHR must develop metrics that strategically evaluate recruitment efforts in terms of their impact on organizational effectiveness and strategic success.

An effectiveness measure frequently overlooked is that of customer satisfaction with the recruitment process and results. In this case, customers can be defined in a number of ways. First, management satisfaction should be evaluated. Managers should be questioned as to their overall satisfaction with the recruitment process and the timeliness of actions and the quality of recruits in particular. Because managers at different levels often have different expectations, satisfaction should be surveyed at multiple levels in the organization. The second, and probably more important, customer group is the actual recruits themselves. This includes both those who were hired and those who were rejected for employment. They should be questioned about their perspectives regarding the various stages of the recruitment and selection process. These data often provide valuable information regarding recruitment effectiveness and identify areas that might need improvement.

The effectiveness of recruitment efforts should be evaluated in terms of eventual employee performance and retention. Therefore, the SPHR should lead the HR function in engaging in longitudinal studies in these areas. In the press of current requirements historical research is often ignored. Yet these data are the ones that allow the organization to fine-tune current operations. Organizations that have effective recruitment evaluation programs periodically (usually yearly) evaluate a sample of hires from previous years, correlating retention, promotion rates, and performance data with recruitment sources, selection tests, and other employment practices. Evaluation of individual recruiters can also be done using the same process. These data provide rich information as to the long-term effectiveness of recruitment programs. The potential value of these types of evaluations is, however, moderated by the nature of the organizational environment and the organizational strategies. These data have the greatest impact in planning and engaging in activities to improve the recruitment program when the environment is relatively stable.

> **NOTE**
>
> Remember that almost all employment practices are *tests* under EEOC regulations and the Uniform Guidelines for Employee Selection Procedures. Any recruitment practice that creates adverse impact must be a business necessity under either job-relatedness or bona fide occupational qualifications.

NOTE

An important effectiveness metric for many organizations is tracking the capabilities of the organization to attract and retain minority and female candidates.

EXAM ALERT

The SPHR should be familiar with the types of metrics that can be used to evaluate the effectiveness and efficiency of recruitment efforts.

Contingent Workforce

Objective:
Gain an Understanding of the Contingent Workforce

The contingent workforce is composed of those individuals who work for an organization but are not permanent full-time employees. Use of a contingent workforce is increasing and it is estimated that contingent workers represent more than 20% of the total United States workforce. The dynamics of today's organizational and business environment often drive employers to use contingent workers to achieve a strategic advantage. These drivers of change are discussed extensively in this chapter and in others, but a brief summary is appropriate.

Increased competition and the need for cost-efficiency require that employers have flexibility in adjusting employment levels and employment costs to demand for its product or services and in relationship to its level of operations, both of which might be constantly changing and volatile. A permanent full-time workforce does not permit that. The changing psychological contract encourages lack of permanency of relationships, both in employee and employer expectations.

Contingent workers are in alignment with those expectations. Changing technology often requires new skills that permanent full-time employees might not have and might not be capable of developing. Downsizing and rightsizing could result in the loss of organizational capability, which can be augmented with the use of contingent workers. The increasing difficulty of compliance with the complexity of employment laws and the cost associated with them can be largely avoided by having workers that are employees of other organizations. Finally, significant cost savings can often accrue from outsourcing the organization's work to organizations located in foreign countries in which the wage rates are low.

However, the use of contingent workers does not come without some organizational concerns and disadvantages. Increased flexibility often brings about loss of control. The employer might be able to control only the outcome of work, not the means used to obtain it. This issue is further discussed in Chapter 5. Use of some types of contingent workers might, in the long run, be more expensive than permanent employees because the source of those workers must not only be reimbursed for compensation and benefit costs but must also be paid a fee in addition.

There is a concern regarding the loyalty of employees that are not employed on a full-time basis. Will the employee act in the best interest of the organization or of the actual employer? Another issue of substantial concern is the impact of this strategy on the remaining permanent full-time workforce. Does the practice lower overall morale and induce stress and concern among the remaining workers who might become worried about their own job security?

A final issue is one of ethics and social responsibility. The SPHR must lead the organization in balancing its obligations to its employees, the community or communities in which it operates, and society as a whole against the organization's legitimate desire to maximize its profits for stockholders. The advantages and disadvantages of use of the contingent workforce are summarized in Table 3.8.

TABLE 3.8   Advantages and Disadvantages of Using the Contingent Workforce

Advantages	Disadvantages
► Flexibility	► Perceived lack of loyalty
► Savings in the cost of taxes and benefits	► Lack of knowledge of the organization's culture, policies, and procedures
► Access to expertise not internally available	
► Potential savings in overall compensation costs	► Potential for overall higher costs, depending on the situation
	► Concern with disclosure of organizational proprietary information
	► Impact on morale of permanent workforce
	► Loss of internal capabilities
	► Potential for increased training costs when contingent workers must be trained on unique or unusual processes or procedures used by the organization

A contingent workforce can be composed of many types of workers. Employers often use several sources simultaneously. Common types or sources of contingent workers include the following:

> ► **Part-time workers**   Part-time workers can be obtained from a temporary employment agency, in which case flexibility is maximized and the organization avoids liability for taxes and benefits. Part-time workers can be employees of the organization. Although that arrangement might be somewhat permanent in nature and of limited

flexibility, organizations often provide no or a limited range of benefits, resulting in cost savings.

▶ **Temporary workers**   Traditional temporary workers are obtained from employment agencies that specialize in providing these types of workers. However, the employer can also hire temporary workers internally.

NOTE

The employer that hires temporary workers must do so based on some rational basis such as temporary or seasonal increases in operations, the need to replace workers during the peak vacation period, and so forth. The temporary workers should be terminated when the temporary demand for additional workforce ceases. Continued employment of temporary workers for extended amounts of time might negate their temporary status and obligate the employer to provide expensive benefits. Microsoft Corporation paid a 97-million dollar settlement to workers that it had mischaracterized as temporary workers.

NOTE

Hiring temporary labor from a temporary employment agency can also pose potential legal problems for the employer. If the organization exercises control over the temporary employees, provides training, negotiates compensation, or engages in other employment-related practices, the temporary employee is likely to be considered by the courts as an employee of both the organization and the temporary employment agency (referred to as *dual employment*).

In such cases the organization might be obligated to provide certain benefits. In addition, as a dual employer, the organization must comply with all employment laws in its relationship with the temporary workers. For example, the organization might have an obligation to provide reasonable accommodation to a temporary worker under the Americans with Disabilities Act and can be found liable for illegal discrimination or harassment under the Civil Rights Act of 1964.

NOTE

Temporary employees in many situations have the right to join unions that are the certified bargaining agent either of the temporary employment agency or of the organization.

EXAM ALERT

The SPHR should understand the concept of dual employment. As the contingent workforce grows and organizations increasingly use temporary employment agencies, this issue is likely to take on more importance.

▶ **Consultants**   Often consultants are contracted with to provide expertise not currently available to the organization and not needed on a permanent and continuing basis.

▶ **Contract workers**   Contract workers are often hired on a project basis. After the project is complete, the organization has no further obligation to the individual.

▶ **Outsourcing**   *Outsourcing* is the process of contracting for services or products with external vendors rather than producing them internally. Frequently outsourcing results in substantial compensation savings because of the economies of scale that are created when an organization specializes in a particular type of work and/or employs specialized software. Outsourcing often permits access to specialize expertise not available internally to the organization.

▶ **Offshoring**   *Offshoring* refers to hiring workers in foreign countries to perform tasks previously done in the United States. Oftentimes, substantial cost savings can be realized because of the lower compensation rates in those countries.

▶ **Leasing**   Leasing typically involves a contract with a professional employer organization *(PEO)*. A *PEO* is an organization that assumes the employer rights and responsibilities for employees that it provides to its clients. An employer wanting to lease its currently employees signs a contract with a PEO and the PEO hires the employees. The organization then leases them back, with the PEO assuming the responsibilities of an employer. Employee leasing tends to be particularly suited for small employers that do not have internal expertise to comply with the complexities of today's employment laws. Also, because the PEO has a much larger workforce, it might be able to provide the former organizational employees with much better benefit packages. Obviously these services do not come without a cost, and it is estimated that leasing raises total labor costs by about 5%. For many employers this is additional money well spent.

EXAM ALERT

The contingency workforce is growing and the SPHR must understand what workers are included in the definition of contingent workforce and the advantages and disadvantages of using a contingent workforce strategy. Expect a question in this area.

Selection

Objective:
Gain an Understanding of Selection

Selection is the commonly used term, but probably a misnomer for what the organization attempts to accomplish during this stage of the employment process. *Selection* is the process used to choose individuals with the right qualifications to fill job openings in the organization. The more strategic term is *placement*, which means the process of ensuring that the right person is placed in the right job. Placement includes two separate but integrated concepts:

▶ **Person-job fit**   This is the process of ensuring that the knowledge, skills, and abilities of the individual match the requirements of the essential functions of the job.

▶ **Person-organization fit**   This is the process of ensuring that the personality and value system of the individual match the culture and objectives of the organization.

Person-job fit is especially critical when jobs and organizations are stable and the emphasis is on quality, productivity, and efficiency. However organizations and jobs are often not stable in today's dynamic and volatile world. If the nature of the job is constantly changing and the goals of the organization are flexible and fluid, person-job fit does not provide the workforce flexibility needed. In such situations, person-organization fit becomes increasingly important and facilitates creativity, innovation, and organizational and workforce flexibility and adaptability. In reality, both are important and the relative importance of each in the placement process depends on the situation.

EXAM ALERT

The concepts of person-job and person-organization fit are strategic issues with which the SPHR should be familiar. Expect a question.

The selection process follows a relatively consistent pattern in most organizations, although the complexity and number of steps vary based on the sophistication and needs of the organization. However, prior to the start of the selection process, a determination must be made as to the basis on which selection and placement is to be made. To do this, the organization must develop selection criteria that link those criteria to on-the-job performance. Finally, the organization must evaluate its selection processes. These topics are discussed in the following sections:

▶ Development of selection criteria

▶ The selection process

▶ Evaluation of the selection process

Development of Selection Criteria

As previously discussed in this chapter, the selection process and all its components are *tests* in terms of the Uniform Guidelines for Employee Selection Procedures. Criteria used for selection must be both job-related (discussed in this chapter) and valid (discussed in Chapter 2).

The question then becomes how to achieve compliance with the law, avoid adverse impact on protected classes, and develop a process that accurately predicts on-the-job performance.

As discussed earlier in this chapter, the process begins with quality job analysis. Job analysis provides information necessary to determine what the critical elements of performance are with respect to the job. Those elements can be defined in terms of quality of work, quantity of work, and so forth. In general, the selection process cannot directly measure job performance because the individual would have to actually be in the position, often for an extended period of time, to be able to measure that individual's performance. However, the organization can develop selection criteria that are believed to be correlated with the job performance elements. Criteria are often defined in terms of characteristics that the individual must possess such as knowledge, motivation, ability, intelligence, interpersonal skills, and so forth.

Unfortunately, selection criteria are not often directly observable, so the organization must develop predictors that can be used to evaluate whether the desired criteria are present in the individual. Predictors are such items as experience, education, certifications, test scores, references, background checks, past performance, interview results, and so forth. The predictors are used in the selection process as depicted in Figure 3.2. *Predictors* are those items used to determine the presence of desired attributes (selection criteria) in an individual because those selection criteria are directly correlated with job performance. Each step in this linkage must be a valid predictor of the next step.

| Predictors $\longrightarrow$ Selection Criteria $\longrightarrow$ Job Performance |

FIGURE 3.2 Relationship of predictors, selection criteria, and job performance.

The selection process should be designed to make correct decision and avoid incorrect ones. Appropriate selection and validation of predictors, selection criteria, and job performance elements facilitates the acceptance of qualified candidates and the rejection of unqualified ones, but also prevents the acceptance of unqualified candidates and the rejection of those that are qualified.

EXAM ALERT

You should understand the concept of predictors and selection criteria and their linkage, ultimately, with the elements of job performance.

The Selection Process

A threshold question in designing the selection process is determining how the applicant should proceed through the process. Two options are most frequently used:

▶ **Multiple hurdle approach**   In a multiple hurdle approach, the applicant must pass each step in the selection process. Failure at any step disqualifies the applicant from further consideration.

▶ **Compensatory approach**   In the compensatory approach, applicants complete the whole selection process and their scores in each stage are added up to determine final ranking.

There are advantages and disadvantages to both approaches. The multiple hurdle approach is efficient, eliminating candidates at each step of the process. However, it might result in the elimination of outstanding candidates who are excellent in all areas except for one. The compensatory approach allows for a fuller examination of every candidate and enables a candidate to compensate for a weakness or poor performance in one stage. However, it is more time-consuming and expensive. The ultimate decision as to which type of approach to use likely revolves around the importance of the job, the availability of candidates, and organizational time and resource constraints. Most organizations use the multiple hurdle approach.

Figure 3.1 earlier in this chapter can be used as a broad outline of a typical selection process that includes

▶ Initial applicant contact

▶ Prescreening

▶ Application forms

▶ Applicant testing

▶ Interviews

▶ Background and reference checking

▶ Conditional job offer

▶ Medical/drug testing

▶ Offer and acceptance

Each stage in the process is discussed in the following sections.

Initial Applicant Contact

Recruitment methods were discussed earlier in this chapter. Often candidates express interest by showing up at the employer (such candidates are called *walk-ins*) or by telephoning and inquiring as to current or potential job openings. Other candidates might mail or fax unsolicited resumes. These types of inquiries must be handled appropriately by the organization. Employer branding concerns (discussed earlier in this chapter) require that these inquiries or submissions be handled in a professional and courteous manner. Yet the requirements for applicant flow tracking (also discussed earlier in the chapter) make additional clerical work. Many employers do not accept unsolicited resumes and require all applicants to follow standard application procedures, accepting applications only when openings are currently available.

Prescreening

Prescreening is the process of determining whether candidates meet the basic qualifications for the position. Many employers prescreen applicants prior to the application process. For example, if the employer accepts walk-in applications, it might determine at that time whether the candidate is qualified for its jobs. If not, the walk-in is not provided with a job application. In that way, the employer does not incur the time and expense of processing the application and can avoid the need to track the candidate for applicant flow purposes.

Other organizations prescreen on receipt of the application. They then reject those candidates that do not meet the minimum qualification standards for the job.

Application Forms

Application forms serve multiple purposes:

- ▶ Provides a record of interest in employment
- ▶ Provides information to determine the qualifications of the individual
- ▶ Provides information that can be used in the employment interview
- ▶ Provides the basic data needed for initial preparation of the personnel file
- ▶ Clearly puts the employee on notice regarding the selection process and the nature of the employment relationship in that it typically contains one or more of the following notices:
  - ▶ That employment is at-will and either the employee or employer may terminate the relationship for any legal reason at any time
  - ▶ Notifies the applicant that falsification of information on the application is grounds for immediate termination
  - ▶ Notifies the applicant of any tests, including medical and drug tests, that will be required during the selection process
  - ▶ Advises the applicant that references will be checked

Application forms are tests and must not be discriminatory. Unless there is a business necessity or bona fide occupational qualification applications must yield information that would permit the identification of the applicant's protected class status.

It is possible to use applications to rank order applicants in terms of qualifications for the job. This type of applications is called a *weighted* or *biodata* application form. Scores are assigned to specific answers on the application form. Those scores are then added together to come up with an overall score that can be used to rank candidates. These processes often can be done by computer software that scans the application for key words and assigns points when they appear. Although these types of systems are efficient, they must be valid predictors of performance and job related to avoid adverse impact issues.

Employers must make a determination as to whether to accept resumes as applications. Even though resumes could contain rich data about the candidate, they might also contain information such as age, race, or religion—information that the selecting official should not know. Frequently, candidates attach pictures to their resumes, again providing information that cannot legally be used in most selection processes. Good HR practice, if resumes are to be accepted, is to

▶ Redact (black out) information that cannot be used in the selection process.

▶ Require the applicant to also complete an application. In that way, the candidate is provided with the notifications described earlier and the organization is assured of getting the required information necessary to consider the qualifications of the individual.

Applicant Testing

Many organizations use a variety of types of tests to improve the validity of the selection process. Valid tests that are job-related can be powerful predictors of subsequent on-the-job performance. Types of tests used in the selection process are discussed in the following sections.

Cognitive Ability Tests

These types of tests measure an individual's mental abilities and acquired knowledge. Examples of cognitive ability tests are those that test memory, analytical ability, verbal capabilities, mathematical ability, and reasoning.

Physical Ability Tests

These test measure an individual's physical skills and mobility. They are often important indicators of the ability to perform manual types of jobs, such as work on assembly lines. Examples of physical ability tests are those that measure strength, flexibility, balance, and stamina.

Work Simulation Tests

These tests require the applicant to perform a representative sample of the tasks that are part of the responsibility of the job. To the extent that the test is representative of the actual job, these types of test can be excellent predictors of future performance.

Personality Tests

Certain personality traits can be specifically correlated with performance on the job. If predictive validity has been proven, these tests are excellent tools.

Assessment Centers

Assessment centers are processes not places. They consist of a variety of tests and exercises that are scored, often by multiple raters. Assessment centers can be used as developmental tools or in the selection process. Because of the expense involved, they are frequently used only for selection and development of higher-level positions.

Honesty / Integrity Tests

Although polygraph tests are generally prohibited as pre-employment tests in the private sector, honesty and integrity tests are not. They are particularly useful in the selection process when individuals will have access to money, such as retail cashiers and bank tellers. The downside to using such tests is that they send the message to the applicant that he or she is not trusted.

Drug Tests

Drug tests can be used as a pre-employment test. Many employers elect to wait until a conditional offer of employment is made. Drug testing is discussed in the following section on post-offer employment practices.

Interviews

Organizations might use one or more interviews in the selection process. The purpose of interviews is to determine both person-job and person-organization fit, and to clarify information found on the application or gathered throughout the application process. If an organizations uses more than one interview, the first interview is normally used as a screen early in the selection process. HR is frequently responsible for performing the initial interview, and it is used to screen out those candidates who are obviously unsuitable for the position for which they applied. Subsequent interviews are conducted at higher levels of the organization, usually with management participation. They are used to evaluate the potential of viable candidates.

The interview is a traditional mainstay in the selection process. However, its validity is questionable. Yet few managers feel comfortable in selecting individuals without an interview. To maximize validity, interviews should be structured, directive, behavioral, or situational, and conducted by more than one interviewer. There are numerous common problems in the interview process that could lead to incorrect determinations. Also there are certain types of questions that either do not elicit the responses required to evaluate the candidate or should not be asked because they might create the potential for adverse impact and EEO complaints. These issues are discussed in the following sections.

Types of Interviews

There are numerous types of interviews that can be used in the selection process. It is up to the SPHR to guide the organization in selecting the type(s) of interview that best allows it to make a determination as to the potential of candidates to perform on the job. Types of interviews include the following.

Structured Interview

Structured interviews are those that include prescripted questions that are asked of all candidates. Interview structure runs on a continuum from highly structured to unstructured. At the far end of the structured interview continuum, the interview is totally scripted and the interviewer is not free to divert from the script. In addition, potential answers to each of the mandatory questions are often evaluated and given a score. The interviewer then must determine which of the potential answers is most like the one that the interviewee gave and assign it the predetermined score. At the other end of the continuum, the interviewer is free to ask any questions that come to mind. In practice, structured interviews tend to be less restrictive than the example given, but still require that a number of prescripted questions be asked. A structured interview is more valid and defensible than other interview types when making selection decisions because all candidates are asked the same questions and comparisons can be made between the answers given.

Directive Interview

An analogous but somewhat different concept to structured interviews is the concept of directive interviews. *Directive interviews* are those in which the interviewer maintains control of the flow of the questioning. It also is on a continuum from strict control by the interviewer to a nondirective approach at the other end, which is essentially a free-flowing conversation with little or no direction. In this situation, the interviewer essentially relinquishes control of the interview to the interviewee. Obviously, there is some correlation between the concepts of directive and structured interviews. A structured interview must also be directive.

Behavioral Interview

Although the term *behavioral interview* is commonly used, the term *behavioral* refers more to the type of questions than to the type of interview. For example, a behavioral interview might be structured and directive, using behavioral questions. *Behavioral questions* are those that ask the individual how the individual handled a particular situation in the past. For example, a candidate for a managerial position could be asked how he or she handled a situation in the past when an employee was habitually late for work. The concept behind behavioral questioning is that past behavior is the best indicator of future behavior in the same or similar situation. The weakness in this approach is that behavioral questions do not take into account any learning that might have occurred after the situation.

Situational Interview

Situational interviews, like behavioral interviews, also refer to the type of questions being asked. *Situational interviews* ask candidates to explain how they would handle a particular situation when confronted with it on the job. The concept behind situational questions is that answers to these types of theoretical scenarios are good predictors of future performance. The weakness in this approach is that candidates can often fake it by giving the answer they believe the interviewer wants.

Stress Interview

Stress interviews are appropriate when the essential functions of the job are performed under demanding conditions that require quick thinking and control of one's emotions. A *stress interview* is one designed to create anxiety and place pressure on the interviewees to determine how they respond. Stress interviews are appropriate for certain types of jobs such as public safety and customer complaint-handling. The risk in this type of interview is the negative image that the interviewees might get about the organization, leading them to withdraw from consideration or refuse a subsequent offer of employment.

Mass Interview

A *mass interview* is one in which more than one interviewee is interviewed at the same time. The mass interview is infrequently used, but when used, often involves some sort of problem-solving exercise that is given to the interviewees to work through. Each candidate is evaluated on characteristics such as leadership, interpersonal skills, and teamwork.

360° Interview

A 360° interview is one that is conducted by a panel of interviewers representing various constituencies in order to get a broad perspective in the evaluation of the candidate. For example, this type of interview might include the supervisor, a peer, a customer, and a subordinate if the interview is for a supervisory position. The concept behind the 360° interview is that the candidate is evaluated from a broad perspective. The potential problem with this concept is that each of the stakeholders might come to the interview with a different perspective as to the characteristic needed to do the job effectively.

Panel Interview

A panel interview is one in which more than one interviewer conducts the interview. Panel interviews are generally considered to be more valid than other types because more than one perspective is included in the evaluation process.

EXAM ALERT

You should be familiar with the various types of interviews and their advantages and disadvantages.

Problem with Interviews

There are common problems in perception that occur in interview that might cause the interviewer to make an incorrect determination of the candidate's potential. Interviewers receive training regarding these errors so that they can avoid them in the interview process. Common perceptual errors include the following:

- **Snap judgments** Interviewers often make up their minds regarding a candidate in the first few minutes of the interview. Such a quick decision precludes a full evaluation of the candidate's characteristics.

- **Stereotyping** *Stereotyping* involves evaluating persons based on their demographic characteristics rather than their individual capabilities.

- **Similar to me** The candidate is evaluated based on having a similar characteristic to the interviewer. For example, candidates from the same college as the interviewer are evaluated higher than those from other colleges.

- **Negative emphasis** Unfortunately, in the culture of the United States negative information is given more credence than positive information. One negative piece of information often precludes selection for the position and cannot be offset by many positive characteristics.

- **Halo/horn effect** Frequently all the candidate's characteristics are evaluated based on an evaluation of only one characteristic or trait. A positive evaluation is referred to as the *halo effect*, whereas a negative evaluation on all traits based on a negative evaluation of one trait is referred to as the *horn effect*.

- **Contrast error** It is important that candidates be evaluated against objective criteria related to job performance (predictors). However, interviewers frequently evaluate candidates against the prior candidate rather than the objective criteria. This can cause errors in the evaluation. For example, an average candidate interviewed after a poor candidate might be evaluated higher than average.

Interview Questions

Questions used in interviews should be designed to gather information need to make a determination as to whether to offer the individual a position. Questions that are poorly formulated do not assist in that endeavor. Questions that lead to answers that would identify the protected class of an individual, in the absence of BFOQ or business necessity, are illegal and should be avoided. The following types of questions do not lead to responses that facilitate evaluation of the candidate:

- **Questions that are not job-related** Questions not directly related to the job decrease the validity of the interview and do not assist in gather information regarding the candidate.

- **Bipolar questions**   Bipolar questions are those that can be answered with yes or no. They provide little or no definitive information.

- **Leading questions**   Leading questions guide the respondent to the answer. The interviewer then does not know whether or not the answer is truthful.

- **Illegal questions**   Questions that would identify protected class status are illegal. The following areas of questioning should be avoided unless they constitute a BFOQ for the specific job or are directly job-related:

  - Age

  - Sex

  - Race

  - National origin

  - Disability

  - Ancestry

  - Number of children

  - Marital status

  - Arrests

  - Height and weight

  - Date of college degree or high school graduation

  - Religious holidays observed

  - Birthplace

  - Medical history

Background Investigations

Background investigations are frequently the last step in the selection process prior to making a job offer or conditional job offer to the applicant. Background investigations serve two purposes. First they provide accurate information on the individual that is needed to make a final decision regarding employment. Second they provide evidence that the employer conducted due diligence in its hiring practices, which could be beneficial in the event the organization is sued for negligent hiring. A side benefit of background investigations is that candidates are less likely to apply or to falsify applications when they know background checks will be done. Background investigations incorporate one of more of the following processes:

- **Reference checks**   Employers typically attempt to get information from prior employers regarding the nature of the applicant's prior employment. Former employers frequently are reluctant to provide any derogatory information on prior employees because of fear of litigation for defamation of character, libel, and slander. Checking of personal references is also usually done, but is unlikely to reveal information of value.

▶ **Criminal record checks**   Limited criminal background checks are available through local or state law enforcement agencies. Decisions based on criminal record checks must be job-related because certain protected classes have disproportionately higher criminal conviction rates and decisions that are clearly not job-related might create adverse impact.

▶ **Credit checks**   Credit checks should be performed when the nature of the job involves responsibilities of a financial nature (payroll, accounts receivable, and so forth) or handling money (cashiers, bank tellers, and so forth). As is the case with criminal record checks, certain protective classes have higher incidences of bad credit than others.

▶ **Third-party background checks**   Many organizations elect to have reference, criminal history, and credit checks done by third parties.

NOTE

Remember that the provisions of the Fair Credit Reporting Act are applicable when the organization conducts credit checks. The act also covers most types of background checks if the organization contracts with a third party to perform them.

Conditional Job Offers, Medical Exams / Drug Testing, and Offers and Acceptance

These issues are discussed in the section on post-offer employment practices. In addition, medical examinations and drug testing were discussed in relation to the provisions of the Americans with Disability Act earlier in this chapter.

Evaluation of the Selection Process

Strategies and methods used to evaluate the selection process are essentially the same as those used to evaluate the recruitment process, which was discussed earlier in this chapter and is repeated here. The selection process should be continually evaluated in terms of its impact on protected classes. The Uniform Guidelines on Employee Selection Procedures calls for a bottom-up approach to evaluation. If adverse impact is indicated at the end of the selection process, the whole process must be dissected into its various stages to determine at what level or levels adverse impact occurs.

The organization should evaluate its selection process effectiveness in terms of the performance and retention of individuals hired. Predictors and criteria should be consistently evaluated for validity and predictive capacity.

NOTE

Two issues are allied with selection and are important determinants of the ultimate effectiveness of the process. The first is realistic job previews, which were discussed previously in this chapter. There are multiple opportunities throughout the selection process to provide the applicant with accurate information as to the exact nature of the job and the characteristics of the organization. The other issue is orientation. Orientation is discussed in Chapter 4. The selection process is an opportunity to begin the orientation process by providing the individual information on the terms, conditions, and benefits of employment with the organization. The accuracy and quality of both realistic job previews and employee orientation are positively correlated with employee retention.

Post-Offer Employment Practices

Objective:

Gain an Understanding of Post-Offer Employment Practices

There are several commons employment practices that the organization might want to use after a determination has been made to hire an individual. First is the employment offer itself. Next the organization must decide whether it is in its best interest to formalize the employment relationship with a formal employment contract. In addition, the organization must determine its employment practice with respect to medical examinations and, finally, whether to offer relocation benefits. Each of these practices is discussed in the sections that follow.

Employment Offers

Often the hiring process is a long and intensive process frequently characterized by considerable stress, particularly on the part of the employee. This can lead to miscommunication and misunderstandings as to the parameters of the proposed employment relationship. Therefore, many organizations consider it good practice to place their employment offers, often referred to as *job offers*, in writing. It is recommended that employment offer letters be reviewed by legal counsel to ensure that the organization does not create a legal obligation that it did not intend. The offer should clearly delineate the terms and conditions of employment. Care should be taken to avoid vague language that might be interpreted by the employee to promise any future benefit such as job security, pay raises or bonuses, particular work schedules, and so forth. Especially important is a clear identification that the employment relationship is "at-will" (an issue discussed in further detail in Chapter 6), and can be terminated by either party at any time for any legal reason.

The employee should be required to sign one copy of the offer and return it to the employer prior to or simultaneously with reporting for work. The signed offer should be retained in the employee's personnel file.

> **NOTE**
>
> If the employee is to be paid by the hour or by some type of piece-rate or commission basis (issues further discussed in Chapter 5), the employment offer should clearly delineate how the employee is to be compensated. However, if the employee is to be paid by salary, it is good practice to for the employment offer to align the salary offer with the current compensation payment practice. In other words, whether the employer pays weekly, biweekly, or monthly, the offer should be for the gross amount to be paid during a pay period. Some courts have interpreted employment offers that quote annual salaries as creating an implied contract for that amount of compensation.

Employment Contracts

The legal concepts associated with contracts are discussed in additional depth in Chapter 4. Organizations might want to negotiate a formal contract with employees that goes beyond the normal employment offer or agreement and clearly identifies additional terms and conditions of employment. Employment contracts are often used to negate the employment-at-will condition of employment and to establish fixed terms and conditions of employment—including length of employment and restrictions on employee activities should they leave the organization. Employment contracts provide protection, rights, and obligations for both the organization and the employee. A more in-depth discussion of employment contracts is contained in Chapter 6.

Medical Tests

Medical tests can be administered after a conditional offer of employment. The subject of medical tests is covered in depth earlier in this chapter as part of the discussion of the Americans with Disabilities Act.

An allied issue is the emerging and somewhat complex issue of genetic testing. *Genetics* is a branch of biology that studies the transmission of hereditary characteristic from parents to offspring. Medical tests are now available that can identify the genetic markers for certain debilitating diseases. Employers could use these test results to discriminate against individuals that have an increased potential for developing serious illnesses that might require expensive medical treatment and, ultimately, affect the employer's health insurance costs. On the other hand, this information could be valuable to the employee. The employee could be advised of the potential for certain diseases and take preventative measures. In addition, the employer might be able to place the employee in certain jobs that would lessen the potential for certain types of diseases. For example, the employee could be placed in a job that does not come into contact with certain types of hazardous chemicals.

As stated before, this issue is emerging as the genetic technology improves. Taking employment-related actions based on genetic information that negatively affects the employee should not be done. The SPHR can expect legislation and additional case law in this area.

Relocation

Many employers provide some assistance with the expenses of moving should the employee be relocating from a different geographical area to accept employment. Relocation benefits often involve issues of taxability and real estate law. For those reasons, many organizations elect to outsource this program. Concepts associated with managing outsourced programs were discussed in Chapter 2, and the subject of relocation benefits is discussed further in Chapter 5.

Organizational Exit

Objective:
Gain an Understanding of Organizational Exit

It is up to the SPHR to strategically manage organizational exit so that it is, to the extent possible, controllable, involuntary, and functional. Organizational exit is controllable when it is the employer that determines when employees leave the organization. It is involuntary when employees leave the organization because of organizational mandates, not the employees' desire to do so. Voluntary organizational exit (also called *turnover*) is frequently a significant problem in organizations, and often it is the best employees that leave. Involuntary organization exit involves termination for poor performance or layoffs or termination of excess employees when they are no longer needed by the organization. *Functional* organizational exit means that the organization is more efficient and/or effective after the exit occurs. Dysfunctional organizational exit results in a decrease in the human capital of the organization and decreased organizational capacity.

Organizational exit is the process of managing the conditions under which employees leave the organization and is often referred to as *decruitment*. An employee might be required to leave the organization because of his or her own actions, or the exit might be mandated based on organizational strategy that is beyond the control of the individual. Layoffs are discussed in the first section, along with strategies that can be employed to either avert the layoff or lessen its impact on the employee. After that, discussion moves on to involuntary terminations based on employee performance or conduct. If organizational exit is to be controllable, involuntary, and functional, the organization must know why exit occurs, particularly voluntary exit. One of the ways of determining this is by conducting exit interviews. Strategies and practices associated with exit interviews are discussed. Finally, this section addresses the issue of wrongful terminations.

Layoffs

There are a number of reasons why an employer might desire to reduce the total number of employees. Some of the more common reasons include the following:

- Downturns in overall operations caused by economic conditions or drop in product or service demand; commonly referred to as *downsizing*

- Concentrating on core competencies; commonly referred to as *rightsizing*

- Mergers or acquisitions that create redundant or duplicate positions

- Increases in production or introduction of new technology requiring fewer employees

- Competitive decisions, such as movement of plants to lower cost labor areas domestically or internationally (*offshoring*)

- Competitive decisions to outsource work currently being done internally

Any of these reasons might result in a decruitment situation in which the employer has a surplus of employees and must reduce the overall size of its workforce or must change the composition of its workforce in terms of employee capabilities.

Decisions to terminate or lay off employees have significant organizational implications. First the organization should evaluate the impact of layoffs on its diversity programs and the potential for creating adverse impact. Although seniority is generally considered to be a defense in adverse impact situations, the organization might be able to craft a layoff scenario that avoids adverse impact. Next the organization must consider the impact of layoffs on its important stakeholders. Layoffs send a mixed message to customers and investors. Even though the process might be perceived by these constituencies as prudent business decision-making, there is equal likelihood that it could be considered a sign of organizational, product, or service weakness, impacting demand and access to capital. The organization must consider the impact that such activities might have on the communities in which it operates, balancing business goals with social responsibilities. Finally, and most importantly, organizations should consider the impact of layoffs both on those employees directly affected and those who remain.

Because of these factors, the SPHR must be able to lead the organization in the development of programs that might permit the organization to avoid layoffs entirely or reduce the total number of employees that are laid off and programs that lessen the impact personal impact if an employee is in fact laid off. They are discussed the following sections.

> **NOTE**
>
> It is not only the employees that are laid off that are affected, but also those who remain. Often they have to endure increased workloads, having to both perform their current duties and assume the duties of those who have left. The remaining employees often are affected by increased stress based on concerns for their future in the organization and a bit of guilt associated with still being employed while their former coworkers have been laid off. The organization can lessen these impacts by communicating honestly with employees as to organizational plans and providing programs such as counseling to assist in development to the new condition.

> **NOTE**
>
> Layoffs by definition imply that the employee is to be returned to work. This might or might not occur. It is good practice to advise employees in writing that the layoff is considered permanent and end in a termination at the end of a specified period of time.

> **NOTE**
>
> Remember requirements under the WARN, discussed earlier in this chapter, when implementing layoffs and plant shutdowns.

Strategies to Avoid Layoffs

Even though the organization has decided to reduce the total size of the workforce, there are many strategies for accomplishing this goal without involuntarily laying off or terminating employees. These strategies frequently take some time to have impact; consequently, they might not be feasible if the immediacy of action is critical. However, in other situations the strategies discussed in the following section might avoid it totally or reduce the number of layoffs required.

Early Retirement Incentives

Many workers are willing to retire early if provided with the right incentives. Early retirement options that provide added benefits and that do not violate the Older Workers Benefit Protection Act, discussed in Chapter 5, can facilitate reductions in workforce levels. However, a major concern with this strategy is that it is often the best workers that are attracted by the offer. They are those who have additional options, such as second careers.

Part-time Work and Job Sharing

Many employees are interested in reducing the total number of hours worked, either through part-time work or job-sharing arrangements. This strategy can often accommodate family lifestyle needs and reduce total compensation costs.

Leaves of Absence

Organizations have had surprising success with offering unpaid leaves of absence. If the conditions requiring reductions in workforce levels are projected to be temporary, offering leaves of absence might assist in avoiding the need to involuntarily lay off employees.

Attrition and Hiring Freezes

Attrition is the reduction of workforce levels caused by the normal processes of retirement, resignation, termination, and so forth. *Hiring freezes* prohibit the hiring of new and additional employees and the replacement of current employees that leave the organization.

Voluntary Resignation Programs

Employers might offer bonuses for employees that want to leave the organization voluntarily. Many employees might have other options available to them, but are not eligible for early retirement. Some sort of bonus might be sufficient to motivate them to leave the organization voluntarily. As with early retirements, these types of programs must be crafted to avoid the loss of critical individuals and serious impact on critical departments.

EXAM ALERT

The SPHR should be familiar with strategies to avoid actually having to lay off employees when decreases in overall workforce size are required. Expect a question in this area.

Strategies to Minimize the Impact of Layoffs on Individuals

Two common strategies that can be used to minimize the impact of layoffs on individuals are severance pay and outplacement services. They are discussed in the following sections.

Severance Pay

There is no federal legal requirement for severance pay. However, many organizations offer this benefit to provide former employees with income continuation in the event of involuntary termination. Severance pay is either a one-time lump sum payment or a temporary continuation of salary provided by the employer to terminated workers. Calculations of the total amount to be received are typically based on length of service, and frequently involve one week's pay for every year of service. Severance pay often makes good business sense because it serves both a humanitarian and public relations purpose.

Outplacement Services

Outplacement services are provided to assist terminated individuals in obtaining new employment. Services provided frequently include employment counseling, assistance with resume preparation, training in job search skills, training to improve interviewing skills, and job referral assistance. Generally, these services are outsourced to vendors that specialize in this area.

As discussed earlier in this chapter, outsourcing vendors are often good sources of external recruits.

Exit Interviews

Many, in fact most, employers use exit interviews, which are conducted in an attempt to determine why individuals are leaving the organization. The objective is to determine what is good and what is bad about the organization in order to provide management with information that assists in developing or modifying programs to improve organizational performance.

These interviews are typically conducted by the HR function. There is an assumption that the individual has no reasons to guard his or her remarks and is forthright in observations about the organization when leaving. However, recent research has revealed that changes in the psychological contract may be modifying that paradigm. In today's environment, employees often do not consider their termination of the employment relationship to be permanent and might want to retain their option to return at some future date. In these situations they are not likely to be totally forthright in evaluating the organization and its programs. To overcome this reluctance current exit interview practice often involves delaying the interview for about 30 days after termination and conducting it via phone, guaranteeing anonymity.

Wrongful Termination

The subject of wrongful termination is also discussed in Chapter 6. Wrongful termination occurs when the termination violates statutory or common law. Wrongful termination actions can be pursued as tort actions in court or under the provisions of the applicable employment law, but generally not both. Three types of wrongful terminations are discussed in this section: terminations that violate law, constructive discharge, and retaliatory discharge.

Terminations That Violate Law

The concept of employment-at-will is discussed in Chapter 6 along with exceptions to the concept. Terminations that violate public policy and implied contracts (both discussed in Chapter 6) and those that violate contract law could be wrongful terminations. Disagreements of this type are tort actions under common law and the former employee can sue for damages of various types.

Constructive Discharge

Constructive discharge occurs when employer actions make the employment relationship so untenable that a reasonable person would have no obligation but to resign. In this case, the resignation is coerced and the employee might have recourse under either common law or certain employment laws. Recourse under common law is typically limited to situations in which the individual gives up a legal property interest in the employment relationship, such as when the individual has an employment contract. Constructive discharge might be another form of illegal discrimination under various employment laws.

Retaliatory Discharge

Retaliatory discharge occurs when the employer terminates the employee for exercising right or obligations under the law. This typically occurs under one of two scenarios:

▶ The employee is terminated for filing a complaint or otherwise exercising rights guaranteed under employment legislation. Examples are filing an EEO complaint, reporting OSHA violations, and so forth.

▶ The employee is terminated for fulfilling obligations under the law, such as testifying against the employer when summoned to do so in a court of law or reporting employer violations of law.

EXAM ALERT

The SPHR should be familiar with prohibitions on wrongful termination, and constructive and retaliatory discharge. This is often the subject of a question on the exam.

NOTE

The employer can avoid allegations of wrongful termination actions by engaging in good HR practice such as the following:

▶ Providing internal complaint resolution processes and grievance procedures

▶ Training all managers on employment law

▶ Thoroughly documenting the reasons for all terminations

▶ Evaluating employment practices for adverse impact

▶ Engaging in the workplace strategies discussed earlier in the chapter to avoid the necessity for involuntary termination

Management of Employment Records

Objective:

Gain an Understanding of the Management of Employment Records

To a large extent, the management of employment records is part of the administrative role of HR and an in-depth discussion of this issue is more appropriate in preparation for the PHR examination. However, the SPHR should have some familiarity with the records retention requirements of the many laws and regulations with which the HR function must deal. A threshold issue is the determination as to whether the law requiring employment record retention actually applies to the organization. Various laws might apply only if the organization has a stated number of employees and/or federal contracts of more than certain dollar amounts. The information as to which organizations are covered by a law is contained in the discussion of that law in this chapter and others. It is not repeated in this section.

It is not unusual for the same record to have different record retention requirements in different laws. In that case, the retention period for that particular record should be the one corresponding to the longest period. It is often prudent, and in some instances required, to keep records longer than mandatory retention period. If, for example, the records in question are part of litigation or a proceeding in front of a third party, such as the EEOC or OSHA, the records must be retained until final disposition of the complaint or lawsuit. In addition, it often is prudent to keep employment records until the statute of limitations for filing a complaint or lawsuit has expired if there is some potential that the employee might do so.

Table 3.9 contains a brief summary of records retention requirements. It has been adapted from a more detailed summary prepared by Wallace Bonapart and Cornella Gamiem, which is available on the Society for Human Resource Management website at http://www.shrm.org/. The SPHR should use this table only as a broad guideline and consult a more detailed source such as agency regulations and guidance when determining the need for retention of employment records.

TABLE 3.9   Summary of Employment Record Retention Requirements

Law	Record Retention Requirements
Age Discrimination in Employment Act *(ADEA)*	Payroll records—**3 years**. Employment records (promotions, applications, layoff, recall, terminations and so forth)—**1 year**.
Americans with Disabilities Act *(ADA)*	Employment records (applications, requests for reasonable accommodations, promotions, selections for training, terminations and so forth)—**1 year from record creation or taking of the action**.
Title VII of the Civil Rights Act of 1964	Employment records (applications, promotions, transfers, layoffs, terminations and so forth)—**1 year from record creation of taking of the action**. A copy of the current EEO-1 Report must be kept in the files.
Consolidated Omnibus Budget Reconciliation Act *(COBRA)*	Notices, payroll actions, and so forth—**6 years**.* *COBRA does not mandate retention requirements, *per se*. However, COBRA amends ERISA and its retention requirements apply.
Davis-Bacon, Service Contract, and Walsh-Healy Public Contract Acts	Employment and payroll records—**3 years from end of the contract**.

(continues)

TABLE 3.9 *Continued*

Law	Record Retention Requirements
Employee Retirement Income Security Act *(ERISA)*	Annual reports, summary plan descriptions, plan changes, required reports to the Department of Labor and the Pension Benefit Guarantee Corporation, along with related materials to prepare such reports—**6 years**. Information necessary to determine benefits for participants—**As long as they are relevant**.
Employee Polygraph Protection Act	Test results and reason for administration—**3 years**.
Equal Pay Act	Payroll records—**3 years**.
Executive Order 11246	Affirmative action plans—**2 years**.
Fair and Accurate Credit Transactions Act *(FACTA)*	Documents containing information from credit reports—**Must be shredded on completion of action/determination**.
Fair Labor Standards Act *(FLSA)*	Payroll records—**3 years**. *
Family and Medical Leave Act *(FMLA)*	Employment records, payroll records, leave records, employee notices, and so forth—**3 years**.
Federal Insurance Contribution Act *(FICA)* Federal Unemployment Tax Act *(FUTA)* Internal Revenue Code (Federal Income Tax Withholding)	Employment and payroll records—**4 years from the date the tax is due or the tax is paid, whichever is later**.
Immigration Reform and Control Act	Form I-9—**3 years from date of hire or 1 year from date of termination, whichever is later**.
Occupational Safety and Health Act *(OSHA)*	Logs and reports—**5 years**. Medical records and records of exposure to toxic substances for each employee—**30 years from the date the employee leaves employment with the organization**.
Rehabilitation Act of 1973	Employment and payroll records—**2 years**. A copy of the current affirmative action plan developed under the act must be kept in the files.
Uniform Guidelines on Employee Selection Procedures *(UGESP)*	Recruitment and selection documents, including the analysis of adverse selection based on these documents—**2 years after the adverse impact is eliminated where analysis indicated adverse impact**.
Vietnam Era Readjustment Assistance Act	Employment and payroll records—**2 years** A copy of the current affirmative action plan must be kept in the file. A copy of the current VETS-100 must be retained.

NOTE

State laws might impose additional requirements regarding retention of certain employment records beyond that required by federal law and regulations.

Strategic Considerations for the SPHR

Where appropriate, the strategic implication of various workforce planning and employment issues have already been discussed in this chapter. However, a brief review is appropriate. If an organization provides services or knowledge, that output is created and delivered largely by its employees. Thus, organizational success, distinctiveness in the market, and the core competency of many organizations is dependent on the capacity of its human capital. The SPHR must be able to lead the organization in developing programs that enable it to determine its current and future workforce needs and to develop and implement programs that satisfy those needs in an effective and efficient manner.

Chapter Summary

This chapter covered a wide array of issues associated with workforce planning and employment. First discussed was the critical importance of these issues in today's organizational environment, where the success of the organization is more and more dependent on the capabilities of its workforce. The complex maze of employment law, federal regulations, and precedent case law was discussed. Concepts associated with affirmative action, equal employment opportunity, and gender discrimination were introduced.

An organization must be able to forecast its needs for employees and then develop recruitment and selection programs to satisfy those needs. These processes were fully introduced and discussed. However, prior to recruiting and selecting employees for jobs, the organization must know what the functions of those jobs are and what kinds of employees—in terms of knowledge, skills, and abilities—to place in them. This is accomplished through the process of job analysis. Processes and methods regarding job analysis were discussed.

Sometimes the organization might want to depart from the philosophy of having only full-time permanent employees on their roles and, instead, use a contingent workforce. The components of a contingent workforce and the strategic reasons for doing so were covered.

After an organization decides to hire an individual a number of potential options can be pursued that affect the employment situation, such as requirement for medical examinations, providing reimbursement for relocation expenses, formalizing the relationship through an employment contract, and so forth. These issues were also discussed briefly.

Although most of the discussion in this chapter assumes that the organization is adding to, or at least replacing, its workforce, that is not always the case. The concept of organizational exit and associated program considerations was introduced. Finally, workforce planning and employment activities generate huge amounts of paper and electronic data. Legal requirements for retention of this data were discussed in the final section of the chapter.

Key Terms

- ▶ Core competency
- ▶ Equal Pay Act (1963)
- ▶ Civil Rights Act of 1964
- ▶ Protected classes
- ▶ Business necessity
- ▶ Bona fide occupational requirement
- ▶ Executive Order 11246

- ▸ Executive Order 11478

- ▸ Office of Federal Contract Compliance Programs (OFCCP)

- ▸ Age Discrimination in Employment Act of 1967

- ▸ Consumer Credit Protection Act (1968)

- ▸ Fair Credit Reporting Act (1970)

- ▸ Vocational Rehabilitation Act of 1973

- ▸ Vietnam Veterans' Readjustment Assistance Act (1974)

- ▸ Pregnancy Discrimination Act (1978)

- ▸ Uniform Guidelines for Employee Selection Procedures (1978)

- ▸ Disparate treatment

- ▸ Adverse impact

- ▸ Immigration Reform and Control Act (1986)

- ▸ Worker Adjustment and Retraining Notification Act (1988)

- ▸ Employee Polygraph Protection Act (1988)

- ▸ Americans with Disabilities Act (1990)

- ▸ Qualified individual

- ▸ Reasonable accommodation

- ▸ Fitness for duty exam

- ▸ Civil Rights Act of 1991

- ▸ Compensatory damages

- ▸ Punitive damages

- ▸ Uniformed Services Employment and Reemployment Act (1994)

- ▸ Congressional Accountability Act (1995)

- ▸ Fair and Accurate Credit Transactions Act (2003)

- ▸ *Griggs v. Duke Power* (1971)

- ▸ *McDonnell-Douglas Corp. v. Green* (1973)

- ▸ *Abermarle Paper Company v. Moody* (1975)

- ▸ *Chandler v. Roudebush* (1976)

- *Regents of the University of California v. Bakke* (1978)
- *United Steelworkers v. Weber* (1979)
- *Meritor Savings Bank v. Vinson* (1986)
- *Johnson v. Santa Clara County Transportation Agency* (1987)
- *Martin v. Wilks* (1988)
- *City of Richmond v. J. A. Croson Company* (1989)
- *Taxman v. Board of Education of Piscataway* (1993)
- *Harris v. Forklift Systems, Inc.* (1993)
- *Hopwood v. State of Texas* (1996)
- *Ocale v. Sundowner Offshore Services, Inc.* (1998)
- *Faragher v. City of Boca Raton* (1998)
- *Ellerth v. Burlington Northern* (1998)
- *Grutter v. Bollinger et al.* (2003)
- *Gratz et al. v. Bollinger et al.* (2003)
- *General Dynamics Land Systems, Inc. v. Cline* (2004)
- Affirmative action
- Affirmative action plan
- Reverse discrimination
- Quota
- Dismissal and notification of rights letter
- Letter of determination
- Right-to-sue letter
- Sexual harassment
- Quid pro quo
- Hostile environment
- Constructive discharge
- Affirmative defense
- Workforce planning

- ► Trend analysis
- ► Ratio analysis
- ► Nominal group technique
- ► Delphi technique
- ► Yield rates
- ► Job analysis
- ► Job description
- ► Job specifications
- ► Recruitment
- ► Job posting
- ► Job bidding
- ► Employment agencies
- ► Contingency workforce
- ► Professional employer organization
- ► Offshoring
- ► Selection
- ► Placement
- ► Person-job fit
- ► Person-organization fit
- ► Selection criteria
- ► Predictor
- ► Multiple hurdle approach
- ► Compensatory approach
- ► Prescreening
- ► Assessment center
- ► Structured interview
- ► Directive interviews
- ► Behavioral interview

- ▶ Situational interview

- ▶ Stress interview

- ▶ Mass interview

- ▶ 360° interview

- ▶ Panel interview

- ▶ Stereotyping

- ▶ Employment offer

- ▶ Employment contract

- ▶ Attrition

- ▶ Hiring freeze

- ▶ Severance pay

- ▶ Outplacement services

Apply Your Knowledge

Exercises

3.1 Employment Law

Fill in the missing cells in the following table without referring back to the text.

Legislation/Regulation	Provisions
	Requires employers to provide 60-day advance notice for certain plant closings or mass layoffs
Executive Order 11246	
	Federal regulations that assist employers in complying with federal antidiscrimination legislation
	Prohibits discrimination based on race, color, religion, sex, or national origin
Age Discrimination in Employment Act	
	Requires employers to establish the identity and eligibility to work of all employees

3.2 Adverse Impact

The CEO of your organizations asks you to provide her with the answer to two questions. First, she wants to know the results of recent expansion efforts in which the organization hired 100 new employees. Specifically, she wants to know whether the organization's hiring practices resulted in any adverse impact for protected classes. Second, she wants to know about the overall composition of the organization's workforce in terms of the labor market. She wants to know whether any protected class is under-represented in relation to the local population. Answer her two questions using the following data.

Expansion Hire

Group	# Interviewed	# Hired
Hispanic-American	50	30
African-American	50	25
White	60	40
Asian-American	9	5

Comparison of Workforce with External Labor Market

Group	% of Workforce	% of Labor Market
Hispanic-American	17	20
African-American	20	18
White	60	56
Asian-American	3	6

Review Questions

1. You are the first HR Director of a small but growing philanthropic organization. The organization does not have job descriptions. You mention to the executive director that one of your first projects is to begin a job analysis project so that you can obtain data to write job descriptions and job specifications. The executive director is not familiar with job analysis and asks you to brief him on the process. What do you tell him?

2. You are the HR Director of a small not-for-profit social service organization that has just received its first notification and request for information ever from EEOC that a complaint of illegal discrimination has been received. The President of the organization is unfamiliar with the process and asks you to brief her on how the process proceeds. What do you tell her?

3. You are the VP of HR for an organization that is increasingly being affected by foreign competitors that have substantially lower compensation costs. The CEO is contemplating a recommendation to the board of directors that the organization explore a strategy of using contingent versus permanent full-time workers. He has asked you to brief him on what the advantages and disadvantages of such a strategy might be. How do you respond?

4. You are the HR Director of a medium-sized manufacturing firm that has recently refused accommodation to several individuals based on a determination that they were not disabled. This resulted in formal complaints under the Americans with Disabilities Act. The board of directors was briefed by the CEO on the complaints and the directors would like you to brief them on the definition of disability under the act. What do you tell them?

5. The CEO of your organization just came back from a meeting in which the terms *quid pro quo* and *hostile environment* were used in a discussion regarding preventing sexual harassment. He asks you to define them for him. How would you define the two terms?

Exam Questions

1. The judicial concept of adverse impact was created in which Supreme Court decision?

   ○ **A.** *Griggs v. Duke Power*

   ○ **B.** *McConnell-Douglas Corp. v. Green*

   ○ **C.** *Regents of the University of California v. Bakke*

   ○ **D.** *Meritor Savings Bank v. Vinson*

2. The utilization analysis section of an affirmative action plan:

   ○ **A.** Displays information on the composition of the organization by gender and ethnicity for each organizational unit

   ○ **B.** Aggregates the information from the organizational profile

   ○ **C.** Evaluates the availability of workers for jobs internally and externally

   ○ **D.** Compares the availability analysis with the job group analysis

3. Replacement charting can be used in workforce planning to:

   ○ **A.** Forecast the need for employees

   ○ **B.** Forecast turnover

   ○ **C.** Forecast external supply of employees

   ○ **D.** Forecast internal supply of employees

4. All the following are advantages of recruiting internally except for:

   ○ **A.** Brings new ideas and methods into the workplace

   ○ **B.** Promotes high morale

   ○ **C.** Provides a career path for employees

   ○ **D.** Reduces recruiting costs

5. Which of the following is not a protected class under Title VII of the Civil Rights Act of 1964?

   ○ **A.** Women

   ○ **B.** African-Americans

   ○ **C.** Gay Americans

   ○ **D.** Workers over 40 years of age

6. A candidate for a supervisory job opening is asked how she would handle a particular situation involving a subordinate. What type of interview is being conducted?

   ○ **A.** Nondirective

   ○ **B.** Unstructured

   ○ **C.** Behavioral

   ○ **D.** Situational

7. When may medical examinations be administered during the selection process?

   ○ **A.** As a prescreen to determine whether the individual has a disability

   ○ **B.** Anytime there is an obvious physical or mental disability

   ○ **C.** Only after a conditional offer of employment

   ○ **D.** Only when the employee reports to work after being hired

8. All the following are considered to be disadvantages of using the contingent workforce except for:

   ○ **A.** Lack of loyalty

   ○ **B.** Impact on morale of permanent workforce

   ○ **C.** Flexibility

   ○ **D.** Loss of internal capabilities

9. You have been assigned a project to develop a new job description for about 200 truck drivers employed by your organization, all of whom perform similar duties. Which of the following job analysis data collection methods might be most appropriate?

   ○ **A.** Observation

   ○ **B.** Interviews

   ○ **C.** Questionnaire

   ○ **D.** Employee logs

10. Quid pro quo sexual harassment occurs when:

- ○ **A.** An employee is refused a promotion because she is perceived to be too old

- ○ **B.** An employee is refused a promotion because she has cancer

- ○ **C.** An employee is refused a promotion because she refuses to go out on dates with the supervisor

- ○ **D.** An employee cannot do her work properly because of the constant horseplay, dirty jokes, and sexual innuendo pervasive in her work area

Answers to Exercises

3.1 Employment Law

Legislation/Regulation	Provisions
Worker Adjustment and Retraining Notification Ace (1988)	Requires employers to provide 60-day advance notice for certain plant closings or mass layoffs
Executive Order 11246	Requires federal contractors with contracts of at $50,000 and 50 or more employees to prepare and implement affirmative action plans
Uniform Guidelines on Employee Selection Procedures	Federal regulations that assist employers in complying with federal antidiscrimination legislation
Title VII of the Civil Rights Act of 1964	Prohibits discrimination based on race, color, religion, sex, or national origin
Age Discrimination in Employment Act (1967)	Prohibits, with certain exceptions, discrimination in employment for employees 40 and over
Immigration and Reform Control Act (1986	Requires employers to establish the identity and eligibility to work of all employees

3.2 Adverse Impact

The answer to the first question is that the recent expansion hire resulted in adverse impact for African-Americans. As shown in the following table, the highest selection rate was for whites at 67%. The adverse impact threshold is computed by using the 4/5ths rule (.80 ¥ .67) and is 54%. African-Americans were selected at a rate (50%) below the adverse impact threshold.

Expansion Hire

Group	# Interviewed	# Hired	Selection Rate
Hispanic-American	50	30	60%
African-American	50	25	50%
White	60	40	67%
Asian-American	9	5	56%
Totals	169	100	

The answer to the second question is that Asian-Americans are under-represented and experiencing adverse impact. This is determined by comparing their percentage of the internal workforce by their percentage is the external labor market, again using the 4/5ths rule to calculate an adverse impact threshold. The following table includes the adverse impact threshold calculations. Only Asian-Americans are represented less in the workforce population than the adverse threshold (3% versus 4.6%).

Comparison of Workforce with External Labor Market

Group	% of Workforce	% of Labor Market	4/5ths of Labor Market
Hispanic-American	17	20	16%
African-American	20	18	14.4%
White	60	56	44.8%
Asian-American	3	6	4.6%

Answers to Review Questions

1. You remind him that *job analysis* is the systematic process of gathering information regarding the duties required of a job and the human characteristics necessary to successfully perform those duties. Job analysis can be described as a six-step process:

   1. **Determination of the purpose for conducting the job analysis**. In this case, the purpose is to begin documentation of job descriptions and job specifications because the organization currently has none.

   2. **Identify jobs to be analyzed**. Again, in this case all jobs need to be analyzed because no job descriptions exist.

   3. **Review relevant background data**. There is not likely to be much to review in the organization because this is the first job analysis project. An organization chart might exist, which would be a start.

   4. **Plan and execute the job analysis**. This step involves collecting data from employees regarding what they do and what knowledge, skills, and abilities that they use.

5. **Write the job descriptions and specifications**. The documents are written and verified with the employees and their managers prior to finalization.

6. **Periodic review**. In this step, a system is developed to review the job specifications and job descriptions for accuracy and to update them as needed.

2. You can tell her that EEOC has made a determination that the organization is covered under the Civil Rights Act of 1964 and the request for information is used to make an initial determination as to whether there is reasonable cause to believe that illegal discrimination has occurred. The process will continue from this point as follows:

1. The EEOC investigates the allegation. During this period the organization is required to respond to the allegation by providing its defense and is required to provide information requested by the EEOC. If the investigation reveals that no illegal discrimination has occurred, EEOC dismisses the case.

2. If investigation reveals that it appears that illegal discrimination has occurred, the EEOC issues a cause letter (letter of determination) and attempts conciliation and settlement. The organization must determine whether it is in its best interest to offer a full or partial settlement.

3. If a settlement is not reached, the EEOC either files suit against the organization or issues a right-to-sue letter to the complainant. You can tell the President that, being a small organization with few employees, the EEOC is unlikely to file suit itself.

3. You can respond as follows:

The advantages are

▶ Flexibility

▶ Savings in the cost of taxes and benefits

▶ Access to expertise not internally available

▶ Potential savings in overall compensation costs

The disadvantages are

▶ Perceived lack of loyalty

▶ Lack of knowledge of the organization's culture, policies, and procedures

▶ Potential for overall higher costs, depending on the situation

▶ Concern with disclosure of organizational proprietary information

▶ Impact on morale of permanent workforce

▶ Loss of internal capabilities

▶ Potential for increased training costs when contingent workers must be trained on unique or unusual processes or procedures used by the organization

4. You can tell them that a disabled individual has a physical or mental impairment that substantially limits one or more major life functions, has a record of such impairment, or is regarded or treated as having an impairment.

▶ *Physical impairment* refers to any physiological condition or loss of one or more body systems (neurological, respiratory, speech organs, cardiovascular, digestive, and so forth). Mental impairment encompasses such conditions as mental retardation, mental or emotional illness, and learning disabilities.

▶ *Major life functions* include

   ▶ Caring for oneself

   ▶ Reproduction

   ▶ Performing manual tasks

   ▶ Walking

   ▶ Seeing

   ▶ Hearing

   ▶ Speaking

   ▶ Breathing

   ▶ Learning

   ▶ Sitting or standing

   ▶ Lifting or reaching

   ▶ Thinking or concentrating

   ▶ Interacting with others

However, certain conditions are specifically exempted from the definition of disability in the act. They are

   ▶ Homosexuality and bisexuality

   ▶ Sexual behavior disorders

   ▶ Gender identity disorders not resulting from physical impairments

   ▶ Compulsive gambling

   ▶ Pyromania

   ▶ Kleptomania

   ▶ Current illegal use of drugs

5. You can tell him the following:

> ▶ *Quid pro quo* means *this for that* and occurs when an employee is forced to choose between submitting to sexual advances or forfeiting employment opportunities or benefits. It is harassment in which employment outcomes are linked to the granting of sexual favors. By definition, the harasser must be in a position or perceived to be in a position to, in fact, create the employment opportunities and tangible employments promised. Consequently, quid pro quo harassment must be perpetrated by a supervisor or manager. EEOC guidelines provide that the employer is strictly responsible for the actions of its supervisors regardless of whether the employer knew or should have known of their occurrence. Nevertheless, it is possible for the employer to avoid legal liability in some cases of quid pro quo sexual harassment by using an affirmative defense.

> ▶ A hostile workplace environment can violate Title VII even if there is no employment or economic effects if that environment unreasonably interferes with an individual's work or work performance or creates an intimidating, hostile, or offensive working environment. As opposed to quid pro quo sexual harassment, the employer is liable only if it knew or should have known that the conditions existed. Also as opposed to quid pro quo, the harassers do not have to be supervisors for the organization to be found guilty. In fact, the harassers do not even have to be employees of the organization. Customers, suppliers, independent contractors, and so forth can all create a hostile work environment. Activities such as sexual or derogatory jokes or remarks, offensive physical contact, sexually oriented horseplay, posting of offensive or pornographic material, inappropriate emails, solicitation of sexual favors, and so forth could lead to hostile environment claims.

Answers to Exam Questions

1. The correct answer is **A**. *Griggs v. Duke Power* created the judicial concept of adverse impact. *McDonnell-Douglas Corp. v. Green* (answer B) created the judicial concept of disparate treatment. *Regents of the University of California v. Bakke* (answer C) created the judicial concept of reverse discrimination. *Meritor Savings Bank v. Vinson* (answer D) created the judicial concept of hostile environment.

2. The correct answer is **D**. The utilization analysis compares the job group analysis with the availability analysis to determine whether underutilization exists. The organization profile displays information on the composition of the organization by gender and ethnicity (answer A). The job group analysis aggregates the information from the organizational profile (answer B). The availability analysis evaluates the availability of workers internally and externally (answer C).

3. The correct answer is **D**. Replacement charts provide information on internal employees who are currently ready for a promotion should a job become open. Replacement charts will not assist in forecasting turnover (answer A) nor can they be used to forecast either internal (answer B) or external (answer C) overall supply of employees.

4. The correct answer is **A**. Bringing new ideas and methods into the workplace is an advantage of external recruiting not internal recruiting. Promoting high morale (answer B), providing a career path (answer C), and reducing recruiting costs (answer D) are all advantages of internal recruiting.

5. The correct answer is **C**. Sexual preference is not protected under federal law. It might, however be protected under state or local law. Sex (answer A), race (answer B), and age (answer D) are all protected classes under Title VII of the Civil Rights Act of 1964.

6. The correct answer is **D**. Situational interviews ask candidates how they would likely respond in theoretical situations. A nondirective (answer A) interview occurs when the interviewer relinquishes control of the flow of the interview to the interviewee. An unstructured interview (answer B) occurs when there are no predetermined questions. A behavioral interview (answer C) occurs when the interviewee is asked how she handled a situation in the past.

7. The correct answer is **C**. Medical examinations under the Americans with Disabilities Act may be administered only after a conditional offer of employment. Using medical examinations as a pre-screening device (answer A) and when there is an obvious disability (answer B) violates ADA. Requiring a medical examination after the employee reports to work (answer D) does not violate ADA, but might is not, in general, considered to be a good business practice because it might obligate the employer to pay compensation to employees that are incapable of performing the essential functions of the job. Furthermore, it might open up the organization to potential discrimination complaints because it terminated those individuals.

8. The correct answer is **C**. Flexibility is an advantage, not a disadvantage, of using contingent rather and full-time permanent workers. Lack of loyalty (answer A), impact on the morale of the permanent workforce (answer B), and loss of internal capabilities (answer D) are all considered to be disadvantages associated with use of the contingent workforce.

9. The correct answer is **C**. Questionnaires are appropriate for collecting data from a large number of employees. Observation (answer A) would likely be too time-consuming to capture the necessary data because truck drivers do not do repetitive short-cycle work. Interviews (answer B) are staff-intensive and would likely incur too much cost in this case because of the large number of employees. Employee logs (answer D) are not viable because of the large amount of time that would be required to analyze the data from the 200 employees and because employees frequently do not complete the logs in a timely and accurate manner.

10. The correct answer is **C**. Quid pro quo sexual harassment occurs when an employee is forced to choose between submitting to sexual advances and forfeiting employment opportunities. Answer A is an example of age discrimination. Answer B is an example of discrimination based on disability. Answer C is an example of sexual discrimination based on a hostile environment.

Suggested Readings and Resources

1. Books and Articles

▶ Brannick, M. T. & Levine, E. L. (2002). *Job Analysis: Methods, Research, and Applications for Human Resource Management in the New Millennium*. Thousand Oaks, CA: Sage Publications.

▶ Buford, J. A. Jr. & Lindner, J. R. (2002). *Human Resource Management: Concepts and Applications for HRM Students and Practitioners*. Cincinnati, OH: South-Western.

▶ Cook, M. (2004). *Personnel Selection: Adding Value Through People* (4th edition). West Sussex, England: John Wiley & Sons.

▶ Dessler, G. (2005). *Human Resource Management* (10th edition). Upper Saddle River, NJ: Pearson Education.

▶ Jackson, S. E. & Schuler, R. S. (2003). *Managing Human Resources Through Strategic Partnerships* (8th edition). Mason, OH: Thomson South-Western.

▶ Mathis, R. L. & Jackson, J. H. (2006). *Human Resource Management* (11th edition). Mason, OH: Thomson South-Western.

▶ Naffziger, F. & Phillips, L. (2004). "Conducting Employee Investigations Prior to Imposition of Discipline." *Midwest Law Review*. 19 153-176.

▶ Robinson, R. H., Franklin, G. M. & Wayland, R. (2002). *The Regulatory Environment of Human Resource Management*. Forth Worth, TX: Harcourt.

▶ Wendover, R. W. (1998). *Smart Hiring: The Complete Guide to Finding and Hiring the Best Employees* (2nd edition). Naperville, IL: Sourcebooks.

▶ Yorks, L. (2005). *Strategic Human Resource Development*. Mason, OH: Thompson South-Western.

2. Websites

▶ http://www.bls.gov/

▶ http://www.dol.gov/

▶ http://www.eeoc.gov/

▶ http://www.ftc.gov/

▶ http://www.onetcenter.org/

CHAPTER FOUR

Human Resource Development

Objectives

This chapter helps you to prepare for the SPHR examination by covering the concepts and strategies associated with human resource development. This section composes **13%** of the SPHR examination.

Gain a Strategic Understanding of Human Resource Development

▶ Understand the importance of human resource development (HRD) to organizational success

▶ Understand how to align human resource development programs with organizational strategy and goals

▶ Understand the difference between training and development and when each is strategically appropriate

Gain an Understanding of Human Resource Development Law

▶ Understand the implication of these laws in the design of human resource development programs

Gain an Understanding of Human Learning and Motivation

▶ Understand basic concepts regarding adult learning, learning styles, and learning rates, and their implications for HRD program development and design

▶ Understand the basic concepts associated with a variety of theories of motivation and their impact on HRD program design

Gain an Understanding of the Human Resource Development Process (ADDIE)

▶ Understand concepts and activities associated with HRD:

Needs assessment

Program design

Program development

Program implementation

Program evaluation

Gain an Understanding of Career Development

▶ Understand the components of career development programs

▶ Understand special issues in career development and their implications for career development

Gain an Understanding of Leadership Development

▶ Understand the various types of leadership

▶ Understand the basic concepts associated with a variety of theories of motivation and their impact on HRD program design

Gain an Understanding of Organizational Development

▶ Understand the organizational development process

▶ Understand organizational change, including designing and implementing change and overcoming resistance to change

▶ Understand concepts associated with learning organizations

Gain an Understanding of the Performance Management Program

▶ Understand the process of setting performance standards

▶ Understand the performance appraisal process, its purposes, methods used, and the activities associated with preparing the appraisal and sharing it with the employee

Outline

Study Strategies

▶ Human resource development consists of a variety of diverse yet related programs. It will help, as you go through the chapter, to initially think about the programs as separate entities. Try to grasp the concepts of the basic law, and then motivation and learning, and then the HRD process (ADDIE), and then organizational development, and finally performance management. At some point, you will begin to discern the interrelationships among the programs and start to think in terms of commonalities and differences. That's when your study efforts will become both efficient and effective.

▶ Try to understand the programs from a strategic point of view. Develop a big-picture concept based on basic understanding of the parts. The exam alerts provide guidance in areas where in-depth knowledge or memorization might be appropriate.

Introduction

Gain a Strategic Understanding of Human Resource Development

Human resource development can trace its roots in the United States to apprentice programs among the skilled trade guilds in the early eighteenth century. On a global scale, training programs can be traced back literally to the beginning of time, when skills were passed from one person to another via coaching and mentoring. However, much has changed since then.

We can define human resource development (HRD) as a systematic organizational program designed to provide its members with the necessary knowledge, skills, and abilities to meet current and future job requirements to facilitate the achievement of organizational goals. This definition encompasses two distinct but related concepts: *training* and *development*. Training and development can be thought of as the two opposite ends of the HRD continuum. Yet at the middle of the continuum the two concepts merge and programmatic activities are designed to achieve both goals.

At one end of the continuum, training provides employees with the necessary skills to perform the job to which they are assigned and only that job. At the other end of the continuum, development programs are concerned with the organization's future and, specifically, in growing its human capital (the current and potential capabilities of the workforce) to be able to adapt to an increasingly complex environment. Inherent in both training and development is the requirement to assist employees in managing their careers, particularly in today's vibrant atmosphere in which both the technology of work and the structure of the organization might be in constant flux.

HRD includes not only programs designed to improve the current and future capabilities of organizational members, but also the organization itself. Organizational development *(OD)* programs are designed to improve the effectiveness of the organization. Two major emphases in OD are managing change and facilitating organizational adaptation to a dynamic environment (organizational learning).

Increasingly, the core competencies and competitiveness of an organization depend on the capabilities of its workforce. HRD programs are critical to maintaining and improving those capabilities, and the SPHR must have a strategic appreciation and understanding of these concepts to help the organization be successful both now and in the future. This chapter will discuss the HRD process and associated programs, such as career planning and management, leadership development, organization development, and performance management. Because HRD programs are designed to change behavior, create learning, and develop management skills, underlying theories of motivation, learning, and leadership are also discussed as the basis from which many of the programmatic activities are built.

Human Resource Development Law

Objective:
Gain an Understanding of Human Resource Development Law

HRD has a body of law that you must understand for both on-the-job realities as well as for the SPHR exam. The following subsections will discuss various acts, copyrights, patents, and other legal issues related to HRD.

Common Law

Training and development programs must provide sufficient skills and knowledge to perform the duties of the job in such a way that innocent third parties are not harmed. If improper training results in the injury of a third party or damage to a third party's property, the employer could incur tort liability for negligent training under common law. The same is true if the performance management system does not permit the identification of unacceptable performers and that unacceptable performance leads to the injury of a third party. A more complete discussion of common law is contained in Chapter 6, "Employee and Labor Relations."

Patents

A *patent* is a grant from the federal government giving the owner the exclusive right to sell, manufacture, and benefit from an invention. The right of the federal government to grant patents flows from the United States Constitution. Congress created the United States Patent and Trademark Office to oversee its granting rights. Patents are granted for 20 years for inventions and 14 years for designs. Patent rights are enforceable in the courts with patent infringement torts. Inventions made by employees in the normal course of their employment are usually patented by the employer not the employee.

Workers' Compensation

Employees undergoing training and development activities are generally covered under state workers' compensation laws. Injuries and illnesses resulting from these activities are compensable under the law and would negatively affect the employer's experience rate, potentially increasing insurance costs. A more comprehensive discussion of workers' compensation is contained in Chapter 7, "Occupational Health, Safety, and Security."

Civil Rights Act (1964)

Title VII of the Civil Rights Act (1964) prohibits discrimination in employment decisions based on race, color, religion, sex, or national origin. This includes training and development programs. Employees must be provided equal access to these programs because such programs are frequently required for promotion or otherwise provide an advantage when employment decisions are being made. The act is comprehensively discussed in Chapter 3, "Workforce Planning and Employment."

Age Discrimination in Employment Act (1976)

The act prohibits employment discrimination, based on age, against employees who are 40 years of age or older. This includes discrimination in training and development programs. The act is comprehensively discussed in Chapter 3.

Copyright Act (1976)

This act governs the granting of copyrights. A *copyright* is an intangible property right granted to the author or originator of literary, musical, or artistic works to exclude others from copying their work. The copyright may be transferred to others and bequeathed. The process of obtaining a copyright, length of the copyright, what can and cannot be copyrighted, copyright infringement, fair use, public domain, and ownership of the copyright are discussed in the sections that follow.

Obtaining a Copyright

Any original work produced after January 1, 1978 is automatically protected by the Copyright Act after it is fixed in a durable medium (paper, digital, film, tape, and so on). Copyrights can be registered with the Untied States Copyright Office, but doing so is not required to protect the work. The copyright symbol or the term *copyright* does not have to be affixed to the work.

Length of Copyright

The length of copyright is based on rather complicated regulations depending on the date of creation and whether or not the work was registered. Works created after January 1, 1978 are protected for the author's life plus 70 years. If there are joint authors, the protection continues for 70 years after the death of the last surviving author. For works that were created for hire and for works of anonymous authors or authors using a pseudonym (unless registered with the Copyright Office), the protection is for 95 years from the date of publication or 120 years from the date of creation, whichever is the shorter time period.

What Can and Cannot Be Copyrighted

The following types of original work can be copyrighted:

▶ Literary works, including computer software

▶ Musical works, including lyrics

- ▶ Dramatic works, including accompanying music

- ▶ Pantomimes and choreographic works

- ▶ Pictorial, graphic, and sculptural works

- ▶ Motion pictures and audiovisual works

- ▶ Sound recordings

- ▶ Architectural works

The following types of works are not generally eligible for copyright:

- ▶ Works that have not been placed in a fixed durable medium

- ▶ Titles, names, short phrases, and slogans

- ▶ Familiar symbols and designs, and so on

- ▶ Ideas, procedures, methods, systems, processes, concepts, principles, discoveries, and devices (although some of these might be patentable)

- ▶ Works consisting entirely of information that is common property and containing no original authorship (for example, a compilation of public documents without analysis)

> **NOTE**
>
> The expression of a work that is not eligible for copyright might itself be eligible. For example, an idea cannot be protected by copyright, but the larger document in which that idea appears—a book, for example—can be.

Copyright Infringement

It is an infringement of copyright to engage in the following activities without permission of the copyright owner:

- ▶ To reproduce the copyrighted material

- ▶ To prepare derivative works based on the copyrighted material

- ▶ To distribute copies of the material to the public

- ▶ To perform the copyrighted material publicly

- ▶ To display the copyrighted material publicly

- ▶ In the case of sound recordings, to perform the copyrighted work publicly by means of digital audio transmission

Penalties for copyright infringement can be rather severe. These penalties could include actual damages, statutory damages, and attorney costs. In some circumstances, criminal prosecution is possible.

Fair Use

Fair use is a statutory provision of the Copyright Act that allows limited use of copyrighted material for such purposes as criticism, comment, news reporting, teaching (including multiple copies for classroom use), scholarship, and research. The determination as to whether the use is fair use is situational and depends on the following:

- The purpose and character of the use, including whether such use is of a commercial nature or is for nonprofit educational uses

- The nature of the copyrighted work

- The amount or substantiality of the portion used in relation to the copyrighted material as a whole

- The effect of the use on the potential market for or value of the copyrighted works

Public Domain

Works that are not protected by the copyright laws, either because the copyright has expired or because the material itself is not of a type that can be copyrighted, and works produced by the United States government are considered to be in the public domain. This means that they can be copied, distributed, and used for other purposes.

Ownership of the Copyright

The copyright belongs to the creator from the time the work is created in a fixed durable medium. Authors of joint works are co-owners unless there is some other agreement between them. Copyrights may be conveyed to other parties by the copyright owner.

If the work was made for hire, the employer, not the employee, is considered the author and owns the copyright. Work made for hire encompasses

- Work that was created by the employee within the scope of employment

- Work specifically ordered or commissioned in one of the following categories and for which there is an agreement specifically indicating that the work was made for hire:

  - A contribution to a collective work

  - A part of a motion picture or other audiovisual work

  - A translation

  - A supplementary work

  - A compilation

▶ An instructional text

▶ A test

▶ Answer material to a test

▶ An atlas

Americans with Disabilities Act (1990)

The act prohibits discrimination against a qualified employee who is disabled. The act also requires reasonable accommodation. Selection for training and development programs cannot discriminate against disabled employees, and training facilities must be handicapped accessible. The act is comprehensively discussed in Chapter 3.

Learning and Motivation

Objective:
Gain an Understanding of Human Learning and Motivation

The purpose of HRD programs is to improve the capability of the organization to achieve its goals through improved performance and human capacity. These increases in capability are achieved through permanent changes in behavior, which is the definition of *learning*. Because we most frequently deal with adults in organizations, HRD programs and professionals must design programs around the way adults learn. Learning is affected by individual motivation. This section discusses adult learning, concepts associated with learning, and motivation.

Adult Learning

The writings of Malcolm Knowles, much of which was done in the 1960s and 1970s, still form the basis for our understanding of adult learning. To differentiate the way adults learn and should be taught from the way children learn and should be taught, Knowles used the term *adragogy* as opposed to *pedagogy*. Adragogy is based on several assumptions:

▶ Adults are self-directed learners.

▶ Adults have knowledge and experience that can be utilized to facilitate learning.

- Adults need to know the relevancy of what they are learning. They need to know why they need to learn whatever is being taught.

- Adults want to learn things that can be applied on the job and that can be used to solve problems.

- Adults are motivated to learn by both intrinsic and extrinsic rewards.

These assumptions lead to implications for the development of HRD programs designed for adults. Some of theses implications are

- Employees should be involved in the planning and implementation of HRD programs.

- Programs should build on current knowledge and experience. Learners with greater knowledge and experience should be able to be exempt from or test out of certain sections based on pre-assessments.

- The importance of learning the material should be clearly indicated before the training or development occurs.

- The learning should occur within the context of actual job content and problems, and practice application of the new learning should be built into the content.

- Interim tests and exercises should be built into the program to provide intrinsic reward.

In addition, adults present several other challenges not usually experienced when teaching children. For many adults, training and development experiences bring about anxiety. Many workers might not have had successful experiences in grade and high school. To overcome this issue, HRD program developers should build in activities that bring quick and early success in a learning environment. Easy exercises and tests at the beginning of a program might build confidence and help employees overcome their resistance and stress.

Unfortunately, training programs are often developed based on what is popular at a particular time. The training program for this quarter might be emotional intelligence, whereas a program regarding cultural awareness might be the subject for the next quarter—all based on fads or what either upper-level management or the HRD leadership perceive as being relevant at the time rather than on an analysis of what types of training the organization actually needs. When this happens HRD programs might develop the reputation of being a waste of time; employees might resist attending. If forced to attend, they might actively resist participating and learning. These types of training programs generally have little impact on changing employee behavior or facilitating organizational success because they are largely pro forma activities to which the organization is not committed and to which it will provide little ongoing support. On the other hand, HRD activities that are a result of planned changes in the work environment or work processes are often resisted because the employees are comfortable with the current situation and learning new ways of doing things is threatening. In these cases, the relevancy and importance of the program must be explained and employees should be assisted in adapting to the associated changes.

Learning

How humans learn is a complex discipline and the subject of much research. An overview of some of the concepts is presented in this section. This information facilitates decision-making because the SPHR, with the assistance of HRD professionals, guides the development of HRD programs in the organization. An SPHR should have a basic understanding of a few core concepts, including learning styles, learning curves, and levels of learning in order to make informed decisions regarding the development and delivery of HRD programs that accommodate the diversity of learners and achieve the proper level of understanding required of a particular HRD program.

Learning Styles

Individuals differ in the way they learn. These are called *learning styles*. Although we all learn in a variety of ways, we tend to have a dominant or preferred style. HRD programs, to be effective, must accommodate a variety of styles so that all participants have a chance to learn in an effective and efficient manner. Learning is facilitated if multiple styles are accommodated and learners are required to use the new learning as soon as they return to their job. There are various ways to categorize the way humans learn, but a common method is based on the types of material a student prefers to use in the learning environment. The various learning styles are briefly discussed in the following sections.

Visual

Visual learners prefer print material, graphs, charts, PowerPoint presentations, overhead transparencies, videotapes, and other types of visual material. The inclusion of this type of material in the HRD program assists the visual learner to process the material.

Auditory

Auditory learners process the information best by listening. HRD programs based on interactive discussion, lectures, audiotapes, and other types of aural instructional material are appropriate.

Psychomotor/Kinesthetic

This type of learner benefits from hands-on experience. Role-playing, on-the-job training, and work simulation experiences facilitate the learning process for psychomotor/kinesthetic learners.

Learning Curves

Learning *styles* indicate how an individual prefers to learn, whereas learning *curves* describe the rate at which an individual learns. Accommodating learning style preferences increases the rate of learning, but the type of material to be learned also affects the rate. Factors such as motivation, intelligence, and learning style can affect the slope of the curve, but the overall shape might be more a factor of the type of material being learned. The important points here are that HRD programs should be designed to anticipate the likely learning curves that result from teaching various types of materials, and use those expected curves to maximize the effectiveness of the learning event. A variety of potential learning curves exist, but the three common curves displayed in Figure 4.1 should be sufficient to grasp the concept and its implications.

Figure 4.1(a) shows a curve that results from learning a simple process, such as filling out a form or doing a task with only a few steps. The learning curve is quick and then levels off or plateaus. Increasing training beyond the point at which the curve plateaus does not result in improved performance and is an inefficient HRD program design.

Figure 4.1(b) is a learning curve indicative of learning something completely new, such as a new job or running a new, relatively complex process. The learning is slow at first but when the basic concepts are grasped, the learning accelerates. The implication for HRD programs is to design sufficient time to grasp the basic new concepts, building in practice and feedback, before proceeding with higher-level concepts. Another implication is to break down the training into phases, teaching the basic concepts and returning the employee to the workplace to practice. The employee then later attends more advanced training, where skill and knowledge levels are built on through the introduction of more complex material.

Figure 4.1(c) represents a learning curve on which the learning is relatively quick but tapers off. The difference between 4.1(a) and 4.1(c) is that some additional learning is possible along with improved performance. The implication for HRD programs is to design a program in which there is initial training at the steep part of the curve and then some sort of support to facilitate continued learning as the slope of the curve declines. The additional support could take many forms such as on-the-job coaching, additional self-study modules, or mini training sessions.

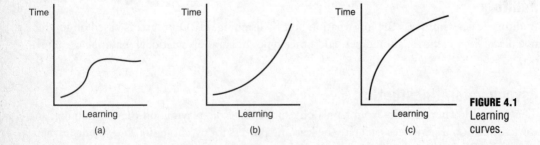

FIGURE 4.1
Learning curves.

Levels of Learning

Levels of learning describe how much is to be learned as opposed to how fast it is to be learned (learning curve) or how it is to be learned (learning style). Bloom's Taxonomy is the classic work with respect to this issue and delineates a hierarchy of learning behaviors or outcomes. The taxonomy describes six levels of learning from knowledge at the lower level to evaluation at the highest level. The levels are

- **Knowledge** This level requires the learner to be able to recall facts. An example might be to list the speed, capacity, and major parts of the machine on which the employee will be working.

- **Comprehension** This level requires understanding of the information. Continuing with the preceding example, the learner could explain the purpose of the machine, what it does, and, to some extent, how it works.

- **Application** This level requires that the learner not only understand the information but also be able to apply it in a new situation. The learner should be able to operate the machine.

- **Analysis** This level requires the learner to take the information received and break it into its component parts. The learner should be able to perform common repair and maintenance items on the machine, and understand how the various parts fit together to create a working unit.

- **Synthesis** This level requires the learner to be able to take information from multiple sources and create new meaning by reaching a conclusion of his or her own. The learner understands how the machine fits into the whole system or production line, can fix the machine when unusual or unique breakdowns occur, and could train others in how to use the machine.

- **Evaluation** The learner is able to make informed judgments. In this example, the learner is able to determine what type of machines will be needed in the future.

The importance of learning levels is that the HRD program must be designed to achieve certain learner behaviors or outcomes based on the need of the organization. If a worker is required to have only knowledge, for example, programs designed to produce outcomes at the evaluation level would likely be a waste of resources. Furthermore, it is typically demotivating to an employee to be trained at one level but be required to work at a level significantly below that. If the philosophy of the organization is merely to provide job training for lower-level employees, HRD programs should be developed at the application level. Anything above this level would likely increase costs unnecessarily. However, if the philosophy of the organization is toward the development end of the continuum, HRD programs should be designed at levels above the requirements of the current job.

Motivation

Motivation, in its simplest terms, is that which causes a person to act. Motivation is need-driven, goal-oriented, and situational. Motivation is discussed in this section because motivation affects learning. HRD programs must be designed to harness the motivation of employees to achieve the programmatic goals. A wide variety of theories of motivation are discussed in this section but, because human beings are extremely complex, no one theory explains human behavior in every situation. Therefore the SPHR must be able to integrate a variety of theories into program design and delivery. We will start with earlier motivation theories, such as Maslow's Hierarchy of Needs, and proceed to discussion of more modern theories, such as Vroom's Expectancy Theory.

EXAM ALERT

You should expect several questions regarding the motivation theories discussed in this section. You should understand the basic concept of a theory and its implications on the development of HR and HRD programs.

Maslow's Hierarchy of Needs

Abraham Maslow theorized that there are five human needs arranged hierarchically in rigid, lock-step fashion. These needs are

1. **Physiological**   Food, water, shelter, and so on

2. **Safety**   Freedom from physical, emotional, and psychological harm

3. **Social**   Being accepted, belonging to a group, having friends, and so forth

4. **Esteem**   Consists of internal self-respect and external respect from others

5. **Self-actualization**   Achieving one's full potential

Figure 4.2 is a depiction of the theoretical model.

Maslow hypothesized that a need would not be motivating until all needs below it were substantially fulfilled. However, continued research in human motivation has identified a number of problems with Maslow's theory. The premise that the five needs Maslow identified were all-inclusive has been disproved, as has his belief that a higher-level need would be motivating only if all lower-level needs were substantially satisfied. Humans are motivated by a large number of needs, and many of these needs can simultaneously affect behavior.

Maslow's Hierarchy of Needs is still important because it reminds HRD professionals and managers that behavior in the workplace is need-based and that programs can be designed to satisfy those needs. Furthermore, because employees are affected by multiple needs at the same time, the SPHR must design programs that address needs at many levels. Examples of programmatic implications at each level are

- **Physiological**   Adequate compensation to provide basic living necessities
- **Safety**   Safe working conditions, job security
- **Social**   Break rooms, social events, work teams, employee organizations
- **Esteem**   Performance management programs, employee recognition programs, praise
- **Self-actualization**   Employee development programs, challenging work and assignments

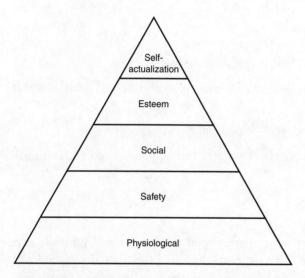

FIGURE 4.2   Maslow's Hierarchy of Needs.

EXAM ALERT

Expect a question on Maslow's theory, memorize the hierarchy, and consider how each need might be satisfied in the workplace.

Theory X and Theory Y

Theory X and Theory Y is the work of Douglas McGregor. He proposed that managers essentially view the nature of human beings in one of two distinct ways. Theory X is a negative view and Theory Y a positive one. A different set of management practices and HRD programs, designed to motivate employees, is indicated depending on which of the two theories the organization subscribes to. Current research does not support Theory X and Theory Y as a comprehensive theory of human motivation because it does not recognize the full range of human behavior. However, it is applicable in certain situations and gives the SPHR a framework in which to consider program and strategic implications under two diverse scenarios. Assumptions held by managers as to the nature of employees under the two theories are as follows:

Theory X

- ▶ Human beings are lazy, dislike work, and avoid it when possible.

- ▶ Because of their dislike for work, employees must be coerced, tightly controlled and directed, and threatened with punishment to motivate them to put forth effort to achieve organizational goals.

- ▶ Employees want to be directed, avoid taking responsibility for their work, and desire security above other factors associated with the workplace.

Theory Y

- ▶ Employees view work as one of the natural functions of life.

- ▶ Employees are self-motivated and self-directed to achieve organizational goals to which they are committed.

- ▶ Workers can learn to accept and even seek responsibility in their jobs.

- ▶ Workers are capable of contributing to the workplace through innovation and imaginative new ideas.

Herzberg's Two-Factor Theory

Frederick Herzberg's Two-Factor Theory (also referred to as the *Motivation-Hygiene Theory*) postulates that there are two separate characteristics of the workplace that affect employee behavior and job satisfaction. Herzberg called the two characteristics *motivation* factors and *hygiene* factors. Motivation factors are intrinsic to the individual, such as growth, achievement, increased responsibility, and challenging work. Hygiene factors are characteristics of the workplace that are extrinsic to the person, such as compensation, company policies, work conditions, management practices, and relationships with peers. Herzberg believed that hygiene factors could lead to job dissatisfaction but not job satisfaction, whereas motivation factors could lead to job satisfaction but not dissatisfaction. In other words, the opposite of job satisfaction is not dissatisfaction but no satisfaction, and the opposite of job dissatisfaction is not satisfaction but no dissatisfaction.

Although there are many problems with the theory, particularly with respect to its methodology, it does have implications for the practice of both HR and HRD. Job satisfaction is linked to positive outcomes, such as employee retention and improved work quality, and job dissatisfaction is linked to some negative work behaviors, such as tardiness and absenteeism. HRD programs, particularly training programs, must therefore be designed not to create job dissatisfaction by the inclusion of appropriate hygiene factors, whereas other programs, particularly development types of programs, can be developed to facilitate job satisfaction by the inclusion of motivation factors.

ERG Theory

Clayton Alderfer's ERG Theory is a reworking of Maslow's Hierarchy of Needs Theory and reflects more recent research in motivation theory. Alderfer believed that there were three, not five categories of needs. He called them *existence*, *relatedness*, and *growth* needs (hence the acronym ERG). Existence needs include Maslow's physiological and safety needs. Relatedness needs include Maslow's social need and the extrinsic reward portion of the esteem need. Growth needs include the intrinsic reward portion of Maslow's esteem need and the self-actualization need.

ERG theory differs from Maslow's theory in that a lower-level need does not have to be substantially fulfilled before another need affects motivation. ERG theory recognizes that needs are not rigidly hierarchically arranged and that multiple needs can be motivating the individual at one time.

McClelland's Theory of Needs

David McClelland developed a theory of motivation based around three needs. The need for achievement (nAch) motivates people to excel and to do something better than it has been done before. High achievers are highly motivated to succeed, but are not great risk takers because they do not want to fail. Consequently, risk taking is limited to those situations in which they have about a 50/50 chance of success. The need for power (nPow) is the need to influence people and to control others. The need for affiliation (nAff) is the need to be liked and to establish relationships and friendships.

Although the theory does not explain the wide range of human behavior, some research partially validates it and instruments are available to test the individual's strength of need in each area. The theory has practical application in employee selection and placement and in HRD because research indicates that training programs can affect the strength of some needs.

Goal-Setting Theory

Goal-setting theory is based on the work of Edward Locke and Gary Lanham. The theory postulates that motivation and performance is increased when goals are set. Maximization of motivation and performance are achieved when

- ▸ Goals are clear and specific.

- ▸ Goals are challenging. Theoretically, the more challenging the goal the higher the motivation and performance level, assuming that the goal is accepted by the person.

- ▸ Progress toward the goal is facilitated by performance feedback.

- ▸ Commitment increases motivation and performance.

There is mixed research as to whether participation in goal-setting increases motivation. The issue really seems to be commitment. If participation increases commitment, it has a positive effect. If commitment is obtained without participation, participation is not necessary.

Research in goal-setting theory tends to validate it. Management by Objectives *(MBO)* is an effective program based on the theory.

> **NOTE**
>
> Goal-setting theory and McClelland's theory differ a bit. Goal-setting theory indicates that goals, when accepted, have an unlimited capacity to motivate, whereas McClelland believes that high achievers (nAch) are motivated only by goals in which they have at least a 50/50 chance of achieving.

Self-Efficacy

Self-efficacy is a construct rather than a theory that is applicable to motivation. Self-efficacy is the belief that a person has that he or she can accomplish a task. Self-efficacy can be influenced by training and by management. The mere statement by a manager indicating the belief that the employee can perform a certain task can have a positive impact on self-efficacy. Self-efficacy is particularly important as one aspect of goal-setting theory in that a person with high self-efficacy is more likely to accept and commit to difficult and challenging goals, and will likely persist longer in attempting to achieve the goal than a person with lower self-efficacy.

Expectancy Theory

Expectancy theory is largely the work of Victor Vroom. The basic premise is that, in the work setting, motivation is determined by the importance of an outcome to the individual and the belief that increased effort will lead to a positive outcome. Expectancy theory can be expressed as a formula:

$M = E¥I¥V$

where

M Motivation.

E Expectancy that a certain amount of effort will lead to a first-level outcome.

I *Instrumentality* is the probability that a first-level outcome will lead to a second-level outcome.

V The valance or value placed on the second-level outcome.

Although the preceding information seems a bit complex, a simple example explains it quite clearly. A person's motivation (M) in the work setting can be explained and influenced by the expectancy (E) that if the employee expends a certain amount of effort, that effort will lead to a first-level outcome (an outstanding performance award, for example) and the probability (I) that the first-level outcome will lead to a second-level outcome (a merit increase, for example) and the value of that second-level outcome (the merit increase in this example) to the person. The actual theory is a bit more complex because the formula can include multiple levels of effort (M), multiple potential first-level outcomes (E), multiple second-level outcomes (I) and values (V) associated with each.

The formula can be further explained in that expectancy (E) can be defined as the effort-performance relationship. Instrumentality (I) is the performance-reward relationship and valence (V) reflects the employee's personal evaluation of the worth of the reward. Both E and I are under the control of management, whereas management must determine V to craft programs that appeal to many employees.

Substantial research supports this theory. It has practical application in HR and HRD program management and the linkage of performance to compensation.

EXAM ALERT

Expectancy theory has substantial research support. Expect a question asking you to link the theory to application in performance management and compensation programs.

Reinforcement Theory

Reinforcement theory has evolved from B. F. Skinner's work on operant conditioning. The theory essentially states that behavior is a result of the consequences of the behavior and is externally imposed. Because the impetus to act is external instead of internal, reinforcement theory might be better described as a theory of learning instead of motivation. However the theory does explain some types of behavior and the ability to shape behavior, so its discussion is appropriate in this section.

Reinforcement is used to shape behavior, either increasing the likelihood of its reoccurrence or the likelihood that it will not occur again, depending on the desired end result. There are four types of reinforcement:

▶ **Positive reinforcement**   A person is given a reward or something pleasant when the desired behavior is displayed. This reward increases the likelihood that the behavior will be repeated. An example is praise given to an employee that exhibits a desired work behavior in order to increase the likelihood of that behavior being repeated.

▶ **Negative reinforcement**   Something unpleasant is terminated when a desired behavior is displayed. This removal increases the likelihood that the behavior will be repeated. An example is the termination of criticism when the employee begins performing a certain task correctly.

▶ **Punishment**   Negative consequences occur when a particular unwanted behavior is displayed in order to reduce the likelihood of a repeat of the behavior. An example is giving an employee an unpaid suspension for repeated tardiness in order to attempt to reduce the reoccurrence of that type of behavior.

▶ **Extinction**   The behavior elicits neither positive nor negative consequences. Behavior that is not reinforced tends to dissipate. An example is refusing to acknowledge negative comments by one employee about another. The lack of reinforcement of this activity will likely result in the termination of the comments.

The frequency or schedule of reinforcement is important. *Continuous* reinforcement, in which reinforcement is given each time the behavior occurs, tends to lose its impact because of satiation. *Variable* or *intermittent* reinforcement tends to be more effective than continuous reinforcement in shaping behavior over the long run, although continuous reinforcement might be preferable at the beginning when the behavior is being initially shaped. Noncontinuous reinforcement can be either ratio or interval in pattern. *Ratio* refers to reinforcement that is based on the number of times the desired behavior is displayed, whereas *interval* refers to reinforcement that is based on the amount of time that elapses between reinforcements. Either type can be fixed, in that a reinforcement schedule is set and consistent, or variable, in which the reinforcement schedule changes from one reinforcement to the next. Table 4.1 gives examples and further explanation of the various types of intermittent reinforcement.

TABLE 4.1   Types of Intermittent Reinforcement

Reinforcement Schedule	Explanation	Example
Fixed-ratio	Reinforcement is given when a set number of desired behaviors occur.	Commissioned sales, piecework
Variable-ratio	Reinforcement is given at varying numbers of occurrences of the desired behavior.	Random call monitoring in call site with praise for good work
Fixed-interval	Reinforcement is given at consistent time intervals.	Salary check every two weeks
Variable-interval	Reinforcement is given at varying time intervals.	Pizza parties at irregular intervals for making weekly quota

Among the types of intermittent reinforcement, variable reinforcement tends to have more impact on increasing the desired behavior and is less subject to extinction than fixed intermittent reinforcement. Positive and negative reinforcement result in learning, in that a desired behavior is elicited. In general they are preferable to punishment and extinction because those types of reinforcement eliminate undesired behavior but do not elicit the desired behavior. Reinforcement theory has practical application in the workplace in terms of compensation and rewards systems. A common application of the theory is the process of behavior modification.

Equity Theory

Equity theory is based on the work of J. Stacy Adams and is often called *Adams' Equity Theory*. The theory postulates that employees compare the ratio of their inputs:outcomes to the ratio of inputs:outcomes of others to determine whether they are being treated fairly. This is a perceptual and personal process and each individual might approach it a bit differently. Inputs can be such things as how many hours the person works, educational level, experience level, skill and performance level, and so on. Outcomes can be defined in terms of compensation, benefits, performance ratings, working conditions, perks, and so forth. The comparison point (frequently called the *referent*) can be another person in the same job in the organization, another person in a similar job in another organization, or the referent can be the employee him or herself comparing current inputs and outputs with those of other jobs the employee held in the same organization or in another organization.

After the mental comparison is made there are three possible outcomes. If the ratio is equal to the referent, a perception of equity is created and is not motivating. If the ratio is unequal, however, a perception of unfairness is created regardless of whether the perception is that the employee is treated better or worse than the comparison point and the employee is motivated to act to create equity. Potential behaviors resulting from a perceived inequitable situation are

- ▶ Re-evaluate or distort the estimates of outcomes and inputs either of themselves or of the referent. This forces the equation into equity.

- ▶ Influence others to change their behaviors.

- ▶ Quit.

- ▶ Choose a more appropriate referent.

- ▶ Change their behavior to change either their inputs or outputs.
  - ▶ Over-rewarded employees might reduce their output or increase quality to create perceived equity.
  - ▶ Under-rewarded employees might reduce production or increase production, but reduce quality to create perceived equity.

Equity theory is supported by research. Compensation programs attempt to create perceived equity as discussed in Chapter 5, "Compensation and Benefits."

Job Characteristics Model

The *job characteristics model*, often referred to as the *JCM*, links job design to motivation and is derived from the research of J. R. Hackman and G. R. Oldham. The JCM indicates that all jobs consist of five characteristics that can be manipulated to create varying effects. The five characteristics are

▸ **Skill variety**   The number of different skills required to do the job.

▸ **Task identity**   The extent to which the work output of the job is a whole or identifiable piece of work. A job that requires assembling the whole product rather than just part of it has higher task identity.

▸ **Task significance**   The degree to which the job has an impact on others. For example, the executive director of a philanthropic organization would have greater task significance than the custodian who cleans the organization's offices.

▸ **Autonomy**   The extent to which the individual has freedom, independence, and discretion in making job-related decisions.

▸ **Feedback**   The extent to which the individual receives information regarding the effectiveness of his or her performance.

The extent to which these characteristics are present in the job are theorized to create varying amounts of three psychological states:

▸ Skill variety, task identity, and task significance combine to create the psychological state of experienced *meaningfulness of work*.

▸ Autonomy creates the psychological state of experienced *responsibility for work outcomes*.

▸ Feedback creates the psychological state of knowledge of work results.

NOTE

The ability to create the psychological states is also affected by the person's need for growth. Increasing skill variety, task identity, and so on have a greater impact on creating the three psychological states on those with a high growth need than those with a low growth need.

The psychological states are combined to create work outcomes. The greater the strength of the psychological states, the greater impact on motivation and work outcomes such as job satisfaction, low turnover, low absenteeism, and high quality work. Job designs such as job enrichment and job enlargement are practical applications of the JCM. Note, however, that increasing the strength of the psychological states does not result in increased productivity. Job simplification is another practical application of the theory, but it increases productivity by reducing the amount of skill variety, task identity, task significance, autonomy, and feedback and the strength of the associated psychological states. However, a negative outcome of designing simplified jobs is that job satisfaction will likely be reduced.

Linkage of Theory to Practice

Practical application of the various theories of motivation was integrated with the earlier discussion of the concepts associated with each theory. Table 4.2 summarizes potential program applications for each theory. These applications are examples, not all inclusive, because many of the theories have multiple potential applications in a variety of HR and HRD program areas.

TABLE 4.2   Applications of Motivational Theories

Motivation Theory	Potential Application
Maslow's Hierarchy of Needs	A wide variety of programs such as compensation, work environment, performance management, and training and development
Theory X and Theory Y	Management practices, employee relations
Herzberg's Two-Factor Theory	Job satisfaction, training and development, compensation, employee relations
ERG Theory	Same as Maslow's Hierarchy of Needs
McClelland's Theory of Needs	Employee and management selection, training
Goal-Setting Theory	MBO, performance management
Self-Efficacy	Performance management, training programs
Expectancy Theory	Performance management, compensation, and benefits
Reinforcement Theory	Training, incentive programs, compensation
Equity Theory	Compensation, internal, external and individual equity, benefits
Job Characteristic Model	Job analysis and design, job enrichment, job rotation, job simplification, job enlargement

NOTE

Motivation theory is largely based on research done in the United States or in cultures that are relatively similar. The theories might not have the capability to be generalized to other cultures.

HRD Process

Objective:

Gain an Understanding of the Human Resource Development Process (ADDIE)

The HRD process can be described in terms of the following five steps:

- ▶ Needs assessment
- ▶ Program design

- ▶ Program development
- ▶ Program implementation
- ▶ Program evaluation

Each of these steps will be discussed separately for ease of explanation and understanding. The steps are, however, interdependent and often simultaneous. For example, implementation considerations might dictate program development, even though development occurs before implementation in the process.

Furthermore, the process is circular. Issues arising in any step might require the process to revert to a prior step for further work. In addition, the process is not only circular but also frequently iterative. The evaluation step might reveal that the HRD program did not adequately address a problem, requiring a circle back to the needs analysis step and a second iteration of the whole process. In fact, many iterations might be necessary.

SHRM/HRCI uses the acronym ADDIE (shown next) to facilitate recall of the process. The process described in ADDIE is not limited just to HRD, but is a standard process model that can be used with any HR program. For example, you could use the same process in compensation and benefits to assess the needs, design a compensation and benefits program concept, develop the program, implement it, and then evaluate it in terms of the needs that were determined in the needs assessment step.

To remember ADDIE, note the following example:

A   Needs **A**ssessment
D   Program **D**esign
D   Program **D**evelopment
I   Program **I**mplementation
E   Program **E**valuation

EXAM ALERT

Expect a question on ADDIE. You should memorize the acronym to remember the steps in the HRD process. You should also have a basic understanding of what activities are undertaken at each step.

The HRD process is discussed in the following sections. Explanations of the major activities conducted in each section are also provided.

Needs Assessment

Needs assessment (also called *needs analysis*) is the process of determining whether HRD programs are needed to achieve organizational goals. Needs assessment is the critical first step in the HRD process. In fact, it could be argued that this is the most important step. Unless the needs of the organization are accurately determined and clearly articulated, all subsequent steps will be based on inaccurate assumptions and could potentially lead to wasteful and ineffective program activities.

Needs assessment is performed at three levels: *organizational*, *task*, and *person*. Further discussion of these levels follows, but it is important to understand the underlying concepts of the purposes of these analyses first. Needs assessment begins with the strategic goals of the organization and the objectives derived from those goals. An assessment is then made of the current performance in relation to the performance that is needed to achieve the goals and objectives. If there are gaps between the current and required (desired) performance, these gaps (needs) are further analyzed to determine what programmatic activities are appropriate. Unfortunately, there is often considerable pressure to bypass this step and go immediately to design and development. The classic statement is "We have a training problem," indicating the belief that the performance gap can be resolved by rolling out some sort of HRD program. In reality HRD programs are the solution to the problem, but the problem can be fully defined and described only through the assessment process. It is often difficult to sell management on the criticality of needs assessment because

▸ Managers do not understand its importance.

▸ The performance data seem to clearly indicate that some sort of HRD program is required.

▸ Needs assessment takes time and managers prefer immediate action to research and in-depth analysis.

Levels of Assessment

As previously stated, needs assessment can be conducted at three levels: *organizational*, *task*, and *person*. Each level is discussed in the following sections.

Organizational Assessment

At the organizational level, assessment is made in terms of current performance against strategic objectives and in terms of the organization's current capabilities to deal with future challenges and goals. Turnover, grievance rates, profitability, productivity, quality, scrap rates, customer satisfaction, customer complaints, employee skill and education levels, recruitment yield rates, and accidents are examples of the types of data used at this level of analysis. If gaps are found in current performance or potential when compared to the desired performance or future capabilities, those gaps are further analyzed to identify the root cause and programmatic activity needed to resolve them.

Task Assessment

Task assessment involves the analysis of the job requirements of current or future jobs against the current knowledge, skills, and ability levels of employees. Much of this data can be determined by analysis of job descriptions, job specifications, and information contained in employee personnel files or human resource information systems. A determination can then be made as to the implications of gaps found for HRD programs, now and in the future.

Person Assessments

At this level assessments are made of individual employees and their need for current or future HRD programs. Current performance evaluations, test scores, assessment centers, individual production data, and managerial and employee surveys and interviews can all be used as the source of data analysis.

Needs Assessment Process

The process can be explained rather simply in terms of five steps:

1. Gathering necessary data

2. Analyzing the data to determine whether gaps exist that can be resolved by HRD programs

3. Proposing HRD program solutions

4. Evaluating the cost-benefit of each solution

5. Selecting a solution for design, development, and implementation

Each of the steps is discussed in more detail next.

Gathering Data

The first determination in this stage is to decide the level of assessment to be used: organizational, task, or person. That decision dictates which types of data-gathering methods are most appropriate. Next, a data-gathering plan must be developed that includes not only the methods to be used but also a determination as to the population from which the data is to be gathered. If the population is small, the data is likely to be gathered from all. If the population is large, a representative sample must be chosen. An action plan should be developed, listing action items and due dates. The action plan should incorporate necessary communications to both participants and their supervisors. Participants must be clearly advised as to the purpose of the data gathering. Supervisors need this information also and must be consulted regarding both timeframes and methodology so that the process does not unnecessarily interrupt work activities, particularly at critical times.

Data-gathering sources are, in many cases, the same as are used in both the job analysis and job evaluation processes. Most data-gathering projects use more than one method because each individual method tends to yield different types of data. Typical methods of data gathering, along with their advantages and disadvantages, are contained in Table 4.3.

TABLE 4.3 Data-Gathering Methods

Method	Advantages	Disadvantages
Observations	Little interruption of work	Expensive
	Directly job relevant	Requires trained observer
		Might affect employees' behavior
		Data subject to observer's interpretation
Questionnaires/surveys	Inexpensive	Low return rates
	Can be statistically analyzed	Limits issues to be explored
	Can gather data from large number of people	Might limit answers to only those listed in survey
Focus groups	In-depth data	Group think
	Can explore issues as they are raised	Time-consuming
Interviews	Rich data	Expensive and time-consuming
	Allows exploration of many issues	Difficult to analyze themes
		Requires trained interviewer
Document reviews (organization charts, technical manuals, policies, grievances, and so on)	Does not interfere with production	Might require expert to understand material
	Provides task requirements	Historical; could be obsolete
	Objective	
Test results	Objective	Does not indicate on-the-job use of knowledge
	Can be statistically analyzed	
	Might indicate problem areas	Might not be reliable or valid
Assessment centers	Might provide comprehensive data	Expensive
Advisory committees	Increases commitment to decisions	Subject to the bias and personal agendas of those participating
	Includes participation of those who might be affected	
	Includes input from those having special knowledge	

Data Analysis

After the data is gathered, it must be analyzed to determine whether gaps exist between actual and desired performance. More importantly, a gap must be evaluated in terms of whether it can be affected by the development and implementation of HRD programs. The concept of *performance consulting*, largely developed by Robinson and Robinson, is instructive here.

The old adage is that the organization should engage in training or development only if the employee does not know how to do something. Performance-consulting processes look at the gap in a more holistic way. Gaps often are the result of issues that cannot be addressed by HRD programs. If that is the case, the HRD process is terminated and the issue is referred to another area of HR or to another department. For example, if the issue is poor equipment, lack of resources, inappropriate compensation plans, or employee negligence, the gap cannot be addressed by HRD programs and should be referred elsewhere.

Proposing Solutions

Assuming that a determination is made that HRD program intervention is indicated, various potential programmatic activities that might address the problem must be identified. Options might include creating a new program internally, purchasing an already-developed program, or contracting with an external vendor for the development of a customized program.

Determining Cost-Benefit of Alternative Solutions

It is the goal of HRD to be considered revenue enhancing rather than a cost center and for HRD programs to be considered investments in human capital, much the same as investments in plant and equipment, rather than merely costs. To accomplish this goal, HRD programs must be evaluated in terms of the projected benefits to be derived in comparison with costs. Cost-benefit analysis is comprehensively discussed in Chapter 2, "Strategic Management." Potential costs and benefits are listed in Table 4.4.

TABLE 4.4   Cost and Benefits of HRD Processes

Costs	Benefits
Lost productivity of those in program	Improved quality
Salary of participants	Reduced errors
Salary of trainer, developers, and so on	Increased productivity
Cost of travel for those in program	Increased job satisfaction
Cost of classroom space and equipment	Reduced turnover
Cost of contractors	Increased customer satisfaction
Clerical, technical, and managerial costs of program administration	Reduced managerial oversight
	Increased managerial flexibility

Selecting a Solution

Based on the cost-benefit analysis and other considerations, a decision is made as to which, if any, solution to proceed with. At this point, the assessment stage is complete and design begins.

Competencies

We have been discussing needs assessment in terms of gaps in performance related to deficiencies in skills, knowledge, or ability. However, this process assumes that requirements are static. What if the skills required are rapidly changing? Any needs assessment done today based on knowledge, skills, and ability might be invalid tomorrow. Consequently, many organizations now are basing needs assessment on the competencies required at the three levels of analysis. What are the competencies needed to make the organization successful now and in the future? What are the competencies needed to achieve work outcomes? And what are the competencies needed by individual employees to be successful?

Competencies are personal or organizational capabilities that are linked to successful performance outcomes. Competencies at the individual level are a combination of knowledge, skills, abilities, behaviors, motivation, and other characteristics that contribute to job-related outcomes. Competencies at the organizational level are those characteristics of the organization that are linked to organizational success. Examples might be innovation, capability to adapt, and technical excellence.

Needs assessment using competencies follows the same process. Instead of analyzing performance or skill gaps, the analysis centers on gaps between current competency Levels and needed competency levels.

Program Design

Program design and development are frequently considered one step in the HRD process because they are so intertwined. We will continue using SHRM/HRCI's ADDIE process and discuss program design and development as separate steps. However, the distinction between the two steps is arbitrary. HRD design involves the establishment of training goals and objectives, determining the target audience for the program, and selecting a developer.

Goals and Objectives

A problem well defined is a problem well on its way to being solved. Well-stated goals and objectives, like a good problem statement, facilitate the rest of the HRD process immeasurably. The *goal* is a very succinct statement of what the program is about, who it is for, and why it is being conducted. An example is *This program is designed to improve the communications skills of all managers to increase employee job satisfaction and retention.*

Objectives are supporting statements that define what the outcome of the program is to be in terms of

▶ What the participant will be able to do after program completion

▶ In what timeframe the participant will be able to do it

▶ How well the participant will be able to do it

▶ Under what conditions the participant will be able to do it

An example is *After the completion of training the participant will be able to*

▶ Completely assemble the XYZ widget using its component parts

▶ Within two weeks of on-the-job experience

▶ At a quality reject rate of less than 5% and a minimum production rate of 100 XYZ widgets per hour

▶ While working independently on the XYZ production line

Another way of looking at objectives is that they should be SMART, as described in the following acronym:

▶ **S**pecific   A clear statement of what the program is to accomplish.

▶ **M**easurable   To evaluate whether the objective has been achieved.

▶ **A**ction-oriented   The objective should clearly describe what the participant will be able to do on completion of the program.

▶ **R**easonable   The objective should be challenging but achievable.

▶ **T**imely   The objective must specify a timeframe in which the objective is to be accomplished.

Target Audience

The needs assessment step will have identified the gap and organizationally where the gap is located: organization, task, or person. The target audience then becomes those persons or groups experiencing the gap and who can benefit from a program designed to impact the gap. Here the design and development steps are intertwined. Such issues as learning styles, adult learning principles, Bloom's Taxonomy, and employee capabilities and motivation (issues discussed elsewhere in this chapter) must all be considered in selecting the target audience. These are, effectively, simultaneous considerations rather than distinct ones.

The level at which the program operates must be appropriate to the aptitude and motivation of the participant. To attempt to raise the level of capability of the participants to synthesis (Bloom's Taxonomy) requires that they have the aptitude and capability of performing at that level, that they have a reason for doing so (adult learning), and that they want to or can be persuaded to (motivation). In addition, the selection of the target audience is also integrally intertwined with the development stage so that learning curves, current knowledge or skill levels, and various learning styles are considered before selection and accommodated in the development.

Selection of Developer

Before the process can go from design to development, a decision must be made as to who will perform the actual development. In fact, this decision might actually be required in the cost-benefit stage of needs assessment. There are three options, whose advantages and disadvantages are described in Table 4.5.

TABLE 4.5 Types of Program Developers

Developer	Advantages	Disadvantages
In-house	Program is customized to needs of organization Knowledge of organization, mission, culture, and so on	Might take considerable time to develop Might be more expensive than buying something already developed Organization might not have expertise to do so Bias against in-house expertise (expertise is evaluated in terms of how far they have to travel and how much they cost)
Off-the-shelf	Quick Might be less expensive Access to expertise and support	Not initially customized to organization Customization either by the vendor or the organization requires additional time and expenditure of resources Might not address specific gaps identified
Third-party developer (consultant, academic organization, and so on)	Access to expertise Program customized to the needs of the organization	Could be expensive and time-consuming Developer might not understand organizational needs and culture

Program Development

During the program development stage, the actual methods of delivery are determined and the program materials are produced. In addition, the type of HRD program to be delivered is decided.

Delivery Methods

The course content can be delivered in a number of ways. The determination of the appropriate method is based on a number of variables including, but not limited to, the type of material, needs of the participant, availability and proximity of the participant, technology available, and type of program being delivered. There is a very fine line between delivery methods, program materials, and types of HRD programs. Some of the activities discussed in the following sections could fall into more than one category. Various delivery methods include

▶ **Lecture**   Good for delivery to a large number of persons, but it might not permit questions and discussion.

▶ **Computer-based training**   Enables delivery at any time and any place, but it might not be appropriate for some types of programs, such as interpersonal training and some types of managerial training. Computer-based training includes training that is resident on an employee's personal computer or available through either the organization's intranet or the Internet.

▶ **Group discussion**   Facilitates the exchange of knowledge and experience, but might be dominated by a few participants if not facilitated.

▶ **Role-plays**   Allows participants to practice new learning, but is sometimes viewed as fake.

▶ **Case studies**   Allows participants to work through various theoretical situations, but innovation might be thwarted by the "book answer" or instructor preferences.

▶ **Demonstration**   Provides guidance on the right way to accomplish a task, but might not allow for hands-on experience.

The choice of delivery methods is not an either/or decision. Effective delivery often incorporates multiple delivery methods.

Program Materials

Program materials are the actual content of the program. As with methods, a wide variety of options are available depending on the purpose the materials are to serve. Types of materials are

▶ **Print materials**   Textbooks, manuals, written handouts, workbooks, and so on

▶ **Visual materials**   DVDs, videotapes, overhead transparencies, writing on black/whiteboards, PowerPoint slides, and so on

▶ **Audio materials**   CDs, audiotapes, and so on

▶ **Tangible objects**   Models, simulators, machines, and equipment

Effective program delivery frequently requires the use of multiple types of program materials. This facilitates learning in that it accommodates various types of learning styles.

Types of Programs

There are a wide variety of HRD programs designed to accomplish various purposes. Types of programs are

- **Job instruction training**   *JIT*, not to be confused with just-in-time training, is a type of on-the-job training used to train employees when the nature of the work is not complex and consists of relatively few repetitive motions. It consists of telling and showing the trainee what to do, having the trainee tell the trainer what to do and then having the trainer do it, and finally the trainee tells the trainer what to do and then is allowed to do it him or herself.

- **Orientation**   This is a program to socialize the new employee into the workplace. Multiple research studies clearly link effective orientation with employee retention. During orientation, new employees are briefed on the organization's mission, culture, policies, and work rules. They are familiarized with benefits, working environment, and introduced to fellow workers.

- **Basic skills/remediation**   Work and basic work requirements often rapidly change in high-tech (or technologically advanced) industries. Workers either come to the organization without the necessary skills and knowledge or their current skills and knowledge become outdated. Employers frequently must provide programs to update these work skills or to improve mathematical and literacy skills.

- **On-the-job training**   These programs are designed to give the employee actual work experience either in the workplace or in a simulated workplace setting (vestibule training).

- **Skill development programs**   These programs are designed to improve the skills of employees already working in the organization. Skill development is used to update skills as job requirements change or to develop skills for future job requirements. Examples are team member training, interpersonal skills training, computer training, quality training, sales training, and technology training.

- **Executive and management development programs**   These include a wide variety of programs designed to improve the effectiveness of current managers or to develop the potential of managers to assume increased responsibility. Examples are assessment centers, graduate degree or executive degree programs, and various seminars and conferences.

- **Wellness programs**   Although wellness programs are part of the occupational health, safety, and security program, an important component of such a program is employee awareness and education.

▶ **Harassment program**   Harassment prevention is part of an effective EEO (*equal employment opportunity*) program. The EEO has interpreted United States law to mean that employers have an obligation to engage in communicating harassment policies and basic requirements of the law to all employees and to train managers on harassment recognition and prevention.

▶ **Workplace violence**   Prevention of violence in the workplace is discussed in Chapter 7. Workplace violence prevention programs include programmatic activities to increase awareness of the issues and recognize and deal with potentially violent employees in the early stages of a problem.

▶ **Diversity programs**   Effective diversity programs include diversity training and awareness initiatives.

Implementation of Programs

Excellent design and development of HRD programs can be negated by poor execution in the implementation stage. Important issues in implementation of programs are

▶ Piloting of the program

▶ Selection of a facilitator

▶ Selection and arrangement of the facility

▶ Communication and marketing

▶ Final launching of the program

Piloting of Program

Diligent design and development do not necessarily guarantee program effectiveness. Frequently it is good practice to pilot test the program prior to full implementation. This is especially true if the program is designed to be given many times, to many people, and if the program's desired outcomes are critical to the success of the organization. To the extent possible, the pilot test should be presented to a representative sample of the target population so that feedback received can be generalized. The pilot test can be used to

▶ Test the timing and sequencing of the presentation

▶ Verify the accuracy of information presented

▶ Test the effectiveness of program materials, exercises, and simulations

▶ Verify the expected learning outcomes

- ▶ Verify the appropriateness of physical environment layout
- ▶ Gain support from upper management

The information gained from the pilot test is then used to modify the program before actual implementation. Pilot testing often results in comments and suggestions that were not considered in the design and development stages, resulting in overall improvement in the effectiveness of the program.

Selecting the Facilitator

Selecting the correct facilitator is critical to the success of the program. Facilitator skills must be appropriately matched to the type of program, program materials being used, and type of delivery. For example, a facilitator that is an outstanding lecturer might not be appropriate as a facilitator for group discussion, or a subject matter expert in manufacturing technology might be an excellent facilitator for a theoretical discussion of a work process design but not as a facilitator for on-the-job training.

Selection and Arrangement of the Facility

Selection and arrangement of the facility must be in alignment with the type of program and delivery methods. The facility must enhance the potential for achievement of program goals, not detract from it. Facility layout must permit the type of delivery methods determined in the development stage.

The facility must be conducive to learning and the achievement of program goals. The first decision to be made is whether the program is to be held in the organization's space or offsite. The decision will be based on a number of considerations: cost, availability of appropriate equipment, participant comfort, and message that the program wants to convey.

Cost

It is generally less expensive to hold programs in the organization's own space. However, many organizations do not have appropriate space. To hold a program in a space not conducive to learning negates all the excellent design and development work. For example, to hold a diversity program event in vacant space on the production floor in noisy and dirty surroundings would not likely facilitate the achievement of the program's goals.

Availability of Equipment

The space must have the appropriate equipment or equipment must be easily moved to the facility. For example, if the program requires actual practice or work on a production machine, that program generally must be held where the equipment is located or a facility specifically designed to conduct training on that particular type of equipment. If the program requires a computer terminal for each participant, the program event must be held in a facility that can accommodate the need.

Participant Comfort

Program effectiveness will be negatively affected by physical and psychological discomfort. The facility must be clean and comfortable. The temperature must be maintained at an appropriate temperature (around 70°) and the system must be capable of providing fresh, odor-free air. Desks, tables, and workspaces must be appropriate to the activities being undertaken and provide sufficient working room for participants. Chairs should be comfortable and provide ergonomic support. The space must be ADA compliant and provide adequate lighting. External noise should not be distracting and windows should have drapes or blinds, both to control the light when visual presentations are being made and to prevent distractions from the outside. Large rooms will generally require voice amplification systems.

Program Message

A program held onsite in a dirty room with inadequate equipment where participants can easily be contacted for mundane job-related issues sends a message that the program is really not important. Spending a bit more to conduct the program in an offsite space with excellent equipment sends the opposite message. The organization must decide how important the program is when selecting the facility.

Arrangement of the Facility

The facility's arrangement must complement the program delivery. The space must be large enough or have associated small rooms to accommodate breakout groups if that is part of the delivery process. The actual furniture arrangement of the room is critical to achieving delivery objectives. Figure 4.3 provides examples of several common furniture arrangements, each designed to support a particular type of delivery method.

These arrangements are discussed in more depth in the following list:

- ▶ **Classroom/theater** Classroom and theater arrangements are appropriate for lecture or discussion presentations to larger groups. The difference between the two types of set-ups is that classroom arrangements usually contain a writing surface, whereas theater arrangements usually don't. In the design, the circles represent desks in the classroom arrangement and chairs in the theater arrangement. The classroom arrangement could also include writing tables in front of each row of chairs. Although these arrangements can accommodate larger numbers of people and allow for discussion between the facilitator and participants, they do not encourage interaction and discussion between participants.

- ▶ **Banquet** The banquet arrangement is appropriate when the delivery method includes breakout groups or small group discussion and projects. It is also appropriate when the event includes meals. Banquet arrangements do not maximize use of available space and limit the number of participants. Also, the orientation of some participants precludes contact with the facilitator and they must turn their chairs around to do so.

▶ **Rectangle**   Having participants seated around a rectangular table facilitates intra-group interaction and discussion if that is part of the delivery methodology. The number of participants per table should be limited to fewer than 20 and the arrangement takes more space per participant than some other styles (theater style, for example).

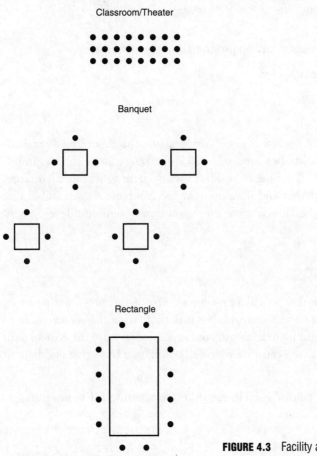

FIGURE 4.3   Facility arrangement possibilities.

TIP

A circular table serves the same purposes as a rectangular table.

EXAM ALERT

You should be familiar with types of arrangements and their advantages and disadvantages.

Program Communication and Marketing

It is important that HRD programs be communicated to interested and affected parties, and that they be marketed to the target population. These activities are undertaken with the following objectives in mind:

- Provides participants with advance information as to the purpose, length, and agenda of the program

- Generates interest in and enthusiasm for the program among participants

- Reinforces support from key stakeholders

Program Launch

After the program has been tested and revised as necessary, decisions have been made regarding selection of the facilitator, the facility has been selected and arranged, and the communication and marketing plan is in place, it is time to roll out the program to its intended target audience. This does not mean that design and development are complete. It is possible that feedback from stakeholders during the launch stage might require design and development changes along the way.

Evaluation of Programs

It is important that the organization know whether expenditure of resources for program implementation is having the desired impact and whether it is facilitating the achievement of organizational goals. Evaluation should include all affected stakeholders, and the cost-benefit analysis used in the needs assessment step must be revisited to validate both cost and benefit assumptions.

Several concepts and processes must be discussed in relation to evaluating HRD programs:

- Transfer of training/learning

- Evaluation models

- Evaluation methods

- Sources to be used in the collection of evaluation data

Transfer of Training/Learning

The purpose of HRD training programs is to impart the necessary skills and knowledge for the person to do the job. Transfer of training occurs when what is learned in the training is actually utilized on the job. Although certain HRD programs might be conducted for the express purpose of improvement of human capital, even then there is a belief that these programs, although not directly job-related, will result in performance improvement.

For training to have organizational benefits, it must be utilized on the job. Research indicates, however, that much of the training money spent is wasted because of a lack of transfer. Why does this occur? The HRD function, unfortunately, has only partial control over training transfer. The HRD function can ensure that the participants have the skills and knowledge to do the job. Testing and observation can determine this. The HRD function can also facilitate participant confidence in his/her ability to perform the tasks though practice in the training framework. What HRD cannot guarantee is transfer of the training to the job site; only management can do that. It is up to management to ensure that the participant is actually permitted to use what is learned on the job and to provide the participant with the required tools, resources, and support to do so. Failure of management to adequately support these activities precludes transfer of training to the job.

The same can be said for developmental activities. Again, the HRD function can provide new skills and knowledge, but management might not be receptive to implementation of these concepts after the participant returns from the developmental program. This phenomenon is referred to as *encapsulated development*.

Whether it is encapsulated development or lack of transfer of training, billions of dollars of HRD program expenditures are wasted each year. It is therefore critical as an HRD professional to be able to evaluate HRD programs, determine impact, and make changes as necessary.

> **EXAM ALERT**
>
> Expect a question on transfer of training; probably regarding why training is not transferred to the workplace.

Evaluation Models

The best-known and most influential model for evaluating HRD programs was developed by Donald Kirkpatrick. Although the model was specifically developed to evaluate training, expansion to other HRD program evaluation is appropriate. Robert Brinkerhoff has extended the evaluation model to six stages. Kirkpatrick's and Brinkerhoff's models are discussed next. The actual evaluation methods used, particularly in Kirkpatrick's model, are discussed in the next section.

Kirkpatrick's Four Levels of Evaluation

Donald Kirkpatrick proposed that training effectiveness could be evaluated according to four levels or criteria: *reaction*, *learning*, *behavior*, and *results*.

▶ **Reaction** Reaction data measure the participant's attitude and perceptions regarding the program. Did they like it? Did they think the facilitator did a good job? Were the facilities OK? All are measured at this level. Reaction is easy to measure and is usually done with a checklist or brief survey at the end of the program (called *smile sheets* by

HRD professionals). However, reaction information tells us little about the effectiveness of the program: It merely tells us whether the participants enjoyed it. Does this mean that reaction data is useless? The answer is no. Reaction data indicates whether the right climate was set for learning. Participants who are unhappy are less likely to learn than those who value the program they are attending. In addition, positive reaction to the program by participants might generate interest in it by others and might encourage others to attend.

▶ **Learning** Learning data tells us whether program objectives, in terms of knowledge or skill acquisition, were achieved. Learning data is typically collected by administration of tests or quizzes or by observation and demonstration. Learning data is important but it does not tell us whether the learning was actually used in the workplace or whether the learning impacted organizational goal achievement.

▶ **Behavior** Behavior data indicate whether the program has affected on-the-job behavior or performance. Managerial observations and feedback from others are among a variety of means of collecting data at this level. Behavior data indicate changes in performance but do not indicate whether those changes in behavior contribute to the achievement of organizational goals.

▶ **Results** Results data provide the evaluator with information as to the impact the program had on the organization. The type of data to be collected is determined by the gap identified in the needs analysis stage of the HRD process. If a gap was found between desired productivity and actual productivity and an HRD program was developed to address that gap, data collection at the results level must be production information and statistics.

NOTE

The ease with which data is collected is (for the most part) inversely proportional to its usefulness. Reaction data is easy to collect but has limited value. On the other hand, results data is the most valuable but the hardest to collect.

EXAM ALERT

Expect a question regarding Kirkpatrick's four levels of evaluation. The question will likely have you link the collection of a particular type of data with its level. Methods of collecting data for each level are discussed in the next section.

Brinkerhoff's Six Stages of Evaluation

Robert Brinkerhoff expanded the Kirkpatrick model to six overlapping stages. He suggests that data indicating a problem collected at one step might have been caused by activities occurring in a previous step or stage. The six stages are

▶ **Goal Setting**   What are the needs that can be resolved by HRD intervention and programs?

▶ **Program Design**   What programmatic activities and design will satisfy the need?

▶ **Program Implementation**   Does the design work?

▶ **Immediate Outcomes**   Were learning objectives achieved?

▶ **Intermediate Outcomes**   Was the learning applied on the job?

▶ **Impacts and Worth**   Did the program affect the organization in a meaningful and cost-effective way?

NOTE

Evaluation, unless the scientific method is used with a control group, proves only *correlation* not *causation*. The HRD should be careful in generalizing results of a program or unequivocally attributing results to program activities.

Evaluation Methods

Although the models discussed provide a framework for evaluation, they do not dictate what data should be collected or the method of collection. Evaluation methods are discussed later and are keyed to Kirkpatrick's model. However, the Brinkerhoff model is basically an expansion of the Kirkpatrick model, so the discussion is applicable to that model also. It is important to collect data from a number of sources: *the participant*, *the facilitator*, and *management*. Because these three groups might have different desired outcomes from the program, differences in evaluation scores are likely. When this occurs, evaluators should analyze the differences for insights to program effectiveness and, if the program is still active, recommend program modifications as appropriate.

Reaction

Reaction data can be collected using the following methods:

▶ **Interviews**   They provide rich data, but are time-consuming. If the number of participants is small, this might be the best data collection method. If the number is large, interviews can be used as the basis for developing surveys/questionnaires.

▶ **Check sheets**   This is the most frequently used method in which different facets of the program are evaluated on a continuum. They are easy to fill out, but do not provide in-depth information and are often considered to be *pro forma* by those asked to fill them out.

▸ **Surveys/questionnaires** These allow evaluators to gather information from a large number of people in a timely and inexpensive manner. Data can be analyzed statistically. However, this method often results in low participation rates and the results can be affected if the questions or the response protocol is not clear to the respondent.

Learning

Learning data is typically collected based on some sort of test, either written (paper or digital) or demonstration. Using some sort of experimental design facilitates the collection of learning data. To the extent possible, the data should reveal the difference in knowledge or skills after the program was completed. Various types of experimental design are discussed next.

Post-Measure

A test is given at the completion of the program to determine whether learning objectives have been achieved. The obvious weakness to this methodology is that the data does not tell us whether the performance is a result of the program or could have been achieved without it.

Pre-/Post-Measure

Tests are given before the program begins and at its conclusion. Although this data give an indication of a change in performance, it cannot be concluded unequivocally that the program caused the change. It is possible that the change in performance was a result of some other variable, not the program itself.

Pre-/Post Measure with Control Group

This method uses two statistically similar groups. Each group is given a pre-test and a post-test, but the control group does not participate in the program. Statistically significant differences in performance between the two groups can then be attributed to the program and causation is scientifically established. Use of a control group is not always appropriate. For example, giving safety training to one group but not to the control group raises ethical questions. Is it appropriate to allow one group to incur injuries just to prove that the program is effective?

Behavior

There are a number of ways to measure whether on-the-job behavior has changed after exposure to the program. Some of these ways are

▸ **Observations** Is the change observable by the evaluator? Often checklists are used and either the manager or an HRD person observes performance, making note of proper behaviors.

▸ **Simulations** Does the participant perform in a new and appropriate way in a simulated job environment?

> ▶ **Managerial feedback**   The manager is asked to observe performance and provide observations back to HRD as to improvements in performance.

> ▶ **Self-statements**   The participant reports back to HRD as to changes in on-the-job behavior and performance.

> ▶ **360° feedback**   Managers, subordinates, peers, and customers of the participant provide feedback to HRD as to changes in the participant's performance.

Results

As stated earlier, the most critical evaluation measures are those that report results. They also are often the most difficult to obtain. Unfortunately, HRD professionals, because of a variety of reasons, tend to evaluate at lower levels of the Kirkpatrick model while forgoing evaluation at the fourth level. Often this is based on time or resource constraints that are beyond HRD control. However, the extent to which results are measured is the extent to which HRD can prove its usefulness to the organization.

It is the gap that was identified that must be measured. Baseline data is critical to show performance improvement. Some examples of results data collection methods are

> ▶ **Financial reports**   ROI *(return on investment)*, profitability, and so on

> ▶ **Production records**   Productivity, scrap, quality data, and so on

> ▶ **Compensation records**   Gainsharing results, merit or incentive pay

> ▶ **Progress toward organizational goals**   Meeting of milestones or subobjectives

> ▶ **Performance management data**   Overall rise in performance evaluation scores

> ▶ **Cost-benefit data**   Indicators of benefits derived from the program as opposed to costs

Sources of Evaluation Data

All stakeholders must be included as sources of data in the HRD program evaluation process. Programs are often designed to solve multiple needs of different groups of stakeholders. Different stakeholders might view gaps identified in the needs analysis stage differently. The objectives of the program might be differentially valued and there might be differences among the stakeholders as to the appropriateness of the program design, development, and implementation.

Input from those affected allows for a fuller and more accurate evaluation of program success. Data sources should include

> ▶ **Participants**   That is, those who are most directly affected by the program and can provide significant information as to the effectiveness of the program and

recommendations for improvement. Participants can provide data at the reaction, learning, and behavior levels of evaluation.

- ▶ **Management** Input from a variety of management officials (executives, supervisors, finance directors, production directors, and so on) can best provide information as to the organizational and performance impact of the program.

- ▶ **Facilitator** Trained facilitators are experts in conducting program activities and can provide valuable professional input into evaluation at the reaction and learning levels.

Career Development

Objective:
Gain an Understanding of Career Development

A *career* is a series or sequence of work-related positions and experiences held by a person over the span of their working life. HRCI and SHRM use definitions that are somewhat different from those typically found in the literature, and this section uses the same definitions for consistency with the SPHR test.

Career development is defined as a combination of career management and career planning. *Career development* is an umbrella concept that includes decisions regarding occupational choices and activities to facilitate the achievement of career goals that are of mutual benefit of the employee and the employer. *Career management* is a process conducted by the employer to identify current and future staffing needs and to engage in activities to fulfill those needs. *Career planning* is the process by which an individual sets career objectives and engages in activities to attain those goals.

Career development, planning, and management are undergoing a significant change in direction because of the changing dynamics of the work environment. The *psychological contract*—an unwritten agreement between the employer and employee regarding work expectations and obligations—has changed dramatically in the last several decades from the concept of employment security to one of employability security. Changes in the nature of the contract are shown in Table 4.6.

TABLE 4.6   Changes in the Psychological Contract

Traditional		Current	
Employer	**Employee**	**Employer**	**Employee**
Career-long loyalty	Job security	High levels of performance	Competetive wages
Competent performance	Annual pay raises	Extra effort when required	Portable benefits
Employee retention	Steady career progression	Reasonable length of retention	Developmental opportunities
	Retirement plan		Challenging work
	Benefits based on seniority		Growth

Traditionally employees expected to stay with one company until retirement. Throughout their time with the company, they expected to receive annual pay raises, a retirement plan that guarantees a certain amount of retirement income based on years of service, and career progression up the hierarchy. In return the employer expected employee loyalty and retention and competent performance. Today, employees can expect to work for many organizations during their career. To facilitate that movement, they expect portable benefits such as 401(k) retirement plans. They also expect competitive wages and opportunities to improve their skills through challenging work and developmental activities. In return, the employer expects high levels of performance, increased hours, or extra effort as needed to get the work done. The employer does not expect the employee to stay with it forever because that employee's skills might not always be needed, but it does expect the employee to remain for a reasonable amount of time.

Increasingly, career development is a process that has changed from a primarily employer-driven one to one that is primarily driven by the employee. As labor mobility increases and employers pursue a strategy of buying talent rather than developing it, the employee must plan, manage, and develop his/her own career and negotiate career development opportunities and benefits on entrance to the organization. In the new work world, responsibilities are divided as follows:

- ▶ Employer responsibilities

  - ▶ Create growth opportunities in terms of work assignments

  - ▶ Support employee developmental activities, such as paid travel to professional conferences or tuition reimbursement

  - ▶ Clearly articulate the organization's strategic plan and its implications for future employment, including the types of jobs that will be needed

▶ Employee responsibilities

  ▶ Individual career planning

  ▶ Assess individual KSAs *(knowledge-skills-abilities)* and interests

  ▶ Engage in career-long developmental activities

Using the SHRM/HRCI nomenclature, Table 4.7 depicts those activities that are associated with career management, which is organization centered, and those that are employee centered, or associated with career planning. It is to the benefit of both the organization and the employee that the two sets of activities are correlated and coordinated. When combined, they constitute career development.

TABLE 4.7 Activities Associated with Career Management, Planning, and Development

Career Management (Organization Centered)	Career Development	Career Planning (Employee Centered)
Identification of future staffing needs	Intersection of career management and career planning	Identifying personal KSAs and interests
Planning career ladders		Developing and periodically reassessing career goals
Coordinating compensation plans with career progression		Engaging in development activities to facilitate career goal attainment
Matching organizational needs with individual KSAs		
Assessing HRD needs		

The following sections discuss important issues associated with career development. They are career stages, career development programs, and special issues and challenges in career development.

Career Stages

Careers typically follow predictable patterns or stages; at least, they used to. In today's workplace environment, careers do not necessarily follow the typical progression, with many individuals delaying retirement or re-entering the workforce after retirement. However, discussion of career stages still captures the experience of the majority of workers. Table 4.8 has a five-stage model of career development that links the major tasks to be accomplished at each stage.

TABLE 4.8   Five-Stage Model of Career Development

Career Stage	Age	Major Tasks
Occupational preparation	0–18	Pursue education Identify career interests Make initial career choices Develop occupational self-image
Organizational entry	18–25	Apply and interview for jobs Accept job offer and enter workforce Explore several jobs
Early career	18–40	Learn job and organizational rules Pursue career goals Career advancement and promotions Improve competence
Middle career	40–55	Reevaluate early career choice and goals Reaffirm or modify goals Lead others Make decisions based on goals Update skills
Late career	55+	Prepare for retirement Examine nonwork interests and options Maintain productivity

Career Development Programs

There is a virtually endless list of developmental programs that an organization can engage in. It is up to the SPHR to lead the organization in deciding, based on analysis and organizational goals, which categories of career development programs best meet its needs and, within each category, which specific types of activities should be undertaken. Career development programs can be broken down into five major areas. These areas, which are discussed in the following sections, are not mutually exclusive. Program activities in one area might often also serve the purposes of another area.

Employee Self-Assessment

These activities allow the employee to identify interests, career aspirations, aptitudes, and abilities. Examples are

▶ **Retirement workshops**   Assists employees in the transition to retirement and to discover nonwork-related interests.

▶ **Career planning workshops**   Provides information on various career fields and a variety of self-assessment exercises.

- ▶ **Self-assessment workbooks**   Allows employees to determine their interests and abilities on their own, without professional assistance.

- ▶ **Computer-based assessment**   Many interactive computer programs are available for self-assessment.

Individual Career Counseling

Many organizations provide one-on-one career counseling. Examples are

- ▶ **Supervisory counseling**   Coaching from immediate supervisor regarding career aspirations and career potential

- ▶ **Mentoring**   Counseling from someone not in the employee's immediate chain of command regarding career goals

- ▶ **Professional career counselors**   In-house or subcontracted specialists that provide career counseling

- ▶ **Executive coaching**   Provided for top-level executives, usually by a consultant, to assist them in improving performance

Internal Labor Market and Job-Matching Programs

These programs are designed to provide employees with information regarding career options within the organization and to place the correct employee in the correct position. Examples are

- ▶ **Career pathing**   Employees are provided with information regarding the series of jobs that employees in their career field typically move through during their careers. This allows employees to better plan and prepare for future promotions.

- ▶ **Job posting and job bidding**   Jobs currently available or expected to be available are advertised internally.

- ▶ **Career resource centers**   Provide a variety of career services, including information on jobs within the organization.

- ▶ **Replacement charting**   Used to identify employees who are currently ready for promotion should a vacancy occur.

- ▶ **Dual career ladders**   The traditional way to move to higher levels of the organization is to move into management. However, many highly talented employees either do not have the appropriate skill sets for management or do not want to leave their technical field. Dual career paths permit employees to choose between two career paths, one technical and one managerial, both leading to relatively senior positions and associated compensation. Figure 4.4 shows an example of a dual career path.

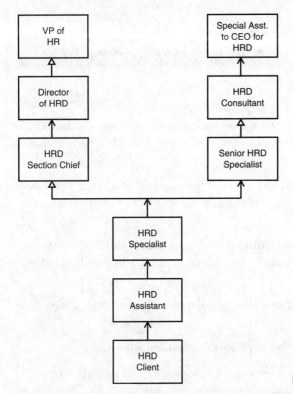

FIGURE 4.4 A dual career path.

Organizational Potential Assessments

These are career development programs designed to assess the individual's potential for assuming greater responsibilities within the organization itself. Examples are

- ▶ **Succession planning**   This is a process used to determine potential candidates for executive-level jobs, although it is increasingly being used for jobs lower in the organization. Employees are assessed on current performance and potential for advancement. High-potential candidates are provided with developmental activities to address gaps in current skill and performance levels.

- ▶ **Assessment centers**   This is a process, not a place, consisting of multiple exercises, tests, and role-plays to determine an individual's potential for advancement.

NOTE

Succession planning and replacement charting are somewhat similar concepts. Replacement charting is the identification of individuals who are currently ready for promotion, whereas succession planning is identification of those who have the potential for promotion at some future date. Replacement charting is short-term and tactical, whereas succession planning is long-term and strategic. Replacement charting tends to be associated with mid- to lower-level jobs, whereas succession planning is associated with senior-level and executive jobs.

EXAM ALERT

Expect a question regarding the differences between succession planning and replacement charting.

Developmental Programs

Developmental programs are designed to provide the opportunity for employees to learn new ideas and develop new skills to prepare them for new challenges and job responsibilities. Examples are

- **Job rotation**   Moving employees from one job or department to another in a planned series. This allows the employee to develop new skills and a broader perspective on the organization and its component parts.

- **Committee, task force and project assignments**   Allows the employee to work on new tasks and develop new skills, particularly interpersonal, team, and decision-making skills.

- **External seminars, conferences, and workshops**   Exposes the employee to new ideas and new ways of doing things.

- **Tuition reimbursement**   Facilitates the acquisition of new knowledge.

- **Job enrichment and job enlargement**   Permits employees to gain new skills or undertake new responsibilities in their current positions.

Special Issues in Career Development

There are many special issues with respect to career development. Careers are not always made up of progressive steps up the hierarchical ladder. People retire, organizations downsize and rightsize, careers reach an apex through no fault of the employee, and women and minorities still have difficulties in reaching top positions. These issues are discussed in the following sections.

Retirement

Career development programs regarding planned retirement were discussed earlier, but what are the implications for organizations and their employees when early retirement options are offered in attempts to reduce the workforce? Employers who want to reduce employment levels through early retirement options must walk a fine line between aggressively promoting these plans to eligible workers and engaging in coercive practices that violate the law. The Older Workers' Benefit Protection Act (1990) prohibits such actions and provides substantial protection for covered workers in these situations. This act was covered in Chapter 5.

Workers facing a major, and sometimes unanticipated, retirement decision require substantial career development support during this period. They often need help in evaluating the financial implications of early retirement. Special counseling might be required to assist these younger workers' transition into early retirement and evaluate nonwork related interests.

Layoffs

In today's volatile environment, it often becomes necessary for organizations to reduce the overall level of operations (downsize) or concentrate on its core competencies (rightsize). In both cases, layoffs frequently result. Many companies provide outplacement services to these employees in an attempt to facilitate new employment. Although some larger organizations might have capabilities to provide these services internally, most organizations obtain the services of outside vendors. Outplacement services typically include help with job searches, interviewing skills, and resume writing. Some outplacement programs provide training assistance to help employees update their work skills.

Plateaued Careers

To be more flexible and adaptive, many organizations have flattened their organizational structure, empowering workers at the lower levels and eliminating layers of middle management. The impact of these flattened hierarchies is that there are fewer promotion opportunities. The career development challenge then becomes how to keep an employee engaged and satisfied when there are few or no future opportunities for promotion and the employee has many years left until retirement. Options in these cases include

- ▸ Job enrichment and job enlargement.
- ▸ Job rotation.
- ▸ Broadbanding to recognize superior performance and build flexibility in the work environment. (Broadbanding is discussed in more detail in Chapter 5.)

Glass Ceilings and Glass Walls

These issues were discussed in Chapter 3, and particular emphasis was given to illegal discrimination and adverse impact. However, they also raise significant career development issues. Organizations can engage in developmental activities that prepare individuals to break through the walls and ceilings. Activities such as mentoring, tuition assistance, and providing developmental assignments are all appropriate.

Leadership Development

Objective:

Gain an Understanding of Leadership Development

This section discusses the concepts of leadership and leadership development. Organizations must be managed so that the day-to-day activities are conducted efficiently. But management is not leadership. Leadership incorporates the concepts of change and adaptation, and is increasingly important to organizational survival and success. It is critical to many organizations that HRD programs be developed to identify, train, and nurture leaders. To understand leadership development, you must understand what leadership is and how it differs from management, what leaders do, different types of leadership, leadership theory, and some special issues affecting the issue of leadership.

Leadership Versus Management

Leadership can be defined as the ability to influence others toward the achievement of goals. Leadership and power are closely aligned concepts, and power is certainly a component of leadership. However, *power* is the ability to influence others to do something that they would not otherwise do and does not include a goal orientation.

Management is the process of working with both people and resources to achieve organizational goals. Management is concerned with the direction of people and the efficient use of resources in day-to-day operations. Management is concerned with doing the thing right, whereas leadership is doing the right thing. Management is concerned with maintaining stability, whereas leadership involves adaptation and change. Management deals with control, whereas leadership deals with inspiration and motivation.

Types of Leadership

Leadership can be thought of as a continuum ranging from transactional leadership to visionary leadership with interim levels of transformational and charismatic leadership (as follows):

Transactional Æ Transformational Æ Charismatic Æ Visionary

Notice that this is a continuum, not a hierarchical arrangement; each type of leadership is critical at certain times if the organization is to grow and survive. For example, visionary and charismatic leadership might be important in the early life cycle of an organization to attract followers and resources. But as the organization grows, it must function efficiently, which requires transactional leadership; it also might need to change and adapt to a dynamic environment, requiring transformational leadership. Keep in mind that there are no distinct start and end points on a continuum that distinguish one type of leadership from another. The four types of leadership are

- ▶ Transactional leadership
- ▶ Transformational leadership
- ▶ Charismatic leadership
- ▶ Visionary leadership

The following subsections describe these leadership types in further detail.

Transactional Leadership

Transactional leadership is essentially management, leading the group toward established organizational goals by providing direction and guidance regarding work requirements. Transactional leaders use contingent reward, management by exception, and other techniques (TQM, for example) to ensure that work is efficiently completed.

Transformational Leadership

Transformational leadership is adaptive leadership. Transformational leaders bring about change and superior performance by consensus building and concern for employee welfare. They pay attention to the needs of their subordinates and followers and attempt to help them develop to their fullest potential. *Transformational leadership* is a broad term that incorporates the concepts of both charismatic and visionary leadership.

Charismatic Leadership

Charisma is an attribution that followers give to leaders. Charismatic leaders are able to articulate a desirable future that appeals to those being led. Charismatic leaders engage in unconventional behavior that brings attention to both the leader and the cause. This type of leader takes risks (personal, career, and financial) to achieve his or her objectives. Charismatic leaders are very perceptive of how to be responsive to the needs and wants of their followers, and in terms of what can be accomplished relative to the constraints of the environment. Charismatic leaders communicate high expectations to their followers and express confidence in their ability to reach high performance levels, the result of which is, in fact, high performance.

Visionary Leadership

Visionary leaders exhibit the characteristics of charismatic leaders, but have taken it to a different plane. They are able to articulate a vision that evokes strong emotions in their followers and appeals to their basic value systems. The vision is drawn from the needs of the individuals and the visionary leader is able to adapt the vision so that it becomes compelling for a wide base of followers. The vision becomes a road map for action and provides a sense of identity for followers.

Leadership Theory

Leadership theory can be grouped into three categories. They are

- ▶ Trait theories
- ▶ Behavioral theories
- ▶ Contingency theories

Trait Theories

Trait theories assume that leadership is the result of personal characteristics and that the leader is born as opposed to being developed. If that were the case, HRD programs designed to develop leaders would be for naught.

Researchers have historically looked for a common set of characteristics, or even one characteristic, that is consistently associated with successful leadership. Traits investigated include intelligence, integrity, self-confidence, conscientiousness, extroversion, charisma, decisiveness, and many others. Although some traits seem to be associated with leadership, research has not yielded any one trait or characteristic that always differentiates leaders from nonleaders. In fact, traits might better predict the emergence of leadership rather than the effectiveness of a leader.

Behavioral Theories

Because researchers were unable to identify specific traits associated with effective leadership, they began inquiries as to whether specific behaviors were associated with effective leadership. Findings based on studies run at both The Ohio State University and the University of Michigan led to the development of the managerial grid.

Ohio State Studies

This research began in the late 1940s. Researchers attempted to identify and catalog leadership behaviors, ending up with two categories that covered most of the leadership behaviors that they observed. They called the two categories *initiating structure* and *consideration*.

Initiating structure behaviors are those that attempt to define roles and formalize processes. Activities such as organizing roles and processes, assigning work tasks, establishing performance standards, and deadlines are all associated with initiating structure.

Consideration behaviors are those that establish a trusting and respectful relationship between the manager and subordinates. Interest in an employee's personal life, treating all employees equally, showing genuine concern for employees' welfare, and being friendly and approachable are examples of consideration behaviors.

Extensive research revealed that those managers rated high in both initiating structure and consideration tended to achieve both high productivity and high job satisfaction in their subordinates. However, there were sufficient exceptions to indicate that other factors in addition to managerial behavior that affect group performance.

University of Michigan Studies

The University of Michigan studies were occurring at the same time as the Ohio State research, had the same research goals, and came up with similar findings. The University of Michigan researchers also came up with two categories of leadership behavior: production-oriented behavior and employee-oriented behavior. Production-oriented behaviors were directed toward accomplishment of the group's work objectives. Employee-oriented behaviors emphasized interpersonal relationships and taking an interest in group members.

The University of Michigan research found that leaders who were employee-oriented in their behaviors achieved higher group productivity and job satisfaction than those who were production-oriented. Again, however, there were sufficient exceptions to indicate that additional factors must be included.

The Managerial Grid

Blake and Mouton developed the managerial grid, which is a 9¥9 matrix (see Figure 4.5) depicting managerial behavior or style with concern for people on the vertical axis and concern for production on the horizontal axis. Based on their research, Blake and Mouton found that 9,9 managers (those high in both concern for productivity and concern for people) were the most effective.

Subsequent research does not substantiate their conclusions. The managerial grid is a useful visual tool to consider managerial leadership style, but does not answer the question of what types of leadership behavior are most effective.

EXAM ALERT

The managerial grid is frequently a question item.

Contingency Theories

The behavioral theories failed to identify behaviors that are effective in all leadership situations. It became clear to researchers that it was the situation itself, the contingency, which was a critical intervening variable between the behaviors and traits of the leader and leader effectiveness. This led to a variety of contingency theories:

▶ Fiedler's Contingency Theory

▶ Leader-Member Exchange Theory

▶ Path-Goal Theory

▶ Hersey and Blanchard's Situational Theory

▶ The Leader-Participation Model

These theories are discussed more fully in the upcoming sections.

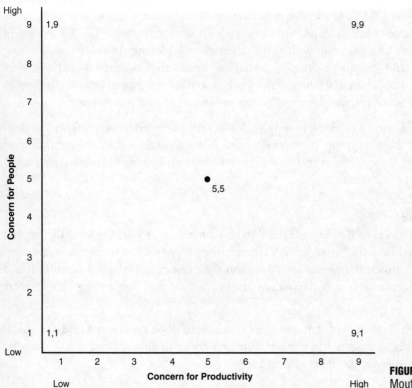

FIGURE 4.5 Blake and Mouton's managerial grid.

Fiedler's Contingency Theory

The first comprehensive leadership model to take contingencies into account was Fiedler's Contingency Theory, developed by Fred Fiedler. The theory proposes that leadership effectiveness is based on a match between the leader's leadership style and the contingencies of the workplace. Through research, Fiedler categorized two styles of leader behavior: task-oriented and relationship-oriented. He defined the situation in terms of three contingencies described here:

- ▶ **Leader-member relations** How much trust and respect the members have in the leader

- ▶ **Task structure** How formalized and structured the work environment and processes are

- ▶ **Position power** The amount of authority the leader has over the group members in terms of hiring, discipline, control over salary, and so on

The leader has maximum control over the leadership situation when the three contingencies are favorable: leader-member relations are good, task structure is high, and position power is strong. When the three contingencies are combined in all possible ways, the result is eight situations ranging from highly favorable to highly unfavorable to the leader. Based on his research, Fiedler concluded that task-oriented leaders produced better results in five of the eight situations, both those that were favorable to the leader and those that were unfavorable to the leader. The relationship-oriented leader produced better results in the three situations that were neither favorable nor unfavorable.

Subsequent research largely supports the theory. However, there are some glaring weaknesses in its capability to predict success. Fiedler considered leadership style to be fixed. If there was a mismatch between style and the situation, one of two things had to happen: either the leader had to be changed to one with the other leadership style or the contingencies had to change to alter the situation. The theory does not recognize that leaders can adjust their leadership style. Fiedler also did not consider that there might be more than two leadership styles.

EXAM ALERT

Expect a question regarding Fiedler's model. Remember that directive leadership was found to be most effective in five of eight possible situations—those in which conditions were most favorable and least favorable for the leader.

Leader-Member Exchange Theory

Leader-member exchange theory is an example of the Pygmalion effect or the self-fulfilling prophecy. The theory proposes that leaders quickly make a decision about a new employee and place that employee in the "in" group or the "out" group. The research is not totally clear as to how that decision is made, but it likely has to do with whether the employee shares common values, perspectives, and personality traits with the leader. The leader treats the "in" group differently, providing greater interaction, better support, and more challenging assignments and assumes that those employees will be highly productive and happy. The result is as expected and supported by research. The "in" group's employees tend to be more productive, have lower turnover and absenteeism, and higher job satisfaction. Employees in the "out" group tend to be less productive, have higher rates of turnover and absenteeism, and lower job satisfaction.

Path-Goal Theory

Path-goal theory is derived from the work of Robert House and essentially states that the leader's job is to provide that which is missing in either the subordinates or the environment so that the group's task and goals can be accomplished. This might include information, direction, or other types of support that clarify the goal and assist in its achievement.

The path-goal theory includes two types of contingency variables. The first deals with the capabilities and motivation of the subordinates. The second contingency variable is the work environment itself in terms of the formality of task structure and the power of the leader. Depending on the status of the two contingencies, a particular type of leadership is indicated. If the leader behaves in the indicated way, goal achievement is facilitated. The theory uses four styles of leadership: directive, participative, achievement-oriented, and supportive. A full discussion of this theory is beyond the scope of this book, but several examples should prove instructive and allow the prospective SPHR to grasp the concept:

▶ Directive leader behavior is indicated when the work environment is ambiguous with unclear rules and/or the subordinates lack motivation, skill, and experience.

▶ Supportive leader behavior is indicated when the work tasks are mundane, repetitive, and unchallenging and/or the subordinates have low job satisfaction and desire affiliation.

Path-goal theory is generally supported by research. Leader behavior that compensates for what is missing either in the work environment or lacking in the subordinates tends to improve group performance and goal achievement.

Hersey and Blanchard's Situational Leadership Theory

Paul Hersey and Ken Blanchard developed a contingency theory of leadership, called the *situational leadership theory*, which is predicated on using the right style of leadership based on the followers' readiness to accomplish a certain task. Readiness has two elements: employee skill or ability, and motivation or willingness. These two elements lead to four possible readiness levels (high skill-high motivation, high skill-low motivation, low skill-low motivation, and low skill-high motivation) that require the four different leadership styles illustrated here:

▶ **Directing**   Leader provides specific instructions and close monitoring when employees have both low skill and low motivation levels.

▶ **Coaching**   Leader provides both specific task guidance and a high level of support when employees have low skill but high motivation.

▶ **Supportive**   Leader provides little task direction but a participative style of support when employees have high skill levels but low motivation.

▶ **Delegating**   Leader turns over decision-making to employees when they have both high skill levels and high motivation.

Situational leadership theory has considerable appeal, however, research does not generally support its validity.

EXAM ALERT

Despite its lack of research support, SHRM/HRCI seem to like the approach. Expect a question regarding situational leadership.

Leader-Participation Model

The leader-participation model was developed by Victor Vroom (who also developed expectancy theory) and Phillip Yetton. It is really a model used to determine how much participation subordinates should have in making decisions. The model takes the leader through an algorithm in which the leader answers a series of question, either yes or no, until reaching the end. The final question leads the leader to one of five alternative styles, indicating how much participation the leader should allow with respect to that particular decision. For example, if the decision is unimportant, time is not an issue, and subordinate commitment is important, participation by the subordinates is indicated. Although the model has received some research validation, it is a bit too cumbersome and time-consuming to be practical.

Special Issues in Leadership

Leadership style can be affected by a great number of factors. Gender differences and cultural appropriateness are discussed next.

Gender Differences

The two genders are more alike than different in terms of leadership style. However, research does indicate that women tend to approach leadership from a more transformational style. That is, they tend to engage in supportive behaviors and consensus building more than men.

Culture

National and ethnic culture influences what type of leadership is appropriate and inappropriate. For example, authoritarian/directive leadership might be preferred in countries and cultures high in power-distance (China and Russia, for example) but not in other countries or cultures. The leader must be familiar with the culture of those being led and adjust to an appropriate leadership style. Furthermore, the leadership theories discussed earlier have been generally developed in North America and might not be generalized to other areas of the world.

Organizational Development

Objective:

Gain an Understanding of Organizational Development

Organizational development (OD) is a strategy and process to improve the effectiveness of an organization through planned programmatic activities and interventions. As opposed to the concepts of training and development, which deal with individuals, OD is concerned with the functioning of the organization as a whole. OD is an adaptive process concerned with the management of planned change based on the dynamics of both the internal (organizational culture) and external environments. Organizational development is based on research in the social sciences and can be traced back to the initial work of Kurt Lewin and others on laboratory training (referred to as *T-groups*). The practice of OD has incorporated the concepts of action research, participative management, quality of work life programs, strategic change, and organizational learning as it has evolved. The sections that follow discuss organizational culture, OD process, various types of OD interventions, and change management.

Organizational Culture

Organizational culture refers to the system of shared values and norms held by organizational members. It is descriptive of the organization much the same as personality is descriptive of the individual, and provides organizational members with guidance as to how to interpret events and behaviors that are organizationally acceptable. Organizational cultures can be strong or weak. In strong cultures, the values and norms are intensely held by organizational members. These types of cultures have a significant impact on the behavior and commitment of organizational members. Just as individual personalities are an aggregation of a number of concepts (openness, agreeableness, extroversion, and so on), so too are organizational cultures. Characteristics associated with organizational cultures are production orientation, people orientation, team orientation, risk taking versus stability orientation, and so forth. Furthermore, organizations can have a shared common culture but many subcultures typically associated with organizational subentities. For example, although the organization might have a strong organizational culture that is widely held, each department (marketing, production, and so on) might have an underlying subculture of its own.

Cultures are created by the founder of the organization and can be modified by subsequent leaders. The founder creates the culture through his or her vision of the organization in terms of values and orientation. The day-to-day decisions and activities of the founder provide a guide to appropriate behavior. These behaviors subsequently become the legends, sagas, symbols, and traditions of the organization, and they often guide member behavior well after the founder is gone. In the beginning, founders tend to hire those people who have similar beliefs and this homogeneity facilitates culture creation.

The culture is sustained by the continued selection of members who fit; that is, persons who already share common values with the organization. These new members are then oriented to the culture through formal and informal socialization processes. Top management models the acceptable cultural behavior, sending strong messages throughout the organization as to what is appropriate and valued.

Culture is critical to an organization's survival and provides a framework of identity for organizational members. The culture differentiates one organization from another and provides important cues for members as to acceptable behavior. The commonly shared values and norms appeal to members and generate organizational commitment and cohesion.

However, culture is not always positive. Strong cultures might actively resist change and could prevent or inhibit the organization from making necessary adaptations. Cultures might also become counterproductive if the shared values and norms no longer contribute to organizational success.

> **EXAM ALERT**
>
> You should expect one or more questions regarding organizational culture. You should be able to define culture, explain the benefits and disadvantages of culture, and how culture is created and sustained.

The OD Process

The OD process in some ways is similar to the HRD process. It involves assessment of organizational needs, development and implementation of appropriate intervention strategies, and evaluation of the effectiveness of the intervention. The OD process is one of planned organizational change and can be described as follows:

▶ **Initial entry**   OD specialists tend to follow a similar protocol whether they are outside consultants or professionals employed by the organization. The first stage involves preliminary inquiry into the nature of problem and potential change methodologies. When that is done, the professional meets with organizational management to discuss the change process and suggests methodologies, resource commitments, and proposed outcomes. An agreement or contract is then negotiated to formalize commitments and responsibilities.

▶ **Research/diagnoses**   In-depth inquiry is made into the problems being experienced by the organization and the need for change. This data is then discussed with organizational members so that they better understand the nature and causes of the problems and the implications for change.

- ▶ **Intervention**   The OD professional and organizational members work together to develop, design, and implement intervention strategies. It is in this stage that the change process is managed.

- ▶ **Evaluation**   The change process is evaluated in terms of outcomes and the information fed back to organizational members. If successful, the changes are institutionalized through appropriate processes and systems (policies, organizational structure, compensation, performance management program, and so on). If the interventions are unsuccessful, the process begins again. Like many processes, OD is circular in design and practice.

Organizational Change

Today's organizations often face a volatile environment that requires them to adapt. The goals of OD are to facilitate the change (as a change agent) in a controlled and planned way and to evaluate the impact and success of the change effort. Some changes are unanticipated and forced on the organization. This is unplanned change and the organization can merely react. Planned change, however, is proactive and managed. Effective organizations monitor changes in the environment, as discussed in Chapter 2, and engage in adaptive strategies. The process of designing and implementing change and strategies for overcoming change are discussed next along with an allied concept, the learning organization.

Designing and Implementing Change

There are several models for managing organizational change. However, the work of Kurt Lewin is the best known. Lewin proposed that planned organizational change follows a three-step process and that change can be initiated through force field analysis. Both of these concepts (the three-step change process and force field analysis) are depicted in Figure 4.6.

Lewin argued that organizational change incorporates three steps:

1. The status quo situation is disturbed by a process called *unfreezing*. Organizations attempt to maintain a homeostatic condition. Unfreezing disturbs the homeostasis by removing the equilibrium of the forces causing instability.

2. After the equilibrium is removed, the organization can be moved to a new, desired state. Lewin called this step *movement*.

3. The new desired state is stabilized through the process of *refreezing*. This is done by reestablishing the equilibrium of forces affecting the organization.

The question not answered in the model itself is how equilibrium is disturbed and then reestablished. For that, Lewin proposed the process of force field analysis. This is illustrated in Figure 4.6 by the restraining and driving forces. As long as those two forces are equal, the organization remains at status quo in an equilibrium state. The process of force field analysis involves determining the major restraining forces and driving forces that are currently affecting the organization and then analyzing which of them can be changed to create an imbalance.

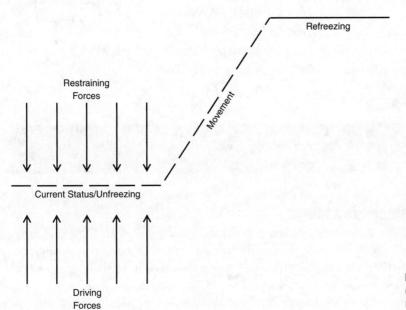

FIGURE 4.6 Lewin's organizational change model.

Table 4.9 is an example of a theoretical force field analysis matrix. There are three ways of creating movement: increasing the driving forces, decreasing the restraining forces, and both increasing the driving forces and decreasing the restraining forces. Both convention and research favor decreasing the resisting forces. Increasing the driving forces tends to bring about substantial increased resistance. In the example that follows, the restraining forces can be reduced using the practices regarding decreasing both organizational and individual resistance to change discussed in the next section. In addition, attempting to raise capital at favorable rates or to encourage union acceptance and participation in the change initiative might result in decreased restraining forces. After the organization is moved to the desired new condition, status quo must again be reestablished. This is again done through force field analysis by readjusting the opposing forces until equilibrium is achieved. Table 4.9 demonstrates a force field analysis.

TABLE 4.9   Force Field Analysis

Driving Forces	Restraining Forces
New federal regulations	Lack of capital
Downturn in economy	Union resistance
Increase in interest rates	Tradition
Stockholder unrest	Culture
New management	Concern for power
Increased competition	Fear of change
Decreased profitability	Organizational structure and policies
Change in technology in the industry	Fear of economic loss

> **EXAM ALERT**
>
> You should be familiar with Lewin's concepts: three-step change process and force field analysis. You should be able to determine likely driving and restraining forces given a scenario.

Overcoming Resistance to Change

Change, particularly cultural change, is difficult. Both the organization as an entity and organizational members are likely to resist change. Individuals resist change because they are comfortable with what they are currently doing. Change brings fear of the unknown and potentially affects their financial and employment security. Organizational resistance often comes through processes built to ensure stability. Formalized policies, procedures, job descriptions, orientation programs, and employee selection criteria are all designed to provide stability and are hard to change. Organizational subentities will resist change if that change is perceived to threaten the status quo; such changes include resource allocation, power relationships, or expertise.

There are a number of models and strategies that can be used to attempt to overcome resistance to change both at the individual and organizational level. These can be categorized into the following types:

▶ **Forcing**   Using power, coercion, cooptation, and/or manipulation to bring about the change. Although this might be the only alternative in certain situations, forcing strategies often result in negative outcomes such as subversive resistance, distrust, and lowered employee morale and organizational commitment.

▶ **Reward**   Resistance can be reduced if the reward for changing is sufficient. The reward costs, however, might be significant.

▶ **Communication**   This is the rational approach and assumes that explaining the need for change and education on the change process will reduce or eliminate resistance.

However, change is often an emotional issue that is not addressed by a rational approach. In addition, communication efforts will be successful only where there is a culture of trust.

- ▶ **Participation**   Assisting in the design and implementation of change often reduces resistance to the change and improves commitment. The challenge here is in the time it takes to develop a change initiative and the fact that the participants might not have sufficient experience or knowledge to make quality decisions.

- ▶ **Counseling**   Dealing with the emotional aspects of change. Employees and groups are provided with assistance to understand change and its psychological impact. However, this could be an involved, lengthy, and expensive process. Organizations might not have the time or resources to proceed with a counseling approach.

No one of the approaches just mentioned is likely to address all issues surrounding resistance to change. Therefore, successfully overcoming resistance typically requires a variety of strategies.

> **EXAM ALERT**
>
> Expect a question on either the causes of resistance to change or the strategies for overcoming that resistance.

Learning Organization

Are there organizations that actively engage in adaptation without intervention? Today, many organizations find themselves in a constant state of change and adaptation. In this case, planned change might not result in the real-time adaptation that is required. What is needed is an organization that is specifically designed to be continually adaptive. The concept of the learning organization is attributed to Peter Senge and originally discussed in his book, *The Fifth Discipline*. A true learning organization is probably more of a theoretical construct than a reality. However, some organizations are moving in that direction. Characteristics that describe a learning organization are

- ▶ Strong member commitment to a vision.

- ▶ Organizational culture that values adaptation, change, and risk-taking and accepts failures as part of the risk of change.

- ▶ Organizational members think in terms of systems and outcomes rather jobs and departments.

- ▶ All members of the organization are environmental scanners.

- ▶ Members feel comfortable in communicating both laterally and vertically.

▶ Members sublimate their personal desires for the good of the organization.

▶ Organizations engage in double-loop learning. Most organizations establish goals and track performance towards those goals, making mid-course corrections as necessary. This is *single-loop learning*. Learning organizations re-evaluate the goal itself at periodic intervals, which often results in new conceptualization of goals and modifications of the organization's methods of operation.

▶ The organizational structure is free of unnecessary boundaries that inhibit internal communication and interaction with the environment.

EXAM ALERT

Strategies to make the organization more adaptable are becoming an increasingly important issue in HRD. Expect a question regarding learning organizations.

OD Interventions

A wide variety of interventions can be used to create change and improve organizational effectiveness. The choice of the proper intervention is based on the nature of the problem observed, the characteristics of the organization, the desired outcome, and the capabilities of those who will be managing the intervention. The major categories of interventions and examples of interventions from each category are listed next and discussed further in the following sections.

▶ Process interventions

▶ Technostructural interventions

▶ Human resource management interventions

▶ Strategic interventions

Process Interventions

Process interventions are designed to improve interpersonal and intergroup working relationships. Examples are

▶ **T-groups**   Also called *sensitivity training*, the purpose of T-groups is to have participants

  ▶ Better understand group dynamics so that they engage in activities that facilitate group effectiveness

  ▶ Better understand how their behavior affects others

  ▶ Better understand and interpret the behavior of others

▶ **Process consultation**   Designed to help individuals and groups improve processes such as decision-making, communication, interpersonal relations, and so on to improve performance

▶ **Conflict resolution**   Assistance in working out conflict situations

▶ **Team building**   A broad range of activities and training designed to improve the effectiveness of teams

Technostructural Interventions

Technostructural interventions are designed to improve the effectiveness of the organization and its processes. Technostructural interventions include design of the organizational structure, employee involvement programs, and design of work processes. Examples are

▶ **Organizational structure**   Design of the organization to increase effectiveness and adaptability. This includes the use of alternative departmentalization, matrix, and organic structures that were extensively discussed in Chapter 2.

▶ **Downsizing and rightsizing**   Resizing the organization and its processes to increase efficiency and effectiveness.

▶ **Process reengineering**   Rethinking and redesign of business processes. Outcomes are frequently large improvements in productivity, elimination of work that does not add value, movement from specialized to generalized jobs, and team-based concepts.

▶ **Quality circles**   Small groups of employees who meet to identify and resolve quality and productivity problems.

▶ **Total quality management**   Based on the work of Deming, Juran, and Crosby. These are processes of continuous improvement, producing products or services designed to meet or exceed customers' expectations. Quality standards are developed and monitored. Statistical process techniques and employee involvement are used to get at and correct the root causes of poor quality.

▶ **Job characteristic model**   The JCM, previously discussed, is used to enrich and enlarge jobs.

▶ **Self-directed work teams**   One of several approaches to integrating the social and technical systems of the workplace. Teams are responsible for making most of the decisions previously made by managers regarding the work environment. Results have generally been increases in both productivity and job satisfaction.

Human Resource Management Interventions

Human resource management interventions are designed to improve organizational effectiveness by managing individual and group performance and providing supportive programs designed to help employees deal with job and home pressures. Examples are

- **Performance management systems** These are discussed extensively in the next section.

- **Incentive compensation systems** Designed to align employee and group behavior and performance with organizational goals.

- **Career management** Designed to prepare employees for future organizational needs.

- **Quality of work-life programs** These programs help employees balance their family and work obligations.

- **Diversity initiatives** Designed to facilitate individual and group adjustment to an increasingly diverse workforce.

- **Wellness and employee assistance programs** Programs designed to improve organizational effectiveness by facilitating physical, mental, and emotional health and assisting employees in dealing with personal problems and stressors.

Strategic Interventions

Strategic interventions are designed to enable the organization to properly position itself in its environment and to institute practices that will enable it to adapt as necessary. Examples are

- **Strategic planning** Interventions that assist the organization in planning its future and properly alignment with the market and environment.

- **Transorganizational strategies** Designed to assist organizations in the planning and implementation of joint ventures, acquisitions, and mergers.

- **Transformational change** Interventions designed to assist organizations when major changes in mission or organizational structure are required because of significant changes in the environment.

- **Culture change** Interventions to facilitate major organizational culture change when the current culture becomes counterproductive to organizational success and survival.

- **Learning organizations** This concept was discussed earlier in this section. Interventions can be designed to facilitate the development of a learning organization.

Performance Management

Objective:
Gain an Understanding of the Performance Management Program

Performance management is the process of linking organizational goals to employee performance. It includes strategic goal setting, development of performance standards, performance appraisal, development and coaching, and discipline and reward; all integrated to achieve organizational goals. Strategic goal setting was discussed in the Chapter 2, discipline in Chapter 6, "Employee and Labor Relations," and rewards and incentive programs in Chapter 5. Coaching and development activities are discussed elsewhere in this chapter. Consequently, the major emphasis in this section will be on the processes of developing performance objectives and performance feedback, including the actual performance appraisal.

Setting Performance Standards

Performance standards are derived from the critical duties of the job found in the job description and are frequently called *performance dimensions*. These dimensions are chosen because they are aligned with organizational goals and values and are critical to successful job performance. After the dimensions are selected, performance standards must be developed that define the expected or acceptable level of performance. The evaluation of the employee's performance level is then based on a comparison of the performance information collected on the employee against the performance standard for the dimension. There are three types of performance information that can be obtained: outcomes, behaviors, and traits.

Outcomes

Outcomes are the most useful of the three types of information because they are generally measurable and can be most easily evaluated against achievement of organizational goals. Quantity and quality of production, achievement of specific goals, customer satisfaction ratings, budget execution, completion of projects, and so on are outcome-related performance information.

Behaviors

Behavior information is the second-most useful type of performance information. It is often difficult to measure the outcomes of specific jobs, particularly if the job duties involve thinking and decision-making as opposed to production. In these cases, it is often behavior information that is available as opposed to outcome information. The rationale behind evaluating behaviors is that certain behaviors are believed to be directly correlated with the achievement of desired outcomes. Examples of behaviors might be timeliness of decisions or actions, sales calls or customer contacts, or the coaching activities engaged in by a manager.

Traits

Traits are constructs such a dependability, commitment, and integrity. They are the least useful and defensible and the most subjective of the three types of performance information. The rationale for using traits is that they are believed to lead to behaviors that are valued by the organization and are further linked to the achievement of desired outcomes.

Performance Appraisals

There are critical decisions to be made regarding the performance appraisal process. First, the organization must decide what it wants to accomplish through the performance appraisal process. It must determine who will do the appraisals and what types of appraisal methods will be used.

Goals of Performance Appraisals

Performance appraisals are used for two distinct purposes: *administrative* and *developmental*. These two purposes are often at odds (referred to as the *paradox of performance appraisal*) and require different types of measures. The two uses of performance appraisals are shown in Table 4.10.

TABLE 4.10   The Two Uses of Performance Appraisals

Developmental	Administrative
Identifying strengths	Pay raises
Identifying career goals	Promotions
Creating career plans	Determining eligibility for and amount of bonuses and awards
Identifying areas for improvement	
Developing individual development plans	Selection for training
Coaching	Selection for projects/teams/task forces
Identifying need for additional work experiences	Placement on layoff/recall lists
Identifying training and educational needs	Discipline
	Termination

Developmental purposes require absolute measures; that is, measures that evaluate the employee's performance against some predefined performance standard. This relationship between the employee's current performance and the performance standard is critical in determining strengths, defining areas for improvement, developing improvement plans, determining realistic career goals, and so on.

Administrative purposes require relative measures. The performance appraisal must provide some relative measure of the individual's performance against others in the same job. This information is critical when making decisions regarding pay raises, promotions, selection for training and developmental projects and programs, determining eligibility for and amount of bonuses and awards, and so on.

The development of an appraisal system that provides both absolute and relative measures is critical if the appraisal system is to fulfill all of its intended functions. As will be discussed in the section on appraisal methods, combinations of approaches are often needed.

NOTE

The paradox of performance appraisal puts the manager in juxtaposed roles: that of evaluator (often adversarial) and that of coach/mentor (a trusting relationship). It also creates a dilemma for the employee. It might not be in the employee's best interest to discuss developmental needs with the manager if that discussion might identify performance deficiencies that could potentially affect managerial ratings on the performance appraisal. To overcome this, some companies have separated the performance management program into two processes: appraisal and development.

Who Does the Appraisal?

It would seem that the obvious answer to the question of who performs the appraisal is the supervisor, but what if the supervisor is biased, has not observed the employee's performance, or does not possess sufficient expertise regarding the employee's job responsibilities to perform an accurate assessment? In today's digitally connected, globalized, and flattened organizations, new options are being explored regarding who actually conducts the evaluations. The following list highlights the options in who does the performance appraisal. Each option will be covered in more depth throughout the following subsections.

▸ Supervisor rates employees

▸ Employee rates manager

▸ Self-rating

▸ Peer-team ratings

▸ Outside ratings

▸ 360° ratings

Supervisor Rates Employees

This is the standard and most used method. Theoretically it should be the supervisor's duty. Generally, it also is the supervisor's responsibility to recommend pay raises, awards, promotions, and other personnel actions based on performance. The advantages and disadvantages of supervisory ratings are shown in Table 4.11.

TABLE 4.11   Advantages and Disadvantages of Supervisory Ratings

Advantages	Disadvantages
Traditional role of manager.	Manager might be biased.
Accepted by employees.	Manager might not observe employee.
Managers are trained to do so.	Manager might not have technical expertise.
Managers often have close contact with employees.	

Employee Rates Manager

Subordinate employees generally have the most intimate knowledge of the managerial skills of their supervisor, and their input into the appraisal process might be important. Generally, employee input is not the sole determinant of the manager's performance appraisal. Advantages and disadvantages are shown in Table 4.12.

TABLE 4.12   Advantages and Disadvantages of Employee Rating Managers

Advantages	Disadvantages
Employees are familiar with manager's skills.	Might not be acceptable to the manager.
Might influence manager to improve.	Employees might consider it "payback time."
Might provide information to higher level management regarding developmental needs of manager.	Employees might not have knowledge of the manager's performance in all aspects of job.

Self-Rating

Self-ratings are often used as input into the performance appraisal process and as a developmental tool. They are rarely used as the final appraisal rating. Advantages and disadvantages are shown in Table 4.13.

TABLE 4.13   Advantages and Disadvantages of Self-Ratings

Advantages	Disadvantages
Person has intimate knowledge of accomplishments.	Employee might not have skill to do so.
Provides a basis for introspection and determination of development needs.	Employee might overrate or underrate themselves.

Peer-Team Ratings

These ratings are often used when the employee works in a team-based environment, has spent substantial time during the rating period working on cross-functional projects or taskforces, or in situations in which the manager cannot closely observe the employee or does not possess technical expertise regarding the employee's job responsibilities. Fellow employees might have the best information with which to prepare an appraisal. Advantages and disadvantages are discussed in Table 4.14.

TABLE 4.14   Advantages and Disadvantages of Peer-Team Ratings

Advantages	Disadvantages
Peers have close contact.	Peers might unfairly give high or low ratings based on nonwork criteria.
Peers may be best able to evaluate performance.	
Useful when manager does not have opportunity to observe employee.	Peers might collude to give everybody high ratings.
	Might have negative impact on teamwork.
Useful when manager does not have technical expertise to evaluate employee.	

Outside Ratings

Input on the appraisal process might be requested from those external to the organization or those in other departments within the organization. This often includes suppliers and both external and internal customers. Advantages and disadvantages are discussed in Table 4.15.

TABLE 4.15   Advantages and Disadvantages of Outside Ratings

Advantages	Disadvantages
Provides external perspective on performance.	Performance observation occurs only in a limited context.
Provides information regarding customer service responsibilities.	
	Expectations of external raters might not be aligned with internal goals.
Identifies what is important to customers, both internal and external.	

360° Ratings

360° appraisals include input from all or many of the sources discussed earlier. This process has gained in popularity over the years and is used by a growing number of organizations. Advantages and disadvantages are shown in Table 4.16.

TABLE 4.16   Advantages and Disadvantages of 360∞ Appraisals

Advantages	Disadvantages
Provides performance feedback from many aspects.	Creates administrative burden of requesting, gathering, and analyzing the input.
Can provide excellent information for developmental purposes.	Raters have various expectations regarding performance, which often leads to high variability in the ratings.

What Appraisal Method to Use?

Appraisal methods fall under three majors headings (*category ranking*, *comparative*, and *narrative*) plus a fourth miscellaneous category that includes methods using a combination of the major methods or special types of appraisals (behavioral scales and MBO). Each will be discussed, along with its advantages and disadvantages, in the sections that follow.

Category Rating Scales

Category rating scales are the simplest and most frequently used appraisal methods and require the rater to merely check the appropriate box or statement that best describes the characteristics or level of performance of the person being evaluated. Category rating scales include *graphic rating scales*, *checklists*, and *forced choice*.

- ▶ **Graphic rating scales** The graphic rating scaled is the most used method, allowing the rater to mark the employee's performance on each dimension based on a continuum. A representative five-point category rating scale is shown below. Each of the points on the scale can either be represented by a number (1, 2, 3, 4 5) as in the example or as a descriptive word or phrase (unacceptable, needs improvement, meets expectations, exceeds expectations, outstanding, for example) or both. The following graph demonstrates an example of a graphic rating scale.

Performance Dimension	1	2	3	4	5
Performance Dimension 1					
Performance Dimension 2					
Performance Dimension 3					
Performance Dimension 4					

- ▶ **Checklists** The rater is provided with a list of narrative statements that describe performance, often a list for each performance dimension. The rater then must choose the statement that best describes the person being appraised.

- ▶ **Forced choice** The forced choice is a variation of the checklist in which the rater is provided a list of narrative statements, some positive and some negative, for each performance dimension. The rater is then forced to choose two of those statements: one that is most like the employee being appraised and one that is least like the employee.

Table 4.17 highlights some advantages and disadvantages found with category rating scales.

TABLE 4.17   Advantages and Disadvantages of Category Rating Scales

Advantages	Disadvantages
Simple and easy to use.	Does not provide relative measures.
Provides absolute measures.	Raters interpret rating categories differently (for example, the meaning of *outstanding*).
	Checklist and forced choice narrative statements might not be directly job related.

Comparative Methods

Comparative methods require the rater to compare performance of one employee with that of others. Comparative methods include *ranking*, *forced distribution*, and *paired comparison*.

▶ **Ranking**   The ranking method requires the rater to evaluate all employees in terms of their performance from the highest performer to the lowest performer. For example, if the manager has 10 subordinates, the ranking method requires that all 10 subordinates be listed in order from the best performer to the worst performer.

▶ **Forced distribution**   In its simplest form, forced distribution merely requires the rater to evaluate the employee's performance in one of several categories. For example, the rater might be required to rate 15% of their employees as outstanding, 80% as meeting expectations, and 5% as needing improvement. The forced distribution method is often used in conjunction with other appraisal methods.

▶ **Paired comparison**   The paired comparison method requires that the rater compare the performance of each employee with the performance of every other employee, determining whether that employee's performance is better or worse. The outcome of the process is a ranking of all employees based on how many times that employee's performance was determined to be better than that of the employee to which the first employee was compared.

Table 4.18 highlights some advantages and disadvantages found with comparative methods.

TABLE 4.18   Advantages and Disadvantages of Comparative Methods

Advantages	Disadvantages
Provides relative measures	Does not provide absolute measures
Makes manager differentiate between employees	Does not indicate the relative difference between those ranked higher and lower
Prevents rater leniency or strictness	
	Might force overrating and underrating of employees

(continues)

TABLE 4.18 *Continued*

Advantages	Disadvantages
	Not based on performance dimensions
	May be time-consuming if there are many employees
	Assumes performance is equally distributed (standard bell curve)

> **NOTE**
>
> Ranking and paired comparison methodologies are more fully described in the discussion of job evaluations in Chapter 5.

Narrative Methods

Narrative methods require the rater to provide a written appraisal of the employee's performance. Narrative methods include the *essay* and *critical incidents*.

▶ **Essay**   The essay method means just what its name implies. The rater writes a short essay that describes the employee's performance.

▶ **Critical incidents**   Critical incident methodology is both an appraisal and performance documentation methodology. The manager keeps a written chronology of the employee's performance, recording incidents of both good performance and substandard performance. As an appraisal, these critical incidents are collected in one document that provides performance feedback to the employee.

Table 4.19 highlights some advantages and disadvantages found with narrative methods.

TABLE 4.19   Advantages and Disadvantages of Narrative Methods

Advantages	Disadvantages
Can provide absolute measures if narrative is written in relation to performance standard for the dimension	Does not provide relative measures
	Might not be job-related if not clearly linked to performance dimensions
Provides in-depth feedback for development purposes	Impact of appraisal might be based more on rater's writing ability than employee's performance

Special Types of Methods

There are many combinations of the three types of appraisal methods, in addition to special types of appraisal systems developed by organizations or consulting firms. Examples of these types of appraisal methods are behaviorally anchored rating scales (BARS) and management by objectives (MBO). Because these types of methods do not share common characteristics, their advantages and disadvantages are discussed separately.

▶ **Behaviorally anchored rating scale (BARS)** BARS is a combination of the graphic rating scale and critical incidents methodology. The development of a BARS appraisal usually involves a committee or taskforce. The committee first produces a large list of critical incidents associated with the particular job. Those incidents are then categorized as being characteristic of performance at one of the levels of performance contained in the graphic rating scale. An appraisal instrument is then developed, which lists examples of critical incidents associated with each level of performance on the graphic rating scale as shown in the following grid. A separate rating scale and a list of critical incidents are developed for each performance dimension. The grid that follows is an example of a BARS rating scale for one performance dimension.

Performance Dimension 1

Rating	Performance Examples
5 (outstanding)	Critical incidents representative of performance at that level
4	Critical incidents representative of performance at that level
3 (satisfactory)	Critical incidents representative of performance at that level
2	Critical incidents representative of performance at that level
1 (unacceptable)	Critical incidents representative of performance at that level

Among the myriad appraisal methods, BARS is considered one of the most valid and defensible. Advantages and disadvantages of BARS are shown in Table 4.20.

TABLE 4.20 Advantages and Disadvantages of BARS

Advantages	Disadvantages
Job related.	Very time-consuming and difficult to develop.
Defensible.	Doesn't provide relative measures unless scores on each performance measure are aggregated, averaged, and ranked against scores given other employees in the job.
Provides good absolute measures.	
Provides good guidelines on which to base the evaluation.	
Increases validity and consistency of appraisal.	Critical incidents are specific to the job and require developing a separate BARS for each job.

▶ **Management by objectives (MBO)** MBO is both a goal-setting and performance appraisal system that is based on goal-setting theory. At each level of the organization, the employee and manager jointly decide on employee performance goals based on the organization's overall goals. Progress toward achievement of the goals is periodically reviewed during the rating period and performance feedback is provided. The employee receives a performance appraisal based on goal achievement at the end of the rating period. MBO appraisals are frequently linked to compensation decisions.

Advantages and disadvantages of MBO are shown in Table 4.21.

TABLE 4.21   Advantages and Disadvantages of MBO

Advantages	Disadvantages
Links individual performance to organizational goals.	Does not provide relative measures.
Builds in periodic performance feedback.	Employee might concentrate on specific goal achievement as opposed to overall performance (suboptimization).
Motivates performance and goal achievement.	
Objectives are specific and measurable.	
Provides absolute measures.	

EXAM ALERT

You can expect one or more exam questions on the various types of performance appraisal methods. You should have a general concept of the advantages and disadvantages of each method.

NOTE

No single appraisal method totally satisfies all the goals of the performance management program. In the end, some combination of one or more methods is required.

Potential Performance Appraisal Errors

Because raters are human beings, no appraisal system, regardless of how well designed it is, can eliminate the human factor (perceptions, likes and dislikes, prejudice, and so forth.). Common potential errors that can affect the accuracy of the appraisal are discussed in the following list:

▸ **Different understanding of the performance dimension**   Vague wording and lack of explanation of the meanings of ratings at each level might lead to inconsistencies among raters. For example, raters might have differing understandings of what the term *acceptable* means.

▸ **Leniency**   Managers rate most employees at the higher end of the scale regardless of actual performance.

▸ **Strictness**   Managers rate most employees at the lower end of the scale regardless of actual performance.

- ▶ **Central tendency** Managers rate most employee at the middle of the scale regardless of actual performance.

- ▶ **Bias** Rater's values or prejudices affect the rating.

- ▶ **Primacy** Greater weight is given to examples of performance that occur early on in the rating period.

- ▶ **Recency** Greater weight is given to examples of performance that occur at the end of the rating period (most recent performance).

- ▶ **Vividness** Greater weight is given to examples of particularly good or particularly bad performance.

- ▶ **Halo effect** Rater scores the employee high on all performance dimensions based on high performance on only one performance dimension.

- ▶ **Horn effect** Opposite of halo effect in that the rater scores the employee low on all performance dimensions based on low performance on only one performance dimension.

- ▶ **Contrast error** Rater rates the employee's performance relative to the performance of other employees when the appraisal requires the performance be rated against the performance standard set for the performance dimension.

- ▶ **Similar to me/different from me** Rater is unduly influenced by a nonperformance characteristic. For example, a rater might give higher ratings to employees who attended the same college as the rater (similar to me) as opposed to those who did not (different from me).

NOTE

Many of the errors in performance appraisal are the same ones that occur in the evaluation of a job interview as discussed in Chapter 3.

EXAM ALERT

Expect a question regarding these errors either in relation to performance appraisal or job interviews.

Documenting the Performance

It is critical for the manager to maintain an accurate and timely record of employee performance. The information is necessary to prepare the performance appraisal and to justify the ratings given during the appraisal interview. Another compelling reason for maintaining this documentation it that it is essential in the defense of the appraisal and any personnel actions or decisions made either partially or wholly on the basis of that appraisal should those issues come before a third party (grievance arbitrator, EEOC, courts, and so on). Performance documentation itself is rather simple. The challenge for managers is to remember to take the time to do it when there are seemingly many more important managerial issues to be deal with. Some suggestions for ensuring that accurate and timely employee performance documentation is maintained are

▶ Maintain a very simple critical incidents log, either manually or on the computer, for each employee. It can consist of merely two columns: one for the date and the second for the critical incident.

▶ Religiously set aside a small amount of time each day to devote to the maintenance of the logs.

▶ Record both positive and negative critical incidents. Many managers tend to record only negative ones.

▶ Merely record the facts as you know them; do not try to evaluate the underlying cause.

▶ In some situations, it might be best to record the critical incident immediately rather than waiting.

▶ Collect any supporting documentation for the entry. The documentation could be examples of work products, production or quality records, communications from customers or other managers, and so on.

The Appraisal Interview

The appraisal interview is the capstone event of the performance evaluation cycle. But, in many ways, it should be the least important part of the process. The process should have started with a clear understanding of the performance dimensions and associated performance standards. Most crucial in the process is continual dialogue and performance feedback with the employee during the cycle, informing the employee of critical incidents, both good and bad, as they are observed. This feedback, combined with accurate and timely documentation during the evaluation period, permits the manager to prepare an accurate and balanced performance appraisal and precludes surprises for the employee at the appraisal interview. Guidelines for conducting the appraisal interview are

▶ Schedule the interview far enough in advance for the employee to prepare for it.

▶ Hold the interview in privacy; neutral territory might be preferable to the manager's office.

▶ Consider giving the employee a draft copy prior to the interview.

▶ Explain the ratings in a nonjudgmental fashion. It is the performance of the employee that is at issue, not the employee's character.

▶ Praise areas of excellence.

▶ Discuss areas of potential improvement and attempt to reach mutual agreement.

▶ Set specific performance goals for the next cycle, including developmental activities and any assistance the manager will give.

Performance Appraisal Best Practices

Listed here are the characteristics of a defensible, equitable, and fair performance appraisal system:

▶ Aligned with organizational goals and organizational culture.

▶ Performance dimensions are clearly job related and performance standards are reasonable.

▶ Performance expectations are clearly communicated to the employees.

▶ Managers are trained in the performance appraisal system and how to fairly and consistently evaluate performance in relation to the standards (referred to as *frame of reference training*).

▶ Employees generally view the system as fair.

▶ Appraisals provide relative measures to make administrative decisions.

▶ Appraisals provide absolute measures to provide developmental feedback.

▶ Feedback is provided throughout the evaluation cycle, not just at the appraisal interview.

▶ There is a process in place for the employee to appeal the appraisal: grievance, discussion with next higher-level manager, and so on.

▶ There are multiple inputs to the appraisal (peers, subordinates, customers, and so forth).

▶ There is at least one higher level of review (for example, immediate manager's supervisor).

▶ Performance appraisals are prepared and shared with the employee in a timely manner.

EXAM ALERT

Expect a question regarding the design of an effective and defensible performance management program. Be familiar with the best practices discussed earlier and be prepared to choose appropriate elements to be included in a good performance management program given a scenario asking you to do so.

NOTE

Personnel decisions and actions based on in part or whole on the performance appraisal must be compliant with the various employment laws discussed at the beginning of this chapter and in other chapters of this book. In particular, the appraisal process must not result in illegal discrimination against protected classes. Adherence to the best practices list given earlier will assist in avoiding problems.

Strategic Considerations for the SPHR

It is the strategic responsibility of the SPHR to design and implement HRD programs that are aligned with the organization's strategic objectives, business strategy, environment, and culture. Selection and implementation of the appropriate HRD activities assists the organization in achieving short-term goals while facilitating change and long-term adaptation, growth, and survival. An emphasis on training might be more appropriate where the environment is relatively constant, the organization pursues goals based on productivity and cost-minimization, and the technology of work is stable. On the other hand, an organizational culture valuing innovation and change, a dynamic environment, a business strategy of being first to the market, rapid fluctuations in market demand, and involvement in a high-tech industry all are indicators of an HRD program slanted towards the development end of the continuum. However, no organization can totally engage in development or training alone. It is up to the SPHR to determine the appropriate mix.

Regardless of the organizational strategy, the SPHR must be able to discern when there is a need to improve overall organizational performance and when development interventions and change initiatives are appropriate. Finally, the SPHR must be able to lead the organization in designing and implementing a performance management system that is aligned with and supports the organization's strategic goals and objectives.

Chapter Summary

This chapter discussed the concepts and practices of human resource development. In fact, many HRD programs require specialized knowledge and training. This chapter provided a broad perspective of HRD and HRD practices and to the strategic importance of HRD programs.

As with all HR programs, HRD activities must be compliant with a variety of laws and regulations. HRD program outcomes often depend on an understanding and effective application of adult learning and motivation.

Two major functions of HRD are management and leadership development and organizational change. Both functions were discussed extensively. Finally, underlying many HRD programs is the organization's performance management system. This system is one way of implementing change, motivating performance, determining developmental needs at the individual, group, and organizational level, and evaluating the impact of HRD program initiatives.

The approach has to be strategic, providing a perspective as to the effect of HRD activities on the organization. Yet strategic understanding is often based on knowledge of operational activities and the underlying concepts, theory, and law that drive them.

Key Terms

- Patent
- Copyright
- Training
- Development
- Human capital
- Andragogy
- Learning styles
- Learning curves
- Bloom's Taxonomy
- Maslow's Hierarchy of Needs
- Theory X and Theory Y
- Herzberg's Two-Factor Theory
- McClelland's Theory of Needs
- Goal-Setting Theory

- Expectancy Theory
- Reinforcement Theory
- Equity Theory
- Job Characteristics Model
- ADDIE
- Needs assessment
- Career
- Career development
- Career management
- Career planning
- Leadership
- Transactional leadership
- Transformational leadership
- Managerial grid

▶ Fiedler's Contingency Theory

▶ Force field analysis

▶ Learning organization

▶ Performance management

▶ Performance dimension

▶ Performance standard

▶ Category rating scales

▶ Comparative methods

▶ Narrative methods

▶ Behaviorally anchored rating scales

▶ Management by objectives

▶ Leniency

▶ Strictness

▶ Central tendency

▶ Bias

▶ Primacy

▶ Vividness

▶ Halo effect

▶ Horn effect

▶ Contrast error

Apply Your Knowledge

Exercises

4.1 Motivation Theory

Without referring back to the text, fill in the blank cells in the following table.

Motivation Theory	Associated Concept
	There are five building blocks of a job that can be manipulated to create various outcomes.
Reinforcement Theory	
Self-Efficacy	
	Specific, challenging goals when accepted and accompanied by feedback are motivating.
	M = E¥I¥V
Theory X	
	Hygiene and motivating factors.
	Employees like to work, are self-motivated, and can bring innovation and creativity to the job.
	Needs are aligned in a hierarchy and lower needs must be substantially satisfied before a higher one becomes a motivator.
	Existence, relationship, and growth needs.
Equity Theory	
	Achievement, power, and affiliation needs.

4.2 Performance Appraisal Methods

Fill in the empty cells in the following table without referring to the text material. In the two columns to the right, indicate whether the appraisal method primarily yields relative or absolute measures of performance.

Appraisal Method	Description	Relative Measures	Absolute Measures
Graphic Rating Scales	Performance dimensions are rated on a continuum.		X
	Goals are set based on discussion between employee and management. Feedback on performance is provided during the year.		
Critical Incidents			
	The performance of each employee is compared against the performance of every other employee.		
	A written narrative is prepared describing the employee's performance.		
Ranking			
	Requires the rater to evaluate the employee's performance in one of several set categories.		
BARS			
	Requires the rater to check the statement that best describes the performance of the employee being evaluated.		
Forced Choice			

Review Questions

1. You are the HR Director for a small city that has no performance management program. The mayor is contemplating going to the city council to propose that the city develop and implement a program that is effective and defensible. The mayor asks you to research best practices and brief her on the characteristics of a good system. How do you respond?

2. The CEO is planning a retreat for the board of directors and wants to center one morning's discussion around Maslow's Hierarchy of Needs Theory and how it applies to the workplace. Specifically, he wants to know what sorts of organizational activities and programs might satisfy needs at the various hierarchical levels. What do you tell him?

3. You are the Director of Human Resource Development for a not-for-profit organization. Your Director of Human Resource Management returns from a conference at which she heard the term *ADDIE* used in reference to training and development. She comes to you and asks you to refresh her memory on what ADDIE means. What do you say?

4. The board of directors of your organization would like a briefing on organizational change. In particular, the chairman indicated that the board would like you to discuss Lewin's three-step model of change. What would you tell them?

5. You are the Director of HRD for a midsize publicly traded corporation. The VP for HR is currently completing his executive MBA and has suddenly become aware of the need to footnote material when writing papers for his courses. He is aware that your shop creates a lot of training materials using copyrighted material and knows there is something called *fair use*. He asks you to brief him on the concept. What can you tell him?

Exam Questions

1. Participants in an HRD program are given a test to measure their knowledge of standard bookkeeping practices prior to beginning a bookkeeping training program and then are given another test at the end of the program to determine current knowledge of bookkeeping. This is an example of what type of experimental design?

   ○ **A.** Post-measure

   ○ **B.** Pre-/post-measure

   ○ **C.** Pre-/post-measure with control group

   ○ **D.** Results

2. Two authors publish a book and register the copyright with the United States Copyright Office. What is the length of that copyright?

   ○ **A.** 70 years after the death of the last surviving author

   ○ **B.** 95 years after the death of the last surviving author

   ○ **C.** 120 years after the death of the last surviving author

   ○ **D.** 70 years after the death of first author to die

3. Bill Smith is a manager of 10 engineers who are evaluated using a graphic rating scale appraisal. The scale runs from 1 to 5, with 1 indicating unsatisfactory and 5 outstanding. Bill rates all the engineers either 4 or 5 on each performance dimension because he does not want to deal with the hassle of having to explain lower ratings to them. This is an example of what type of performance appraisal error?

   ○ **A.** Contrast error

   ○ **B.** Halo effect

   ○ **C.** Central tendency

   ○ **D.** Leniency

4. Which of the following statements is not an assumption of andragogy (adult learning)?

○ **A.** Adults are motivated to reward only by extrinsic rewards.

○ **B.** Adults are self-directed learners.

○ **C.** Adults have knowledge and experience that they bring to the learning experience.

○ **D.** Adults want to learn things that can be applied on the job and that can be used to solve real life problems.

5. Mary seems to learn best when the instruction contains lots of graphs, PowerPoint slides, and videotapes. Mary is most likely a _____.

○ **A.** Visual learner

○ **B.** Auditory learner

○ **C.** Kinesthetic learner

○ **D.** Psychomotor learner

6. Based on Herzberg's Two-Factor Theory, a weekly paycheck is a:

○ **A.** Motivation factor

○ **B.** Fixed-interval reinforcement

○ **C.** Hygiene factor

○ **D.** Fixed-ratio reinforcement

7. The behaviorally anchored rating scale (BARS) is a combination of the _____ and the _____ methods of performance appraisals.

○ **A.** Essay and ranking

○ **B.** Forced distribution and forced choice

○ **C.** Category rating scale and critical incidents

○ **D.** Checklist and MBO

8. Advantages of selecting an off-the-shelf training program, as opposed to developing it internally, include all the following except:

○ **A.** It is usually quicker than developing it internally.

○ **B.** It might be less expensive than developing it internally.

○ **C.** It can provide access to expertise and support.

○ **D.** It is customized to the needs of the organization.

9. Participants in an HRD program are asked to fill out a quick questionnaire at the completion of the program. This is most likely an evaluation tool at which level of evaluation based on Kirkpatrick's model?

- ○ **A.** Reaction
- ○ **B.** Learning
- ○ **C.** Behavior
- ○ **D.** Results

10. A leader engages in behavior that is intended to move the group toward established goals by providing direction and clarifying work requirements. This is an example of _____ leadership.

- ○ **A.** Transformational
- ○ **B.** Charismatic
- ○ **C.** Transactional
- ○ **D.** Visionary

Answers to Exercises

4.1 Motivation Theory

Motivation Theory	Associated Concept
Job Characteristics Model	There are five building blocks of a job that can be manipulated to create various outcomes.
Reinforcement Theory	Behavior is the result of consequences of prior behavior and can be shaped by the application of reinforcement.
Self-Efficacy	Belief by an individual that he/she can accomplish a task.
Goal-Setting Theory	Specific, challenging goals when accepted and accompanied by feedback are motivating.
Expectancy Theory	$M = E \yen I \yen V$
Theory X	Employees dislike work and must be coerced and threatened to achieve organizational goals.
Herzberg's Two-Factor Theory	Hygiene and motivating factors.
Theory Y	Employees like to work, are self-motivated, and can bring innovation and creativity to the job.
Maslow's Hierarchy of Needs	Needs are aligned in a hierarchy and lower needs must be substantially satisfied before a higher one becomes a motivator.
McClelland's Theory of Needs	Existence, relationship, and growth needs.

Motivation Theory	Associated Concept
Equity Theory	Employees compare their ratio of inputs to outcomes with the ratio of inputs to outputs of others. Perceived inequity creates motivation to achieve equity.
ERG	Achievement, power, and affiliation needsn.

4.2 Performance Appraisal Methods

Appraisal Method	Description	Relative Measures	Absolute Measures
Graphic rating scales	Performance dimensions are rated on a continuum.		X
MBO	Goals are set based on discussion between employee and management. Feedback on performance is provided during the year.		X
Critical incidents	The appraisal consists of narrative statements describing examples of performance at, above, and below the performance standard.		X
Paired comparison	The performance of each employee is compared against the performance of every other employee.	X	
Essay	A written narrative is prepared describing the employee's performance.		X
Ranking	All employees are placed in rank order from the best performer to the worst.	X	
Graphic rating scale	Requires the rater to evaluate the employee's performance in one of several set categories.		X
BARS	A combination of graphic rating scale and critical incidents methods		X
Checklist	Requires the rater to check the statement that best describes the performance of the employee being evaluated.		X
Forced choice	Requires the rater to choose the statement that is most characteristic of the employee's performance and the statement that is least characteristic of the performance.		X

Answers to Review Questions

1. You can respond by indicating that best practice indicates a defensible and effective performance management system should include the following:

- ▶ Alignment with organizational goals and organizational culture.

- ▶ Performance dimensions are clearly job related and performance standards are reasonable.

- ▶ Performance expectations are clearly communicated to the employees.

- ▶ Managers are trained in the performance appraisal system and how to fairly and consistently evaluate performance in relation to the standards (referred to as frame of reference training).

- ▶ Employees generally view the system as fair.

- ▶ Appraisals provide relative measures to make administrative decisions.

- ▶ Appraisals provide absolute measures to provide developmental feedback.

- ▶ Feedback is provided throughout the evaluation cycle, not just at the appraisal interview.

- ▶ There is a process in place for the employee to appeal the appraisal: grievance, discussion with next higher-level manager, and so on.

- ▶ There are multiple inputs to the appraisal (peers, subordinates, customers, and so forth).

- ▶ There is at least one higher level of review (for example, immediate manager's supervisor).

- ▶ Performance appraisals are prepared and shared with the employee in a timely manner.

2. You might tell him that current research does not support much of the theory but that it is a good framework in which to look at the concept of human needs and how they may be satisfied in the workplace. Specific programs at the various levels might include:

- ▶ Physiological   Adequate compensation to provide basic living necessities. Facilities in the workplace to accommodate basic needs (restrooms, vending machines, water fountains, cafeterias).

- ▶ Safety   Safe working conditions, job security, OSHA compliance programs, security guards, and so on.

- ▶ Social   Break rooms, social events, work teams, employee organizations, and so forth.

- ▶ Esteem   Performance management programs, employee recognition programs, praise, employee of the month, spot awards, merit pay, and other recognition programs.

- ▶ Self-actualization   Employee development programs, challenging work and assignments, tuition reimbursement, sabbaticals, and so on.

3. You say that ADDIE is an acronym used by HRD professionals to describe the HRD process. ADDIE stands for:

A   Needs **A**ssessment

D   Program **D**esign

D   Program **D**evelopment

I Program **I**mplementation

E Program **E**valuation

4. Lewin proposed a three-step model for change. The first step in the model is *unfreezing*, which disturbs the organization's homeostatic condition and creates an imbalance of forces. The second step is moving the organization to a new, changed condition. Lewin called this step *movement*. The third step is *refreezing*, which involves bringing the organization back into a homeostasis at the new condition by again rebalancing the forces impacting the organization. The board is also likely to want to know how the imbalance is created to move the organization to the new condition. You can explain this by use of Lewin's force field analysis theory. Lewin believed that an organization has a number of forces operating on it. Some of the forces are driving forces for change, whereas others are restraining forces that resist change. In a stable organization, those forces are in balance. To create change, an imbalance of the forces must be brought about. This can be done in three ways: increasing the driving forces, decreasing the restraining forces, or both increasing the driving forces while at the same time decreasing the restraining forces.

5. You can tell him that *fair use* is a statutory provision of the Copyright Act of 1976 that allows limited use of copyrighted material for such purposes as criticism, comment, news reporting, teaching (including multiple copies for classroom use), scholarship, or research. A determination as to whether the material's utilization is fair use is situational and depends on

   ▶ The purpose and character of the use, including whether such use is of a commercial nature or is for nonprofit educational uses

   ▶ The nature of the copyrighted work

   ▶ The amount or substantiality of the portion used in relation to the copyrighted material as a whole

   ▶ The effect of the use on the potential market for or value of the copyrighted works

Answers to Exam Questions

1. The correct answer is **B**. A pre-/post-measure experimental design involves testing both before and after the program event. Post-measure (answer A) is only giving the test after then event. Pre-/post-measure with control group (answer C) involves using two statistically similar groups, testing both groups before and after the program event, but only having one of the groups actually attend the event. Results (answer D) is not an experimental design but one of the four levels of evaluation in Kirkpatrick's model.

2. The correct answer is **A**. In the case of joint authors, the copyright protection continues for 70 years after the death of the last surviving author. The copyright for anonymous authors and authors using pseudonyms (unless registered with the Copyright Office) extends for 95 years from the date of publication (answer B) or 120 years from the date of creation (answer C), whichever is sooner. Answer D is incorrect because the copyright runs from the date of the last surviving author's death, not the first.

3. The correct answer is **D**. Leniency error is evaluating all employees at or near the top of the scale. Contrast error (answer A) is evaluating employee performance against the performance of another employee rather than against the performance standard. The halo effect (answer B) is rating an employee high in all performance dimensions based on a high rating on one dimension. Central tendency (answer C) is evaluating employees in the middle of the range which, in this case, would be a rating of 3.

4. The correct answer is **A**. Adult learners are motivated to learn by both intrinsic and extrinsic rewards, not extrinsic rewards alone. Answers B, C, and D are all assumptions of adult learning theory.

5. The correct answer is **A**. Auditory learners (answer B) prefer to learn through the presentation of aural material such as lectures, discussions, and audiotapes. Kinesthetic learners (answer C) and psychomotor learners (answer D) learn best through simulation and hands-on practice.

6. The correct answer is **C**. Hygiene factors are extrinsic characteristics of the workplace such as compensation and benefits. Motivation factors (answer A) are intrinsic to the individual, such as growth and achievement. A weekly paycheck is a fixed-interval reinforcement (answer B) under reinforcement theory, but the question deals with Herzberg's theory. Fixed-ratio reinforcement (answer D) deals with reinforcement theory, not Herzberg. Even under reinforcement theory, the answer would be wrong because a weekly paycheck is based on time (interval reinforcement) not the number of occurrences of the desired behavior.

7. The correct answer is **C**. BARS combines the category rating scale and critical incident methods of performance appraisal. Answers A, B, and D are incorrect.

8. The correct answer is **D**. Off-the-shelf materials are not customized to the needs of the organization and that might be a disadvantage. Answers A, B, and C are advantages of purchasing an off-the-shelf training program instead of developing it internally.

9. The correct answer is **A**. A questionnaire given at the end of the program is most likely attempting to determine what the participants thought of the program and that is reaction level data. Learning evaluation data (answer B) is normally collected by tests and observation. Behavior evaluation data (answer C) and results evaluation data (answer D) cannot be collected until the participant returns to the job and engages in new types of behavior as a result of the program (behavior) that impacts organizational success (results).

10. The correct answer is **C**. Transactional leadership is essentially management. Transformational leadership (answer B) is adaptive leadership that brings about change. Charismatic leadership (answer C) is an attribution given by followers to a leader based on a number of factors, such as an appealing vision of the future and unconventional leader behavior. Visionary leaders (answer D) are able to articulate a vision that evokes strong emotion, appealing to the basic values of followers.

Suggested Readings and Resources

1. Books

▶ Bateman, T. S. & Snell, S. A. (2004). *Management: The New Competitive Landscape* (6th edition). New York: McGraw-Hill/Irwin.

▶ Cummings, T. G. & Worley, C. G. (2001). *Organizational Development and Change* (7th edition). Cincinnati: South-Western.

▶ Dessler, G. (2005). *Human Resource Management* (10th edition). Upper Saddle River, NJ: Pearson Education.

▶ Hellriegel, D., Slocum, J. W., Jr. & Woodman, R. W. (2001). *Organizational Behavior* (9th edition). Cincinnati: South-Western.

▶ Knowles, M. S. (1970). *The Modern Practice of Adult Education: Adragogy Vs. Pedagogy*. New York: Association Press.

▶ Mager, R. F. (1992). *What Every Manager Should Know About Training*. Belmont, CA: Lake Publishing.

▶ Mathis, R. L. & Jackson, J. H. (2006). *Human Resource Management* (11th edition). Mason, OH: Thomson South-Western.

▶ Mohrman, A. M. Jr., Resnick-West, S. M. & Lawler, E. E. III (1989). *Designing Performance Appraisal Systems: Aligning Appraisals And Organizational Realities*. San Francisco: Jossey-Bass.

▶ Noe, R. A. (2005). *Employee Training and Development*. New York: McGraw-Hill/Irwin.

▶ Northouse, P. G. (2004). *Leadership: Theory and Practice* (3rd edition). Thousand Oaks, CA: Sage Publications.

▶ Robbins, S. P. (2005). *Organizational Behavior* (11th edition). Upper Saddle River, NJ: Pearson Education.

▶ Robinson, D. G. & Robinson, J. C. (1995). *Performance Consulting: Going Beyond Training*. San Francisco: Barrett-Koehler.

▶ Senge, P. M. (1990). *The Fifth Discipline: The Art and Practice of the Learning Organization*. New York: Doubleday/Currency.

▶ Werner, J. M. & DeSimone, R. L. (2006). *Human Resource Development* (4th edition). Mason, OH: Thompson South-Western.

▶ Yorks, L. (2005). *Strategic Human Resource Development*. Mason, OH: Thompson South-Western.

2. Website

▶ http://www.copyright.gov/

CHAPTER FIVE

Compensation and Benefits

Objectives

This chapter helps you to prepare for the SPHR examination by covering the concepts and strategies associated with compensation and benefit programs. This section composes **16%** of the SPHR examination.

Gain a Strategic Understanding of Compensation and Benefits

▶ Understand the purposes of compensation and benefits

▶ Understand the importance of compensation and benefits

▶ Understand how to align compensation and benefit programs with the organizational strategy and culture

Gain an Understanding of Compensation and Benefits Law

▶ Understand the provisions of the multitude of compensation and benefit laws

▶ Understand the implications of these laws in the development and implementation of the compensation and benefit strategies

▶ Understand the interdependencies of the various laws

Gain an Understanding of the Development of a Compensation Structure

▶ Understand the concept and practice of job evaluation

▶ Understand concepts associated with salary surveys

▶ Understand how to integrate the job evaluation and salary survey outcomes into a compensation policy and structure

▶ Understand incentive pay systems

▶ Understand special types of compensation used for various types of employees

Gain an Understanding of Employee Benefit Programs

▶ Understand the types of benefits that are legislatively mandated

▶ Understand the types of benefits that may be voluntarily offered by the employer

▶ Understand flexibility options and the tax implications of the various benefit programs

Outline

Study Strategies

▶ The SPHR should study this chapter with a dual purpose. First, you need to understand the major provisions of the laws that affect compensation programs and the basic processes and building blocks of a compensation system. Second, you should endeavor to understand the interrelatedness of the law and building blocks in developing a comprehensive strategy.

▶ As you proceed through the material:

Stop after each major subsection and try to articulate how that subsection applies to compensation decision-making and how that concept might facilitate organizational goals.

Try to understand how the process of building a compensation structure might relate to your organization and its particular challenges and situation.

Attempt to understand the myriad potential benefits and how they are related to facilitating organizational success in various organizations with different types of external environments and workforce demographics.

Introduction

Compensation and benefits are increasingly important in today's dynamic and competitive environment. Compensation and benefit costs, as a percentage of the total expense of operating the organization, vary from industry to industry. However, these costs can be 80% or more of total organizational expenditures, particularly in the service and knowledge industries.

In the private sector, where markets are increasingly globalized and competitive, effective strategic management of these costs might mean the difference between profit and loss and even determine survivability of the firm. Increasingly, the SPHR responsible for compensation management must look for ways to design compensation systems that more closely align costs with organizational performance.

In the public sector, the effective strategic management of compensation and benefit costs greatly affects the capability of the organization to fulfill its mission and service its constituencies. Rising benefit costs—particularly those of health care—and flat governmental income present significant challenges to the SPHR.

What exactly is meant by the terms *compensation* and *benefits*? What are the goals and purposes of a strategic compensation and benefit system? What are the outcomes of these systems and what are some of the strategic decisions that must be made before a compensation and benefit system can be designed and implemented?

Definition of Compensation and Benefits

Objective:
Gain a Strategic Understanding of Compensation and Benefits

Compensation is a broad term that includes all the extrinsic and intrinsic rewards an employee receives as a result of employment. Benefits are a component of a total compensation system that is composed of

- ▶ **Wages or salary** This is the basic component of compensation consisting of direct financial payments. Employees receive cash payments for either their time (salary or hourly rate) or their production (piecework, commissions, and so on), or a combination of both.

- ▶ **Benefits** These are indirect financial rewards, usually received by virtue of employment with the organization. Examples are health insurance, retirement systems, paid time off, and so forth. The law mandates many benefits, whereas the employer provides others voluntarily.

- ▶ **Nonrecurring or intermittent extrinsic rewards**   These are awards of cash or items having cash value given to the employee based on individual, group, or organizational performance. They are not guaranteed. Examples include merit pay, bonuses, profit sharing, gainsharing, sales promotion incentives, and the like.

- ▶ **Intrinsic rewards**   These are dividends that have no financial value but contribute to the total compensation an employee receives from employment. Examples are praise, pride in belonging to the organization, pleasant working conditions, professional growth and challenge, and so on.

EXAM ALERT

Expect a question regarding the components that make up total compensation.

NOTE

For the remainder of this chapter, the term *compensation* will be used to include all the components in the preceding list.

Goals and Purposes of Compensation

The goals and purposes of compensation are to attract, retain, and motivate employees to achieve organizational goals in a cost-effective manner. The SPHR must strategically design a compensation system that achieves each of these distinct elements of the goals and purposes in alignment with the strategic plans, business strategy, and organizational culture. In doing so, compensation decision makers attempt to achieve three types of equity:

- ▶ External
- ▶ Internal
- ▶ Individual

Equity

Recall from the discussion of equity theory in Chapter 4, "Human Resource Development," that employees will compare their perception of the ratio of their outcomes (in this case, compensation) and inputs (experience, education, work quality, and quantity) to the ratio of outcomes and inputs of others. Perceptions of inequality can lead to negative behaviors such as poor quality work, job and organizational dissatisfaction, and even leaving the organization. All of these potential behaviors directly relate to the purposes and goals of compensation: to attract, retain, and motivate employees. Consequently, compensation systems must be designed with equity in mind. Furthermore, as discussed later in this chapter, different organizational strategies dictate a differential emphasis on the three types of equity.

External Equity

External equity refers to the employees' perception of the fairness of their compensation in relationship to compensation available in the external labor market. External equity is particularly important in attracting individuals to the organization. The compensation system must offer attractive compensation at its portals of entry. *Portals of entry* are those levels at which the organization typically hires individuals from the external labor market. If an organization normally hires employees at only the bottom or entry level positions and then promotes from within, external equity is particularly important at that level. However, if the organization elects to buy expertise from the external market rather than to develop its own and promote accordingly, external equity will be critical at all levels of the compensation schedule.

External equity is created by the process of surveying the external labor market(s) from which the employer recruits.

Internal Equity

Internal equity refers to the employees' perception of the fairness of their compensation in relationship to compensation available to other positions within the organization. Internal equity can be critical to employee retention but is less related to attracting employees to the organization. In large organizations, jobs tend to become specialized to the organization. This often makes it difficult for the employee to compare the job and associated compensation with similar jobs in the external world. Therefore, the important comparison and, hence, the important equity, is internal.

Job evaluation is the process used to create internal equity.

Individual Equity

Individual equity refers to the employees' perception of the fairness of their compensation in relationship to other persons in the same pay scale. The comparison in this case is the relative positioning of the employee's pay rate on the range of rates available for the job. This obviously is not an issue when only one rate is available, as is often the case in a manufacturing environment.

EXAM ALERT

You should be able to define external and internal equity and the process of achieving them. You are less likely to get a question regarding individual equity.

You should be able to relate the concepts of compensation equity to equity theory.

Compensation and Benefits Law

Objective:

Gain an Understanding of Compensation and Benefits Law

The following sections discuss the key compensation and benefits laws and regulations that you should understand for the exam. Specifically, the following are discussed:

- ▶ Workers' Compensation (1911+)

- ▶ Davis-Bacon Act (1931)

- ▶ Copeland Act (1934)

- ▶ Social Security Act (1935)

- ▶ Walsh-Healy Public Contacts Act (1936)

- ▶ Fair Labor Standards Act (1938)

- ▶ Portal-to-Portal Act (1947)

- ▶ Equal Pay Act (1963)

- ▶ Civil Rights Act (1964)

- ▶ McNamara-O'Hara Service Contract Act (1965)

- ▶ Age Discrimination in Employment Act (1967)

- ▶ Employee Retirement Income Security Act (1974)

- ▶ Revenue Act (1978)

- ▶ Consolidated Omnibus Budget Reconciliation Act (1985)

- ▶ Civil Rights Act (1991)

- ▶ Family and Medical Leave Act (1993)

- ▶ Uniformed Services Employment and Reemployment Act (1994)

- ▶ Health Insurance Portability and Accountability Act (1996)

- ▶ Miscellaneous Laws and Regulations Impacting Compensation

Workers' Compensation (1911+)

The first workers' compensation laws were passed by the states of Wisconsin, Washington, and Kansas in 1911. Other states plus Washington, D.C., Puerto Rico, and the Virgin Islands followed suit. These are state laws that provide protection for employees in case of job-related injury or illness. Workers' compensation is covered extensively in Chapter 7, "Occupational Health, Safety, and Security."

Davis-Bacon Act (1931)

The act requires employers with federal construction contracts valued at more than $2,000 to pay prevailing wage rates and benefits (or equivalent increases to the basic wage rate) to certain workers. Prevailing rate determinations are made by the Department of Labor (*DOL*).

Copeland Act (1934)

The act is often referred to as the "anti-kickback act" and prohibits contractors from requiring employees to pay back a portion of their wages to the firm as a condition of employment when working on federally funded projects. It was passed in response to actions of certain contractors in reaction to the Davis-Bacon Act.

Social Security Act (1935)

The act provides a broad array of income continuation protection for most workers in the United States as well as hospital and medical insurance. It is funded by a tax on wages with both the employer and employee paying 6.2% for Social Security and 1.45% for Medicare. Wages of more than $90,000 are not currently taxed for Social Security but the Medicare tax is uncapped. Self-employed individuals pay a self-employment tax that is equivalent to both the employer and employee portions of the tax. Taxes are collected by the Internal Revenue Service and transmitted to the Social Security Administration (*SSA*). Major provisions of the act are

- ▶ Retirement benefits for covered employees

- ▶ Disability benefits for covered employees who become severely disabled

- ▶ Survivor benefits for the family of a covered employee

- ▶ Health insurance (Medicare)

- ▶ Benefits for the indigent (SSI [*Supplemental Security Income*] and Medicaid)

- ▶ Unemployment insurance

NOTE

The Social Security Trust Fund has a large unfunded liability. The SPHR should be alert for legislative action in this area.

Walsh-Healy Public Contacts Act (1936)

The act essentially extended the Davis-Bacon Act provisions to other types of contracts in excess of $10,000 for providing equipment, machines, and supplies to the federal government.

Fair Labor Standards Act (1938)

The act is commonly referred to as *FLSA* and was passed to assist in recovery from the Great Depression. It is the major compensation legislative act in the United States. It covers most private and public employers and is administered and enforced by the Wage and Hour Division of the Department of Labor. The act provides for a minimum wage, overtime, restriction on employment of workers less than 18 years of age, maintenance of compensation related records, and equal pay. In addition there are penalties for noncompliance. These provisions are discussed in the sections that follow.

Minimum Wage

The current minimum wage is $5.15 per hour for most workers. There are exceptions to the minimum wage for certain training programs, for exempt employees, and for employees who receive tips. Tipped employees must be paid $2.13 per hour and their total compensation including reported tips must equal the minimum wage. If not, the employer must make up the difference. The definition of exempt and non-exempt employees has recently changed and is discussed in the following subsection.

> **NOTE**
>
> Some states and/or local governments have passed higher minimum wage or living wage laws.

Nonexempt and Exempt Employees

Nonexempt employees are covered by the minimum wage and overtime provisions of FLSA. Exempt employees are not covered. The issue of which employees are exempt and which are not has historically been problematic, with employers obviously using a very broad definition of exemption to preclude having to comply with FLSA provisions—particularly the overtime provision. To be exempt under FLSA, employees must meet all parts of a three-part test: They must be paid on a salary basis, the salary must exceed a prescribed weekly amount, and their primary duties must be in certain categories. Exemptions are described in the following list:

▶ Exempt employees must be paid on a salary basis.

▶ The salary of exempt employees must be at least $455 per week. However, certain computer personnel paid on an hourly basis meet this test if their hourly rate is at least $27.63 per hour.

▶ Exempt employees must be engaged in exempt duties as their primary function. Categories of exempt duties are

Executive employees primarily engaged in the management of a firm or major component of the firm.

Administrative employees primarily engaged in nonmanual tasks related to management or operations of a firm.

Learned professionals engaged in work that is primarily intellectual in nature (engineers, accountants, scientists, and so on) and that requires either specialized academic degrees or a combination of education and specialized experience.

Creative professionals engaging in work requiring innovation or creativity (writers, artists, graphic designers, and so forth).

Computer employees (computer programmers, analysts, and other skilled computer positions).

Outside sales employees engaged in sales normally away from the employer's place of business. These employees are often compensated on a commission basis and are not subject to the FLSA salary test.

Highly compensated employees making more than $100,000 per year who perform at least one executive, administrative, or professional task.

NOTE

The employer can destroy the exemption from minimum wage and overtime if it takes certain types of actions. The complexity of this issue is beyond the scope of the discussion but the SPHR should be aware that certain types of deductions from pay are not permitted. Examples might include suspensions for minor infractions and deductions for short absences.

Overtime

Nonexempt employees must be paid time and one-half for any hours worked beyond 40 in any workweek, which is defined as a fixed period of 168 consecutive hours. The employer defines and sets the workweek. In computing overtime, the employer must include not only the basic rate of pay but also certain other nondiscretionary compensation items such as commissions, shift differentials, and production bonuses. Overtime is paid only for work time. Therefore, compensated paid time off (holiday, sick, vacation, and so on) is not included for the purposes of determining eligibility for overtime. The Portal-to-Portal Act defines time worked.

> **NOTE**
>
> State and local laws might require payment of overtime for any work of more than eight hours in a day. Federal employees are paid overtime for any work of more than eight hours in a day unless covered by some sort of alternative work schedule.

> **NOTE**
>
> Some occupations are exempt from overtime but not minimum wage. Examples include certain motor carrier employees, certain airline employees, and certain agricultural employees.

Compensatory Time

Congress has frequently attempted to pass legislation dealing with compensatory time for FLSA nonexempt employees. Compensatory time is defined as paid time off from work in lieu of cash compensation for overtime hours worked and is frequently referred to as *comp time*. Absent new legislation, compensatory time is, in general, permissible only in the public sector. There, employees can elect to receive additional time off from work in lieu of compensation for overtime hours. The reimbursement rate is one and one-half compensatory hours for each hour worked beyond forty in a workweek. There are limits to the number of hours of compensatory time that can be accrued.

> **CAUTION**
>
> Keep alert for federal legislative action in this area.

Child Labor

FLSA regulates the employment of workers under the age of eighteen. Restrictions differ depending on the age of the worker and are summarized in the following list:

- ▶ **Children under 14**   Children 14 and under may, within limits, be employed in agricultural work when school is not in session if the work is nonhazardous. Parents of 12- and 13-year-olds must give written permission. Children of 10 and 11 may work on a family farm and on other farms for up to eight weeks during a harvest, but they must get a waiver from the Department of Labor.

  There are limited exceptions in which a 14-year-old may be employed in nonagricultural work. Examples are acting, babysitting, and delivering newspapers.

- ▶ **Children 14 and 15**   Children of 14 and 15 are prohibited from working in a long list of jobs that could be hazardous (manufacturing, construction, using power tools, and so on). They are permitted to work in nonhazardous agricultural jobs and in service types of operations, such as retail stores, gas stations, and restaurants. There are limits to the number of hours and the time of the day they can work depending on whether or not school is in session.

▶ **Children 16 and 17**   There is a long list of occupations that the DOL has found to be hazardous or potentially detrimental to the health of children under 18. Children under eighteen may not be employed in any of these occupations. Examples include logging, excavation, meatpacking, mining, operating a wide range of power equipment, driving large trucks, and demolition. Otherwise, there is no FLSA limitation on the number of hours or time of day that they can work. Children under 17 cannot drive on public highways while working; however, 17-year-olds may drive light cars and trucks under limited conditions as part of their job assignments.

> **NOTE**
>
> State and local laws may place additional restrictions and employer obligations when employing persons younger than 18.

Record Keeping

The law requires that employers keep the following records on all employees. Generally employers are required to keep this information for three years, which corresponds with the statute of limitations regarding complaints under the act.

▶ Employee's full name and address

▶ Employee's identifying number used in the payroll system

▶ Employee's birth date if under the age of 19

▶ Employee's sex and occupation in which employed

▶ When the employee's workweek begins (day and time of day)

▶ Hours worked per day and total hours worked per week

▶ Basis on which the employee is paid (piece work, hourly, salary, and so on)

▶ Hourly rate

▶ Total earnings not including overtime

▶ Overtime payments

▶ Total wages including overtime

▶ Other additions or deductions from wages

▶ Date of payment and period covered

Equal Pay Act

The Equal Pay Act (1963) is an amendment to FLSA and prohibits discrimination in compensation matters based on sex. Its provisions are covered separately later in the chapter.

Penalties for Noncompliance

FLSA authorizes the Wage and Hour Division of the Department of Labor to conduct investigations regarding compliance with the act. The act prohibits employers from discriminating against employees for filing a complaint or testifying in a proceeding.

Employers who do not comply could be liable to the affected employee for

▶ The amount of unpaid minimum wages or overtime

▶ Additional damages equal to the unpaid wages and overtime

▶ Court costs and attorney's fees

Additional penalties may be assessed against not only the employer but also individually against the official who was responsible for making the decisions that resulted in noncompliance. These can range from civil fines up to and including criminal fines and imprisonment.

EXAM ALERT

You should expect one or more question regarding FLSA. In particular, you are likely to get a question regarding the new guidance on exempt and nonexempt employees.

Portal-to-Portal Act (1947)

The Portal-to-Portal Act amended FLSA. It, along with voluminous associated case law, defines what are hours worked (hours subject to compensation and used in determination for eligibility of overtime). Although each situation is different, some general guidelines are as follows:

▶ Time spent at the request of the employer or for the benefit of the employer is generally hours worked. This might include preparatory time before work or cleanup time after work.

▶ Break periods, including meal periods, of more than 20 minutes are not normally considered hours worked.

▶ Commuting time is not normally hours worked.

▶ On-call time might be hours worked if there are substantial restrictions on the employee.

▶ Travel time during work hours is compensable.

▶ Employer directed travel time during nonworkdays might be compensable if that time occurs during the hours that the employee would work on a workday. For example: The employee is directed to travel to a training class beginning on Monday morning and, to get there on time, takes a flight on Sunday from 3:00 to 5:00 p.m. If the employee's normal work hours are Monday through Friday from 9:00 a.m. to 5:00 p.m., the two hours spent traveling on Sunday are work hours.

> **NOTE**
>
> Work that is "suffered and permitted" is hours worked regardless of whether the employer expressly requested the employee to work. For example, if a nonexempt employee tells the employer that he or she is staying a bit late to finish up some task voluntarily, that time is compensable. If the employer knew or should have known that the employee was working, the work is compensable.

Equal Pay Act (1963)

The Equal Pay Act amended FLSA. The act prohibits paying lower wages to one sex than the other for jobs that are similar in terms of

▶ Skill

▶ Effort

▶ Responsibility

▶ Working conditions

Differentials in compensation are allowed under the following circumstances:

▶ Seniority systems

▶ Merit systems

▶ System based on quantity or quality of production

▶ Any other factors other than sex

The act only covers pay, not benefits. However, discrimination in benefits is covered under Title VII of the Civil Rights Act of 1964. Enforcement of the act falls under the responsibilities of the Equal Employment Opportunity Commission (EEOC). Employees filing claims under that act can be awarded back pay for up to two years prior to the date of the complaint. In egregious situations, where the employer willfully violated the act, the employee can be awarded up to double the amount of back pay due for up to three years prior to the date of filing the complaint.

Civil Rights Act (1964)

Title VII of the Civil Rights Act prohibits discrimination against an individual with respect to compensation based on race, color, religion, sex, or national origin. The act is extensively discussed in Chapter 3, "Workforce Planning and Employment," earlier in this book.

McNamara-O'Hara Service Contract Act (1965)

The act requires that contractors providing services with costs in excess of $2,500 to the federal government pay the prevailing rate. It also requires that these contractors provide benefits equivalent to the prevailing benefits in the geographic area and to ensure a safe and healthy working environment.

> **NOTE**
>
> Taken together, the Davis-Bacon, Walsh-Healy, and McNamara-O'Hara acts require the payment of prevailing rates and prevailing benefits (or a cash equivalent) on most federal contracts. The Department of Labor determines what these rates are but they approximate rates negotiated under union contracts in the area. This can cause a potential issue, particularly under Davis-Bacon, where the employer transfers employees from one project to another (some of which are federal contracts and some of which are not) and pays different wages for essentially the same work.

Age Discrimination in Employment Act (1967)

Commonly referred to as *ADEA*, the act was discussed extensively in Chapter 3. It prohibits illegal discrimination in compensation based on age.

Employee Retirement Income Security Act (1974)

Commonly referred to as *ERISA*, the act was passed to protect employees against abuses in the administration of benefit plans. ERISA is an extremely comprehensive and complex law that regulates most private sector pension plans and employee benefit plans (health insurance, life insurance, disability, severance, and so on) if those plans require ongoing administration by the employer. The determination of which plans are covered and which are not requires the assistance of an expert in this area of the law. The act does not require employers to provide benefits but, if they do, many of the plans come under the provisions of ERISA. Plans that meet the requirements of ERISA and of the Internal Revenue Code are considered *qualified* plans and are tax deductible by the employer. Contributions to qualified plans also may accumulate tax-free. Major provisions of the act are

▶ It is administered and enforced by the DOL, whereas the IRS enforces tax aspects.

▶ Prohibits discrimination within plans in favor of highly paid employees.

▶ Requires employers to exercise fiduciary responsibility in the management of plans based on the "prudent person rule" and provides penalties for the employer's violation of its fiduciary responsibilities.

▶ Created the Pension Benefit Guaranty Corporation (*PBGC*) that insures benefits under defined benefit pension plans. Employers having these plans are required to pay a per-participant insurance premium to the PBGC. In the case of plan termination or insolvency, the PBGC takes over the pension plan and pays out retiree benefits, although those benefits might not be equal to those provided under the original plan.

▶ Requires employers to provide certain information to participants in plans, called a *Summary Plan Description (SPD)*, and advise participants of any major modifications to the plan.

▶ Establishes minimum standards for employee eligibility and vesting in retirement plans. Employees at least 21 years of age with a minimum of one year of employment with the firm must be eligible for the employer's retirement plan. *Vesting* is defined as the process by which the employee becomes entitled to nonforfeitable benefits they have accrued under a retirement plan and to the employer contributions to that plan, if any. Vesting can occur in one of two ways depending on the type of plan and the option that the employer selects. *Cliff vesting* occurs when the employee becomes 100% vested in benefits after a set number of years (five years of service, for example), whereas *graded vesting* is incremental. An example of graded vesting is 20% vested after three years of service under the plan, 40% after four, 60% vested after five, 80% after six, and full vesting after seven. Vesting schedules are dependent on whether the plan is defined benefit or defined contribution. Different vesting regulations apply to the employer matching contributions to a defined contribution plan as opposed to non-matching contributions. Defined benefit plans must vest quicker if the majority of benefits go to "key" employees than if they do not. Employees are always fully vested in the funds that they contribute to a retirement system.

NOTE

Benefits payable by PBGC are limited. As major corporations have declared bankruptcy or threatened to declare bankruptcy, their defined benefit retirement plans often become the obligation of PBGC. Maximum per-person benefits are indexed and limited to approximately $45,000 dollars per year. Several major airlines have threatened bankruptcy. For airline pilots, the available maximum yearly benefit is even less because they must retire by law at age 60 and that is considered an early retirement under PBGC rules, which reduces the pension amount.

Revenue Act (1978)

The act added two new sections to the Internal Revenue Code that are pertinent to compensation. Section 125 allows employees to pay for certain benefits with before tax dollars. Section 401(k) allows employees to make tax deferred contributions to a retirement savings account.

Consolidated Omnibus Budget Reconciliation Act (1985)

Better known as *COBRA*, the act provides for continuation of employer health coverage in certain conditions. It is technically an amendment to ERISA. COBRA does not require that an employer provide health insurance, but requires certain actions if it does. It covers employers that have twenty or more employees and provide a group health plan. Major provisions of the act are

- Jointly enforced by the DOL and IRS.

- Requires that group health insurance remain available to a former employer or covered spouse or dependent for certain qualifying events:

  Qualifying events for the employee

  Employee quits or is terminated for reasons other than gross misconduct.

  Reduction of work hours makes the employee ineligible for group health insurance.

  Qualifying events for spouse or dependents

  Death of employee.

  Spouse is divorced or legally separated from employee.

  Dependent child ceases to be eligible under the regular health insurance plan.

  Duration of continuation of coverage

  Termination or reduction in hours: 18 months.

  If the employee is disabled at the time of loss of coverage: 29 months.

  Death, divorce, separation, or dependent child loses eligibility: 36 months.

- During the continuation of coverage period, the employee is required to pay both the employer and employee portions of the premium plus a 2% surcharge for administration.

- The employer must provide notification of the availability of continuation of coverage for qualifying events. These notification requirements were significantly changed in 2004 and require a general notice within 90 days of becoming covered under a health plan subject to COBRA and an election notice that must be provided to the employee within 14 days of receipt of notification that a qualifying event has occurred. It is the employee, spouse, or dependent's responsibility to notify the employer that a qualifying event has taken place, but the employer must have procedures in place for doing so.

- The employer may terminate coverage if the employee fails to pay the premiums in a timely manner.

> **NOTE**
>
> Some states have health insurance continuation laws that expand the employee's rights and benefits.

> **EXAM ALERT**
>
> Expect a question regarding employer obligations under COBRA.

Civil Rights Act (1991)

The act provides for compensatory and punitive damages for illegal discrimination, including discriminatory compensation practices. This act is more fully discussed in Chapter 3, earlier in this book.

Family and Medical Leave Act (1993)

Generally referred to as *FMLA*, the act provides for up to 12 weeks of unpaid leave each 12 months for the birth or adoption of a child, to care for an immediate family member experiencing a serious health condition and/or for recuperation of the employee from a serious health condition. The DOL is the responsible agency for administering the act. Important provisions of the act are

▶ Covers public and private employers that have 50 or more employees within a 75-mile radius during 20 or more weeks during the current or previous year.

▶ Employees are eligible if they have worked for the organization for a total of 12 months (does not have to be continuous employment) and have worked for at least 1,250 hours during the year before the beginning of FMLA leave.

▶ Leave to recuperate from a serious health condition or to care for a spouse (relationship must be legally recognized by the state), child (under 18 or disabled if over 18, adopted, foster, or step-children), or parent (but not parents-in-law) can be taken intermittently, whereas parental leave must be taken consecutively. If both the husband and wife work for the same firm, parental leave and leave to take care of family members is limited to a total of 12 weeks for both employees and can be divided any way they choose.

▶ Employees must give a 30-day notice of intent to take FMLA leave if the leave can be reasonably anticipated.

▶ Employees must be returned to the same or similar position upon return from the leave. An employee is not entitled to return to a position if the employee would have been terminated or laid off during the period in which he or she was on FMLA leave.

Additionally, an employer, under certain conditions, might not be required to return highly compensated employees—that is, salaried employees who are among the highest-paid 10% of all employees within a 75-mile radius—to their regular positions.

▶ Benefits and seniority must continue to accrue during the FMLA leave as if the employee were actually working.

▶ Employers may require the employee to take paid leave (sick, annual, personal) simultaneously with FMLA leave. Workers' compensation and disability benefits may also be used simultaneously. (See Chapter 6 for additional discussion of the issue of FMLA and workers' compensation.)

▶ The employer may require medical documentation that a serious health condition exists for either the employee or a family member, and may require documentation that a covered family relationship exists if the leave is requested to care for a family member. The employer can request a second opinion as to whether a serious medical condition exists. If the second opinion differs from the medical documentation provided by the employee, a third opinion can be requested from a mutually acceptable medical practitioner and that opinion becomes final and binding. The employer must pay for the second and third opinions.

▶ The employer may not retaliate against the employee for exercising any rights under the act.

▶ It is the responsibility of the employer to notify the employee that the absence is being taken as FMLA leave, generally within two business days. The purpose of the notification is to make sure that the employee clearly knows that he/she is using FMLA leave, often simultaneously with other available paid leave. The employee cannot use up paid leave and then request an additional 12 weeks of unpaid FMLA leave.

NOTE

FMLA is a rather complex law and an in-depth discussion is beyond the scope of this chapter. Defining *serious health condition* and counting the 12-month period during which the leave may be taken are issues frequently involved in judicial interpretation. In addition, individual states might have their own family and medical leave laws that provide additional benefits. This is an active legislative issue in many states. FMLA continues to be a controversial law and legislative changes are frequently proposed.

EXAM ALERT

You should be familiar with employer obligations in this area because they are almost certain to be the subject of one or more test questions.

Uniformed Services Employment and Reemployment Rights Act (1994)

Known as *USERRA*, this act prohibits employment discrimination based on military service, providing a broad array of protections including rights to employment and benefits. The act covers all employers and provides protections for members of all uniformed services, including the military, National Guard units, and the Public Health Service, but not those who are discharged under other than honorable conditions. It is administered by the DOL. Major provisions of the act are

▶ Requires the granting of military leave up to a cumulative amount of five years with certain exceptions to the cumulative total amount that include, among others, active duty for war.

▶ Prohibits discrimination in employment decisions based on the employee's military service or potential military service. The employer may not fail to hire, terminate, or fail to provide any benefit the employee would be entitled to if that decision is based on military service or the possibility of military service.

▶ Requires the posting of a notice advising employees of their rights under the act.

▶ Requires re-employment to a position that the employee would normally have obtained had military service not occurred. The employee must apply for re-employment within certain time periods depending on the length of time the employee was away performing military service.

▶ Employers are required to provide reasonable accommodation to employees who become disabled during their military duty.

▶ Reemployed employees are entitled to benefits that would have accrued had they been continuously employed. This includes seniority, pay raises that occurred during their duty time, and retirement benefits. The employees must be allowed to make up contributions to defined contribution plans and the employer must make required payments, if any.

▶ Employees are entitled to continue health insurance through the employer's plan for a period up to two years, essentially under COBRA provisions, even if they are eligible for military health insurance.

EXAM ALERT

USERRA is a relatively new act that many employers do not understand well. Expect a question regarding employer obligations under the act.

Health Insurance Portability and Accountability Act (1996)

The act, generally referred to as *HIPAA*, restricts the ability of health plans and employers to deny or limit health insurance coverage for pre-existing conditions and protects the privacy of medical records. The act is enforced and administered by both the DOL and the Department of Health and Human Services (*HHS*) in conjunction with state insurance agencies. Major provisions of the law are

▶ Provides for portability of health insurance for employees who change employers by restricting the capability of the new health care plan to deny or limit coverage because of a pre-existing medical condition. In general, the insurance carrier can limit or deny coverage of a pre-existing condition for only a 12-month period and that period can be reduced by prior continuous coverage under a former employer's plan.

▶ Prohibits discrimination in terms of eligibility or premium amounts based on genetic information or prior medical history.

▶ Requires the prior health plan to provide a certificate indicating the periods of coverage under the plan.

▶ Provides comprehensive regulations on the transmission, use, and disclosure of health information to protect its privacy.

▶ Requires that individuals receive information on how their medical information will be used and protected.

▶ Amendments to the act require health plans to provide coverage for certain minimum levels of hospitalization during child birth and, if plans cover mental illness, annual and lifetime benefits must be the same as those for other illnesses (Mental Health Parity Act).

Miscellaneous Laws and Regulations Affecting Compensation

The following bulleted list details some other key laws and regulations that deal with compensation:

▶ **Consumer Credit Protection Act (1968)**   The act provides certain protections for employees whose wages have been garnished and applies to private and public employers except for the federal government. A federal employee's wages cannot be garnished for consumer debts. *Garnishment* is a legal action to attach the wages of an employee by a creditor. The employer is obligated to deduct funds from the employee's wages and transmit them to the creditor. The act limits the amount that can be deducted from wages to approximately 25% of the net wages (gross wages less legally required deductions). It also prohibits the employer from terminating or disciplining an employee for a single debt, even if that debt results in multiple garnishments. However, the employee can be disciplined for garnishments resulting from debts owed more than one creditor.

> **NOTE**
>
> The SPHR should be aware of several issues with respect to garnishment:
>
> ▶ Many garnishment actions are not subject to the limitations of the act. Child support, bankruptcy, and state, local, and federal taxes are a few examples.
>
> ▶ Most states have separate garnishment laws and procedures with which the employer must comply.
>
> ▶ Not only is the employer prohibited from disciplining the employee for garnishment of wages by a single creditor, federal and state law provides penalties for failure to hire an individual because of specified garnishment actions.

▶ **Retirement Equity Act (1985)** The act provides additional protection and benefits for spouses and former spouses of retirement plan participants.

▶ **Older Worker's Benefit Protection Act (1990)** The act is an amendment to ADEA and prohibits illegal discrimination in benefits based on age. Employers must provide employees over the age of 40 with the same benefits it provides those under 40 except in the case when those benefits cost more. In that situation, the employer must provide benefits of equal cost. The act also provides certain procedural protections for early retirement programs and waiver of rights under the ADEA.

▶ **Unemployment Compensation Amendments (1992)** Among other provisions, the act requires a 20% income tax withholding rate on withdrawals from qualified benefit plans. However, rollovers to another qualified plan are exempt from the withholding requirements.

▶ **Omnibus Budget Reconciliation Act (1993)** Prohibits firms from deducting compensation in excess of $1,000,000 as a business expense for its top five executives unless the compensation is based on performance. The definition of what is considered performance-based compensation is relatively strict. The act also limits the amount of compensation that can be used in calculating benefits under a qualified plan.

▶ **Taxpayer Relief Act (1997)** Among other provisions, the act created the Roth and Education individual retirement accounts (*IRAs*).

▶ **Tax and Trade Relief Extension Act (1998)** The act extended tax credits for compensation paid to certain targeted workers (Work Opportunity Tax Credit) and to long-term welfare recipients (Welfare-to-Work Tax Credit) to encourage employers to hire these individuals.

▶ **Economic Growth and Tax Relief Reconciliation Act (2001)**   The act made numerous changes to qualified benefit plan regulations. Among them is a change in vesting requirements for the employer portion of defined contribution plans and a provision for catch up contributions to qualified plans for employees who are age 50 and older.

▶ **Sarbanes-Oxley Act (2002)**   Sarbanes-Oxley is a broad act that regulates certain activities of publicly traded companies. This act was passed in response to the Enron scandal. It requires executive certification of financial statements and provides whistle-blower protection for those reporting violations of securities regulations. It also regulates blackout periods in which employees cannot make certain transactions within their defined contribution plans. The employer must provide advance notice of these periods.

Basic Strategic and Compensation Philosophy Considerations

Prior to the overall design and development of a compensation system, the SPHR must guide the employer through a number of questions and areas of analysis so that the eventual compensation system will be aligned with the overall strategy and culture of the organization. Discussed in this section are the following strategic and philosophical decisions that must be considered before the actual design of a compensation system:

▶ Should the workers be considered employees or independent contractors?

▶ Does the employer want to pay at, above, or below market rates for compensation?

▶ Should the compensation system reflect an entitlement-based or performance-based philosophy?

▶ Is the compensation system properly aligned with the business strategy?

▶ Is the compensation system properly aligned with the organizational or product life cycle?

Employee Versus Independent Contractor

It is often appealing to hire independent contractors rather than employees. Using independent contractors relieves the employer from having to comply with FLSA and many IRS rules regarding the withholding of Social Security and federal, state, and local income taxes. In addition the expense of providing benefits is eliminated. However, control of the methods and means of work are also lost. If the employer is satisfied with merely directing the outcome of the work and leaving how the outcome is achieved to the independent contractor, the strategy might be appropriate.

However, many employers try to have the best of both worlds, relieving themselves of the many obligations that are incurred with employees yet maintaining control of methods and means of getting the job done. Workers are either employees or independent contractors and the employer cannot have it both ways. Attempting to call workers independent contractors when they are, in fact, employees is likely to ultimately result in the accumulation of tax liabilities among other potential problems.

Guidance as to whether a worker is an employee or independent contractor can be found in the IRS's Publication 15-A, *Employer's Supplemental Tax Guide*, which is available on its website: www.irs.gov. The determination of the status of a worker is based on three factors: the amount of behavioral control the employer exerts over the worker, the amount of financial control, and the nature of the relationship.

- *Behavioral control* is determined by the amount of authority the employer has to direct how the worker accomplishes the task.

   Employees are generally subject to employer control of how, when, where, in what sequence, with what tools, and so on the worker does the task.

   Employees are often trained to do the work, whereas independent contractors use their own methods and means.

- *Financial control* refers to whether the employer controls the business aspects of the worker's job.

   Independent contractors are more likely to have ongoing unreimbursed business expenses.

   Independent contractors often have significant investments in facilities or equipment.

   Independent contractors are available to work in the relevant market, seek other business opportunities, and advertise their services.

   Employees are typically paid by the hour, week, or some other period of time. Independent contractors, on the other hand, are paid a flat fee for completing the job.

   Independent contractors can make a profit or loss.

- The nature of the relationship refers to

   Whether there is a written contract.

   Whether the employer provides the worker with employee-type benefits.

The permanency of the relationship. If the relationship is for the duration of a specific project or a specific time, this is characteristic of an independent contractor. If the relationship is for long periods, the intent appears to be to create an employee-employer relationship.

The extent to which the work that is provided is a key or critical aspect of the business is important. If the worker provides critical work, it is more likely that the employer will retain some control with respect to that work. This control indicates an employer-employee relationship.

NOTE

If the employer would like the IRS to make the determination as to whether the worker is an employee or independent contractor, it can file IRS Form SS-8, *Determination of Worker Status for Purposes of Federal Employment Taxes and Income Tax Withholding.*

EXAM ALERT

Given a scenario describing the relationship between a worker and an employer, you should be able to determine whether the worker is an employee or an independent contractor.

Lead or Lag the External Labor Market

The employer has to decide whether to pay at, above, or below the external labor market prices for employees. This decision is often a multifaceted one in that the employer might want to pay above market for some jobs (those requiring critical skills essential to the core competencies of the organization) and below market for others (less critical jobs in which the employer is willing to accept higher turnover levels). The decision is also based on the nature of the organizational or product life cycle and the employer's overall business strategy. The advantages and disadvantages of paying either over or below labor market rates are discussed in Table 5.1.

TABLE 5.1   Paying Above or Below Market Prices

Above or Below External Labor Market	Advantages and Disadvantages of Each
Paying above the market	Advantages: ▶ Recruitment is easier and retention is typically higher. ▶ Higher-quality candidates. ▶ Higher quality and quantity of production. ▶ Reduced training costs. Disadvantage: ▶ Higher compensation costs.

TABLE 5.1 *Continued*

Above or Below External Labor Market	Advantages and Disadvantages of Each
Paying below the market	Advantage: ▶ Lower compensation costs. Disadvantages: ▶ Lower quality and quantity of production. ▶ Higher turnover. ▶ Increased training costs.

NOTE

Higher wages do not necessarily mean higher total compensation costs. In some situations, it is possible that the higher quantity and quality of production can offset the increased costs of compensation.

NOTE

Paying below market rates might be appropriate, particularly if the employer is competing on cost. Higher turnover might not be a particular concern if the jobs are simplified and the training time is minimal.

EXAM ALERT

You should expect a question regarding the strategic implications, benefits, and disadvantages of leading, lagging, or mirroring external labor market rates.

Entitlement-Based or Performance-Based Philosophy

The decision is really not either/or. Compensation philosophies run on a continuum from pure entitlement at one end to pure performance based at the other. In reality, most organizations embrace a philosophy that is somewhat in the middle.

Entitlement-Based Philosophy

This is the more traditional approach to compensation and is based on the concept that an employee is entitled to raises and benefits strictly based on continued employment with the organization and the expectation that performance improves with experience. Characteristics of compensation based on entitlement are

▶ Across-the-board annual raises or cost of living adjustments.

▶ Promotion based on seniority.

▶ Movement through the pay range based on seniority.

▶ Any type of merit pay or bonus is *pro forma* and shared by all, usually on a seniority basis.

▶ Compensation costs are fixed and increasing regardless of organizational performance.

▶ Benefits accrue with organizational membership and increase with seniority.

Performance-Based Philosophy

Under this philosophy, compensation costs are more closely aligned with organizational performance and are variable. The philosophy is based on the concept that individual employees bring different skills and work ethics to the job. Employees should be rewarded based on their performance and the success of the organization. Characteristics of compensation based on performance are

▶ Any across-the-board raise is based on either organizational or group performance.

▶ Individual raises are based on employee performance.

▶ Although benefits still are largely given based on membership, certain increases in benefits and some benefits are based on employee performance.

▶ Promotion is based on merit and potential.

Alignment with the Business Strategy

The business strategy that an organization pursues has major implications for the compensation strategy. The compensation strategy must support the business strategy and facilitate its achievement. Although there are many business strategies, examples of their compensation implications at two ends of the spectrum should suffice.

Organizations at one end of the continuum might pursue a cost minimization strategy, attempting to be the cost leader in the industry or market. To support this business strategy, the compensation strategy must be one that minimizes overall payroll costs and encourages high productivity. Depending on the nature of work and the economy, a compensation system built on slightly below market wages and benefits, piecework, gainsharing, and short-term bonuses based on cost reduction or productivity might be appropriate.

At the other end of the continuum, an organization might pursue a strategy of innovation and differentiation in the market, attempting to beat competitors in the introduction of new products. In this case, the compensation system should encourage creativity and growth. A system that compensates above the market to attract and retain the best and brightest, benefits customized to the employee demographics (development, conference travel, concierge services, and so on), stock options and grants based on organizational performance, and other types of long-term incentives might properly align compensation with organizational strategy.

Alignment with the Organizational or Product Life Cycle

To some extent, both organizations and products can be considered as organic entities having a life cycle that follows a predictable path that is much the same as that of a living organism. The cycle can be described as initiation, growth, maturity, and decline. The difference between organizations and products as organisms is that the former can be reinvented, thus beginning the cycle over again. Organizations can adapt to the changing environment, adjusting their product or service to the new demands of the market, and new uses can be found for old products. The compensation strategies in the reinvention stage are essentially the same as in the initiation stage and will not be discussed separately.

In the initiation stage, there is little or no profit, generally low amounts of cash available, and what cash is available is required to grow the business or product market share. Compensation systems that offer low wages and benefits but high equity incentives are appropriate. Stock options and grants based on the potential for future growth and profitability might motivate employees to achieve organizational goals.

In the growth stage, additional cash is available but sales and market share increases are still the predominant goal. Wages can be raised to market levels; long-term equity incentives are appropriate but now need to be balanced with shorter-term incentives (bonuses, awards) to encourage efficiencies in the operations.

In the mature stage, growth has essentially stopped and maximization of cash flow and efficiency become increasingly important. Long-term equity incentives are less important in the mix and short-term incentives based on operational efficiency become more important. The compensation mix moves toward fixed salaries rather than incentives to stabilize costs.

In the decline stage, wages become fixed with some small short-term incentives in the mix. These short-term incentives are based on maximizing cash flow and reducing costs.

Design and Development of the Compensation System

Objective:

Gain an Understanding of the Development of a Compensation Structure

After the overall strategic and philosophical decisions are made, the SPHR can begin leading the organization and actually designing and developing the compensation system. Although the discussion that follows breaks the process into distinct steps, this is for simplicity only. The steps are interdependent and often simultaneous. The process begins with job analysis and the writing of job descriptions and job specifications. Next is job evaluation, which creates a hierarchy of all jobs in the organization based on a determination of the worth of the job to the organization. Then the jobs are priced in an appropriate external labor market. Finally the results of job evaluation and job pricing are compared and the compensation system is finalized.

Job Analysis

Job analysis was discussed at length in Chapter 3. Job analysis is a critical beginning step to the development of a compensation system. Job descriptions and job specifications are necessary to perform most types of job evaluation. They are also required to compare internal jobs to those found in the labor market in order to determine externally equitable rates of pay.

Job Evaluation

Job evaluation is the process by which the relative worth of a job to the organization is determined. The result is a hierarchy of all jobs in the organization from the one with the greatest importance to the one with the least importance. This process considers neither the compensation being paid for the job nor the skills of the individuals performing the job. The goal is to develop a hierarchy that is perceived to be fair by the employees, creating internal equity, and to develop pay scales in alignment with the job evaluation results. In other words, jobs positioned higher on the hierarchy will be paid more than jobs lower on the hierarchy.

Job evaluation is a critical process to the overall development of the compensation system. A variety of methods can be used to create the hierarchy of jobs representing the relative worth of those jobs to the organization. These methods can range from very simplistic to very complex. The methodology can be developed in-house or purchased from an outside vendor. Inherent in many methods are the concepts of *compensable factors* and *benchmark* or *key jobs*. All of these issues are discussed in the following sections.

Compensable Factors

Compensable factors are those characteristics or dimensions of a job that are valued by the organization and used to determine its relative worth. Compensable factors are not required or specified in the law, but the Equal Pay Act provides some guidance as to the essential characteristics of a job: skill, effort, responsibility, and working conditions. Consequently, many organizations use this broad guidance in crafting their compensable factors. Skill, effort, responsibility, and working conditions are largely constructs. The issue then becomes one of defining these compensable factors in an observable and measurable way. Commonly used observable and measurable criteria for compensable factors are

▶ Licenses/credentials

▶ Education

- ▶ Work experience

- ▶ Impact of the work on the organization

- ▶ How closely the job is supervised

- ▶ The kinds and number of employees the job supervises and the nature of that supervision

- ▶ Physical demands

- ▶ Temperature of the workplace, exposure to weather, fumes, dangerous machinery, and so on

The factors should reflect the business plan, strategic objectives, values, and culture of the organization because they will determine what jobs are highly valued by the organization and how the jobs contribute to the achievement of organizational goals. Therefore, different organizations might value essentially the same job differently. For example, a manufacturing firm and an advertising agency might both have a job titled *recruiter* and the job description might be relatively similar along with the compensable factors used in the job evaluation. Yet the relative importance of the job might be much greater in the advertising agency because the core competency of the firm requires talented people, whereas the manufacturing firm can use less-talented employees because the technology used in the manufacturing process, not the people, comprises the core competency.

The selection of compensable factors is a decision left to the organization based on a determination of what it believes to be important to its success. Some organizations might want to use one set of compensable factors for all jobs, whereas other organizations might elect to have separate job evaluation systems for various types of jobs. Using one set of compensable factors for all positions creates uniformity and sends a clear message that these are the job dimensions valued by the organization. However, it is often difficult to find one set of factors that can be used to evaluate all of an organization's jobs. Using multiple sets of compensable factors might allow for more accurate job evaluation, but doing so creates difficulty and potential confusion among employees when evaluating internal equity across multiple evaluation systems.

Whatever the organization decides, compensable factors should be

- ▶ Acceptable to employees. Employees should believe that the compensable factors used result in a fair comparison of jobs.

- ▶ Job related and apply to all jobs being evaluated.

- ▶ Independent of each other. Otherwise, the system could double-count certain job characteristics.

- ▶ Measurable and clearly differentiate between

Different jobs (secretary versus human resource management clerk).

Differences relative to the importance of the work of similar jobs (secretary to first-level supervisor versus secretary to the CEO).

> **NOTE**
>
> Job evaluation systems have historically resulted in adverse impact on protected classes, particularly women. Whatever job evaluation system is used must be defensible in terms of the business needs of the organization.

Benchmark Jobs

Both job evaluation and job pricing use the concept of *benchmark jobs* in many of their processes. In organizations with many jobs, it might be initially difficult to deal with all of them. Consequently, benchmark jobs (sometimes called *key jobs*) are used to build the job evaluation system and as the source of data for external salary information. Many jobs, particularly in larger organizations, become specific to the organization and are not readily identifiable in the external labor market. However, benchmark jobs are chosen based on their comparability to those readily found in the external labor market. When data is known about the benchmark jobs, other jobs can be evaluated and priced based on their similarity to the benchmark jobs. Criteria for selecting benchmark jobs are

▶ Should be comparable to those readily found in the external labor market.

▶ Should cover the range of the pay scale. In other words, there should be benchmark jobs selected all along the continuum from the lowest-priced to the highest-priced jobs.

Job Evaluation Methods

Many methods are available to perform job evaluation, but they tend to fall into four main categories:

▶ Ranking

▶ Job classification

▶ Point factor

▶ Factor comparison

Ranking and job classification are essentially whole job nonquantitative evaluations, whereas point factor and factor comparison are quantitative and rely on the use of compensable factors, as shown in Table 5.2.

TABLE 5.2   Types of Job Evaluation Methods

	Whole Job	Compensable Factors
Nonquantitative	Ranking	
	Job classification	
Quantitative		Point factor
		Factor comparison

Ranking

Ranking is the simplest of the four methods and merely involves ranking all jobs in the organization from the most valuable to least valuable. In its basic form, the ranker makes a subjective determination, based on the whole job, as to that job's value in relation to the other jobs in the organization. There are several procedures that are often used:

▶ **Deck of cards**   All jobs are listed individually on pieces of paper, often index cards. The ranker goes through the deck and selects the most important job and removes it from the deck. The ranker then goes through the cards again, selecting the secondmost important job, and the process is continued until all jobs are ranked.

▶ **Alternation ranking**   This process is similar to the deck of cards method but after the most important job is chosen, the next step is to select the least important job. The process continues, selecting the next most important job and then the next least important job until all jobs are ranked.

▶ **Paired comparison method**   This process involves creating a matrix with all jobs listed both on the vertical and horizontal axis. Each job is then compared to every other job in the organization and a determination is made as to whether the job being ranked is more valuable or less valuable to the organization than the job to which it is being compared. Typically a check mark is made if the job is more important than the comparison job. After each job is compared to every other job, the number of check marks is totaled. The job with the most check marks is then ranked the highest in the hierarchy and those with a lesser number of check marks ranked lower until the job with no check marks is ranked at the bottom.

The ranking method might be appropriate for very small organizations that do not have the internal capacity to develop a job evaluation system and do not want to purchase one from an outside vendor. The resulting job hierarchy might, in fact, be the same as what would have been created by a sophisticated job evaluation system, and at far less cost to the organization. However, there are several disadvantages to using this method. They are as follows:

▶ The ranking method is often based on some vague criteria, largely the subjective evaluation of the ranker, making it difficult to justify both to the employees and to a third party (EEOC, courts, arbitrator, and so on) should a complaint or grievance arise.

▶ It provides only a ranking, not an indication of the relative difference in the value of jobs. As such, jobs ranked one and two might be very close in value to the organization whereas the job ranked number three might be far less important.

▶ In large organizations with many jobs, the ranking method becomes quite involved and cumbersome.

Job Classification

The job classification method of job evaluation requires a definition of several terms used in compensation before proceeding. Consistent with the purposes of this book, the terms, along with the explanation of the various types of job evaluation, will be broadly defined so that the SPHR understands the concept without necessarily being burdened with the minutia of the process itself.

To understand the process of job classification, the following terms are important:

▶ **Position**   The totality of tasks, duties, and responsibilities of one employee.

▶ **Jobs**   A group of positions sharing the same job description.

▶ **Class**   A group of jobs having similar duties. An example might be all secretaries.

▶ **Grades**   A group of jobs sharing similar amounts of compensable factors. Pay scales are often broken down into several pay grades with persons in those grades having the same range of pay.

▶ **Job family**   A broad classification of jobs. If there is only one pay system in an organization, all jobs are in the same family. However, employers often have several compensation plans. In this case, each compensation plan would represent a job family. A firm might have a separate plan for production workers, administrative employees, and managerial/executive employees, which would create three job families.

> **NOTE**
>
> A job class normally includes several pay grades, whereas a pay grade normally includes several job classes. For example: The job class of *secretary* might incorporate pay grades 1, 2, and 3, depending on the job evaluation of the various jobs contained in the class. In addition, pay grade 1 might include not only secretaries, but also other job classes such as clerks and production workers.

Job classification involves comparing the job description of the job to be classified with generic descriptions of the classes contained in the compensation system. These generic descriptions might take the form of very general job descriptions or of a classification guide document. In either case, the initial question is what is the closest match between the duties of the job to be evaluated and the duties of the classes? For example, the rater might decide that the job duties most closely approximate the description of duties contained in the class labeled *secretary*. After the class determination is made, the second determination involves deciding into which grade of that class the job falls. Again, there are either generic job descriptions or classification guides that describe the characteristics of the duties and responsibilities of the class at each grade level. The description is generally broken down into separate descriptions of each compensable factor. The final outcome of job classification is a whole job determination as to the best fit between the job description of the job being evaluated and the generic descriptions of the class and grade (for example: secretary, pay grade 2). Whereas ranking places each job in its appropriate place in the hierarchy, job classification groups jobs hierarchically in pay grades.

Job classification is a widely used and accepted method of job evaluation. The Factor Evaluation System of the federal government is a real-world example of this method. However, there are some disadvantages associated with this methodology. The writing of generic job descriptions in terms of both class and grade is an art form in itself. It is very difficult and time-intensive to write descriptions that clearly differentiate one class and grade from another. Just as difficult is the determination of the best fit between the job description of the job to be evaluated and the generic descriptions. Often the job appears to fall in more than one grade or class. This frequently becomes a source of contention between the rater and the job incumbent or manager of the job incumbent.

Point Factor Method

The *point factor system*, also called the *point system*, involves placing jobs into a hierarchy of pay grades based on the number of points assigned to the job in the evaluation process. Points are assigned based on the level or degree of compensable factors found in the job. The point factor system is the most frequently used job evaluation method.

To develop the point factor method, some design issues must be decided. They include the following:

▶ What compensable factors are to be used and what is the relative importance/weighting of each? For example, it might be decided that one of the compensable factors is twice as important to the organization as the others. If that is the case, that factor will be assigned twice the number of points.

▶ What is the total number of points that can be awarded? Although this determination can be rather complex, the number of total points is largely dependent on the number of grades in the compensation system. The larger the number of grades, the more points needed to differentiate between them.

▶ How many points are to be assigned to each compensable factor? This is based on the determination of the relative importance of the compensable factors discussed in the first bullet point.

▶ What are the subfactors (if any) of the compensable factor, and what is the weighting or importance of the subfactor? Based on this determination, the total number of points assigned to the compensable factor is allocated to the subfactors.

▶ How many degrees should be described for the compensable factor or subfactor? For example, compensable factor number one is allocated 600 of the 3,000 total points that can be assigned. It has no subfactors. A determination is made to describe the presence of the compensable factor in terms of three degrees. At the first-degree level, there is only a small portion of the compensable factor present in the job and it is assigned 200 points. Degree level two is dependent on a moderate amount of the compensable factor being present in the job and is assigned 400 points, whereas degree level three indicates substantial amounts of the compensable factor and is assigned the full 600 points.

After the decisions are made and the point factor method is designed, the rater must compare the job description of the job to be rated against the compensable factors used in the evaluation. A determination is made as to the degree of each compensable factor that is present in the job and points are assigned on that basis. As described earlier, if the rater determines that degree level two of compensable factor one is present in the job, 400 points will be assigned. If there are subfactors, each subfactor must be evaluated and points assigned. The points are then totaled to determine the number of points to be awarded for that compensable factor. The number of points for each factor is then added together to determine the total number of points assigned to the job. The total number of points determines the pay grade to be assigned to the job.

The point factor method, although difficult to design, generally provides for a stable, defensible, and acceptable job evaluation process. After the compensable factors, subfactors, and allocation of points are determined, the system might remain unchanged for a long period of time unless the goals or values of the organization change. The use of compensable factors that are directly job related tends to increase validity, making the method more defensible in case of grievances or litigation. The point factor method is generally acceptable to employees, unions, and management.

Factor Comparison Method

The *factor comparison method* is a more sophisticated variation of ranking. It is the only method in which hourly rates for benchmark jobs are determined in advance. The process begins with the selection of compensable factors and the pricing of benchmark jobs in the external labor market. The actual evaluation is somewhat complex, particularly if there are many benchmark jobs. Each benchmark job is ranked on each of the compensable factors. If there are five compensable factors, there will be five separate rankings of the benchmark jobs based on the amount of compensable factor contained in the job as determined by a review of the job description.

When the ranking is complete, the known wage rate for that job must be allocated among the various compensable factors both horizontally and vertically. The amount allocated to each compensable factor must add up to the hourly rate for the job (horizontal allocation). Also, the amount allocated to each compensable factor must be in alignment with its ranking (vertical allocation). In other words, the job that was ranked number one in terms of compensable factor number one must have more of the hourly rate allocated to it than the job that was ranked number two.

Shown in Table 5.3 is a simple allocation for three jobs. The number in parentheses is the ranking of that job on the particular compensable factor. The amount of money allocated to each compensable factor, when added up, equals the hourly rate (horizontal allocation) and the amount allocated to each compensable factor is aligned with the ranking of that job on the compensable factor (vertical allocation). After this is completed for all benchmark jobs, all other jobs can be evaluated and priced by comparison, compensable factor by compensable factor, with the benchmark jobs. For example, the job description of Job D is evaluated in terms of its compensable factors in relation to the benchmark jobs and is found to require more skill than Job C but less than Job B (allocation $4.00), more effort than B but less than C (allocation $3.50), more responsibility than B but less than A (allocation $10.00), and less severe working conditions than B but more than A (allocation $2.50). When that allocation is complete the hourly wage is determined by adding up all the allocations ($20.00).

TABLE 5.3   Factor Comparison Method

Benchmark Job	Skill	Effort	Responsibility	Working Conditions	Hourly Rate
A	$2.00 (3)	$2.00 (3)	$16.00 (1)	$2.00 (3)	$22.00
B	$8.00 (1)	$3.00 (2)	$3.00 (2)	$4.00(2)	$18.00
C	$3.00 (2)	$4.00(1)	$1.00 (3)	$7.00 (1)	$15.00
D	$4.00	$3.50	$10.00	$2.50	$20.00

The advantage to this system is that after the allocations are made for the benchmark jobs, it is a fairly simple process to price all other jobs. In addition, the evaluation is totally customized to jobs in the organization. However, this method of job evaluation is rarely used because of the complexity of its development and its limited applicability to primarily blue-collar jobs. An obvious problem is that the whole pricing structure is destroyed if wage rates change in the external market. However, indices rather than dollars can be used to overcome this limitation.

EXAM ALERT

Expect one or more questions in this area. You should be familiar with the four basic types of job evaluation.

Other Job Evaluation Methods

There are literally hundreds of job evaluation systems marketed by consulting firms or developed by governmental or not-for-profit organizations. The *PAQ* (discussed in Chapter 3) and the *Hay System* are two of the better-known systems. Increasingly, vendors are developing automated systems that integrate the job analysis, job evaluation, and job pricing processes.

The organization might decide to purchase one of these systems or to develop its own job evaluation system. Developing job evaluation methodology internally customizes the process for the organization and its needs, but is likely to be more time-consuming and costly. Purchasing a system from a vendor might cut costs and development time, but might not be modifiable to the particular needs of the organization.

Who Does Job Evaluation?

There is no set answer to this question. Any answer is dependent on the size of the organization, the complexity of the job evaluation method, whether the process is automated, whether there is a negotiated labor agreement, and many other factors. In small firms, job evaluation might be outsourced or performed by managers using an automated system purchased from a vendor. Larger organizations might have professional HR employees perform the evaluation, or a job evaluation committee created by the labor contract might do it.

Job Pricing

The outcome of job evaluation is a hierarchy of jobs, based on their relative value or worth to the organization, creating internal equity. However, job evaluation (except for the factor comparison method) does not provide the data on which to actually determine how much to pay for each job. To price jobs and create external equity, information is required regarding wages being paid in the appropriate labor market. The selection of the labor market from which the data are to be derived is critical. The appropriate labor market is that market from which the organization recruits for the jobs of interest. For lower-level jobs, that is probably a local labor market. However, for many professional and managerial jobs, the appropriate labor market might be regional, national, or even international for certain hard-to-fill positions that require special expertise.

After a determination is made regarding the appropriate labor market containing the jobs of interest, a decision must be made as to how to obtain the data. There are essentially three options: use consultants, use third-party data, or develop the salary survey internally.

Using Consultants

Often firms do not have either the expertise or staff resources to conduct salary surveys. A viable option in such a case might be to hire a consulting firm to do the work. An advantage to this strategy is that the firm gets instant expertise in a somewhat complex area of HR practice. However, there are several potential disadvantages that the firm must weigh during the decision-making process. The first is that the process might be quite expensive in relation to the value of the data obtained. The second disadvantage is that consulting firms often use boilerplate surveys that might not meet the particular needs of the organization.

Using Third-Party Data

There are many sources of labor or product market salary data available at no cost or minimal cost to the organization. The Bureau of Labor Statistics (*BLS*) and the Federal Reserve System do extensive wage surveying, the results of which are available on their websites and through their offices. Professional organizations (accounting, engineering associations, and SHRM, for example) conduct salary surveys for their professions. Chambers of commerce and industry organizations conduct salary surveys that are made available to their members. In addition, there are many web-based services from which data on individual jobs can be obtained. The obvious advantage of using these data sources is that they are inexpensive and immediately available. However, there are also some potential disadvantages. The data might be summarized or aggregated in a manner that does not provide the specificity required to make compensation decisions. Data collection sources and methods might not be published, bringing into question its accuracy. The survey data might be out of date and no longer reflect current market rates, or the data required by the firm for its specific jobs might not be available in the survey.

Conducting the Salary Survey Internally

If only a few specific jobs are being surveyed, a telephone or in-person interview might suffice to gather the required information. However, considerable information is usually necessary, and the most efficient way to collect that information is by questionnaire. The timeliness of the information is critical. Although salary surveys are typically completed once a year, more frequent data might be required in periods of rapid economic change or for jobs that are in high demand. On return of the survey, the data must be analyzed and placed in a format from which compensation decisions can be made.

The Questionnaire

After the questionnaire is prepared and a sample of organizations selected from the appropriate labor market, the initial step is likely to be a phone call to an appropriate official of the organization to request its participation in the survey. Next, the survey is sent to those organizations that appear willing to participate with a cover letter referencing the initial call, requesting response by a certain date and an offer to provide the results of the survey to those who do respond. One or more follow-up contacts, letters, or personal calls should be built into the process to ensure adequate response rates. The following information should be collected via the questionnaire:

- ▶ Wage data on benchmark jobs (minimum, maximum, and average pay; number of persons performing each benchmark job).

> ▶ Organizational compensation policies (how are wage increases determined: seniority, performance, or combination; how often are they given).

> ▶ Types of benefits, eligibility of benefits, and costs of benefits.

NOTE

Many benefit policies remain constant and data are not required each survey period; the number of paid holidays is one such example. However, other benefits are volatile and data are needed every survey period (health insurance, for example). The questionnaire can be shortened and participation improved by asking questions on noncritical, nonvolatile benefits only every several years.

Data Analysis

The data should be presented in a way that facilitates compensation decision-making. Although it might be desirable to request the actual pay rate for every person occupying a benchmark position, such a request would likely result in low response rates because of the amount of work involved and huge amounts of data to be analyzed from those who do respond. Therefore, a determination must be made in the planning stages of the salary survey as to what data will be requested.

Typically the data should include, at the very least, the maximum, minimum, mean, and median wage rate for each benchmark job. However, the mean (average) and median (middle) rates for the job can be unduly influenced if the employer's actual wages paid are not equally distributed around the mean. To use the mean wage rate of all employers reporting tends to lessen the impact of extreme scores, but using a weighted mean will provide better information from which to make a decision. Therefore, the survey data should include the number of incumbents in each benchmark job. An example of weighted average calculation is provided in Table 5.4.

TABLE 5.4   Weighted Average Calculation: Benchmark Job #1

Employer	Number of Incumbents	Mean Salary	Total Salary
1	22	$45,000	$990,000
2	10	$50,000	$500,000
3	1	$60,000	$60,000
4	2	$65,000	$130,000
Totals	35	$220,000	$1,680,000

The mean salary of the four reporting employers is 220,000/4 = $55,000. However, the weighted mean of the four reporting employers is 1,680,000/35 = $48,000. The two employers paying relatively high wages for their three employees had a disproportionate impact on the mean salary. The weighted mean provides a more realistic view of the appropriate salary for benchmark job #1.

Quartiles are frequently used to report wage data. A *quartile* represents 25% of the data. In other words, 25% of all wage rates would be contained in the first quartile, 50% in the second, 75% in the third, and 100% in the fourth. Organizations often look at what is referred to as the *interquartile range*, which is the range between the first and third quartiles. This provides a good indication of the distribution of wage rates and guidance as to what rate might be used to lead, lag, or mirror the market rate.

Another statistic, less frequently used in reporting wage data, is the *standard deviation*. It is a measure of the dispersion of data around the mean, either above or below. In other words, it provides an indication of how closely grouped together the data is; in this case, the wage rates. Using the mean salary of $48,000 from the preceding example , if the standard deviation is $2,000 and the data approximates a normal distribution (bell curve), about 68% of all employees' wage rates fall between $46,000 and $50,000, which is +/– one standard deviation. About 95% of all employees' wage rates fall between $44,000 and $52,000, which is +/– two standard deviations. The concept of standard deviations was discussed in greater depth in Chapter 1.

NOTE

A survey of the appropriate labor market provides information as to what level of compensation will be required to attract and retain workers. The data allows the organization to determine the minimal level of compensation needed. However, many organizations need additional critical data: the compensation levels being paid by their competitors. This is referred to as *product market data*, and it provides an indication of the maximum amount of compensation that the firm can pay and still remain competitive. In many industries, the technology of work and cost of raw materials and supplies are similar for all competitors. If that is the case, paying above the product market rate will affect competitiveness. The data are derived by including competitors as part of the survey.

NOTE

Often employers join together in conducting salary surveys. Implications that this process results in joint compensation decision-making must be avoided. Such activities could be considered a violation of the Sherman Antitrust Act as a restraint on market pricing of labor. Avoiding face-to-face meetings of survey participants and discussing the decision-making implications of the data are ways to minimize potential problems.

Developing the Pay Structure

The pay structure is the final pricing of the jobs and represents the integration of two processes: job evaluation and job pricing. Essentially the process involves overlaying the job evaluation results with the salary survey data. Ideally, there will be a perfect correlation between the two with the job evaluation hierarchy perfectly correlating with the salary survey. However, this is not likely to happen and some decisions will have to be made regarding the final development of the pay structure.

Figure 5.1 represents a plot of the results of the job evaluation overlaid with the salary survey. In this example, a point factor system is represented with the points converted to pay grades. As you can see, the salary data for benchmarks jobs do not fall exactly on the job evaluation line. Although there are mathematical ways of making the two lines fit, the typical way is merely fitting by sight. The job evaluation line represents internal equity and the circles external equity. Similar jobs might be valued higher by one organization than another. When this occurs, the results of job evaluation and the salary survey might differ. At this point, the SPHR must lead the organization in making a determination as to what is most important. Does the organization want to maintain its culture and internal equity as reflected in the job evaluation results and either overpay or underpay the job, or does it want to create external equity? The resulting pay structure will be a line (often called the *pay policy line*) that displays actual pay rates, as depicted in Figure 5.2. For simplicity purposes the pay line is depicted as straight, but it could, in fact, be curvilinear in many pay structures.

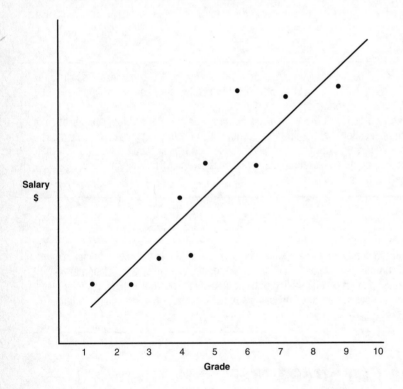

— Job evaluation
● Salary survey data

FIGURE 5.1 Comparison of job evaluation and salary survey results.

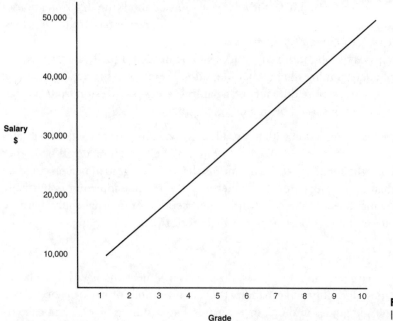

FIGURE 5.2 Pay policy line.

There are two other major decisions that have to be made as the pay structure is developed. This first is whether to use grades, and the second is whether to pay a flat rate for each job or pay grade or to allow for variation in pay (a pay range).

Pay Grades

The pay policy line depicted in Figure 5.2 represents all jobs in the pay structure. The employer could elect to pay a different rate for each job based on where the job fell on the line. However, it is generally easier to use pay grades that pay the same amount to jobs of similar relative worth to the organization. This is generally acceptable to employees and viewed as internally equitable. Another justification is that all job evaluation systems, no matter how complex, are subjective and are not accurate enough to make fine differentiations between the amounts of compensable factors in each particular job.

As covered in the discussion of the point factor job evaluation method, the determination of how many grades to have depends on a number of factors. If increases in pay are to be primarily based on promotions, a larger number of grades will be required. If the pay structure includes many different types of jobs, more pay grades will be needed. Finally, internal equity must be considered when determining the number of grades. If employees generally view one job (human resources assistant) as more difficult and a natural career progression from another job (human resources clerk), each should be in a different grade.

When pay ranges are used in conjunction with pay grades, the pay rates for two adjacent grades will normally overlap. In other words, the maximum rate for the lower grade will be higher than the minimum rate for the higher grade. This means that a lower-graded person could be paid at a higher rate than an employee in the higher grade. This phenomenon is normally acceptable to employees and does not interfere with the perception of internal equity because the higher rates are paid on the basis of seniority or high performance in the job.

Broad Banding

Pay grades, particularly a large number of grades, do not always meet the needs of management in terms of the grades' flexibility and capability to recognize superior performance. *Broad banding* is collapsing multiple grades into one broad band. The resulting broad band encompasses a pay range from the minimum rate on the lowest collapsed pay grade to the maximum pay rate for the highest collapsed pay grade. In a broad band, employees can easily be assigned a variety of duties without consideration of the need to promote from one grade to another. This promotes flexibility in job assignments and facilitates employee growth. It also allows management to give greater pay increases for superior performance without the hindrance of the narrower ranges associated with multiple pay grades. Broad banding might better align the compensation system with today's flattened organizations and dynamic environments.

> **EXAM ALERT**
>
> Expect a question regarding the benefits of broad banding.

Pay Ranges

Many firms, particularly in unionized environments, pay a flat rate with everyone in the particular job receiving the same rate of pay. This most frequently occurs with blue-collar types of jobs. However, employees bring different attributes in terms of skill, ability, and performance to the job. Pay ranges allow employers to pay employees different rates for the same job based on performance, seniority, or both.

Figure 5.3 shows a pay structure with a pay range. The pay policy line reflects the midpoint of the range. Notice that the pay range increases both in terms of absolute amount and in terms of percentage as the grade levels increase. Although pay ranges could be constructed using a fixed dollar amount or a fixed percentage for all pay grades, increasing the percentage at the higher grade levels is more typical. This represents the greater variability of performance and impact on the organization of jobs in the higher grade levels.

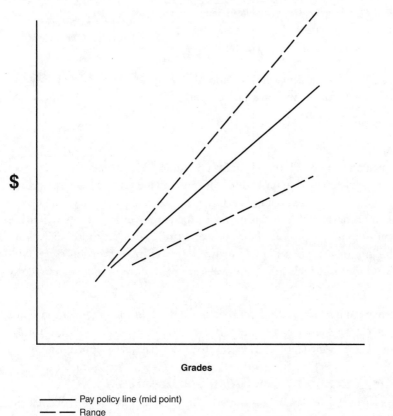

Grades

Pay policy line (mid point)
Range

FIGURE 5.3 Pay structure using a pay range.

A final determination is how an employee will progress through the range. Depending on the compensation philosophy of the organization, there are essentially three ways to move employees from the minimum to the maximum pay rate for the range: seniority, performance, or a combination of both. These three basic methods are depicted in Figure 5.4. Figure 5.4 (a) depicts a step range, and it is used to move employees through the range based on seniority. Assuming satisfactory performance, the employee's wages are raised from step to step at some periodic interval, usually every year. Seniority pay raises are justified based on the rationale that they encourage employee retention and that performance increases with experience. Figure 5.4 (b) depicts an open range, and it is characteristic of performance-based systems. The employee moves through the pay range based on increases that are determined by performance. Figure 5.4 (c) represents a combination of both performance and seniority. The employee's wage rate is raised to the midpoint by seniority. If additional increases in pay are granted, they are based on the employee's performance.

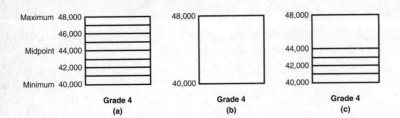

FIGURE 5.4 Movement through the pay range.

Two additional issues associated with the implementation of the pay structure, particularly pay ranges, have to be considered. Those issues are pay compression and pay rates outside the range.

Pay Compression

Pay compression occurs when the pay differential between employees with different levels of skill, performance, or seniority becomes small. It disturbs individual equity. There are several reasons why this might occur, but the most common is that the internal pay scale does not rise as rapidly as the external labor market. When this happens, the employer is forced to offer the external rate to attract new employees, placing their compensation at or near those of employees who have been in the job for extended periods of time. In fact, pay inversion can sometimes occur in high-demand jobs in which new employees are paid more than those currently occupying the job.

The obvious solution to pay compression problems, particularly when the organization tends to fill its positions from the external labor market rather than promoting from within, is to collect pay information from the relevant labor market and to adjust pay levels appropriately.

Pay Rates Outside the Range: Red and Green Circle Rates

Sometimes an employee's current rate of pay falls outside the range of pay for the job that the employee occupies. This can happen in certain circumstances in existing pay structures, but is more likely to occur when a new structure is being implemented. If a large number of employees' wages fall outside the range, an analysis of the situation, including a determination of the organization's capability to pay, should be done. If many employees are being paid below the new range, the employer should review its capability to bring them all up to the new pay policy at one time. This is most likely to occur when the employer's pay policy has not kept in alignment with external rates. If many employees' rates are above the new range, it indicates that the employer has historically, whether purposely or not, paid above market rates. In this case, the employer would need to analyze the effect of a decision to implement a pay policy incorporating market comparability.

More typically, only a small number of employees' rates are out of the range and the issue becomes less strategic and more individual as to how to handle the situation with that particular employee.

Red Circle Rates

A *red circle rate* occurs when the employee's current rate of pay is above the range for the job. Although one solution is to immediately lower the rate of pay to the maximum for the range, most employers are hesitant to do so. There are several other ways of handling the situation:

▶ Freeze the employee's rate of pay until the pay scale rises enough to capture the employee's current rate. This assumes that the employer periodically adjusts the pay structure through cost of living or across-the-board raises.

▶ Allow only partial cost of living or across-the-board raises until the rate is captured.

▶ Promote the employee noncompetitively into a pay grade in which the current pay rate can be captured.

Green Circle Rates

A *green circle rate* occurs when the employee's current rate of pay falls below the minimum rate for that job. In this case, the common practice is to increase the pay to the minimum rate.

Incentive Pay

Incentive programs are designed to achieve organizational goals by motivating employees to perform above the standard. Increasing competition requires optimal employee performance in many industries. Incentive systems to improve performance are becoming an integral part of many compensation strategies.

The design of such programs is critical to ensure that they are in alignment with organizational goals and the organizational culture, and that they will produce the work-related behaviors that the organization wants. The old axiom "you get what you pay for" should be considered when contemplating variable pay types of programs. For example, if the organization values teamwork yet implements an individual incentive pay plan, the plan is likely to create behaviors that are inappropriate.

Some general guidelines in the design of incentive systems are

▶ Provide base pay at or near externally equitable rates. Incentive pay should be separately identified from base pay and should be designed to motivate employees to perform above the standard.

▶ Align the incentive system with organizational culture and goals.

▶ Make sure that the performance for which the incentive is offered is measurable and independent, and that the employee is capable of performing above standard. All of these are often challenges. For many employees, it is difficult to measure output. Incentive programs should be planned around output over which the employee has control; that is, output that is independent of other employees. If the output is not independent or measurable at one level, it is more appropriate to design a program at a different level. For example, if output is not measurable and independent at the individual level, the SPHR should look at designing a program at the group or organizational level. Also, it is possible that the output of work is not variable because of the system, not the employee. In that case, an incentive based on production is not appropriate.

▶ The plan must be balanced between short-term and long-term incentives, particularly at the managerial and executive levels. If the incentive is strong, employees are likely to "suboptimize" to that objective, doing whatever it takes to achieve the incentive and disregarding other performance requirements of their job. This could result in decisions that are not in the best interest of the organization and, in fact, could be unethical and/or illegal. This issue is discussed later in the chapter.

▶ Effectiveness is enhanced when employees are involved in the design of the plan. Employees might not believe in differential compensation based on productivity or they might not value it. In those situations, employee involvement will assist in developing a system or, in some cases, not developing a system, whichever is appropriate.

▶ There must be a method of revising the plan as the situation dictates. The introduction of new technology and systems or changing market or economic conditions might require modification of the plan's design.

▶ Employees must understand the plan, what behaviors will lead to reward, and how this reward is calculated. Clear communications between management and employees is required.

Incentive systems can be categorized into three types for the purposes of discussion: individual, group, and organizational.

Individual Incentives

Individual incentive plans are designed to motivate individual performance by giving employees the ability to control, at least to some extent, the amount of their compensation. Piece rates, standard hour plans, bonuses and awards, commissions, and recognition plans are all considered to be individual incentive programs.

Piece Rates

Piece rate plans pay the individual for their work output. The more they produce, the more they earn. Design of piece rates systems really goes back to the concepts of scientific management. Most piece rate systems are designed so that the average worker doing an average day's work earns the externally equitable rate of pay. For example, if the average worker can produce 80 work output units in an eight-hour day and the externally equitable rate of pay for that type of job is $10.00 per hour, the piece rate becomes $1.00 for each unit of work output ((8 hours per day ¥ $10.00 per hour)/80 work units in a standard day's work). In a pure piece rate plan, the employee would make more than the going rate for the job if production was above 80 work units and less than the going rate if production was below 80 works units. However, under FLSA, the worker could not be paid less than minimum wage. There is a wide variety of piece rate systems—too many to discuss within the context of the purpose of this book.

Recall our discussion of wage ranges; a piece rate plan should be designed so that the average worker doing an average day's work would be at the midpoint of the range (that is, $80.00 per day in the preceding example). A highly productive worker should not, however, make more than the maximum of the range. The piece rate plan should be designed so that a small percentage of the most productive workers can achieve the maximum of the range. Often this is achieved through differential piece rates. Differential piece rates pay a different rate for the production of work units above standard. These rates can be increasing or decreasing. Continuing with the earlier example, an increasing rate system would pay the employee more than a $1.00 for each work unit above the standard. The rationale behind an increasing rate is that the selling price of the item, along with its cost of production, is calculated on the standard rate of production. Therefore, fixed costs are allocated based on the standard rate and anything above standard really costs less to produce and theoretically is more profitable. An increasing rate, say $1.10 for all work units above standard, shares this decreased cost with the employee. It might be appropriate to use a decreasing rate for production above standard if the most productive employees could sustain a rate that would consistently put them above the maximum rate for the compensation range. In our example, the midpoint of the range is $10.00 and the standard piece rate is $1.00 per work unit. Let us assume that the maximum rate for the range is $14.00 dollars per hour and that the best employees can consistently produce 15 work units per hour, placing their potential earnings at $15.00 per hour, which is above the range. In this case, it might be appropriate to pay $1.00 per work unit for the first ten units and $.80 for all units above the standard production rate. This would position these highly productive workers at the maximum of the pay range.

Standard Hour Plans

Whereas piece rate programs are based on exceeding a standard rate of production, standard hour plans are based on completing a certain unit of work output in less than the standard time allotted for that work. A common application of these plans is in the automobile repair business in which an employee is paid the regular rate of pay for the standard time allocated to doing that particular task. In its simplest form, an employee earning $10.00 per hour would be paid $5.00 for a job with a standard of .5 hours whether the job took 10 minutes or 50 minutes. There is a wide variety of standard hour plans, varying in complexity. In many plans, the employee does not keep all the labor savings generated, but the increased productivity is shared with the employer.

Bonuses/Rewards

There is a wide variety of individual incentive plans in which the employee receives either a cash payment or an increase in salary based on the individual's performance. Annual cash bonuses and merit pay increases are two examples.

Commissions

Commission-based compensation is discussed later in the section covering special types of compensation.

Recognition Programs

Recognition programs are nonrecurring incentives designed to recognize the employee for special achievements or superior performance. Examples are spot awards, employee of the month, length of service awards, and merchandise given for a particular act.

Advantages and Disadvantages of Individual Incentive Plans

The advantages of individual incentive plans are

- ▶ Encourages performance above standard
- ▶ Aligns employee behavior with organizational goals

However, the following can be seen as disadvantages with this compensation strategy structure.

- ▶ Does not encourage teamwork
- ▶ Might result in unbalanced behavior not in the best interest of the organization in order to achieve the performance objective
- ▶ Might create dysfunctional internal competition

NOTE

Employers often provide incentive plans to encourage appropriate work-related behaviors. Examples are attendance and safety bonuses. Obviously, these types of programs do not fit our definition of creating incentives for only behaviors or performance that are beyond standard. The SPHR must provide leadership in this area by helping the organization to determine whether these types of incentives are the best way to achieve organizational goals.

Group Incentives

Group incentives are designed to reward performance at the group, department, or plant level. They are appropriate when output can be measured at that level and when that performance is independent of other groups yet individual performance is interdependent within the group. Some examples of group incentive plans are group awards, gainsharing, and goalsharing.

Group Awards

It is possible to essentially implement a piece rate incentive plan at the group level where the group is paid based on the number of work output units produced. This is particularly applicable to self-directed work teams or cell production units. The development of this type of program follows the same basic steps as an individual piece rate plan except that a group rather than an individual is the entity around which the incentive system is built.

Gainsharing

Gainsharing is perhaps the most common incentive at the group level. These are plans that share cost reduction savings or the value of increased productivity with employees. There are a number of ways of designing the gainsharing plan. The Scanlon Plan, Rucker Plan, and Improshare (Improved Productivity Through Sharing) are gainsharing plans. However, the concept of all these plans is relatively similar. Baseline production and labor costs are determined. Improvements from these baselines are evaluated in terms of monetary cost savings, and those savings are shared with the employees on a periodic basis as cash bonuses. Inherent in the process is ongoing employee input and suggestions as to how to achieve continuing cost savings.

Advantages and Disadvantages of Group Incentive Programs

The advantages of group incentive programs are

- ▶ Improvement of teamwork

- ▶ Alignment of group goals with organizational goals

The following are disadvantages with group incentive programs that you should be aware of:

- ▶ They might undermine intergroup cooperation and create dysfunctional competition.

- ▶ It is difficult to develop baseline data in dynamic environments.

- ▶ Gainsharing payout formulae might be complex and difficult for the worker to understand; therefore, they do not provide guidance as to what behaviors lead to reward.

- ▶ Does not acknowledge differences in individual performance within the group. It might be viewed as rewarding those who do not contribute.

- ▶ Group effort might not be valued in the workplace culture.

Organizationwide Incentive Plans

If work at the individual and group level cannot be measured and/or is not independent, organizationwide incentive plans might be the most appropriate method of motivating above-standard performance. Types of organization-wide incentive plans are goalsharing, profit sharing, and employee stock ownership plans (*ESOPs*).

Goalsharing Plans

Goalsharing is a method of aligning employees with organizational goals. Although design and implementation varies from organization to organization, a typical goalsharing incentive plan has the following characteristics:

▶ A committee starts with the overall organizational objectives and determines what employee behaviors and work outcomes would contribute to the achievement of those goals focusing on performance improvement.

▶ The committee determines appropriate yearly goals for organizational subentities that would contribute to achievement of overall goals.

▶ A baseline of current performance is developed and overall organizational and subentity performance improvement goals are formulated. These goals can be related to a variety of organizational performance metrics determined to be necessary for organizational success: profitability, quality, productivity, market share, sales, employee turnover, and so on.

▶ Both the performance of the organization and the subentity are monitored in relation to achievement of the goals and the results are periodically provided to employees.

▶ Cash awards are given out at the end of the goalsharing plan year, based on overall achievement of the organizational goals and based on the subentity's achievement of its subgoals.

Profit-Sharing

Profit-sharing incentive plans distribute a percentage of the firm's yearly profit to employees. There are many methods used to determine the allocation of available funds to employees, including equal amounts to all employees or differential amounts based on individual performance, seniority, or current pay rate. There are also options as to where the money actually goes. The profit might be paid as a yearly cash bonus, distributed to a retirement plan in the employee's account, or a combination of both.

Employee Stock Plans

There is a wide variety of employee stock plans. A more in-depth discussion of stock plans is included in the discussion of executive compensation later in the chapter. The employee stock ownership plan is an organizationwide incentive plan in which the employer purchases and deposits stock in each employee's account in an employee stock ownership trust (*ESOT*) where it stays until the employee retires or leaves the company. The design and ongoing management of these plans is very complex in terms of compliance with the tax law and, to a lesser extent, with ERISA. The amount of stock deposited for each employee is typically based either on the employee's salary or on seniority. Plans can be leveraged, where the money to purchase the stock is borrowed, or not leveraged. Because of the special tax laws for ESOPs, they may be used as a method of raising capital for the firm and for employees to gain partial or total ownership.

Advantages and Disadvantages of Organizationwide Incentives

The following list highlights some advantages found with organization-wide incentives:

▶ Might promote a sense of belonging and commitment to the organization

▶ Might increase employee retention

▶ Might have tax benefits to both the firm and the employee

The following disadvantages highlight potential problems with this incentive method:

▶ Does not recognize superior individual performance.

▶ Might be viewed as rewarding slackers.

▶ Difficult for employees to determine the impact of their work on achievement of the incentive.

▶ Payout might be too far removed in time to provide a linkage between individual performance and the reward.

▶ Achievement of the incentive might be based on issues other than employee performance; that is, profitability might be affected by the economy or poor decisions by the CEO.

▶ Retirement plans funded by stock are dependent on the value of that stock. If the stock declines, the value of the ultimate retirement does so also.

EXAM ALERT

You should be familiar with the types of incentives typically used at the individual, group, and organizationwide levels, when each is appropriate, and their respective advantages and disadvantages.

TIP

You should not forget the motivating power of incentives such as recognition, praise, and a pleasant working environment.

Special Types of Compensation

Often there are special situations or particular types of jobs that require separate compensation strategies, but that do not quite fit the methods discussed previously in this chapter. They are

- Work being performed in high-cost geographic areas
- Compensation of salespersons
- Executive compensation
- Compensation of highly specialized professionals
- Compensation of members of the board of directors
- Compensation of employees on foreign assignment

High-Rate Geographical Areas

Employees in high-cost areas are often paid a higher rate to compensate them for the increased cost of living and to attract and retain them in those areas. For national employers that have an established nationwide system, this higher rate is a differential based on the cost of living in that particular area and not part of basic pay. Employees who move from one geographic area to another retain their basic pay rate and then, if appropriate, might receive a differential based on costs where they are employed.

Salespersons

Salespersons are paid on commission only, salary, or salary plus commission.

Commission-Only Plans

Commission-only plans provide the maximum level of incentive to sell but have a number of drawbacks:

- Commission-only plans do not provide any security or stability of income for the employee. To offset this problem, many employers place their commissioned salespersons on a draw against commission. The employee then receives a certain amount of money on a periodic basis against future commissions. The draw is normally recoverable in that it is deducted from future commission earnings, but it could also be nonrecoverable in which case the employee does not have to pay back the excess draw if commissions are insufficient to cover it during the pay period.

- Commission-only plans could lead to suboptimization in which the employee concentrates only on making sales and sales quotas, and fails to make decisions that are in the best long-term interest of the employer. For example:

Employee engages in unethical behavior to make a sale.

Employee only sells high-commission items, failing to try to sell the employer's other products or services.

Employee does not worry about service after the sale or long-term customer relationships.

▶ Commission-only plans do not encourage teamwork within the organization.

Salary Only

Salary-only plans provide stability and predictability for the employee, but little incentive to sell. These types of plans might be appropriate for trainees and for salespersons that are primarily order-takers or customer service employees.

Salary Plus Commission

Salary-plus-commission plans provide both some stability and some incentive. The mix between the salary component and the commission component is the key to the effectiveness of these plans and is dependent on the product or service being sold, economic conditions, and the market being served.

Executives

Executive compensation, particularly CEO compensation, is one of the hot topics in compensation today. High profile CEOs could make millions of dollars a year while their company's stock is rapidly decreasing in value and there are allegations of both ethical and legal violations in order to achieve incentive goals. Unions, employees, investors, and the government all question these high rates, yet executive compensation continues to climb. The ratio between the average salary of the rank and file and the CEO has increased exponentially in the past 25 years from approximately 40:1 in the early 1980s to a ratio approaching 500:1 today. In other words, CEO salaries of the nation's largest firms are approaching 500 times the average salary of the typical blue-collar worker. However, if a firm is to attract and retain a competent CEO, it will likely be forced to pay market rates.

Executive compensation is typically composed of base salary, short-term incentives, long-term incentives, benefits, and perquisites. The mix of these components has changed substantially over the past several decades. Base salary is increasingly becoming a smaller percentage with the majority of compensation being composed of short-term and long-term incentives.

Base Salary

As previously discussed, base salary is limited to $1,000,000 for the firm's CEO and highest-paid executives. Salaries above that figure can be paid if they are performance based, but the law is rather strict in defining performance-based compensation. In publicly held companies, the compensation committee of the board of directors normally determines the CEO's salary. Because this committee is often composed of CEOs from other firms, there is concern that setting the salary and other compensation as high as possible is in the best interest of the committee members, allowing them to negotiate similar numbers with their boards.

Short-Term Incentives

Short-term incentives typically take the form of bonuses for meeting annual (short-term) objectives. One of the major issues in executive compensation today is the extent to which executives will make decisions that allow them to meet these short-term objectives but might be to the detriment of the organization's long-term well being.

Long-Term Incentives

Long-term incentives are earned by achieving long-term strategic objectives, usually in terms of sustained profitability, increased market share, or growth in stock price. These incentives balance short-term incentives, motivating the executive to engage in strategies that balance the need for short-term success with the goal of long-term growth. Long-term incentives usually take the form of equity (stock). Stock incentives are a complex area of the practice of compensation decision-making and compensation and tax law. Although equity incentives have historically been reserved for the very top levels of the organization, they are increasingly being offered at lower levels. Therefore, discussion of various types of stock-related incentives is more and more frequently applicable to many levels of the organization. Some examples of the various types of stock incentives are

▶ **Stock options** The right to purchase a stated number of shares of stock at a set price (normally the market price at the time of issuance of the option) for a stated period of time (can be up to ten years).

▶ **Nonqualified stock options** Similar to standard options, but the tax treatment is different and there are fewer legal restrictions.

▶ **Stock purchase plans** Allows the executive to purchase stock within a short window of time. Firms may assist the executive in the purchase through low cost loans.

▶ **Restricted stock** Grants of stock predicated on the executive fulfilling some obligation, usually continued employment or achievement of certain performance objectives. The executive normally can vote the stock and receive dividends, if any, but does not actually receive the stock certificates until the obligation is met.

▶ **Phantom stock** Executives are awarded phantom stock units that mirror the value and performance of the regular stock. These units cannot be voted but can earn dividends equal to the regular stock. On completion of certain conditions, the units may be converted to cash or to actual stock.

▶ **Performance units/performance shares**   The executive is allocated a certain number of units or shares but cannot cash these in until certain performance goals are achieved. These plans are based on long-term goals, typically three to five years.

▶ **Stock appreciation rights/book value plans**   The executive receives an award of cash or stock based on the increase in value of the firm's stock during the plan period. The executive can normally exercise the right to receive the value of this increase in stock price anytime during the plan period and doing so does not require the actual purchase and subsequent sale of the actual stock.

EXAM ALERT

Executive salaries are a hot topic at this time, particularly in light of recent scandals in which CEOs were able to garner huge rewards by illegal and unethical activities. Expect a question as to how to best craft executive compensation. See the discussion on agency theory in the following note.

NOTE

Executive compensation decisions are often based on agency theory. *Agency theory* postulates that the interests of the principal (owners or stockholders) and the agent (managers and workers) are not aligned, with the principal wanting maximum growth and profitability and the agents wanting maximum personal income. These two purposes are at odds. The theory further postulates that one way to align these conflicting interests is to connect agent compensation to the achievement of organizational goals.

Benefits

Executives receive those benefits allocated to all other employees. However, benefits of qualified plans are capped by various ERISA and tax code regulations. Although these regulations protect the rank and file, they limit benefit levels that can be given to executives. Therefore, CEOs typically are provided with corresponding nonqualified benefit plans such as retirement, life insurance, and disability coverage. These are often extremely lucrative arrangements, allowing for multimillion dollar coverage and retirement income of seven figures. One benefit often provided CEOs and other top-level executives is an extremely generous severance plan; this is often referred to as a *golden parachute*.

Golden Parachute

A *golden parachute* is a type of executive compensation that protects the individual in case of termination. In times of frequent acquisitions and mergers, CEO employment security is threatened. Golden parachutes protect these executives with lucrative continuation of income arrangements, guaranteed bonuses, immediate vesting of stock options, and other arrangements. The magnitude of severance packages received by executives in recent years brought about federal legislation placing limits on corporate tax deductions for these payouts and imposed additional taxes on the executives in certain situations.

Perquisites

Commonly referred to as *perks*, these are additional components of compensation that are available to the CEO or executive because of rank. Perks are often very lucrative financially and frequently very controversial when the magnitude becomes known by investors or the public through media publication. Examples are

- ▶ Club memberships

- ▶ Use of corporate aircraft, yachts, and vehicles

- ▶ Chauffeurs and domestic help

- ▶ Corporate-provided housing and/or vacation properties

- ▶ Travel of spouse

- ▶ Personal security/bodyguards

- ▶ Generous allowances for entertainment

- ▶ Tickets to exclusive sporting or entertainment events

- ▶ Financial, tax, and legal counseling

- ▶ Low or no-interest loans

Professionals

Professionals, those requiring considerable education, credentialing, or experience, typically receive relatively high compensation. Often their work involves research and development or projects of long duration. Frequently, an important component of recurring compensation or of an incentive package for these employees includes opportunities for professional development (for example, travel to professional conferences) or allocations to improve their work capabilities (for example, allowances for additional laboratory equipment or specialized software packages).

Directors

Typical boards of directors contain several corporate officers (CEO, CFO, COO, for example) and 10 or so outside directors (current or retired executives of other firms, representatives of constituencies, large shareholders, and so on). These outside directors are compensated, sometimes handsomely, for their participation. Directors of large corporations often exceed compensation levels of $100,000 per year. Although each firm is different, components of director compensation are usually:

- Annual salary or retainer

- Travel, lodging, and stipend for each board meeting

- Additional stipend for chairing and/or attending a committee meeting

- Incentives, usually in stock, based on corporate performance

- Benefits and perks such as retirement plans, health insurance, use of corporate aircraft and facilities, and so on

The trend in director compensation is to link it with corporate performance. This is frequently done with stock incentives linked to the long-term growth and profitability of the corporation.

International Employees

In today's global market, many organizations have employees in foreign countries and determinations have to be made as to the appropriate compensation rates. Although an in-depth discussion of this issue is more appropriate for an examination preparation text for the GPHR, the SPHR must have some basic knowledge of these concepts.

Many organizations do not begin by having employees in foreign countries but follow a more conservative process of exporting product, negotiating with a foreign firm for production, licensing, or franchising, and finally establishing their own foreign operations. It is at the point when the organization actually begins to have or contemplates having employees in a foreign country that decisions must be made as to the mix of types of employees and appropriate compensation. Let us begin by defining the type of employees that an organization might have.

- **Expatriates**   Employees that are citizens of the country in which the company is headquartered but working in another country; for example, employees of a U.S. firm who are citizens of the United States but work in France.

- **Third-country nationals (*TCNs*)**   Employees that work for a firm based in one country working in a second country, but are citizens of a third country.

- **Local nationals (locals)**   Employees who are citizens of the country in which they are employed.

- **Transpatriates**   Employees of any country who spend long periods of time stationed in countries other than the country in which the firm is headquartered or the country of which the employee is a citizen.

Expatriates

Expatriates have traditionally been executives, managers, or technicians with specifically needed skills who are sent to the foreign location for relatively short periods of time (one to five years). There are a variety of reasons for sending an expatriate to the foreign location which include

- ▶ Need for international experience
- ▶ Represent the company's interest in the foreign location
- ▶ Requisite skills are not perceived to be available in the foreign country
- ▶ Desire to export the company culture to the new country

However, expatriate compensation is typically very expensive, often running many times the compensation that the employee would earn in the headquarters country. The reason is that many firms compensate based on a *balance-sheet approach*. The employee is compensated so that, to the extent possible, the employee is not financially harmed and can maintain a similar standard of living in the foreign post. The balance sheet can be based on comparable head-quarters office compensation (the *home approach*), or comparable compensation in the host country where the employee is to be stationed (*host approach*, which is generally used only if compensation is higher in the host country), the higher of the two (better of home or host approach), or on some reference point (the *international approach*). An example of the international approach would be basing all compensation for expatriates stationed in the European Union on comparable wages for Belgium. Expatriate compensation often includes the following components:

- ▶ Salary based on what the position would pay in the headquarters country.
- ▶ Taxes, often based on a tax equalization principle. The firm deducts taxes from the employee's salary based on what he or she would pay in the home country, and the employer pays whatever taxes are imposed in the country in which the employee is located or any additional taxes in the home country because of allowances paid for the overseas assignment.
- ▶ Housing costs for maintaining a residence in the country of employment.
- ▶ Allowances for the hardship and extra costs associated with the expatriate assignment:

    Hardship allowance if being assigned to remote or dangerous areas or expatriate premium to compensate for being away from the home country

    Cost of living allowance

    Allowance for children's education

    Bonus for completion of assignment

    Allowance for domestic help, drivers, and so on, if they are expectations in the country based on the position occupied.

Security for employee and family

Home leave and associated transportation for employee and family

Club memberships

Adjustment for loss of spousal income and assistance with spousal employment

Organizations must be careful to plan the expatriate assignment and make sure that the cost is justified. Expatriate assignments are subject to high failure rates and early return from the assignment if both the employee and family are not thoroughly prepared and if ongoing support is not provided. In addition, both the expatriate and family must be provided support on repatriation because the home country culture could have experienced considerable change during the assignment.

Third-Country Nationals

Third-country nationals may be paid based on the compensation rates of either the headquarters country or their home country. They often receive similar types of allowances to those received by expatriates, but the costs are typically less because of the lower standard of living and compensation rates in their home country as opposed to the United States. In some rather rare instances, compensation rates for third-country nationals could be more based on their home country rates. In that case, organizations typically compensate them based on the headquarters rate.

Firms must be careful to avoid assigning expatriates and TCNs to the same positions but paying different compensation rates.

Locals

Locals are typically paid based on the going rates of salary and benefits for their country. Again, as with TCNs, problems can emerge if either expatriates or TCNs occupy the same jobs as locals and are paid at much higher rates. It is frequently advisable to manage foreign operations with locals because they are most familiar with the culture and employment laws of the host country.

Transpatriates

Expatriate and, to a lesser extent, TCN assignments are extremely expensive. As business becomes more and more globalized, there is an increasing need for employees to serve in many foreign countries and to effectively become citizens of the world (*transpatriates*). Many employees can now expect to spend a good portion of their careers in foreign assignments. With this expectation comes a change in compensation strategy to avoid the often exorbitant costs of these foreign assignments. Transpatriate compensation will increasingly be based on rates paid in the host country with limited allowances for additional benefits.

Skill-, Knowledge-, or Competency-Based Pay

The discussion of compensation up to this point (other than individual incentive plans) has been centered on the rate of pay for the job. This is referred to as *job-based pay (JBP)*. The process of job evaluation, job pricing, and the establishment of a pay structure do not consider the attributes that individuals bring to the job but only the relative worth of the job and the human characteristics necessary to do the job successfully. However, pay rates can be based on the attributes of the person in terms of skills, knowledge, or competencies. This inclusion of human characteristics usually is in conjunction with JBP and is used in addition to, not separate from, that process.

Skill-Based Pay

Skill-based pay (*SBP*) provides increased compensation as the employee acquires additional skills, often whether or not those skills are used. The employee is paid based on the job that he/she was hired to do (JBP) plus an additional amount based on additional skills (SBP). For example, an employee is hired in a hotel as a reservation clerk at $10.00 per hour. The employee trains and is certified to also perform front desk clerk duties and is paid an additional $1.50 per hour because of that skill. The employee could also learn additional skills, such as restaurant hostess or bartender, each adding another increment to pay. There are several advantages to this type of compensation plan in that it provides employees with motivation to improve skills and increases management's flexibility in job assignments and in handling periods of peak workload or employee absences. However, among the disadvantages is the fact that the employee is paid this additional increment whether or not the skill is ever actually used, raising overall compensation costs. However, some compensation experts would argue that the increased flexibility actually allows the employer to hire fewer employees, thus offsetting the increased per-employee compensation. Besides the service sector example, skill-based pay is frequently used in manufacturing environments where employees are taught to run more than one machine or to do tasks other than those for which the employee was hired.

Knowledge-Based Pay

Knowledge-based pay (*KBP*) is frequently used in addition to job-based pay for professionals. Professionals are given additional compensation as they gain new credentials, academic degrees, or licenses. An example is teachers who receive additional pay when they receive their masters degree and at certain levels of education beyond the masters. The assumption with knowledge-based pay is that this additional knowledge, as represented by education, licensure, or certification, increases the employee's performance and justifies additional compensation.

Competency-Based Pay

Competencies in terms of hiring and evaluating were discussed in Chapter 3. Competencies, like skills and knowledge, can be used in compensation. Employees are given increased compensation when they achieve a higher level of a particular competency. The rationale is that competencies are related to the achievement of organizational goals. Therefore, the greater the competency an employee has, the greater value the employee has to the organization and compensation should be adjusted to reflect that.

Benefits

Objective:
Gain an Understanding of Employee Benefit Programs

Benefits can be categorized into those that are mandated by law and those that the employer voluntarily provides. Traditionally, benefits have been provided as an entitlement of employment and therefore serve to both attract and retain employees. Increasingly, compensation decision makers are looking at the motivational aspects of certain benefits and developing strategies in which benefits levels are linked to employee performance.

Benefits comprise a substantial portion of total payroll costs in many organizations, often in the neighborhood of 40%. For that reason it is extremely important that the benefit strategy cost-effectively provide those benefits that are valued by the employee. A similar process (needs analysis) to that discussed in Chapter 4 is used in developing the benefit compensation structure. Employees are typically surveyed as to what additional benefits they need or desire (gap analysis) and what current benefits they find to be critical. In addition, usage data are generated to evaluate employee usage of currently available programs. Decisions are then made as to the benefit strategy that best serves the needs of employees while facilitating the achievement of organizational goals in a cost-effective manner.

Legislatively Mandated Benefits

Many benefits are required by law and are discussed in this section. Benefits such as Social Security, unemployment insurance, workers' compensation, and others must be provided by the employer.

Social Security

The basic provisions of the Social Security Act (1935) were discussed in the "Compensation and Benefits Law" section of this chapter. That discussion will be expanded here. Most benefits accrue to an individual, spouse, or dependent children if the worker has sufficient earnings over a specified time. These requirements vary, depending on the type of benefit and age of the beneficiary. Social Security benefits discussed in the following sections are retirement, disability benefits, death benefit, benefits for survivors, Medicare, and unemployment insurance (which is covered later in the chapter as a separate benefit).

Retirement

Social Security provides monthly retirement payments to covered individuals who have earned 40 quarter credits. Reduced retirement benefits are available at age 62, whereas full benefits depend on the date of birth of the recipient. Individuals who were born in 1937 or earlier are eligible for full benefits at age 65. Those born after 1937 become eligible based on an increasing scale so that the minimum retirement age for full benefits becomes 67 for those born in 1960 or later. The amount of monthly retirement benefits is dependent on the age at which the individual starts to draw the benefits and average earnings during their work life.

Disability

Workers who have earned at least 21 quarter credits, 20 of which must have been earned in the preceding 10 years, are eligible for monthly benefits if they are severely disabled. There is a five-month waiting period for benefits and the employee must have medical documentation of a disability that prevents work for at least 12 months.

Death

Social Security provides a lump-sum death benefit to help defer the costs of a funeral or other final arrangements. The death benefit is $255.

Survivor Benefits

Qualified dependents of a worker who dies and has as least 21 quarters of credit are eligible to receive survivor benefits. Those eligible are

▶ Spouse at age 60 or 50 if disabled

▶ Unmarried children under the age of 18 (19 if still in high school)

▶ Disabled children if they became disabled before the age of 22

▶ Spouse at any age if caring for a dependent child

▶ Dependent parents age 62 or older

Medicare

Medicare serves nearly all citizens age 65 and older, providing major medical insurance. The work status of individuals over 65 controls whether Medicare is the primary or secondary insurance. For persons over 65 who are still working and have employer provided health insurance, the employer insurance is primary. However, after the person retires, even if covered under the employer's plan, Medicare becomes the primary insurance. The programs consist of two separate plans: Part A and Part B.

Part A

Part A is compulsory and provides hospitalization insurance for up to 90 days per event. An event begins on the first day of hospitalization and ends after 60 consecutive days of not being hospitalized. There is also a lifetime reserve of an additional 60 days of hospitalization, which is available if necessary. The covered individual pays a portion of the total charges. Part A also covers certain in-home, nursing home, and hospice services. Virtually all persons over 65 are covered by Part A and there is no insurance premium for this benefit.

Part B

Part B is optional, and is supplementary medical insurance that covers physician fees and some medical services, supplies, and medications. Medicare pays 80% of covered charges after a $100 annual deductible. There is a monthly insurance premium.

Workers' Compensation

Workers' compensation is covered by state law and provides protection in the event of an on-the-job illness, injury, or death. Workers' compensation is more fully covered in Chapter 7.

Unemployment Compensation

Unemployment compensation provides partial income continuation in the event that a worker becomes unemployed. Unemployment compensation is a joint effort between the federal and state governments and was established by the Social Security Act of 1935. Most employers are covered by the regulations, but each state exempts certain types of employers and those exemptions vary depending on state law.

Eligibility for Unemployment Compensation

Eligibility for compensation depends on state law. However, in general, the individual must have become unemployed involuntarily, be available for work, and meet certain earnings standards during the period before unemployment. Individuals are likely to be ruled ineligible for benefits or for continuation of benefits if

- ▶ They quit their job without good reason.

- ▶ They were fired for just cause. However, many states have rather strict guidelines for the definition of *just cause* and the action causing termination has to be somewhat egregious.

- ▶ Unemployment is not the result of a labor dispute. With certain exceptions, striking workers are not eligible for unemployment. However, nonbargaining unit employees who become unemployed as a result of a strike are eligible.

- ▶ They fail to pursue employment while receiving unemployment compensation.

Individuals must be available for work and be physically and mentally capable of work. Individuals must seek work in comparable positions within reasonable commuting time from their residence.

Eligible workers must have earned a specified amount of compensation during a base period. The amount of compensation and the definition of base period depend on state law.

Funding of Unemployment Compensation

Unemployment compensation is funded by the Federal Unemployment Tax (*FUTA*) and by state taxes. FUTA is assessed on the first $7,000 of wages paid to each employee at the rate of 6.2%. However, if the employer pays the state unemployment taxes, it receives a credit of 5.4%, making the effective tax rate 0.8%. The federal tax is largely used to pay for federal and state administrative costs while the state tax is used to fund benefits.

State unemployment tax laws vary but, in general, apply to the first $7,000 of wages paid to each employee. The tax rate is variable depending on the experience rate of the employer. The experience rate is based on the number of unemployment compensation claims against the employer in relation to its employee population size. Tax rates can vary from extremely low rates (1% or 2%, or even 0% in some cases) to a much higher rate (8–10%) if there are many unemployment claims against the employer.

Unemployment Benefits

Benefits to qualified individuals are normally available after a short waiting period (1 week) for periods up to 26 weeks. Congress can extend benefits beyond the 26 weeks in certain unusual circumstances. Benefit levels are dependent on state law but are usually a percentage of the employee's average wages during a defined period, replacing 50%–75% of average wages limited to some maximum rate.

Management of Unemployment Costs

High experience rates can result in substantial tax liability for the employer. Practices for managing/minimizing these costs are

- ▶ Challenging unemployment claims from former employees that quit voluntarily or were terminated for misconduct

- ▶ Verifying experience and tax rate calculations, challenging them when appropriate

- ▶ Where appropriate, using contingent workers (temporary agencies, subcontractors, and so on)

- ▶ Considering alternatives to termination and layoffs (part-time work, transfer to other departments, and so forth)

Health Insurance

Health insurance is not legislatively mandated. However, if the employer voluntarily provides health insurance, it must comply with various laws including HIPAA, ERISA, and COBRA.

Retirement

The law does not mandate retirement plans other than Social Security. However, once a employer voluntarily provides a retirement plan, it must comply with various laws, including ERISA and Older Workers Benefit Protection Act (*OWBPA*).

Family and Medical Leave

Unpaid family and medical leave is mandated by the Family and Medical Leave Act (1993). Provisions of the act were discussed in the "Compensation and Benefits Law" section earlier in this chapter.

Court Appearances

In most instances, both state and federal law protect employees that are required to appear in court for testimony or serve on juries. The employer must grant time off to perform these duties, but does not have to pay the individual for work time lost and is generally prohibited from terminating or otherwise disciplining the employee based on absences to perform a civic duty.

Military Duty

The USERRA, discussed in the "Compensation and Benefits Law" section earlier in this chapter, and state law require leaves of absence and other benefits for employees performing military duty.

Voluntary Benefits

Although many benefits are required by law, the list of possible benefits that can be voluntarily provided by the employer is limited only by the employer's willingness to do so and its capability to pay.

Retirement Plans

In general, retirement plans can be categorized into two types:

▶ **Defined benefit plans** *Defined benefit plans* are what have been traditionally thought of as a *pension*. In these plans, the employer guarantees a certain level of payment on retirement. Plans may be contributory (the employee contributes toward the funding of the pension) or noncontributory. The plan is funded by contributions that are actuarially determined based on potential obligations and ERISA requirements.

Pension benefits are either specified as a specific dollar amount (for example, $5.00 a month in retirement annuity for every month worked for the company) or the method or formula for computing the pension benefit is specified (for example, yearly pension equals number of years of service multiplied by 1.5% multiplied by the average of the employee's highest five years of earnings).

Defined benefit pension plans are never fully funded because there is a continuing liability that cannot be predicted and is dependent on the plan, death rates, and other issues. In general, the plans are not portable in that they can be transferred to another employer only under certain conditions.

▶ **Defined contribution plans**   A defined contribution retirement plan specifies the amount of contribution that the employer is obligated to make to the plan. The actual benefit the employee receives is based on the amount of contributions made and the performance of the investments made with those contributions. Defined contribution retirement plans are not subject to many of the regulatory requirements of ERISA. Examples of defined contribution plans are 401(k) in the private sector, 403(b) for employees of tax-exempt organizations, 457 for state and local governmental entities, deferred profit sharing, and employee stock ownership plans (ESOPs). Regulations limit the amount of contributions both the employee and employer can make to these plans. Individuals over 50 are permitted to make additional contributions under catch-up provisions. Because a profit-sharing plan is, by definition, dependent on profits, no contribution may be required in nonprofitable years under such a plan.

Defined contribution plans are fully funded when the contribution is made. Most of these plans are portable to the next employer or can be rolled into an IRA. In general, defined contribution plans better meet the need for flexibility in the current workplace environment where employees are not likely to remain with one employer for their entire career.

EXAM ALERT

Expect questions regarding the difference between defined benefit and defined contribution retirement plans, in particular, how the final benefits are derived and the employer's obligation with respect to each type of plan.

NOTE

Many companies, to avoid the long-term funding liabilities of defined benefit plans, terminated those plans beginning in the early 1990s, converting them to cash balance plans. A *cash balance plan* can be thought of as a combination, or hybrid, of a defined benefit and a defined contribution plan. It provides a guaranteed cash amount based on employer contributions (defined benefit), yet is portable and the amount of actual benefit could exceed the guaranteed amount based on the performance of the funds invested (defined contribution). In theory, a cash balance plan could provide better benefits for younger workers, but the conversion has been found to result in lower benefits for older workers, thus violating ADEA. Currently, conversions to cash balance plans are on hold pending IRS regulation.

Other Retirement Plans

There are a wide variety of retirement vehicles other than defined benefit and defined contribution plans. Examples are

▶ **Individual retirement accounts** There are several types of plans that allow wage earners, under certain conditions and within prescribed limits, to contribute amounts to tax deferred accounts.

▶ **Simplified employee pensions (*SEP*)** Allows self-employed individuals to set up individual retirement accounts.

▶ **Nonqualified plans** Because of limitations imposed by ERISA and the tax code, many organizations set up nonqualified retirement plans for their highest-paid executives to provide additional retirement income.

Life Insurance

Many employers provide group life insurance, often equal to the employee's salary or multiples thereof, either at no cost or shared cost to the employee. The employee frequently has the option of electing, for a fee, to cover family members.

Accidental Death and Dismemberment

Accidental death and dismemberment insurance might be offered in conjunction with life insurance or as a separate option. The insurance pays additional amounts if the death of the covered individual is by accident and also provides lump-sum benefits for the loss of limbs, sight, or other qualifying events.

NOTE

Life insurance in excess of $50,000 is taxable imputed income to the employee. The income in based on the cost of insurance premiums paid on behalf of the employee and is determined by reference to tables contained in IRS documents.

Health Insurance

Most employers offer some type of health insurance to attract and retain employees. Health insurance can be categorized into three types: fee-for-service, health maintenance organization, and a combination of the two (preferred provider organizations). Health maintenance organizations (*HMOs*) and preferred provider organizations (*PPOs*) are referred to as *managed care programs* and emphasize primary and preventive care along with cost savings initiatives and strategies.

Fee-for-Service Plans

Fee-for-service health insurance generally provides the maximum flexibility in terms of selecting health care providers, but may be more expensive and often does not cover preventive care. Characteristics of these types of plans are

▶ Covers hospital, surgical, and physician's fees based on a schedule of covered medical services.

▶ Policyholders are usually subject to a deductible. The deductible is an amount of money that policyholders must pay out each year before insurance coverage begins ($500, for example).

▶ Policyholders are also subject to coinsurance. *Coinsurance* is the percentage of the costs of insured medical costs that the policyholder must personally pay. A typical fee-for-service plan might pay 80% of the covered charges and the policyholder must pay the remaining 20% (the coinsurance).

▶ Policies also have an out-of-pocket maximum. This maximum places a limit on the total amount of coinsurance costs that the employee is obligated to pay during each year in case of a major medical event that results in large medical bills.

Health Maintenance Organizations

HMOs provide complete medical care to enrollees for a set fee and a copayment (referred to as a *copay*) when services are used. The copay is generally a small fee ($15–$20). Employees must use medical providers and facilities within the plan in order to be covered. A limited exception is made if the employee requires emergency treatment while traveling out of the service area.

Preferred Provider Organizations

PPOs are a compromise between the other two major health insurance arrangements. Employees pay small copays, as with an HMO, when using services of medical providers belonging to the PPO. However, employees also have the freedom to go outside the network to obtain medical treatment. If they do so, coinsurance payments are required, similar to a fee-for-service plan.

Employer Funding of Health Insurance

There is a wide variety of methods by which employers fund their obligations under a health insurance plan that is provided to their employees. These options are complex and beyond the scope of this book. But, in general, the firm can elect to self-insure, fully insure, or partly insure. Under a self-insured arrangement, the employer acts as the health insurance company, paying all claims and assuming all risks. Under a fully insured arrangement, the company contracts with an insurance company that assumes the risks and pays the claims. Under a partly insured arrangement, the company pays the claims but protects itself from large individual medical claims by purchasing stop-loss insurance.

There is a wide variety of administrative arrangements if the employer elects to self-insure or partly self-insure. Companies will frequently contract with third-party administrators to administer the health insurance program.

> **EXAM ALERT**
>
> Expect a question asking you to differentiate between fee-for-service, HMO, and PPO plans.

> **NOTE**
>
> Although an employer does not have to offer health insurance, if it does, many regulations come into effect. ERISA regulates the provisions of most plans, whereas state insurance agencies often regulate the insurance aspects of such plans.

Dental Insurance

Although dental insurance can be a part of the primary health insurance plan, employers often offer separate dental insurance or dental health maintenance organization coverage.

Vision Insurance

As with dental insurance, employers might offer vision insurance separately.

Prescription Drug Plans

Prescription drug insurance coverage might be provided under a separate arrangement that typically requires the employee to pay a small copay for each prescription.

Long-Term and Short-Term Disability Insurance

Long-term and short-term disability insurance provides for income continuation if an employee becomes disabled and unable to work. Short-term disability insurance provides protection for limited time periods (disabilities up to six months, for example) and might not take effect until all sick leave is used. Long-term disability protects against longer or permanent disability (six months to life). Both plans are usually integrated with other benefits, such as Social Security and workers' compensation, so that other types of benefits received reduce the amount of insurance payment. The insurance provides partial income protection (typically 50%–70% of the employee's predisability compensation).

Long-Term Care Insurance

Custodial care for the elderly and disabled is not covered by medical insurance except under specific conditions. Long-term care insurance covers nursing home and in-home services.

Legal Insurance

Legal insurance provides for prepaid legal assistance. Typically the program provides for a set amount of assistance time that is available per month or on some other periodic basis.

Paid Time Off

Paid time off is provided by the employer for a variety of reasons. Various categories of paid time off are discussed in the sections that follow. They are

- ▸ Vacation leave

- ▸ Sick leave

- ▸ Holiday pay

- ▸ Personal days off

- ▸ Paid time off

- ▸ Sabbaticals

- ▸ Miscellaneous types of paid time off

- ▸ Bereavement leave

Paid Time Off

Many employers have elected to combine all paid time off into one allocation which is frequently referred to as *PTO*. This philosophy eliminates the administrative burden of having to account for paid time off in multiple allocations and provides more flexibility for the employee. Examples of types of leave that might be included in PTO are in the following bulleted list.

- ▸ **Vacation leave**   Vacation leave is provided for the employee to get away from the stress of work and to rejuvenate him or herself. This type of leave is believed to be correlated with increased productivity on the employee's return to work. The amount of vacation leave is usually awarded based on seniority. In comparison with many industrialized countries, particularly European countries where vacation time might be mandated by law, the amount of vacation leave granted in the United States is rather small.

   The employer must decide on appropriate policy for use of this type of leave. Generally it must be scheduled in advance to not interfere with critical work or peak demand periods. Some employers allow employees to accumulate a prescribed number of vacation days and carry them over to the next leave year. Doing so allows the employee to take a longer vacation but might present work-scheduling problems for the employer. In addition, such a policy allows employees to earn leave at one rate of pay and take at another, usually higher, rate of pay. Some firms have a use-or-lose policy in which the employee loses the leave if it is not used by the end of the leave year. This can become a work-scheduling problem if many employees wait until the end of the year to take leave. Another option is to pay employees for unused leave at the end of the leave year. However, vacation leave is designed to provide the employee with rest, relaxation, and renewal, not additional income.

▶ **Sick leave**   Sick leave is provided for the employee to recuperate from illness and injury and to seek medical attention including preventative checkups and procedures. Some employers allow sick leave to be used for the care of family members. As with vacation leave, policies must be developed with respect to the use and approval of sick leave along with how to handle any leave that is left at the end of the year.

▶ **Holidays**   Most employers provide paid time off for major national holidays, although the number of total holidays varies from employer to employer. Many employers require that employees be at work on the workday immediately preceding and immediately following the holiday to be eligible for the holiday paid time off. Employees required to work on holidays are frequently paid a holiday premium rate for the time worked, often double their normal rate.

▶ **Personal days off**   Some employers grant personal days off in addition to sick and vacation leave. This is normally only a few days a year. Personal days are to be used for personal business that cannot be conducted during normal working hours such as renewing a driver's license, consulting an attorney or financial planner, and so on.

▶ **Sabbatical**   Some organizations provide paid time off for a lengthy period of renewal. Most common in academia, it is increasingly a benefit in the for-profit sector. Traditionally, sabbaticals are granted every seventh year, but the frequency varies from employer to employer. The length of sabbaticals can vary from a few weeks to a year. Some employers require the employee to be engaged in development activities such as job-related study, travel, or research during the year, whereas other employers do not.

▶ **Miscellaneous**   Employers might grant paid time off for a variety of activities such as engaging in fitness activities, serving as an officer in a civic organization, or doing other types of public or community service.

▶ **Bereavement**   Many employers provide for a short period of paid time off for the death of a close relative.

Leaves of Absence

Employers approve extended periods of unpaid time off for a variety of reasons. Examples might be to pursue an advanced degree or to care for a terminally ill friend or relative not covered under FMLA.

Supplemental Unemployment Benefits

Supplemental unemployment benefits (*SUBs*) provide additional income continuation beyond state-provided unemployment compensation. SUBs are most likely to be found in unionized environments where employees are subject to cyclical layoffs (the automobile industry, for example).

Relocation Benefits

Employees transferred or relocating for the benefit of the organization might be provided an array of relocation benefits. Because of the high cost of such arrangements, only higher-level employees might be eligible. Benefits might include travel to the new destination, house-hunting trips, job-hunting trips for a spouse, movement of the household goods, assistance with the purchase of a house at new location and selling of house at the former location, temporary lodging at the new location, and so on.

Educational Assistance

Employers often pay for some or all the expenses of formal education programs. Educational assistance above certain limits is taxable to the employee. The 2005 limit is $5,200 per year.

Severance Package

Severance payments and other services such as outplacement assistance are employer benefits that can be provided to employees who lose their jobs. The pay itself may be a lump sum or monthly payments for a prescribed period. The amount of payment is generally based on the employee's current salary and years of service.

In addition, a severance package might include outplacement assistance. This typically includes job-search, resume-writing, and interview-skill training.

> **NOTE**
>
> Many foreign countries mandate extensive severance payments. Some states have laws addressing severance benefits in certain situations.

Family Friendly and Convenience Benefits

The list of benefits to assist employees in performing their duties and coping with their obligations to family is endless. Only the more common benefit programs are discussed in this list:

▶ **Childcare** There is a wide range of benefits that can be provided from onsite childcare to financial assistance with childcare costs to referral services.

▶ **Eldercare** Employees could be responsible for not only children but also for parents or grandparents. Services provided are similar to those for child care.

▶ **Flexible schedule and work locations** Alternative work schedules and alternative work places can be offered to give employees flexibility in hours worked and locations of work. This can be especially helpful to employees who have life situations that don't cater to a typical 9-to-5 workday or to being in one office or other location everyday.

▶ **Concierge services** Laundry pickup, assistance with entertainment tickets, restaurant reservations, and so forth are some of the services that can be provided to assist employees working long hours for the firm.

▶ **Commuting benefits** Firms often assist employees by underwriting the cost of parking, public transportation, facilitating vanpools and car-pooling arrangements and, in fewer instances, providing company-owned vehicles.

▶ **Adoption assistance** Referral services and reimbursement of costs associated with the adoption

▶ **Employee assistance and wellness programs** As discussed in Chapter 7, these programs offer employees various services for mental and physical well-being, along with other resources employees might find helpful in their lives.

NOTE

Many of the benefits mentioned in the list could be taxable, depending on the value of the benefit. Reimbursement of commuting expenses and parking and personal use of a company vehicle, including commuting, fall into this category, as does reimbursement for adoption expenses. The SPHR should consult the most recent limitations before offering benefits that create a taxable event for the employee and are not deductible by the employer.

Benefit Cost Containment and Flexibility

The major issue in employee benefits today is the rapidly increasing costs of medical services, which is causing health insurance rates to rise at unprecedented rates. Employers engage in all sorts of strategies to reduce the impact of increased costs, both on the employer itself and on the employee. Many of the strategies are discussed in the following sections. They are

▶ Transferring the cost burden to the employee

▶ Carving out certain services

▶ Pretax programs

Transferring the Cost Burden to the Employee

Employers have been forced to increase the proportion of health insurance and medical services costs incurred by the employee. This includes

▶ Increasing insurance premiums and the proportion of premiums paid by the employee. Firms that have previously provided free health insurance have had to require employees to pay a portion of the premium.

▶ Decreasing benefits and covered services under the health insurance plan.

▶ Changing the proportion of coinsurance (from 20% to 30%, for example).

▶ Increasing the deductible before health insurance begins covering medical services.

▶ Increasing copay amounts.

Carving Out Services

It is frequently more cost effective to "carve out" certain benefits from other plans and make them a separate benefit. Some examples are health and dental insurance. Other examples are disease management programs in which special programs are developed to assist with the treatment and management of chronic illnesses. Employers often find that creating specialized benefit programs such as these brings about better health outcomes with decreased overall expense to the employer.

Pretax Programs

There are a number of programs in which both the employer and employee can receive tax advantages resulting in more cost-effective benefit programs.

▶ **Pretax health insurance** Section 125 of the tax code permits several arrangements for employees to pay health insurance premiums (premium-only plans) and out of pocket medical expenses (flexible spending accounts) up to a prescribed limit with pretax dollars.

▶ **Pretax childcare expenses** Section 129 of the tax code allows employees to pay for childcare expenses up to a prescribed limit with pretax dollars.

▶ **Health reimbursement accounts** These are accounts established by the employer to reimburse employees for medical expenses. The account is funded entirely by the employer and is used to pay for substantial medical expenses and the cost of health insurance premiums. The plan is somewhat complex but essentially, the employer purchases high-deductible insurance for the employee and also deposits a designated amount in an account for the employee to cover part of the deductible amount. The combination of the two employer-paid items is often much cheaper than paying for traditional insurance.

▶ **Health savings accounts**   Under these arrangements, the employee or employer (or both) purchases a catastrophic health insurance policy (a high-deductible health plan, referred to as an *HDHP*). These plans must have a deductible of at least $1,000 for an individual or $2,000 for a family. Additional funds are contributed to the plan by the employer, employee, or both, up to the deductible amount. Those funds can then be used for out of pocket medical expenses. If not used, they accumulate indefinitely. Funds can be withdrawn for certain other purposes, but the employee incurs a withdrawal penalty and must pay income tax. Funds that are contributed by the employee are with before-tax monies. These plans are portable, can be taken into retirement, and often result in substantial savings for both the employer and employee.

▶ *Cafeteria plans*   This term is an umbrella for a multitude of plans, including those qualifying under Section 125 of the tax code. Within limits, employees can select the benefits that best meet their needs. Although cafeteria plans have a number of advantages, there are also some disadvantages.

Advantages

Employees can customize benefits based on individual and family needs.

Employer can cap total benefit expenditures. Employees can select benefits only up to a certain dollar level and then must pay for additional benefits.

Employees become more aware of benefit costs and do not select benefits that are not needed.

Disadvantages

Multiple benefit programs and individual selection increases the administrative burden on the employer.

Adverse selection in that employees select only those benefits that they know they will use. High usage rates, particularly on health-related insurance plans, drive up premium rates.

Employees make bad decisions and do not select the types of coverage that are needed.

NOTE

Funds deposited in flexible spending accounts are "use or lose." Unspent funds are forfeited.

Strategic Considerations for the SPHR

The SPHR must develop a strategic compensation plan that meets the goals of the organization. Furthermore, that plan must be constantly monitored to ensure that objectives are being achieved.

Strategic Development

The development of a compensation plan in many organizations is one of the most important, if not the most important, strategic responsibility that the SPHR has. The complexity of this task is enormous and, in larger organizations, often requires the assistance of either external or internal experts. This is particularly true with respect to benefits where the regulatory requirements and tax implications present many challenges.

The SPHR must ultimately develop a strategy that attracts, retains, and motivates employees to engage in behaviors that facilitate the achievement of organizational goals. All of this must be accomplished within a number of constraints or parameters:

▶ The plan must be in alignment with the business strategy and organizational and product life cycle of the organization.

▶ The plan must be developed within the constraint of the organization's ability to pay.

▶ The plan must be cost effective in that the costs must generate results in terms of desired employee behavior and organizational success.

▶ The plan must be in alignment with the organizational culture. Even the most brilliantly crafted compensation strategy will not yield results if it violates the norms and values of the organization and is not accepted by the workforce.

Strategic Monitoring

How does the SPHR know that the compensation strategy is effective? There is a wide variety of metrics that should be used to track the implementation, impact, and workforce acceptance of the compensation strategy.

Implementation

To judge the effectiveness of a compensation strategy, that strategy must first be implemented in accordance with the plan. Most compensation strategies, by their very design, have built-in controls. The processes of job analysis, job evaluation, job pricing, and pay structure development create a structure with defined limits in terms of compensation ranges and the integration of both internal job worth and external job pricing. Assuming that the structure includes ranges of compensation for each job or pay grade and is not a flat rate system, one critical issue is where actual pay rates fall with respect to the midpoint of the range. The midpoint, as you will recall, reflects the employer's pay policy. It is the average pay the employer desires to pay for a particular job or pay grade. A common metric used to evaluate this issue is the compa-ratio, which is calculated as follows:

Actual rate paid / Midpoint of range

The compa-ratio will be 1 when the actual rate of compensation is on the policy line at midpoint of the range, above 1 when it is above the range, and below 1 when it is below the range.

The actual rates of pay for employees can be aggregated at any level for analysis. Thus the SPHR could aggregate the average rate of pay and average midpoint (weighted appropriately) for all employees in a group, a division, or the whole corporation. HRIS systems or integrated payroll systems can frequently provide this calculation. When done, it can be used for analysis in a number of ways. First, at the organizational level, it can provide data on organizational performance in maintaining the pay policy. If the goal is to have average compensation at the pay policy line, an organizationwide compa-ratio above or below 1 would be cause for further analysis to assess why this is occurring. Compa-ratios above 1 might result in substantial increases in overall compensation costs, affecting profitability and capability to compete in the market. On the other hand, such a ratio might indicate a senior and highly productive workforce. Compa-ratios below 1 might result in an inability to retain employees because this could be an indication of below-market pay rates. However, it could also indicate a relatively junior workforce if there has recently been much hiring at the low end of the range.

Compa-ratios can be used to evaluate compliance with equal pay and equal employment opportunity law. Comp-ratios can be computed by race and sex of employee. These compa-ratios would need to be evaluated to make sure that protected groups are not being adversely affected by the compensation strategy.

Finally, compa-ratios can be computed for individual organizational subentities. These data can be used to evaluate the manager's compliance with the pay strategy.

> **EXAM ALERT**
>
> Expect a question regarding compa-ratios. Know the formula and how it can be utilized in analyzing compliance with the compensation strategy.

Impact

Analysis of the impact of the compensation strategy on organizational goals can take many forms. The SPHR must determine which organizational goals are affected by the compensation strategy and track results in terms of goal achievement in relationship to changes in compensation strategy. For example, if the organization is experiencing high turnover and a change in compensation is initiated to improve retention, new turnover rates need to be compared with baseline rates occurring before the implementation of the compensation changes. If it is believed that a new individual incentive program can improve productivity, productivity rates should be compared with the baseline prior to implementation of the variable pay plan.

> **NOTE**
>
> As with virtually all HR programs and strategies, the metrics deal with correlations and do not prove or disprove cause and effect. Because the SPHR cannot control external factors, organizational results could be a result of influences other than the compensation strategy itself, and that must be kept in mind when analyzing the impact of the compensation strategy.

Workforce Acceptance

If compensation strategies are to affect employee behavior and, ultimately, organizational performance, those strategies must be clearly communicated to employees and employees must buy in to them. Employees must perceive the strategies are equitable. It is critical to the SPHR to know exactly how employees perceive the compensation program. Typically this is accomplished via an employee climate or opinion survey. Other methods of getting the information are through exit interviews and focus groups. These data can often provide valuable insights as to the effectiveness of the strategy and ways to improve it.

Chapter Summary

An organization's compensation and benefits strategy is increasingly important as the human capital of the organization is recognized as its core competency and distinctiveness in the market.

The legislative environment of compensation and benefits is extremely complex, but the chapter covered the major laws and regulations.

There is a variety of ways to develop a pay structure. The chapter covered the major processes involved in determining the relative worth of a job to the organization (job evaluation), the external compensation rates of job (salary surveys), and how to develop a compensation structure by integrating the two (job pricing).

Benefits are either mandated by law or voluntary on the part of the employer. Various types of benefits were introduced and discussed.

Throughout the chapter, the emphasis has been on understanding compensation and benefits at the strategic level. The compensation strategy and structure must be developed in light of its cost-effectiveness in achieving organizational goals.

Key Terms

- Prevailing rate
- Exempt employee
- Compensatory time
- Compensation
- Benefits
- External equity
- Internal equity
- Individual equity
- Garnishment
- Vesting
- Job evaluation
- Compensable factors
- Benchmark jobs
- Ranking

- ▶ Job classification

- ▶ Point factor method

- ▶ Factor comparison method

- ▶ Pay grade

- ▶ Pay range

- ▶ Golden parachute

- ▶ Expatriates

- ▶ Third-country nationals

- ▶ Local nationals

- ▶ Transpatriates

- ▶ Medicare

- ▶ Defined benefit plan

- ▶ Defined contribution plan

- ▶ Fee-for-service plans

- ▶ Health maintenance organizations

- ▶ Preferred provider organizations

- ▶ Compa-ratio

Apply Your Knowledge

Exercises

5.1 Using the Factor Comparison Method

You have been given the assignment of evaluating Job D using the employer's already developed factor comparison method of job evaluation. A matrix showing the three benchmark jobs, money amounts, and ranking assigned to the four compensable factors is shown in the table that follows.

Benchmark Job	Skill	Effort	Responsibility	Working Conditions	Hourly Rate
A	$5.00 (1)	$3.00 (3)	$7.00 (1)	$1.00 (3)	$16.00
B	$4.00 (3)	$4.00 (1)	$5.00 (2)	$1.50 (2)	$14.50
C	$4.50 (2)	$3.50 (2)	$3.00 (3)	$3.00 (1)	$14.00

The employer's policy is to price the compensable factor at the midpoint between the benchmark jobs when a compensable factor of a job under evaluation is estimated to lie between two benchmark jobs. For example, using the matrix, if the working conditions of a job under evaluation were rated between the working conditions of Job A and Job B, it would be assigned a rate of $1.25. When the compensable factor is determined to be equal to the benchmark job, it is assigned the same rate.

Determine the hourly rate for Job D when you evaluate the following:

▶ The skill required of Job D is greater than B but less than C.

▶ The effort required of Job D is equal to B.

▶ The responsibility of Job D is greater than C but less than B.

▶ The working conditions of Job D are equal to C.

5.2 Using the Point Factor Method

Your organization uses the point factor method of job evaluation with four compensable factors, each having sub factors. The maximum number of available points is 3,000. Using this system, you have evaluated Job A as follows:

Compensable Factor	Subfactor	Points
Skill	1	50
	2	100
	3	200
Effort	1	200
	2	100
Responsibility	1	50
	2	100
	3	0
Working Conditions	1	200
	2	50

The compensation structure contains 10 pay grades. The points assigned to each grade are as follows:

Grade 1	001–300
Grade 2	301–600
Grade 3	601–900
Grade 4	901–1200
Grade 5	1201–1500
Grade 6	1501–1800
Grade 7	1801–2100
Grade 8	2101–2400
Grade 9	2401–2700
Grade 10	2701–3000

Based on this information, to which pay grade should you assign Job A?

Review Questions

1. You are the HR manager of a mid-sized manufacturing firm. The production department consists of a Director of Production and five subordinate managers. You believe that J. Brown, one of the subordinate managers in the production department, has historically been overly liberal with pay raises in relation to the other managers. What might be one way to determine whether this is the case?

2. There are rumblings from the rank and file regarding the compensation system currently in place. How might you, as the HR Director, get a better handle on exactly what the issues are?

3. You are asked by your CEO to very succinctly describe how a compensation structure is developed. What do you tell the CEO?

4. You are the HR Director of a relatively new business in a volatile, low-margin market. The CEO wants to implement a defined benefit retirement program. Would you recommend such a program? Why or why not?

5. The compensation committee of the board of directors of your firm has asked you for recommendations as to how to restructure the CEO's compensation plan. The plan was originally formulated when the organization was in its infancy and consists of a low salary with a large component of stock options and stock grants. The organization is now well into its growth stage. What recommendations would you make?

Exam Questions

1. The process of determining the relative value of a job to the organization is referred to as which of the following?

   ○ **A.** Job analysis

   ○ **B.** Job evaluation

   ○ **C.** Job pricing

   ○ **D.** Strategic planning

2. Which of the following employees would most likely not be considered an exempt employee under the Fair Labor Standards Act?

   ○ **A.** Physicist performing research and development work

   ○ **B.** An assembly line worker making $110,000 per year

   ○ **C.** The general manager of a large division

   ○ **D.** A political columnist for a major metropolitan newspaper

3. Which method of job evaluation involves creating generic class and pay grade descriptions and then comparing those descriptions to the job description of the job under evaluation?

   ○ **A.** Ranking

   ○ **B.** Job classification

   ○ **C.** Point factor

   ○ **D.** Factor comparison

4. Multiplying the number of years of service by a set percentage amount for each year and then multiplying that amount by the average of his or her wages for the highest five years of earnings determines an employee's pension benefit. This calculation is characteristic of which of the following plans?

   ○ **A.** Defined benefit plan

   ○ **B.** Defined contribution plan

   ○ **C.** Cash balance plan

   ○ **D.** Social security plan

5. Which of the following is not a provision of the Fair Labor Standards Act?

   ○ **A.** Equal pay

   ○ **B.** Overtime

   ○ **C.** Minimum wage

   ○ **D.** Workers' compensation

6. The deck of cards method is associated with which type of job evaluation?

   ○ **A.** Ranking

   ○ **B.** Job classification

   ○ **C.** Point factor

   ○ **D.** Factor comparison

7. Which federal act provides for continuing health insurance coverage for former employees, their spouses, and their dependents when certain qualifying events occur?

   ○ **A.** ERISA

   ○ **B.** COBRA

   ○ **C.** HIPAA

   ○ **D.** FLSA

8. A male employee requests leave under the Family and Medical Leave Act (1993) to care for a family member experiencing a serious medical condition. Which of the following relatives would not be covered under the act?

   ○ **A.** Foster son

   ○ **B.** Adopted daughter

   ○ **C.** Common law wife in a state that recognizes common law marriage

   ○ **D.** Parent-in-law

9. The purpose of a product market survey is to do which of the following?

   ○ **A.** Provide data on wage levels being paid by employers in the local labor market

   ○ **B.** Provide data on prices being charged for products by competitors in the same industry

   ○ **C.** Provide data on market share of competitors

   ○ **D.** Provide data on wage levels being paid by competitors in the same industry

10. An employer is particularly interested in maintaining external equity with respect to its compensation system because it rarely promotes from within and recruits from the external labor market throughout all levels of the organization. What of the following processes is most associated with creating external equity?

   ○ **A.** Job analysis

   ○ **B.** Job evaluation

   ○ **C.** Salary surveys

   ○ **D.** Employee input

Answers to Exercises

5.1 Using the Factor Comparison Method

Based on the employer's policy, you would assign the following rates to the compensable factors resulting in an hourly rate of $15.25.

Skill	$4.25
Effort	$4.00
Responsibility	$4.00
Working Conditions	$3.00
Hourly Rate	$15.25

5.2 Using the Point Factor Method

The total number of points assigned to the job is 1,050, which equates to pay grade 4.

Answers to Review Questions

1. You should consider calculating the overall compa-ratio of the production department and then the compa-ratios of each individual manager. These data will provide you with an indication of the positioning of the salaries of J. Brown's employees in relationship to the pay policy line and can be compared with the other managers in the department and with the department as a whole.

2. There are many ways to accomplish this. The most obvious answer is to ask the employees in exit interviews and through employee surveys. It might also be appropriate to conduct some focus groups interviews. Finally, the SPHR should determine whether it appears that employee behavior is being negatively affected. Data such as turnover, productivity, and quality metrics should be reviewed.

3. To keep it simple, you would indicate that the whole process begins with the development of a job description (job analysis). Next the job descriptions are used to evaluate the relative worth of the various jobs to the organization (job evaluation). When that is complete, a determination has to be made as to an appropriate rate of pay (salary survey). Finally, the relative worth of the job to the organization and the rate being paid in the external market are combined to determine a final rate of pay for the jobs in the organizations (job pricing).

4. Although the question provides limited information on which to formulate a recommendation, today's predominant retirement strategies are formulated around defined contribution plans, not defined benefit plans. Defined benefit plans commit the organization to long-term funding of the retirement system based on actuarial assumptions and ERISA regulations. Defined benefit programs no longer fit the realities of many employment situations in which there could be a great deal of market volatility and uncertain income streams. Defined benefit programs do not align the costs of such programs with organizational success, and they often do not meet the needs of employees in terms of portability in today's labor environment. For these reasons and others, a defined contribution retirement program is likely to better meet the needs of both the employer and employees.

5. A change in compensation is indicated to better align the CEO's compensation with the life cycle of the firm. The current plan is too heavy on equity-based long-term incentives and should be balanced by shorter-term incentives. Assuming that the firm is in a better cash position than when it was first formed, the CEO's salary should be raised to an externally equitable level. Because the firm is now in its growth stage, it is likely that some stabilizing processes have to be introduced. The short-term incentives should be tied to these. Incentives based on formalizing processes and procedures and in developing internal cost control and cost savings measures are likely appropriate. Finally, the long-term equity incentives should be reduced and balanced by the short-term incentives. Long-term incentives might be based on achievement of strategic objectives and dependent on the CEO remaining with the organization.

Answers to Exam Questions

1. The correct answer is **B**. Job analysis (answer A) is the process used to determine the duties of the job and the human characteristics necessary to successfully perform those duties. Job pricing (answer C) is used to determine the appropriate compensation for the job, and strategic planning (answer D) is a broad concept used to determine the direction of the organization.

2. The correct answer is **B**. The assembly worker is not a highly compensated employee as defined in the regulations because it is assumed that the person does not perform executive, administrative, or professional duties. The physicist (answer A) is exempt under the learned professional exception. The general manager (answer C) is exempt under the executive exception, and the columnist (answer D) is exempt under the creative professional exception.

3. The correct answer is **B**. Job classification involves comparing generic descriptions to the actual job description and deciding on the best fit.

4. The correct answer is **A**. A defined contribution plan (answer B) does not guarantee a set amount of pension at retirement because the final benefit is determined by the performance of investments made with contributions to the plan. Cash balance plans (answer C) guarantee a certain cash amount that would be available at retirement. That cash amount could, at the election of the employee, be converted to an annuity but the amount of the annuity would be determined by actuarial calculations at the time of retirement. Currently, cash balance plans are essentially illegal. Social Security (answer D) is a totally different calculation based on quarters earned and wage levels.

5. The correct answer is **D**. Equal pay is part of the Equal Pay Act, which is an amendment to FLSA (answer A). Overtime and minimum wage provisions (answers B and C) are covered in FLSA.

6. The correct answer is **A**. Job classification (answer B), point factor (answer C), and factor comparison (answer D) arrive at the job evaluation hierarchy by using other methods.

7. The correct answer is **B**. The Consolidated Budget Reconciliation Act (1985) (COBRA) provides for continuation of health insurance for former employees and their spouses and dependents under certain conditions. ERISA, the Employee Retirement Income Security Act (1974) (answer A) is a comprehensive act governing pension and certain benefit programs. HIPPA, the Health Insurance Portability and Accountability Act (1996) (answer C), increases the portability of health insurance through limitations on pre-existing condition clauses. FLSA, the Fair Labor Standards Act (1938) (answer D), is a broad-ranging compensation law covering minimum wage, child labor, overtime, and equal pay.

8. The correct answer is **D**. Foster and adopted children (answers A and B) and a common law spouse in states recognizing common law marriage (answer C) are all covered under the act. Parents, but not parents-in-law, are covered.

9. The correct answer is **D**. The product market survey data provides data on what the firm's competitors are paying. Assuming that productivity, technology, and costs of raw materials and supplies are roughly the same for all competitors, the product market wage data provides an indication of the maximum wage levels that can be paid and remain competitive. The labor market survey data provide an indication of the minimum level of wages necessary to attract and retain workers.

10. The correct answer is **C**. Job analysis (answer A) is the basic process on which compensation systems are built. Job evaluation (answer B) is used to create internal equity. Employee input (answer D) is critical to the design of the compensation system, but is not particularly associated with external equity.

Suggested Readings and Resources

1. Books

   ▶ Bergman, T. J. & Scarpello, V. G. (2001). *Compensation Decision Making* (4th edition). Orlando, FL: Harcourt.

   ▶ Henderson, R. I. (2000). *Compensation Management in a Knowledge-Based World* (5th edition). Upper Saddle River, NJ: Prentice Hall.

▶ Martocchio, J. J. (2001). *Strategic Compensation: A Human Resource Management Approach* (2nd edition). Upper Saddle River, NJ: Prentice Hall.

▶ Milkovich, G. T., Newman, J. M, with the assistance of Milkovich, C. (2005). *Compensation* (8th edition) New York: McGraw-Hill Irwin.

▶ Phillips, L. W. & Fox, M. A. (2003). Compensation strategy in transnational corporations. *Management Decision*. 41(5), 465-476.

▶ Robinson, R. H., Franklin, G. M. & Wayland, R. (2002). *The Regulatory Environment of Human Resource Management*. Fort Worth, TX: Harcourt.

2. Websites

▶ http://www.bls.gov/

▶ http://www.dol.gov/

▶ http://www.hhs.gov/

▶ http://www.irs.gov/

▶ http://www.ssa.gov/

C H A P T E R SIX

Employee and Labor Relations

Objectives

This chapter helps you to prepare for the SPHR examination by covering the concepts and strategies associated with employee and labor relations. This section composes **24%** of the SPHR examination.

Gain a Strategic Understanding of Employee and Labor Relations

➤ Understand the importance of employee and labor relations

➤ Understand the historical precedents in employee and labor relations that have contributed to the development of both regulations and practice

➤ Understand the reasons why employees vote for unions and the effect that unionism has on the employer

Gain an Understanding of Employee and Labor Relations Law

➤ Understand the provisions of the multitude of employee and labor relations laws, NLRB rulings, and court decisions

➤ Understand the implications of these laws, rulings, and decisions in the development of employee and labor relations strategies

➤ Understand the interdependencies of these laws, rulings, and court decisions

Gain an Understanding of the Union Certification Process

➤ Understand what tactics and strategies are likely to be used by the union and by management, and which of those are permissible and which constitute unfair labor practices

➤ Understand the mechanics and process of the certification election

Gain an Understanding of the Collective Bargaining Process

➤ Understand what is bargainable and not bargainable and what is and is not good faith bargaining

➤ Understand the concepts associated with distributive and integrative bargaining

➤ Understand the tactics that can be used by either management or the union to apply pressure on the opposition to settle the contract

➤ Be familiar with the various commonly negotiated contract provisions

Gain an Understanding of Contract Administration

➤ Understand the grievance process

➤ Understand the grievance arbitration process

➤ Understand the ULP complaint process

Gain an Understanding of Employee and Labor Relations in a Nonunion Environment

➤ Understand the concept of employee rights and obligations

➤ Understand the concepts and implications of various types of employee involvement and high performance work systems programs

Outline

Study Strategies

▶ The SPHR should study this chapter with the purpose of gaining a strategic perspective regarding unionism and its impact on the organization. To do that, you have to understand the basic building blocks of unionism, such as the certification election, collective bargaining, and contract negotiations.

▶ Stop after each major subsection and attempt to relate its content to prior subsection trying to develop an overall "big picture" understanding of the material. At this point, reflect on what you have learned and what additional information you want to know. Then read the next subsection and repeat the process.

▶ Reflect on the fact that employee and labor relations are not separate concepts, but are related on a continuum. How does each of the concepts discussed affect your organization, regardless of whether it is unionized?

▶ Read the section on employee relations, employee involvement, and high performance work systems and analyze the various programs and consider their applicability to your organization. The process of connecting these abstracts to a real organization will help your understanding of them and improve your ability to retain the material.

Introduction

The SPHR must understand employee and labor relations from a strategic standpoint. It is essential to effectively manage the relationship between the employer and employee whether in a union or nonunion setting. If the organization is unionized, it is critical to effectively manage the union relationship and negotiate and administer labor agreements in order to facilitate the achievement of organizational goals. In this era of increasing global competition, arrangements that accommodate the needs of labor and/or labor unions, but maintain management flexibility and competitive productivity, are essential for organizational success.

In a nonunion environment, the SPHR must develop strategies regarding potential union organizing, whether the goal is avoidance or acceptance. The SPHR must understand the impact that unionization has on the relevant industry and labor market to develop effective strategies for the organization. Finally, the SPHR must develop strategies and programs to create a productive work environment in which employees are committed to exhibiting proper work and citizenship behaviors.

A Brief History of Employee and Labor Relations

Objective:
Gain a Strategic Understanding of Employee and Labor Relations

To gather a better understanding of employee and labor relations, it might be helpful to review its history to see how the current status of employee and labor relations has developed. The following four sections will brief you on some of the watershed events in the labor and employee relations history.

Employee and Labor Relations: 1776–1819

There have been labor organizations since the inception of this country. Early labor organizations were largely made up of skilled craftsman. These organizations were loosely formed and attempted, among other objectives, to maintain wages and prices of their product. However, as transportation improved, making markets larger, employers expanded their operations engaging in practices to minimize labor costs. These brought about the formation of the first formal union organizations. Common law was utilized to keep these organizations in control by use of the *conspiracy doctrine*. The courts interpreted unions as groups of individuals gathered together to conspire to restrain trade.

> **NOTE**
>
> **1790**—The first union was formed by cordwainers (shoemakers) in Philadelphia.

Employee and Labor Relations: 1820–1869

As markets continued to grow, employers began building large factories to bring workers together. These organizations were largely craft unions (representing skilled craftsmen), but some organizations of unskilled workers emerged in the northeastern factories. Although this was a time of increased organization, it was also a period of increased violence as employers aggressively resisted unionization. Unions grew in size and the first national federation of unions, the National Labor Union, was formed to include unions representing a diverse array of crafts.

> **NOTE**
>
> **1866**—The National Labor Union was founded.

Employee and Labor Relations: 1870–1934

The Industrial Revolution, mass production, and scientific management fueled a surge in manufacturing resulting in large factories, long work hours, child labor, physically demanding and simplified jobs, unsafe working conditions, and employer domination. These conditions resulted in labor unrest and violence as employers resisted labor organization with force, often using armed protective forces (such as the Pinkerton National Detective Agency) and frequently resulting in numerous deaths. Large-scale strikes began occurring, the first of which was the Great Uprising in 1877 directed against the railroads. The Knights of Labor, a labor organization committed to social change, emerged as a national union. Although the Knights of Labor gained a large membership in the 1870s and 1880s, it all but ceased to exist by the 1890s, largely because powerful employers violently put down strikes and because the Haymarket Tragedy of 1886 turned public opinion against the labor movement. Many craft unions abandoned the Knights of Labor during this period and joined the *American Federation of Labor (AFL)* led by Samuel Gompers. The AFL was committed to business unionism, stressing collective bargaining rather than social change.

The period was marked by the use of the injunction by employers to prevent labor union activity and the court's and government's general support of employer actions against unions. The Industrial Workers of the World (IWW, or *Wobblies*) was formed in 1905 and was a radical reform labor organization, stressing violent opposition to employer domination and espousing class struggle. In attempt to reduce violence, some employers engaged in open shop and welfare capitalism practices, improving working conditions and creating employer-dominated unions, but maintaining a strong anti-union posture. The Sherman Antitrust Act was used to prevent union activities because the courts viewed these activities as restraint of trade. During WWI the government protected unions, but withdrew that protection after the war. The first permanent government protection of the right to organize was the Railway Labor Act of 1926.

NOTE

1877—The Great Uprising was the first coordinated, large-scale strike.

1888—The Haymarket Tragedy, a labor protest against employer and government violence on strikers, resulted in the death of several policemen and turned public opinion against the labor movement.

1908—The Sherman Antitrust Act was determined by the Supreme Court to cover union activities. Boycotts, and potentially other union activities, were determined to be illegal, and union members could be held personally liable for damages caused by their union activities. The Clayton Act of 1914 removed unions from coverage under the act.

1926—Congress passed the Railway Labor Act, which was the first federal legislation that guaranteed a portion of the labor force the right to form unions and bargain collectively. Airlines were included in 1936.

1932—Congress passed the Norris-LaGuardia Act to limit management's capability to obtain injunctions prohibiting activities of unions. It also made yellow dog contracts unenforceable. (A *yellow dog contract* is an employment condition requiring a potential employee not to join or support a union.) However, the act was largely passive in nature and did not guarantee labor the right to form unions.

Employee and Labor Relations: 1935–Present

Following the Great Depression, or what is often referred to as the *New Deal era*, great strides were made in terms of labor and employment legislation. Among the first of these initiatives were the Social Security Act of 1935 and the Fair Labor Standards Act of 1938. These acts were designed to protect employees and to assist in economic recovery. The Wagner Act, passed in 1935, marks the beginning of strong support for unionization. Initially there was employer resistance and noncompliance as organizations questioned its constitutionality. The Supreme Court resolved the issue in 1937, firmly declaring the law to be constitutional. The act led to a huge increase in union membership, which reached its peak in the 1950s with approximately 35% of the private sector workforce unionized. The Wagner Act shifted, to some extent, the balance of power between the employee and employer. A strike at General Motors in 1936 and 1937 would establish the tone of future labor relations in the United States: retention of management rights to manage as modified by restrictive labor agreements bargained in an aggressive, adversarial environment.

In 1938, industrial unions led by John L. Lewis of the United Mine Workers withdrew from the AFL, which was an organization of craft unions, eventually forming the *Congress of Industrial Organizations (CIO)*. This event is significant in labor history because it represents the beginning of the movement away from craft unionism to industrial unionism. Industrial unions became a powerful labor movement better organized to exert power in an industrialized economy. The two labor organizations were eventually reunited in 1955, forming the *AFL-CIO*.

After a series of strikes following WWII, Congress passed the Taft-Hartley Act in 1947 to rebalance power between labor and employers. The Landrum-Griffin Act was passed in 1959 after a series of hearings in Congress, which brought forth significant allegations of union leaderships' misuse of power and corruption. This act provided a bill of rights for union members and controls, particularly financial, for unions. By 1959 United States labor law was largely in place, and there has been no major legislation since. Since that date, federal legislative action has been largely in the employee relations/employment arena with the Equal Pay Act of 1963, Civil Rights Act of 1964, Age Discrimination in Employment Act of 1967, Occupational Health and Safety Act of 1970, Americans with Disabilities Act of 1990, Civil Rights Act of 1991, Family and Medical Leave Act of 1993, and others.

The latter part of the twentieth century and early part of the twenty-first century have been times of substantial change in the labor relations landscape. An eroding manufacturing base, globalization, increasingly competitive environments, and changes in the demographics of the work force have presented significant issues. Labor unions have had to overcome negative public relations while attempting to organize industries previously not organized (service and knowledge), and to attract demographic groups typically less inclined to join a union (women, professionals, minorities). At times, unions have had to engage in concession bargaining, giving up previously negotiated benefits for job security and an additional voice in decision-making (seats on the board of directors). At the same time, employers have had to deal with restrictive negotiated contracts and labor practices that restrain the flexibility necessary in a dynamic market and environment.

NOTE

1935—Congress passed the Wagner Act, which is the major labor relations legislation in the United States. It guarantees employees the right to form and join unions and to engage in collective bargaining. This act also created the National Labor Relations Board to administer the act and established guidelines for what constitutes employer unfair labor practices (ULPs).

1936–1937—A strike at General Motors established the basic relationship of management and the union in the United States.

1937—The Wagner Act was declared constitutional by the Supreme Court in *NLRB v. Jones and Laughlin Steel Corp.*

1947—Congress passed the Taft-Hartley Act to rebalance the relationship between labor and management. It created unfair union labor practices, provided for employer free speech during certification elections, created the Federal Mediation and Conciliation Service (FMCS), outlawed the closed shop, and included provisions for injunctions in labor disagreements that might affect the safety or health of the country.

1959—Congress passed the Landrum-Griffin Act, largely to control the internal procedures of labor unions and guarantee certain rights for employees as union members.

1963–Present—Most legislation has been in the employee relations arena (Civil Rights Acts, ADA, ADEA, and so on).

EXAM ALERT

You should expect several questions regarding the history of employee and labor relations. Particularly significant is the initial influence of the Sherman Antitrust Act, the formation of the AFL, passage of the Wagner Act, and the rise of industrial unions by the formation of the CIO.

EXAM ALERT

Remember that you are not required to memorize dates.

Union Organizational Structure

Unions can be organized in a variety of ways. Historically unions have been classified as either *craft* or *industrial*. Craft unions represent workers in a particular type of job (carpenters, electricians, and so on) regardless of the industry in which they are employed. Industrial unions represent workers in a particular industry regardless of the jobs the workers perform (auto workers, mine workers, and so forth). Because of decreasing union density and increasing competition for members, however, many unions can now be better characterized as *general* unions that seek to organize workers in many occupations in many industries.

The late twentieth century and early twenty-first century have been periods of reduction in the total number of unions, often through mergers. These unions are frequently called *amalgamated unions*.

Union organization structure is hierarchical in nature. A typical structure could include local unions, national unions, federations, and international organizations. Each level will be discussed further in the following subsections.

Local Unions

Local unions (*locals*) are largely responsible for the day-to-day administration of the labor agreement and relationship with union members. Locals generally have an elected president and elected stewards who represent the workers in the workplace. A larger local union might have a full-time paid business agent. Most locals belong to and are chartered by a larger national union. Negotiations are increasingly conducted and managed by the national union. At a minimum, most national unions retain the right to approve locally negotiated contracts.

National Unions

National unions are the power centers of United States labor relations. They charter the local unions, negotiate on a broad basis with larger employers, approve local agreements, hold overall responsibility for organizing, might manage national benefits plans (retirement, health insurance, and so on), develop strategic initiatives, lobby legislatures, and provide overall guidance and support to the local unions. National unions are led by elected officials. Some national unions title themselves *international* unions because they have local unions in other countries, primarily Canada. National unions might also have an intermediate organizational structure that divides the country into regions or districts.

Federations

Most national unions belong to a federation of unions, such as the AFL-CIO. The AFL-CIO is largely a support organization and does not involve itself with negotiations or contract administration. The AFL-CIO acts as the voice of all organized labor on the national level, lobbies national officials on behalf of labor, and provides support services such as research and education.

International Organizations

The AFL-CIO and many national unions belong to international labor organizations. The AFL-CIO belongs to the *International Confederation of Free Trade Unions (ICFTU)*, which is a federation of national federations, or a *confederation*. The ICFTU operates in the international arena, much as the AFL-CIO operates on a national scale: by providing support. The ICFTU attempts to work on labor's behalf internationally and to assist in communication and collaboration of unions worldwide.

Employee and Labor Relations Law

Objective:
Gain an Understanding of Employee and Labor Relations Law

The SPHR must be familiar with the large body of legislation that affects and regulates the practice of employee and labor relations. Particularly important is an in-depth understanding of the Wagner Act and its major amendments, the Taft-Hartley and Landrum-Griffin Acts.

Sherman Antitrust Act (1890)

The purpose of the act is to prevent monopolies and other activities considered to be a restraint of trade. In 1908, the Supreme Court ruled that the act covered unions, that a boycott conducted by the National Hatters of North America violated the act, and held individual members personally responsible. The Sherman Antitrust Act was subsequently amended by the Clayton Act of 1914, which effectively removed unions from coverage.

Railway Labor Act (1926)

The act provided for the right of railroad employees to form unions for the purpose of collective bargaining and establishes procedures for mediation and arbitration of disputes. The act was amended and strengthened in 1934 to prohibit the establishment of company unions and provide for secret ballot certification elections. The airlines were included in coverage under the act in 1936. Major provisions of the act were

➤ Establishment of the *National Mediation Board (NMB)* to administer the act.

➤ Establishment of resolution procedures under the NMB for disputes arising during contract negotiations. If the parties cannot agree on contract language, they must submit to mandatory mediation. If mediation fails, the NMB must offer binding arbitration. If either party rejects arbitration, it may not strike or lock out until after a 30-day cooling off period.

If a strike would threaten transportation services critical to the economy of a region or the nation, the NMB is required to notify the president, who might appoint a Presidential Emergency Board. The board is a fact-finding body that must issue a report within 30 days. The union and employer then have 30 days to consider the report and its recommendations and attempt to resolve the issue before a lockout or strike can occur.

➤ Establishment of the National Railroad Adjustment Board (*NRAB*) to adjudicate disputes arising from contract interpretation. The NRAB deals with these issues in only the railroad industry, not the airlines.

Norris-LaGuardia Act (1932)

Also called the *Federal Anti-Injunction Act*, it severely limited the power of federal courts to issue injunctions against unions. It also made yellow dog contracts unenforceable in federal courts. A *yellow dog contract* is an employment condition requiring a potential employee to not join or support a union.

National Industrial Recovery Act (1933)

The major purpose of the act was to regulate the economy and promote recovery from the Great Depression. It contained a provision guaranteeing employees the right to organize and bargain collectively. However, the act was ruled unconstitutional in 1935 because the Supreme Court found it to be beyond Congress's authority to regulate interstate commerce.

Wagner Act (1935)

The Wagner Act, officially the *National Labor Relations Act*, is the major labor relations law of the land, covering most employers in the private sector. It does not cover federal, state, or local governments. Important provisions were

➤ **Sections 3–6** Creates the *National Labor Relations Board (NLRB)* to administer the act, conduct and certify representation elections, and investigate and adjudicate alleged violations (unfair labor practices).

➤ **Section 7** Gives employees the right to join and form labor organizations, to bargain collectively, and to engage in concerted activities for mutual aid or protection.

➤ **Section 8** Delineates employer unfair labor practices as follows:

  ➤ Interfering with, constraining, or coercing employees in the exercise of their rights guaranteed under Section 7

  ➤ Dominating or interfering with the formation of a labor organization

  ➤ Discriminating against employees with respect to employment decisions based on membership or nonmembership in a labor organization, subject to legally negotiated security clauses (that is, union or agency shop clauses)

  ➤ Encouraging or discouraging membership in any labor organization

  ➤ Retaliating against an employee because he or she has filed charges or given testimony under the act

  ➤ Refusing to bargain collectively

➤ **Section 9** Gives a properly certified labor organization exclusive representation of all employees in the bargaining unit for the purposes of collective bargaining and empowers the NLRB to determine the proper constitution of a bargaining unit.

NOTE

Notice that the Wagner Act only delineated employer unfair labor practices. Union ULPs did not become law until the Taft-Hartley Act, discussed next.

Taft-Hartley Act (1947)

The Taft-Hartley Act, officially named the *Labor Management Relations Act,* amended the Wagner Act and sought to rebalance the power between the employer and labor. Major provisions

➤ Outlawed the *closed shop*, which requires a prospective employee to be a member of a labor organization prior to being hired.

➤ Created six union unfair labor practices.

  ➤ To restrain or coerce employees in the exercise of their rights as defined in Section 7 of the Wagner Act.

➤ To cause or attempt to cause an employer to discriminate against an employee with respect to employment decisions based on membership or nonmembership in a union, except in accordance with negotiated union security clauses.

➤ To refuse to bargain collectively.

➤ To engage in secondary boycotts and certain types of strikes.

➤ To charge excessive or discriminatory fees or dues.

➤ To cause or attempt to cause the employer to pay for services not rendered (known as *featherbedding*).

➤ Allowed individual states to pass right-to-work laws that outlaw the union shop and, in some states, the agency shop security agreements. Twenty-one states have done so: Alabama, Arizona, Arkansas, Florida, Georgia, Idaho, Iowa, Kansas, Louisiana, Mississippi, Nebraska, Nevada, North Carolina, North Dakota, South Carolina, South Dakota, Tennessee, Texas, Utah, Virginia, and Wyoming.

➤ Guaranteed free speech for employers during representation campaigns so long as that speech does not contain threats of reprisal or promises of benefit.

➤ Clarified that employees also have the right to refrain from exercising their rights under the act.

➤ Allowed the President of the United States to seek an injunction against certain strikes that imperil national health or safety. The President must create a board of inquiry to investigate the causes and circumstances regarding a labor dispute. On receipt of the board's report, the President can direct the Attorney General to request a 60-day injunction through the federal courts system. The parties are required to meet to try to resolve the disagreement during the injunction. If the dispute is not resolved, the NLRB has 15 days to hold a secret ballot of employees to determine whether they want to accept the last offer of the employer and then another 5 days to certify the election results. If the dispute is still not resolved, the strike may ensue.

➤ Created the *Federal Mediation and Conciliation Service* to assist in resolving labor/management disputes.

Landrum-Griffin Act (1959)

The Landrum-Griffin Act, officially the *Labor Management Reporting and Disclosure Act*, amended the Wagner Act and was precipitated by Senate committee hearings that revealed significant corruption and dishonesty within some unions. Major provisions of the act

➤ Created a bill of rights for union members, including secret ballots, guaranteed due process in internal union discipline matters, and allowed members to sue the union.

➤ Required that unions adopt a constitution and bylaws, and file annual financial reports.

➤ Restricted the use of *trusteeships*. This is the process by which the national union can take over control of a local union. This is permitted only in certain restricted circumstances (for example, corruption in the local union).

➤ Required periodic (every three years) elections of union officers, using secret ballots.

➤ Prescribed the financial duties of union officials and limited eligibility of certain individuals for office.

➤ Placed limits on secondary boycotts, organizational picketing, and prohibited *hot cargo clauses* (contractual agreements between the employer and union not to use or handle the products of a third party with which the union is having a labor disagreement).

EXAM ALERT

Expect several questions on the law. You should have a good understanding of the Wagner, Taft-Hartley, and Landrum-Griffin Acts. In particular, you should be know the basic rights granted employees, activities that are prohibited to employers and the union (unfair labor practices), right-to-work provisions, and the presidential injunction process in national emergency strikes.

Significant NLRB and Judicial Decisions

Employee and labor relations law is a constantly evolving process as both the NLRB and the courts interpret and reinterpret legislation. The following sections discuss some of these bodies' more important and relevant decisions that affect human resource management practices in these areas.

Beck Rights

Beck rights are the rights for bargaining unit members to pay only that portion of union dues that are attributable to mainline union responsibilities, such as collective bargaining, organizing in the same industry, and contract administration. These rights were established by the Supreme Court's decision in *Communication Workers of America v. Beck* (1988).

Circuit City

Circuit City is the common name for the Supreme Court decision, in *Circuit City Stores, Inc. v. Adams* (2001), which determined compulsory arbitration, as a condition of employment, is legal.

Borg-Warner Doctrine

The Borg-Warner doctrine empowers the NLRB to categorize bargaining issues into the categories of mandatory, permissive, and illegal. The doctrine derives its name from the Supreme Court decision in *NLRB v. Wooster Division of Borg-Warner Corporation* (1958).

Excelsior List

The *Excelsior list* is a register of the names and addresses of all employees eligible to vote in a union certification election. The list must be provided to the NLRB, which in turn provides it to the union. The list derives its name from the *Excelsior Underwear, Inc. v.NLRB* decision in 1966.

Mackay Doctrine

The *Mackay doctrine* is the right of an employer to permanently replace striking workers during an economic strike. It derives its name from the Supreme Court decision in *NLRB v. Mackay Radio and Telegraph Co. (1938)*.

Weingarten Rights

Weingarten rights are an employee's entitlement to have a representative at an investigatory interview with management if the employee reasonably believes that discipline might result from that meeting. It is derived from the Supreme Court decision in *NLRB v. Weingarten* (1975). Although it is clear that bargaining unit employees are entitled to representation, the issue of nonbargaining-unit employees in a unionized setting and all employees in a nonunionized setting has flip-flopped as the composition of the NLRB has changed. The board's most recent decision in June 2004 (*IBM Corp.*) allows representation for bargaining unit employees only.

> **EXAM ALERT**
>
> You should be familiar with the NLRB and court decisions discussed in the previous sections. Of these, *Circuit City*, *Weingarten*, and the *Excelsior list* are the most likely subjects of test questions.

The Union Certification Process

Objective:

Gain an Understanding of the Union Certification Process

Union certification is the process under which employees can elect a union to be their exclusive representative to deal with the employer regarding wages, hours of work, and other terms and conditions of employment. The steps in the process are heavily regulated by the Wagner Act as amended. For purposes of explanation, the process can be broken down into several stages. The stages are

> ➤ Initial contact and interest building

> ➤ Election campaign

> ➤ Election

Initial Contact and Interest Building

The process usually begins in one of two ways. Either one or more employees contact the union, indicating some potential interest in organizing their employer, or the union makes contact with employees of the organization. The reasons why employees might contact the union are discussed in the later section titled "Appeal and Impact of Unionism."

There are several reasons why the union might contact employees. The primary reason is that the union views the organization as primed for organizing: employees are unhappy, the firm is in an industry typically represented by the union, and there is a sufficient number of potential members. Another reason the union might be interested in organizing the firm is to gain a foothold in a geographic area or industry that the union views as important to its strategic goals. Finally, a union might simply view the firm as an easy target and quick win even though it does not fit with its strategic objectives. As the unions' traditional base, manufacturing, has eroded, they have had to take what's available in order to survive, becoming less selective in the types of employees and the industries that they are willing to represent and target for organizing activities. Increasingly, unions are becoming general in nature and will represent interested employees in virtually any industry.

After the contact is made and a decision is reached to begin exploration of the potential for organizing, the union will attempt to develop interest among employees in the proposed bargaining unit. This interest is expressed by signing an authorization card. When 30% of the prospective bargaining unit has signed authorization cards, the union may petition the NLRB to hold a certification election. In practice, unions attempt to obtain signed authorization cards from at least 50% of the proposed bargaining unit and then attempt to get the employer to view these cards and voluntarily agree to bargain with the union. This is called a *card-check election*, but is rarely used because employers typically do not voluntarily recognize the union. A card-check election must be approved by the NLRB to verify that a majority of the bargaining unit wants to be represented by the union.

Another potential union action at this time is to call a recognition strike to force the organization to bargain with the union. Although this occurred frequently in the early twentieth century, it is relatively rare now. Most unions prefer to petition for a certification election.

In general, petitions from the union will not be accepted if an election has been held within the prior year, if a union has been certified within the past year but has not successfully negotiated a contract, or if there is a valid contract (not to exceed three years) in effect.

After the petition is filed, the employer essentially has two options. The first is to agree that the authorization cards are valid and that they have been signed by at least 30% of the proposed bargaining unit. If that occurs, the NLRB will proceed to schedule an election, called a *consent election*.

The second option is to request a hearing with the NLRB, alleging that the election should not be held. The employer may request the hearing based on a number of grounds. Typical reasons for requesting the hearing are

➤ The union committed a ULP during the organizing process.

➤ The authorization cards are not valid in that the signatures were not collected in a timely manner (that is, they are more than a year old), or the person signing the card is not an employee or is not part of the proposed bargaining unit.

➤ The bargaining unit is not properly constituted. The bargaining unit comprises all employees who will be represented by the labor organization. Certain types of employees are, by regulation, not permitted to be in a bargaining unit. Examples are managers, supervisors, confidential employees (essentially secretaries and administrative assistants to managers who can make labor relations decisions), and several others. Beyond this regulatory exclusion, management can claim that those positions proposed to be in the bargaining unit do not share a "community of interest." It is then incumbent on the NLRB to make a determination as to the proper constitution of the unit. In making that determination, it will typically consider the following issues:

➤ Geographical dispersion of employees

➤ Similarity of working conditions and duties

➤ Standard/historical organizing arrangements in the industry

➤ Mobility of employees between organizational units contained in the proposed unit

➤ Requests of the employees

➤ The employer's organizational structure

After the hearing process is completed and any issues are resolved, the NLRB may then direct that an election be held. The election typically will be held 30–60 days after the date of the petition.

On issuance of the directed election order, the employer has seven days to provide a list of the names and addresses of all employees eligible to vote. This is called the *Excelsior list* and must be given to the NLRB, which will in turn provide it to the union.

EXAM ALERT

Expect a question regarding the initial contact stage. You should be familiar with the rules surrounding authorization cards, the NLRB hearing process, and reasons for objecting to an election.

Election Campaign

It is the responsibility of the NLRB to conduct the election to ensure that the requests of the bargaining unit are carried out. In doing this, the board attempts to maintain "laboratory conditions" so that the employees are free to choose without being influenced by illegal activities of either the union or management. The election campaign is similar to other democratic elections in that both parties try to influence the employees' decision-making and gain their vote.

Union Strategy and Tactics for Influencing Votes

In attempting to influence votes, the union can use a number of strategies and tactics similar to the strategies found in almost any election. Some strategies and tactics, however, cross the boundary between aggressiveness and violation of the law, and become unfair labor practices. The following two sections highlight the strategies and tactics that unions can and cannot use.

Permissible Activities

The union typically mails campaign literature to the bargaining unit and distributes leaflets and flyers either off the premises or in common areas within the organization's premises, if so permitted. Organizers may meet with employees in their homes or conduct group meetings and rallies at offsite locations. Unions may use local media (newspapers, radio, and so on) both to reach the employees and to attempt to gain public sentiment for a positive vote. These advertisements are often in cooperation with various public interest groups who support unionization.

The union may use *salting* in both the organizing and election campaigns. *Salting* is a legally protected process in which paid union organizers attempt to get hired by the target employer for the express purpose of facilitating the organizing/certification process. It is an unfair labor practice for the employer to terminate these employees strictly on the basis of their organizing activities.

Although the employer may not promise benefits if the employees do not vote for the union, the union can promise benefits if employees vote for it. This is the union's strongest tactic and most persuasive argument. The union must convince employees that they will be better off being represented by the union.

The union may engage in organizational picketing to attempt to interest employees in voting for the union. It may also engage in recognition picketing to attempt to get the employer to recognize the union, but such picketing is limited to 30 days, after which the union must petition the NLRB for an election. Picketing is also commonly used during strikes and boycotts. Although picketing is constitutionally protected as free speech, there are prescribed limits. In general, picketing must be conducted off the employer's property and the activities of picketers must not damage the employer's property or result in violence or injury.

Unfair Labor Practices

The union may use neither coercive nor threatening pressure against an employee to gain his or her vote, nor threaten retaliation if the employee votes against the union and the union subsequently wins.

EXAM ALERT

Expect a question regarding permissible union tactics. Remember that unions can visit the employee at home, but management cannot.

Employer Strategy and Tactics

The employer has many tactics at its disposal to attempt to influence the employee's vote. Many believe that the process is a bit unbalanced, favoring management over the union during the campaign. Just as with unions, there are permissible strategies and tactics and unfair labor practices.

Permissible Employer Strategies and Tactics

Research shows that delaying tactics are effective in improving the chance of management defeating the union in a certification election. Consequently, management will often request a hearing with the NLRB to try to prevent the election from occurring. The longer that the election can be delayed, the more likely it is that the union will lose some of the momentum it has built up in piquing employee interest and enthusiasm in unionization, which culminated in sufficient signed authorization cards to petition for an election. It is often in management's best interest to question the composition of the bargaining unit. Management's odds of winning the election are improved by attempting to make the bargaining unit as large and heterogeneous as possible. Such bargaining units tend to be less cohesive and less committed to the union cause because of their diversity of interests.

A typical tactic used by management is to hire an election consultant to guide the organization through the process. Most often, the employer has not experienced a certification election before and does not have internal expertise with regard to the issue. The consultant, who is experienced and an expert in the area of certification elections, can be an invaluable asset in developing strategy and tactics to defeat the union in the certification election.

The employer can use its communication capabilities to provide employees with anti-union information through bulletin boards, emails, one-on-one supervisor and employee meetings, various mailings to the employees' home address, and stuffers in the pay check. It may also use "captive audience" meetings in the workplace during regular working hours. This is a contentious tactic opposed by the union because it forces employees to listen to anti-union rhetoric by attending a mandatory presentation by management officials. Unions do not have this capability and believe it provides an unfair advantage to the employer. Captive audience meetings are prohibited within 24 hours of the actual election.

The employer may convey anti-union and/or pro-management information during any of these communication activities so long as they are factual and are not threatening or coercive in nature. For example, the employer may cite factual statistics—on job losses in an industry after unionization or the actual rise in wages after paying union dues, for example—if such data are accurate and make the employer's case.

The employer may prevent union organizing activities in the workplace during work periods alleging that it affects productivity. The employer may also institute a no-solicitation policy throughout its premises which, in effect, prohibits union organizing activities in nonwork areas. However, this a bit risky because the policy must be universally applied and monitored. For example, such a policy would likely prevent solicitation for the sale of items in support of the local Little League team on company premises.

ULPs on the Part of Employers

An easy way to remember what the employer is prohibited from doing is the mnemonic TIPS, which stands for *threat, interrogate, promise, surveil*. An employer cannot threaten to take some negative action if the employees vote for the union. For example, the employer cannot threaten to close the plant. An employer cannot interrogate the employee regarding how he plans to vote or what activities she engaged in during the campaign. An employer cannot promise benefits for voting against union certification. For example, the employer could not promise to lower health care deductibles in return for a vote against the union. Finally, an employer cannot engage in surveillance of the employee, such as taking pictures of all persons entering an offsite union organizing meeting. Although union organizers can visit an employee at home during the campaign, management cannot.

EXAM ALERT

Expect a question, probably based on a scenario, in which you must differentiate between permissible tactics and employer ULPs. Remember that captive audience meetings are a big advantage for the employer. Also remember TIPS when dealing with activities that the employer is not permitted to engage in.

Determination of Results

The NLRB conducts the actual election, generally at the work site. Both management and the union can have observers present. These observers can object to a vote if they believe the individual is voting illegally. The NLRB resolves voter eligibility issues prior to the final count.

The NLRB counts the votes and certifies the election. A simple majority of those voting is required to win.

> **NOTE**
>
> Certification requires only a majority of those voting, not a majority of the proposed bargaining unit. It is assumed that those who do not vote are in agreement with those who did.

If activities are engaged in that the NLRB believes disturbed the "laboratory conditions" and affected the outcome of the election, the board can order a new election. For example, if the union lost but the employer committed one or more ULPs, a new election might be ordered. If the behavior of the employer was extremely egregious and so tainted the process that a fair election could not be held, the NLRB could require the employer to recognize the union and bargain. This called a *bargaining order* and is a relatively rare occurrence.

Decertification

Employees might become dissatisfied with the union and want to remove its representation rights. This is called *decertification* and the process is similar to that of certification. The decertification process begins with a petition to decertify being sent to the NLRB. The petition must be signed by 30% of the bargaining unit. Decertification cannot occur until 12 months after certification if an initial contract has not been negotiated or until the expiration of a contract if one has been negotiated. If the petition is in order, the NLRB will conduct a decertification election. If a majority of those voting choose to remove the union, decertification occurs. A tie vote also removes the union.

Deauthorization

Another type of election is the deauthorization election, which is rarely used. Deauthorization revokes the union security clause of the existing contract (union or agency shop), effectively making the security one of an open shop. Unlike decertification, deauthorization does not remove the union; it retains its authority to represent the bargaining unit with the employer. Deauthorization requires a majority vote of the entire bargaining unit. In this case, a tie vote retains the current clause.

> **NOTE**
>
> Unlike certification and decertification elections, which require a majority of those voting, deauthorization requires a majority vote of the entire bargaining unit to remove the security clause.

The Collective Bargaining Process

Objective:

Gain an Understanding of the Collective Bargaining Process

After the union is certified, the next important task is to negotiate a labor contract through a collective bargaining process between the union, the employees, and the employer. This bargaining process is done to establish the terms and conditions of employment for the bargaining unit.

Good Faith Bargaining

Both sides are required to bargain in good faith. Failure to do so is a ULP. However, there is neither a requirement to reach an agreement nor to make concessions. The NLRB takes a comprehensive look at the activities of both sides when evaluating an unfair labor charge for failing to engage in good faith bargaining.

There is no specific regulatory guidance regarding the characteristics of good faith bargaining. In general, it is characterized as an honest attempt on both sides to reach agreement. This usually includes introducing contract language, discussion of the language, and discussion of possible compromise or movement on the issues. Good faith bargaining probably is better described in the negative. Characteristics of not bargaining in good faith are

➤ Either party engaging in *surface bargaining*. This is merely going through the process with no intent to reach an agreement.

➤ Management bypassing the union bargaining team and presenting proposals directly to the employees (*direct dealing*).

➤ Refusing to meet at reasonable times and locations.

➤ Presenting proposals as "take it or leave it."

➤ Insisting on bargaining on illegal or permissive items, or refusing to bargain on a mandatory item.

➤ Making unilateral changes in hours, wages, and other terms and conditions of employment while negotiations are being held.

➤ Not providing sufficient information to the opposition to enable it to make informed proposals and counterproposals. It is usually the union that requests information, and this is often a contentious area. It should be noted that if the employer indicates an inability to fund a specific proposal, it is obligated to provide financial documentation to support the statement. Consequently the employer will normally respond to a proposal with an unwillingness to fund it, which does not obligate the employer to provide financial data.

➤ Committing ULPs while bargaining is being conducted.

➤ Although there is no requirement to make concessions, failure to advance proposals or counter proposals and/or to make concessions can be viewed within the larger context as bad faith bargaining.

Bargaining Items

The Supreme Court, in *Borg-Warner*, authorized the NLRB to categorize bargaining items into three areas. The three areas include

➤ Mandatory bargaining items

➤ Permissive bargaining items

➤ Illegal items

Mandatory Bargaining Items

These are the items or topics that must be negotiated to agreement or impasse, and are the meat of any labor agreement. The list of mandatory topics is extensive and management must provide relevant information to the union for it to negotiate these items. Examples of mandatory items are

➤ Regular wages

➤ Work hours

➤ Overtime

➤ Discipline procedures

➤ Paid and non-paid time off

➤ Union security

➤ Layoffs and recalls

➤ Seniority

➤ Work rules

➤ Work assignments

Although an item might not fall in the category of mandatory and might be a right reserved for management, the impact and implementation of decisions arising from that right on bargaining unit employees might be negotiable. This is also called *effects bargaining*. For example, although management has the right to determine the type of technology it employs (machines, automation, and so on), issues regarding how that technology is implemented and their impact on employees are negotiable.

Permissive Bargaining Items

Permissive bargaining items are topics that can only be negotiated on agreement to do so by both parties. It is illegal to strike or go to impasse on these issues. The process is often referred to as *voluntary bargaining*. Examples of permissive topics might be representation of the union on the board of directors, benefits for retired employees, and so forth.

Illegal Items

These are items that would violate the law. To insist on negotiating these items is a ULP. Examples include insisting on a closed shop, or proposing work rules or procedures that would violate the Civil Rights Act.

EXAM ALERT

You should expect a question that asks you to determine whether a bargaining topic is mandatory.

Distributive Bargaining

Distributive bargaining is the traditional and prevalent way of negotiating and involves the advancing of positions; an example of this would be a demand for a 5% across-the-board raise. It is often called *positional bargaining*. Distributive bargaining is often adversarial and is win/lose in nature. The basic assumption is that there is a fixed amount of resources available (fixed pie) and that every concession or movement away from a previously held position is a win for one side and a loss for the other. In other words, it involves the distribution of resources.

Distributive bargaining is not conducive to mutual problem-solving or long-term relationship-building. Movement to integrative bargaining (discussed next) has been hindered by the expectations of both sides that hard positional bargaining is the best way to maximize each side's respective interests.

Integrative Bargaining

Integrative bargaining is a mutual problem-solving process that discusses interests and issues, rather than positions, in an attempt to resolve them in a collaborative manner. For example, how can the standard of living of union members be maintained or increased while, at the same time, improving organizational profitability? This approach is often called *interest-based bargaining*. Integrative bargaining is predicated on a win/win philosophy and assumes that resources are flexible (the pie can be made larger). It is believed to facilitate long-term relationship-building between the parties and to result in contractual language that better serves both parties.

Integrative bargaining requires a different mindset and substantial understanding of this type of negotiating. The innovative results of integrative bargaining often must be further negotiated in a distributive process (dividing up the larger pie). In general, neither unions nor management have embraced this type of bargaining.

Bargaining Tactics

The bargaining tactics used in these two styles, for both the union and employer, are similar yet different. The commonality is that each side is trying to convince the other to agree to its proposal. In integrative bargaining, the tactic is essentially to improve the situation for both parties; in essence, to convince the other party that it will be better off. In distributive bargaining, however, the tactic is essentially opposite. It is to convince the opposite party that it will be worse off by not agreeing to the proposal. The tactic is to apply pressure to convince the opposite side that the cost of agreeing is less than the cost of disagreeing.

Successful bargaining is based on selection of an effective bargaining team. Appointment of the spokesperson is most critical because that person will speak for the team during the process. Critical to success is effective preparation in terms of defining both sides' interests and creating proposals and counterproposals based on those interests. Although it is easy to believe that each side will respond rationally to reasonable proposals, this is not always the case. Effective negotiators understand that their opposition has numerous constituencies with conflicting priorities. They evaluate what tactics and proposals might be most effective in such an environment. Distinct tactics used by labor or management are discussed in the sections that follow.

Union Tactics in Bargaining

The following list describes some common tactics unions might use to influence a bargaining session with management:

➤ **Economic strike** The ultimate weapon to apply pressure on management is the strike and threat of a strike. A *strike* is an employee-initiated work stoppage of temporary duration. An economic strike occurs when workers strike during the contract negotiations over mandatory bargaining topics. A strike imposes significant economic costs to the employer and might incur other substantial costs in terms of public opinion and public pressure to resolve the conflict. However, workers can be permanently replaced during an economic strike, meaning the employer does not have to bring the workers back following resolution of the strike. However, workers are entitled to priority status as the employer hires new employees. For reasons explained in the following item, the more frequent strategy is to call the economic strike an unfair labor practice strike.

The use of the economic strike has diminished over the years and there are relatively few strikes in relation to the total number of negotiations occurring each year.

➤ **Unfair labor practice strike** The union can protect jobs by alleging that the employer has committed an unfair labor practice during contract negotiations, making an economic strike an unfair labor practice strike instead. Permanent strike replacements are not permitted and the strikers must be returned to work upon resolution of the strike. The union, however, must be able to prove that a ULP has been committed.

➤ **Strike benefits**   Generally, employees cannot receive unemployment benefits during a strike. To offset the loss of income, many unions have funds set aside to partially replace lost wages during a strike.

➤ **Work slowdowns**   Unions can engage in a variety of activities to reduce productivity for the purpose of applying economic pressure on the employer. Workers can refuse to work overtime during critical production periods. They can call in sick or show up late for work. They can file huge numbers of grievances to bog down the system. They can follow very precisely the work rules and safety requirements of their jobs, frequently asking for direction and guidance from their supervisors. Whether employees can be disciplined for these activities is situational and depends on the employer's policies and the nature of the employee's conditions of employment.

➤ **Corporate campaigns**   Corporate campaigns include a variety of activities designed to exert external pressure on the employer. Unions might enlist the help of customers who would be affected by the strike or local governmental officials. They can file numerous complaints with regulatory bodies such as the EEOC, OSHA, or the Department of Labor. Unions can appeal to outside directors on the board or to investors to apply pressure on management to settle.

➤ **Picketing and boycotts**   Picketing is a common strategy. It is used for several reasons, including to inform the public, to prevent workers from entering the workplace, and to encourage a boycott of the company's services or products. Picketing is lawful but heavily regulated by state and federal law. Unions must control those on the picket line to prevent violence or property damage.

Picketing of the struck employer for the purposes just mentioned, including a boycott, is generally permissible. Picketing or secondary boycotting of a neutral third party is not. The law is very complex in this area. For example, it would generally be illegal (an unfair labor practice) to picket or encourage boycotting of the financial institution used by the target company of the strike. However, it might be legal to picket an employer that is now doing the work previously done by the striking employees or a company essentially owned by the employer. Likewise, a nonunion subsidiary of the primary employer (commonly called *double breasting*) may be picketed.

A common issue, particularly in the construction industry, is many employers working at the same work location. The union may picket the struck employer (commonly called *common situs picketing*), but must not prohibit other neutral employers from conducting their business. Specific entrance gates are often reserved for the strike-targeted employer (referred to as the *primary* employer) and the secondary employers. Picketing may only occur at the gate used by the primary employer.

➤ **Sympathy strike**   Members of a different union may refuse to cross the picket line of another union during a strike. This is a protected activity under labor law, but the employee generally may be replaced (not fired). However, an employee can be fired for refusing to cross the picket line of another union if that employee's labor contract prohibits sympathy strikes.

Management Tactics in Bargaining

The following list describes some common tactics management may use to influence a bargaining session with unions:

➤ **Lockout**   The opposite of a strike is a *lockout*, in which the employer prohibits workers from working in order to put economic pressure on the union and employees to resolve disputes. In general, lockouts are legal. However, if it is clear that the purpose of the lockout is to destroy the union, the lockout would be an unfair labor practice. In a lockout, employers may replace workers only temporarily, not permanently replace them.

➤ **Strike replacements**   Employers can maintain operations during a strike by using nonbargaining employees or by hiring replacement workers. In economic strikes, the employer can permanently replace striking workers under the *Mackay doctrine*. The employer must advise these new employees, at the time of hiring, whether they are temporary or replacement workers. Permanently replaced workers are not entitled to reinstatement following resolution of the strike but are put on a priority list. The employer is required to offer jobs to replaced workers on this list as openings become available.

NOTE

Strike replacements are a particularly contentious issue with labor. Unions argue that strike replacements lessen the impact of a strike, or the threat of a strike, and gives employers an unfair advantage in the contract negotiation process.

➤ **Strike insurance**   Employers can purchase private insurance to partially offset losses incurred during a strike.

➤ **Strike preparations**   Employers can engage in a number of activities designed to negate the potential economic impact and pressure caused by a strike. In addition to maintaining operations, employers can take other actions such as stockpiling inventory, moving production to other plants, or subcontracting the work.

Bargaining Structure

It cannot be assumed that the bargaining unit established under a union certification election will be the only unit included in negotiation of a contract. Both the employer and the union, for various tactical and strategic reasons, might want to include multiple bargaining units in one negotiation process. In general, the employer would typically prefer to negotiate at the local level and include only one bargaining unit, believing that its negotiating effectiveness is improved by negotiating with local union officials who are presumably less trained and experienced. In general, the union would prefer to negotiate on a multiple-unit level, believing there is power in the number of employees affected by the negotiations, which provides greater leverage. In addition, union members in various bargaining units look to the union to provide similar contractual arrangements for all members. The challenge in this case for unions is to balance the power of numbers with the need for customization to meet local specific needs. Some common bargaining structures are

➤ **Decentralized** Local management and union officials negotiate the labor contract.

➤ **Centralized** The employer negotiates with multiple bargaining units at once, often on a companywide basis.

➤ **Multi-employer** More than one employer negotiates with the union at the same time. This is often found in highly competitive industries in which multiple small employers are located in the same geographical area and can, effectively, occur industrywide.

➤ **Pattern** The union selects a major employer in an industry and negotiates a contract that then becomes the pattern for other contracts in the same industry. The automobile industry is an example of where this type of bargaining is used.

➤ **Multiple unions** Either a single employer or multiple employers negotiate with multiple unions at the same time.

Impasse and Third-Party Resolution

The obligation of both parties is to bargain to impasse. *Impasse* is not specifically defined in the law but occurs when it is apparent that future bargaining, based on the current environment, is not likely to result in agreement on the contract. At this point, a strike or lockouts could occur and the employer may legally implement the terms and conditions of its latest contract offer. However, strikes and lockout pose considerable costs to both sides and it is often better to try to resolve the issues. There are a variety of techniques and services available to assist in the resolution of issues, which include

➤ Mediation

➤ Interest arbitration

➤ Med-arb

➤ Fact finding

➤ Legislative intervention/governmental seizure

Mediation

Mediation is a process in which a neutral third party, a mediator, attempts to assist the parties to reach an agreement. Mediation services are offered by the *Federal Mediation and Conciliation Service* and by agencies in many of the states. Under the Taft-Hartley Act, the parties must advise FMCS that negotiations are underway. FMCS will contact the parties and offer mediation during the negotiations; however, these services are most likely to be requested when impasse has been declared or appears imminent. The mediator does not have the authority to impose settlement, but rather tries to facilitate communication. The mediator helps each side understand the other's position and interests, and he or she raises new alternatives not previously considered by the parties.

Mediation is generally voluntary, particularly in the private sector. However it is required for railways and airlines, under the Railway Labor Act, and by many state laws.

Interest Arbitration

Interest arbitration is the process by which a neutral third party, an arbitrator or arbitration panel, makes a binding decision as to the provisions to be included in a contract. Interest arbitration is a resolution to a dispute arising in the negotiations process. Another type of arbitration, *rights arbitration*, is discussed later in this chapter and involves the resolution of grievances arising under interpretation of the agreement after it has been signed.

There are essentially two types of interest arbitration. In *conventional interest arbitration*, the arbitrator can write the contract as he or she chooses after reviewing the positions of the two parties. In *"final offer" interest arbitration*, the arbitrator is constrained to picking the final offer of either labor or the employer and cannot amend or change the provisions of that offer. Final offer interest arbitration can be either *total package* or *issue-by-issue*. Under final offer total package interest arbitration, the arbitrator must select the final offer of one of the two parties in its totality. Under final offer issue-by-issue interest arbitration, the arbitrator is free to select either party's final offer on an item-by-item basis.

Interest arbitration is rarely used in the private sector where the parties want to keep their options open to use economic pressure to force resolution. It is more frequently used in the public sector where economic pressures such as a strike are often less available.

Med-Arb

Med-arb (mediation-arbitration) is the combination of mediation and arbitration and is conducted by the same neutral third party. This neutral person acts first as a mediator attempting to assist the parties to reach resolution. If mediation fails, the neutral person changes roles and becomes an arbitrator rendering a final and binding decision. Med-arb is more common in the public sector than in the private sector because it leads to arbitration, and most private sector employers and unions want to preserve the right to resolve negotiation conflicts through the use of economic pressure on the opposing party.

Med-arb is only infrequently used as a major way of resolving bargaining disputes. There are two inherent challenges with this process. Mediation and arbitration involve separate skill sets and techniques. It is often difficult to find an individual who possesses both. In addition, parties are often reluctant to reveal too much information that would facilitate the mediation because they fear that same information could be used against them in formulating a decision at the arbitration stage.

Fact-Finding

Fact-finding is a dispute-resolution process in which a neutral third party, fact-finder, or board of inquiry investigates the disagreement and issues a report of findings that frequently contain recommendations. These recommendations are nonbinding on the parties, but often contain guidance as to what is an appropriate compromise. Publication of the report frequently results in public pressure to resolve the dispute in terms of the recommendations.

Fact-finding is more prevalent in the public sector and, in some cases, might be mandated by state or public law. Fact-finding, in essence, is required in the private sector by the Railway Labor Act and the national emergency and health care provisions of the Taft-Hartley Act.

Legislative Intervention/Governmental Seizure

Although relatively rare, it is possible that either Congress or a state or local legislative body will resolve the dispute through legislative action. The seizure of organizations or even the entire industry by the President of the United States is also possible. This is rarely done and typically occurs only in times of war.

EXAM ALERT

You should be familiar with third-party impasse-resolution methods, particularly interest arbitration, mediation, and fact-finding because there is likely to be a test question in this area.

Bargaining History

It is critical that copious notes be kept at the bargaining table. These will chronicle the events as they take place and clarify the intent behind what is often somewhat vague contract language. Both labor and management typically compile a bargaining book or contract interpretation guide for administering the contract on an article-by-article basis. As will be discussed in the contract administration section, even though both parties have signed the agreement, there will likely be disagreements over the actual meaning of the language.

Ratification

The negotiation process typically assumes that the employer negotiating team can approve and sign the contract agreement. If that is not the case, the group must point out that fact to the union bargaining team at the beginning of the negotiations. It is also assumed that any tentative agreement must be submitted to union membership prior to final approval. The internal union ratification process is the privy of each union. The contract may be submitted to all union members for a vote of approval or to a group of elected representatives acting on behalf of all members. Approval may require a simple majority or some higher-level percentage. If the agreement is not ratified, the negotiation process is resumed.

On ratification, the union is obligated to fairly represent all employees without discrimination, whether or not they are union members. In exchange for designation as the exclusive bargaining agent, the union must undertake the obligation of representing all bargaining unit employees.

Typical Contract Provisions

Although each labor agreement is different, the overall content tends to have some commonality. The following items are contract provisions that are included in most or many labor contracts:

➤ Union security

➤ Management rights clause

➤ No strike clause

➤ Employee representatives/employer-provided items

➤ No lockout clause

➤ Discipline and discharge

➤ Grievance procedure

➤ Wages, hours, and other terms and conditions of employment

➤ Seniority

> **NOTE**
>
> These clauses often become rather complex and extensively limit management's flexibility in the organizational assignment of employees. To the extent possible, management will try to bargain for only one definition of seniority, that being firmwide seniority.

Union Security

Union security clauses are used to protect the interests of the union in terms of bargaining unit employee requirements regarding union membership and the payment of dues. There are numerous forms of union security provisions. Only the more prevalent ones are discussed in the following list:

► **Closed shop** The closed shop requires that an employee be a member of the union prior to being hired. This security arrangement was outlawed by the Taft-Hartley Act, but still effectively exists in some industries through union hiring hall provisions. This practice is relatively common, for example, in the construction industry. Although unions are required to refer both union and nonunion members to the employer, the extent to which this occurs is questionable.

► **Union shop** Bargaining unit employees must join the union after a specified period of time, usually 30 days, and must remain a member as a condition of employment. Employers must terminate employees who are not union members. As previously discussed, the *Beck* decision modified the union shop provisions so that employees do not have to join the union, but must pay that portion of union dues attributable to union costs of negotiations, contract administration, and some organizing costs. The union shop is illegal in right-to-work states, and the *Beck* ruling effectively makes the union shop provision enforceable only as an agency shop. However, the union shop remains a powerful and desirable security arrangement for the union to negotiate. It is up to the employee to exercise *Beck* rights and, for a number of reasons, he or she is often reluctant to do so.

► **Agency shop** Employees are not required to join the union, but must pay a fee each month that is typically equivalent to union dues. The agency shop is illegal in right-to-work states.

► **Maintenance of membership** Although used infrequently, *maintenance of membership* requires that bargaining unit employees who voluntarily join the union must maintain that membership for the duration of the labor contract. The employee may terminate membership, but only during a rather small window of opportunity at the beginning of the next contract period. Again, this arrangement is illegal in right-to-work states.

► **Open shop** An employee need not join the union nor pay union dues. This is the only security provision legal in right-to-work states and in the federal government.

➤ **Dues checkoff** The union will usually attempt to get the employer to collect union dues and agency fees via payroll deduction and transmit them to the union. An employee must voluntarily agree to this in writing before the employer can deduct the amount from the employee's pay.

Management Rights Clause

The purpose of this clause is to reserve for management the right to manage the organization as it sees fit unless those rights have been specifically modified in the labor contract (the reserved rights doctrine). This article of the agreement can be general in nature or very specific, enumerating all management rights.

No Strike Clause

The union agrees to not strike for the duration of the contract. This is usually associated with, and in return for, a grievance procedure that includes submitting unresolved contract administration issues to binding arbitration.

Union Representatives/Employer-Provided Items

The contract may indicate the number of stewards or other union officials and/or the amount of paid hours that will be allocated to the union for administration of the contract. It can also specify the types of facilities, equipment, and services the employer will provide to the union (bulletin boards, office space, telephone, and so on). Some agreements might provide for super seniority or other job protections for a limited number of union officials.

No Lockout Clause

The employer agrees to not lock out employees for the duration of the contract. This is usually associated with, and in return for, a union agreement not to strike during the duration of the contract.

Discipline and Discharge

Most contracts limit management's rights to impose discipline up to and including discharge to those instances involving *cause* or *just cause*. Many contracts specifically list employee behaviors that may result in discipline and the normal level of discipline associated with those behaviors (table of penalties).

Grievance Procedure

A *grievance procedure* is a formal process used to resolve disagreements arising from the administration of the labor agreement.

Wages, Hours, and Other Terms and Conditions of Employment

This is the meat of the agreement and specifies, frequently in great detail, the wage rates, work hours, and other terms and conditions of employment.

Seniority

Seniority is typically defined by an employee's length of service with the employer. It is often used as a factor in employment decisions such as promotion, layoff and recall, transfer or reassignment, and other types of personnel actions, including the rights to benefits. Seniority could result in a process called *bumping*, which allows senior qualified employees to replace less senior ones during a layoff. Contracts can, in some instances, differ in the way seniority is defined and might have different types of seniority for different purposes. Seniority could be defined in terms of organization, plant, and department seniority or other definitions.

> **EXAM ALERT**
>
> You should be familiar with the typical clauses in a labor agreement. Expect one or more clause-related questions, particularly on the union security and management rights clauses.

Contract Administration

Objective:
Gain an Understanding of Contract Administration

After the labor agreement is signed, it must be implemented and administered. Contract administration is really the heart of labor relations and reflects the day-to-day management of that relationship.

Contract administration is critical for two reasons:

➤ The contract does not administer itself. Activities that violate the provisions of the contract could be engaged in by either the union or employer. These violations might be unintentional because of a lack of knowledge of contract requirements, or they might be purposeful to test the limits of the other party's understanding of the language or to attempt to create a new meaning of the specific provision.

➤ Contract language is often vague and might be interpreted differently by each side when applied in the worksite.

Contract administration is the process of determining the proper application of the agreement in specific situations. In most cases, contracts are administered through the grievance procedure process.

Grievance Procedure

The *grievance procedure* is the formal process of resolving differences in interpretation of contract language or the perceived unfair application of the language related to employee personnel actions, usually discipline or discharge decisions. It provides procedural due process.

Although both management and labor have the right to use the process, management rarely does so. The process is initiated by an employee or union filing a complaint (grievance) alleging that the labor contract has been violated. Grievance procedures vary widely, but consist of a series of steps and prescribed time limits for action at each step and for appeal to the next step. A generic four-step grievance procedure is described next. The following example assumes the allegation is that management violated the contract:

1. If either the union or an employee believes that the contract has been violated, a complaint must be initiated within a prescribed time period after the alleged violation has occurred or the employee or union became aware of the violation. Depending on the contract, the first step might be either formal (a written complaint is filed) or informal (the complaint is verbal). The complaint is normally filed with the first-level supervisor, who has a prescribed number of days to meet with the employee and union steward to discuss the issue. After that meeting, the supervisor has a prescribed number of days to render a decision, either denying relief or granting relief, either in part or in full. If the proposed resolution is acceptable, the grievance is settled. If the proposed resolution is not acceptable, the union has a prescribed number of days to appeal the grievance to the next step. Failure of management to abide by the contractual time limits is often grounds for an immediate appeal to the next step, whereas failure of the union to meet the time limits often results in termination of the grievance process.

2. Step two follows the same procedures as step one, but involves a meeting between higher levels of leadership of both the union and management. An example might be that the local union chapter president and the plant manager meet at this step. Again, time limits apply as in step one and, if the resolution offered by management is not acceptable, an appeal can be made to step three.

3. Step three follows the same process but the parties involved are at even higher levels. The union might be represented by someone from its national office, whereas management might be represented by someone from its corporate headquarters—frequently the director or vice president of human resources. If the resolution offered is not acceptable, the union must contemplate whether to appeal to binding arbitration. It has a prescribed amount of time to do so.

4. Step four is arbitration in which the disagreement is referred to a third party for a decision that is binding on both parties. The submission to the arbitration process is contained in most labor contracts.

It is up to the union as to how aggressively to pursue the grievance and whether to appeal it to arbitration. The decision must be based on the merits of the grievance and not the union's relationship with the grievant. The union has an obligation to fairly represent all bargaining union employees regardless of union membership.

> **EXAM ALERT**
>
> Expect a question regarding a typical grievance process. You should know the basic procedures associated with the process and who would normally be present at each of the steps.

Arbitration

As discussed earlier, *arbitration* is the submission of a labor dispute to a neutral third party (an arbitrator or an arbitration panel) for resolution. There are two types of arbitration: *interest arbitration* and *rights arbitration*. Interest arbitration was discussed earlier and refers to settlement of contract language during the bargaining process. Rights arbitration is used in the contract administration process to resolve grievances. The decision reached by the arbitrator or arbitration panel is usually binding on both parties.

Selection of the Arbitrator

After a decision is reached to submit the grievance to arbitration, the arbitrator must be chosen. The process of doing this is normally specified in the contract and usually involves selection from one of two sources: lists of qualified arbitrators maintained by the FMCS or lists maintained by the *American Arbitration Association (AAA)*. The arbitration itself may be conducted by one individual arbitrator or a panel of arbitrators.

➤ Arbitration panels are usually composed of three arbitrators, one of whom is selected by management, one by the union, and one jointly (the neutral arbitrator).

➤ Permanent arbitrators are selected for a fixed period of time, frequently for the duration of the contract, and hear all arbitration cases between the parties. The chief advantage of this arrangement is that the arbitrator becomes very familiar with the contract and issues between the parties and the decisions will be consistent from issue to issue in terms of interpretation of the contract. A disadvantage is that the parties are essentially stuck with the arbitrator for an extended period of time.

➤ The most common way of selecting arbitrators is on an ad hoc basis. Therefore, each arbitration involves a separate selection process. There are several advantages for this method. The arbitrator might be a specialist in the particular issue involved in the arbitration, the parties are not required to pay a retainer fee as in a permanent arrangement, and, if either party does not like the arbitrator, he or she can be struck from the next selection process. Disadvantages are that there might be a lack of consistency in decisions on the same or similar issues and the process of selection is time-consuming.

Arbitration Hearing

The hearing is a somewhat formal, quasi-judicial process in which each side presents an opening statement, brings forward evidence and witnesses, and summarizes its arguments in a closing statement. Often lawyers are used by both sides.

Obligation to Arbitrate

There is a substantial body of law surrounding the obligation to litigate when a labor contract requiring resolution of disagreements by binding arbitration is in effect. The employer must arbitrate if the union elects to do so and that requirement can be enforced in court. In a series of 1960 Supreme Court decisions, commonly referred to as the *Steelworkers Trilogy*, the basic requirements for employers were set. The first case determined that the employer cannot refuse to arbitrate an issue based on a claim that the grievance has no merit, nor can the courts rule on the merits of a grievance. The employer must arbitrate the case when the union appeals to arbitration, and it is the sole authority of the arbitrator to determine the merits. The second case determined that the employer cannot refuse to arbitrate based on a declaration that the issue was not specifically covered in the contract, nor can the courts make that determination. The employer must arbitrate the case and the arbitrator must make the decision as to whether the issue can be arbitrated. In the third case, the Supreme Court determined that courts cannot reverse the decision of an arbitrator except in extremely limited conditions.

In addition, the NLRB will allow arbitrators to handle grievances that go beyond issues of contract administration alone. This includes not only alleged violations of the contract but also alleged unfair labor practices (*Collyer doctrine*).

Decision/Award

The arbitrator is not free to modify or write the contract in rights arbitration. The arbitrator must resolve the dispute based on strict interpretation of the contract language. If the language is not clear, the arbitrator may look at intent of the parties, often by referring to the bargaining history. The arbitrator may also look at past practice of the parties in similar situations. Past practice can have the effect of interpreting ambiguous language or of modifying the contract language.

Just Cause

In deciding disciplinary cases, the arbitrator must determine whether the action taken was for *just cause*, which means that there was sufficient justification for taking the disciplinary action and that it was appropriate to the seriousness of the infraction. There are no specific guidelines that define just cause and it is determined on a case-by-case basis based on an evaluation of actions taken. A seven-part test (enumerated by Arbitrator Daugherty in his decision in *Enterprise Wire Company*) is commonly used in that evaluation process. Indicators of just cause are

➤ The employee was warned that certain types of conduct would lead to discipline.

➤ The conduct leading to discipline is job related.

➤ The employer conducted a thorough investigation.

➤ The investigation was fair and impartial.

➤ The investigation indicated that the employee was guilty of the infraction.

➤ The penalty was consistent with past practice.

➤ The penalty was appropriate for the severity of the conduct in accordance with the concept of progressive discipline.

Arbitrators provide a written decision to both parties. If the grievance is sustained either in part or in whole, the arbitrator will also indicate what actions are required (back pay, retroactive promotion, seniority adjustments, and so on).

NOTE

Past practice (the common law of the workplace or shop floor) is extremely important in influencing the arbitrator's decision. If an issue is frequently handled in a certain way, even though that way is a violation of the contract, that consistent practice will have the effect of modifying the contract. The SPHR must ensure that all managers are thoroughly familiar with contract provisions and that they do not engage in practices that might have the impact of nullifying or changing those provisions.

Appeal and Enforcement of an Arbitration Decision

Courts will defer to the decision of an arbitrator, and appeal of a decision is allowable only in very rare circumstances. If, however, one of the parties refuses to implement the decisions, the courts will enforce it.

EXAM ALERT

You should anticipate a question on rights arbitration. Be familiar with arbitrator selection procedures, just cause determinations, and the limited appeal rights.

Appeal and Impact of Unionism

Two issues are of critical importance with respect to unionism. The first is why employees join unions—why do they vote for union certification in the workplace? The second is what is the impact of a union to the organization and its management?

Why Do Employees Vote for Unions?

Obviously there are many reasons that drive different individuals to vote for union certification. The quick answer is that employees believe that unions will provide them better working conditions.

Employees who desire union representation are seeking a better working environment. In essence, this means that current organizational practices and management are not meeting their needs. Therefore, a major reason that employees want unions is bad management. Employees might feel alienated from the workplace because of lack of involvement in decisions affecting their work, overbearing management practices, high productivity standards, and lack of job security; in other words, lack of job satisfaction.

Another major reason is the utility the union can provide in terms of higher wages, better benefits, and greater workplace protections. Compensation is generally better in a unionized environment. Labor agreements almost always include a grievance procedure and just cause and due process protections for discipline and termination.

A third reason is social. The union facilitates social relationships among its constituency and a sense of belonging.

EXAM ALERT

Know the reasons why an employee would vote for union certification and expect a question in this area.

What Is the Effect of Unionization for the Employer?

A major impact will almost always be higher labor costs. Studies vary and the impact is different in different industries, but the differential in wages and benefits for union employees versus nonunion employees is significant. A conservative estimate would be in the 10% range in terms of wages. In addition, employees covered by a union contract typically receive health insurance, a retirement package, and paid time off.

Another major impact to the organization is the restriction of management rights in terms of the flexibility to assign work and to conduct other management actions such as discipline. Many management decisions are subject to collective bargaining and those that are not are typically subject to bargaining in terms of their impact and implementation. The grievance process is typically adversarial and legalistic in nature, and the collective bargaining process, in most instances, does not engender improved long-term relationships.

There is an interesting paradox as to the impact of unionization on the attitudes and behavior of the workforce. Many studies reveal that unionized employees experience relatively low job satisfaction but relatively high retention. One explanation is that the low job satisfaction is related to better knowledge regarding the problems in the workplace combined with rather restrictive workplace rules that affect the employee as well as the employer. The high retention can be explained by the differential in benefits and wages experienced by the unionized worker.

Are there benefits to unionization for the employer? Yes, in some instances, the presence of a union allows the employer to provide better benefits at the same or lower cost. Labor contracts provide some consistency and a guide for management actions. As stated earlier, employee retention is improved.

Whether unionization improves productivity depends on the industry and the nature of the relationship with the union and the provisions of the labor contract. Typically, the restrictive work assignment rules have not resulted in productivity improvements over nonunion organizations. However, new cooperative relationships and partnering between unions and management driven by increased global competition have resulted in productivity differentials. In general though, these productivity increases have not been sufficient to offset the increased labor costs. Consequently, unionized firms tend to be less profitable than their nonunionized competitors.

> **EXAM ALERT**
>
> Expect a question regarding the impact of unionization on the firm. The paradox of improved retention and decreased job satisfaction is likely subject matter for a question.

Strikes

Economic, sympathy, and unfair labor strikes have been discussed in terms of union tactics during the bargaining process. There are other types of strikes that unions might use legally or illegally. It is useful to discuss the various types of potential strike activity in one section so that the various types of strikes are clearly differentiated and employee protections delineated. There are two major issues with respect to strikes. The first is whether the activity is protected under labor law. If the employee is engaged in a protected activity, the employer may not terminate or otherwise discipline the employee for doing so. To do so would be an unfair labor practice. The other issue is whether the employer may permanently replace the employee even though the employee is engaged in a protected activity. Strikes can be categorized as follows:

➤ **Recognition strike**   This is a strike that is rarely used today. Its purpose is to get the employer to recognize and bargain with the union. This activity is protected, but the employee can be permanently replaced.

➤ **Economic strike**   This is a strike during contract negotiations to place additional economic pressure on the employer to agree to union proposed language. The activity is protected but the employee may be permanently replaced.

➤ **Unfair labor practice strike**   This is a strike to protest the alleged unfair labor practice of an employer. The activity is protected and the employee cannot be permanently replaced.

➤ **Jurisdictional strike**   This is a strike to force the employer to assign work to bargaining unit employees as opposed to some other work group, and is not a protected activity. It is a ULP for the union to engage in this type of strike and strikers can be disciplined up to and including termination.

➤ **Wildcat strike**   This is a strike over a dispute while a labor agreement is in effect, often without the approval or knowledge of the union. It is a strike over a grievance. Technically, this type of strike is protected. However, most labor agreements include a union no-strike clause in exchange for a grievance procedure and binding arbitration. Therefore, in most cases the strike is not protected and the striking employees may be disciplined.

➤ **Sympathy strike**   This is a strike in support of other striking unions. Refusal to cross a picket line is considered a sympathy strike. Sympathy strikes are protected but the employee can be permanently replaced. However, the strike is unprotected if the current labor contract contains a no-strike clause and, in that case, the strikers can be disciplined.

EXAM ALERT

You should expect at least one question, probably more, on whether a particular type of strike is a protected activity, and if it is, whether the striking employees can be permanently replaced.

The NLRB ULP Complaint Process

Unfair labor practices have been defined and discussed elsewhere in this chapter. The purpose of this section is to describe the process involved in adjudicating allegations of unfair labor practices and the potential remedies for violations. The process consists of

➤ Initiation

➤ Investigation

➤ Hearing

➤ Cease and desist order

➤ Appeal/enforcement

Initiation

A union, employer, or employee can initiate the complaint process by filing a charge with the NLRB's regional director. The charge must be filed within six months of the alleged ULP.

Investigation

An investigation will then ensue and the regional director must make a determination as to the merit of the charge. If the charge is determined to be without merit, it is dismissed. The charging party may appeal the regional director's decision to the Office of General Counsel. Dismissal by the Office of General Counsel cannot be appealed. If the charge alleges an unlawful boycott or strike, the regional director must request a temporary restraining order from the federal district court having jurisdiction.

It should be noted that ongoing informal resolution discussions often occur between the charging party and the *respondent* (the party alleged to have committed the ULP). The charge may be withdrawn or settled at any point up to final board action. The regional director must approve informal settlements between the parties after a complaint has been filed.

If the investigation reveals there is reason to believe a ULP has been committed, the regional director will attempt to get the parties to resolve the issue. If that does not occur, the director will issue a formal complaint and schedule a hearing. The respondent then has 10 days to respond to the complaint.

Hearing

A hearing is scheduled before an administrative law judge (*ALJ*). During the hearing the NLRB general counsel office will present evidence that a ULP has occurred, whereas the respondent will argue that no violation occurred. On completion of the testimony and proceedings, the ALJ will issue to the NLRB and the respondent a report either recommending dismissal of the charge or an order to cease and desist the illegal activity. The ALJ will also include recommendations for remedial action, if appropriate. If there are no timely exceptions filed regarding the ALJ's report, it becomes the board's order. If either party appeals to the board, the board will make a final decision.

Cease and Desist Order

If the board determines that a ULP has been committed, it will issue a cease and desist order along with any remedial actions required to be taken by the respondent. The order will require the respondent to immediately stop the illegal activity and to refrain from engaging in it in the future. The board has considerable latitude to fashion appropriate remedies, but cannot punish the respondent through punitive damages or fines. Examples of remedies the board might order are

➤ Return to work and back pay for lost wages. However, a terminated employee is under an obligation to seek work after termination and the remedy is limited to the difference between what he employee would have earned had he not been terminated and what he did actually earn.

➤ Retroactive promotion and back pay.

➤ Restitution of seniority.

➤ An order to recognize the union and bargain collectively.

➤ An order requiring another election in a union certification.

➤ An order to bargain in good faith.

The board will normally order the respondent to post the order in prominent places throughout the workplace.

> **NOTE**
>
> Organized labor has traditionally argued that the law does not provide sufficient punishment for engaging in unfair labor practices. It argues that the NLRB should have the authority to punish offenders in terms of fines or other sanctions as opposed to ordering remedial action and posting of a notice.

Appeal/Enforcement

Either party can appeal the final board decision to the federal appeals court having jurisdiction. The decision of the federal appeals court can be appealed to the Supreme Court.

If the respondent fails to honor the order to cease and desist and implement remedial action, the board may request enforcement by a federal appeals court.

> **EXAM ALERT**
>
> You most certainly will get at least one question regarding the ULP process, cease and desist orders, or appeal and enforcement of the cease and desist orders.

Public Sector Employee and Labor Relations

Although there are certainly many federal employment laws that cover all or most public sector employees, employee and labor relations in the public sector varies considerably among the many governmental entities. This is especially true when evaluating labor relations. Consequently, this section will largely deal with the issue of public sector employee rights with respect to union representation. Public sector union density is almost three times that of the private sector (approximately 37% versus 13%). However, unions are often restricted in terms of the actions they can take and in the types of issues that are can be bargained.

State and Local Government Employees

There are 50 states and 50 different sets of laws, regulations, and executive orders affecting employee and labor relations in these states. The first state to allow bargaining by public employees was Wisconsin in 1959. In some states virtually all state and local employees have bargaining rights, whereas in other states those rights are restricted to a specific group of employees—usually teachers, fire fighters, and police. In a few states, the law is silent as to bargaining rights and in one state (North Carolina) bargaining is prohibited.

In those states in which collective bargaining is permitted, bargaining is generally allowed on the same topics as in the private sector: wages, hours, and other terms and conditions of employment. However, many states limit or prohibit strikes as being contrary to the public interest and safety. In exchange for the limitation to strike, interest arbitration is much more prevalent in the public sector.

Federal Employees

There have been unions of federal employees since the early 1800s. However, their activities were largely limited to lobbying until 1962 when President Kennedy signed Executive Order 10988, extending limited bargaining rights to federal employees. Those provisions, among others, were codified into law with the passage of the *Civil Service Reform Act (CSRA)* in 1974. Labor relations in the federal sector essentially follow the private sector NLRA model in that there are unfair labor practices, exclusive recognition, and an agency was created to administer the provisions of the act. The *Federal Labor Relations Authority (FLRA)* has somewhat similar responsibilities as the NLRA. It has jurisdiction over ULPs, determines the appropriateness of bargaining units, supervises certification elections, and rules on exceptions to arbitrator awards. The act also created the *Federal Services Impasse Panel (FSIP)*, which has a similar role to FMCS.

However, there are significant differences between private and federal sector law. Federal employees, in general, cannot bargain over wages and benefits. Federal employees cannot strike, and issue arbitration is under the authority of the FSIP. The Postal Service is covered under the NLRA, whereas the military is excluded from CSRA as are certain other arms of the government—the FBI, for example.

International Employee and Labor Relations

In-depth coverage of comparative employee and labor relations is beyond the scope of this book. Extensive knowledge of these issues is tested in the GPHR exam, not the SPHR. However, the SPHR must work in an ever-expanding globalized environment and some knowledge of international employee and labor relations is a must. Some aspects, such as international compensation, are covered in other portions of the book.

International Law

The SPHR must be familiar not only with United States law but also with the laws of other nations in which their organizations have operations. For example, as discussed in a prior chapter, the Civil Rights Act of 1991 applies to United States citizens working for a United

States corporation overseas unless application of that law would violate the local law. Therefore knowledge of both sets of laws is required.

There is little international law regarding employee and labor relations per se in terms of laws that apply across national boundaries, with the exception of the European Union. There are, however, agreements among nations that, although nonbinding, influence the practice of HR in an international environment. Examples are

➤ **North American Free Trade Agreement (*NAFTA*)**   NAFTA is a binding agreement between the United States, Canada, and Mexico with respect to trade, goods and services, and capital, but does not expressly deal with employee or labor relations. However, the participating countries signed a side agreement that took effect on January 1, 1994 and deals with employee and labor relations issues. The agreement is titled the *North American Agreement on Labor Cooperation (NAALC)*. The agreement provides 11 guiding principles regarding many employee and labor issues such as minimum wage, child labor, equal employment, occupational safety and health, workers' compensation, and the right to form unions and bargain collectively. The agreement does not require any new laws or consistency of laws among the nations. Its goal is to achieve the guiding principles through enforcement of current national law. An organization, the *National Administrative Office (NAO)*, was established to monitor and enforce the agreement, but to this point its effectiveness has been minimal.

➤ **World Trade Organization (*WTO*)**   The WTO is a worldwide organization for negotiating and enforcing trade agreements. The WTO has the authority to enforce agreements, assess damages, and impose sanctions. Unions and other interest groups have long worked to attach employee and labor relations standards to these trade agreements so that participating countries must abide by the same or similar employment standards. To date, these efforts have not been successful. The WTO is primarily a proponent of free trade as opposed to *fair trade*, a concept that requires all countries to compete based on equal standards of worker and environment protection.

➤ **International Labor Organization (*ILO*)**   The ILO is a specialized agency of the United Nations. Its mission is to promote minimum standard basic labor rights throughout the world. The ILO does so through the adoption of conventions and recommendations that are approved by its members (nearly 180 nations). In 1998, it adopted the *Declaration of Fundamental Principles and Rights at Work*, which consists of a set of core standards of employment. The core standards include many of the same standards cited in the NAALC agreement. However, the ILO really has no enforcement authority.

➤ **European Union (*EU*)**   The EU, consisting of 25 countries, is a comprehensive approach to international trade and capital and labor mobility. The EU has a centralized structure for passing regulations that are binding on all member nations. As yet, the actual number of binding directives and regulations are minimal in terms of employee and labor relations, but the structure is in place.

International Labor Relations

To assume that the United States' structure of labor relations is a model for the rest of the world would be incorrect. In fact, the United States structure is atypical. Characteristics such as exclusive representation, tightly drawn, legally enforceable labor agreements, strong management opposition to unionization, and permanent replacement of striking workers are relatively rare in the rest of the world.

In many nations, unions are broad social movements rather than organizations devoted to improve the terms and conditions in the workplace. Unions might in fact be political parties or closely allied with a particular political party. Unions could be closely linked with the company whose employees they represent, such as the enterprise unions in Japan. Unions might be largely operatives of the government or closely regulated by the government, as in Mexico and many third-world countries. Bargaining might take place centrally through employer associations rather than on an employer-by-employer basis, as in western Europe. Employees might be legally entitled to a voice in managerial decisions, independent of unions, along with seats on the board of directors, as in Germany. Countries vary as to the *density* of union membership (percentage of the labor force that belongs to a union) and the percentage of the workforce covered by a labor agreement. Some countries have high union density but low contract coverage, whereas others have extremely high coverage and low density as in France.

To understand labor relations in an international environment, you almost have to make an analysis on a country-by-country basis. You also have to look at the trends in that country because the labor relations structures in many third-world countries and countries in eastern Europe are emerging and changing rapidly.

Transnational Bargaining

Multinational and transnational corporations are a considerable problem for unions. Imposing economic pressures or striking these corporations often has little impact because operations and production can be shifted to another country. One obvious potential for unions would be to bargain collectively with these firms and reach agreement on wages, hours, and other terms and conditions of employment on an international basis either by representing all bargaining unit employees of the organization or by bargaining in collaboration with other unions in other nations. Even though unions continue to think about and pursue this initiative, as yet there has been little success. The reasons for lack of progress are

➤ Labor laws vary significantly from nation to nation, and there is no overarching international law that applies.

➤ Labor unions themselves vary as to purposes, philosophies, and goals, and there are differing cultural values among the employees they represent.

➤ Multinational and transnational corporations have opposed this type of bargaining.

Unionism in the Twenty-First Century

The composition and strategy of private sector unions are evolving as a result of the changing dynamics of the economy. Union density in the private sector has dropped from a high of approximately 35% in the 1950s to about 13% today, but it is relatively stable at about 37% in the public sector. The economy has changed from one of manufacturing to one and service and knowledge. The demographics of the work force are changing to include more minorities and women, and the workforce is aging. The traditional union membership base of white, male, blue-collar workers has eroded. Increased competition caused by technology and globalization has reduced the competitiveness of United States firms burdened with restrictive labor contracts and high union-negotiated employee benefits, particularly health insurance and defined benefit retirement plans.

Unions are beginning to adapt their strategies to better accommodate the dynamics discussed earlier. They are reaching out to minorities, women, and white-collar employees. They are organizing in industries in the service and knowledge economy. They have engaged in concession bargaining, giving up previously hard-earned gains for better job security or greater input in corporate decisions. They are increasingly involved in new and creative work structures and arrangements involving greater employee empowerment. They have created new types of memberships, such as associate memberships, to increase the membership base and provide union exposure to groups not normally inclined to join unions. In addition, unions have engaged in a concerted public relations campaign to improve their image and get their message out.

> **NOTE**
>
> The SPHR must not assume that an organization, industry, or geographical region that has remained largely union-free will not be the subject of union organizing in the future.

Employee and Labor Relations in a Nonunion Environment

Objective:

Gain an Understanding of Employee and Labor Relations in a Nonunion Environment

Employee and employer rights and obligations are delineated by the labor agreement in a unionized setting. But what are the rights and obligations of employees in a nonunion environment? What happens if the employee does not live up to obligations? What are the characteristics of a positive employee-relations environment that will allow the employer to remain union-free?

Employee Rights and Obligations in a Nonunion Setting

Employees derive rights and obligations from a number of sources: common law, employment contracts, and legislative acts.

Common Law

Common law is the body of legislation that is based on tradition and judicial rulings through the ages. It was imported from England (except for Louisiana law, which is based on the Napoleonic Code) during the colonial period and is the foundation for many of the basic concepts affecting the employer-employee relationship. Common law includes property rights, torts, defamation of character, and the concept of employment-at-will, among other legal concepts.

Common law also includes both employer and employee obligations. The basic concepts of employee obligations are derived from common law. An employee is expected to do the job, show up for work in a timely manner, abide by employer rules, and not harm the employer. *Causing harm* includes not only damaging the employer's property or equipment but also its reputation, competing with the employer, or disclosing its business practices and processes. One of the most controversial concepts of common law is that of employment-at-will.

Employment-at-Will

Employment-at-will means that either the employee or the employer can terminate the employment relationship for any reason at any time. Although the concept appears neutral, the power relationship between the employee and the employer usually favors the latter. However, there are several exceptions to employment-at-will that provide additional protection for the employee. Exceptions to employment-at-will are

➤ Employment law of the federal, state, or local government.

➤ Employment contracts.

➤ Implied contracts. In general, implied contracts can by created in two ways:

  ➤ When an employer document or publication, usually the employee handbook, implies some benefit or right, that language might be sufficient to create a contract even though it is not the intent to do so. For example, a statement in the employee handbook indicating that employees will be fired only for good reasons might be interpreted by the courts as obligating the employer to terminate only for just cause.

  ➤ When an agent of the employer promises some benefit or right, that agent might be creating an implied contract. As in the earlier example, if a recruiter indicates to a prospective employee that the employer terminates employees only for good reason, that recruiter, acting as an agent of the employer, has likely created an implied contract.

➤ Public policy. An employee cannot be fired for refusing to violate a law or for engaging in activities required by the law. This would be against the public policy. Examples might be refusing to lie in a court of law for the employer or refusing not to show up for jury duty because the employer requires the employee to work. The public policy exception is broadly accepted in state courts. In addition, many federal laws protect the person from termination for exercising their rights under the law. For example, an employee cannot be fired for reporting a safety violation to OSHA or filing a discrimination report with EEOC.

➤ Good faith and fair dealing. This exception is less frequently accepted in the court systems, and involves failure to treat the employee fairly or to provide some benefit. Terminating an employee so that the employer does not have to pay a year-end bonus or terminating an employee just prior to being eligible for a benefit are examples.

> **EXAM ALERT**
>
> Expect a question on the exceptions to the employment-at-will doctrine.

Torts

Torts are wrongful acts that harm a person and are actionable in court. Torts are also derived from common law. Employees and others who have been harmed have recourse in the court system to seek restitution. Common employment related torts are

➤ **Wrongful termination**   An employee might be able to pursue a wrongful termination tort action under certain circumstances. Terminations under the employee-at-will exceptions or termination in violation of an employment contract are examples. In general, an employee covered by a labor contract would not be able to pursue a wrongful termination claim, but would have to use the negotiated grievance procedure.

➤ **Defamation**   An employee can sue for libel or slander committed by the employer.

➤ **Invasion of privacy**   This is a very complex issue in today's electronic world, but certain activities by employers might go beyond the line of what is required for prudent conduct of business. For example, drug testing is likely not to be considered by the courts as invasion of privacy, but releasing an employee's disciplinary record to the newspaper might be.

➤ **Negligent hiring, retention, and training**   The employer might incur tort liability if it hired a person without due diligence, retained a person that it clearly should not have, or inappropriately trained a person for the job and the result of one of these activities was that another person was harmed.

➤ **Negligent referencing**   Employers typically are very wary about releasing information about a current or former employee to a prospective employer because of the potential of a defamation suit. However, if the current or former employer clearly had information that the employee could pose a danger to another party and failed to provide that information to the prospective employer, the current or former employer might be liable if the employee was subsequently hired and then harmed a third party. For example, suppose that an employee is fired for being intoxicated on the job and applies to the city to be a bus driver. The city requests information regarding the nature of the former employee's employment, and the former employer does not reveal the reason for discharge. The city hires the employee as a bus driver and that employee is later involved in a serious accident while driving under the influence of alcohol. The courts might very well transfer the tort liability (negligent hiring) associated with the accident from the city to the former employer.

Employment Contracts

Employment contracts are individual agreements between the employee and employer as to the conditions of employment. These are bilateral agreements between the parties, which typically delineate the term or length of employment, compensation, job responsibilities, termination and cancellation procedures, and other obligations and rights of both parties. These types of contracts amend the employment-at-will relationship. Employment contracts increasingly include mandatory arbitration, noncompete clauses, or both. These are somewhat controversial issues and must be crafted carefully to be legal.

Mandatory Arbitration

As a condition of employment, employees can be required to waive their rights to employment law complaint processes and to the court system and submit all employment disagreements to compulsory arbitration. There are certainly some advantages to this type of arrangement for both parties. For the employee, there is a guarantee that a neutral third party will settle employment decisions. In return, the employer avoids an expensive, long, and drawn-out process in front of regulatory agencies or in the courts.

Mandatory arbitration was found to be legal by the Supreme Court in its *Circuit City* decision. However, the process must be balanced and fair for both parties. Mandatory arbitration that provides little due process or imposes onerous financial or other conditions on the employee will not be acceptable to the courts. Although the employee might be prohibited from filing a discrimination complaint with the EEOC, contracts cannot legally modify a third party's rights, so the EEOC might be able to intervene on its own with respect to issues under its jurisdiction.

Noncompete Agreement

This agreement takes many forms, but its intent is to impose an obligation by prohibiting current or departed employees from competing against their former employer, from soliciting that employer's clients, or from enticing other employees of the former employer away from the firm. To be legal, the agreement must have a reasonable limit to duration of the prohibition, and define any geographical restrictions and any prohibited activities. The limitations must not be so restrictive that the former employee is unable to engage in the profession or reasonably earn a living.

Confidentiality

The contract may contain provisions that prohibit the employee from divulging trade secrets, patent information, and other proprietary information.

Legislative Acts

Employees and employers have specific rights and obligations guaranteed them in the United States Constitution and in specific federal and local laws. These laws are discussed comprehensively throughout this and other chapters of the book.

Employee Discipline

In the private sector, employees are disciplined for either substandard performance of their assigned tasks or for failure to follow the employer's work rules, often referred to as *citizenship behaviors* (absenteeism, tardiness, insubordination, substance abuse, sexual harassment, and so on). In a nonunion environment, those citizenship expectations are communicated to the employee in the form of policies, procedures, and rules as either individual documents or compiled in an employee handbook. In a union environment, policies, procedures, and rules may exist separately, be in an employee handbook, or be included in the negotiated agreement or a combination of all three. It is HR's responsibility in both scenarios to communicate this information to both management and employees.

➤ *Policies* are broad, general statements of the organization's philosophy with respect to an issue.

➤ *Procedures* are more tightly defined and represent guidance to organizational members as to the standard or customary way of dealing with an issue or handling a situation.

➤ *Rules* are specific as to actions to be taken and provide little latitude for individual discretion.

Handbooks

Employee handbooks are the standard method by which the employer sets forth its policies, procedures, and rules, and informs the employee of both the obligations and benefits of employment. It is often important documentation in both the prosecution and defense of disciplinary cases. Good HR practice is to have the employee acknowledge receipt of the employee handbook in writing and also to acknowledge the obligation to abide by the policies included therein. In this way the employee cannot use lack of knowledge as a defense for wrongdoing. Published policies distributed to employees also can be one source of proof that the employer does have an established policy and program in place when having to defend itself in front of third parties (courts, EEOC, OSHA, and so on). On the other side of the ledger is the fact that employee handbooks have frequently had unanticipated consequences when apparently neutral language has been interpreted by the courts as creating an implied contract that affected the intended employment-at-will relationship.

NOTE

It is critical that the employer be able to prove that employees were aware of policies and work rules. HR should keep employee acknowledgement of receipt of the employee handbook, policies, and work rules along with class rosters proving attendance at training sessions on these issues.

If the employer wants to maintain the employment-at-will relationship, the wording of the employee handbook is critical and should be reviewed by an employment attorney. Differentiating between *probationary* and *permanent* employees implies there is some level of protection for permanent employees beyond employment-at-will. Terms such as *due process*, *just cause*, and *progressive discipline* or the publication of a table of penalties for rules violations are likely to be inferred as creating an implied contract. It is best to have an attorney draft a disclaimer to be prominently displayed in the employee handbook, which indicates clearly that employment is at will, that the handbook does not create a contract, and that no agent of the employer other than the one designated in the handbook has the authority to enter into a contract (this could be the HR director, president, CEO, and so on). The acceptability of this disclaimer and appropriate language differs from state to state.

The handbook must be customized to the demographics and skills of the workforce. Increasingly, third parties (courts and regulatory bodies) will insist that employee handbooks and other directives by translated into the language used by the workforce. An employer with a large Spanish-speaking workforce, for example, should ensure that its employee handbook, legally required posters, and other important employee communication be translated accurately into Spanish. In addition, the language of the employee handbook must be appropriate to the reading level of the employee population. An employee handbook written on a college level will not be acceptable for an employee workforce composed largely of high school graduates.

Finally, it is important that the employee handbook be widely communicated and frequently updated. At a minimum, the handbook should be distributed and extensively discussed during new employee orientation. Better yet is an annual all-employee meeting at which the handbook and any changes are discussed. Employees must be advised in a timely manner when changes are made to policies, procedures, and rules. Historically, good practice has been to create the handbook in loose-leaf format and send out printed changes with an employee acknowledgement sheet to be returned to HR. As access to email and intranet technology has increased, many employers now maintain the handbook online and advise employees of changes via email.

Methods of Discipline

Disciplinary procedures, including due process and just cause discipline, are typically in the labor agreement. In a nonunion environment, it is up to the employer to decide how to proceed with discipline. As discussed earlier, written procedures can affect the employment-at-will relationship, but it is often in the employer's best interest to engage in a disciplinary practice that is fair to the employee yet protects the employer's rights. Each employee represents an investment by the employer. In most situations, it is best to try to correct the behavior rather than have to replace the employee. Progressive and positive methods of discipline are discussed in the sections that follow.

Progressive Discipline

The term *discipline* comes from a root word that means to teach. Thus, the purpose of discipline is to correct behavior, informing the employee of what is proper and acceptable, not to punish. *Progressive discipline* is the application of increasingly severe penalties for rules violations in an attempt to encourage proper behaviors. However, there is nothing in this concept that precludes severe punishment up to and including termination in a first instance of particularly egregious behavior. A typical progressive discipline procedure can be described as a four-step process:

1. At the first instance of poor performance or work rules violation, the employee is given a verbal warning by the supervisor and advised as to what is expected in the future.

2. If the behavior is exhibited again, the employee is issued a written warning indicating that the behavior is unacceptable, what behavior is expected, and that future instances will result in more severe discipline.

3. At the third incidence, the employee is suspended without pay for a brief period of time, again given expectations as to appropriate behavior, and advised that future incidents will result in termination.

4. Continuation of the same unacceptable behavior results in termination.

There are two other concepts commonly associated with progressive discipline. The first is some sort or forgiveness for good conduct. Typically, if the employee does not continue the undesirable behavior for a period of time (typically a year), the progressive discipline process is stopped and the clock starts over should the undesirable behavior begin again. The second concept is based on the same or similar inappropriate behavior. For example, a first instance of tardiness might result in a verbal warning. If the employee fails to properly perform a critical job function the next day, the next step in the progressive discipline procedure (a written warning) is not generally appropriate because the two behaviors are not similar. Therefore, an employee could be on more than one progressive discipline track at the same time.

Positive Discipline

Positive discipline is sometimes called *nonpunitive discipline* and is a problem-solving approach to correcting behavior. A typical positive discipline approach includes four steps as in the progressive discipline approach, but without the increasingly severe punishment. Each step, except for the last one, is designed to have the employee work through the issue and come up with a resolution. Positive discipline proceeds as follows:

1. At the first instance of unacceptable behavior, the employee is advised that the behavior is unacceptable, what the organization and supervisor expect, and the employee and supervisor verbally agree to a resolution of the issue.

2. If the employee continues the unacceptable behavior, another meeting occurs with a discussion similar to the one in this first step, but the meeting is documented and the employee agrees in writing to correct the problem.

3. If the behavior continues, another meeting occurs in which the employee is advised that further instances will result in termination. Many organizations give a one-day paid suspension at this point to reiterate the seriousness of the problem. This is often referred to as a *decision day off*, during which the employee is to consider the desirability of continued employment with the organization and what behavior is required to continue to be employed.

4. If the behavior is not corrected, the employee is terminated.

> **EXAM ALERT**
>
> Expect a question on the disciplinary process, most likely on the concept and procedures associated with progressive discipline.

Failure to Discipline

Although some workplaces impartially and consistently impose discipline, many do not. Frequently this is an issue of a culture in which improper behavior is permitted for one reason or another. Often, however, it is a failure of management to understand the importance of maintaining a safe workplace in which rules are uniformly applied, harassment is not permitted, and policies of the organization are enforced. Typical reasons for failure of management to enforce the rules and impose discipline are

➤ Managers do not like the adversity associated with imposing discipline. It is easier to let the improper behavior continue than to confront the employee.

➤ Managers fear the employee will become violent.

➤ The manager has risen from the ranks, exhibited the same kinds of improper behaviors, and does not think it fair to punish someone for something he or she used to do.

➤ The distinction and distance between first-level supervisors and their subordinates is minimal. Often times they are friends and the manager does not want to disturb this relationship by punishing the individual.

➤ Managers fear that they will look silly when the discipline is overturned by an upper-level manager or in the grievance process.

Dispute Resolution

In a nonunion environment, employees who disagree with the discipline imposed, have some other complaint, or otherwise want to communicate with management are often not permitted to do so. Absent a complaint to a regulatory agency or filing suit in a court, employees might have little voice in the workplace. If they do not like the decision or practice, they can quit. However, many employers consistently provide some levels of due process, just cause discipline, and employee complaint resolution, believing it to be in the best interest of the organization to do so. Examples of these types of activities are open door policies, ombudsmen, peer review panels, and nonunion grievance processes.

Open Door Policies

Open door policies are meant to convey the impression that management's door is always open and that employees are always welcome in the manager's office at any time to discuss workplace issues. Typically, there is little formalization to this practice and no appeal rights. Management maintains strict control. However, organizations now frequently formalize the open door policy, building in specific steps and appeal processes, but still maintaining management control. The more formalized this policy becomes, the more it looks like a nonunion grievance process.

Ombudsman

An ombudsman is an employee of the organization whose responsibilities are to facilitate resolution of disputes between employees and management. The person might be authorized to investigate the situation and make recommendations for resolution, often acting in a mediator capacity. However, in these situations, management normally maintains control and the ombudsman rarely has independent authority to take action or to resolve the dispute.

Peer Review Panel

Some organizations have created peer review panels or boards to which the employee can appeal discipline and other management actions. The composition of the board differs depending on the organization. The panel might be composed of all employees (truly a peer board). Others are composed of both management and employees with, at one end of the continuum, management composing a majority of the review panel. Some panels have ultimate decision-making authority whereas others can only issue advisory opinions. Management must be aware of the *Electromation* decision, discussed later in this chapter, to ensure it does not violate the Wagner Act prohibition regarding domination of a labor organization.

Nonunion Grievance Process

Nonunion grievance processes can take many forms. At one extreme is a formal grievance process including binding arbitration typical of those found in labor agreements. At the other end are less formal processes that are merely formalized open door policies.

Employee Involvement Programs

Employers in both union and nonunion environments and the public and private sector are increasingly experimenting with and implementing employee involvement programs and high performance work systems in an attempt to increase productivity, quality, and worker satisfaction. The need for both increased flexibility and cost containment in a dynamic environment necessitates these types of innovations.

Employee involvement programs encompass a wide variety of activities designed to encourage input from employees. These programs range from essentially passive systems, such as suggestion boxes where the employees provide input but have little or no decision-making authority, to active systems, such as self-directed work teams in which employees make many of the day-to-day operational decisions. Some employee involvement programs are also part of the design of high performance work systems, and the terms are sometimes used synonymously. The purpose of these systems is to increase commitment to the organization and the achievement of organizational goals by allowing and encouraging the employee to provide input into the decision-making process. A normal job often utilizes a small portion of an employee's capacity, leaving a large potential untapped. Increasing employee involvement often yields many positive outcomes for the employer including, but not limited to, increased employee commitment, better decision-making, improved communications and cooperation, and increased productivity.

The following discussion is divided into two sections: employee involvement programs and high performance work systems. However, the programs are interrelated, and many types could fall into either category. The distinction is for explanation purposes but is artificial.

Types of Employee Involvement Programs

Employee involvement programs are primarily designed to increase employee participation in their work life by soliciting their input on decisions affecting work processes and the work environment. The employee involvement programs discussed in the following sections are suggestion programs, survey/feedback/action programs, participative management, quality circles, various types of group activities, and special compensation plans.

Suggestion Programs

This is probably the simplest type of involvement program in which there is a system, often a suggestion box, to collect employee suggestions ranging from those involving the work environment to those involving work systems themselves. Effective suggestion programs ensure that all suggestions are quickly acknowledged and analyzed. If appropriate, the suggestion is implemented in a timely manner and the employee making the suggestion receives recognition commensurate with the value of the suggestion to the organization.

Survey/Feedback/Action

Survey/feedback/action (SFA) encompasses a three step process, the first of which is the administration of a survey, often called a *climate survey*, to employees in order to determine their opinions regarding a wide variety of workplace issues ranging from compensation to working conditions to management practices. Employee responses are anonymous but organizational location of the employee is collected. After the data are collected, they are analyzed and disaggregated into organizational sections. Managers are then fed back the data from their employees. They then meet with their employees to discuss the data and develop action items to address the issues identified.

Participative Management

Participative management permits employee input into the decision-making process. The amount of employee input and decision-making authority varies according to the situation and can range from no or little input in a particular situation to authority to unilaterally make the decision in others. The effectiveness of participative management in increasing commitment depends on a number of factors, including the organization's culture and management's commitment to receiving and using input in the decision-making process.

Quality Circles

Quality circles are small groups of employees that meet periodically to discuss quality problems, determine the cause of poor quality, and recommend corrective action. They might or might not be empowered to take remedial action without management approval.

Committees, Project Groups, Teams, and Task Forces

These terms have similar meanings and will be grouped together for the purposes of discussing employee involvement. All are composed of small numbers of employees convened to discuss a particular issue or work on a particular problem. They might be from the same work group or from various work groups (cross-functional). The composition might or might not include managers and multiple hierarchical levels. They could be virtual, meeting via electronic means. The commonality is that the purpose is to obtain employee input for some purpose. Such groups might be empowered only to study the issue and make recommendations to management or they might have the authority to implement the decisions they make.

Compensation Plans

Several types of compensation plans are used in connection with employee involvement. Gainsharing plans frequently use employee committees to suggest methods of improving productivity or reducing costs. The monetary value of the sustainable increases in productivity or decreases in costs is then shared with employees.

Under an employee stock ownership plan (*ESOP*), stock is held in trust for the employee. Equity positions in the organization potentially improve commitment to organizational goals and increased involvement in one's work.

Profit-sharing plans distribute profits to employees either as a lump sum or as a distribution to a retirement system. As in ESOPs, sharing in the profit of the company potentially improves commitment and involvement.

More in-depth discussion of these plans is contained in Chapter 5, "Compensation and Benefits," earlier in this book.

Types of High Performance Work Systems

High performance work systems use employee input in an attempt to improve organizational performance. Although, as stated before, employee involvement programs and high performance work systems are similar concepts, employee involvement programs are primarily concerned with employee commitment, whereas high performance work systems attempt to use employee involvement to raise individual, group, and organizational performance to new levels. The high performance work systems discussed in the following sections are total quality management, lean manufacturing, and self-directed work teams.

Total Quality Management

Total Quality Management (TQM) is a program to improve quality through continuous improvement. TQM uses quality teams (as in quality circles, discussed earlier) to find ways to improve the quality of the organization's services or products. The extent to which these teams are empowered to actually make decisions and implement its suggestions varies.

Lean Manufacturing

Lean manufacturing, also called *lean production*, attempts to maximize quality and productivity by eliminating unnecessary steps in the process and unnecessary in-production and component inventories. Production is often organized into cells or teams responsible for manufacturing all or most of the product. Inherent in the process is employee involvement in the continuous improvement process. Again, the extent to which employees, cells, or teams are empowered varies greatly from organization to organization.

Self-Directed Work Teams

Self-directed work teams, also called *self-managed* and *self-designing teams*, incorporate the concepts of employee involvement and high performance work systems. Teams are essentially self-managed and have authority to make most work decisions on their own, including work design and flow, assignment of work, selection of suppliers, inventory requirements, quality and productivity improvement, selection of team members, and performance evaluation.

> **EXAM ALERT**
>
> High performance work teams are increasingly important in a competitive, globalized market. Expect a question in this area, most likely having to do with cell manufacturing or self-directed work teams.

Electromation

The NLRB's 1992 decision in *Electromation, Inc. and International Brotherhood of Teamsters, Local Union No. 1049, AFL-CIO* presents a challenge when implementing employee involvement programs. The NLRB ruled that certain types of programs created a labor organization as defined by the NLRA, and that Electromation, Inc. had committed an unfair labor practice by dominating them. The outcome of the decision is that an employer can violate the NLRA's section 8(a)(2) prohibition against domination of a labor organization by creating and dealing with employee committees, task forces, or other types of employee involvement programs even if the intentions are to honestly seek employee input and to deal with employee issues. Although *Electromation* deals with a nonunionized environment, the NLRB's 1993 *E. I. du Pont and Co.* decision applied similar thinking in the unionized environment. Therefore, these types of programs must be carefully crafted. The application of the decision depends on the specifics of the program. Suggestions for maintaining compliance with the NLRA are

➤ Programs that deal with issues such as productivity and quality, as opposed to wages, hours, and other terms and conditions of employment, are usually permissible.

➤ Programs in which there is little management intervention are usually permissible. Committees or task forces that have independent authority to make decisions and implement those decisions are usually permissible.

➤ Programs in which it is clear that the employee group is merely making suggestions or providing information are usually permissible.

It should be noted that Congress attempted to lift some of the restrictions of section 8(a)(2) by passing the Teamwork for Employees and Managers Act (*TEAM Act*) in 1995, which would have exempted certain employee involvement activities from coverage. However, under pressure from organized labor, President Clinton vetoed the act in 1996.

EXAM ALERT

Expect a question on *Electromation*. The decision is increasingly an impediment to necessary managerial flexibility in the environment of the twenty-first century.

Strategic Considerations for the SPHR

As the HR strategic leader, the SPHR must assist management in developing an employee and labor relations strategy, along with appropriate programmatic activities that are aligned with the organization's strategic goals and its culture. Although it is easy to say that employee relations should be accommodating and friendly, that is not always effective in a dynamic, globalized, competitive environment, and might not best support the business model of the organization.

If already unionized, the SPHR must develop appropriate strategies to accommodate the needs of the union in ways that facilitate goal achievement of the organization. These strategies range from an extremely adversarial relationship with the union, which could involve hard bargaining and a willingness to take a strike or lockout with the ultimate goal of union decertification, to a collaborative relationship in which the union is accepted as a valued stakeholder in the employer's success.

As unions look at new industries and new types of employees to expand their membership base, the SPHR must develop strategies to deal with potential organizing efforts. Strategies might range from acceptance of the union to attempts to avoid unionization. Each of these options has a wide continuum of HR practices that can be initiated.

Union Acceptance

The employer can accept the inevitability of an organizing attempt by either actively campaigning against it or accepting the legitimacy of the union as a stakeholder and not opposing the certification. Aggressive opposition can utilize all the tactics previously discussed, such as one-on-one supervisory discussions with employees, captive audience meetings, delaying tactics, and so on. The SPHR should guide the employer through these tactics to ensure that ULPs are avoided. At the other end of the continuum, the employer can agree to a consent election and effectively remain neutral during the certification process.

Union Avoidance

Union avoidance strategies are also on a continuum, running from aggressive union suppression to benevolent union substitution. Union suppression activities involve very aggressive strategies to prevent the union from gaining a foothold within the organization and might involve consistent anti-union rhetoric even though no union organizing is underway. They might also include moving plants to right-to-work states with low union density and low union support, including moving operations to another country. At the other end of the continuum, union substitution strategies attempt to make the union irrelevant by providing a positive employee and labor relations environment, compensation equivalent to unionized firms, formal grievance procedures with final step arbitration, due process protections, just cause discipline, and employee involvement programs.

As stated earlier, the SPHR must be able to develop the appropriate strategy for the organization in alignment with the organization's strategic objectives and the environment in which the organization functions. The strategy must be ethically sound while maximizing the organization's potential of achieving its goals in an efficient and effective manner.

EXAM ALERT

Expect a question on union avoidance strategies.

Chapter Summary

As the world moves from a manufacturing-based to a service-and-knowledge-based economy, the success of the organization is increasingly predicated on the productivity of its employees. The nature of the organization's relationship with its employees, either directly or through the exclusive representative, greatly influences the organization's capability to achieve its goals.

This chapter covered the major components of the practice of employee and labor relations, including the complex maze of federal legislation, regulatory decisions and guidance, and judicial precedents.

The critical issues surrounding union certification, collective bargaining, and contract administration were discussed along with strategies to apply economic and other types of pressure on the other party and basic methods of dispute resolution. These concepts are critical for every SPHR even if not practicing in a unionized environment because the threat of unionization is always present.

Also covered in the chapter were concepts and strategies associated with employee relations in a nonunion environment. These included strategies for union avoidance and current practices in employee involvement and high performance workplace programs.

Key Terms

- ➤ Craft union
- ➤ Industrial union
- ➤ General union
- ➤ National Labor Relations Board (NLRB)
- ➤ Unfair labor practices (ULPs)
- ➤ Exclusive representation
- ➤ Bargaining unit
- ➤ Right-to-work laws
- ➤ Federal Mediation and Conciliation Service (FMCS)
- ➤ Beck rights
- ➤ Borg-Warner doctrine
- ➤ Excelsior list

- ➤ Mackay doctrine
- ➤ Weingarten rights
- ➤ Recognition strike
- ➤ Salting
- ➤ Certification
- ➤ Decertification
- ➤ Deauthorization
- ➤ Mandatory bargaining topics
- ➤ Permissive bargaining topics
- ➤ Illegal bargaining topics
- ➤ Distributive bargaining
- ➤ Integrative bargaining
- ➤ Economic strike

➤ Unfair labor practice strike

➤ Sympathy strike

➤ Lockout

➤ Pattern bargaining

➤ Mediation

➤ Interest arbitration

➤ Closed shop

➤ Union shop

➤ Agency shop

➤ Maintenance of membership

➤ Open shop

➤ Management rights clause

➤ Seniority

➤ Just cause

➤ Jurisdictional strike

➤ Wildcat strike

➤ Mediation

➤ Rights arbitration

➤ Cease and desist order

➤ Common law

➤ Employment-at-will

➤ Tort

➤ Progressive discipline

➤ Positive discipline

➤ Employee involvement programs

Apply Your Knowledge

Exercises

6.1 Bargaining Items

Fill in the following table, indicating whether the item is a mandatory, permissive, or illegal bargaining topic in the private sector.

Topic	Mandatory	Permissive	Illegal
Health insurance for retirees			
Christmas bonus			
Drug testing procedures			
Closed shop union security			
Use of union label on products			
Severance pay			
Limiting FMLA leave to union members only			
Seniority provisions			
Overtime pay provisions			
Profit-sharing plans			

6.2 Strikes

The following table lists several different types of strikes. Complete the table by indicating in the middle column whether that type of strike is a protected activity; that is, whether the employee can be disciplined, up to and including termination, for engaging in the strike. In the next column, indicate whether striking employees can be permanently replaced. Your answers should reflect private sector law. You might want to qualify some of your answers because they might depend on the situation.

Type of Strike	Protected Activity	Can Be Permanently Replaced
Recognition		
Economic		
Unfair labor practice		
Jurisdictional		
Wildcat		
Sympathy		

Review Questions

1. You are the HR director of an organization in the private sector and are not unionized. The CEO asks you to give her a very brief explanation of the process by which a union is certified to be the sole representative of the employees. What do you tell her?

2. The CEO has just been advised by NLRB that an unfair labor practice has been filed against the organization by the union. He calls you to his office and asks that you briefly explain the complaint process to him. How do you respond?

3. You have been asked to brief the management bargaining team regarding the requirements of good faith bargaining. What do you tell them?

4. The CEO would like to get the employees more involved in their work and more committed to the organization, and asks you for options as to how this might be accomplished. The organization is in the service sector and the nature of the work does not lend itself to a team approach. What options can you provide?

5. You are the HR director of a private sector organization that is in the middle of collective bargaining. The bargaining is not going well and the union is threatening a strike. You have been asked to brief the board of directors on legal tactics that are available to either prevent the strike or minimize its impact. The board does not want to offer any further concessions to the union. What do you tell the board?

Exam Questions

1. An employee can be disciplined for participating in which of the following types of strikes?

   ○ **A.** Economic strike

   ○ **B.** Unfair labor practice strike

   ○ **C.** Recognition strike

   ○ **D.** Jurisdictional strike

2. A union negotiates a contract with a major employer in an industry and then attempts to negotiate similar contracts with other employers in the same industry. Which of the following bargaining structures does this represent?

   ○ **A.** Centralized

   ○ **B.** Decentralized

   ○ **C.** Pattern

   ○ **D.** Multi-employer

3. Which of the following was not a provision of the Taft-Hartley Act amendments to the Wagner Act?

   ○ **A.** Employer unfair labor practices

   ○ **B.** Prohibition of the closed shop

   ○ **C.** Procedures for obtaining injunctions in national emergency strikes

   ○ **D.** Permission for states to pass right-to-work laws

4. Which of the following activities would be illegal for an employer to engage in during the pre-election campaign leading up to a union certification election?

   ○ **A.** One-on-one discussions with the bargaining unit employee and the supervisor regarding the cost of union dues

   ○ **B.** A captive audience meeting that employees are forced to attend during normal working hours in which the vice president of HR attempts to persuade employees to vote against certification of the union

   ○ **C.** Visiting the employee at home to try to convince that employee not to vote for union certification

   ○ **D.** A mass email to all potential bargaining unit employees, encouraging them to not vote for union certification

5. An arbitrator often uses a seven-part test to determine whether a disciplinary action meets the threshold of just cause. Which of the following would not normally be considered by the arbitrator in making this determination?

   ○ **A.** A thorough investigation was conducted.

   ○ **B.** The manager was new and had never imposed discipline before.

   ○ **C.** The penalty was appropriate to the severity of the infraction.

   ○ **D.** The employee was on notice that the behavior could lead to disciplinary action.

6. Which of the following federal legislative acts governs labor relations in the airline industry?

   ○ **A.** Railway Labor Act (1926)

   ○ **B.** Norris-LaGuardia Act (1932)

   ○ **C.** National Industrial Recovery Act (1933)

   ○ **D.** Landrum-Griffin Act (1959)

7. Which of the following bargaining topics would not be a mandatory topic under the Wagner Act?

   ○ **A.** Overtime

   ○ **B.** Sick leave

   ○ **C.** Seniority

   ○ **D.** Benefits for retired employees

8. Which Supreme Court decision validated the legality of mandatory arbitration employment contracts?

   ○ **A.** *Mackay*

   ○ **B.** *Borg-Warner*

   ○ **C.** *Circuit City*

   ○ **D.** *Weingarten*

9. Orders of the National Labor Relations Board are enforced by which of the following?

   ○ **A.** Fines and other sanctions imposed by the board

   ○ **B.** The federal appeals court having jurisdiction

   ○ **C.** The appropriate state court in which the firm is located

   ○ **D.** The Supreme Court

10. Which of the following actions would be legal under the employment-at-will doctrine?

   ○ **A.** An employee is discharged for filing an EEO complaint.

   ○ **B.** An employee is discharged because she refused to lie under oath on the employer's behalf in a civil suit.

   ○ **C.** An employee is discharged on the first instance of tardiness when the employee contract indicates a progressive discipline system for tardiness issues.

   ○ **D.** An employee is discharged because he comes to work in jeans at an organization that does not have a dress code.

Answers to Exercises

6.1 Bargaining Items

Topic	Mandatory	Permissive	Illegal
Health insurance for retirees		X	
Christmas bonus	X		
Drug testing procedures	X		
Closed shop union security			X
Use of union label on products		X	
Severance pay	X		
Limiting FMLA leave to union members only			X
Seniority provisions	X		
Overtime pay provisions	X		
Profit-sharing plans	X		

All the mandatory items are wages, hours, and other terms and conditions of employment. There is no obligation to agree to reach agreement on any of these items, but they must be bargained. Issues regarding former employees and retirees may be bargained only if both parties agree to do so. Placing the union label on products that the employer makes is also only a permissive item. Both bargaining on a closed shop union security arrangement and not providing a benefit guaranteed in law are illegal.

6.2 Strikes

Type of Strike	Protected Activity	Can Be Permanently Replaced
Recognition	Yes	Yes
Economic	Yes	Yes
Unfair labor practice	Yes	No
Jurisdictional	No	Yes*
Wildcat	Yes**	Yes**
Sympathy	Yes**	Yes**

Because jurisdictional strikes are not a protected activity, striking employees can be terminated or otherwise disciplined for engaging in the strike. Sympathy and wildcat strikes are protected activities unless they are prohibited by a no-strike clause in the bargaining agreement. In that case, the contract prevails, the activity is unprotected, and striking employees may be terminated or otherwise disciplined.

Answers to Review Questions

1. You can advise her that the union certification process consists of three stages.

    1. **Initial contact and interest building**—In this stage, the union and employees attempt get the workforce interested in and committed to unionization and to sign an authorization card indicating that interest. After 30% of the employees of the proposed bargaining unit have signed, the union can request that the NLRB hold a certification election. Generally, however, the union will try to obtain at least a 50% signature rate before requesting the election.

    2. **Election campaign**—After the NLRB has directed that a certification election be held, both management and the union will begin campaign to convince employees to support them in the election. The campaign is very similar to other types of political campaigns with each side engaging in a variety of tactics to influence voters.

    3. **Election**—A secret ballot election is held. If the union gets the majority of votes cast, it becomes the exclusive bargaining agent. The employer must then recognize the union and bargain in good faith to achieve a negotiated agreement.

2. To keep the explanation relatively concise, you can explain the process as follows:

    1. The union files a complaint with the appropriate Regional Director of the NLRB within six months of the alleged violation.

    2. The regional director makes a determination on the merits of the charge. If it is determined to be without merit it is dismissed. Dismissals may be appealed to the Office of General Counsel. Further appeals of dismissal are not permitted. If there appears to be merit, the regional director will attempt to get the two parties to resolve the issue. If it is not resolved, a formal complaint is issued and a hearing is scheduled.

3. A hearing is held before an ALJ who will issue a ruling including any remedial actions to be taken, if any. If the ruling is not timely appealed to the NLRB, it becomes the board's order.

4. If either party appeals to the board, it will issue a final decision.

5. Decisions of the board can be appealed initially to a federal appeals court and then to the Supreme Court.

3. You can tell them that it is up to the NLRB, on receipt of a unfair labor practice charge, to determine whether one of the parties to the negotiations has not engaged in good faith bargaining. There is nothing in the law that defines good faith bargaining. The NLRB will look at the totality of the management team's action in making that determination. In doing so, the NLRB would consider the following as being indicators of bargaining in good faith:

➤ The management team appears to be seriously intent on reaching an agreement.

➤ The team deals directly with the union bargaining team, and does not try to circumvent that team by presenting proposals directly to the bargaining unit.

➤ The management team is willing to meet at reasonable times and places.

➤ Management proposals are presented as being negotiable, not absolute "take or leave it."

➤ Management does not insist on bargaining on illegal or permissive items and does not refuse to bargain on mandatory ones.

➤ Management does not make unilateral changes in hours, wages, or other terms and conditions of employment during the negotiations.

➤ The management team provides sufficient information for the union to craft and respond to proposals.

➤ The employer does not commit ULPs during the negotiations.

➤ The management team advances proposals, responds to union proposals, and offers concessions or compromises.

4. A number of options can lead to increased employee involvement and organizational commitment. They are

➤ Suggestion programs.

➤ Survey/feedback/action in which employee surveys are administered to determine employee opinions regarding a wide variety of issues. The data from the surveys are analyzed and the results provided to both the manager and subordinates. Meetings are held between management and workers to deal with issues identified in the survey.

➤ Participative management in which employees are given greater input into decision making.

➤ Quality circles in which employees meet to discuss ways of improving the quality of the organization's products or services.

➤ Employee participation on various committees, taskforces, and project groups.

➤ Compensations arrangements such as ESOPs and profit-sharing plans.

5. You can advise the board that there are several options. The employer can be proactive and pre-emptive and institute a lockout, preventing bargaining unit employees from working and applying economic pressure through the loss of wages. The employer can threaten the union with continuing to operate during the strike. Continuation of operations could potentially be accomplished by using managerial workers, bargaining unit workers who cross the picket line, and/or temporary workers. However, the biggest threat is to tell the union that the employer is going to use permanent strike replacements that will retain their jobs after the completion of the strike. The employer can also initiate actions now that would minimize the potential financial impact of the strike. Examples include building up inventories of finished product, gearing up for increased production at other employer locations, and beginning preparations for potentially subcontracting out the work. You should also advise the board of whether the organization has strike insurance.

Answers to Exam Questions

1. The correct answer is **D**. Jurisdictional strikes are unfair labor practices by the union. As such, they are not a protected activity and the employee can be disciplined for failure to report to work. Economic (answer A), unfair labor practice (answer B), and recognition strikes (answer C) are all protected activities for which the employee cannot be disciplined. However, the striking employee can be permanently replaced in economic and recognition strikes and temporarily replaced in unfair labor practice strikes.

2. The correct answer is **C**. Pattern negotiating structure occurs when the union negotiates a contract with one employer in an industry and then attempts to negotiate a similar one with other employers. Centralized bargaining (answer A) occurs when the employer negotiates with multiple bargaining units at the same time, often on a companywide basis. Decentralized bargaining (answer B) occurs when the negotiations occur at the local level, whereas multi-employer negotiations (answer D) occur when more than one employer negotiates with one union at the same time.

3. The correct answer is **B**. Employer unfair labor practices were included in the Wagner Act in 1935. The other three items (answers A, C, and D) were provisions of the Taft-Hartley Act of 1947, which amended the Wagner Act.

4. The correct answer is **C**. Employers are not allowed to visit voting-eligible employees at their residence during the election campaign. The other activities (answers A, B, and D) are legal, assuming that the employer provides accurate information and does not try to coerce the employee to vote against the union.

5. The correct answer is **B**. Whether the manager is new is largely irrelevant in that the arbitrator will look at consistency of practice organizationwide. The other three answers (answers A, C, and D) are clearly part of the seven-part test.

6. The correct answer is **A**. Airlines were included in the act's coverage in 1936. Norris-LaGuardia (answer B) limited injunctions against labor union activities. The National Industrial Recovery Act (answer C) contained a provision dealing with the right of employees to form unions but was found to be unconstitutional. Landrum-Griffin (answer D) largely dealt with regulation of internal union matters.

7. The correct answer is **D**. Overtime (answer A), sick leave (answer B), and seniority (answer C) are mandatory topics. Retiree benefits is a permissive topic.

8. The correct answer is **C**. The *Mackay* (answer A) decision validated the use of permanent strike replacements. *Borg-Warner* (answer B) empowers the NLRB to categorize bargaining issues into mandatory, permissive, and illegal. *Weingarten* (answer D) deals with the right of an employee to have a representative present at investigatory interviews.

9. The correct answer is **B**. The NLRB does not have the authority to issue fines or other sanctions (answer A) for noncompliance. The state courts (answer C) have no jurisdiction. Decisions of the NLRB are appealed to a federal appeals court; decisions of the appeals court can be appealed to the Supreme Court (answer D). Enforcement of the decision is the responsibility of the appeals court.

10. The correct answer is **D**. Answer A is prohibited by protection against retaliation in the federal statue itself. Answer B is prohibited under the public policy exception. Answer C is prohibited under the implied contract exception.

Suggested Readings and Resources

➤ Boyer, R. O. & Morais, H. M. (1955). *Labor's Untold Story*. New York: Cameron and Associates. Budd, J. W. (2005). *Labor Relations: Striking a Balance*. New York: McGraw-Hill/Irwin.

➤ Fisher, R. & Ury, W. (1991). *Getting to Yes: Negotiating Agreement Without Giving In* (2nd edition). New York: Penguin.

➤ Holley, W. H., Jr., Jennings, K. M. & Wolters, R. S. (2005). *The Labor Relations Process* (8th edition). Mason, OH: South-Western.

➤ Heneman, H. G. & Judge, T. A. (2003). *Staffing Organizations* (4th edition). Burr Ridge, IL:McGraw-Hill

➤ Mathis, R. L. & Jackson, J. H. (2006). *Human Resource Management* (11th edition). Mason, OH: Thomson South-Western

➤ Overby, J. (editor). (2006). *Annual Editions: Labor Management Relations 2005/2006*. Dubuque, IA: McGraw-Hill/Dushkin.

➤ Robinson, R. H., Franklin, G. M. & Wayland, R. (2002). *The Regulatory Environment of Human Resource Management*. Fort Worth, TX: Harcourt.

➤ Sauer, R. L. & Voelker, K. E. (1993). *Labor relations: Structure and Process* (2nd edition). New York: Macmillan.

➤ Tompkins, J. (1995). *Human Resource Management in Government*. New York: HarperCollins.

7

Occupational Health, Safety, and Security

Objectives

This chapter helps you to prepare for the SPHR examination by covering the concepts and strategies associated with occupational health, safety, and security. This section composes **5%** of the SPHR examination.

Gain a Strategic Understanding of Occupational Health, Safety, and Security

▶ **Understand the historical development of health, safety, and security programs**

▶ **Understand the importance of health, safety, and security programs**

Gain an Understanding of Health, Safety, and Security Laws and Regulations

▶ **Understand the provisions of the major laws and associated regulations regarding health, safety, and security**

▶ **Understand the impact of these laws on the development of health, safety, and security programs**

Gain an Understanding of Safety Programs

▶ **Understand the basic characteristics of a safety program that complies with laws and regulations**

Gain an Understanding of Occupational Health Programs

▶ **Understand the characteristics of wellness and employee assistance programs**

▶ **Understand issues surrounding health related challenges in the workplace such as stress, tobacco use, substance abuse, indoor air quality, and obesity**

Gain an Understanding of Security Programs

▶ **Understand the components of a security plan**

▶ **Understand issues surrounding workplace violence**

Outline

Study Strategies

▶ This chapter should be studied from a strategic point of view. There will be only approximately eleven questions from this area on the whole test. Consequently a top-level understanding of the concepts of health and security will be required.

▶ The law and regulation around safety is, however, a bit more comprehensive and prescriptive. The SPHR should study that section a bit more intensely with the goal in mind of understanding the strategic implication of the safety program based on a good understanding of the requirements of law, particularly OSHA.

Introduction

Objective:
Gain a Strategic Understanding of Occupational Health, Safety, and Security

Health, safety, and security are increasingly important issues in the workplace with which the SPHR must deal. Health and safety are frequently used together as one concept because the same federal law covers them both. However, *health* is the broader term and refers to the employee's overall physical and psychological well-being. *Safety* is concerned with the prevention of injury due to working conditions, processes, and procedures, whereas health deals with injuries and both physical and psychological illnesses. *Security* is, to some extent, a separate, yet allied, program dealing with the protection of physical, human, and intellectual assets from harm, including unwanted disclosure.

Currently, there are more than 5,000 workers killed each year in the workplace and more than 4,000,000 reported job-related accidents and illnesses. Injury and illness rates are around five cases per one hundred workers and the death rate hovers around four deaths per one hundred thousand workers. Workers' compensation insurance is a major business-related expense for some organizations. Although you might usually think of accidents in terms of manufacturing, this is not necessarily the case. An increasing number of workers from the nonmanufacturing sector are filing claims for cumulative trauma disorder problems resulting from computer use. All types of employees are subject to injury and illness as a result of exposure to the workplace environment, whether it be to toxic chemicals, reaction to mold, or other conditions present in the working environment.

September 11, 2001 and the anthrax terrorism that followed brought about an unparalleled increase in workplace security efforts in terms of access to facilities, emergency preparedness, and mailroom security. In addition, constant attacks by computer hackers and rampant theft of digitized information has resulted in a relentless upgrading of computer security systems.

In addition to the obvious cost in terms of lost time, decreased productivity, training and replacing sick and injured workers, and increased workers' compensation insurance premiums, the SPHR should also be aware of the human costs involved in workplace accidents, illnesses, and violence. Workers are subject to pain and suffering, lost wages, permanent or temporary disability, psychological maladies, and death. Not only is the employee affected; so, too, are the employee's friends and family.

The capability of an employer to remain profitable, to efficiently and effectively produce goods or services, and to attract and retain excellent employees is dependent to some extent on its ability to provide a safe and healthy work environment for its employees. The SPHR must develop and implement health, safety, and security programs to assist in achieving the organization's goals.

A Brief History of Health, Safety, and Security

During most of the history of this country, issues of health, safety, and security were largely those of the employee and employer independently. Workplace injuries and illnesses were considered to be an outcome of the employment relationship, and employees were largely responsible for their own health and safety. Generally, the only recourse that the employee had regarding an on-the-job injury or illness was to sue the employer under common law, largely on the grounds of employer negligence. This was a one-sided battle with the employer possessing superior capabilities in terms of resources to defend itself from tort claims. Although workers could seek relief in the courts, employers had multiple defenses available to them. The employer could argue that the employee knowingly accepted the dangerous job and assumed the risks associated with that type of work, that the employee contributed to the injury or illness through negligent behavior, or that the injury or illness was the fault of another employee, not of the employer.

In terms of security, the employer was responsible for protecting its property. Employees were largely responsible for their own protection. Violence in the workplace resulting in employee injury or death, again, was considered to be part of the normal risks associated with the work environment. Employee recourse was limited to the courts either by suing the employer for negligence or the perpetrator for the harm caused.

As the Industrial Revolution ensued and huge manufacturing plants were built, the dangers of the workplace increased. This was due, in large part, to the mechanization of the work, which introduced machines that could cause serious injury or death, and because of the poor working environment in terms of heat, fumes, and caustic chemicals that could cause serious medical conditions. In the early 1900s, states began passing workers' compensation laws that provided protections for workers who were the victims of on-the-job injuries or illnesses. This action was driven by increasing public awareness of the dangers of factory work and of the abuses by employers. Three states (Wisconsin, Kansas, and Washington) passed workers' compensation laws in 1911. Today, all 50 states plus Washington, D.C., Puerto Rico, and the Virgin Islands have these laws.

The incidence of injury and death in the workplace declined significantly after the passage of the workers' compensation laws making employers responsible for on-the-job injuries and illnesses. Although the method of funding the program differs among the states, a commonality is that the employers' cost associated with its liability is based on the number of incidences of claims by employees. To reduce exposure, employers began to develop programs to reduce employee injury and illness.

Even though workers' compensation programs had an initial dramatic impact on the health, safety, and security of employees, injuries and illnesses began to increase again in the middle of the twentieth century, resulting in heightened congressional and public interest. This led to the passage of the Occupational Safety and Health Act in 1970.

Security has become an increasing concern after the events of September 11, 2001 and the continued threat of terrorism. Computer security has also become a major issue. Computer systems must be protected from being compromised by sophisticated and technically savvy hackers.

Health, Safety, and Security Law

A number of federal, state, and, in some instances, local laws and regulations affect the practice of HR in the areas of health, safety, and security. The two laws that have the most impact are the Workers' Compensation Act and the Occupational Safety and Health Act of 1970. They, along with other applicable laws and regulations, are covered in the following section.

Workers' Compensation

Workers' compensation is covered by state law and compensates employees for on-the-job injuries or illnesses. Illnesses can be either physical or mental, as long as they are work-related. In most states the employer is required to obtain workers' compensation insurance through a private insurance carrier. However, in a few states the employer must participate in an insurance fund administered by the state. Most states allow the employer to self-insure upon proof of financial capability to do so. In general, the laws cover both public and private employees.

Workers' compensation is essentially no-fault. Except in extreme cases, the employee's only recourse is through the workers' compensation program. The employee may not sue the employer even in the case of employer negligence. Also, the employee is covered in most instances even if the injury or illness is the result of the employee's own negligence or the negligence of a co-worker.

Workers' compensation payments are determined by state regulations. There are limits as to the amount of compensation payment that can be received and as to the total number of weeks or months that an employee can receive the payments. Thus there is an element of coinsurance in that the employee must absorb those costs or loss of income not covered by the payments. Benefits are also normally coordinated with other types of income protection such as short- and long-term disability insurance and Social Security. Compensation payments are normally reduced or limited by the amount of money received from other programs.

Compensation is usually available as follows:

▸ Medical treatment costs incurred as a result of the injury or illness

▸ Survivor benefits in case of death

▸ The expenses associated with rehabilitation

▸ Income loss during permanent or partial disability

▸ Lump-sum payments for permanent partial disability (loss of a limb or eye, for example)

The company's costs are typically determined by the firm's experience rate. In other words, the greater the number of claims, the higher the premium rates that the employer must pay. Thus it is in the organization's best interest to provide a safe and healthy work environment.

EXAM ALERT

> Expect several questions regarding workers' compensation. The most likely question topics are the no-fault provisions, what benefits are provided, and how benefits are funded (typically private insurance).

NOTE

> Workers' compensation, ADA (*Americans with Disabilities Act*), and FMLA (*Family and Medical Leave Act*) sometimes present a strategy problem for the SPHR. Under workers' compensation, it is often to the employer's benefit to bring the employee back to work, either full or part time, as soon as possible to limit utilization under the employer's insurance coverage or from the state fund. This could also mean bringing the employee back to light duty by modifying the nature of the tasks required to be performed. Conflicts can occur in two ways:
>
> ▶ Under FMLA, the employee must be returned to the same or similar position. Consequently, assuming continuing medical conditions, the employee might be legally able to refuse to return to a modified position for the entire twelve weeks, continuing to draw workers' compensation payments.
>
> ▶ Light duty frequently involves eliminating or modifying one or more essential functions of the job to temporarily accommodate the injured or ill employee so that the employee can return to work. If the light duty continues for a lengthy period of time, a future applicant (and the EEOC) could argue that the job has been permanently changed. Thus, applicants that the employer would not normally considered qualified for the position might be now eligible for the modified position, and not to consider them would be a violation of ADA.

Fair Labor Standards Act (1938)

The Fair Labor Standards Act, discussed in Chapter 5, "Compensation and Benefits," earlier in this book, limits the types of jobs that can be performed and the number of hours that can be worked by those under 18 years of age in order to protect younger workers from potential injury or illness.

Occupational Safety and Health Act (1970)

The major legislation affecting safety and health is the Occupational Safety and Health Act, which was passed in 1970 to ensure that all workers are provided a safe and healthy work environment. The act covers virtually all private employers except for those that are covered by a different act (mining, for example). It does not cover local, state, or federal employees. However, the act allows states to set up their own agencies to manage safety and health. Twenty-six states and territories have done so. Under those circumstances, the state must also cover its public sector employees in addition to private sector workers. Federal employees are covered by an executive order that requires agencies to maintain a safe and healthy workplace in alignment with protections provided for workers in the private sector.

The major provisions of the act are as follows:

▶ Establishes the Occupational Safety and Health Administration (*OSHA*) under the Department of Labor to administer the act. OSHA has the authority to set and enforce safety standards, inspect work sites, and issue penalties for non-compliance.

▶ Establishes the National Institute of Occupational Safety and Health (*NIOSH*) under the Department of Health and Human Services to research safety and health issues in the workplace and to assist OSHA in developing standards.

▶ Establishes the Occupational Safety and Health Review Commission (*OSHRC*) under the Department of Labor to adjudicate challenges to OSHA enforcement activities.

▶ Requires employers to maintain a safe and healthy environment and to comply with OSHA standards.

▶ Requires employers with more than 10 employees to keep health and safety records.

▶ Requires employees to comply with health and safety standards but does not impose penalties for failure to do so.

▶ Requires employers to publish posters advising employees of their rights under the act.

▶ Prohibits the employer from retaliating against an employee for exercising rights under the act (requesting an inspection by OSHA, reporting health and safety violations to OSHA, refusing to work in unsafe conditions, and so forth).

▶ Permits OSHA to inspect worksites and to issue citations for violations.

▶ Permits states to operate their own plans to regulate health and safety in the workplace.

EXAM ALERT

You should expect several questions on the basic law. You should know what NIOSH and OSHRC do and know which employers are covered by the Occupational Safety and Health Act. You should also expect a question regarding the basic responsibilities of the Occupational Safety and Health Administration.

NOTE

Twenty-six states and territories have developed their own occupational health and safety plans and regulatory agencies. In those states and territories, OSHA has, in effect, transferred authority to those entities to administer the Occupational Safety and Health Act. Therefore inspections and other contacts initially will likely be with state officials. As with most federal laws, the states are allowed to pass additional legislation regarding health, safety, and security so long as they provide greater employee protections than the federal law. The appeal process of citations and penalties eventually leads to the federal process through OSHA and OSHRC, although an initial appeal might be made at the state level.

Superfund Amendments and Reauthorization Act of 1986

The Superfund Amendments and Reauthorization Act of 1986 is frequently referred to merely as *SARA*. Title III of SARA (community right to know and emergency response regulations) places requirements on firms that store toxic chemicals or release them into the environment. When certain thresholds are reached in terms of the amount of chemical stored or released, the employer might be obligated to make reports and provide inventories to state and local emergency planning organizations and to the local fire department. The organization might also be required to develop an emergency response plan, designate an emergency response coordinator, and provide site plans indicating where toxic chemicals are located. SARA is administered and enforced by the federal Environmental Protection Agency (*EPA*) and state environmental management agencies.

Drug-Free Workplace Act of 1988

This act requires employers who receive federal contracts of at least $100,000 or federal grants of any amount to maintain a drug-free workplace. The act itself does not require that the employer perform employee drug testing nor does it require that the employer pay for drug rehabilitation. The act is monitored and enforced by the contracting agency, and failure to abide by its provisions can lead to termination of the current contract and debarment from future contracts. Major provisions of the act are to

▶ Publish a drug policy prohibiting illegal substances in the workplace and provide a copy to each employee

▶ Create and publicize a drug-free awareness program

▶ Advise employees of the availability of assistance programs such as counseling, rehabilitation, EAP, and so on

▶ Inform employees of the consequences of workplace use of illegal substances

▶ Require employees to report to the employer any conviction for workplace drug activity within five days of the conviction

▶ Report the employee conviction to the contracting agency within 10 days after being notified by the employee and discipline the employee within 30 days of being notified

Other Acts and Regulations

Although the SPHR exam will not test you on state laws, it is important to note that individual states might have additional laws and regulations regarding all facets of health, safety, and security in the workplace. The Department of Transportation requires random and incident related drug testing for many categories of transportation workers (truck and bus drivers, airline pilots and mechanics, train crews, and so forth).

OSHA Standards

Objective:
Gain an Understanding of Health, Safety, and Security Laws and Regulations

As you learned previously, OSHA has responsibility under the Occupational Safety and Health Act to develop and issue health and safety standards to protect workers. When they're issued, these standards become obligatory for employers and require actions in order to become compliant. The employer must not only implement certain practices or procedures, but it must also publicize those to employees and train them. Proposed or amended standards are published in the *Federal Register* for review and comment and hearings may be held if requested by an interested party. After this review process, OSHA publishes the final standard and its effective date. If an employer still does not agree with the final standard, it may appeal the standard to the United States Court of Appeals within 60 days of final issuance. In certain circumstances, emergency standards can be issued but the permanent issuance process must then be followed to finalize the standard. Even if there is not a particular standard covering a work process or procedure, the general duty clause of the Occupational Safety and Health Act provides an overarching requirement to provide a safe and healthy workplace.

The General Duty Clause

It is virtually impossible to issue specific standards for all tasks and processes performed in the workplace, yet citations can be issued only for violations of standards. The general duty clause provides a standard in those instances when another specific standard does not apply. The clause obligates the employer to provide a workplace that is free from recognized hazards that might cause death, serious injury, or illness.

EXAM ALERT
Expect a question regarding the general duty clause.

Examples of Standards

A huge number of standards have been issued by OSHA. A few of the more common standards are listed later in this section to provide an indication of the types of issues covered and employer obligations associated with them.

EXAM ALERT
You should expect a question requiring you to identify a standard from a list, given a scenario describing the type of work being done; or, vice versa, to identify what types of activities would be generally subject to a standard from a list of activities given the standard's name. It is most likely that the question will address the common standards listed next.

▶ **Control of Hazardous Energy**   This standard is usually referred to as *lockout* or *tagout*. The purpose of the standard is to prevent the accidental operation of equipment during maintenance. *Lockout* means to physically prevent the inadvertent operation by denying access to the activation switch. Locking a cap over the on/off switch is an example of lockout. *Tagout* means to attach a tag to the activation device, warning employees to not activate it.

▶ **Hazard Communication**   Hazard communication is commonly referred to as the *employee right to know standard*. The standard requires that manufacturers and users of hazardous chemicals label those products and provide information regarding the substances in material safety data sheets (*MSDSs*). MSDSs contain information as to the nature of hazard the substance is composed of and what the appropriate treatment is for employees who come in contact with it. These chemicals must be inventoried and a hazard communication plan established in the workplace. MSDSs must be readily available to employees, and training must be provided as to how to read the MSDS and what to do in case of exposure to hazardous substances.

> **NOTE**
>
> The hazard communication standard presents a bit of a problem in terms of its application in the workplace, particularly with respect to pregnancy. The standard requires that employees be provided information regarding the hazards and protection requirements associated with various chemicals. There are some chemicals that do not affect the adult but do affect the fetus. To transfer an employee away from those chemicals when the employee is pregnant might assist in compliance with the standard but subject the employer to a violation of the Pregnancy Discrimination Act.

▶ **Personal Protective Equipment**   The standard requires that the employer analyze the hazards associated with a job and provide appropriate equipment to prevent injury or illness. Equipment might include hard hats, safety glasses, breathing masks, and steel-toed shoes.

▶ **Bloodborne Pathogens**   The standard is designed to protect employees who are regularly in contact with blood and bodily fluids or subject to needle sticks from contracting bloodborne diseases such as HIV or hepatitis. The standard requires training as to how to avoid exposure and the proper response should exposure occur.

▶ **Others**   Other common standards are Forklift Operation, Confined Space, Emergency Exit, Noise Exposure, and Machine Guarding.

Ergonomics

Ergonomics is the study of the physical impact of work on the body and the design of work processes and the work environment to minimize them. It would seem logical, particularly with the large number of back injuries and cases of carpal tunnel syndrome, that there would be one or more standards dealing directly with ergonomics. This is not the case. An ergonomic standard was issued by OSHA in 2000 but was repealed by Congress. However, the debate and publicity surrounding the standard and its subsequent repeal did focus employer, employee, and public attention on the issue. OSHA has not been totally silent since the repeal with respect to ergonomics and the resultant cumulative trauma disorders (*CTDs*), but has approached the issue through training and nonbinding guidance. Employers have increasingly developed ergonomic programs in an attempt to reduce CTDs. A typical ergonomic program should include

- Upper management commitment to minimizing CTDs

- Development of a formal program and/or policy and communication of that policy to employees

- Ergonomic analysis of job tasks and worksite environment

- Job design and redesign to minimize muscle stress, strain, and fatigue and to improve worksite environment

- Training of employees in proper performance of ergonomically designed tasks

- Medical monitoring and intervention of employees affected by CTDs

- Follow-up and analysis of program results, and modifying the program if necessary

EXAM ALERT

Ergonomics is likely to be covered in a question because it is a controversial area. Expect a question regarding the components of an ergonomic program.

Exemption from Standards

An employer may request an exemption from compliance with a standard under limited conditions. Such an exemption is called a *variance*. The following items describe *temporary variance* and *permanent variance*.

- **Temporary variance**   The Secretary of Labor can grant a temporary variance from the standard if a firm cannot reach compliance by the standard's implementation date, but can show that it is working toward compliance and will attain it in a reasonable amount of time. Employees must be advised of the temporary variance and the fact that the employer is not yet in compliance. Temporary variances may be extended if the employer is making progress but still cannot become compliant during the initial temporary variance. In general, temporary variances can be granted for a total of only two years, including extensions.

▶ **Permanent variance** The Secretary of Labor can grant a permanent variance from a standard if the employer can prove that its processes, procedures, and/or safety precautions provide employee protection equal to or better than those provided by the standard. Employees must be advised of the permanent variance, have a right to a hearing before the variance is actually issued, and have a window to request revocation or modification of the variance after it has been issued.

OSHA Inspection Process

The Occupational Safety and Health Act permits OSHA to enter and inspect the workplace to determine compliance with standards. OSHA inspections must occur during normal working hours or other convenient times and the inspectors are permitted to talk to and question employees during the inspection. Both the employer and a representative of employees are permitted to accompany the inspector during the inspection. Employers are protected against warrantless inspections and do not have to permit OSHA access to the worksite. In that case, OSHA must petition the U.S. district court for a search warrant to conduct the inspection. Reasons for inspections and the inspection process are discussed in the sections that follow.

Reasons for OSHA Inspections

OSHA conducts inspections for a number of reasons. The following list highlights the priority list of potential OSHA inspections:

▶ The highest priority inspections are for conditions that cause imminent danger of injury or death to employees.

▶ The second priority is inspection after a serious incident involving death or serious injury.

▶ The third priority is as a result of employee complaints.

▶ The fourth priority is targeted OSHA program inspections. These inspections might involve industries with high incidence rates, dangerous jobs, or special emphasis programs where OSHA believes there is high noncompliance and wants to send a message to a particular industry.

▶ The final priority for inspections is reinspections and random inspections. Although the percentage of reasons for inspections might vary from year to year, the majority occur in high-hazard targeted industries.

EXAM ALERT

Expect a question regarding OSHA inspection priorities.

The Inspection

A typical inspection can be described as follows:

▶ An OSHA or state officer shows up at the place of business. At this time the inspector will display appropriate credentials and request to speak with the owner or manager.

▶ An opening conference is held in which the inspector explains the purpose of the inspection, how it will proceed, and gives an overview of the standards that are likely to apply. If the inspector is likely to become aware of trade secrets or proprietary information during the inspection, the issue of protection of this information is discussed.

▶ The inspection is conducted with both an employer and employee representative accompanying the inspector. The inspection is likely to include the following:

  ▶ Physical inspection of the worksite

  ▶ Check of employer-required OSHA records

  ▶ Check to ensure that mandatory posters are properly displayed

  ▶ Review of the employer safety program

▶ A closing conference is held in which the employer and employee representative are presented with the results of the inspection and any proposed citations and penalties.

EXAM ALERT

You should expect a question regarding the inspection process. A favorite item is the fact that employers are protected from warrant-less inspections and can require OSHA to get a judicial warrant to proceed.

Citations and Penalties

Inspectors have the authority to issue citations and recommend penalties depending on the severity of the violation and the potential for injury. In extreme cases, where there is immediate danger of serious injury or death, the inspector can seek an injunction to prevent the employer from operating until the violation is corrected. The types of citations and associated penalties are provided in Table 7.1.

TABLE 7.1   Types of OSHA Citations and Penalties

Type of Citation	Civil Penalty
Willful: The employer intentionally and knowingly violates a standard.	$5,000–$70,000 Willful violations that result in the death of an employee could also result in criminal prosecution resulting in fines of up to $10,000 and imprisonment up to six months. Fines and imprisonment terms are doubled for repeat offenders.
Serious: Violation of a standard where there is substantial probability that death or serious injury could result and that the employer knew or should have known that the hazard existed.	Up to $7,000 per violation.
Repeat: Continued violation of a standard upon OSHA reinspection.	Up to $70,000.
Failure to Abate: The employer fails to correct a violation found in an inspection.	Up to $7,000 per day beyond the prescribed abatement period.
Other: Violation that is not likely to cause death or serious harm.	Up to $7,000.

There are additional criminal penalties for knowingly providing false information to OSHA or for divulging the fact that OSHA is planning an inspection at a particular work location.

Appeal of Citations and Penalties

Proposed citations and penalties are discussed during the closing conference. This is the first chance for the employer to reach agreement and negotiate. If resolution cannot be reached, the appeal process differs a bit depending on whether the inspection was done by the federal or state government. In either case, the process will eventually merge with the federal process. For state inspections, the next step is an appeal to a higher-level state official, either at the closing conference or soon thereafter. For federal inspections, an appeal must be made to the area director within 15 days of the inspection. If resolution of the issue in either state or federal inspections cannot be reached, the appeal goes to the OSHRC, which will assign an administrative law judge (*ALJ*) to hear the case. Decisions of the ALJ can then be appealed to the OSHRC. Decisions of the OSHRC can be appealed through the federal court system.

EXAM ALERT

Expect a question regarding the types of citations, their definitions and associated penalties, and on the appeal process.

OSHA Record Keeping Requirements

The Occupational Safety and Health Act imposes recordkeeping and reporting requirements on employers with more than 10 employees unless the employer is in certain industries that are exempt from these provisions (generally service industries where the nature of work is not hazardous). All occupational illnesses must be recorded. Occupational injuries, except for those that involve minor first aid, also must be recorded. Recordation is required if the injury results in lost days from work, restricted work (light duty) or job transfer, loss of consciousness, or death. All employers, even those with 10 or fewer employees and those that are exempt, must report incidents that result in the death of an employee or hospitalization of three or more employees. These events must be reported to OSHA within eight hours of their occurrence.

In-depth discussion of the recording and reporting process is beyond the scope of this section. There are numerous rules as to what is recordable and what is not, what is job related and what is not, and what is first aid and what is more than first aid. However, each recordable instance must be recorded on OSHA Form 301 (*Injury and Illness Incident Report*) and certain information transferred in summary fashion to OSHA Form 300 (*Log of Work-Related Injuries and Illnesses*). The recordation must be done within seven calendar days of becoming aware of the incident. Form 301 must be kept for five years and must be available for employee review in most instances. Form 300 must, in all cases, be made available to employees.

Once a year, the employer is required to complete and post OSHA Form 300A (*Summary of Work-Related Injuries and Illnesses*). The form must be signed by a company executive, indicating that the information is correct and posted during the period February 1 to April 30 following the year covered by the report.

All forms must be available to OSHA on request.

Safety Programs

Objective:

Gain an Understanding of Safety Programs

Regardless of the requirements of law, it is important that the employer maintain a viable safety program with the intention of promoting safety awareness and preventing injuries and illness. To develop an effective program, the SPHR must know the major reasons why accidents occur and then develop a program around prevention.

Why Do Accidents Occur?

Accidents occur for two main reasons. The first is unsafe working conditions and improper work design. An effective safety program addresses this issue through compliance with OSHA standards, frequent safety inspections, immediate correction of potential safety hazards, and proper work design, including ergonomic design of the work tasks and work environment. A critical component of maintaining safe working conditions is a culture that values safety and encourages employees to report unsafe working conditions.

The second cause of accidents is unsafe acts by employees. An effective safety program addresses this issue through continuous job and safety awareness training. The program encourages safe acts and a culture of safety among management and employees. Incentives are provided for safety and corrective action, and discipline is imposed for unsafe acts. Recruitment, selection, orientation, training, and performance evaluation are components of preventing unsafe acts.

Components of the Program

Critical to the success of a safety program is the strong support of management, particularly top management. Components of an effective safety program include

▶ A strong policy statement contained in the employee handbook, separate document, or negotiated agreement (or any combination thereof) that indicates management's commitment to a safe and healthy working environment and places obligations on both management and employees to comply with the policy.

▶ A consistent and aggressive effort to implement and comply with OSHA standards, including the general duty clause.

▶ Frequent safety training covering both OSHA standards and proper safety procedures and encouraging a culture of safety and safety awareness.

▶ Consistent inspection for safety hazards at the shop level. This can be done by a safety committee established by the employer or negotiated in the labor agreement, and is augmented by a culture in which employees are encouraged to report hazards.

▶ Immediate resolution of dangerous conditions and timely resolution of less dangerous ones.

▶ Immediate response to accidents, including a thorough investigation.

▶ Timely implementation of recommendations resulting from accident investigations.

▶ Incentive programs consisting of both intrinsic and extrinsic rewards. Recognition can be at the individual, group, or plant level.

▶ Both ongoing and periodic evaluation of the safety program and its results. Injuries and illness rates should be analyzed for trends and the cost effectiveness of various programmatic activities.

> **NOTE**
>
> Remember the *Electromation* decision and carefully craft any safety committee that you create. Refer to Chapter 6, "Employee and Labor Relations," to review this decision.

> **NOTE**
>
> Be careful with the design and implementation of recognition systems. The culture should always value reporting of injuries and illnesses so that the cause can be determined and preventive actions undertaken, as opposed to valuing the failure to report because doing so results in not earning recognition.

Accident Investigation Procedures

Accident investigations should be immediate, thorough, and conducted in a professional manner. Safety committee members, designated employees, or managers can complete investigations. The critical issue is that they be trained in proper investigatory techniques and analysis. The steps in an effective investigation are

▶ **Immediate response to the accident scene**   The accident investigator should take charge and ensure that medical treatment is provided to injured employees as necessary and that everything possible is done to minimize damage to property and equipment.

▶ **Secure the accident scene and begin the investigation**   Normally the investigator will take pictures or videotape the scene as soon as possible. This might provide valuable insights later.

▶ **Interview all witnesses**   Videotaping is a good way to ensure that information is captured for further analysis. If videotaping is not possible, the investigator should take copious notes or have someone assist in doing so. Accident victims should be interviewed as soon as possible and medically permissible.

▶ **All the information is accumulated and analyzed**   Analysis should also include secondary sources, such as accident reports available from third parties and the review of technical manuals and appropriate professional journals.

▶ **A formal report is prepared that describes the accident**   This report should include the accident's cause(s) and recommendations to prevent a reoccurrence. The report is presented to management and/or the safety committee.

▶ **Recommendations**   All recommendations are considered in a timely manner and implemented as appropriate.

Occupational Health Programs

Objective:

Gain an Understanding of Occupational Health Programs

Occupational health programs are a growing and increasingly complex area. The responsibilities of the SPHR are strategic in nature, ensuring that appropriate programs are in place and that various federal, state, or local laws and regulations are complied with. Development of occupational health programs often requires the assistance of certified industrial hygienists or other appropriate health and environmental professionals. Some of the major components of occupational health programs are discussed briefly in the sections following this one, along with several of the more important workplace health-related issues. Such components include

- Employee assistance programs
- Wellness programs
- Stress reduction programs
- Smoking cessation programs
- Drug testing including substance abuse
- Obesity control and prevention
- Indoor air quality

Employee Assistance Programs

Employee Assistance Programs (*EAPs*) provide a variety of counseling and assistance services. Issues that EAPs are prepared to deal with typically include health and wellness (mental and physical), drug and alcohol abuse, financial problems, relationship problems (marital, family, and job related), childcare, eldercare, legal problems, retirement transitions, and many others. Although some firms might provide the program in-house, many EAP programs are contracted out. Employees using the program are generally guaranteed confidentiality and are provided toll-free numbers to access the program. EAP services are often integrated with health insurance benefits if the issue is one that requires long-term care or counseling. Most research evaluating EAPs indicates substantial cost-effectiveness in providing these types of programs.

Wellness Programs

Wellness programs consist of a variety of efforts to improve the overall physical and mental health and fitness of the employee population. The term is really a catchall phrase for a wide variety of efforts ranging from one end of the continuum with minimal activities, such as providing health promotion brochures to a comprehensive culture of health and fitness promotion, to activities and facilities at the other end. EAPs are often integrated with and a part of a broader wellness program. Wellness programs might include

▶ Providing health promotion and information brochures

▶ Providing health screenings and health risk assessments

▶ Providing health related training and programs dealing with such issues as obesity, smoking cessation and stress management

▶ Providing an employee assistance program

▶ Providing incentives (intrinsic and extrinsic) for healthy lifestyles

▶ Providing onsite fitness and health facilities or underwriting all or a portion of the cost of offsite facilities

Stress Reduction Programs

Stress is an employee's reaction to events, job-related or otherwise. Stress is not necessarily bad and can produce enhanced performance. However, stress can result in "job burnout," undesirable workplace behaviors, and serious or debilitating illness. Symptoms of high stress levels of workers might be an inability to make decisions, irritability, tardiness or absenteeism, decrease in productivity or work quality, or an increase in accident rates. Physiologically, stress has been correlated with ulcers, high blood pressure, strokes, and heart attacks. These costs of stress to employers are estimated to be in the hundreds of billions of dollars each year.

Effective EAPs and wellness programs can be of great assistance in preventing and treating stress and its related symptoms. Also effective are a number of management related practices that can help reduce the potential for the workplace to be stressful. Job design, clear performance expectations, equitable work assignments, clear managerial communications, and effective selection and placement of workers all can contribute to the reduction of stress in the workplace.

Smoking Cessation Programs

Many private sector employers have banned smoking in the workplace, and there are numerous federal, state, and local regulations governing smoking in the public sector, all with the intent of protecting both smokers and nonsmokers from being subject to dangerous fumes. This ban in the private sector is legal and does not violate an employee's rights, although the implementation of the ban would be negotiable in a unionized environment. Good HR practice is to provide counseling through an EAP, if available, and smoking cessation programs for employees when a no smoking policy is introduced. Some employers have made abstention from tobacco a condition of employment, requiring employees to refrain from using tobacco products outside of work and testing them for compliance. Such a provision has been upheld by the courts, but might violate state law. See the following note for more information.

> **NOTE**
>
> Although banning smoking in the workplace is legal, requiring employees to be tobacco free or making employment decisions based on the legal use of tobacco might violate state law. This same caution applies to banning or making employment decisions based on the use of other legal substances.

Drug Testing

Drug testing, either as an employment prescreen, on a random basis, or following an incident in the workplace, is legal and often part of an occupational health program. It is required by the Department of Transportation for certain categories of workers. When instituting these types of programs, there are numerous procedural requirements for maintaining privacy of the results, implementing appropriate safeguards for the chain of custody of the specimen, and ensuring the accuracy of the results. The SPHR must determine whether such a program, unless mandated by law or regulation, is in alignment with the goals and culture of the organization. Some firms have found that the cost-effectiveness of such a program in terms of the number of positive results does not justify the cost, whereas others have found testing to be a valuable part of an overall occupational health program.

Substance Abuse

Illegal use of substances and abuse of legal substances is not a protected employee right under ADA. These employees are at much greater risk (some studies show three to four times) of being involved in a workplace accident. In addition, productivity and work quality are also negatively affected. Employees who use illegal substances or are impaired by the use of legal substances should be dealt with in accordance with the employer's disciplinary procedures. The employee should be advised of the existence of an EAP program and given procedures for contacting the program if the employer has one.

Obesity Prevention and Control

Increasingly, health officials are warning that obesity and its related health problems are a major health challenge in the United States. Many companies have developed programs stressing proper nutrition and exercise to try to combat this problem. The programs can be contained within a larger wellness program or can be standalones.

Indoor Air Quality

The use of noxious chemicals and processes, poor building maintenance, improper heating, ventilation, and air conditioning systems design or maintenance, and numerous other problems frequently result in temporary or permanent employee health problems. Although compliance with the various OSHA standards frequently prevents such problems, compliance does not guarantee that such issues as "sick building syndrome" will be totally alleviated. In these times of high energy costs, efficiency might be traded off for proper airflow, resulting in improperly treated and conditioned workplace air (stale air, mold, and so forth). The employer should ensure that processes, procedures, and systems provide safe indoor air quality.

Security Programs

Objective:
Gain an Understanding of Security Programs

It seems that every day brings new media accounts of failures of computer security systems to prevent the theft of huge amounts of data, particularly personal information maintained on employees or customers that could be used for identity theft or some other illegal purpose. Frequently, employer proprietary information and other types of property are either stolen or damaged by outsiders or current or former employees.

Workplace violence creates havoc in the workplace and in such a case, injury or death is just the beginning. Studies frequently show that productivity at plants where a serious violent incident has occurred takes years to get back to its pre-incident levels.

Security is a comprehensive term for programs designed to protect the physical and intellectual property of the firm and the employees, clients, and suppliers of an organization. In this post-9/11 world, with increasingly complex data systems and the threat of terrorism, both physical and electronic security programs have taken on new importance. The sophistication of programs now required for protection are beyond the scope of this chapter and, very often, beyond the expertise of the typical SPHR. More and more, successful security programs require technical experts, either in-house or contracted.

The basic concepts behind the development of a security plan that an SPHR needs to understand are discussed in the following sections. Also discussed are issues with respect to computer and physical security and workplace violence.

Security Plans

The concept behind developing effective security plans is *risk assessment*. What are the potential risks, what is the cost to the organization if a particular incident occurs, and what is the cost of implementing programs to eliminate or minimize the risk? The issue then becomes, effectively, one of cost-benefit analysis and the determination of how to allocate resources to best protect the interests of the firm. The development of a security plan can be thought of in terms of a three-step process as discussed next.

Security Audit/Risk Analysis

This is a determination of the potential risks that a firm could face (natural disasters, theft, computer theft and fraud, workplace violence, fire, terrorism, and so on). After the potential risks have been enumerated, the probability of those risks must be determined. Are they extremely likely, likely, or unlikely?

Impact of Risks Should They Occur

How likely is it that a particular event will occur and what is the impact of that event on the organization? The likelihood of an employee stealing a ballpoint pen, for example, is extremely high, but the impact of that theft on the organization is *de minimus*. However, the likelihood of a major fire or of terrorism might be relatively low, but the impact devastating.

Cost-Benefit Analysis and Determination of Security Measures

The security plan is then developed based on an analysis of the likelihood and impact of an event in relation to the cost of preventing or minimizing the impact of the event. To carry the scenarios just discussed a bit further, the impact on the organization of employee theft of ballpoint pens would not likely justify the cost of developing and implementing a plan to prevent petty theft, whereas the impact of a major fire or a major act of terrorism would likely justify substantial expenditure of funds to prevent such an event or to minimize the impact of that event.

Computer Security

Computer security is a technically challenging and dynamic issue. Hackers seem to be able to quickly overcome the latest in security protocols and software protections. It is critical that proprietary information and employee records data be protected. The increasing use of Internet- and intranet-based applications increases the potential of illegal access to data. Development of computer security systems, firewalls, and access protection requires the assistance of experts in the field.

Physical Security

Physical security involves the protection of property from damage and employees from harm through limited access to physical facilities. Protection might include limited access to the parking lot or workspace through guards, key cards, or other systems; the installation of panic buttons in public use spaces, such as reception areas; employee name badges; and the development of evacuation plans and emergency response plans in coordination with local law enforcement and fire protection agencies. Development of physical security programs requires the advice and assistance of experts professionally trained in these areas.

Workplace Violence

Workplace violence is a major problem in the work environment today. Homicide is the second biggest cause of death in the workplace, occurring on average more than 10 times a week. Proportionally, women are the victims of violence at much higher rates than men. It is estimated that more than a million instances of violence take place in the workplace each year, resulting in hundreds of thousands of lost workdays and lost productivity.

Prevention of Workplace Violence

Employers can be proactive in their attempts to prevent workplace violence and to minimize the consequences if violence does occur. Some activities associated with effective workplace violence prevention and post-incident management are

- Managerial training in recognizing the potential for violence and how to deal with it

- Development of and training on emergency action plans and emergency response teams

- Investigation of workplace violence incidents, analysis of findings, determination of causes, and recommendations as to preventative measures

- Installation of security measures, including improved perimeter and parking lot lighting, cash-handling procedures to minimize the amount of cash on hand, security cameras, building security, and so on

- Improved employee selection procedures to screen out persons with a history or potential for violent behavior

- Use of EAP and counseling services for quick intervention at the first sign of potential violence

- Consistent application of discipline in the event of violent behavior or threats

Profile of Violent Employees

A profile is, obviously, a very general description of the characteristics or background of an individual who has a higher potential than others to engage in violent behavior. These are gross indicators that the SPHR should be aware of. This information should obviously be shared with managers in violence prevention training. Almost invariably, when an analysis is made of a violent incident, there were indicators that the perpetrator had violent tendencies.

Whether managerial awareness and intervention could have prevented the incident is the question. The following are characteristics frequently associated with those who have committed violence in the workplace:

- ▶ Caucasian.

- ▶ Male.

- ▶ Work is the only constant in the person's life.

- ▶ Person is somewhat of a loner.

- ▶ Interest in guns and/or military history.

- ▶ History of minor problems at work, including aggressiveness and prior threatening behavior or verbal threats.

- ▶ Recent event in the workplace or outside that pushed the person over the edge (termination, potential layoff, disciplinary action, domestic problems, and so on).

- ▶ Person blames others and holds grudges.

Employee Privacy

There is frequently a tradeoff between employee privacy and successful safety, health, and security programs. The SPHR must balance these two goals. Does the invasiveness of drug and alcohol testing justify the program? Do security cameras on the production line sufficiently prevent theft and other improper behaviors to justify the lack of privacy and the impression of lack of trust that they might create? Does the monitoring of telephone calls, Internet use, and computer keystrokes promote the goals of the organization or unnecessarily invade the privacy of employees? Even though all these activities are likely to be legal, are they appropriate? The answer is situational and depends on a host of issues, including the nature of the work being done and the culture of the organization. It is the job of the SPHR to balance these often conflicting and competing issues.

Strategic Considerations for the SPHR

The SPHR must develop strategic safety, health, and security plans, and associated programmatic activities that are effective and efficient. The plans must facilitate the achievement of organizational goals and align properly with the organizational culture. Finally, the plans must provide maximum protection within the constraints of resources available.

Very often the SPHR will find that organizational culture and solid safety, health, and security planning are not in alignment. A culture of "get the product out at any cost" will not be conducive to the implementation of highly effective safety and health protections in the workplace. The SPHR must often work in the margins, implementing organizational change initiatives while at the same time attempting to become compliant with safe and healthy work environment laws and regulations.

Today's work environment is extremely competitive, dynamic, and increasingly complex. Safety, health, and security programs often require expertise not normally found in the HR department. Consequently, the use of consultants and contracting of program design, implementation, and maintenance is often indicated.

Finally, the SPHR must guide the organization in making the right choices to maximize protection of human, physical, and intellectual assets in a cost-effective way. The SPHR must analyze past practices and experiences and convince organizational leadership that current and planned programmatic activities positively affect the success of the organization and facilitate achievement of organizational goals.

Chapter Summary

The health, safety, and security of an organization's employees and property are of major importance. This is becoming more important because organizational success is increasingly dependent on the abilities of its employees and the protection of its intellectual property.

The development of an effective safety program is mandated by the Occupational Safety and Health Act, a complex law. It is also a strategic advantage decreasing workers' compensation insurance costs.

Occupational health programs increase employee productivity and decrease related costs such as health insurance and sick leave usage. There are significant challenges to implementing successful programs because of employee lifestyle choices.

Security programs involve balancing risks, costs, and employee privacy. Much of the current security program needs involve the protection computer systems and proprietary data.

Key Terms

▶ Health

▶ Safety

▶ Security

▶ Workers' compensation

▶ General duty clause

▶ OSHA standards

▶ Ergonomics

▶ Employee Assistance Programs (EAPs)

▶ Wellness programs

▶ Provisions of the Occupational Safety and Health Act (1970)

▶ OSHA inspection procedures

▶ Citation and appeal process

▶ Components of a safety program

▶ Components of an occupational health program

▶ Development of a security plan

▶ Security planning

Apply Your Knowledge

Exercises

7.1 OSHA Citations

The following is a partly completed table. Fill in the blank cells without referring back to the chapter.

Citation	Definition	Penalty
Willful	Employer intentionally and knowingly violates a standard.	Up to $70,000 per violation. Potential criminal penalties including fines and imprisonment.
	Violation of a standard where there is substantial probability of death or injury and the employer knew or should have known about the hazard.	
Repeat		
		Up to $7,000 per day beyond prescribed abatement period.
	Violation is not likely to cause death or serious harm.	

7.2 Health, Safety, and Security Laws and Regulations

In the following table are two columns. The first column contains either a law or OSHA standard, whereas the second column contains the provisions of that law or standard. Without referring back to the chapter, fill in the blank cells.

Law or OSHA Standard	Provisions
	A state law that compensates workers for on-the-job illness.
Superfund Amendments and Reauthorization Act	
General duty clause	
	Contains lockout/tagout requirements.
Hazard Communication standard	
	Federal law that protects the safety and health of workers under 18 by limiting the types of jobs they can do.
Drug-Free Workplace Act	
	Protects employees who are subject to needle sticks.
	Federal law that created NIOSH.

Review Questions

1. The CEO has been reading about the deplorable safety and health conditions found in factories during the Industrial Revolution, and asks you to give her a brief history of the transition of responsibility of safety and health from the employee to the employer under the current OSHA standards. What do you tell her?

2. Your organization is inspected by OSHA and receives a citation and fine even though there is no specific standard that covers the situation that is the subject of the citation. Is this legal?

3. The board of directors of your organization would like you, as the director of HR, to brief them on procedures that should be followed in the event that an employee is involved in a serious on-the-job accident. What can you tell them about proper accident investigation procedures?

4. The president of your organization was reading an article in a management magazine that continually referred to NIOSH, which he believes is some sort of governmental agency. He asks whether you are familiar with NIOSH and its purposes. What do you tell him?

5. A group of employees has approached the CEO and requested that the organization implement an EAP. The CEO admits that he is not familiar with the term and asks you to brief him on the concept. What can you tell him?

Exam Questions

1. Workers' compensation is designed to provide certain benefits for an employee who incurs a job-related injury on illness. How is the program funded?

   ○ **A.** Through employer provided private insurance or payments to a state insurance fund

   ○ **B.** Through payroll deduction from the employee's wages

   ○ **C.** Through sharing of the costs equally by the employer and the employee (through payroll deduction) with each paying 6.75% of the first $7,000 in wages earned each year

   ○ **D.** Through a tax paid by the employer based on experience rates and filed annually with the federal government

2. The OSHA standard that is often referred to as lockout/tagout is

   ○ **A.** Control of Hazardous Energy

   ○ **B.** Hazard Communication

   ○ **C.** Personal Protective Equipment

   ○ **D.** Forklift Operation

3. Employer programs that provide counseling and other services for a variety of issues such as substance abuse, financial problems, child and elder care, and legal problems are referred to as

◯ **A.** Employee Assistance Programs (EAPs)

◯ **B.** Wellness Programs (WPs)

◯ **C.** Employee Welfare Programs (EWPs)

◯ **D.** Stress Reduction Programs (SRPs)

4. The federal agency established to research safety and health issues in the workplace and to assist in developing OSHA standards is

◯ **A.** The Department of Labor (DOL)

◯ **B.** The Occupational Safety and Health Administration (OSHA)

◯ **C.** The National Institute for Occupational Safety and Health (NIOSH)

◯ **D.** The Occupational Safety and Health Review Commission (OSHRC)

5. A violation of an OSHA standard which the employer intentionally and knowingly commits and that is punishable with fines up to $70,000 is called a(n):

◯ **A.** Serious Violation

◯ **B.** Willful Violation

◯ **C.** Egregious Violation

◯ **D.** Category 1

6. The profile of an employee most likely to engage in violent workplace behavior includes all the following except for

◯ **A.** White female.

◯ **B.** Work is the only constant in the person's life.

◯ **C.** Person is a loner.

◯ **D.** Interest in guns and military history.

7. Data indicates that there are more than _____ workers killed and more than _____ reported job-related accidents and illnesses each year.

◯ **A.** 10,000 / 4,000,000

◯ **B.** 5,000 / 10,000,000

◯ **C.** 10,000 / 10,000,000

◯ **D.** 5,000 / 4,000,000

8. Compliance with the Fair Labor Standards Act of 1938 is an important component of safety, health, and security because it

   ○ **A.** Requires employer to provide a safe and healthy work environment

   ○ **B.** Requires employers to compensate employees for work-related injuries and illnesses

   ○ **C.** Regulates the types of jobs that employees under the age of 18 can do

   ○ **D.** Requires that certain employers provide the local fire department with the location of toxic chemicals

9. To receive a permanent variance from the requirements to comply with an OSHA standard, an employer must prove

   ○ **A.** Compliance with the standard would place an onerous burden on the employer

   ○ **B.** That the employer is working toward becoming compliant

   ○ **C.** The process or procedures that the employer uses protects employees as well or better than those mandated by the standard

   ○ **D.** That the standard is not applicable to the work in which the employer is engaged

10. There is no specific OSHA standard covering a particular process used by a manufacturing firm, yet OSHA can still issue citations and penalties based on unsafe practices conducted by the firm during the process. On what does OSHA base these citations and penalties?

    ○ **A.** Common law

    ○ **B.** The general duty clause

    ○ **C.** NIOSH guidance

    ○ **D.** OSHRC regulations

Answers to Exercises

7.1. OSHA Citations

Citation	Definition	Penalty
Willful	Employer intentionally and knowingly violates a standard.	Up to $70,000 per violation. Potential criminal penalties including fines and imprisonment.
Serious	Violation of a standard where there is substantial probability of death or injury and the employer knew or should have known about the hazard.	Up to $70,000 per violation.

(continues)

Citation	Definition	Penalty
Repeat	Continued violation of a standard upon OSHA reinspection.	Up to $70,000 per violation.
Failure to Abate	Failure to correct a violation found in an inspection.	Up to $7,000 per day beyond prescribed abatement period.
Other	Violation is not likely to cause death or serious harm.	Up to $7,000 per violation.

7.2 Health, Safety, and Security Laws and Regulations

Law or OSHA Standard	Provisions
Workers' compensation	A state law that compensates workers for on-the-job illnesses.
Superfund Amendments and Reauthorization Act (1986)	Requires certain users of hazardous chemicals to reports amounts and locations of these chemicals to emergency planning organizations and to develop emergency response plans.
General duty clause	Requires employers to maintain a workplace free of recognized hazards that might cause death of serious injury or illness. Governs situations in which a specific standard has not been developed.
Control of Hazardous Energy standard	Contains lockout/tagout requirements.
Hazard Communication standard	Requires manufacturers and users of certain hazardous chemicals to label them and provide information on MSDSs. The chemicals must be inventoried and a hazard communication plan developed.
Fair Labor Standards Act (1938)	Federal law that protects the safety and health of workers under 18 by limited the types of jobs they can do.
Drug-Free Workplace Act (1988)	Requires employers with at least $100,000 in federal contracts to maintain a drug-free workplace.
Bloodborne Pathogens standard	Protects employees who are subject to needle sticks.
Occupational Safety and Health Act (1970)	Federal law that created NIOSH.

Answers to Review Questions

1. You can tell her that on-the-job injuries and illnesses were historically considered to be part of the risks of employment to be borne by the employee. The employee's only recourse in such instances was to attempt to obtain justice through the courts. This rarely occurred, however, because the employer had access to superior resources to defend these lawsuits. However, beginning in 1911, the states began passing workers' compensation laws. These laws made the employer responsible for on-the-job injuries and illnesses and required either private insurance or payments to a state

maintained workers' compensation fund to compensate employees for medical expenses, lost wages during temporary or permanent disability, survivor benefits in case of death, and lump-sum payments in case of permanent partial disability. Workers' compensation laws are no-fault. The worker is covered if the accident or illness is caused by negligence on his/her part and cannot sue the employer if the cause is negligence on its part. Although workers' compensation laws provided an incentive for employers to improve working conditions to reduce insurance premium costs or lower payments to the state fund, they did not mandate health and safety programs or standards. The Occupational Safety and Health Act of 1970 was passed to mandate healthy and safe working conditions for employees and to set up standards of practice to protect workers.

2. Yes. The general duty clause requires that an employer provide a workplace that is free from recognized hazards that might cause injury or illness. Because it is virtually impossible to issue specific standards for all work processes and work environments, the overarching general duty clause is used to issue citations and fines when unsafe or unhealthy conditions are found but there are no specific standards that apply.

3. The accident investigation should be immediate, thorough, and professional. The desired outcome of the investigation is determination of its cause and recommendations for changes to prevent a reoccurrence. The steps in the investigation are

    A. Immediately respond to the scene to ensure treatment for the injured and protect property from further damage.

    B. Secure the accident site so that an investigation can begin. Photograph or videotape the accident scene as soon as possible.

    C. Interview all witnesses including the victim. Interview the victim as soon as medically permissible.

    D. Accumulate all data, including information from secondary sources (similar accident reports, technical manuals and journals, and so forth) and analyze it.

    E. Prepare a report based on the analysis, indicating the cause of the accident and any recommendations to prevent a reoccurrence.

    F. Follow through to ensure that recommendations are implemented and have the desired effect.

4. You tell him that NIOSH stands for the National Institute of Occupational Safety and Health. It was set up under the Occupational Safety and Health Act of 1970 to research safety and health issues and to assist the Occupational Safety and Health Administration with the development of new safety and safety standards.

5. *EAP* is a common term used to refer to employee assistance programs. EAPs provide a variety of counseling and assistance services to employees. Services provided might include family and marital counseling, wellness education, substance abuse counseling, financial counseling, legal counseling, and assistance with child and elder care. These programs typically provide a limited number of assistance sessions, and are often integrated with existing insurance programs if long-term assistance is needed.

Answers to Exam Prep Questions

1. The correct answer is **A**. Answer B is incorrect because the employee does not pay for this benefit. Answer C describes the process by which Social Security is funded. Answer D is descriptive of unemployment insurance.

2. The correct answer is **A**. The Control of Hazardous Energy standard requires the locking out or tagging out of the activation switch during maintenance and repair of equipment to prevent accidental operation. The Hazard Communication standard (answer B) requires employers to label and provide employees information with respect to certain hazardous substances present in the workplace. The Personal Protective Equipment standard (answer C) requires that employers analyze the work environment and provide appropriate protective equipment to prevent injury or illness. The Forklift Operation standard (answer D) requires the employer to develop procedures and provide training on safe operation of forklifts.

3. The correct answer is **A**. Wellness programs (answer B) are broader in scope, including health screening, disease prevention, nutrition information, and fitness programs. *Employee welfare programs* (answer C) is not a standard term used in the HR literature. Stress reduction programs (answer D) may be provided by an EAP contractor, but EAPs are much broader in scope.

4. The correct answer is **C**. The DOL (answer A) is the department in which OSHA and OSHRC reside. OSHA (answer B) has overall responsibility for administering the Occupational Safety and Health Act and OSHRC (answer D) adjudicates certain actions taken by OSHA.

5. The correct answer is **B**. Serious violations (answer A) can incur penalties of no more than $7,000 per violation. There are no violations categorized as Egregious (answer C) or Category 1 (answer D).

6. The correct answer is **A**. The profile of a potentially violent employee is that of a Caucasian male, not female. Answers B, C, and D are all part of the profile.

7. The correct answer is **D**. There have been, in recent years, more than 5,000 work-related deaths and more than 4,000,000 reported work-related injuries and illnesses. Answers A, B, and C do include the accurate data on deaths, injuries and illnesses.

8. Answer **C** is correct. Answer A is a requirement of the Occupational Safety and Health Act of 1970. Answer B is a requirement of workers' compensation laws. Answer D is a requirement of Title III of the Superfund Amendments and Reauthorization Act of 1986.

9. The correct answer is **C**. A permanent variance is based on providing employee protection equal to or better than the standard. If the standard causes an onerous burden, that issue should be raised during the comment period before the standard is permanently adopted (answer A). If the employer is working toward compliance in a reasonable amount of time, it might be entitled to a temporary but not permanent variance (answer B). If the standard does not apply, no variance would be required (answer D).

10. The correct answer is **B**. If there is no specific standard covering a process or procedure, the employer is obligated to provide a safe and healthy workplace under the general duty clause. Failure to do so can result in citations and penalties. OSHA does not get its authority from common law (answer A). NIOSH (answer C) provides guidance on the writing of standards, but does not have the authority to enforce them. OSHRC regulations (answer D) deal with the appeal of citations and fines not with the authority to issue them.

Suggested Readings and Resources

1. Books

   ▶ Bergman, T. J. & Scarpello, V. G. (2001). *Compensation Decision Making* (4th Edition). Orlando, FL: Harcourt.

   ▶ Buford, J. A. & Linder, J. R. (2002). *Human Resource Management in Local Government*. Cincinnati, OH: Thomas South-Western.

   ▶ Dessler, G. (2005). *Human Resource Management* (10th Edition). Upper Saddle River, NJ: Pearson Education.

   ▶ Jackson, S. E. & Schuler, R. S. (2003). *Managing Human Resources Through Strategic Partnerships* (8th Edition). Mason, OH: Thomson South-Western.

   ▶ Mathis, R. L. & Jackson, J. H. (2006). *Human Resource Management* (11th Edition). Mason, OH: Thomson South-Western.

   ▶ Robinson, R. H., Franklin, G. M. & Wayland, R. (2002). *The Regulatory Environment of Human Resource Management*. Fort Worth, TX: Harcourt.

2. Website

   ▶ http://www.osha.gov/

PART II

Final Review

Practice Exam

Senior Professional in Human Resources Examination

This practice exam consists of 225 questions that are representative of what you should expect on the actual exam. The subject matter of the questions is in the same proportions as those on the SPHR exam. In other words, 26% of the questions relate to strategic management, 16% to workforce planning and employment, 13% to human resource development, 16% to compensation and benefits, 24% to employee and labor relations, and 5% to occupational health, safety, and security. The practice exam contains the same number of questions as the real exam.

You should take the practice exam all at one time, allowing four hours for completion. Doing so will give you a feeling for timing when taking the actual exam. The answers and their explanations are in "Practice Exam Answers," which follows this exam. Your performance on the practice exam should guide you in your future preparation efforts, particularly in terms of specific subject areas in which additional concentrated study might be appropriate.

Exam Questions

1. The *Electromation* decision affects the employer's capability to:

   - **A.** Talk to employees during the election campaign

   - **B.** Create employee involvement programs

   - **C.** Permanently replace strikers during an economic strike

   - **D.** Maintain the employment-at-will relationship

2. In which of the following scenarios would the employee not likely be entitled to benefits under state workers' compensation laws?

   - **A.** The employee trips and breaks a leg while engaging in horseplay in the workplace.

   - **B.** The employee sustains a laceration requiring stitches because of the employer's failure to properly cover a jagged edge on a machine.

   - **C.** The employee is severely injured when hit by a forklift due to the negligence of the forklift driver.

   - **D.** The employee is injured in an automobile accident while driving to work.

3. Compa-ratio is a commonly used statistic to evaluate adherence to the pay policy. How is it calculated?

    ○ **A.** Midpoint of range / actual rate paid

    ○ **B.** Actual rate paid / midpoint of range

    ○ **C.** Actual rate paid / range

    ○ **D.** Range / actual rate paid

4. Bill Jones has the same job as Mary Smith but is paid about 10% less. Bill evaluates his experience, education, skills, and performance against Mary's and comes to the conclusion that he is underpaid. As a result, Bill decides to do less work. This is an example of which motivation theory?

    ○ **A.** Goal-setting theory

    ○ **B.** Equity theory

    ○ **C.** Job characteristics model

    ○ **D.** Expectancy theory

5. NAALC is:

    ○ **A.** A worldwide organization for negotiating and enforcing trade agreements

    ○ **B.** An agency of the United Nations whose mission is to promote minimal standards of employment throughout the world

    ○ **C.** An organization of European countries

    ○ **D.** An agreement between the United States, Canada, and Mexico regarding employee and labor issues

Use the following scenario to answer questions 6, 7, and 8:

An organization is developing its first performance management program and wants to design an appraisal process and appraisal form that provides the necessary data, is job-related, and defensible.

6. Which of the following appraisal methods provides relative data to assist management in making administrative decisions?

    ○ **A.** Graphic rating scales

    ○ **B.** Checklists

    ○ **C.** Forced choice

    ○ **D.** Paired comparison

7. Which of the following types of performance information would be normally considered the most useful, job related, and valid?

    ⃝ **A.** Outcomes

    ⃝ **B.** Behaviors

    ⃝ **C.** Traits

    ⃝ **D.** Dependability

8. The organization has done research on performance management best practices to guide its development efforts. Which of the following would not be included in the list of best practices?

    ⃝ **A.** Performance management program supports organizational goals.

    ⃝ **B.** Performance dimensions are clearly job related.

    ⃝ **C.** Immediate supervisor's appraisal is final.

    ⃝ **D.** Feedback is provided throughout the evaluation period.

9. The FLRA is a federal agency created to:

    ⃝ **A.** Administer the Civil Service Reform Act of 1974

    ⃝ **B.** Administer the National Labor Relations Act of 1935

    ⃝ **C.** Administer state and local legislative acts regarding labor relations

    ⃝ **D.** Assist in the resolution of labor management relations disputes in the private sector

10. You are using a procedure called "Deck of Cards." What method of job evaluation are you using?

    ⃝ **A.** Ranking

    ⃝ **B.** Classification

    ⃝ **C.** Point factor

    ⃝ **D.** Factor comparison

11. The A in the acronym ADDIE, which describes the HRD process, stands for:

    ⃝ **A.** Achievement measurement

    ⃝ **B.** Action implementation

    ⃝ **C.** Needs assessment

    ⃝ **D.** Active development

12. All the following statements regarding organizational culture are true except for:

  ○ **A.** It is the system of shared values and norms held by organizational members.

  ○ **B.** Organizational cultures are created by the founder and may be modified by subsequent leaders.

  ○ **C.** Weak cultures strongly resist organizational change.

  ○ **D.** Strong cultures have a great influence on employee behavior.

13. Historically, HR began as a(n) _____ function.

  ○ **A.** Strategic

  ○ **B.** Operational

  ○ **C.** Administrative/clerical

  ○ **D.** Employee advocate

14. Under a four-step progressive discipline process, what would be a typical disciplinary action at step three?

  ○ **A.** Verbal warning

  ○ **B.** Written warning

  ○ **C.** Decision day off

  ○ **D.** Suspension without pay

15. Which of the following statements is not correct regarding contract law?

  ○ **A.** An offer must be made and accepted.

  ○ **B.** At least one of the parties must give and receive something of value.

  ○ **C.** Both parties must be competent.

  ○ **D.** The contract must be for legal purposes.

16. What provision is shared by the Davis-Bacon Act, Walsh-Healy Public Contracts Act, and McNamara-O'Hara Service Contract Act?

  ○ **A.** Equal pay for men and women

  ○ **B.** Payment of the prevailing wage rate

  ○ **C.** Limits jobs that children under the age of 18 can perform

  ○ **D.** Provides for continuation of health insurance if employment is terminated

17. The philosophy behind positive discipline is:

    ○ A. The application of increasingly severe penalties teaches the employee to quit doing the improper behavior.

    ○ B. Employees should not be terminated for continuing to engage in improper behaviors, but should be trained to restrain themselves.

    ○ C. Employees should be able to work through an issue, engage in problem-solving, and be able to come up with a resolution to their conduct or performance deficiency.

    ○ D. Progressive discipline is inhumane and should be abolished in the workplace.

18. If assets equal $100,000 and liabilities equal $75,000, what must the owners' equity be according to the fundamental accounting equation?

    ○ A. $175,000

    ○ B. Unable to determine because enough data is not provided

    ○ C. $25,000

    ○ D. ($25,000)

19. As the Director of HR, you are directed to develop a strategy of union substitution with the hope of diverting any potential union-organizing activity. Which of the following actions is appropriate under this strategy?

    ○ A. Moving the firm to a right-to-work state

    ○ B. Instituting a formal grievance procedure with binding arbitration as the final step

    ○ C. Contracting out the work normally done by the potential bargaining unit

    ○ D. Engaging in a constant barrage of anti-union rhetoric

20. Although cafeteria benefit plans have a number of advantages for both the employee and the employer, there are also some disadvantages. Which of the following is not considered a disadvantage of cafeteria plans?

    ○ A. Employees become more aware of the costs of benefits.

    ○ B. Multiple benefit programs and individual selection increase the administrative burden on the employer.

    ○ C. Employees select only those benefits that they intend to use. This raises usage rates, which cause increases in premium rates.

    ○ D. Employees do not make wise selections, leaving themselves or their families vulnerable.

Use the following sample distribution to answer questions 21, 22, and 23:

6

7

7

7

8

9

10

11

12

15

18

21. What is the mean of the distribution?

   ○ **A.** 6

   ○ **B.** 7

   ○ **C.** 9

   ○ **D.** 10

22. What is the mode of the distribution?

   ○ **A.** 6

   ○ **B.** 7

   ○ **C.** 8

   ○ **D.** 10

23. What is the median of the distribution?

   ○ **A.** 6

   ○ **B.** 7

   ○ **C.** 8

   ○ **D.** 10

24. The Federal Mediation and Conciliation Service was created by which legislative act?

   ◯ **A.** The Wagner Act

   ◯ **B.** The Taft-Hartley Act

   ◯ **C.** The Landrum-Griffin Act

   ◯ **D.** The Norris-LaGuardia Act

25. The hierarchical arrangement of authority in an organization is called:

   ◯ **A.** Span of control

   ◯ **B.** Centralization

   ◯ **C.** Departmentation

   ◯ **D.** Chain of command

26. A research study that uses both inductive and deductive reasoning to analyze data from observations and interviews in order to develop themes is referred to as:

   ◯ **A.** Quantitative research

   ◯ **B.** Basic research

   ◯ **C.** Qualitative research

   ◯ **D.** Applied research

27. Which of the following statements is not correct regarding the impact that technology has on the HR function?

   ◯ **A.** It facilitates the strategic role of HR.

   ◯ **B.** It makes outsourcing more difficult.

   ◯ **C.** It enhances rational decision-making.

   ◯ **D.** It improves productivity.

28. The *Excelsior* list is:

   ◯ **A.** A list of mandatory bargaining topics determined by the NLRB

   ◯ **B.** The list of striking employees that are being permanently replaced

   ◯ **C.** Those activities that are considered to be unfair labor practices during the election campaign

   ◯ **D.** A list of names and addresses of employees eligible to vote in a union certification election

29. The organization is developing an HRD program to train employees to operate a new robotic weld-
ing machine. Based on Bloom's taxonomy, which of the following levels of learning has to be
achieved to accomplish the organization's goal?

○ **A.** Knowledge

○ **B.** Comprehension

○ **C.** Application

○ **D.** Analysis

30. An employer decides to lead the market by paying above-market wages. All the following are
advantages of this strategy except for:

○ **A.** Lower retention

○ **B.** Higher quality candidates

○ **C.** Easier recruitment of candidates

○ **D.** Higher quality of production

31. Which of the following is the career stage at which the employee typically revaluates earlier career
choices and goals, either by reaffirming them or seeking new goals?

○ **A.** Occupational preparation

○ **B.** Organizational entry

○ **C.** Early career

○ **D.** Mid-career

32. An integrated computer application that collects, processes, stores, and analyzes human resource
data to support HR activities is referred to as a(n) _____.

○ **A.** Service center

○ **B.** Application service provider *(ASP)*

○ **C.** Data warehouse

○ **D.** Human resource management information system *(HRIS)*

33. Which of the following items would not typically be one of the determining factors that the NLRB would consider when determining the proper constitution of a bargaining unit?

   ○ **A.** Mobility of employees between organizational units contained in the proposed bargaining unit

   ○ **B.** Geographical dispersion of the employees

   ○ **C.** Constitution of the bargaining unit in other industries

   ○ **D.** Wishes of the employees contained in the proposed bargaining unit

34. How might compliance with FMLA prevent good practice under workers' compensation laws?

   ○ **A.** The employee's right to return to a same or similar position might interfere with the employer's desire to bring the employee back to a light duty assignment.

   ○ **B.** There is no conflict between the provisions of the two laws.

   ○ **C.** Light duty, if continued for an extended period of time, could be interpreted as a permanent modification of the essential functions of the position.

   ○ **D.** The FMLA leave is without pay, preventing the employee from receiving workers' compensation.

35. ABC Corporation began business six months ago in an emerging high-technology industry. As with most firms in their infancy, ABC has little excess capital. All the following are appropriate elements of a compensation strategy for this firm at its current life cycle stage except for:

   ○ **A.** Generous stock options

   ○ **B.** Limited benefits

   ○ **C.** Below-market wages

   ○ **D.** Short-term bonuses to encourage efficiencies in operations

36. Economic resources owned by the organization are:

   ○ **A.** Owners' equity

   ○ **B.** Human capital

   ○ **C.** Liabilities

   ○ **D.** Assets

37. Which of the following is generally not true regarding the impact of unions on the employee in relation to a nonunion environment?

   ○ **A.** Job satisfaction is higher.

   ○ **B.** Wages are higher.

   ○ **C.** Benefits are higher.

   ○ **D.** Retention is higher.

38. A sample distribution consists of the following scores: 10, 10, 10, 12, 13, 14, 15, 18, 19, 22. What is the range of the distribution?

   ○ **A.** 10

   ○ **B.** 12

   ○ **C.** 13

   ○ **D.** 14

39. An organization has tightly written job descriptions, specific standard operating procedures, and policy statements on almost every issue. The organization is said to be:

   ○ **A.** Highly departmentalized

   ○ **B.** Highly formulized

   ○ **C.** Highly centralized

   ○ **D.** Highly job specialized

40. The Director of HR decides to conduct a wage survey of the local labor market by using a questionnaire. Which of the following is not information normally requested in such a questionnaire?

   ○ **A.** Organizational policy on sexual harassment

   ○ **B.** Organizational policy on wage increase determinations

   ○ **C.** Types of benefits provided

   ○ **D.** Compensation data on benchmark jobs

41. Which of the following is not a reason why *transnational bargaining* (that is, bargaining across national borders) has not become a significant factor in international labor relations?

   ○ **A.** Multinational and transnational corporations have opposed this type of bargaining.

   ○ **B.** Labor laws of different countries vary considerably.

   ○ **C.** Labor unions differ as to purposes, philosophy, and values.

   ○ **D.** The International Confederation of Free Trade Unions *(ICFTU)* specifically bans member federations from engaging in this kind of bargaining.

42. Which antidiscrimination act dealt only with the prohibition of discrimination based on race or ethnicity in the formulation and enforcement of contacts?

- ○ **A.** Civil Rights Act of 1866
- ○ **B.** Equal Pay Act (1963)
- ○ **C.** Civil Rights Act of 1964
- ○ **D.** Civil Rights Act of 1991

43. A "Right to Sue" letter issued by the Equal Employment Opportunity Commission indicates that:

- ○ **A.** The investigation is complete and there is no indication that illegal discrimination has taken place.
- ○ **B.** There appears to be reasonable cause to believe that illegal discrimination occurred.
- ○ **C.** The investigation is complete and there is reasonable cause to believe that illegal discrimination has occurred, but EEOC has determined not to pursue litigation.
- ○ **D.** The investigation is complete, there is reasonable cause to believe that illegal discrimination has occurred, and the EEOC is planning to sue the employer in court.

44. It is critical that the employer communicate behavior expectations to the employee. Expectations are often communicated in terms of policies, procedures, and rules. Which of the following statements is not correct?

- ○ **A.** Rules represent the traditional way of doing something.
- ○ **B.** Policies are broad general statements of the organization's philosophy with respect to an issue.
- ○ **C.** Rules are specific as to actions to be taken and provide little or no latitude.
- ○ **D.** Procedures represent guidance to organizational members as to the standard or customary way of doing things.

45. ABC, Inc. has an organizational structure that can be described as lacking departmentalization, wide spans of control, little formalization, few levels of hierarchy, broad and flexible work assignments, and a very centralized decision-making process. This describes what type of organizational model?

- ○ **A.** Mechanistic
- ○ **B.** Bureaucracy
- ○ **C.** Simple
- ○ **D.** Concentrated Structure

46. All the following are considered to be external employee recruitment methods except for:

- ○ **A.** School recruiting
- ○ **B.** Media advertising
- ○ **C.** Walk-ins
- ○ **D.** Employee referrals

47. Components of the contingent workforce include all the following except for:

- ○ **A.** Part-time workers
- ○ **B.** Workers on sabbatical
- ○ **C.** Temporary workers
- ○ **D.** Contract workers

48. A statement that describes the organization's desired future state is referred to as a:

- ○ **A.** Vision statement
- ○ **B.** Mission statement
- ○ **C.** Values statement
- ○ **D.** Strategic statement

49. All the following are considered good practice when writing an employee handbook except for:

- ○ **A.** Distributing the handbook at new employee orientation and getting a signed receipt acknowledging an obligation to abide by the provisions contained in it.
- ○ **B.** Providing the handbook in Spanish for Spanish-speaking employees.
- ○ **C.** Requesting, as a courtesy, employees provide a two-week notice prior to resignation so that the employer has sufficient time to fill the job.
- ○ **D.** Making sure that the language of the handbook is aligned with the reading level of the employees.

50. Patents for inventions are good for _____ years from the date of filing:

- ○ **A.** 20
- ○ **B.** 14
- ○ **C.** Life of the inventor plus 70
- ○ **D.** 95

51. The Wagner Act marks the beginning of:

    ◯ **A.** Strong governmental support of unions

    ◯ **B.** Attempts to readjust the balance of power between labor and management by imposing restrictions on union activities and enumerating rights of management

    ◯ **C.** Attempts to regulate the internal operations of unions because of the perception of substantial corruption

    ◯ **D.** Major employee relations legislation in the United States

52. The HR function is involved in the planning, implementation, and evaluation of various HR programmatic activities to support the achievement of organizational goals. Which role is HR performing?

    ◯ **A.** Administrative

    ◯ **B.** Operational

    ◯ **C.** Employee Advocate

    ◯ **D.** Strategic

53. The Civil Rights Act of 1964 covers most employers who have:

    ◯ **A.** Fifteen or more employees for each working day in each of 20 or more weeks in the current or preceding calendar year

    ◯ **B.** Twenty or more employees for each working day in each of 20 or more weeks in the current or preceding calendar year

    ◯ **C.** Any number of employees

    ◯ **D.** One hundred or more employees that, in the aggregate, work 4,000 hours per week

54. Quid quo pro sexual discrimination occurs when:

    ◯ **A.** An employee propositions a co-worker

    ◯ **B.** A supervisor offers an employment benefit in exchange for sexual favors

    ◯ **C.** A customer constantly tells an employee lewd jokes and engages in suggestive behavior

    ◯ **D.** A supplier constantly asks an employee of the client organization for dates

55. Which of the following statements is true regarding union ratification of the negotiated labor agreement?

   ○ **A.** Ratification requires a majority vote of all union members

   ○ **B.** Ratification requires a majority vote of all bargaining unit employees

   ○ **C.** Ratification requires that 30% of the bargaining unit sign a card indicating they accept the newly negotiated agreement

   ○ **D.** Ratification is dependent on the internal procedures set up by that particular union

56. Which of the following is not a provision of the Social Security Act of 1935?

   ○ **A.** Retirement benefits for covered employees

   ○ **B.** Medicare

   ○ **C.** Twelve weeks of nonpaid leave for covered family medical emergencies

   ○ **D.** Unemployment insurance

57. Changing the organizational structure to improve organizational performance is an example of what type of organizational development intervention?

   ○ **A.** Process

   ○ **B.** Technostructural

   ○ **C.** Human resource management

   ○ **D.** Strategic

58. The financial statement that reports the profitability of the organization is called the:

   ○ **A.** Fundamental accounting equation

   ○ **B.** Balance sheet

   ○ **C.** Income statement

   ○ **D.** Statement of cash flows

59. In a normal distribution, _____% of all scores fall within plus or minus two standard deviations of the mean.

   ○ **A.** 34%

   ○ **B.** 68%

   ○ **C.** 95%

   ○ **D.** 99%

60. Although there are a wide variety of negotiated grievance procedures, who would typically meet in the step 1 grievance meeting, assuming that the grievance was filed by a production worker against the first-level supervisor?

○ **A.** First-level supervisor and steward

○ **B.** Second-level supervisor and chapter president

○ **C.** Director of HR and national office attorney

○ **D.** Arbitrator and attorneys from both parties

Use the following scenario to answer questions 61, 62, 63, and 64:

A manufacturing organization uses large presses in its process. These presses produce thousands of pounds of force and are used to mold thick metal. A worker is killed while performing preventative maintenance on the press when the control switch is turned on by another worker, resulting in activation of the press and the crushing of the worker. The worker, who is married with no children, took no actions to deactivate the system prior to beginning work, and the organization has no safety procedure or policy regarding deactivation of machines during maintenance. In fact, the Vice President of Production refuses to implement policy and procedure for most workplace processes because of fear that they would slow down production.

61. What law, if any, would provide benefits for the deceased worker's spouse?

○ **A.** OSHA

○ **B.** WARN

○ **C.** Common law tort

○ **D.** Workers' compensation

62. What OSHA standard was violated?

○ **A.** Hazard Communication

○ **B.** Control of Hazardous Energy

○ **C.** Personal Protective Equipment

○ **D.** Bloodborne Pathogens

63. Under OSHA reporting requirements, what is the obligation of the employer?

○ **A.** None. Only events involving the death of three or more employees must be reported.

○ **B.** It must be recorded in the log, but no formal report is required.

○ **C.** The employer must report the death to OSHA within eight hours.

○ **D.** The employer must report the death to OSHA within three work days.

64. What type of citation is the employer most likely to receive?

○ **A.** None. There is no reason to advise OSHA of the incident and the likelihood of an inspection is small.

○ **B.** Serious

○ **C.** Willful

○ **D.** Repeat

65. The HR professional association, originally founded in 1948 as the American Society for Personnel Administration *(ASPA)*, is now known as _____.

○ **A.** ASTD

○ **B.** SHRM

○ **C.** IMPA

○ **D.** World at Work

66. A union contacts members of an organization's board of directors to try to influence the board members to put pressure on the organization's bargaining team to agree to the union's proposals. This is an example of a(n):

○ **A.** Boycott

○ **B.** Work slowdown

○ **C.** Corporate campaign

○ **D.** Unfair labor practice

67. Which federal law amends another federal law and defines what are hours worked that must be compensated and used to determine eligibility for overtime?

○ **A.** Equal Pay Act

○ **B.** FLSA

○ **C.** Portal-to-Portal Act

○ **D.** Workers' compensation laws

68. Which of the following is not one of the four steps of the strategic-planning process described in this book?

○ **A.** Strategy formulation

○ **B.** Development of strategic objectives

○ **C.** Strategy implementation

○ **D.** Strategy reformulation

69. Quick Thinking, Inc. pursues a strategy of innovation and creativity, attempting to be first in the market with new products. What type of business strategy is the organization pursuing?

   ○ **A.** Cost leadership

   ○ **B.** Differentiation

   ○ **C.** Cost minimization

   ○ **D.** Dynamic

70. Striking employees can be permanently replaced by the employer in all the following types of strikes except for:

   ○ **A.** Economic

   ○ **B.** Unfair labor practice

   ○ **C.** Recognition

   ○ **D.** Sympathy

71. Employees reporting employer improprieties with respect to securities regulations are likely to be protected from retaliation by the _____.

   ○ **A.** Sarbanes-Oxley Act of 2002

   ○ **B.** False Claims Act of 1863

   ○ **C.** State whistle-blowing acts

   ○ **D.** Wagner Act of 1935

72. Executive Order 11246 requires that:

   ○ **A.** All state government agencies comply with the WARN Act.

   ○ **B.** Contractors with $50,000 in federal contracts and 50 or more employees develop and implement a written affirmative action plan.

   ○ **C.** Federal agencies prepare and implement affirmative action plans.

   ○ **D.** Contractors with $100,000 in federal contacts and 100 or more employees develop and implement a written affirmative action plan.

73. All the following are characteristics of an affirmative defense against allegations of sexual harassment except for:

   ○ **A.** The employer took aggressive disciplinary action against the perpetrator of sexual harassment when it found out that a tangible employment action had occurred.

   ○ **B.** The organization exercised reasonable care to prevent and promptly correct any harassing behavior.

   ○ **C.** The complainant unreasonably failed to take advantage of any preventive or corrective opportunities provided.

   ○ **D.** The organization has a proactive harassment prevention program.

74. A workforce-needs forecasting method that studies historical organizational employment levels to forecast future employment levels is referred to as:

   ○ **A.** Turnover

   ○ **B.** Ratio analysis

   ○ **C.** Trend analysis

   ○ **D.** Nominal group technique

75. If the NLRB finds that an unfair labor practice has been committed, it has the authority to:

   ○ **A.** Fine the party that committed the unfair labor practice

   ○ **B.** Issue a cease and desist order including requirements for remedial action

   ○ **C.** Issue punitive sanctions for the party's misdeeds

   ○ **D.** Charge the party with criminal violations in the federal district court

Use the following scenario to answer questions 76, 77, 78, and 79:

A family-owned manufacturing firm employs 51 full-time and 4 part-time employees, all at the same plant. Joe Smith, an entry-level production worker who has been working full time for 9 months, has just found out that his common-law wife has terminal cancer and requires extensive care. Common-law marriages are legal in the state and Joe's relationship qualifies under state law. Several years ago, Joe worked for the business for 5 months. Joe has accrued 10 days of vacation time and 5 days of sick leave. Company policy is to allow employees to use sick leave to care for close relatives.

76. Is the employer a covered employer under FMLA?

   ○ **A.** No. FMLA only covers public employers.

   ○ **B.** No. FMLA requires that the employer have 75 employees within a 50-mile radius.

   ○ **C.** Yes.

   ○ **D.** No. Family-owned businesses are specifically exempted from coverage under FMLA.

77. Joe asks to immediately take twelve weeks of FMLA leave and provides a doctor's statement indicating that his common-law wife needs immediate homebound care. Is Joe eligible for FMLA leave?

   ○ **A.** No. Common-law marriages are not recognized under FMLA.

   ○ **B.** No. He has not worked continuously for the firm for one year.

   ○ **C.** No. FMLA leave requires an advance-notice period of at least 30 days.

   ○ **D.** Yes.

78. How many days of paid leave can the employer require Joe to take simultaneously with the FMLA?

   ○ **A.** None. FMLA specifically prohibits simultaneous usage of paid and unpaid leave.

   ○ **B.** Ten days of vacation. FMLA does not permit the employer to require the employee to use sick leave to care for a family member.

   ○ **C.** Five days. FMLA specifically allows for the employer to require the employee to use any accrued sick leave to care for a family member if the employer's policy permits it. However, the employer cannot require an employee to use vacation time simultaneously with FMLA leave.

   ○ **D.** Fifteen days. FMLA permits the employer to require the employee to use all qualifying paid leave simultaneously with the FMLA leave.

79. Which of the following is not a benefit to which Joe is entitled while on FMLA leave?

   ○ **A.** Continuation of health insurance under the same conditions as before he began leave

   ○ **B.** Payment for overtime he would have earned had he been on the job

   ○ **C.** Continuation of seniority accrual

   ○ **D.** Reinstatement to the same or similar position

80. The wage data from a wage survey has been collected and analyzed. The CEO would like a report giving the compensation rates for all benchmark jobs that reflect the rate that includes 25% of the rates being paid and 75% of the rates being paid. What statistic is the employer requesting?

   ○ **A.** Mean

   ○ **B.** Mode

   ○ **C.** Median

   ○ **D.** Quartile

81. Learning curves describe the:

  ○ **A.** Permanent changes in behavior

  ○ **B.** Way different individuals prefer to learn

  ○ **C.** Rate at which material is learned

  ○ **D.** How much is to be learned

82. A major problem in developing compensation strategy today is the rapidly increasing costs of benefits, particularly health insurance. Employers are constantly seeking ways to reduce their portion of health insurance costs. Which of the following is not a method used to reduce employer health insurance costs?

  ○ **A.** Increasing deductibles

  ○ **B.** Decreasing copays

  ○ **C.** Decreasing the number of covered services

  ○ **D.** Increasing the proportion of insurance premium paid by the employee

83. Because of flatter organizations, rightsizing, and contracting out, many employees face the prospect of careers that reach a plateau. These workers might have a number of years of service left before they are eligible for retirement. Organizations have found all the following strategies effective in keeping employees in this situation engaged except for:

  ○ **A.** Job enlargement

  ○ **B.** Job rotation

  ○ **C.** Job simplification

  ○ **D.** Job enrichment

84. An HR manager allocates staff and resources to a particular project. Which management function is being performed?

  ○ **A.** Planning

  ○ **B.** Organizing

  ○ **C.** Leading

  ○ **D.** Controlling

85. The financial ratio that measures the extent to which an organization is leveraged—that is, relies on borrowed money—is called:

   ○ **A.** Inventory turnover

   ○ **B.** Debt of owners' equity

   ○ **C.** Current ratio

   ○ **D.** Acid-test

86. Which of the following is not an advantage of strategic planning?

   ○ **A.** Provides guidance for action

   ○ **B.** Provides rigid statement of goals

   ○ **C.** Forces organizational leaders to be forward-thinking

   ○ **D.** When properly done, correlates with organizational success

87. An employer makes a strategic decision to lag the market by paying below-market wages. All the following are likely outcomes of this strategy except for:

   ○ **A.** Lower quality of production

   ○ **B.** Lower quantity of production

   ○ **C.** Decreased turnover

   ○ **D.** Decreased compensation costs

88. ABC Corporation provides in-home installation of electronic systems. Jan Jones, one of ABC's installers and a 15-year employee, has had a series of convictions for assault, including one within the last month. In addition, Jan has received numerous disciplinary actions within the organization for a series of insubordinate actions, including several threats against his supervisor. Last week Jan got in a physical altercation with a customer at the customer's home, resulting in the customer requiring medical attention. ABC could be the subject of tort action based on:

   ○ **A.** Negligent training

   ○ **B.** Defamation

   ○ **C.** Negligent retention

   ○ **D.** Negligent hiring

89. A critical step, perhaps the most critical step in the HRD process, is that of assessment of needs. However, needs assessment is often overlooked in the rush to develop new and exciting HRD programs. Which of the following is not a factor contributing to this omission?

- ○ **A.** HRD professionals believe that managerial insight and preference are superior to research.
- ○ **B.** Managers do not understand the importance of needs assessment.
- ○ **C.** Performance data seems to clearly indicate the nature of the program to be conducted.
- ○ **D.** Managers prefer immediate action to in-depth analysis.

90. All the following are characteristics of appropriate choices for compensable factors except for:

- ○ **A.** Should be acceptable to employees
- ○ **B.** Should be interdependent
- ○ **C.** Should apply to all jobs being evaluated
- ○ **D.** Should differentiate between the relative importances of jobs

91. Which of the following is not a measure included in the balanced scorecard?

- ○ **A.** Financial
- ○ **B.** Customers
- ○ **C.** Internal business processes
- ○ **D.** Environmental impact

92. United States organizations are prevented from engaging in such practices as bribery and payoffs (with certain exceptions) when operating in foreign countries even if that is the standard way of doing business in that country. What act prohibits such practices?

- ○ **A.** Sarbanes-Oxley Act of 2002
- ○ **B.** False Claims Act of 1863
- ○ **C.** Foreign Corrupt Practices Act of 1977
- ○ **D.** Civil Rights Act of 1991

93. All the following are exemptions from the Age Discrimination in Employment Act except for:

- ○ **A.** Bona fide seniority systems
- ○ **B.** BFOQ
- ○ **C.** Valid disciplinary actions
- ○ **D.** Mandatory retirement requirements

94. Mandatory arbitration of all employment disagreements has been a controversial issue in employment law. However, if properly crafted, mandatory arbitration was found to be legal by the Supreme Court in its _____ decision.

    ○ **A.** *Mackay*

    ○ **B.** *Circuit City*

    ○ **C.** *Beck*

    ○ **D.** *Weingarten*

95. The act that regulates the process of obtaining and using credit and other types of information on employees is called the:

    ○ **A.** Consumer Credit Protection Act (1968)

    ○ **B.** Fair Credit Reporting Act (1970)

    ○ **C.** Rehabilitation Act (1973)

    ○ **D.** Privacy Act (1974)

96. A group of experts is assembled to forecast workforce employment levels. The experts never meet face-to-face, but independently develop forecasts that are shared with other members of the group. The process is continued with the experts reviewing and revising their forecasts until a consensus is reached. This is an example of:

    ○ **A.** Nominal group technique

    ○ **B.** Statistical forecasts

    ○ **C.** Delphi technique

    ○ **D.** Managerial judgment

97. To win a certification election, a union must have how many votes?

    ○ **A.** A simple majority of the bargaining unit, with a tie going to the union

    ○ **B.** A simple majority of those voting, with a tie going to the union

    ○ **C.** A simple majority of the bargaining unit, with a tie going to the employer

    ○ **D.** A simple majority of those voting, with a tied going to the employer

98. Manual or automated records indicating which employees are currently ready for promotion to a specific position are referred to as:

○ **A.** Succession planning data

○ **B.** Human resource management systems *(HRIS)*

○ **C.** Replacement charts

○ **D.** Promotion ledgers

99. The process of ensuring that the personality and value system of the individual matches the culture and objectives of the organization is called:

○ **A.** Selection

○ **B.** Placement

○ **C.** Person-job fit

○ **D.** Person-organization fit

100. What is the standard practice in pay-setting when encountering an isolated green circle rate?

○ **A.** Freezing the employee's rate of pay until the pay scale raises enough to capture the rate within the appropriate range

○ **B.** Raising the pay rate to the minimum rate for the range

○ **C.** Reducing the pay rate to the maximum rate for the range

○ **D.** Noncompetitively promoting the employee to a higher pay grade

101. Which of the following uses would not generally be considered a copyright infringement?

○ **A.** Distributing copies of the copyrighted material to the public without permission

○ **B.** Using the copyrighted material publicly in a theatrical or musical performance without permission

○ **C.** Quoting from the copyrighted material in a newspaper article reviewing the work without permission

○ **D.** Preparing derivative works based on the copyrighted material without permission

102. In which of the following high-performance work systems are the employees typically the most involved in making decisions and empowered to implement those decisions?

○ **A.** Self-directed work teams

○ **B.** TQM teams

○ **C.** Lean manufacturing teams

○ **D.** Cross-functional task forces

103. All the following are disadvantages of 360° performance appraisal ratings except for:

   ○ **A.** Creates an administrative burden requesting, gathering, and analyzing the input from a wide variety of raters.

   ○ **B.** Raters have differing expectations regarding performance.

   ○ **C.** There is a potential for high variability among the raters and ratings.

   ○ **D.** Provides feedback from many points of view or aspects.

104. Which of the following is not a trend in the demographics of today's workforce?

   ○ **A.** More women

   ○ **B.** More diverse

   ○ **C.** Younger

   ○ **D.** Older

105. Which of the following statements is not true about the Congress of Industrial Organizations?

   ○ **A.** Its origin was as a committee of the AFL *(American Federation of Labor)*.

   ○ **B.** It was a federation of craft unions.

   ○ **C.** It affiliated with the AFL to form the AFL-CIO in 1955.

   ○ **D.** John L. Lewis of the United Mine Workers was its first leader.

106. The Occupational Safety and Health Review Commission *(OSHRC)* is to the Occupational Safety and Health Act as the _____ is to the National Labor Relations Act.

   ○ **A.** FLRA

   ○ **B.** FSIP

   ○ **C.** NIOSH

   ○ **D.** NLRB

107. The FLSA test for exemption from its minimum wage and overtime provisions is a three-part test. One of the parts is a prescribed weekly amount of wages. What is that amount?

   ○ **A.** $455 per week

   ○ **B.** $34.00, if a computer professional is paid on an hourly basis

   ○ **C.** $100,000 per year, if a blue-collar worker is doing production work

   ○ **D.** $1,000 per week for learned professionals

108. Which of the following statements is not true regarding the HR strategic-planning process?

   ○ **A.** Procedurally, it is very similar to the organizational strategic process.

   ○ **B.** It has traditionally been a proactive process performed simultaneously with the organizational strategic-planning process.

   ○ **C.** It involves a SWOT type of analysis.

   ○ **D.** It involves a determination of HR strategic objectives that are aligned with the strategic objectives of the organization.

109. Which of the following statements is not correct regarding the provisions of the Wagner Act?

   ○ **A.** It created the NLRB.

   ○ **B.** It provided for employer unfair labor practices.

   ○ **C.** It gave unions the right to bargain collectively and engage in concerted activity.

   ○ **D.** It provided for exclusive representation of all employees in the bargaining unit by a properly certified labor organization.

110. A budget that allocates resources to individual processes or projects is referred to as a(n):

   ○ **A.** Incremental budget

   ○ **B.** Formula budget

   ○ **C.** Zero-based budget

   ○ **D.** Activity-based budget

111. The organization decides to invest in an outsourced training program that will cost $100,000 in total and $25,000 the first year. The estimated benefits from the program are expected to be $200,000 in total, but only $12,500 during the first year of the program. What is the return on investment *(ROI)* for the first year of operation and what return is expected for the total project?

   ○ **A.** 200% first year, 50% for total project

   ○ **B.** 50% first year, 200% for total project

   ○ **C.** 25% first year, 4% for the total project

   ○ **D.** 4% first year, 25% for the total project

112. Which of the following statements is not true regarding an effective organizational ethics program?

   ○ **A.** It must be a grassroots effort driven by lower levels of the organization.

   ○ **B.** The organization should have a clearly written code of ethics and/or code of contact that articulates the values of the organization and provides guidance as to appropriate and inappropriate behavior.

   ○ **C.** All levels of the organization must be trained on the code of ethics and code of conduct.

   ○ **D.** There should be a way for employees to anonymously report allegations of ethical violations and to obtain guidance and advice regarding ethical issues.

113. A union may petition the NLRB for a certification election when:

   ○ **A.** Fifty-one percent of the prospective bargaining unit has signed an authorization card.

   ○ **B.** The employer has refused to view the authorization cards.

   ○ **C.** Thirty percent of the prospective bargaining unit has signed an authorization card.

   ○ **D.** Not more than two months have expired after having lost a prior certification election.

114. Which of the following is not a violation of the Pregnancy Act (1978)?

   ○ **A.** Transferring a pregnant employee to a new job because of fears that the current position is dangerous to the fetus

   ○ **B.** Failing to consider pregnancy as a temporary disability under the employer's short-term disability insurance benefit, which it provides to all employees

   ○ **C.** Laying off a pregnant employee based on seniority

   ○ **D.** Failure to hire an applicant because she is pregnant

115. Which of the following factors would not be considered one that affects the availability of external candidates for the organization's positions?

   ○ **A.** Unemployment rates

   ○ **B.** Net migration of in or out of the area in which the organization is located

   ○ **C.** Organizational employee development programs

   ○ **D.** Economic conditions

116. Which of the following statements is not true regarding the Equal Pay Act of 1963?

   ○ **A.** An exception to the act is differentials in pay between the sexes based on quality of quantity of production.

   ○ **B.** The act requires payment of equal wages and benefits to both sexes.

   ○ **C.** To be covered under the act, jobs must be similar in terms of skill, effort, responsibility, and working conditions.

   ○ **D.** The act is enforced by EEOC.

117. Salting is:

   ○ **A.** A union unfair labor practice in which the union uses coercive tactics in an attempt to influence employee votes during a certification election.

   ○ **B.** An employer unfair labor practice in which the employer attempts to infiltrate the union in order to dominate it.

   ○ **C.** A legal practice by the employer of promising increases in benefits if the employees do not vote for the union.

   ○ **D.** A legal practice by the union in which it attempts to get union organizers hired by the target company for the purpose of conducting organizing activities internally.

118. The systematic process of gathering information regarding the duties required of a job and the human characteristics necessary to successfully perform those duties is referred to as:

   ○ **A.** Job evaluation

   ○ **B.** Job analysis

   ○ **C.** Workforce planning

   ○ **D.** Job pricing

119. Surface bargaining is one indication of failure to bargain in good faith. Which of the following answers describes surface bargaining?

   ○ **A.** Bypassing the union and presenting proposals directly to the employees

   ○ **B.** Merely going through the process of bargaining with no intent to reach an agreement

   ○ **C.** Refusing to meet at convenient times and locations

   ○ **D.** Not providing sufficient information to the opposition to enable it to make informed proposals and counterproposals

120. To which federal agency are appeals of OSHA citations made?

- ○ **A.** NLRB
- ○ **B.** NIOSH
- ○ **C.** FMCS
- ○ **D.** OSHRC

Use the following table to answer questions 121 and 122:

Selection Rates

Group	# Interviewed	# Selected	
Hispanic Males	50	20	40%
African-American Males	75	37	49%
Caucasian Males	50	30	60%
Native-American Males	25	14	56%

121. What is the adverse impact threshold?

- ○ **A.** 40%
- ○ **B.** 48%
- ○ **C.** 56%
- ○ **D.** 60%

122. Does the selection rate indicate that adverse impact has occurred, and if so, which protected class(es) was affected?

- ○ **A.** There is no adverse impact.
- ○ **B.** There is adverse impact affecting Native-American males.
- ○ **C.** There is adverse impact affecting Hispanic males.
- ○ **D.** There is adverse impact affecting African-American males.

123. Which of the following statements is not descriptive of distributive bargaining?

- ○ **A.** Win/lose
- ○ **B.** Position based
- ○ **C.** Fix resources
- ○ **D.** Interest based

124. A manager believes that all employees are lazy, dislike work, and avoid taking responsibility. What motivation theory is depicted in the manager's beliefs?

  ○ **A.** Maslow's Hierarchy of Needs

  ○ **B.** Theory X and Theory Y

  ○ **C.** Herzberg's Two-Factor Theory

  ○ **D.** ERG Theory

125. The Uniformed Services Employment and Reemployment Act (1994) provides substantial benefits to employees who are called to active duty. Which of the following statements is not correct?

  ○ **A.** Prohibits discrimination in employment decisions based on the employee's military service or potential for military service

  ○ **B.** Requires reemployment to a position that the employee would normally have attained had military service not occurred

  ○ **C.** Employers are required to provide reasonable accommodation to employees who become disabled during their military duty

  ○ **D.** Employees cannot continue the employer's health insurance because they will be covered under the federal system while on active duty

126. Trait leadership theories assume:

  ○ **A.** Leaders can be trained.

  ○ **B.** Leaders are born.

  ○ **C.** Leader behaviors can be categorized into two main types: initiating structure and consideration.

  ○ **D.** Leader behaviors can be categorized into two main types: production oriented and employee oriented.

127. During which of the following activities are permanent strike replacements not permitted?

  ○ **A.** Economic strike

  ○ **B.** Lockout

  ○ **C.** Recognition strike

  ○ **D.** Sympathy strike

128. Which of the following statements is not true regarding the environmental scanning process?

○ **A.** It involves evaluating the internal strengths and weaknesses of the organization.

○ **B.** It involves collecting and interpreting information regarding the environment.

○ **C.** It is integral to the SWOT analysis.

○ **D.** It attempts to evaluate trends and changes in the environment.

129. The process of developing, pricing, promoting, and distributing products, services, or knowledge is called:

○ **A.** Operations management

○ **B.** Financial management

○ **C.** Sales and marketing

○ **D.** Information technology

130. _____ are internal quantitative measures of performance.

○ **A.** Benchmarks

○ **B.** Forecasts

○ **C.** Metrics

○ **D.** Scenarios

131. Which of the following is not true regarding rights arbitration?

○ **A.** The arbitrator is free to rewrite the portion of the contract that is the subject of the agreement to be consistent common practice in the industry.

○ **B.** The arbitrator must strictly interpret the contract language.

○ **C.** In cases in which the language is ambiguous, the arbitrator may look at the intent of the parties, often by referring to the bargaining history.

○ **D.** The arbitrator may rule that past practice has modified the contract language.

132. The Drug-Free Workplace Act of 1988 applies to:

○ **A.** Only federal, state, and local governmental employers

○ **B.** All public sector employers with over ten employees

○ **C.** Employers who have federal contracts of at least $100,000

○ **D.** All private universities, regardless of whether they receive federal monies

133. At the highest level of social responsibility, an organization:

   ○ **A.** Operates on an ethical imperative to make society better

   ○ **B.** Not only obeys the letter of the law, but also engages in activities in the spirit and intent of the law

   ○ **C.** Meets legal obligations and no more

   ○ **D.** Tries to not get caught

134. An employer bases promotion and movement through the pay range on seniority, gives across-the-board raises based on cost of living, provides benefits based totally on organizational member-ship with benefit levels rising with length of service, and has a merit pay system that is largely *pro forma* with most employees receiving a merit bonus without regard to actual performance. This compensation strategy can be best described as:

   ○ **A.** Performance-based

   ○ **B.** Entitlement-based

   ○ **C.** Lead the market

   ○ **D.** Lag the market

135. Which of the following statements is true?

   ○ **A.** Union density in the public sector peaked at about 35% in the 1950s and has been declining since then.

   ○ **B.** Union density in the public sector is about three times that of the private sector.

   ○ **C.** Union density in the private sector has been increasing since the 1960s and is now at about 37%.

   ○ **D.** Union density in the private sector is about twice that of the public sector.

136. Under the Immigration Reform and Control Act (1986), Form I-9 must be completed within _____ of hiring and kept for a minimum of _____ years.

   ○ **A.** 24; 2

   ○ **B.** 48; 2

   ○ **C.** 72; 3

   ○ **D.** 96; 3

137. All the following information is collected during the job analysis process except for:

   ○ **A.** Tasks needed to perform the job

   ○ **B.** Worker behaviors, such as decision-making, that are required by the job

   ○ **C.** Compensation levels for the job in the external labor market

   ○ **D.** Machines used in the performance of the job

138. Judging all characteristics of an individual positively because of a positive impression on one characteristic during the interview is referred to as:

   ○ **A.** Snap judgment

   ○ **B.** Horn effect

   ○ **C.** Halo effect

   ○ **D.** Contrast error

139. Under which scenario might an employee most likely be able to pursue a wrongful termination tort?

   ○ **A.** A bargaining unit employee is terminated improperly while covered by a negotiated agreement.

   ○ **B.** An at-will employee is terminated due to lack of work.

   ○ **C.** An employee under an employment contract is terminated for just cause.

   ○ **D.** An at-will employee is terminated for absenteeism while serving on a jury.

140. Which types of job evaluation methods are both quantitative and use compensable factors?

   ○ **A.** Point factor and factor comparison

   ○ **B.** Point factor and ranking

   ○ **C.** Point factor and job classification

   ○ **D.** Factor comparison and ranking

141. Under the Worker Adjustment and Retraining Notification Act (1988), the employer must provide a minimum of _____ days of advance notice under which of the following conditions?

   ○ **A.** 30; layoff of 300 of the organization's 1,000 employees

   ○ **B.** 60; layoff of 550 of the organization's 10,000 employees

   ○ **C.** 30; layoff of 25 of the organization's 50 employees

   ○ **D.** 60; anytime there is a layoff of 50 or more employees

142. You are planning an HRD event that will feature a lunch before the program and a number of small group exercises. The lunch and program must be held in the same room due to lack of space availability. What room arrangement type would be best in this situation?

- ○ **A.** Classroom
- ○ **B.** Banquet
- ○ **C.** Rectangle
- ○ **D.** Theatre

143. The United Auto Workers *(UAW)* would be considered a(n):

- ○ **A.** Local union
- ○ **B.** National union
- ○ **C.** Federation
- ○ **D.** International union

144. A financial ratio that measures an organization's capability to turn resources into profits is:

- ○ **A.** Inventory turnover ratio
- ○ **B.** Return on investment
- ○ **C.** Debt of owners' equity
- ○ **D.** Current ratio

145. In the _____ stage of the organizational lifecycle, revenue is a maximum but profitability might be declining because of increased competition. At this stage, organizations may become somewhat inflexible and bureaucratic.

- ○ **A.** Introduction
- ○ **B.** Growth
- ○ **C.** Maturity
- ○ **D.** Decline

146. Management by objectives *(MBO)* is the practical application of which motivation theory?

- ○ **A.** Equity Theory
- ○ **B.** Goal-Setting Theory
- ○ **C.** Fiedler's Contingency Theory
- ○ **D.** Leader-Member Exchange Theory

147. Which of the following is not a provision of the Landrum-Griffin Act (1959)?

◯ **A.** Created union unfair labor practices

◯ **B.** Created a bill of rights for union members

◯ **C.** Required periodic elections of union officers

◯ **D.** Required that unions adopt a constitution and bylaws

148. An employee pays a monthly health insurance premium and then 20% of the cost of any medical services received after a $200 deductible. Maximum out-of-pocket medical expenses are capped at $5,000 per year and the employee can select the medical provider to be used. There is no discount on costs for using a particular provider. What type of health insurance plan does the employee have?

◯ **A.** HMO

◯ **B.** PPO

◯ **C.** Fee-for-service

◯ **D.** HDHP

149. At the completion of an HRD training program, HRD can guarantee:

◯ **A.** Skills or knowledge and confidence, but not transfer nor a supportive job environment or opportunity to perform on the job

◯ **B.** Skills or knowledge and supportive job environment, but not confidence or opportunity to perform

◯ **C.** An opportunity to perform and supportive job environment, but not skills or knowledge or confidence

◯ **D.** Confidence and a supportive job environment, but not skills or knowledge or an opportunity to perform on the job

150. Which of the following incentive plans is not considered an individual incentive plan?

◯ **A.** Piece rates

◯ **B.** Sales commissions

◯ **C.** Gainsharing plans

◯ **D.** Standard hour plans

151. What is the importance of the Supreme Court decision in *NLRB v. Jones and Laughlin Steel Corp.*?

- ○ **A.** Determined that bargaining unit members have to pay only that portion of union dues that pertain to its mainline representational duties
- ○ **B.** Determined that compulsory arbitration is legal
- ○ **C.** Empowered the NLRB to determine what topics are mandatory, permissive, or illegal bargaining items
- ○ **D.** Determined that the Wagner Act was constitutional

152. Employer provided life insurance in excess of _____ is taxable income to the employee.

- ○ **A.** $5,000
- ○ **B.** $10,000
- ○ **C.** $25,000
- ○ **D.** $50,000

153. Works on the copyright has expired and works produced by the United States government are considered to be:

- ○ **A.** Fair use items
- ○ **B.** In the public domain
- ○ **C.** Protected for an additional 20 years from the date of expiration of copyright and in the case of United States government publications, copyright-protected for 120 years from the date of creation
- ○ **D.** Protected for an additional 14 years from the date of expiration of copyright and in the case of United States government publications, copyright-protected for 95 years from the date of publication

154. A bargaining team made up of the plant manager, two subordinate managers, and the Director of HR negotiates a labor agreement with a union bargaining team composed of union officials from the Production Employee's Union, Local 10. This is an example of what type of bargaining?

- ○ **A.** Pattern
- ○ **B.** Centralized
- ○ **C.** Decentralized
- ○ **D.** Multi-employer

155. All the following are components of the environment except for:

    ◯ **A.** Federal laws and regulations.

    ◯ **B.** Societal expectations

    ◯ **C.** Competitors

    ◯ **D.** Organizational mission statement

156. The scientific method is composed of five steps. Which of the following is not one of the steps?

    ◯ **A.** Problem identification

    ◯ **B.** Hypothesis development

    ◯ **C.** Research design

    ◯ **D.** Data collection and analysis

157. Under FLSA, nonexempt employees must be paid overtime:

    ◯ **A.** At the rate of time and one-half for any hours worked over 8 in any workday

    ◯ **B.** At the rate of double time for any hours worked over 8 in any workday

    ◯ **C.** At the rate of time and one-half for any hours worked beyond 40 in any workweek that is defined as 168 consecutive hours

    ◯ **D.** At the rate of double time for any work performed on a national holiday

158. If the president does not sign a bill sent by Congress during the period that Congress is not in session, the bill:

    ◯ **A.** Becomes law

    ◯ **B.** Dies due to a "pocket veto"

    ◯ **C.** Is sent to the Supreme Court for a determination as to its constitutionality

    ◯ **D.** Is sent back to the chamber in which it was originally submitted

159. Which of the following employers is not exempt from the pre-employment restrictions on the administration of lie detector tests under the Employer Polygraph Protection Act (1988)?

    ◯ **A.** Federal government

    ◯ **B.** Banks

    ◯ **C.** Drug manufacturers

    ◯ **D.** Armored car providers

160. Marie Smith is hired by ABC Corporation as a bargaining unit employee. She refuses to join the union and pay any union dues or representational fees within the timeframe prescribed in the labor agreement and the employer is forced to terminate her. What type of security agreement does the union have?

   ○ **A.** Closed shop

   ○ **B.** Union shop

   ○ **C.** Agency shop

   ○ **D.** Open shop

Use the following scenario to answer questions 161, 162, and 163:

You are assigned to be the project manager for the design, development, implementation, and evaluation of a training initiative that involves training all employees from the CEO to lowest level of the organization.

161. In your initial planning you divide the project into tasks that need to be performed, identifying the time that will be needed on each task and who will be responsible for completing the task. What planning tool are you using?

   ○ **A.** Statement of work

   ○ **B.** Work breakdown structure

   ○ **C.** PERT

   ○ **D.** CPM

162. You use a planning tool that visually shows the planned starting and ending times of all tasks, how the tasks fit in with the overall schedule, and the actual beginning and ending times of the tasks. What planning tool are you using?

   ○ **A.** PERT

   ○ **B.** CPM

   ○ **C.** Gantt charts

   ○ **D.** WBS

163. Which of the following statements is not true regarding the critical path as determined by PERT, CPM, or similar project-planning methodologies?

   ○ **A.** It provides the mandatory order in which tasks must be done to complete the project.

   ○ **B.** It represents the least possible time in which the project can be completed.

   ○ **C.** It identifies float or slack, which are projects that are on the critical path but do not have to be done in a mandatory order.

   ○ **D.** It identifies the path of activities that must be most closely monitored.

164. The _____ element of organizational structure is the extent to which work is broken down into its component parts with each part being the primary task assignment of a separate job (commonly referred to as *division of labor*).

- ○ **A.** Job specialization
- ○ **B.** Formalization
- ○ **C.** Departmentation
- ○ **D.** Span of control

165. Which of the following statements was not part of the famous "Steelworkers Trilogy" Supreme Court decisions?

- ○ **A.** Employers cannot refuse to arbitrate an issue based on a claim that the issue has no merit.
- ○ **B.** Arbitrators are allowed to decide claims that allege both a violation of the labor contract and an unfair labor practice.
- ○ **C.** Employers cannot refuse to arbitrate based on a claim that the issue was not specifically covered in the labor contract.
- ○ **D.** The courts cannot reverse the decision of an arbitrator except in extremely limited instances.

166. Which of the following is an example of cliff vesting?

- ○ **A.** The employee is 100% vested in the defined benefit plan after five years of participation.
- ○ **B.** The employee is vested at 20% after three years, 40% after four years, 60% after five years, 80% after six years, and 100% after seven years of participation.
- ○ **C.** The employee is vested at 20% after two years, 40% after three years, 60% after four years, 80% after five years, and 100% after six years of participation.
- ○ **D.** There is no such thing as cliff vesting. ERISA prescribes that vesting must occur using a graded schedule.

167. Which of the following situations does not necessarily qualify an individual as being disabled under the Americans with Disabilities Act (1990)?

- ○ **A.** Currently receiving workers' compensation benefits
- ○ **B.** Has a mental impairment that substantially limits one or more major life functions
- ○ **C.** Has a record of physical or mental impairment that substantially limits one or more major life functions
- ○ **D.** Is regarded or treated as if there is a physical impairment that substantially limits one or more life functions

168. An employee is required to record what tasks are performed at periodic intervals during the work day. This is an example of what type of job analysis data collection methodology?

- ○ **A.** Observation
- ○ **B.** Questionnaire
- ○ **C.** Employee log or diary
- ○ **D.** Critical incidents

169. All the following are strategies that can assist the organization in avoiding having to lay off employees except for:

- ○ **A.** Early retirement incentives
- ○ **B.** Part-time work
- ○ **C.** Hiring freezes
- ○ **D.** Severance pay

170. The current bargaining agreement contains a no-strike clause. Therefore an employee can be terminated for participating in all the following strikes except for:

- ○ **A.** Jurisdictional
- ○ **B.** Wildcat
- ○ **C.** Sympathy
- ○ **D.** Unfair labor practice

171. A weakness of Fiedler's Contingency Theory is:

- ○ **A.** It assumes that the leader has more control over the situation when the three contingencies were favorable.
- ○ **B.** It finds that directive behavior is more effective in five of the eight potential situations.
- ○ **C.** It assumes that leadership behavior could only be task oriented or relationship oriented.
- ○ **D.** It finds that relationship-behavior is more effective when the contingency situation is neither particularly favorable nor particularly unfavorable to the leader.

172. A forecast is which of the following?

   ○ **A.** Prediction as to how a particular measure will change in the future

   ○ **B.** Information regarding competitors that enables the organization to adjust its strategies to better compete in the environment

   ○ **C.** General description of what the future is likely to be

   ○ **D.** Comparison of the organization's internal operations with those of other organizations

173. The consistency of dependability of a measurement is referred to as:

   ○ **A.** Content validity

   ○ **B.** Construct validity

   ○ **C.** Reliability

   ○ **D.** Criterion-related validity

174. An organization has an excellent performance management plan. Performance expectations are clearly delineated and linked to the performance evaluation rating. Performance ratings are clearly linked to financial rewards; for example, an outstanding performance rating results in a bonus of 5% of salary. This bonus arrangement was determined based on extensive input from employees. In terms of Vroom's expectancy theory, what is the term used for the linkage of the performance rating to the bonus?

   ○ **A.** Motivation

   ○ **B.** Expectancy

   ○ **C.** Instrumentality

   ○ **D.** Valence

Use the following information to answer questions 175, 176, and 177:

You are the HR Director of a small manufacturing firm. The ABC Production Workers' Union has just been successful in obtaining a directed election. The CEO has ordered you to take aggressive action within the limits of the law to convince the workforce to vote against union certification during the campaign.

175. How many days do you have to provide the *Excelsior* list to the NLRB?

   ○ **A.** 7 days

   ○ **B.** 1 day

   ○ **C.** 30 days

   ○ **D.** 60 days

176. Which of the following actions of the union might destroy the "laboratory conditions" required by NLRB for an election and serve as the basis for management to file an unfair labor practice?

- ○ **A.** The union places advertising in the newspaper comparing the wages and benefits your firm pays to those of unionized firms in the same industry, and promises to obtain increased compensation once certified as the exclusive representative.

- ○ **B.** The union visits every prospective bargaining unit employee at their home in an effort to convince them to vote in the union's favor.

- ○ **C.** The union has several of its employees apply to your firm for the express purpose of assisting the election campaign after they are hired.

- ○ **D.** The union meets with a group of employees at an offsite hotel and tells the assembly that any employee that does not vote for the union will lose the support of the union, making promotion unlikely and termination a possibility.

177. A distinct advantage that the employer has during the election campaign that the union does not have is?

- ○ **A.** The employer can hire a consultant to help guide it through the election campaign.

- ○ **B.** The employer can hold mandatory meetings of employees during normal work hours to try to influence employee votes.

- ○ **C.** The employer can promise new or increased benefits if the union is defeated in the election.

- ○ **D.** The employer can send materials to the home address of employees.

178. Which federal act restricts the capability of health insurance plans and employers to deny or limit health insurance coverage for preexisting conditions and protects the privacy of medical records?

- ○ **A.** FLSA

- ○ **B.** HIPAA

- ○ **C.** FMLA

- ○ **D.** USERRA

179. The CEO of an organization implements an organizational change initiative by telling employees that they will either comply or be fired. This is an example of what model of overcoming resistance to change?

- ○ **A.** Forcing

- ○ **B.** Reward

- ○ **C.** Communication

- ○ **D.** Participation

180. HR activities involved in workforce planning, change management, and planning and executing mergers and acquisitions are part of the _____ role of HR.

- ○ **A.** Administrative
- ○ **B.** Operational
- ○ **C.** Employee Advocate
- ○ **D.** Strategic

181. All the following are characteristics of essential functions of the job under the Americans with Disabilities Act except for:

- ○ **A.** It is the reason why the job exists.
- ○ **B.** It cannot be assigned to another person.
- ○ **C.** The function requires a great deal of skill not found in employees in other job categories.
- ○ **D.** In-depth job analysis indicates that the incumbent in the position typically performs the function.

182. Which portion of the typical job description contains the knowledge, skills, and abilities needed by the incumbent of the position to successfully perform the job?

- ○ **A.** Identification section
- ○ **B.** Position summary
- ○ **C.** Job specifications
- ○ **D.** Essential functions

183. _____ are personal or organizational capabilities that are linked to successful performance outcomes.

- ○ **A.** Essential functions
- ○ **B.** Competencies
- ○ **C.** Job specifications
- ○ **D.** Nonessential functions

184. The organization is divided into four departments titled Governmental Services, Retail Services, Business Services, and International Services. What type of departmentation is reflected in this arrangement?

- ○ **A.** Functional by customer
- ○ **B.** Functional by geography
- ○ **C.** Divisional by customer
- ○ **D.** Divisional by process

185. You are the HR Director of the Wisconsin State Department of Education and the employees of your department indicate that they want to form a union for the purposes of collective bargaining of wages, hours, and other terms and conditions of employment. What legislative act would you consult to determine the legality of such an act?

- ○ **A.** Wagner Act (1935)
- ○ **B.** Civil Service Reform Act (1974)
- ○ **C.** State law
- ○ **D.** Taft-Hartley Act (1947)

186. Which of the following activities is not typically outsourced?

- ○ **A.** Payroll processing
- ○ **B.** Benefits administration
- ○ **C.** 401(k) administration
- ○ **D.** Strategic planning

187. All job applicants for a particular position are given a test, but the test is not used in the selection process. One year from the date they are hired, productivity data are collected on the employees who were tested. Test scores are compared with performance and found to be positively correlated at a statistically significant level. What type of validity is being determined?

- ○ **A.** Predictive
- ○ **B.** Concurrent
- ○ **C.** Content
- ○ **D.** Construct

188. A firm pursues a business strategy of cost minimization, attempting to be the low-cost provider in the industry. All the following are appropriate compensation strategies except for:

   ○ **A.** Lag the market

   ○ **B.** Piecework

   ○ **C.** Stock grants

   ○ **D.** Short-term bonuses based on achieving efficiency goals

189. Which of the following is not an evolving issue in HR management today?

   ○ **A.** Movement of HR from an administrative to strategic role

   ○ **B.** Aging of the workforce

   ○ **C.** Decrease in the level of outsourcing activities

   ○ **D.** Increased use of contingent workforce

190. Which of the following statements is not true regarding the obligation to provide reasonable accommodation under the Americans with Disabilities Act?

   ○ **A.** All disabled individuals are entitled to reasonable accommodation.

   ○ **B.** The intent of the law is that the process be interactive, with the employee requesting the accommodation and the employer responding in an appropriate manner.

   ○ **C.** The employer may require medical documentation before responding to the request for accommodation.

   ○ **D.** Accommodation is not required if it would create an undue hardship on the employer.

191. The International Labor Organization *(ILO)* is:

   ○ **A.** An agency of the United Nations whose mission is to promote minimal employment standards throughout the world

   ○ **B.** An agreement between Canada, Mexico, and the United States to promulgate 11 guiding principles regarding employee and labor relations

   ○ **C.** A worldwide organization for negotiating and enforcing minimum labor standards

   ○ **D.** The agency formed to monitor and enforce NAALC

192. Constructive discharge occurs when:

   ○ **A.** The termination is in violation of the public policy exclusion of common law.

   ○ **B.** Employer actions make the employment relationship so untenable that a reasonable person would have no alternative but to resign.

   ○ **C.** The employer terminates the individual for exercising rights or obligations under the law.

   ○ **D.** The termination violates an implied contract.

Use the following scenario to answer questions 193 and 194:

The CEO is particularly concerned about workplace violence because a nearby competitor, whose workforce is very similar in composition, has had a series of incidents. You, as the HR Director, are asked to develop a workplace violence prevention program and to provide training for managers in identifying employees most likely to engage in violent behaviors.

193. Which of the following components is not an appropriate component of a violence prevention program?

   ○ **A.** Discipline for violent behavior or threats that is consistent, fair, and timely

   ○ **B.** Creating emergency response teams

   ○ **C.** Termination of EAP because discipline, not counseling, is most effective in thwarting violence

   ○ **D.** Installation of security measures

194. All the following characteristics are commonly associated with a profile of a potential violent employee except for:

   ○ **A.** Carries grudges and blames others.

   ○ **B.** History of minor problems at work, including aggressiveness and threatening behavior.

   ○ **C.** Dislikes guns and military history.

   ○ **D.** Work is the only constant in employee's life.

195. A ranker creates a matrix with all jobs listed on both the horizontal and vertical axis and then compares each job with every other job in terms of the job's relative worth to the organization, placing a check mark in the cell denoting which of the two jobs is most important. The check marks for each job are then added up. What type of job evaluation method is the ranker using?

○ **A.** Ranking

○ **B.** Job classification

○ **C.** Point factor

○ **D.** Factor comparison

196. An HRD program is designed to improve employee retention of the organization. Baseline measures of employee turnover were determined prior to the implementation of the program. Turnover was again measured at the end of the program and there was a significant decrease in turnover. What level of evaluation is being performed using Kirkpatrick's model, and can HRD unequivocally claim that the program intervention caused the dramatic increase in employee retention?

○ **A.** Behavior; yes

○ **B.** Behavior; no

○ **C.** Results; yes

○ **D.** Results; no

197. The concepts of employment-at-will, wrongful termination, defamation of character, and negligent hiring all come from:

○ **A.** International law

○ **B.** State law

○ **C.** Federal law

○ **D.** Common law

198. The analysis of financial data and preparation of financial statements, such as the balance sheet for regulatory and external use, is referred to as:

○ **A.** Financial accounting

○ **B.** Tax accounting

○ **C.** Managerial accounting

○ **D.** Auditing

199. A description of the basic beliefs of the organization is called a:

○ **A.** Vision statement

○ **B.** Code of conduct

○ **C.** Mission statement

○ **D.** Values statement

200. All the following are considered to be advantages of organizationwide incentive plans except for:

○ **A.** Promotes a sense of belonging and commitment to the organization

○ **B.** Clearly links the performance of the individual and the reward

○ **C.** Increases employee retention

○ **D.** Might have tax benefits to both the employer and the employee

201. Which of the following would not be considered a union tactic to apply pressure to management to agree to proposals during collective bargaining?

○ **A.** Corporate campaign

○ **B.** Work slowdown

○ **C.** Lockout

○ **D.** Boycott

202. *Andragogy* is the study of adult learning. Based on the assumptions of andragogy, which of the following statements is not an implication for the development of HRD programs for adults?

○ **A.** Interim tests and exercises should be built into the program to provide intrinsic rewards.

○ **B.** Programs should assume a *tabula rasa* (clean slate) and teach the basics first.

○ **C.** Adults should be involved in the planning and implementation of the program.

○ **D.** The importance of learning the material should be clearly indicated before the HRD program begins.

203. All the following are provisions of the Civil Rights Act of 1991 except for:

○ **A.** Prohibits the practice of race-norming

○ **B.** Permits jury trials and compensatory and punitive damages up to $500,000 in discrimination cases

○ **C.** Prevents the use of "mixed motive" defenses

○ **D.** Extended the protection of the Civil Rights Act of 1964 to United States citizens working for United States organizations in foreign countries, except where those rights conflict with local law or customs

204. Mary Smith reports to both the Vice President of Human Resources and the Vice President for International Operations. This arrangement represents what type of departmentation and violates what organizing principle?

- ○ **A.** Division; span of control
- ○ **B.** Matrix; span of control
- ○ **C.** Functional; unity of command
- ○ **D.** Matrix; unity of command

205. An arbitrator makes a binding decision on the provisions to be included in a labor agreement using the issue-by-issue method. This is called:

- ○ **A.** Interest arbitration
- ○ **B.** Rights arbitration
- ○ **C.** Mediation
- ○ **D.** Fact-finding

206. The judicial concept of disparate treatment is based on the Supreme Court's decision in:

- ○ **A.** *Griggs v. Duke Power*
- ○ **B.** *McDonnell-Douglas v. Green*
- ○ **C.** *Regents of the University of California v. Bakke*
- ○ **D.** *Meritor Savings Bank v. Vinson*

207. With respect to FLSA limitations on workers less than 18 years of age, which of the following statements is incorrect?

- ○ **A.** A 14-year-old may be employed, with certain restrictions, to deliver newspapers.
- ○ **B.** A 16-year-old may drive a car on public highways as part of his or her job duties.
- ○ **C.** A 15-year-old may work in a restaurant in a nonhazardous job, but there are limitations as to the number of hours and time of day that the employee may work.
- ○ **D.** There is no limitation as to the number of hours that a 17-year-old may work.

208. In general, all the following organizations must submit written affirmative action plans except for:

- ○ **A.** Federal contractors with 50 or more employees and $50,000 in government contracts during any 12-month period
- ○ **B.** Private employers with more than 100 employees
- ○ **C.** Depositories of federal funds
- ○ **D.** An issuing or paying agent for United States savings bonds or savings notes

209. All the following are typically considered advantages of recruiting externally except for:

- ○ **A.** Promotes high morale

- ○ **B.** Brings in new ideas

- ○ **C.** Brings in expertise not available internally

- ○ **D.** Facilitates diversity initiatives

210. The only legal union security clause that can be negotiated in a particular state is an open shop. The state is:

- ○ **A.** In violation of the Wagner Act

- ○ **B.** A right-to-work state

- ○ **C.** In violation of the Sherman Anti-trust Act by giving monopolistic power to the employer

- ○ **D.** In violation of the Civil Rights Act of 1964 by permitting the employer to discriminate against union members

211. Glass walls refer to:

- ○ **A.** A situation is which minorities and women are hired in "nonrevenue-producing" occupations that do not typically lead to high-level positions in the organization and are prevented from transferring to other occupations in the organization

- ○ **B.** A situation in which minorities and women are promoted only so far in the organization and are unable to achieve promotion into the highest levels

- ○ **C.** A situation in which minorities and women are treated differently from other employees

- ○ **D.** A situation in which neutral employment practices of the organization disproportionately affect minorities and women

212. You are conducting an HR research project to determine the job satisfaction levels of 500 production employees in your organization. Which of the following is likely to be the most effective and efficient way of collecting this data?

- ○ **A.** Interviews

- ○ **B.** Observation

- ○ **C.** Questionnaire

- ○ **D.** Organizational records

213. The financial statement that reports all cash receipts and disbursements during a specified time period is called the:

  ○ **A.** Balance sheet

  ○ **B.** Income statement

  ○ **C.** Statement of cash flows

  ○ **D.** Acid-test

214. Which leadership theory incorporates the *Pygmalion Effect* (that is, the self-fulfilling prophecy)?

  ○ **A.** Leader-Member Exchange Theory

  ○ **B.** Path-Goal Theory

  ○ **C.** Situational Leadership Theory

  ○ **D.** Leader-Participation Model

Use the following information to answer questions 215, 216, and 217:

You are the HR Director of a private sector service industry organization that is being targeted for organizing by a union. The founder and CEO of the organization is surprised at the interest the employees are displaying in the union and, to some extent, feels that these long-term employees are being a bit disloyal.

215. The CEO asks what the appeal of a union is to employees and why would they vote for union certification. Which of the following is typically not a reason that employees would vote for union certification?

  ○ **A.** They believe that the union can provide better compensation, benefits, and greater workplace protection in terms of work rules and a grievance procedure.

  ○ **B.** They are attracted by the social aspects of belonging to a union.

  ○ **C.** They believe that they can improve their control over their work and work environment.

  ○ **D.** They believe that the union can get rid of overbearing managers.

216. The CEO asks how union certification would affect the organization. Which of the following statements is not correct?

  ○ **A.** Certification will likely increase compensation costs in terms of both wage rates and benefit levels.

  ○ **B.** Employee retention will likely improve.

  ○ **C.** Productivity will likely improve, bringing with it increased profitability.

  ○ **D.** Management flexibility in the assignment of work and imposition of discipline will likely decrease.

217. The CEO does not want to aggressively oppose the union, but wants to improve the work environment now to make the union irrelevant, knowing that changes must be made quickly before the union-organizing effort becomes more formalized. Which of the following actions would not be appropriate given the CEO's strategy?

○ **A.** Instituting a formal grievance process

○ **B.** Raising compensation levels to be equivalent to those paid by unionized firms

○ **C.** Issuing a policy reaffirming employment-at-will as a term and condition of employment

○ **D.** Offering a health insurance policy equivalent to that being offered in unionized firms

218. An employee loses eligibility for health insurance benefits because a reduction in his or her work hours changes the employee's status to part-time. The employee is not disabled at the time of the loss. Under COBRA, how many months of continuation of health insurance is the employee eligible for?

○ **A.** 36 months.

○ **B.** 29 months.

○ **C.** 18 months.

○ **D.** None. There is no obligation under COBRA for the employer to continue health insurance coverage of part-time employees.

219. Which of the following is not normally considered an advantage of outsourcing an HR program?

○ **A.** Increased control over the means of accomplishing the work

○ **B.** Decreased costs

○ **C.** Access to expertise

○ **D.** Access to sophisticated technology

220. An employee, employer, or union can initiate a complaint that an unfair labor practice has been committed by:

○ **A.** Filing a complaint with DOL headquarters

○ **B.** Contacting any designated NLRB administrative law judge

○ **C.** Filing directly with the NLRB in Washington, D.C.

○ **D.** Filing with the appropriate NLRB regional director

221. All the following are characteristic of the new psychological contract except for:

- ○ **A.** The employee expects portable benefits.
- ○ **B.** The employee expects challenging work leading to individual growth.
- ○ **C.** The employer expects the employee to remain with the firm for his/her entire career.
- ○ **D.** The employee expects externally competitive wages.

222. The organization has instituted a policy of casual dress on Fridays, which permits employees to wear jeans. Marie, one of your employees, feels that this is extremely unprofessional and complains to you each Friday. You have previously explained the rationale and potential benefits of the policy to her, but doing so had no impact. You then begin ignoring her complaints and the complaints ceased. In reinforcement theory terms, what type of reinforcement did you use?

- ○ **A.** Positive reinforcement
- ○ **B.** Negative reinforcement
- ○ **C.** Punishment
- ○ **D.** Extinction

223. Which of the following statements is incorrect regarding the use of independent contractors?

- ○ **A.** Day-to-day control of the means and methods of work is improved.
- ○ **B.** The expense of providing benefits is eliminated.
- ○ **C.** FLSA rules do not apply.
- ○ **D.** The withholding of federal, state, and local taxes is not required.

224. In which type of job evaluation method are the pay rates of benchmark jobs determined prior to the job evaluation being conducted?

- ○ **A.** Ranking
- ○ **B.** Job classification
- ○ **C.** Point factor
- ○ **D.** Factor comparison

225. Unions have, in some cases, had to make dramatic changes in their strategies and practices to adapt to the changing dynamics of the workplace and increased competitiveness in the market in the twenty-first century. Which of the following strategies is not a result of these drivers of change?

- ○ **A.** Increased organizing activity in the service sector

- ○ **B.** Attempts to appeal to minority and female employees

- ○ **C.** Reliance on growth in the manufacturing sector

- ○ **D.** Collaborative projects and arrangements with management

Practice Exam Answers

1. The correct answer is **B**. *Electromation* deals with employee involvement committees by declaring them employee organizations under the Wagner Act which, in this case, were dominated by the employer violating section 8(a)(2). Employers must be careful in how they constitute such committees and the issues with which the committees deal.

2. The correct answer is **D**. Workers' compensation normally covers employees even if the injury or illness is a result of the negligence of the employee (answer A), the organization (answer B), or another employee (answer C).

3. The correct answer is **B**. Compa-ratio indicates the relationship between the actual rate paid and the midpoint of the range (actual rate paid / midpoint of range). A compa-ratio of 1 indicates that the pay is at midpoint, which is commonly referred to as the *pay policy line*. A compa-ratio of <1 indicates actual pay rates below the midpoint and a compa-ratio of >1 indicates actual pay rates above the midpoint.

4. The correct answer is **B**. Equity theory states that an individual compares his or her ratio of outcomes to inputs against those of some other reference, which results in a perception of equality or inequality. Inequality motivates the employee to take action to create an equitable situation. Goal-setting theory states that motivation increases when specific, measurable, and challenging goals are given and accepted and when performance feedback is given (answer A). The job characteristic model states that there are five characteristics of a job that can be manipulated to create motivation (answer C). Expectancy theory's basic premise is that motivation is determined by an individual's belief that increased effort leads to a positive outcome that is important to that individual.

5. The correct answer is **D**. NAALC is a side agreement under NAFTA. Answer A is the World Trade Organization. Answer B is the International Labor Organization and answer C is the European Union.

6. The correct answer is **D**. The paired comparison method requires the rater to compare the performance of each employee with the performance of every other employee. The outcome of the process is a ranking of employees based on performance from best to worst. This is relative data. Graphic rating scales (answer A), checklists (answer B), and forced choice (answer C) are all category rating scales that provide absolute data but not relative data.

7. The correct answer is **A**. Outcomes are, in general, measurable and can be evaluated in terms of goal achievement of the organization. Behavior information (answer B) is the second most useful type of information because certain behaviors are believed to lead to outcomes. Traits (answer C) are constructs that are characteristic of the person. They are the least useful and dependable type of performance information. Dependability (answer D) is a trait.

8. The correct answer is **C**. Best practices dictate that the next level of management reviews the immediate supervisor's evaluation and that the system has a process for employees to appeal the appraisal. The performance management system should support organizational goals (answer A), performance dimensions should be clearly job-related (answer B), and performance feedback should be provided to the employee throughout the evaluation cycle (answer D). These are all best practices.

9. The correct answer is **A**. Answer B is the National Labor Relations Board which administers the National Labor Relations Act. State labor relations statutes are controlled by state agencies (answer C). Answer D is the Federal Mediation and Conciliation Service *(FMCS)* which is an agency that was created to assist in the resolution of labor relations disputes.

10. The correct answer is **A**. The "Deck of Cards" method is a way of ranking jobs from most valuable to least valuable to the organization. Typically, each job is written on an index card. The ranker goes through all cards and selects the job having the most value to the organization and removes it from the deck. The ranker then goes through the deck and selects the second-most valuable job and removes it. The process is completed when all jobs are ranked.

11. The correct answer is **C**. The "A" stands for needs assessment. The other letters in the acronym stand for design, development, implementation, and evaluation. Answers A, B, and D are incorrect.

12. The correct answer is **C**. Weak cultures are less likely to create resistance to change than are strong cultures. *Organizational culture* is the shared values and norms held by members (answer A). Those values and norms are typically created by the organization's founder (answer B). The stronger the culture, the more influence it has over members' behavior (answer D).

13. The correct answer is **C**. Initially HR, or *Personnel* as it was known then, was largely a clerical/administrative function with responsibility for record-keeping and payroll functions. The strategic (answer A), operational (answer C), and employee advocate (answer D) functions did not occur until later in the profession's evolution.

14. The correct answer is **D**. Answer A is typical at the first step, and answer B is typical at the second step. Answer C is a positive discipline, not a progressive discipline action.

15. The correct answer is **B**. Not one but both parties must give and receive something of value. For the contract to be enforceable, an offer must be made and accepted (answer A), both parties must be competent (answer C), and the contract must not be for something illegal (answer D).

16. The correct answer is **B**. All these acts require the payment of prevailing rates to employees working on federal contracts. Equal pay is a provision of the Equal Pay Act of 1963, which amended FLSA (answer A). Limitations on child labor are a provision of the Fair Labor Standards Act of 1938 (answer C). Continuation of health insurance is contained in the Consolidated Omnibus Budget Reconciliation Act of 1985 (answer D).

17. The correct answer is **C**. Answer A is the philosophy behind progressive discipline. Answer B is incorrect because there is nothing in the philosophy of positive discipline that prohibits termination. Termination is, in fact, normally the last step in either a progressive or positive discipline process. Answer D slightly overstates the philosophy of positive discipline. It is merely a different approach to achieving the same goal.

18. The correct answer is **C**. The fundamental accounting equation is Assets = Liabilities + Owners' Liability. If assets are $100,000 and liabilities are $75,000, the equation is balanced when owners' liability equals $25,000. Answers A, B, and D are incorrect.

19. The correct answer is **B**. The other three answers are more characteristic of union suppression than of union substitution.

20. The correct answer is **A**. Increased awareness of benefit costs is an advantage, not a disadvantage, of cafeteria plans because it promotes wise use of the benefit dollars available. Increased benefit burden (answer B), selection of only those benefits that the employee plans on using and in doing so causing premium rates to rise (answer C, commonly referred to as *adverse selection*), and making bad choices (answer D) are all considered disadvantages of cafeteria plans.

21. The correct answer is **D**. The summation of all scores equals 110. When the sum is divided by the number of scores (11), the mean is computed to be 10. Answers A, B, and C are incorrect.

22. The correct answer is **B**. The mode is the most frequently occurring score. In the distribution, the value 7 occurs three times—more than any other value. Answers A, C, and D are incorrect.

23. The correct answer is **C**. The median is that score below which 50% of all scores fall. In the distribution, five scores fall below 9 and five above. Answers A, B, and D are incorrect.

24. The correct answer is **B**. FMCS is a provision of the Taft-Hartley Act of 1947. Neither the Wagner Act (answer A), the Landrum-Griffith Act (answer C), nor the Norris-LaGuardia Act (answer D) created the Federal Mediation and Conciliation Service.

25. The correct answer is **D**. The chain of command is a hierarchical arrangement of authority as it flows from the top of the organization to the bottom. It defines who reports to whom. Span of control (answer A) refers to the number of subordinates that a manager directs. Centralization (answer B) describes at what level in the organization decisions are made. Departmentation (answer C) is the framework by which work and workers are arranged in the organization.

26. The correct answer is **C**. Qualitative research uses observation and interview data to develop themes that are used to attempt to explain the behavior being studied. Basic research (answer A) and applied research (answer D) are normally referred to as types of quantitative research. Quantitative research (answer B) uses statistical analysis to determine relationships between variables.

27. The correct answer is **B**. Technology frequently makes outsourcing more beneficial and easier rather than more difficult. Outsourced applications can be accessed by employees through web portals, and the outsourcing vendor can often directly input data into the organization's systems— saving considerable staff processing time. By automating routine processing tasks, resources are freed up so that the HR function can devote increased time and effort to the strategic role (answer A). Technology provides increased access to relevant information, which facilitates rational decision-making (answer C). Productivity in many program areas has been dramatically increased by automating repetitive processes (answer D).

28. The correct answer is **D**. There is no definitive list of mandatory bargaining topics. Under the *Borg-Warner* Doctrine, the NLRB is empowered to determine what topics are mandatory (answer A). The *Mackay* Doctrine deals with the issue of permanent replacement of striking employees (answer B). There is no exhaustive list of unfair labor practices during an election campaign; this is an evolving issue because NLRB continues to adjudicate unfair labor charges (answer C).

29. The correct answer is **C**. At the application level, the individual can operate the machine. At the knowledge level (answer A), the employee is merely able to recall facts about the machine. At the comprehension level (answer B), the employee can explain the purpose of the machine. At the analysis level (answer D), the employee can perform common repair and maintenance activities. However, if the goal is merely to get the employee to operate the machine, teaching at the analysis level would not be cost-beneficial.

30. The correct answer is **A**. Retention is expected to be higher rather than lower when paying above-market wages. Higher-quality candidates (answer B), easier recruitment of candidates (answer C), and higher-quality production (answer D) are all expected outcomes of leading the market in wage rates.

31. The correct answer is **D**. The occupational preparation stage is where the person pursues education and explores initial career interests (answer A). At the organizational entry stage, the person accepts an initial job offer and enters the workforce (answer B). During the early career stage, the person learns the job and begins to advance in the organization (answer C).

32. The correct answer is **D**. An HRIS is an integrated software system that supports the HR function. A service center (answer A) is used to centralize administrative processing of repetitive actions such as payroll. An application service provider *(ASP)* (answer B) is a vendor that hosts and manages hardware and software for the organization. An ASP might host an HRIS. A data warehouse (answer C) is a large database or databases that contain HR-related information.

33. The correct answer is **C**. Answers A, B, and D are clearly determinants that would be considered by the NLRB. The NLRB also would consider the history/standard practice of constitution of the bargaining unit in the industry under discussion, but not of bargaining units in other industries—particularly if they were greatly dissimilar.

34. The correct answer is **A**. Under FMLA, the employee may refuse return to work in a light duty position. Answer B is incorrect. Answer C alludes to a potential conflict between workers' compensation and ADA. Answer D is incorrect in that an employee can simultaneously be on FMLA leave and collecting workers' compensation.

35. The correct answer is **D**. At the initiation or infancy stage of either product or organizational life cycles, efficiency incentives are not needed because there is likely no cash with which to pay them, no historical data to base them on, and they are not in alignment with the organization's major strategic goals at that time. These types of incentives are, however, viable at later stages in the life-cycle. Generous stock options (answer A), limited benefits (answer B), and below-market wage rates (answer C) are appropriate components of the compensation strategy at the initiation stage.

36. The correct answer is **D**. Assets are economic resources owned by the company. Owners' equity (answer A) is the difference between assets and liabilities of the organization based on the fundamental accounting equation. Human capital (answer B) is the current and potential abilities of the organization's workforce. Liabilities (answer D) are financial obligations of the organization.

37. The correct answer is **A**. Although somewhat paradoxical in that there is usually a positive correlation between job satisfaction and employee retention, this does not seem to hold true in a unionized environment. Wages, benefits, and retention are, in general, higher in a unionized environment, whereas job satisfaction is lower.

38. The correct answer is **B**. The range is difference between the highest score (22) and the lowest (10). Answer A (10) is the mode or most frequently occurring score. Answer C (13) is the mean or average score. Answer D (14) is the median, the score that divides the distribution in half.

39. The correct answer is **B**. Strong guidance to employees that limits employee discretion is formalization. Departmentalization (answer A) refers to the framework by which jobs are grouped. Centralization (answer C) refers to where is the organization's decision authority lies. Job specialization (answer D) refers to how the work of the organization is broken down into its component parts and assigned.

40. The correct answer is **A**. Information regarding organizational policies not related to compensation, such as the sexual harassment policy, is not normally collected in the wage survey process. The organizational policy on how wage increases are determined (answer B), information regarding the types of benefits offered (answer C), and wage rates for benchmark jobs (answer D) are all typically requested when conducting a wage survey.

41. The correct answer is **D**. Answers A, B, and C are all difficulties that are associated with and hinder the effective implementation of transnational bargaining. The ICFTU has no ban on this type of bargaining. In fact, its mission is to support collaboration and cooperation among labor organizations from member companies.

42. The correct answer is **A**. The Civil Rights Act of 1866 prohibits discrimination only with respect to contracts and based only on race or ethnicity. The Equal Pay Act (answer B) prohibits discrimination in compensation based on sex. The Civil Rights Act of 1964 (answer C) prohibits discrimination in employment based on race, color, religion, sex, or national origin. The Civil Rights Act of 1991 (answer D) contains a number of provisions, including the right to a jury trial and potential compensatory and punitive damages in illegal discrimination cases.

43. The correct answer is **C**. The "Right-to-Sue" letter indicates that there is reasonable cause to believe that illegal discrimination occurred, attempts at conciliation with the employer have failed, the EEOC is not going to pursue the matter in court, and the employee may institute a suit on his or her own. If there is no indication of illegal discrimination on completion of the investigation (answer A), a "Dismissal and Notice of Rights Letter" is issued. If there appears to be reasonable cause to believe illegal discrimination has occurred (answer B), the EEOC issues a "Letter of Determination." No letter is issued if the EEOC determines that it is taking the case to court (answer D).

44. The correct answer is **A**. Answer A actually defines procedures, not rules. Rules are much more tightly defined and leave little room for deviation. Answers B, C, and D are correct statements defining policies, rules and procedures respectively.

45. The correct answer is **C**. A simple organization is one characterized by the description in the question. A mechanistic organization (answer A) is one that is rigid and highly structured in terms of a high degree of departmentation, formalization, and job specialization. It also normally has wide spans of control and multiple levels of hierarchy. A bureaucracy (answer B) can be described in the same terms as a mechanistic organization. Concentrated structures (answer D) are substructures of an organization created specifically to make it more organic.

46. The correct answer is **D**. Employee referral of external recruits is considered to be an internal recruitment method. Recruiting at high schools and technical schools (answer A), media advertising (answer B), and walk-ins of applicants (answer C) are all considered external recruiting sources.

47. The correct answer is **B**. Workers on sabbatical typically are receiving compensation and benefits during that period, and are considered traditional employees. However, part-time workers (answer A), temporary workers (answer C), and contract workers (answer D) are considered part of the contingent workforce.

48. The correct answer is **A**. A vision statement describes the organization's desired future state. A mission statement (answer B) describes the fundamental purposes of the organization. A values statement (answer C) describes the basic beliefs of the organization. The phrase *strategic statement* (answer D) is not a standard term used in strategic planning.

49. The correct answer is **C**. Requesting that employees give a two-week notice before quitting has implications on the employment-at-will relationship (assuming that the employer wants to maintain it). A two-week notice for the employee could be interpreted to place the same obligation on the employer when terminating an employee. Answers A, B, and D are all considered to be good practices when publishing an employee handbook.

50. The correct answer is **A**. Patents on inventions are good for 20 years. Patents on designs are good for 14 years (answer B). Copyrights, not patents, are good for the life of the author plus 70 years (answer C), whereas copyrights for an anonymous author are good for 95 years from the date of publication (answer D) or 120 years from the date of creation, whichever is the shorter time period.

51. The correct answer is **A**. The Taft-Hartley Act attempts to rebalance the power between the employer and the unions (answer B). The Landrum-Griffin Act regulates certain internal practices of the unions (answer C). The Wagner Act is a labor relations act, not an employee relations act like the Social Security Act and Workers' Compensation Act (answer D).

52. The correct answer is **B**. The administrative role (answer A) involves clerical functions such as record-keeping and payroll processing and administration. The employee advocate role (answer C) ensures fair treatment of employees. The strategic role of HR (answer D) is a proactive approach in assisting the organization to design its future.

53. The correct answer is **A**. The Age Discrimination in Employment Act requires 20 or more employees (answer B). Answer C is incorrect. The Worker Adjustment and Retraining Notification Act requires 100 or more employees (answer D).

54. The correct answer is **B**. Quid pro quo sexual harassment occurs when submission or rejection of requests for sexual favors is used as the basis for employment decisions affecting the individual. Propositioning by a coworker (answer A), and inappropriate behaviors of customers (answer C) and suppliers (answer D) might create sexual harassment under the concept of hostile environment, but not quid pro quo.

55. The correct answer is **D**. Contract ratification is based on the procedures that each individual union agrees on. It might require a majority vote of union members or of elected representatives chosen by the members or the required vote might be some other higher percentage.

56. The correct answer is **C**. Nonpaid leave for family medical emergencies is a provision of the Family and Medical Leave Act of 1993. Answers A, B, and D are provisions of the Social Security Act. Although state controlled, unemployment insurance is a provision of the Social Security Act.

57. The correct answer is **B**. Technostructural interventions are designed to improve organizational effectiveness through such interventions as redesigning the organizational structure. Process interventions (answer A) are designed to improve interpersonal and intergroup working relationships. Human resource management interventions (answer C) are designed to manage individual and group performance and provide supportive assistance to employees so that they can better deal with the dual stresses of work and family life. Strategic interventions (answer D) are designed to enable organizations to properly align themselves and their mission with the environment.

58. The correct answer is **C**. The income statement is used to show the profit or loss of the organization during a stated time period. The fundamental accounting equation (answer A) is the basis for the balance sheet. The balance sheet (answer B) reports the organization's financial condition as of a certain date. The statement of cash flows (answer D) reports all cash receipts and disbursements during a specified period of time.

59. The correct answer is **C**. Approximately 95% of all scores fall within plus or minus two standard deviations of the mean. Answer A (34%) represents the percentage of scores that fall within one standard deviation of the mean on either side of the mean, whereas answer B (68%) represents the percentage of scores that fall within plus or minus one standard deviation of the mean. Answer D (99%) is the percentage of scores that fall within plus or minus three standard deviations of the mean.

60. The correct answer is **A**. A meeting of the second-level supervisor and the local union president is more characteristic of step 2 (answer B). A meeting of the Director of HR and a representative of the national union frequently occurs at step 3 (answer C). Arbitration is characteristic of step 4 (answer D).

61. The correct answer is **D**. OSHA (the Occupational Safety and Health Act) requires the organization to provide a safe and healthy environment, but does not provide for medical or death benefits for an employee injured on the job (answer A). WARN (Worker Adjustment and Retraining Notification Act of 1988) requires certain employers to give notices of impending mass layoffs or plant shutdowns (answer B). Under Workers' Compensation laws, the worker is generally not permitted to use a common law tort (answer C) in an attempt to recover damages from on-the-job injuries or illnesses.

62. The correct answer is **B**. The Hazard Communication standard (answer A) deals with hazardous chemicals, not machines. The Personal Protective Equipment standard requires the organization to provide equipment such as gloves and safety glasses to protect employees from work hazards (answer C). The Bloodborne Pathogens standard is designed to protect employees that are regularly exposed to bodily fluids, including blood (answer D).

63. The correct answer is **C**. It is the death of an employee or the hospitalization of three or more employees that requires a report to OSHA (answer A). Answer B is clearly wrong because the event requires a report. The report must be made within eight hours, not three workdays (answer D).

64. The correct answer is **C**. The employer clearly intentionally and knowingly violated a standard, which is the criterion for a willful violation citation. Answer A is wrong in that the death must be reported and will likely result in an immediate OSHA response. A citation for a serious violation of a standard is used when there is a substantial change that serious injury or death would result and the employer knew or should have known that the hazard existed (answer B). A repeat violation occurs when there is a continued violation of a standard when that violation was found in a prior inspection (answer D). There is no indication that the employer in this scenario was the subject of a prior OSHA inspection.

65. The correct answer is **B**. The Society for Human Resource Management *(SHRM)* was originally founded as the American Society for Personnel Administration *(ASPA)*. ASTD, which stands for *American Society for Training and Development* (answer A); IMPA, which stands for *International Personnel Management Association* (answer C); and World at Work (answer D) are all incorrect.

66. The correct answer is **C**. A boycott is an attempt to convince others not to use the organization's products or services (answer A). A work slowdown is an attempt to apply pressure on the organization by reducing productivity (answer B). Corporate campaigns are permissible within limits and not unfair labor practices (answer D) unless those limits are exceeded.

67. The correct answer is **C**. The Portal-to-Portal Act (1947), which is actually an amendment to FLSA, defines what activities are hours of work requiring compensation and are used to determine eligibility for overtime. The Equal Pay Act of 1963 prohibits paying lower wages to one sex than the other for jobs that are similar in skill, effort, responsibilities, and working conditions (answer A). The Fair Labor Standards Act of 1938 contains many provisions regarding compensation, but did not in its original form define what work was compensable and what not (answer B). Workers' compensation laws are state regulations that require certain benefits if an employee sustains an on-the-job injury or illness (answer D).

68. The correct answer is **D**. The fourth step in the strategic planning process is strategy evaluation, not strategy formulation. Strategy formulation (answer A) is the first step in the process and involves making basic decisions regarding the organization's vision, mission, and values. The development of strategic objectives (answer B) is the second step and involves a SWOT analysis and the determination of strategic objectives. Strategic implementation (answer C) is the third step and involves the development and execution of operational plans to achieve the strategic objectives.

69. The correct answer is **B**. A differentiation strategy is one in which the organization attempts to be first in the market with new and innovative products or services that are valued by the customer. A cost leadership strategy (answer A) is one in which the organization attempts to be the low-cost provider in the market by concentrating on efficiency. A cost minimization strategy (answer C) is another name for cost leadership. The term *dynamic* (answer D) is not typically used to describe a particular type of business strategy.

70. The correct answer is **B**. Striking workers cannot be permanently replaced if the strike is the result of an employer unfair labor practice. Workers can be permanently replaced in economic, recognition, and sympathy strikes (answers A, C, and D). If the employer and union have negotiated a no-strike clause, workers can be terminated for participating in a sympathy strike.

71. The correct answer is **A**. The Sarbanes-Oxley Act of 2002 protects employees from retaliation when they report employer improprieties with respect to securities regulations to the Securities and Exchange Commission. The False Claims Act of 1863 (answer A) as amended provides rewards for those that report improprieties with respect to federal contracts. Some states have specific legislation that protects employees when they report employer misconduct with respect to state contracts (answer C). The Wagner Act of 1935 (answer D) protects employees from retaliation for reporting unfair labor practices and otherwise exercising their rights under the act.

72. The correct answer is **B**. State governments are exempt from the WARN Act (answer A). The requirement for federal agencies to prepare AAP plans comes from Executive Order 11478 (answer C). Answer D is incorrect.

73. The correct answer is **A**. The organization cannot raise an affirmative defense if a tangible employment action has occurred. Answers B, C, and D are all components of an affirmative defense.

74. The correct answer is **C**. Trend analysis uses historical data to predict future needs. Turnover (answer A) is a subset of trend analysis that allows the organization to predict recruitment needs to maintain the same level of employment. Ratio analysis (answer C) is a forecasting method that assumes there is a set relationship between one variable and another. Nominal group technique (answer D) is a method that requires members of the forecasting group or committed to make independent forecasts prior to the discussion of the topic.

75. The correct answer is **B**. The NLRB may issue a cease and desist order directly to the offending party to stop the unfair labor practice. The Board does not have the authority to fine or impose sanctions (answers A and C). Unfair labor practices are not, in themselves, criminal offenses (answer D).

76. The correct answer is **C**. Answer A is incorrect because both public and private employers are covered under FMLA. Answer B is incorrect because the requirement is 50 employees within a 75-mile radius, which the business meets. Answer D is incorrect because there is no exemption for family-owned businesses under FMLA.

77. The correct answer is **D**. Answer A is incorrect because common-law spouses are qualifying if the state legally recognizes such arrangements. Answer B is incorrect because the 12 months of service does not have to be continuous and Joe has more than a year's total service. Answer C is incorrect because the 30-day advance notice is required only if the need for leave can be reasonably anticipated, which is not the case in this scenario.

78. The correct answer is **D**. Answer A is incorrect because FMLA does permit the employer to require the employee to use paid leave simultaneously with FMLA leave. Answer B is incorrect because FMLA permits the employer to require the employee to use available sick leave if the employer's policy permits it. In this scenario, the employer allows employees to take sick leave to care for a spouse. Answer C is wrong because FMLA permits the employer to require the use of all qualifying paid leave simultaneously with FMLA leave.

79. The correct answer is **C**. There is no entitlement to compensation while on FMLA leave. The employee is entitled to continuation of health insurance under the same conditions as before the leave began (answer A) and continued accrual of seniority (answer B). The employee, with limited exceptions, is entitled to reinstatement at the same or similar job (answer D).

80. The correct answer is **D**. Each quartile captures 25% of the date. In fact, what the CEO is requesting is referred to as the *interquartile range,* which captures the range of compensation rates being paid between the first (25% of the rates) and third (75% of the rates) quartiles. The mean (answer A) is the average rate being paid. The mode (answer B) is the most frequent rate being paid. The median (answer C) is the middle rate being paid.

81. The correct answer is **C**. Learning curves describe the rate at which learning occurs. Answer A is the definition of learning itself: a permanent change in behavior. The way people learn (answer B) is called a *learning style.* The amount that people learn (answer D) is the *learning level* and is frequently described in terms of Bloom's Taxonomy.

82. The correct answer is **B**. A copay is the amount that the employee pays for a covered service. Decreasing that amount would increase premium rates. Increasing the deductible amount before the insurance begins to cover medical services (answer A), decreasing the number of services that the insurance covers (answer C), and raising the proportion of insurance premium that the employee is required to pay (answer D) are all means by which the employer can reduce its health insurance benefit costs.

83. The correct answer is **C**. Job simplification would, in most instances, cause the employee to have even lower job satisfaction, leading to less organizational commitment and engagement. Job enlargement (answer A) is increasing the variety of tasks an individual is responsible for doing. Job rotation (answer B) is a type of job enlargement in which the employee is rotated from job to job. Job enrichment (answer D) is the vertical loading of the job by increasing skill variety, task identity, task significance, autonomy, and feedback. Job enlargement, job rotation, and job enrichment are all strategies used to keep employees facing career plateaus engaged and committed to the organization.

84. The correct answer is **B**. Organizing is the management function in which resources necessary to achieve the goal are allocated. Planning (answer A) involves determining the goals and deciding on activities required to accomplish them. Leading (answer C) involves directing and motivating employees to achieve the goals. Controlling (answer D) requires monitoring progress toward the goals and making changes when necessary.

85. The correct answer is **B**. The debt of owners' equity ratio provides a measure of the extent to which the organization relies on borrowed money and is calculated by dividing the total equity by the owners' equity. Inventory turnover ratio (answer A) is a measure of the organization's efficiency in using its assets. The current ratio (answer C) and the acid-test ratio (answer D) both evaluate the organization's capability to pay its short-term debts.

86. The correct answer is **B**. Rigidity is a disadvantage, not an advantage. Plans, after they're formulated, must be flexible and consistently reviewed. The strategic planning process provides guidance throughout the organization for action (answer A), forces organizational leaders to be forward-thinking (answer C) and is positively correlated with measures of organizational success when properly done (answer D). All these are advantages.

87. The correct answer is **C**. Lagging the market will likely result in increased turnover as employees leave to obtain more externally equitable wages. Lower quality (answer A) and quantity of production (answer B) are likely to occur, assuming that the employees have some control over production. Also overall compensation costs are likely to decrease (answer D).

88. The correct answer is **C**. It seems pretty clear that the employee should have been terminated based on the internal disciplinary record and a clear nexus between the external convictions and the nature of the employee's work. There is nothing in the scenario to indicate that the employer would be liable for negligent training (answer A), defamation (answer B), or negligent hiring (answer D).

89. The correct answer is **A**. HRD professionals often find that managerial first impressions are incorrect and that thorough needs analysis results in a fuller understanding of the performance gap and its causes. A lack of understanding of the importance of needs analysis (answer B), believing that performance data clearly indicate the cause of poor performance and the type of intervention needed (answer C), and a preference for action over analysis (answer D) all are reasons why needs analysis might be overlooked.

90. The correct answer is **B**. Compensable factors should be independent, not interdependent. Interdependent factors effectively result in measuring the same factor twice, giving it double weight. Compensable factors should be acceptable to employees (answer A) and should apply to all jobs being evaluated (answer C). Jobs should vary in the amount of compensable factor that is present so that the compensable factor can assist in determining the relative value of that job to the organization (answer D).

91. The correct answer is **D**. Learning and growth, not environmental impact, is the fourth measure of the balanced scorecard. The others are financial (answer A), customers (answer B), and internal business processes (answer C).

92. The correct answer is **C**. The Foreign Corrupt Practices Act of 1977, in general, prohibits bribes, payoffs, and kickbacks while conducting business in a foreign country. The Sarbanes-Oxley Act of 2002 (answer A) deals with violations of securities regulations. The False Claims Act of 1863 (answer B) deals with improprieties in federal contracts. The Civil Rights Act of 1991 (answer D) provides Title VII protections for United States citizens working for United States organizations in foreign countries.

93. The correct answer is **D**. Mandatory retirement is prohibited by ADEA except in certain limited situations. Seniority systems (answer A), BFOQ (answer B), and valid disciplinary actions (answer C) are exemptions to the act.

94. The correct answer is **B**. *Mackay* validated the right of an employer to permanently replace striking workers during an economic strike (answer A). *Beck* gave the right for bargaining unit employees to only pay that part of union dues directly related to the union's mainline responsibilities (answer C). *Weingarten* allows bargaining unit employees to have a representative present at investigatory interviews (answer D).

95. The correct answer is **B**. The Consumer Credit Protection Act (answer A) regulates, among other things, the garnishment of wages. The Rehabilitation Act (answer C) prohibits discrimination based on disability by federal contractors having contracts of at least $2,500. The Privacy Act (answer D) regulates the release of information about federal employees.

96. The correct answer is **C**. In the nominal group technique (answer A), the members meet face-to-face and each member presents a forecast before any discussion takes place. Statistical forecasts (answer B) use mathematical processes to determine forecasts. Managerial judgment (answer D) uses the experience and knowledge of managers and executives to develop forecasts.

97. The correct answer is **D**. The union must carry only a simple majority of those voting, not of those eligible to vote in the bargaining unit. A tie vote goes to the employer and the union does not become certified.

98. The correct answer is **C**. Succession planning (answer A) is more long-term in nature and identifies those employees who might be ready for promotion to specified jobs in the future. HRIS (answer B) is an integrated database that is much broader than the concept of replacement charts, but might, in fact, have the capability to identify potential candidates for specific job openings. *Promotion ledgers* (answer D) is not a term typically used in the HR function.

99. The correct answer is **D**. Selection (answer A) is the process used to choose individuals with the right qualifications to fill jobs openings in the organization. Placement (answer B) is the process of ensuring that the right person is placed in the right job. Person-job fit (answer C) is the process of ensuring that the knowledge, skills, and abilities of the individual match the requirements of the essential functions of the job.

100. The correct answer is **B**. Green circle rates are those below the minimum rate for the pay range; employers typically raise the rate to the minimum, assuming that the green circle rate is an isolated case. Freezing the employee's pay until captured in the pay range (answer A), reducing the pay to the maximum rate for the pay range (answer C), and noncompetitively promoting the employee to a higher pay grade (answer D) are all actions associated with red circle rates.

101. The correct answer is **C**. Briefly quoting from the copyrighted material for the purposes of criticism and review is considered fair use and does not infringe on the copyright. Distributing copyrighted material to the public without permission (answer A), performing the copyrighted material public without permission (answer B), and preparing derivative works (answer D) without permission all are infringements of the copyright.

102. The correct answer is **A**. TQM teams (answer B) and lean manufacturing teams (answer C) do not necessarily connote the right to make and implement decisions unilaterally. Cross-functional task forces (answer D) are not normally thought of as being high-performance work systems. They are one type of employee involvement activity.

103. The correct answer is **D**. Obtaining performance feedback from multiple raters and perspectives is an advantage, particularly in developing information for development purposes. The increased administrative burden (answer A), the various performance expectations among the raters (answer B), and the potential for considerable variability in ratings (answer C) are all disadvantages of 360° performance appraisal ratings.

104. The correct answer is **C**. The workforce is aging because of the impact of a large demographic cohort, referred to as "Baby Boomers," who were born between 1946 and 1964. The workforce is increasingly composed of women (answer A) and various minority groups (answer B). As already discussed, the workforce is aging (answer D).

105. The correct answer is **B**. The CIO was initially a federation of industrial unions, not craft unions. The rest of the answers are true with respect to the CIO.

106. The correct answer is **D**. Both the NLRB and the OSHRC adjudicate penalties and decisions of ALJ's under their respective acts. Answers A and B refer to the Civil Service Reform Act of 1978. NIOSH (answer C) is largely a research agency created under the Occupational Health and Safety Act.

107. The correct answer is **A**. Certain computer professionals might meet the test if they make $27.63 per hour if paid on an hour basis, not $34.00 per hour (answer B). Highly compensated employees could be exempt if they make more than $100,000 per year, but they must perform at least one executive, administrative, or professional task (answer C). The $455 per week applies to all workers, whether executive, administrative, or professional (answer D).

108. The correct answer is **B**. The HR strategic-planning process has traditionally been reactive and not simultaneous with the organizational strategic planning process. After the organization determines its strategic objectives, HR develops objectives to support those objectives. The HR strategic-planning process is very similar to the organizational strategic process (answer A) and involves a SWOT analysis (answer C). If properly executed, the process results in HR objectives that are in alignment with and support the accomplishment of the organization's strategic objectives (answer D).

109. The correct answer is **C**. It is employees, not unions, that are given these rights. Answers A, B, and D are provisions of the act.

110. The correct answer is **D**. Activity-based budgets allocate resources directly to the process or project, as opposed to the function or division. An incremental budget (answer A) uses the previous budget as a base, making adjustments up or down to individual line items, and is the traditional way of budgeting. A formula budget (answer B) is a type of incremental budget in which a specific percentage is added to or subtracted from each budget line item to create the new budget. A zero-based budget (answer C) is one that is developed from scratch each budgeting cycle with each budget item having to be justified.

111. The correct answer is **B**. The first-year ROI is calculated by dividing the benefits derived from the training in the first year ($12,500) by the first-year costs ($25,000) and multiplying the result by 100. Therefore, first-year ROI (12,500/25,000) ¥ 100 = 50%. Total ROI is calculated in the same manner (200,000/100,000) ¥ 100 = 200%. Answers A, C, and D are incorrect.

112. The correct answer is **A**. Effective ethics programs are driven by commitment at the top of the organization rather than by efforts at the lowest levels. Written codes of ethics and conduct (answer B), training on ethics at all levels of the organization (answer C), and a method of reporting ethical violations and obtaining ethical advice anonymously (answer D) are all elements of an effective ethics program.

113. The correct answer is **C**. Answer A is incorrect because only 30%, not 51%, of the prospective bargaining unit must sign the authorization cards to permit the union to petition for an election. Nothing precludes the union from asking the employer to view the cards at any time, although it would serve little purpose until at least 30%, and preferably 50%, of the prospective bargaining unit has signed the authorization cards (answer B). The union is barred from requesting a new election for a period of one year after a prior election (answer D).

114. The correct answer is **C**. Nothing in the act prohibits taking appropriate personnel actions even if they affect a pregnant employee. Transferring a pregnant employee because of concerns for the fetus (answer A) violates the act because the health of the fetus is the responsibility of the parents. If the employer provides short-term disability insurance (answer B), it must consider pregnancy the same way it considers any other short-term disability. Failing to hire an individual because she is pregnant or could become pregnant (answer D) violates the act.

115. The correct answer is **C**. Employee development programs would affect internal supply but not external supply. Unemployment rates (answer A), net migration in and out of the area (answer B), and economic conditions (answer D) all are factors that could affect the external supply of labor.

116. The correct answer is **B**. The Equal Pay Act of 1963 addresses only wages, not benefits. However, Title VII of the Civil Rights Act of 1964 prohibits illegal discrimination between the sexes in terms of benefits. Employers can pay differential compensation between the sexes if that compensation is based on quality or quantity of work output (answer A). The act does not cover differentials in pay between the sexes for jobs that are not similar (answer C). Although the FLSA is administered by the Department of Labor and the Equal Pay Act is an amendment to FLSA, enforcement of the Equal Pay Act is assigned to the EEOC (answer D).

117. The correct answer is **D**. Salting is a legal practice. Answers A, B, and C are all unfair labor practices.

118. The correct answer is **B**. Job evaluation (answer A) is the process of determining the relative worth of jobs to the organization. Workforce planning (answer C) is the process of determining future organizational employment needs. Job pricing (answer D) is the process of determining the appropriate compensation for the organization's jobs.

119. The correct answer is **B**. All the other answers are indications of failure to bargain in good faith. Answer A is often called *direct dealing*.

120. The correct answer is **D**. Appeals of OSHA citations are made to the Occupational Health and Safety Review Commission *(OSHRC)*. The NLRB, the National Labor Relations Board, deals with administration of the National Labor Relations Act (answer A). NIOSH, the National Institute of Safety and Health, is the agency established to perform research on safety and health matters and to assist OSHA with development of standards (answer B). FMCS, the Federal Mediation and Conciliation Service, was established by the Taft-Hartley Act to assist labor and management in resolving disagreements (answer C).

121. The correct answer is **B**. The adverse impact threshold is calculated by applying the 4/5ths rule to the highest selection rate. In this case, the highest selection rate is that of Caucasian males and is 60%. Applying the 4/5ths rule (.8 ¥ 60) yields an adverse impact threshold of 48%. Answers A, C, and D are incorrect.

122. The correct answer is **C**. The selection rate for Hispanic males of 40% is below the adverse impact threshold of 48%. Answer A is incorrect because there is adverse impact for Hispanic males. The selection rate for Native American males (answer B) is 56%, which is above the adverse impact threshold. The selection rate for African-American males (answer D) is 49%, which is also above the adverse impact threshold.

123. The correct answer is **D**. Answers A, B, and C are all associated with distributive bargaining. Answer D is another term for *integrative bargaining*.

124. The correct answer is **B**. Theory X managers view employees as lazy, disliking work, and avoiding responsibility. Theory Y managers takes the opposite view. Maslow's Hierarchy of Needs (answer A) states that there are five universal human needs arraigned in a hierarchy, and that lower needs must be essentially fulfilled before higher needs become motivating. Herzberg's Two-Factor Theory (answer C) states that there are two separate characteristics of the workplace, one that can create motivation or job satisfaction and another that can be demotivating and create job dissatisfaction. ERG Theory (answer D) is a rework of Maslow's five universal needs into three: existence, related-ness, and growth. ERG theory also states that there can be multiple needs motivating behavior at the same time.

125. The correct answer is **D**. Employees can continue their employer's health insurance for up to two years after being called to duty. Employers are prohibited from discriminating against the employee based on military duty or the potential for military duty (answer A), and they must reinstate the employee to the position that would have been obtained had military duty not interfered (answer B). Employers are required to provide reasonable accommodation if the employee becomes disabled as a result of his or her military duty (answer C).

126. The correct answer is **B**. Trait theories assume that leadership is the result of the personal charac-teristics of the individual. Behavioral and contingency leadership theories assume that leaders can be trained (answer A). Initiating and consideration structures (answer C) come from the Ohio State studies, and production-oriented and employee-oriented (answer D) leadership behaviors come from the University of Michigan studies. Both of these are behavioral theories of leadership.

127. The correct answer is **B**. To attempt to balance power in a lockout, permanent strike replacements are not allowed. They are, however, allowed in economic (answer A), recognition (answer C), and sympathy strikes (answer D).

128. The correct answer is **A**. Environmental scanning is, as its name implies, externally oriented, and does not evaluate the internal strengths and weaknesses of the organization. It does involve collecting and interpreting information from the environment (answer B) to determine changes and trends (answer D). It is integral to the SWOT process because the environmental-scanning information is used to determine opportunities and threats in the environment (answer C).

129. The correct answer is **C**. Sales and marketing is the organizational function that develops, prices, promotes, and distributes products, services, or knowledge that satisfies customer needs while facilitating the achievement of organizational goals. Operations management (answer A) is the organizational function that plans and analyzes activities by which the organization transforms inputs to outcomes. Financial management (answer B) is the organizational function responsible for accounting for and controlling the organization's resources. Information technology (answer D) is the organizational function that plans and manages computer systems.

130. The correct answer is **C**. Metrics are used as internal measures of performance. Benchmarks (answer A) are measures of performance of other organizations, and are used for comparison. Forecasts (answer B) are predictions of how a particular measure will change in the future, whereas scenarios (answer D) are general descriptions of what the future is likely to be.

131. The correct answer is **A**. Although the arbitrator may effectively write the contract in interest arbitration, that is not permissible in rights arbitration. The arbitrator must strictly interpret the contract language (answer B). If the language is ambiguous, the arbitrator may look at the intent of the parties with whom the particular article was negotiated (answer C) or the past practice (answer D) that has been commonly used in similar situations.

132. The correct answer is **C**. The Drug-Free Workplace Act applies to employers that receive federal contracts of at least $100,000 and to those that receive federal grants in any amount.

133. The correct answer is **A**. At the highest level of social responsibility, organizations pursue activities that make society better, even if those activities might not be the best for the organization. Organizations that engage in activities that are within the intent and spirit of the law (answer B) are operating at the second-highest level of social responsibility, often referred to as *social responsiveness*. Organizations that meet their legal obligations and not more (answer C) are operating at the next-to-lowest level, which is often referred to as *social obligation*. Organizations that believe most activities are okay and try to not get caught acting unethically (answer D) operate at the lowest level of social responsibility, sometimes referred to as *indifference*.

134. The correct answer is **B**. A performance-based system would base compensation, raises, and some benefits on individual, group, or organizational performance (answer A). Leading (answer C) or lagging the market (answer D) has to do with the relationship of internal compensation rates to the external market and not with how raises, bonuses, and promotions are determined.

135. The correct answer is **B**. Union density in the public sector is around 37%, whereas it is about 13% in the private sector.

136. The correct answer is **C**. Form I-9 must be completed within 72 hours of hiring and kept for a minimum of three years or one year after the employee leaves employment. Answers A, B, and D are incorrect.

137. The correct answer is **C**. External compensation rate determination is part of the job-pricing process, not job analysis. Determining tasks (answer A) and employee behaviors (answer B) required by the job are part of the job analysis process, as is the determination of machines used on the job (answer D).

138. The correct answer is **C**. Snap judgment (answer A) occurs when the interviewers make up their minds in the first few minutes of the interview. The horn effect (answer B) occurs when a negative impression on one characteristic causes the interviewer to judge all characteristics negatively. Contrast error (answer D) occurs when the interviewer judges the candidate against the prior interviewee rather than against objective criteria.

139. The correct answer is **D**. Answer D appears to violate the public policy exemption of at-will employment. The employee in answer A would normally have to pursue the improper termination through the negotiated grievance procedure. Answers B and C are normally considered proper/legal terminations.

140. The correct answer is **A**. The point factor and factor comparison methods of job evaluation are quantitative methods that use compensable factors. Answers B, C, and D are incorrect because ranking and job classification are whole job, nonquantitative methods of job evaluation.

141. The correct answer is **B**. A 60-day advance notice is required when 500 or more employees are to be laid off. Answer A is incorrect because 60, not 30, days advance notice is required and because 300 employees does not constitute 33% of the organization's workforce. Answer C is incorrect because the layoff is fewer than 50 employees and because the advance notice requirement is 60 days. Answer D is incorrect because a layoff of 50 or more employees must constitute at least 33% of the organization's workforce to come under coverage of the act.

142. The correct answer is **B**. A banquet arrangement facilitates both the meal and the small group exercises. The classroom (answer A) and theatre (answer D) arrangements are more suited for large audiences where the delivery method is a lecture. The rectangle arrangement facilitates inter-group interaction of mid-sized groups (fewer than 20) and does not work as well for meals (answer C).

143. The correct answer is **B**. Technically a local union could be an independent union, serving only one bargaining union (answer A). A federation is an organization of national unions as in the AFL-CIO (answer C). Although a few national unions use the term *international* in their title, international unions are typically federations of various national federated unions or confederations (answer D). An example is the International Confederation of Free Trade Unions *(ICFTU)*.

144. The correct answer is **B**. Return on equity is a measure of profitability and is calculated by dividing net income after taxes by owners' equity. Inventory turnover ratio (answer A) is a measure of the organization's efficiency in using its assets. Debt of owners' equity (answer C) is a measure of the extent to which the organization relies on borrowed money. The current ratio (answer D) evaluates the organization's current assets against its current liabilities.

145. The correct answer is **C**. The maturity stage is characterized by maximum revenue but decreased profits. During this stage, the organization might become somewhat bureaucratic, inflexible, and nonadaptive to the environment. In the introduction stage (answer A), the organization is simple and flat, devoting its energy to surviving and growing. At this stage, the organization begins the process of formalization and attempts to improve the efficiency of internal operations. In the growth stage (answer B), the organization attempts to expand its market share and become profitable. In the decline stage (answer D), the organization is noncompetitive in the market.

146. The correct answer is **B**. MBO is the practical application of Goal-Setting Theory, incorporating the concepts of SMART objectives, feedback, and reward. Equity Theory deals with perceptions of equity of outcomes to inputs between the employee and others and is not a basic premise of MBO (answer A). Fiedler's Contingency Theory (answer C) and Leader-Member Exchange Theory (answer D) are theories of leadership, not motivation.

147. The correct answer is **A**. Unfair labor practices for unions are a provision of the Taft-Hartley Act (1947). Answers B, C, and D are all provisions of the Landrum-Griffin Act (1959).

148. The correct answer is **C**. The scenario clearly depicts a fee-for-service plan. HMOs (health maintenance organizations) require a small copay, but restrict selection of providers to those within the HMO (answer A). A PPO (preferred provider organization) is similar to an HMO when using medical providers belonging to the PPO, but similar to a fee-for-service plan when using providers that are not participants in the plan (answer B). Because the employee did not receive reduced prices for using a particular medical provider, answer B is incorrect. An HDHP (high deductible health plan) is a component of health savings accounts and must have a minimum $1,000 deductible (answer D).

149. The correct answer is **A**. HRD can guarantee skills or knowledge through testing and confidence through the inclusion of practice into the program. However, only management can provide an opportunity to perform what is learned on the job and a supportive environment in terms of the tools, equipment, and encouragement to do so.

150. The correct answer is **C**. Gainsharing plans are considered group incentive, plans not individual incentive plans. Piece rates (answer A), sales commissions (answer B), and standard hour plans (answer D) are all individual incentive plans.

151. The correct answer is **D**. Answer A is *Communication Workers of America v. Beck.* Answer B is *Circuit City Stores, Inc. v. Adams.* Answer C is *NLRB v. Wooster Division of Borg-Warner Corporation.*

152. The correct answer is **D**. Life insurance in excess of $50,000 is taxable imputed income. The amount of the income is based on the theoretical cost of insurance premiums for the additional amount paid on the employee's behalf by the employer. The IRS provides tables used to determine the taxable amount. Life insurance provided by the employer in the amounts of $5,000 (answer A), $10,000 (answer B), and $25,000 (answer C) are not considered taxable income.

153. The correct answer is **B**. United States government works (unless classified) and works on which the copyright has expired are considered to be in the public domain and can be copied, distributed, and used for other purposes. Fair use (answer A) refers to limited use of copyrighted material for certain purposes such as education. Answers C and D are incorrect: Copyrights cannot be extended, and the reference to 120 and 95 years has to do with anonymous and pseudonym authors, not United States government publications.

154. The correct answer is **C**. Pattern bargaining occurs when a union selects a major employer and negotiates a labor agreement using that agreement as a pattern for negotiating with other employers in the industry (answer A). Centralized bargaining occurs at the corporate headquarters level (usually on a companywide basis) with officials of the national union (answer B). Multiemployer bargaining occurs when more than one employer negotiates with a union at the same time (answer D).

155. The correct answer is **D**. The mission statement is internal to the organization and not part of the environment. Federal laws and regulations (answer A), societal expectations (answer B), and competition (answer C) are all components of the environment.

156. The correct answer is **D**. The data collection and data analysis steps are separate, as opposed to one step. Problem identification (answer A), hypothesis development (answer B), and research design (answer C) are all separate steps in the five-step scientific method systematic process.

157. The correct answer is **C**. There is no FLSA requirement to pay either time-and-one-half (answer A) or double time (answer B) for time worked over eight hours in a workday. However, this is a requirement for employees of the federal government and might be a requirement under state or local compensation laws. FLSA does not require payment of a premium for time worked on a holiday unless that time would exceed forty hours in the workweek (answer D). In that case, payment would be at time-and-one-half.

158. The correct answer is **B**. The bill is vetoed by no action of the president and does not become law. Answers A, C, and D are incorrect.

159. The correct answer is **B**. Banks may not use polygraph test as a pre-employment screening device. The federal government, drug manufacturers, and armored car providers, within certain limitations, are all permitted to use polygraph tests as a prescreen under the act.

160. The correct answer is **B**. A closed shop requires the employee to be a union member prior to hire (answer A). This question might be a bit tricky because the employee could effectively make it an agency shop, but she refused to pay any funds to the union (answer C). An open shop (answer D) does not require the employee either to join the union or pay dues.

161. The correct answer is **B**. A work breakdown structure divides the total project into its component parts and identifies how long the task will take and who will be responsible for doing it. A statement of work (answer A) is a broad written description of the project. PERT, which stands for *Performance Evaluation and Review Technique* (answer C), and CPM, which stands for *Critical Path Method* (answer D), are used to determine the proper flow of the work; that is, the order in which the tasks and activities must be performed.

162. The correct answer is **C**. Gantt charts can be used to visually display such information as planned starting and ending times, actual starting and ending times, and how each task or activity fits in with the overall schedule. PERT (answer A) and CPM (answer B) are used to determine the order in which tasks must be done. WBS, the work breakdown structure (answer D), shows the total project divided into its component tasks, time required for the tasks, and who is responsible for the tasks.

163. The correct answer is **C**. Slack or float is created by tasks that are not on the critical path. The mandatory order in which tasks must be completed (answer A) and the least possible time in which the project can be completed (answer B) are both determined by the critical path. The critical path is that path of activities that must be most closely monitored (answer D) because any delay in activities on the critical path will likely delay the entire project.

164. The correct answer is **A**. Job specialization, or division of labor, refers to how much the work of the organization is broken down into its component parts or simplified. Formalization (answer B) is the extent to which work assignments are standardized through job descriptions, policies, and standard operating procedures. Departmentation (answer C) is the framework by which work and workers are organized. Span of control (answer D) is the number of workers assigned to one supervisor.

165. The correct answer is **C**. Allowing arbitrators to deal with alleged violations of the contract and commission of a ULP is known as the *Collyer Doctrine* and is based on an NLRB decision. Answers A, B, and D all flow from the *Steelworkers Trilogy*.

166. The correct answer is **A**. Cliff vesting occurs when employees have no vested rights for a defined number of years, but become 100% vested when the required number of years is obtained. Answer B is the minimum graded vesting system under ERISA for a defined benefit plan that is not considered top heavy. Answer C is the minimum graded vesting schedule for the employer-matching portion of a defined contribution plan. Answer D is wrong in that cliff vesting is permitted under ERISA.

167. The correct answer is **A**. The requirements to qualify for workers' compensation are substantially different from those that define disability under ADA. Employees with either a physical or mental impairment that substantially limits one or more major life functions (answer B), that have a record of such impairment (answer C), or that are regarded or treated as having an impairment (answer D) meet the definition of "disabled individual" under the act.

168. The correct answer is **C**. Employer logs are used to have the worker perform self-observation, recording exactly what tasks are being done at periodic intervals during the day. Observation (answer A) occurs when the person doing job analysis observes the worker and records what tasks are being performed. A questionnaire (answer B) requests that the worker respond to a written survey regarding job duties. Critical incidents (answer D) are recordation of positive and negative job performance.

169. The correct answer is **D**. Severance pay is a strategy for minimizing the impact of a layoff, but not for avoiding one. Early retirement incentives (answer A), part-time work (answer B), and attrition (answer C) are all strategies for avoiding having to lay off employees.

170. The correct answer is **D**. Unfair labor practice strikes are protected activities under the law. Jurisdictional strikes are never protected and are an unfair labor practice on the part of the union (answer A). If a no-strike clause is in the contract, both wildcat and sympathy strikes become unprotected and striking employees are subject to discipline (answers B and C).

171. The correct answer is **C**. The theory assumes that leaders use a fixed style that is either task-oriented or relationship-oriented and that a leader can't change his or her style. Other research has identified a number of potential styles, and the fact that leaders can learn to adjust their style to the contingencies of the situation. That contingencies give the leader more or less control in the work-place (answer A) is a concept associated with Fiedler's Contingency Theory, which has not been broadly disputed. Answers B and D are results of research using the theory, and have been duplicated consistently.

172. The correct answer is **A**. A forecast is used to predict the future value of some measure. Information about competitors that allows the organization to better compete in the environment (answer B) is referred to as *competitive intelligence*. General descriptions of the future (answer C) are scenarios, whereas comparisons of the organization's internal operations to those of other organizations (answer D) are benchmarks.

173. The correct answer is **C**. Reliable measures yield the same results on multiple measurements. Content validity (answer A) is the extent to which the measurement contains actual elements of what it is intended to measure. Construct validity (answer B) is the capability of the measurement to measure theoretical traits or characteristics such as intelligence. Criterion-related validity (answer D) is the extent to which the measurement predicts performance.

174. The correct answer is **C**. The instrumentality is the linkage between a first-level and second-level outcome; in this case, the linkage between the performance first-level outcome of an outstanding performance rating and the second-level reward outcome of a bonus. Motivation (answer A) encompasses the whole expectancy theory formula. Expectancy (answer B) is the effort-performance link-age, which is the expectancy that a certain level of effort leads to a specific performance rating. Valence (answer D) is the value that the employee places on the reward; in this case, the bonus.

175. The correct answer is **A**. The list of employees eligible to vote in the election along with their home addresses must be provided to NLRB within seven days. The NLRB then provides the list to the union. Answers B, C, and D are incorrect.

176. The correct answer is **C**. The union must not coerce votes or threaten reprisal for not voting for the union. To do so is an unfair labor practice. Unions, but not employers, may promise benefits dur-ing the election campaign to entice votes (answer A). Unions, but not management, may visit employees at home (answer B). It is legal for the union to attempt to get paid organizers hired with the firm to assist in the election campaign (answer D). This is called *salting*.

177. The correct answer is **B**. Employers can hold mandatory meetings, referred to as *captive audience meetings*, but the union has no such capability. Both the union and employer can hire consultants to assist with the election campaign (answer A). The employer cannot promise new or increased benefits during the election campaign (answer C). To do so is an unfair labor practice. Both the employer and the union (because of the *Excelsior* List) can send election campaign materials to the employee's home address (answer D).

178. The correct answer is **B**, the Health Insurance Portability and Accountability Act (1996). FLSA, the Fair Labor Standards Act of 1938, provides for minimum wage, overtime, restrictions on child labor, and equal pay (answer A). FMLA, the Family and Medical Leave Act of 1993, provides for up to 12 weeks of unpaid leave for certain qualifying events (answer C). USERRA, the Uniformed Services Employment and Reemployment Act of 1994, provides certain benefits for employees called to duty in the military (answer D).

179. The correct answer is **A**. The forcing strategy of overcoming resistance to change is through the use of power, coercion, and punishment. The reward strategy (answer B) involves offering a reward in exchange for compliance with the change. The communication strategy (answer C) is the rational approach, assuming that resistance can be eliminated by a rational explanation of the need for change. Finally, the participation strategy (answer D) assumes that employee input into the design and implementation of the change effort minimizes resistance.

180. The correct answer is **D**. The strategic role involves proactive planning to assist the organization in planning the future. Workforce planning, change management, and planning and executing mergers and acquisitions are all activities associated with the strategic role. The administrative role (answer A) involves clerical administration, personnel process, and record-keeping. The operational role (answer B) involves the planning, implementing, and evaluating of various HR programmatic activities in support of the organization's goals. The employee advocate role (answer C) deals with treating employees fairly and accommodating various work-related needs.

181. The correct answer is **D**. Simply because the incumbent of the job typically performs a function does not necessarily mean that it is an essential function of that job. If a function is the reason that the job exists (answer A), cannot be assigned to another employee (answer B), and requires skills not found in employees in other job categories (answer C), it is likely to be an essential function.

182. The correct answer is **C**. The identification section (answer A) contains general information about the job, such as the job title and the department in which it is located. The position summary (answer B) is a concise statement that indicates what the job actually does. The essential functions section (answer D) specifies the major or critical duties of the job.

183. The correct answer is **B**. Essential functions (answer A) are those duties that constitute the most important components of the job. Job specifications (answer C) are the KSAs that a job incumbent should possess to perform the job successfully. Nonessential functions (answer D) are other duties of the job, but are of minor importance.

184. The correct answer is **C**. The departmentation is by division, not function, and the division reflects separate customer bases. Functional by customer (answer A) and functional by geography (answer B) are not correct. Departmentation by function structures the organization around common work processes such as finance, operations, and HR. Divisional by process (answer D) is not correct because the four divisions are presumed to be basically the same process that is delivered to different customer bases.

185. The correct answer is **C**. Employee and labor relations rights of state and local government employees are covered by state law, if any. Both the Wagner Act (answer A) and Taft-Hartley (answer D) regulate labor relations in the private sector. The Civil Service Reform Act covers federal employees (answer B).

186. The correct answer is **D**. Strategic planning is central to the organization's success and is typically not outsourced. Payroll processing (answer A), benefits administration (answer B), and administration of the 401(k) plans (answer C) are frequently outsourced because external vendors might be able to offer cost savings through economies of scale and provide expertise that is not available internally.

187. The correct answer is **A**. Predictive validity is one type of criterion-related validity that involves testing employees and then correlating the test with some measure at a later date. Concurrent validity (answer B) is the other type of criterion-related validity, but involves testing current employees and correlating test scores with some measure of performance. Content validity (answer C) is proven if the measurement contains actual examples of what it is intended to measure. Construct validity (answer D) means that the measure is able to gauge a theoretical trait or characteristic, such as intelligence.

188. The correct answer is **C**. Stock grants raise overall compensation costs and are not in alignment with a cost minimization business strategy. Lagging the market (answer A), piecework systems (answer B), and short-term bonuses based on efficiency goals (answer D) are all appropriate with a business strategy of cost minimization.

189. The correct answer is **C**. Increased outsourcing and subcontracting, not decreased usage, is an evolving issue in HR management today. Movement of HR from an administrative to a strategic role (answer A), aging of the workforce (answer B), and increased use of the contingent workforce (answer D) are also evolving issues for HR.

190. The correct answer is **A**. Reasonable accommodation is required only if the employee is both disabled and qualified to perform the essential functions of the job with or without reasonable accommodation. The intent of the law is that the process be interactive (answer B). Prior to making a determination on the request for accommodation, the employer may require medical documentation of the nature and extent of the disability (answer C). The accommodation may not create an undue hardship on the employer's part (answer D).

191. The correct answer is **A**. Answer B is the North American Agreement on Labor Cooperation (NAALC). Unfortunately, there is no worldwide organization for negotiating and enforcing labor standards (answer C). The National Administrative Office was created to monitor and enforce NAALC (answer D).

192. The correct answer is **B**. Answers A, C, and D are examples of likely wrongful terminations.

193. The correct answer is **C**. EAPs are a critical component of workforce violence-prevention programs because early intervention has proven to be effective. Therefore, termination of such programs would not be appropriate. Answers A, B, and D are normal program components.

194. The correct answer is **C**. A common characteristic of employees with a high potential for violence is an intense interest in guns and military history. Answers A, B, and D are all characteristics associated with a potentially violent employee.

195. The correct answer is **A**. The ranker is using the paired comparison method, which is one of the techniques used in the ranking method of job evaluation. Job classification (answer B) compares the job description of the job to be evaluated against generic job descriptions at various grade levels and determines the closest match. The point factor method (answer C) evaluates the amount of each compensable factor in a job and awards points based on that evaluation. The points for the job are totaled and equated to a pay grade. The factor comparison method (answer D) assesses the compensable factors of the job under evaluation with predetermined pay rates for each compensable factor. Each compensable factor is assigned a rate of pay and those rates are added up to determine the total hourly rate of pay.

196. The correct answer is **D**. The program is being evaluated at the results level, directly measuring impact on the gap determined by needs analysis. However, HRD cannot unequivocally claim that the program caused the results without a control group. Answers A, B, and C are incorrect.

197. The correct answer is **D**. All these concepts are based on the traditions and judicial precedents of common law. They do not come from international law (answer A), state law (answer B), or federal law (answer C).

198. The correct answer is **A**. Financial accounting involves analysis of financial data for external use. Tax accounting (answer B) involves the preparation of tax forms and documents. Managerial accounting (answer C) provides financial data for internal use in decision-making. Auditing (answer D) is the process of reviewing the accuracy of internal accounting practices.

199. The correct answer is **D**. A values statement describes the basic beliefs of the organization. A vision statement (answer A) describes the organization's desired future state. A code of conduct (answer B) provides guidance to employees as to what is acceptable and unacceptable behavior. A mission statement (answer C) describes the fundamental purpose of the organization.

200. The correct answer is **B**. Organizationwide incentive plans do not clearly link individual performance to the incentive reward. This occurs for several reasons. The employee might be an outstanding performer but receive no reward at all, as in a profit-sharing plan when there is no profit during the incentive plan year. The length of time between performance and subsequent reward might be too long to clearly link the two. Finally, oftentimes all employees share in the organizationwide reward even if their performance is marginal. Promoting a sense of belonging and commitment to the organization (answer A), increasing employee retention (answer C), and potential tax advantages for both the organization and the employee (answer D) are all considered to be advantages of organizationwide incentive plans.

201. The correct answer is **C**. Lockouts are a management tactic to apply economic pressure on the union and its members to agree to contract provisions. Corporate campaigns, work slowdowns, and boycotts (answers A, B, and D) are all union tactics.

202. The correct answer is **B**. Adults do not come to the program with a clean slate. They have a background of knowledge and experience that should be considered the floor from which the program begins. If there is a variance of knowledge and experience level among the participants, they should be given an opportunity to test out or be exempt from the lower-level training. Providing interim test and exercises (answer A), involving the participants in the planning and implementation of the program (answer C), and explaining the importance of learning the material (answer D) are all implications based on the assumptions of andragogy.

203. The correct answer is **B**. The act permits compensatory and punitive damages up to $300,000, not $500,000. Prohibitions against race-norming (answer A) and "mixed motive" defenses (answer C) are provisions of the act. Extension of the rights protected under the Civil Rights Act of 1964 to United States citizens working for United States organizations in foreign countries unless those rights violate local law or custom (answer D) is also a provision of the Civil Rights Act of 1991.

204. The correct answer is **D**. The departmentation is a matrix structure combining departmentation by function (HR) and by division (International Operations). It violates the unity of command principle, which states that an employee should report to only one supervisor. Answer A is incorrect because the departmentation is a matrix structure and span of control is not an organizing principle *per se*, but one of six elements used to describe organizational structure. Answer B identifies the departmentation correctly but refers to span of control, which is incorrect as described earlier. Answer C is incorrect because the departmentation is not by function alone.

205. The correct answer is **A**. Rights arbitration is used to settle disputes regarding contract administration (answer B). Mediation is the process of attempting to get the two parties to reach a voluntary agreement (answer C). Fact-finding is the process whereby a neutral third party investigates the bargaining dispute and issues a report containing nonbinding recommendations (answer D).

206. The correct answer is **B**. *McDonnell-Douglas v. Green* is the precedent case for adverse treatment. *Griggs v. Duke Power* (answer A) is the precedent case for adverse impact. *Regents of the University of California v. Bakke* (answer C) is the precedent case for reverse discrimination. *Meritor Savings Band v. Vinson* (answer D) is the precedent case for hostile workplace environment.

207. The correct answer is **B**. Employees must be at least 17 years of age to drive a car on public highways as part of their job responsibilities. A 14-year-old may be employed in a limited number of nonagricultural jobs, such as delivering newspapers and acting (answer A). Fourteen- and fifteen-year-olds may work in nonhazardous service industry jobs such as those in restaurants, but there are restrictions on the number of hours and the time of day they can work, depending on whether school is in session (answer C). There are no limitations on the number of hours that 16- and 17-year-olds can work (answer D). These are the FLSA rules, but individual states might have stricter rules for employees under 18.

208. The correct answer is **B**. Employers with more than 100 employees are required to file and EEO-1 report but not an AAP. Federal contractors with 50 or more employees and federal contracts of at least $50,000 (answer A), depositories of federal funds (answer C), and issuing or paying agents for United States savings bonds or notes (answer D) are all required to submit written affirmative action plans.

209. The correct answer is **A**. Because internal employees do not get to compete for the position, external recruiting is thought to reduce internal workforce morale. Bringing in new ideas (answer B), access to expertise not currently available internally (answer C), and facilitating diversity initiatives (answer D) are all considered to be advantages of recruiting externally.

210. The correct answer is **B**. The only union security provision that is legal in right-to-work states is the open shop. The Wagner Act does not prohibit the open shop and specifically permits it under the Taft-Hartley Act amendments (answer A). An open shop does not give monopolistic power to the employer. It is still obligated to abide by the provisions of the labor agreement, which presumably provides numerous protections for employees (answer C). Union members are not a protected class under the civil rights laws (answer D).

211. The correct answer is **A**. A situation in which women are promoted only so far up in the organization is referred to as a *glass ceiling* (answer B). Treating protected classes differently from other classes is disparate treatment (answer C). Neutral employment practices that disproportionately negatively impact protected classes is referred to as *disparate* or *adverse impact* (answer D).

212. The correct answer is **C**. Questionnaires can reach a large number of persons cost-effectively and the process yields quantifiable data that can be analyzed statistically. Interviews (answer A) and observations (answer B) are very time-consuming and expensive for the number of employees involved. In addition, it is doubtful that job satisfaction could be determined by observation. Organizations are not likely to have data regarding job satisfaction in their databases (answer D) and, if so, it would likely be dated.

213. The correct answer is **C**. The statement of cash flows reports cash receipts and disbursements for a defined time period. The balance sheet (answer A) reports the organization's overall financial condition as of a certain date. The income statement (answer B) shows whether the organization is making a profit or loss. The acid-test (answer D) is not a financial test *per se* but a financial ratio. The acid-test is a measure of the organization's capability to pay its short-term debts.

214. The correct answer is **A**. The Leader-Member Exchange Theory states that managers place some employees in an "in" group, treat them differently, provide better developmental opportunities and support and, as a result, the employees are highly productive and have better job satisfaction. Path-Goal Theory (answer B) states that the leader's job is to provide that which is missing in either the characteristics of subordinates or of the environment. Situational Leadership Theory (answer C) is predicated on leaders changing their style of leadership to best fit the readiness of their subordinates to accomplish assigned tasks. The Leader-Participation Model (answer D) is more aligned with decision-making strategy than leadership, and provides a model to determine how much participation followers should have in decisions.

215. The correct answer is **D**. Employees do not typically believe that a union can cause managers to be fired because this is a protected management right. Answers A, B, and C reflect research findings on why employees are attracted to unions and vote for union certification.

216. The correct answer is **C**. The research on improved productivity is mixed but even if productivity is improved, that increase is not likely to offset the increased compensation costs. Therefore profitability is not likely to go up and, in fact, is more likely to go down. Answers A, B, and D are impacts of unionism.

217. The correct answer is **C**. Union labor agreements typically override the employment-at-will doctrine with a just cause discipline and termination provision. Answers A, B, and D are actions that would provide benefits equivalent to the union, and therefore tend to make the union irrelevant.

218. The correct answer is **C**. Termination or reduction of hours resulting in loss of health insurance coverage entitles the employee to continuation of coverage for 18 months. Death of the employee, divorce or separation, or if a dependent child loses eligibility are all events that entitle an eligible individual, depending on the qualifying event, to continuation of coverage for 36 months (answer A). An eligible employee that is disabled at the time of loss of coverage is entitled to 29 months of continuation of coverage (answer B). Answer D is incorrect. Employees that lose coverage because of loss of hours, making them part-time employees, are entitled to continuation of coverage if they had coverage previously.

219. The correct answer is **A**. Outsourcing contracts normally specify only the work that is to be accomplished. It is up to the vendor to determine how the work is to be done. Decreased costs (answer B), access to expertise (answer C), and access to sophisticated technology (answer D) are all considered advantages of outsourcing.

220. The correct answer is **D**. The complaint should be filed directly with the appropriate NLRB Regional Director.

221. The correct answer is **C**. Under the new psychological contract, the employer does not expect, and might not want, the employee to stay with the organization for an entire career. Portable benefits (answer A), challenging work leading to individual growth (answer B), and externally equitable and competitive wages (answer D) are all employee expectations under the new contract.

222. The correct answer is **D**. By ignoring the complaint, you engaged in extinction. Behavior that is not reinforced tends to dissipate. Positive reinforcement (answer A) is rewarding desired behavior. Negative reinforcement (answer B) is the removal of something unpleasant when a particular behavior is displayed. Punishment (answer C) is the imposition of negative consequences when a particular behavior is displayed.

223. The correct answer is **A**. Control of the means and methods of work is the purview of the independent contractor. If the employer attempts to control day-to-day work, it will likely create an employer-employee relationship. The employer-independent contractor relationship eliminates the requirements of providing benefits (answer B), complying with FLSA (answer C), and having to withhold taxes and Social Security (answer D).

224. The correct answer is **D**. The rates of pay for benchmark jobs must be determined before the job evaluation process can begin. Ranking (answer A), job classification (answer B), and point factor (answer C) methods of job evaluation determine the rate of pay for benchmark jobs after the job evaluation process is complete.

225. The correct answer is **C**. The manufacturing sector is largely saturated in terms of union density and is declining in terms of percentage of the workforce it employs. The other answers (A, B, and D) are recent strategies and activities brought about by changes of the twenty-first century.

PART III

Appendixes

APPENDIX A

CD Contents and Installation Instructions

The CD features an innovative practice test engine powered by MeasureUp, giving you yet another effective tool to assess your readiness for the exam.

Multiple Test Modes

MeasureUp practice tests are available in Study, Certification, Custom, Adaptive, Missed Question, and Non-Duplicate question modes.

Study Mode

Tests administered in Study Mode allow you to request the correct answer(s) and explanation to each question during the test. These tests are not timed. You can modify the testing environment *during* the test by selecting the Options button.

Certification Mode

Tests administered in Certification Mode closely simulate the actual testing environment you will encounter when taking a certification exam. These tests do not allow you to request the answer(s) and/or explanation to each question until after the exam.

Custom Mode

Custom Mode allows you to specify your preferred testing environment. Use this mode to specify the objectives you want to include in your test, the timer length, and other test properties. You can also modify the testing environment *during* the test by selecting the Options button.

Adaptive Mode

Tests administered in Adaptive Mode closely simulate the actual testing environment you will encounter when taking an Adaptive exam. After answering a question, you are not allowed to go back; you only are allowed to move forward during the exam.

Missed Question Mode

Missed Question Mode allows you to take a test containing only the questions you have missed previously.

Non-Duplicate Mode

Non-Duplicate Mode allows you to take a test containing only questions not displayed previously.

Question Types

The practice question types simulate the real exam experience. For a complete description of each question type, please visit http://www.microsoft.com/learning/mcpexams/faq/innovations. asp.

The different types of questions you might encounter include

- ▶ Create a Tree Type
- ▶ Select and Place
- ▶ Drop and Connect
- ▶ Build List
- ▶ Reorder List
- ▶ Build and Reorder List
- ▶ Single Hotspot
- ▶ Multiple Hotspots
- ▶ Live Screen
- ▶ Command-Line
- ▶ Hot Area

Random Questions and Order of Answers

This feature helps you learn the material without memorizing questions and answers. Each time you take a practice test, the questions and answers appear in a different randomized order.

Detailed Explanations of Correct and Incorrect Answers

You'll receive automatic feedback on all correct and incorrect answers. The detailed answer explanations are a superb learning tool in their own right.

Attention to Exam Objectives

MeasureUp practice tests are designed to appropriately balance the questions over each technical area covered by a specific exam.

Installing the CD

The minimum system requirements for the CD-ROM are

- ▶ Windows 95, 98, Me, NT4, 2000, or XP

- ▶ 7MB disk space for testing engine

- ▶ An average of 1MB disk space for each test

To install the CD-ROM, follow these instructions:

> **NOTE**
>
> If you need technical support, please contact MeasureUp at 678-356-5050 or email support@ measureup.com. Additionally, you'll find Frequently Asked Questions (FAQs) at www.measureup.com.

1. Close all applications before beginning this installation.

2. Insert the CD into your CD-ROM drive. If the setup starts automatically, go to step 6. If the setup does not start automatically, continue with step 3.

3. From the Start menu, select Run.

4. Click Browse to locate the MeasureUp CD. In the Browse dialog box, from the Look In drop-down list, select the CD-ROM drive.

5. In the Browse dialog box, double-click on `Setup.exe`. In the Run dialog box, click OK to begin the installation.

6. On the Welcome Screen, click MeasureUp Practice Questions to begin installation.

7. Follow the Certification Prep Wizard by clicking Next.

8. To agree to the Software License Agreement, click Yes.

9. On the Choose Destination Location screen, click Next to install the software to C:\Program Files\Certification Preparation.

> **NOTE**
>
> If you cannot locate MeasureUp Practice Tests through the Start menu, see the section later in this appendix titled "Creating a Shortcut to the MeasureUp Practice Tests."

10. On the Setup Type screen, select Typical Setup. Click Next to continue.

11. In the Select Program Folder screen you can name the program folder your tests will be in. To select the default, simply click next and the installation will continue.

12. After the installation is complete, verify that Yes, I Want to Restart My Computer Now is selected. If you select No, I Will Restart My Computer Later, you will not be able to use the program until you restart your computer.

13. Click Finish.

14. After restarting your computer, choose Start, Programs, MeasureUp Practice Tests, Launch.

15. On the MeasureUp Welcome Screen, click Create User Profile.

16. In the User Profile dialog box, complete the mandatory fields and click Create Profile.

17. Select the practice test you want to access and click Start Test.

Creating a Shortcut to the MeasureUp Practice Tests

To create a shortcut to the MeasureUp Practice Tests, follow these steps.

1. Right-click on your Desktop.

2. From the shortcut menu select New, Shortcut.

3. Browse to C:\Program Files\MeasureUp Practice Tests and select the MeasureUpCertification.exe or Localware.exe file.

4. Click OK.

5. Click Next.

6. Rename the shortcut MeasureUp.

7. Click Finish.

After you have completed step 7, use the MeasureUp shortcut on your Desktop to access the MeasureUp products you ordered.

Technical Support

If you encounter problems with the MeasureUp test engine on the CD-ROM, please contact MeasureUp at 678-356-5050, or email support@measureup.com. Technical support hours are from 8 a.m. to 5 p.m. EST Monday through Friday. Additionally, you'll find Frequently Asked Questions (FAQ) at www.measureup.com.

If you'd like to purchase additional MeasureUp products, telephone 678-356-5050 or 800-649-1MUP (1687), or visit www.measureup.com.

Glossary

360° Interview A selection interview that is conducted by a panel of interviewers representing various constituencies in order to get a broad perspective regarding the evaluation of the candidate.

4/5ths Rule A method of proving adverse impact; found in the *Uniform Guidelines for Employee Selection Procedures*.

A

***Abermarle Paper Company v. Moody* (1975)** The Supreme Court decision that expanded the guidance provided in *Griggs* clarifying that employment tests, including performance evaluation systems, used to make employment decisions must not only be job-related but must also be valid predictors of performance on the job.

Accounting The process of collecting, recording, summarizing, and analyzing financial data.

Activity-Based Budget One that allocates resources to processes or projects rather than to organizational functions or departments.

ADDIE The steps in the HRD process: needs **A**ssessment, program **D**esign, program **D**evelopment, program **I**mplementation, and program **E**valuation.

Administrative Role One of the three management roles of HR; involves clerical administration, personnel processing, and record keeping.

Adverse Impact Occurs when the overall impact of an employer's employment practices negatively affects members of a protected class in a significant way. It is also referred to as *disparate impact*.

Affirmative Action A process by which employers engage in employment practices designed to eliminate the present effects of past discrimination.

Affirmative Action Plan A written document required of certain federal contractors that analyzes the internal workforce against the availability of workers by gender and ethnicity. If underutilization of protected classes is determined, the employer must develop action plans and associated programmatic activities to eliminate or reduce the underutilization.

Affirmative Defense A method of avoiding liability in harassment complaints in which the organization must prove that it took reasonable care to prevent such activity.

Andragogy The study of the way adults learn and how they should be taught.

Age Discrimination in Employment Act of 1967 Commonly referred to as *ADEA*, it prohibits employment discrimination against employees who are at least 40 years of age.

Agency Shop A union security arrangement requiring bargaining unit employees who elect not to join the union to pay a fee, which is often equivalent to union dues.

Americans with Disabilities Act (1990) Commonly referred to as *ADA*; the major federal legislative act that prohibits employment discrimination against the disabled.

Arbitration The submission of a labor dispute to a neutral third party (arbitrator or arbitration panel) for resolution. The decision is usually binding on both parties.

Assessment Center A process used in either the selection or developmental processes in an organization consisting of a variety of tests and exercises that are scored, often by multiple raters.

Attrition The reduction of workforce levels caused by the normal processes of retirement, resignation, termination, and so forth.

B

Balance Sheet A financial statement that gives the organization's financial condition at a certain date and is a measure of the organization's overall financial health.

Balanced Scorecard A process for translating strategic goals into operational plans and metrics.

Bargaining Unit Those employees represented by the union and sharing a "community of interest."

Beck Rights The right of bargaining unit employee to pay only that portion of union dues attributable to union costs of bargaining, administering the contract, and certain limited organizing activities.

Behavior Theories Leadership theories that propose leadership effectiveness is based on the types of behaviors that leaders engage in.

Behavioral Interview Selection interview in which the candidate is asked how the individual handled a particular situation in the past.

Behaviorally Anchored Rating Scales An employee performance appraisal method that combines the graphic rating scale and critical incidents methodologies.

Benchmark Jobs Jobs that are common in the external labor market and used as reference points in both the job evaluation and job-pricing processes.

Benchmarking An outcome of environmental scanning that involves comparing the organization's operations against those of other organizations.

Benefits A component of employee compensation consisting of indirect financial rewards, usually received by virtue of employment with the organization.

Bias Judgments based on values or prejudices rather than facts.

Bloom's Taxonomy A hierarchy of learning behaviors/outcomes.

Bona Fide Occupational Qualification An exception to the antidiscrimination laws which permits employers to require an employee to be of a particular sex, religion, or national origin where that requirement is reasonably related to the organization's normal operations.

Boundaryless Organizations An organizational design model that is a construct or concept of how large organizations can become adaptive and organic by removing the vertical boundaries of hierarchy, the horizontal boundaries of rigid functional departmentalization, and the external organizational boundaries that preclude free interaction with suppliers and customers.

Branding A marketing concept referring to customer perceptions of the organization or its products that differentiate it from it competitors. It is increasingly being used as a strategy in recruitment.

Break-Even Analysis Financial analysis technique used to determine at what point the benefits from a particular activity begin to exceed the investment in the activity.

Budgeting The process of estimating revenues and allocating them for specific purposes.

Bureaucracy A organizational model, frequently found in large organizations and in the government, which is characterized by a high degree of job specialization, highly formalized procedures and policies, centralization, rigid departmentation (usually by function), small spans of control, and multiple levels of hierarchy.

Business Necessity A practice that is necessary for the safe and efficient operation of the organization and is a permissible exception to the antidiscrimination laws.

C

Career A series or sequence of work-related positions and experiences held by a person over the span of his or her working life.

Career Development A combination of career management and career planning. Career development is an umbrella concept that includes decisions regarding occupational choices and activities to facilitate the achievement of career goals that are of mutual benefit to the employee and the employer.

Career Management A process conducted by the employer to identify current and future staffing needs and to engage in activities to fulfill those needs.

Career Planning A process in which an individual sets career objectives and engages in activities to attain those goals.

Category Rating Scales Methods of performance appraisals that require the rater to check the appropriate box or statement that best describes the employee's performance. Methods include category rating scales, checklists, and forced choice.

Cease and Desist Order An order issued by the NLRB requiring a party determined to have committed a ULP to cease the illegal activity and refrain from engaging it in the future. The order may also contain requirements for remedial action.

Central Tendency An error caused by raters evaluating all employees in the middle of the evaluation scale, irrespective of the facts.

Centralization The extent to which decision-making authority in concentrated at high levels in the organization.

Certification The process by which a union becomes the exclusive bargaining agent of a designated group of employees.

Chandler v. Roudebush (1976) The Supreme Court ruling indicating that federal employees have the same rights under federal employment discrimination statutes as private sector employees.

Change Alteration of the status quo of an individual, group, or organization.

Chain of Command The hierarchical arrangement of authority.

City of Richmond v. J. A. Croson Company (1989) The Supreme Court ruling indicating that rigid numerical quota systems were unconstitutional when past discrimination was documented.

Civil Rights Act of 1866 Prohibits illegal discrimination based on race or ethnicity in the formation or enforcement of contracts.

Civil Rights Act of 1964 The most comprehensive antidiscrimination law in the United States; prohibits discrimination in employment decisions based on race, color, religion, sex, or national origin.

Civil Rights Act of 1991 An amendment to the Civil Rights Act of 1964 passed largely to reverse the conservative Supreme Court decision of the "Reagan Court" of the late 1980s.

Closed Shop A union security arrangement requiring a bargaining unit employee to be a member of the union prior to being hired. This arrangement was outlawed by the Taft-Hartley Act.

Common Law The body of law based on tradition and judicial precedent inherited from England.

Compa-ratio   A statistic used to analyze compensation policy versus actual practice within the organization. The formula for calculation is compa-ratio = (actual pay / midpoint of the pay range).

Comparative Methods   Methods of performance appraisal that require the rater to compare the performance of one employee with that of others. Methods include ranking, forced distribution, and paired comparison.

Compensable Factors   Those characteristics or dimensions of a job that are valued by the organization and used to determine the job's relative worth.

Compensation   The sum total of extrinsic and intrinsic rewards received by an employee as a result of employment.

Compensatory Approach   A type of employee selection process in which applicants complete the whole selection process and their scores in each stage are totaled to determine their final ranking.

Compensatory Damages   Monetary awards permitted under the Civil Rights Act of 1991 for pain and suffering, mental anguish, and other intangible damages suffered as a result of the employer's discriminatory practices.

Compensatory Time   Paid time off from work in lieu of cash compensation for overtime. In general, this is permissible only in the public sector.

Competencies   Personal or organizational capabilities that are linked to successful performance outcomes.

Competitive Intelligence   An outcome of the environmental-scanning process that provides information about competitors to enable the organization to adjust its strategies to compete in the environment.

Concentrated Structures   Specific organizational substructures created to make mechanistic organizations more organic.

Concurrent Validity   A type of criterion-related validity in a group is simultaneously measured on the independent and dependent variables and the two measures are correlated.

Congressional Accountability Act (1995)   Federal law that brought employees of the United States Congress under coverage of 11 major employee relations– and employment-related laws.

Consolidated Omnibus Budget Reconciliation Act (1985)   Better known as *COBRA*, the law provides for continuation of health insurance coverage for former employees and their spouses and dependents on the occurrence of certain qualifying events.

Construct Validity   The extent to which a measure actually measures that which cannot be directly observed. Constructs are theoretical traits or characteristics, such as intelligence and dependability.

Constructive Discharge   Occurs when the work environment is so hostile that a reasonable person would quit.

Consumer Credit Protection Act (1968)   Provides protections for employees whose wages have been garnished.

Consumer Price Index *(CPI)*   Measures the change in cost of about 400 goods and services and is used to measure inflation.

Content Validity   The extent to which the measurement contains actual elements of what it is intended to measure.

Contingency Theories   Leadership theories that propose leadership effectiveness is based on a proper match between leadership style and the situation.

Contingent Workforce   Those individuals who work for an organization but are not permanent full-time employees.

Contract   A binding and legally enforceable agreement between two or more people or parties.

Contrast Error   A rating error caused by basing the rating on comparison with other employees instead of the objective standard.

Controlling   The management function that involves monitoring progress toward goals and making changes when necessary.

Copyright   An intangible property right granted to the author or originator of literary, musical, or artistic works to exclude others from copying the work.

Copyright Act (1976)   A comprehensive federal law governing copyrighting of literary, musical, or artistic works. The act regulates the types of materials that can be copied, the length of copyright, the copyright process, penalties for copyright infringement, and associated issues.

Core Competency   The unique capability of an organization that distinguishes it from its competitors.

Correlation Coefficient   A measure of the strength of association between two variables.

Cost-Benefit Analysis   A quantitative method of evaluating the financial value of program outcomes in relation to program costs.

Craft Union   A union that seeks to represent workers engaged in a particular type of job regardless of the industry in which the workers are employed (carpenters, electricians, and so on).

Criterion-Related Validity   The degree of correlation between a measure and actual performance.

Critical Path Method   A project-planning technique, developed by DuPont, that indicates the order in which activities must be completed.

D

Deauthorization   The process by which the union security clause is removed from the contract, but the union retains its right to represent the bargaining unit.

Decentralization   The extent to which decision-making authority is dispersed throughout the organization.

Decertification   The process by which a union is removed from being the exclusive bargaining agent for a designated group of employees.

Deductive Reasoning   Data analysis that involves applying the general to the specific.

Defined Benefit Plan   A retirement plan that specifies the dollar amount or formula for determining the amount of pension benefit.

Defined Contribution Plan   A retirement plan that specifies the amount of contribution required by the employer, but the actual amount of pension benefit is determined by the amount of contributions and the performance of the investments made with those funds.

Delivery   The step in the HRD process in which the actual methods of delivery are determined and the program materials are produced.

Delphi Technique   A group workforce needs-forecasting method in which experts independently develop forecasts that are shared with each other, but they never actually meet face to face. Individual forecasts are refined until the group reaches consensus.

Departmentation   Also known as *departmentalization*. The framework by which jobs are grouped in the organization.

Dependent Variable   Something that is affected by or caused by an independent variable.

Descriptive Statistics   Mathematical methods to organize, summarize, and describe the data.

Design   The step in the HRD process that involves the establishment of training goals and objectives, determining the target audience for the program, and deciding how the development stage will be completed.

Development   Programs designed to improve the capability of the organization's workforce (human capital) to be able to adapt to an increasingly complex and dynamic environment and prepare for responsibilities of the future.

Development of Strategic Objectives   The second step in the strategic-planning process in which the organization performs an internal and external analysis to translate its mission and vision into strategic goals and determines a strategy to achieve those goals.

Directive Interview   Selection interview in which the interviewer maintains control of the flow of the questioning.

Disability   Under the Americans with Disability Act, an applicant or employee that

▸ Has a physical or mental impairment that substantially limits one or more major life functions

▸ Has a record of such impairment

▸ Is regarded or treated as having an impairment

Dismissal and Notice of Right Letter   A communication issued by EEOC to the complainant and organization on completion of an investigation indicating that no illegal discrimination has taken place.

Disparate Treatment   Occurs when members of a protected class are treated differently from others.

Distributive Bargaining The traditional way of negotiating labor contracts in a win/lose manner by distributing a fixed amount of resources.

E

Economic Strike A strike occurring during labor contract bargaining over mandatory bargaining items.

Effectiveness The extent to which goals are met and the needs of stakeholders satisfied.

Efficiency The ratio of inputs to outputs.

Electromation An NLRB decision that ruled that certain types of employee involvement activities in labor organizations are protected from domination by the Wagner Act.

Ellerth v. Burlington Northern (1998) The Supreme Court ruling that defined the term *tangible employment action* with respect to sex discrimination cases.

Employee Assistance Program *(EAP)* An employer-provided program that provides employees with counseling and assistance for a variety of personal and work-related issues.

Employee Involvement Programs A wide variety of programs designed to increase commitment to organizational goals through increased employee input into decision-making.

Employee Polygraph Protection Act (1988) An law that restricts most private employers from conducting polygraph (lie detector) tests on prospective and current employees except in certain limited conditions.

Employee Retirement and Income Security Act (1974) Commonly referred to as *ERISA*, this law regulates most private sector pension and benefit plans.

Employment Agencies Firms that recruit and screen applicants for a fee.

Employment Contract A written agreement between the employee and employer to specify the employment relationship.

Employment Offer A written or verbal proposal to establish an employment relationship. The offer should be clear as to the exact terms and conditions of employment.

Employment-at-Will A common law concept that either the employee or employer can terminate the employment relationship at any time for any reason.

Environment Institutions, forces, and stakeholders external to the organization that directly or potentially affect its performance, success, and survivability.

Environmental Scanning The process of collecting and interpreting information to determine conditions, trends, and changes in the environment that might create opportunities for or impose threats on the organization.

Equal Pay Act (1963) An amendment to the Fair Labor Standards Act; prohibits discrimination in compensation on the basis of sex when the jobs are similar in terms of skill, effort, responsibility, and working conditions.

Equity Theory Motivation theory that states that employees compare their ratio of inputs to outcomes with the inputs and outcomes of others. Perceived inequity causes the person to act to bring about an equity condition.

Ergonomics   The study of the physical impact of work on the body and the design of work processes and the work environment to minimize them.

Ethics   System of rules and values that govern the conduct of individuals or groups.

***Excelsior* List**   A list of the names and addresses of eligible voters in a union certification election that the employer must provide to the NLRB, which will in turn provide it to the union.

Exclusive Representation   Only a labor organization that has been properly certified can represent the bargaining unit.

Executive Order 11246   Requires federal contractors with contracts of more than $10,000 to comply with Title VII and contractors with contracts in excess of $50,000 and more than 50 employees to develop and implement affirmative action plans.

Executive Order 11478   Requires federal agencies to develop and implement affirmative action plans for federal employees.

Exempt Employee   Employees not subject to the minimum wage and overtime provisions of FLSA.

Exit Interview   A discussion that is conducted in an attempt to determine why an individual is leaving the organization.

Expatriate   An employee who is a citizen of the country in which the company is headquartered but who works in another country; for example, an employee of a United States firm working in France.

Expectancy Theory   A theory that states motivation is a factor of the expectation that a certain amount of effort will lead to a first-level outcome, the probability that the first-level outcome is linked to a second-level outcome, and the value of that second-level outcome.

External Equity   An employee perception that his or her compensation is equal to that in the external labor market.

F

Factor Comparison Method   A job evaluation method that involves ranking jobs in terms of each compensable factor and then pricing the job based on the rankings in relation to known wage rates for benchmark jobs.

Fair Credit Reporting Act (1970)   An act that regulates the process of obtaining and using credit and other types of information on employees.

Fair Labor Standards Act (1938)   The major federal legislation covering compensation; the act covers minimum wage, overtime, child labor provisions, and equal pay.

Family and Medical Leave Act (1993)   Generally referred to as *FMLA*, the legislation provides for up to 12 weeks of unpaid leave for birth or adoption of a child, for care for an immediate family member experiencing a serious health condition, and for recuperation of the employee from a serious health condition.

***Faragher v. City of Boca Raton* (1998)**   The Supreme Court ruling that establishes the basis for employer affirmative defense.

Federal Mediation and Conciliation Service (FMCS)   A federal agency created by the Taft-Hartley Act. FMCS is responsible for assisting in the resolution of contract-bargaining disputes.

Fee-for-Service Plan   The traditional health insurance indemnity plan incorporating deductibles and coinsurance. This type of plan provides maximum flexibility, but typically costs more.

Fiedler's Contingency Theory   A theory of leadership that proposes leadership effectiveness is based on a match between the leader's leadership style and the contingencies of the workplace.

Financial Accounting Standards Board (FASB)   A private entity that derives its authority from the federal Security and Exchange Commission, which issues rules to be followed by the accounting profession as to how certain transactions are to be recorded and how financial information is to be reported to stockholders and the public.

Financial Management   Those activities designed to account for and control the organization's resources so that it can achieve its goals and objectives.

Financial Ratios   The statistical measures used to evaluate the financial performance of the organization, especially in relationship to other organizations in its particular industry.

Fitness for Duty Examination   A medical examination required by the employer to determine whether the employee is physically or mentally able to perform the essential functions of the job.

Force Field Analysis   A model of organizational change that proposes organizations can be modified by altering the equilibrium of change-driving and change-resisting forces.

Forecasts   An outcome of the environmental-scanning process that attempts to predict how a particular measure will change in the future.

Formalization   The extent to which work assignments in an organization are standardized.

Formula Budget   A type of incremental budgeting in which a specific percentage increase (or, less likely, decrease) is applied to the whole budget.

Fundamental Accounting Equation   Assets = Liabilities + Owners' Equity

G

Gainsharing Plan   A group incentive plan that shares cost reduction savings or the value of increased productivity with employees.

Gantt Charts   A project-planning technique that visually displays the starting and ending times of all activities and shows how each activity fits into the overall schedule.

Garnishment   A legal action to attach the wages of an employee by a creditor. The employer is obligated to deduct funds from the employee's wages and transmit them to the creditor.

General Duty Clause An overarching health and safety standard requiring employers to provide safe and healthy working conditions even if a specific OSHA standard does not apply.

***General Dynamics Land Systems, Inc. v. Cline* (2004)** The Supreme Court ruling indicating that the Age Discrimination in Employment Act does protect younger workers that are more than 40 years of age from employment decisions that favor older workers.

General Union A union that is a combination of a craft and industrial union seeking to represent workers in multiple occupations and multiple industries.

Genetics A branch of biology that studies the transmission of hereditary characteristic from parents to offspring.

Glass Ceiling Occurs when protected-class individuals are promoted only so far in the organization and then reach a seemingly impenetrable barrier in which they can see the top of the organization but cannot achieve promotion into it.

Glass Walls Also referred to as *glass elevators*. It is the phenomenon that occurs when women and minorities are hired into non-revenue-producing staff functions that do not normally lead to high-level executive positions and are prohibited from transferring into other occupations within the organization.

Goal-Setting Theory A theory of motivation that states performance and motivation are increased when employees are provided with specific and challenging goals, when they commit to those goals, and when feedback is provided regarding achievement of those goals.

Golden Parachute Executive compensation benefit that provides often lucrative financial protection if the executive is terminated because of acquisition or merger.

***Gratz et al. v. Bollinger et al.* (2003)** The Supreme Court ruling indicating that giving preference to minorities for admission to a college undergraduate program serves a governmental interest in the educational benefits that result from a racially and ethnically diverse student body. However, the Court ruled that the procedures used in this case violated the Fourteenth Amendment guarantee of equal protection because they were not sufficiently narrowly tailored.

Green Circle Rate A green circle rate occurs when the employee's current rate of pay is below the range for the job held.

Grievance Procedure A formal process used to resolve disagreement arising from the administration of the labor agreement.

***Griggs v. Duke Power* (1971)** The Supreme Court decision that created the judicial concept of adverse impact.

Gross Domestic Product *(GDP)* The total value of goods and services produced by a country in a given year.

Grutter v. Bollinger et al. (2003) The Supreme Court ruling indicating that narrowly tailored use of race in admission decisions to a law school does not violate the Fourteenth Amendment guarantee of equal protection when it is used to further a compelling governmental interest in the educational benefits that flow from a diverse student body. The Court ruled that the admission decision must be made based on a highly individualized review of each applicant, that no decision can be based automatically on one variable (such as race), and that the process must ensure that all factors contributing to diversity are meaningfully considered.

H

Halo Effect A rating error caused by a high rating in one category positively influencing the ratings in other categories.

Harris v. Forklift Systems, Inc. (1993) The Supreme Court ruling indicating that a "reasonable person" test must be used to determine whether a hostile work environment violating Title VII exists.

Health Refers to an employee's overall physical and psychological well-being.

Health Insurance Portability and Accountability Act (1996) Generally referred to as *HIPAA*, the act restricts the capability of health plans and employers to deny or limit health insurance coverage for preexisting conditions and protects the privacy of medical records.

Health Maintenance Organization (HMO) A prepaid managed care system providing regular and preventive medical care. Users typically pay a small copay, but services outside the system are not covered.

Herzberg's Two-Factor Theory Motivation theory stating that characteristics of the workplace can be categorized into intrinsic or motivation factors that can create job satisfaction but not job dissatisfaction, and extrinsic or hygiene factors that can create job dissatisfaction but not job satisfaction.

Hiring Freeze A prohibition on the employment of new and additional employees and the replacement of current employees that leave the organization.

Hopwood v. State of Texas (1996) The United States Court of Appeals ruling that taking race into account, even as a means of achieving diversity, violates the Fourteenth Amendment guarantee of equal protection. The Supreme Court refused to hear this case on appeal.

Horn Effect A rating error caused by a low rating in one category negatively affecting ratings in other categories.

HR Audit A formal and systematic process of evaluating the current effectiveness and efficiency of the HR function and determining what activities must be taken to improve it.

HR Scorecard A method of evaluating the effectiveness and efficiency of the HR function by using a series of measures or metrics of employee behaviors and HR program outcomes that are believed to be related to organizational success.

Human Capital   The total current and potential capabilities of the organization's workforce.

Human Resource Certification Institute *(HRCI)* An organization affiliated with SHRM that collects the body of knowledge of HR and administers HR certification programs.

Human Resource Information System *(HRIS)* An integrated computer application that collects, processes, stores, and analyzes human resource data to support HR activities.

Human Resource Management *(HRM)*   The design and implementation of organizational systems to efficiently and effectively use people to accomplish organizational goals.

Hypothesis   A tentative statement describing the relationship between the independent and dependent variables.

I

Illegal Bargaining Topics   Subjects of negotiation that would violate law.

Immigration Reform and Control Act (1986) Legislation that prohibits the hiring of unauthorized aliens and discrimination in hiring and firing based on national origin or citizenship status.

Implementation   The step in the HRD process in which the program is delivered to its target audience.

Income Statement   A financial statement summarizing all revenue coming into the organization and expenses going out, which results in a net income or net loss.

Incremental Budget   The traditional way of developing a budget, which involves using the previous budget as a base or reference point. The new budget is developed by adjusting individual budget items either upward or downward.

Independent Variable   The factor that is manipulated or measured to determine whether it affects the dependent variable.

Individual Equity   An employee perception that his or her compensation is appropriately positioned within the range available for the position.

Inductive Reasoning   Data analysis that involves creating the whole from its parts.

Industrial Union   A union that seeks to represent workers in a particular industry (auto workers, mine workers, and so on).

Inferential Statistics   Mathematical methods that permit inferences to be made about a larger group based on data collected from a representative subset of that group.

Integrative Bargaining   A mutual problem-solving approach to labor negotiations dealing in interests and not positions.

Interest Arbitration   The process by which a neutral third party makes a binding decision as to the provisions of a labor contract.

Internal Equity   An employee perception that his or her compensation is appropriate based on comparison with other jobs within the organization.

J

Job Analysis The systematic process of gathering information regarding the duties required of a job and the human characteristics necessary to successfully perform those duties.

Job Bidding Permits an employee to apply for a position even if no openings exist. The employee's application is then held for a period of time, usually for a year, and the employee receives automatic consideration should the position come open.

Job Characteristics Model A motivation theory that links the design of a job to motivation and work outcomes.

Job Classification A method of job evaluation in which jobs are classified into pay grades based on comparison of the job description of the job to a generic description for that pay grade.

Job Description A written document that describes the functions and working conditions of a job.

Job Evaluation The process used to determine the relative worth of a job to the organization without consideration of rate of pay or the individual who encumbers it.

Job Posting The process of advising and publicizing job openings to employees.

Job Specialization Also known as *division of labor*. The extent to which work is broken down into its component parts with each part being the primary task assignment of a separate job.

Job Specifications The human characteristics necessary to successfully perform a job, typically included as a subsection of the job description.

***Johnson v. Santa Clara County Transportation Agency* (1987)** The Supreme Court ruling indicating that gender could be used as one factor in an employment decision if under-representation was shown and the affirmative action plan did not have firm quotas.

Jurisdictional Strike A strike with the purpose of forcing the employer to assign work to a bargaining unit work group. It is illegal under labor law.

Just Cause The concept that disciplinary reasons should be taken only for job-related reasons and the severity of the disciplinary action should be commensurate with the level of infraction.

K–L

Leadership The ability to influence others toward the achievement of goals.

Leading The management function that involves directing and motivating employees to achieve goals.

Learning Curve The rate at which an individual learns.

Learning Organization A organization specifically designed to engage in constant adaptation to its environment.

Learning Style The way people learn, usually defined on the basis of the type of learning material that is preferred (visual, auditory, kinesthetic).

Leniency   An error caused by raters evaluating employees or candidates at the high end of the evaluation scale irrespective of the facts.

Letter of Determination   A letter issued by EEOC advising the complainant and the organization that there is reasonable cause to believe that illegal discrimination has occurred.

Linear Regression   Permits the prediction of one variable based on the systematic relationship between it and one or more other variables.

Local National   Also simply *locals*. An employee that is a citizen of the country in which the employee is employed.

Lockout   Management's refusal to let employees work in order to place pressure on the union to resolve a bargaining dispute.

M

Mackay Doctrine   Right of the employer to permanently replace striking workers during an economic strike.

Maintenance of Membership   A union security arrangement requiring an employee that joins the union to maintain membership for the duration of the current labor contract.

Management   The process used to achieve organizational goals through people and resources.

Management by Objectives   A performance management method based on mutual goal-setting, periodic review and feedback, and performance appraisal based on achievement of the goals.

Management Rights Clause   A portion of a typical labor agreement that reserves the right of management to make decisions regarding the business unless those rights have been specifically limited in the negotiated labor contract.

Managerial Grid   A matrix developed by Blake and Mouton that illustrates managerial styles along a vertical axis of concern for people and a horizontal axis of concern for production.

Mandatory Bargaining Topics   Topics that must be negotiated (wages, hours, and other terms and conditions of employment).

Marketing   The process of developing, pricing, promoting, and distributing products, services, and knowledge that satisfy customer needs while facilitating the achievement of organizational goals.

***Martin v. Wilks* (1988)**   The Supreme Court ruling indicating that reverse discrimination could occur if the nonprotected class is not consulted in the negotiations for a consent decree, giving a protected class employment preferences.

Maslow's Hierarchy of Needs   Motivation theory that states there are five categories of human needs arranged in a hierarchy, and that a need does not become a motivator unless the lower-level needs have been substantially satisfied.

Mass Interview   A type of selection interview in which more than one interviewee is interviewed as the same time.

McClelland's Theory of Needs   A motivation theory that states there are three needs that affect motivation and behavior: the need for achievement, the need for power, and the need for affiliation.

McDonnell-Douglas Corp. v. Green (1973)
The Supreme Court ruling that established the concept of disparate treatment and created what is known as the *McDonnell-Douglas test.*

Mean   The average score defined as the sum of all scores divided by the number of scores.

Mechanistic Organizations   An organizational design model that provides for stability and efficiency, but lacks flexibility and capability to adapt to changes in the environment. A bureaucracy is an example of such an organization.

Median   The score below which 50% of all scores fall in a distribution.

Mediation   A dispute resolution technique in which a neutral third party, the mediator, attempts to help the parties come to resolution.

Medicare   Hospitalization and health insurance provided under Social Security and consisting of two plans. Part A requires no premium payment, is mandatory, and provides hospitalization insurance. Part B requires an insurance premium payment, is optional, and provides coverage for physician fees and certain other medical costs.

Meritor Savings Bank v. Vinson (1986)   The Supreme Court decision that created the judicial concept of hostile environment sexual harassment.

Metrics   Quantitative measures of performance.

Mission Statement   A statement that describes the fundamental purposes of the organization.

Mode   The score that is obtained most often in a distribution.

Multiple Hurdle Process   A type of employee selection process in which the applicant must pass each step to proceed to the next step in the progression. Failure at any step disqualifies the applicant from further consideration.

N

Narrative Methods   Methods of performance appraisal that require the rater to provide a written description of the employee's performance.

National Institute for Occupational Safety and Health (NIOSH)   Federal agency that conducts research on workplace safety and health and assists OSHA in developing safety standards.

National Labor Relations Board (NLRB)   The board created by the Wagner Act to administer its provisions as amended.

Needs Assessment   Also called *needs analysis*, it is the process used to determine whether HRD programs are needed to achieve organizational goals.

Nominal Group Technique   A group workforce needs-forecasting method that requires each member of the group to make an independent forecast prior to discussion of any forecasts.

Nonqualified Benefit Plans   Pension and benefit plans that do not comply with the regulatory requirements of ERISA and/or the tax code. They are used to provide additional benefits for executives.

Norris-LaGuardia Act (1932) The act that largely prevented management from getting injunctions against union activities. It also made the yellow dog contract unenforceable in federal courts.

O

***Ocale v. Sundowner Offshore Services, Inc.* (1998)** The Supreme Court ruling indicating that Title VII prohibitions against discrimination based on sex include same sex harassment.

Occupational Safety and Health Act (1970) Federal legislation passed to ensure that all workers are provided a safe and healthy environment in which to work.

Occupational Safety and Health Administration *(OSHA)* The agency that administers the Occupational Safety and Health Act (1970). OSHA has authority to inspect worksites, issue and enforce safety and health standards, and issue penalties for violators.

Occupational Safety and Health Review Commission The quasi-judicial federal agency that adjudicates challenges to OSHA enforcement activities.

Office of Federal Contract Compliance Programs *(OFCCP)* The agency of the Department of Labor that was created to monitor compliance of federal contractors with Executive Order 11246, as amended, requiring contractors to comply with Title VII of the Civil Rights Act of 1964 and to develop and implement affirmative action plans to increase the participation of protected classes in the workforce.

Offshoring The employment practice of hiring workers in foreign countries to perform tasks previously done in the United States.

Open Shop A type of union security in which bargaining unit employees are neither required to join the union nor pay union dues.

Operational Role One of the three roles of HR; involves the planning, implementation, and evaluation of various HR programmatic activities in support of support the organization's strategic goals.

Operations Management The planning and analysis of those activities by which the organization transforms its inputs to outputs.

Organic Organizations An organizational design model that is highly adaptive. They interact with the environment and communicate the dynamics of the environment through rapid lateral and vertical channels, tend to be composed of a loose configuration of cross-functional and cross-hierarchal teams with decentralized decision-making, and have few levels of hierarchy and little formalization.

Organizational Change Transformation of the structure, culture, or work processes in response to internal or external forces.

Organizational Culture A system of shared values and norms held by organizational members.

Organizational Design The process of determining the appropriate organizational structure based on organizational goals and culture.

Organizational Development *(OD)* A strategy and process to improve the effectiveness of an organization through planned programmatic activities and interventions.

Organizational Exit The process of managing the conditions under which employees leave the organization.

Organizational Structure A composition of six descriptive elements that define how an organization functions.

Organizing The management function that involves assembling the resources necessary to achieve goals.

OSHA Standards Regulations published by OSHA requiring certain actions to prevent employee injury or illness. Bloodborne Pathogens and Personal Protective Equipment are examples of OSHA standards.

Outsourcing The process of contracting for services or products externally rather than producing them internally.

Outplacement Services An employee benefit that provides assistance in obtaining new employment to terminated individuals.

P

Panel Interview A type of selection interview in which more than one interviewer conducts the interview.

Patent A grant from the federal government giving the owner the exclusive right to sell, manufacture, and benefit from an invention.

Pattern Bargaining A model of labor-management bargaining in which the union negotiates a contract with one employer and then uses that agreement as a pattern for other agreements in the same industry. The automobile industry is an example of where this is used.

Pay Compression Occurs when the pay differential between employees with different levels of skills, performance, or seniority becomes small, usually because of failure to keep the pay structure in alignment with external labor market rates.

Pay Grade A grouping of jobs of similar relative worth for purposes of determining pay rates.

Pay Range The variability of available pay in a job from the minimum to maximum rate.

Performance Dimension Those critical responsibilities of the job that are evaluated in a performance appraisal.

Performance Management The process of linking organizational goals to employee performance. Performance management includes strategic goal setting, development of performance standards, performance appraisal, development and coaching, and discipline and reward—all integrated to achieve organizational goals.

Performance Standard The acceptable level of performance in a performance dimension.

Permissive Bargaining Topics Subjects that can be negotiated only with the agreement of both parties.

Person-Job Fit The process of ensuring that the knowledge, skills, and abilities of an individual match the requirements of the essential functions of the job.

Person-Organization Fit The process of ensuring that the personality and value system of an individual match the culture and objectives of the organization.

Placement The process of ensuring that the right person is placed in the right job in an organization.

Planning The management function that involves determining the goals of the organization and deciding on activities required to accomplish them.

Point Factor Method A type of job evaluation that involves placing of jobs into a hierarchy of pay grades based on the number of points assigned to the job in the evaluation process. Points are assigned based the level or degree of compensable factors present in the job.

Policies Broad general statements of the organization's philosophy with respect to an issue.

Population The total group to which the research being conducted applies.

Positive Discipline A problem-solving approach to correcting employee behavior.

Predictive Validity A type of criterion-related validity in which a group is measured on the independent variable and on the dependent variable at a later date. The two measures are then correlated.

Predictors Measurable indicators that a particular selection criterion is possessed by a candidate in the employee selection process.

Preferred Provider Organization (*PPO*) A type of medical insurance arrangement in which the firm contracts with medical providers to provide medical coverage at reduced rates (much like an HMO), but also allows employees to choose other providers at increased costs (similar to a fee-for-service plan).

Pregnancy Discrimination Act (1978) The act is an amendment to the Civil Rights Act of 1964 and prohibits discrimination in employment matters based on pregnancy, childbirth, or related medical conditions.

Prescreening A step in the selection process that is used to determine whether a candidate meets the basic qualifications for the position.

Prevailing Rate The rate of wages and benefits generally paid in a geographic area. Prevailing rates are required to be paid by employers under most federal contracts.

Primacy Basing judgments on the first occurrences rather than all occurrences.

Procedures Represent guidance to organizational members as to the standard or customary way of dealing with an issue or handling a situation.

Professional Employer Organization (*PEO*) An organization that leases employees and assumes the employer rights and responsibilities for the employees that it provides to its clients.

Profit Sharing Plans An organizationwide incentive plan in which a percentage of the firm's yearly profit is distributed to the employees.

Program Evaluation and Review Technique (PERT) A project-planning technique first used by the United States Navy in 1958 to plan and monitor huge weapons systems projects. PERT indicates the order in which activities must be completed.

Progressive Discipline The imposition of increasingly severe sanctions to correct employee behavior.

Project A set of coordinated activities and tasks having a definite beginning and ending point.

Project Champion An individual that is committed to the project and communicates its value throughout the organization.

Project Management The process of planning and monitoring project activities.

Project Monitoring The process of tracking project progress, comparing actual results to predicted results, and making corrections.

Project Planning The process of determining project tasks to be accomplished and the resources needed to accomplish those tasks.

Project Sponsor Typically a high-level executive that controls resources and agrees to fund the project.

Protected Classes Groups that are specifically identified in the law for special protection from illegal discrimination

Psychological Contract An unwritten agreement between the employer and employee regarding work expectations and obligations.

Punitive Damages Monetary awards permitted under the Civil Rights Act of 1991 to punish the employer for its discriminatory practices.

Q

Qualified Benefit Plans Pension and benefit plans that comply with both ERISA and the tax code, giving the employer certain tax advantages and allowing the employee to defer compensation.

Qualified Individual Under the Americans with Disabilities Act, a disabled person who is able to perform the essential functions of the job with or without accommodation.

Qualitative Research Type of inquiry that produces findings that are arrived at by neither statistical procedures nor other types of quantification.

Quantitative Research Type of inquiry that produces findings by using statistical procedures.

Quid Pro Quo A type of sexual harassment that occurs when an employee is forced to choose between submitting to sexual advances or forfeiting employment opportunities or benefits.

Quota Created when all individuals that are not members of a targeted protected class are excluded from consideration for a position.

R

Railroad Labor Act (1926) Legislation guaranteeing the right of airline and railroad employees to form unions.

Range   The difference between the highest score and lowest score in the distribution.

Ranking   The simplest method of job evaluation in which jobs are placed in a hierarchy from most valuable to least valuable by an evaluation of the whole job in relation to other jobs found in the organization.

Ratio Analysis   A forecasting technique used in workforce planning that assumes there is a set relationship between one variable and another that enables prediction of workforce needs.

Realistic Job Preview   Provides the applicant with an accurate description of the job and the work environment, and is positively correlated with employee retention.

Reasonable Accommodation   Under the Americans with Disabilities Act, it is the modification of the workplace or work requirements that would permit the individual to perform the essential functions of the job, unless those accommodations would create an undue hardship on the employer.

Recency   Basing judgments on the most recent occurrences rather than all occurrences.

Recognition Strike   A strike to get an employer to recognize and bargain with a union.

Recruitment   The process of attracting qualified applicants for the organization to consider when filling its positions.

Red Circle Rate   Occurs when the employee's current rate of pay is above the range for the job held.

Regents of the University of California v. Bakke (1978)   The Supreme Court ruling on reverse discrimination indicating that a medical school could legitimately consider race in its admission procedures, but that race could not be the only factor.

Rehabilitation Act of 1973   Prohibits employment discrimination based on disability by federal contractors, depositories of federal funds, and employers receiving federal grants or aid. Requires contractors with contracts of $50,000 or more and at least 50 employees to develop and implement written affirmative action plans for the employment of the disabled.

Reinforcement Theory   A motivation/learning theory that states behavior is the result of the consequences of that behavior and can be shaped by the type of reinforcement received.

Reliability   The consistency or dependability of a measurement.

Replacement Charts   Manual or automated records used in workforce planning indicating which employees are currently ready for promotion to a specific position.

Research   The process of finding answers to questions.

Retaliatory Discharge   Occurs when the employer terminates the employee for exercising rights or obligations under the law.

Return on Investment (ROI)   A financial tool that measures the productivity of assets.

Reverse Discrimination   Occurs when an equally qualified or more qualified member of a nonprotected class (generally, a white male) is not hired or promoted in favor of a member of a protected class.

Right-to-Work Laws Laws passed in 21 states prohibiting the use of the union and/or agency shop security clauses in labor agreements.

Right-to-Sue Letter Letter issued by EEOC indicating that the agency is not going to file suit on behalf of the complainant and permitting the complainant to pursue the complaint in the court system.

Rights Arbitration The process by which a neutral third party makes a binding decision regarding a grievance arising from an existing labor agreement.

Rules Provide guidance to organizational members as to specific actions to be taken in a situation, providing little latitude for individual discretion.

S

Safety Prevention of injury due to working conditions, processes, and procedures.

Salting A union tactic involving paid union organizers applying for positions with a target firm for the express purpose of engaging in organizing activities within that firm.

Sample A subset of the population used in research studies.

Scenario An outcome of the environmental-scanning process that describes what the future is likely to be.

Scientific Method A systematic process of testing a hypothesis regarding the relationship between two or more variables.

Security Protection of physical, human, and intellectual assets of an organization from harm.

Selection The process used to choose individuals with the right qualifications to fill job openings in an organization.

Selection Criteria Characteristics of an individual that are believed to be correlated with the job performance elements and used in the employee selection process.

Seniority The employee's length of service with the employer. It is often used as the sole determinant or a factor in employment-related decisions such as promotion, layoff and recall, and reassignment.

Severance Pay Either a one-time lump sum payment or a temporary continuation of salary provided by the employer to terminated workers.

Sexual Harassment Unwelcome sexual advances, requests for sexual favors, and other verbal or physical conduct of a sexual nature that takes place under any of the following conditions:

- ▶ Submission to such conduct is made either explicitly or implicitly a term or condition of employment.

- ▶ Submission to or rejection of such conduct by an individual is used as the basis for employment decision affecting the individual.

- ▶ Such conduct has the purpose or effect of unreasonably interfering with an individual's work performance or creating an intimidating, hostile, or offensive work environment.

Sherman Antitrust Act (1890) Prohibits monopolies and other activities in restraint of trade.

Simple Structure   An organizational model characterized by lack of departmentalization, wide span of control, few levels or hierarchy, low formalization, fluid job responsibilities, and high centralization.

Situational Interviews   A type of selection interview in which candidates are asked to explain how they would handle a particular situation when confronted with it on the job.

Social Responsibility   The organization's long-term commitment to the welfare of society.

Society for Human Resource Management (SHRM)   The largest professional organization devoted to human resource management.

Span of Control   The number of employees a manager directs.

Standard Deviation   An index of the spread of scores in the distribution about the mean.

Statement of Cash Flows   The financial statement that reports all cash receipts and disbursements during a specified period.

Statement of Work   A project-planning document that provides a broad written description of the work required to complete a project.

Statistics   The results of mathematical processes that collect, analyze, interpret, and describe data.

Stereotyping   Evaluating persons based on their demographic characteristics rather than their individual capabilities.

Strategic Planning   The process of making decisions regarding the organization's long-term goals and strategies.

Strategic Role   One of the three roles of HR; involves a proactive planning approach to assist the organization in designing its future.

Strategy   A course of action that directs organizational activities.

Strategy Evaluation   The step in the strategic planning process that involves evaluating progress toward achievement of the strategic objectives and, if required, taking corrective action.

Strategy Formulation   The first step in the strategic planning process in which the organization makes decisions regarding what business it is in and what its basic mission and values are.

Strategy Implementation   The third step in the strategic planning process; involves activities such as creating action plans, committing resources, and motivating organizational members to achieve the strategic objectives.

Stress Interview   A type of selection interview that is designed to create anxiety and place pressure on the interviewees to determine how they respond.

Strictness   An error caused by raters evaluating employees or candidates at the low end of the evaluation scale irrespective of the facts.

Structured Interview   One that includes pre-scripted questions that are asked of all candidates.

SWOT   An acronym standing for *Strengths, Weaknesses, Opportunities, and Threats*. It refers to the process of performing an internal and external analysis during strategic planning.

Sympathy Strike   A refusal to cross the picket lines of another union or a strike by an uninvolved union in an attempt to influence the outcome of a labor dispute in which another union is involved.

T

***Taxman v. Board of Education of Piscataway* (1993)**   The United States Court of Appeals ruling indicating that a nonremedial affirmative action plan cannot violate the nondiscrimination mandate of the Civil Rights Act of 1964.

Theory X, Theory Y   Motivation theory developed by Douglas McGregor stating that managers view human behavior from one of two viewpoints and that different managerial and motivations practices are indicated, depending on which viewpoint is subscribed to.

Third-Country National *(TCN)*   An employee of a firm based in one country that works in a second country, but is a citizen of a third country.

Tort   An act that harms another party and is actionable in the courts.

Total Quality Management   A comprehensive approach to achieving customer satisfaction though the process of continuous improvement.

Training   Programs designed to provide the workforce with the knowledge, skills, and abilities to perform the current work assignment.

Trait Theories   Leadership theories proposing that effective leadership is the result of personal characteristics such as intelligence, self-confidence, and extroversion, among others.

Transactional Leadership   Moving the group toward established organizational goals by providing direction and guidance regarding work requirements.

Transformational Leadership   Bringing about group change. Focuses on increased performance and adaptation through consensus building and concern for employee welfare.

Transpatriate   An employee of any country that spends long periods of time stationed in countries other than the country in which the firm is headquartered.

Trend Analysis   As used in workforce planning, it involves studying historical organizational employment levels to predict future employment levels.

U

Unemployment Compensation   A mandatory benefit under the Social Security Act; provides limited income continuation for employees who involuntarily lose their jobs.

Unfair Labor Practice *(ULP)*   Activities of either the employer or labor organization that are prohibited by the Wagner Act as amended.

Unfair Labor Practice Strike   A strike occurring to protest commission of an unfair labor practice by the employer.

Uniform Guidelines on Employee Selection Procedures (1978)   Guidance published in the *Code of Federal Regulations* that assists employers in complying with federal law and avoiding complaints of illegal discrimination.

Uniformed Services Employment and Reemployment Act (1994)   Also known as *USERRA*. This legislation prohibits employment discrimination based on military service and provides a broad array of protections, including rights to employment and benefits.

Union Shop   A union security arrangement requiring that bargaining unit employees maintain union membership as a condition of employment.

United Steelworkers v. Weber (1979)   The Supreme Court ruling indicating that voluntary affirmative action quotas agreed to by the employer and a union are legal.

V

Validity   The capability of the measurement to measure what it is intended to measure.

Values Statement   Describes the basic beliefs of the organization.

Vesting   The process by which an employee gains nonforfeitable rights to benefits under a retirement plan.

Vietnam Era Veterans' Readjustment Assistance Act (1974)   Legislation that prohibits discrimination in employment against disabled veterans, veterans of the Vietnam era, veterans who served on active duty in during a war, campaign, expedition, or military operation, and recently separated veterans. Contractors holding contracts in excess of $100,000 are required to develop and implement affirmative action plans to hire covered veterans.

Virtual Organization   An organizational design model characterized by largely being composed of rented, leased, or contracted workers and functions.

Vision Statement   A general description of the organization's desired future state.

Vividness   Basing judgments on occurrences that are particularly memorable rather than on all occurrences.

W

Wagner Act (1935)   The major labor relations legislation in the United States, guaranteeing employee rights to form and join unions, engage in collective bargaining and other concerted activities, and delineating unfair labor practices that management is prohibited from engaging in.

Washington v. Davis (1976)   The Supreme Court ruling determining that an employer practice can be job related, even if it creates adverse impact for a protected class, if it validly predicts performance.

Weingarten Rights   The right to have a representative attend an investigatory meeting with management if the employee reasonably believes that discipline could result from the meeting.

Wellness Program   An employer-sponsored benefit that encompasses a variety of services designed to improve the overall health of employees.

Wildcat Strike   A strike over a grievance while a labor contract is in effect.

Work Breakdown Structure   A project-planning document that shows the total project divided into the tasks that must be completed.

Worker Adjustment and Retraining Notification Act (1988)   Legislation, most frequently referred to as the *WARN Act*, that requires advance notification to employees in the event of mass layoffs and plant closings.

Workers' Compensation   A law in each state that provides compensation to workers in the event of on-the-job injury or illness.

Workforce Planning   The process of determining how to staff the organization with the right employees at the right time and in the right place.

X–Z

Yellow Dog Contract   A promise by a worker to not join a union. This type of contract was made unenforceable by the Norris-LaGuardia Act.

Yield Rates   Comparison of the number of applicants or potential applicants at one stage in the recruitment/selection process with the number that remain available at the next stage.

Zero-Based Budget   A budget developed entirely from scratch with each budget item having to be justified each budget cycle.

NUMBERS

A

How can we make this index more useful? Email us at indexes@quepublishing.com

Q - R

S

X - Y - Z